SIGMUND FREUD AS A CRITICAL SOCIAL THEORIST

Studies in Critical Social Sciences Book Series

Haymarket Books is proud to be working with Brill Academic Publishers (www.brill.nl) to republish the *Studies in Critical Social Sciences* book series in paperback editions. This peer-reviewed book series offers insights into our current reality by exploring the content and consequences of power relationships under capitalism, and by considering the spaces of opposition and resistance to these changes that have been defining our new age. Our full catalog of *SCSS* volumes can be viewed at https://www.haymarketbooks.org/series_collections/4-studies-in-critical-social-sciences.

Series Editor
David Fasenfest (York University, Canada)

Editorial Board
Eduardo Bonilla-Silva (Duke University)
Chris Chase-Dunn (University of California–Riverside)
William Carroll (University of Victoria)
Raewyn Connell (University of Sydney)
Kimberlé W. Crenshaw (University of California–LA and Columbia University)
Raju Das (York University, Canada)
Heidi Gottfried (Wayne State University)
Alfredo Saad-Filho (Queen's University Belfast)
Chizuko Ueno (University of Tokyo)
Sylvia Walby (Royal Holloway, University of London)

Sigmund Freud as a Critical Social Theorist

Psychoanalysis and the Neurotic in Contemporary Society

Edited by
Dustin J. Byrd and Seyed Javad Miri

Haymarket Books
Chicago, IL

First published in 2024 by Brill Academic Publishers, The Netherlands
© 2024 Koninklijke Brill NV, Leiden, The Netherlands

Published in paperback in 2025 by
Haymarket Books
P.O. Box 180165
Chicago, IL 60618
773-583-7884
www.haymarketbooks.org

ISBN: 979-8-88890-565-4

Distributed to the trade in the US through Consortium Book Sales and Distribution (www.cbsd.com) and internationally through Ingram Publisher Services International (www.ingramcontent.com).

This book was published with the generous support of Lannan Foundation, Wallace Action Fund, and the Marguerite Casey Foundation.

Special discounts are available for bulk purchases by organizations and institutions. Please call 773-583-7884 or email info@haymarketbooks.org for more information.

Cover design by Jamie Kerry and Ragina Johnson.

Printed in the United States.

Library of Congress Cataloging-in-Publication data is available.

This book is dedicated to all those who have mentored us over the course of decades. May we honor them by the work we do.

Contents

Notes on Contributors XI

Introduction 1
    Dustin J. Byrd and Seyed Javad Miri

PART 1
Reviving Freud

1   Exhuming the Freudian Corpus: On Freud as a Social and Cultural Theorist   21
    Howard L. Kaye

PART 2
Freud and the Frankfurt School

2   Freud's Psychology of Religion: The Frankfurt School, Determinate Negation, and Return to Religion   43
    Dustin J. Byrd

3   Adorno, Freud, and the Dialectic of the Individual and the Social   71
    Gregory Joseph Menillo

4   Marx and Freud, Horkheimer and Adorno: Beyond the Historical Gender Struggle   93
    Rudolf J. Siebert

PART 3
Freud and Religion

5   Critical Social Theory and Religion: Revisiting Sigmund Freud's Discourse on Religion   133
    Seyed Javad Miri

6   Black Power's Deification of the Son: A Freudian Reading of the Reverse Oedipal Relationship between Malcolm X and Elijah Muhammad   162
    Jimmy Butts

PART 4
Freud and the Political

7   Freud's Mass Psychology Today: Psychoanalysis, Politics, and Populism in the Age of Post-truth   185
    Yannis Stavrakakis

8   Freud, Marx, and the Structure of Freedom   208
    Michael J. Thompson

9   How to Conceive of the Unconscious and its Political Significance   240
    Fabio Molinari

PART 5
Freud, Morality, and the Death Drive

10 Beyond the Death-Drive: Psychoanalysis and Social Critique   269
    Delia Popa and Iaan Reynolds

11 "I Know Very Well, but Nevertheless": Moral Immaturity of the 21st Century Humanitarian Witness   296
    Mlado Ivanovic

12 Freud and the Problem of Moral Agency   321
    Alfred I. Tauber

13 "No One Believes in His Own Death." On More and Less Necessary Illusions   350
    Ulrike Kistner

14 Killing in the Name of the Father: Freud and René Girard on the Question of Desire   364
    Clint Jones

PART 6
Freud, Neo-freudians, and Beyond

15 Psychoanalysis and the American Intellectual   385
    Eli Zaretsky

16 A Freudian Analysis of the Competing Groups on Uncorroborated Allegations of Child Sexual Abuse   407
    Michael Naughton

17 No Heart to Feel, No Soul to Steal: Necrophilia and Mass Shootings in America   438
    Joan Braune

18 Freud as a Mythmaker, Scientist, and Critical Social Theorist   469
    Francesco Ranci

19 Psychodynamics and the Public Spheres: Class, Identity, and the Political   502
    Lauren Langman

Index   531

Notes on Contributors

Joan Braune
Ph.D., is Lecturer in Philosophy and Instructor in the Doctoral Program in Leadership Studies at Gonzaga University in Spokane, Washington, USA. Her research lies in Frankfurt School Critical Theory and (Anti)fascism Studies. In addition to numerous shorter works, she has published two books on socialist humanist philosopher and psychoanalyst Erich Fromm's critical theory, and more recently two books on countering fascism: *Understanding and Countering Fascist Movements: From Void to Hope* (Routledge 2024), and the co-edited volume *The Ethics of Researching the Far Right: Critical Approaches and Reflections* (Manchester University Press 2024). She is an activist in addition to her scholarship and a frequently invited speaker to help communities address the threat posed by hate groups. She also serves on the Editorial Board of the *Journal of Hate Studies*.

Jimmy Butts
is a Black Studies scholar and Assistant Professor of African American History at Trinity University. He specializes in Africana history, religion, critical theory, and Malcolm X Studies. His work has been published in various Black Studies journals. The most recent publication is *The Suppression and Liberation of Malcolm's Personal Agency: Malcolm X and His Religio-Racial Understanding of White People* at the *Journal of Black Studies*. His current project highlights Malcolm X as a central figure in the construction of an Africana Critical Theory of Religion.

Dustin J. Byrd
Ph.D. (2017), Michigan State University, is Professor of Philosophy and Religious Studies at The University of Olivet. He is the Founder and Co-Director of the Institute for Critical Social Theory, and the Editor-in-Chief of Ekpyrosis Press. He has published numerous monographs, edited volumes, and articles of the subjects of Psychoanalysis, political philosophy, Critical Theory, and the Critical Theory of Religion. His latest books include: *Syed Hussein Alatas and Critical Social Theory: Decolonizing the Captive Mind,* co-edited with Seyed Javad Miri (Brill 2022); *The Dark Charisma of Donald Trump: Political Psychology and the MAGA Movement* (Ekpyrosis Press 2023); *The Frankfurt School and the Dialectics of Religion: Translating Critical Faith into Critical Theory* (Ekpyrosis Press 2020), *The Critique of Religion and Religion's Critique: On Dialectical Religiology* (Brill

2020), and *Frantz Fanon and Emancipatory Social Theory: A View from the Wretched*, co-Edited with Seyed Javad Miri (Brill 2020). www.dustinjbyrd.org.

Mlado Ivanovic
is an Associate Professor in the Department of Philosophy at Northern Michigan University. His research interests are situated within the intellectual tradition of the Frankfurt School and Poststructuralism, primarily the works of Theodor W. Adorno, Walter Benjamin, and Michel Foucault. His academic focus is currently on moral, political, and environmental challenges tied with the forceful displacement and migration of people, particularly by examining both the socio-historical and political contexts of human vulnerability and exclusion. Mlado was awarded his Ph.D. from the Department of Philosophy at Michigan State University. He has published on humanitarianism, refugees, social and global justice, and human right and the media. He is currently working on a manuscript dealing with the epistemic, moral, and political underpinnings of forceful displacement and humanitarian management of displaced peoples, and their inclusion in Western societies. In addition to his academic commitments, Dr. Ivanovic is also engaged with humanitarian Non-Profit and Non-Governmental communities in Serbia, Greece, and Turkey, and serves as an advisor for various student organizations in Michigan that deal with humanitarianism and social justice. He is one of the directors of the Michigan based NGO, "Refugee Outreach Collective."

Clint Jones
is an instructor of philosophy at Capital University in Columbus, OH. Although he teaches a wide range of classes, his primary research interests are at the intersections of critical social theory (especially Marx, Freud, and Marcuse), religion, popular culture, environmental theory, and utopianism. His recent published works include chapters on *Watchmen and Theology*, *Joker and Philosophy*, *Mad Max and Philosophy*, and the fairytale BlueBeard for *The Philosophical Power of Fairy Tales from Around the World*. His most recent books are edited volumes, *Contemporary Cowboys* (Lexington Books) and a forthcoming title, *Terrorism in Youth Popular Culture* (Lexington Books).

Howard L. Kaye
is Professor of Sociology, Emeritus at Franklin and Marshall College, in Lancaster, PA. He is the author of *The Social Meaning of Modern Biology: From Social Darwinism to Sociobiology* (Yale, 1986; Routledge, 1997) and *Freud as a Social and Cultural Theorist: On Human Nature and the Civilizing Process* (Routledge, 2019)

Ulrike Kistner

is Professor Emerita in the Department of Philosophy at the University of Pretoria. Her teaching and research activities are focused on social theory, psychoanalytic theory, and political philosophy. She has also translated texts from these fields – among others, the first edition of Freud's *Three Essays on a Theory of Sexuality*.

Lauren Langman

is a professor emeritus of sociology at Loyola University of Chicago. He received his Ph.D. from the University of Chicago and analytic training at the Chicago Institute for Psychoanalysis. He has long worked in the Hegelian-Marxist tradition of the Frankfurt School of Critical Theory, especially nationalism and reactionary movements, relationships between culture, identity, and politics/political movements He is the past chair of Marxist Sociology of the American Sociological Assassination where he recently received the Lifetime Achievement Award. In this past, he was the President of Alienation Research and Theory, Research Committee 36, of the International Sociological. He was a founding member and board member of the Global Studies Association, the International Herbert Marcuse Society, and the North American Erich Fromm Society. His recent publications deal with globalization, alienation, global justice movements, the right-wing, the body, nationalism, and national character. His publications include: *The Evolution of Alienation: Trauma, Promise, and the Millennium* with Devorah Kalekin-Fishman; *Alienation and Carnivalization of Society* with Jerome Braun, and a special issue of *Current Sociology* on the Arab Spring, the Indignados and Occupy. His latest books are on American Character (with George Lundskow), *God, Guns, Gold and Glory* (Brill/Haymarket), and *Twenty-First Century Inequality and Capitalism: Marx, Piketty and beyond*, with David A. Smith (Brill). He is on several editorial boards, including *Critical Sociology*, *Current Perspectives in Social Theory*, and *Populism*.

Gregory Joseph Menillo

holds a PhD in music composition from the CUNY Graduate Center where he additionally specialized in the aesthetic theory of Theodor W. Adorno. He is continuing his research on Adorno, aesthetics, and modernism as a doctoral student in philosophy at Stony Brook University. He has contributed to *How to Critique Authoritarian Populism: Methodologies of the Frankfurt School,* edited by Jeremiah Morelock (Brill: 2021), and currently maintains an active composition schedule. His music has been performed by the Argento New Music Project, the Da Capo Chamber Players, Either/Or, the Mivos Quartet, and others. He lives in Queens, New York, and is an Adjunct Assistant Professor of Music at Lehman College.

Seyed Javad Miri
Ph.D. is a Swedish-Iranian sociologist, public intellectual and professor of sociology at the Institute for Humanities and Cultural Studies in Tehran-Iran. He is known for his expertise on social theory and Islamic and critical thinkers. He is also the Co-Director of the Institute for Critical Social Theory. He has published over 100 books in English, Persian and Swedish. His recent publications are *Ali Shariati: Critical Theory and the Struggle for Decolonization* and *Socio-Analysis: A Theory on Emancipation and Pain* (in Persian).

Fabio Molinari
received his PhD from the University of Urbino, Italy. He has been a visiting scholar at the Ruhr-Universität Bochum, and his research interests combine German classical philosophy, psychoanalysis, critical theory, and the philosophical history of concepts, particularly psychological and psychoanalytic ones. Among his recent publications are *Quale inconscio per quale politica?* (What Unconscious for which Politics?) and *Memoria, individuo e Mondo. Percorsi tra Leibniz e Hegel* (Memory, Individual and World. Paths between Leibniz and Hegel).

Michael Naughton
Ph.D. is a Reader in Sociology and Law across the Law School and the School of Sociology, Politics and International Studies (SPAIS) at the University of Bristol, UK. He has researched and written extensively on the limitations and/or outright failings of the criminal justice system. His researches have emphasized the distinction between 'miscarriages of justice' and the wrongful conviction and/or imprisonment of factually innocent victims. He has researched the likely scale, causes and forms of harm associated with miscarriages of justice and wrongful convictions. He has highlighted how the Parole Board, the criminal appeals system and the Criminal Cases Review Commission (CCRC) can also fail innocent victims of wrongful convictions. Michael is known for pioneering the introduction of a total of 36 innocence projects into UK universities, which see students working on alleged wrongful conviction cases to determine their truthfulness or otherwise, and for his efforts to effect changes to the criminal justice system so that innocent victims are guaranteed to be able to make progress through the prison system to release and to overturn their wrongful convictions when they occur. Dr Naughton is author or sole editor of four books: *The Innocent and the Criminal Justice System* (2013, Palgrave

Macmillan); *Claims of Innocence: An introduction to wrongful convictions and how they might be challenged* (2010, University of Bristol. with Tan, G.); *The Criminal Cases Review Commission: Hope for the Innocent?* (2009, Palgrave Macmillan); and, *Rethinking Miscarriages of Justice: Beyond the tip of the 'iceberg'* (2007, Palgrave Macmillan). In addition, he has over 80 further publications in peer-reviewed academic journals, edited book collections, professional journals and broadsheet newspapers.

Délia Popa
is an Associate Professor of Philosophy at Villanova University, where she teaches courses on contemporary phenomenology, philosophy of film and literature, and psychoanalysis. She is the author of *Apparence et réalité. Phénoménologie et psychologie de l'imagination* (Olms, 2012) and co-editor of *La portée pratique de la phénoménologie. Normativité, critique sociale et psychopathologie* (2014), *Approches phénoménologiques de l'inconscient* (2015) and *Describing the Unconscious. Phenomenological Perspectives on the Subject of Psychoanalysis* (2020). She co-edited the special issues "Gestures" of *Studia Phaenomenologica* and "Africana Philosophy" of *Symposium. The Canadian Journal of Continental Philosophy* (2022) and published several articles on the relationship between imagination and political responsibility. Her current research focuses on the problem of becoming a stranger, social exclusion and transclass experiences, with a special interest in the project of a feminist phenomenology of sexual difference.

Francesco Ranci
(Milano, Italy, 1964) earned a doctorate in Sociology at the University of Milano, Italy, and is a member of the editorial staff of "Methodologia – Pensiero Linguaggio Modelli/ Thought Language Models" (www.methodologia.it). In 2010, he moved to the United States of America where he taught at several colleges, including Naugatuck Valley Community College (Waterbury and Danbury, CT), Sacred Heart University (Fairfield, CT), Berkeley College (Manhattan and White Plains), UCONN (Stamford and Waterbuty, CT), and The College of New Rochelle. His recent publications include F. Ranci (2021) "The Unfinished Business of Erving Goffman: From Marginalization Up Towards the Elusive Center of American Sociology." The American Sociologist 52, (May 2021): 390–419; and F. Ranci (2021) "An Alternative to Oppressive Epistemology: the 'Methodological-Operational' View." *GNOSI: An Interdisciplinary Journal of Human Theory and Praxis* 4, no. 3 (2021): 42–57. In Italian, with Felice Accame, he recently co-authored a book about the philosophical origin of Italian grammatical categories (Felice Accame e Francesco Ranci, *I nomi delle categorie*

grammaticali, Milano, Biblion Edizioni, 2023); he wrote a Preface to Silvio Ceccato's book, *La mente vista da un cibernetico*, originally published in 1972 (Silvio Ceccato, *La mente vista da un cibernetico*, Milano, Mimesis, 2017); and he published an Italian translation of Erving Goffman's first two publications (*Symbols of Class Status*, 1951, and *On Cooling the Mark Out*, 1952), together with an introductory essay (F. Ranci, *Simboli di appartenenza a una classe sociale e Sul rinfrescare le idee al pollo*, Milano, Biblion Edizioni, 2016).

Iaan Reynolds

is Assistant Professor in Utah Valley University's Department of Philosophy & Humanities, where he teaches courses in social and political philosophy, critical theory, and continental philosophy. His research concerns the role of concepts of education and development in social and political thought, including in the Frankfurt School and the broader Marxist tradition. His book, *Education for Political Life: Critique, Theory, and Practice in Karl Mannheim's Sociology of Knowledge*, was published by Rowman & Littlefield in 2023. He has recently published articles in *Theory & Event*, *History of the Human Sciences*, *Social Epistemology*, and *Radical Philosophy Review*, and he currently serves as a member of the Radical Philosophy Association's advisory board.

Rudolf J. Siebert

is Professor Emeritus of Religion and Society, Western Michigan University, where he taught for over fifty years. He grew up under fascism in Frankfurt am Main, Germany, where he was part of a Catholic anti-fascism young group. He participated in World War II. With his friends and colleagues, Siebert created the Critical Theory of Religion and Society, or "Dialectical Religiology," based on the Frankfurt School's Critical Theory of Society. He has published over 30 books and over 500 articles on various issues, including the Frankfurt School, Philosophy of Religion, Psychology of Religion, etc. He was the founder and director of the Center for Humanistic Future Studies at Western Michigan University; founder and director of the international course on the "Future of Religion" in the Inter-University Center in Dubrovnik, Croatia, and the founder and director of the international course on "Religion in Civil Society" in Yalta, Ukraine. Siebert's previous works include: the three-volume *Manifesto of the Critical Theory of Society and Religion: The Wholly Other, Liberation, Happiness, and the Rescue of the Hopeless* (Brill 2010); *The Critical Theory of Religion: Frankfurt School* (The Scarecrow Press 2001), and *Hegel and the Critical Theory of Religion* (Ekpyrosis Press 2021).

Yannis Stavrakakis studied political science at Panteion University (Athens) and received his MA degree from the Ideology and Discourse Analysis Programme at the University of Essex, where he also completed his PhD. He has worked at the Universities of Essex and Nottingham before taking up a position at the Aristotle University of Thessaloniki in 2007, where he is currently directing the Postgraduate Programme in Political Theory and the Laboratory for the Study of Democracy (both at the School of Political Sciences). His research primarily focuses on contemporary political theory (with emphasis on psychoanalytic and post-structuralist approaches) and on the analysis of ideology and discourse in late modern societies (with emphasis on populism and anti-populism, environmentalism, post-democracy and the role of artistic practices). He is the author of *Lacan and the Political* (London: Routledge, 1999), *The Lacanian Left* (Edinburgh: Edinburgh University Press/Albany: SUNY Press, 2007), and *Populist Discourse: Recasting Populism Research* (New York: Routledge 2024), editor of the *Routledge Handbook of Psychoanalytic Political Theory* (New York: Routledge, 2020) and co-editor of *Discourse Theory and Political Analysis* (Manchester: Manchester University Press, 2000), *Lacan & Science* (London: Karnac, 2002), *Aspects of Censorship in Greece* (Athens: Nefeli, 2008), *The Political in Contemporary Art* (Athens: Ekkremes, 2008) and the *Research Handbook on Populism* (Cheltenham: Edward Elgar, 2024). He has served two consecutive terms as vice-president of the Hellenic Political Science Association and has been Leverhulme Visiting Professor at Queen Mary University of London (2014–5) and Visiting Professor at the Scuola Normale Superiore in Florence (2019). He was one of the founding co-conveners of the Populism Specialist Group of the Political Studies Association (UK) and since 2014 he is directing the POPULISMUS Observatory: www.populismus.gr.

Alfred I. Tauber is Zoltan Kohn Professor *emeritus* of Medicine, Professor *emeritus* of Philosophy, and former Director of the Center for Philosophy and History of Science at Boston University. His studies of Freud's thought have focused on the ethics of psychoanalytic inquiry and the philosophy of mind framing psychoanalysis: Major works include, *Freud, the Reluctant Philosopher* (Princeton 2010), *Requiem for the Ego: Freud and the Origins of Postmodernism* (Stanford 2013) and *William James and Sigmund Freud on the Mind. Saving Subjectivity* (Routledge 2025)

Michael J. Thompson
is Professor of Political Theory at William Paterson University and a practicing psychoanalyst in New York City. He is the author of numerous books the most recent of which include: *The Specter of Babel: A Reconstruction of Political Judgment* (SUNY, 2020), *Twilight of the Self: The Decline of the Individual in Late Capitalism* (Stanford, 2022), and *Descent of the Dialectic: Phronetic Criticism in an Age of Nihilism* (Routledge, 2024).

Eli Zaretsky
is Professor of History at The New School for Social Research. His interests are in twentieth century cultural history, the theory and history of capitalism (especially its social and cultural dimensions), and the history of the family. His most recent book is *Political Freud,* published in 2017 by Columbia University Press. His earlier works include *Why America Needs a Left: A Historical Argument* (Wiley 2013), *Secrets of the Soul: A Social and Cultural History of Psychoanalysis* (Vintage 2005), and *Capitalism, the Family, and Personal Life* (Harper & Row, 1976). He is currently writing a book entitled, *The Mass Psychology of Liberalism*.

Introduction

Dustin J. Byrd and Seyed Javad Miri

The 2020s are witnessing a resurgence of interest in both Sigmund Freud and Psychoanalysis. While interest in Freud never seems to completely evaporate – witnessed by how many books about him are published each year – it does ebb-and-flow, both in academia and in the broader world of psychology.[1] No matter how often Freud's detractors decry him to a be a "charlatan," a "myth-maker," and a wildly speculative and irresponsible theorist as opposed to a serious man of scientific, sociological, and philosophical thought, people continue to "return to Freud," especially when world events take chaotic turns, inevitably increasing socially-induced anxiety, feelings of alienation, as well as severe disillusionment with life, both personal and social. Indeed, some seem to find the "oceanic feeling" that Freud once rejected by reading Freud himself, as if they're having an enlightenment experience while watching Freud tear away the ideological veils that cover the complex – and bleak – realities of the human condition.[2] In that sense, he has become a means through which individuals reconnect to what is important in life: the search from truth and the meaningful life that comes with that search.[3] In many ways, Psychoanalysis, not only as a method but also through the content of Freud's philosophy, presupposes Viktor Frankl's logotherapy; finding meaning in a world that too often feels meaningless is already a Freudian endeavor.

Indicative of this "return to Freud" trend, Psychoanalysis has once again made it to the big screen. In 2024, the film *Freud's Last Session*, based on Mark St. Germain's stage play of the same name, was released in the United States. While it was not a typical Hollywood blockbuster, it was generally well-received

---

1 Hannah Zeavin, "Psychoanalysis has Returned: Why 2023 brought a new Freud Revival." *The Guardian*, December 29, 2023, https://www.theguardian.com/us-news/2023/dec/29/freuds-last-session-sigmund-freud-film-psychoanalysis.
2 The "oceanic feeling" comes from a letter to Freud from Romain Rolland, a French dramatist and mystic, who thought religion delivered a "sensation of eternity" and a feeling of "being one with the external world as a whole." Freud discusses the "oceanic feeling" both in *The Future of an Illusion* and *Civilization and its Discontents*. See Sigmund Freud, *The Standard Edition of the Complete Psychological Works of Sigmund Freud*, trans. James Strachey (London: The Hogarth Press, 1961).
3 Erich Fromm makes a similar argument regarding Freud's "search for truth" as being a tacit yet substantive form of religiosity in his essay, "Freud and Jung." See Erich Fromm, "Freud and Jung," in *Psychoanalysis and Religion* (New Haven: Yale University Press, 1978): 10–20.

by critics, as Sigmund Freud (played by Anthony Hopkins) sparred with C.S. Lewis (Matthew Goode) over issues of God, religion, science, theodicy, suffering, sexual norms, and war trauma. While some critics found the film's flimsy regarding Freudian thought, the movie is sure to contribute to the current interest in Freud and his "art and science" of Psychoanalysis.[4] In the film, C.S. Lewis seemed at times unsure of his Christian convictions, having once been an atheist and remains afflicted by PTSD and haunted by the theodicy problem, while Freud remained resolute despite the obvious suffering he experienced with his advanced cancer, exile, and the prospect of death drawing near. Despite their mutual traumas, Freud's psychoanalytic worldview seemed to provide him with a certain level of psychological stability, which is lacking in C.S. Lewis, who in many ways symbolizes Christianity and Christian faith in our modern post-Death-of-God societies.

Freud's Last Session was preceded by the German film, *The Tobacconist* (*Der Trafikant*), directed by Nikolaus Leytner, which depicted a young man's friendship with Freud (played by Bruno Ganz). In this 2018 film, Freud helps his young friend's love-life amidst the Austrian *Anschluss*. Centered around Freud's passion for cigars, this was another "Freudian film" that was light on Freudian thought beyond the typical clichés about sex and dreams but was nevertheless a sympathetic depiction of Freud in the second to last chapter of his life. It too depicted Freud as a resolute theorist in an age of uncertainty, someone who's life and work prepared him for both the personal and social afflictions that he experienced during a troubled time in Europe's history.

Off the big screen, 2020 saw the 8-part Netflix series entitled, *Freud,* which depicts a young Freud in 1886, still under the spell of the French neurologist, Jean-Martin Charcot (1825–1893) and his use of hypnosis to treat "hysteria." In this series, Freud investigates a series of bizarre crimes that lead all the way to Emperor Franz Josef and Crown Prince Rudolf, which are shrouded in occult practices. While the series is a psychological thriller, and therefore less explicitly about Psychoanalysis (as in 1886 Freud had yet to join with Josef Breuer and develop the "talking cure"), it does introduce the idea that individuals are partially determined by their unconscious, and that there is world of unexplainable psychological phenomenon that only with Psychoanalysis did we begin to understand.

A year prior to Netflix's *Freud,* the British-Austrian TV series, *Vienna Blood,* aired on BBC Two. Based on the *Liebermann* novels by Frank Tallis, this series tells the story of Max Liebermann (played by Matthew Beard), a medical doctor

---

4 Zeavin, "Psychoanalysis has Returned: Why 2023 brought a new Freud Revival".

and devoted student of Sigmund Freud, who investigates numerous murders through psychoanalytic means. Here too an underlying stream of thought is that Psychoanalysis can give us access to the inner workings of the human psyche that was unavailable before Freud, and that Psychoanalysis can reveal unconscious motivations for violent crimes. Thus, through Freudian thought, Liebermann supplies the investigations of Detective Oskar Reinhardt (Jürgen Maurer) with insights into the psychological motives for the crimes committed in each episode.[5]

This isn't the first time that "Freud mania" hit the big screen. Hannah Zeavin, a historian of psychology, reminds us that in the 1920s, Hollywood attempted to woo Freud into being a film consultant, which he firmly declined, and subsequently urged all other psychoanalysts to follow his example.[6] Freud was not only skeptical of Hollywood, but it is also well documented that he detested mercantile America as a whole. It is no wonder that the artform most associated with America, i.e., Hollywood film, would not interest him. Not only would it trivialize Psychoanalysis, but it would put it to use within the entertainment industry. However, despite Freud's objections, the film industry did not sever their ties with Psychoanalysis nor with Freud. Freud first biographical film, entitled *Freud: The Secret Passion,* starring Montgomery Clift, appeared in 1962, long after psychoanalytic thought had been incorporated into numerous films, including the dream sequence in Alfred Hitchcock's 1945 psychological thriller, *Spellbound.* Regardless of what Freud thought of American film and

---

5 Other recent films that center around Freud or Psychoanalysis include *A Dangerous Method* (2011), which features the tensions between and ultimate breakup of Sigmund Freud (Viggo Mortensen) and Carl G. Jung (Michael Fassbender). 2007 saw Pinchas Perry's film *When Nietzsche Wept*, wherein Freud (Jamie Elman) works with Dr. Josef Breuer to overcome his attachments to his former patient, Bertha Pappenheim, famously referred to by Freud as "Anna O." Simultaneously, Breuer is providing psychological care for the philosopher Friedrich Nietzsche as well as succumbing to an infatuation with Lou Andreas-Salome, whom Nietzsche himself was also infatuated. Freud's role is secondary in this film, but he represents the stable, rational, and clear-sighted analyst to the chaotic, phrenetic, neurotic lives of Breuer, Nietzsche, and Andreas-Salome. In 2002, the British filmmaker Adam Curtis released his 4-part documentary *Century of Self,* which chronicled the ways in which Psychoanalysis was used by Sigmund Freud's nephew, Edward Bernays, to create "public relations." Curtis also documents how Psychoanalysis became engrained in Western culture, especially through consumerism, commodification, marketing, pathological egoism, and political psychology. In 2022, the film *Adieu, Lacan,* directed by Richard Ledes, was also released, which depicts the French Neo-Freudian Jacque Lacan (David Patrick Kelly) within a psychotherapy session with a Brazilian woman who is ambivalent about her therapy; she both specifically sought out Lacan for his help and simultaneously doubts that he can help her.

6 Zeavin, "Psychoanalysis has Returned: Why 2023 brought a new Freud Revival".

the entertainment industry, he and Psychoanalysis would routinely find their way onto the big screen, thus introducing Freud and Psychoanalysis to wider audiences.

To investigate what underlying socio-psychological realities make such films about Freud and Psychoanalysis so appealing at this present time is an endeavor that should be contemplated, as there seems to be an acknowledgement that "something is missing" in modern life that impels many to seek answers in the psychoanalytic realm.[7]

1   Return to Philosophical Freud

Modern philosophers, following in the footsteps of the Frankfurt School and the Lacanian philosopher, Slavoj Žižek, have taken a renewed interest in Psychoanalysis as a means to interrogate an ever-growing dysfunctional world, the maladies of their societies, and the populist movements that are currently threatening the existence of Western democracies. Indeed, the latter sparked many philosophers and social scientists to return to Freud's 1921 *Group Psychology and the Analysis of the Ego* (*Massenpsychologie und Ich-Analyse*) in order to shed light on the nature of the socio-psychological dynamics that were at work in these revolts against the current neoliberal conditions, especially via right-wing authoritarian populism.[8] I myself drew on Freud's understanding of mass psychology when writing my 2023 book, *The Dark Charisma of Donald Trump: Political Psychology and the MAGA Movement*, wherein I attempted to understand why someone with Donald Trump's psychological profile (what I call "Dark Charisma") would be so seductive to millions of culturally alienated and politically aggrieved White Americans.[9] Freud, as well as the Frankfurt School's use of Freud's work, was indispensable in formulating my arguments, even if they had to be supplemented by later studies in personality psychology, social psychology, rhetorical analysis, etc.

At large, Psychoanalytic Political Theory, rooted in Freudian thought, is increasingly developing complex categories, concepts, and principles through

---

7 Jürgen Habermas et al, *An Awareness that Something is Missing: Faith and Reason in a Post-Secular Age,* trans. Ciaran Cronin (Cambridge: Polity Press, 2010).

8 Sigmund Freud, *Group Psychology and the Analysis of the Ego,* trans. James Strachey, in *The Standard Edition of the Complete Psychological Works of Sigmund Freud,* Vol. 18 (London: The Hogarth Press, 1955): 67–143.

9 Dustin J. Byrd, *The Dark Charisma of Donald Trump: Political Psychology and the MAGA Movement* (Kalamazoo: Ekpyrosis Press, 2023).

which social theorists analyze socio-political phenomenon.[10] Many psychoanalytic institutes now offer training programs for scholars who wish to study Psychoanalysis not as a means of becoming psychotherapists, but as a means of incorporating psychoanalytic theory into their political philosophies and social analyses. Additionally, Nick Romeo, writing for *The New Yorker*, profiled the movement of philosophers becoming therapists.[11] Dubbing it the "philosophical-counselling movement," Romeo documents the ways in which philosophy – the 2,500-year-old (in the West) practice of contemplation on the nature of everything – has saturated psychoanalytic practice, thus enriching analysand's experience and connection with their therapist and giving them new ways to think metaphysically, soteriologically, ethically, axiologically, and existentially. In an age of great psychological need, it is becoming increasingly apparent that a coalition of Psychoanalysis and traditional Western philosophy can contribute to the well-being of the individual and the collective within a society that too often creates chronic mental illness. Whether this form of philosophical Psychoanalysis creates malcontent with society-as-it-is within the analysand, or whether it reconciles them to the dysgenic status quo, has yet to be determined. Either way, in this movement Philosophy and Psychoanalysis are inter-penetrating each other, producing a hybrid form of therapy that draws upon the great philosophers of the Western philosophical canon to supplement traditional psychotherapy.

Nevertheless, the adoption of Psychoanalysis into other disciplines and areas of expertise is not without controversy. Much like Philosophy and Sociology, Psychoanalysis has been recruited into "radical" politics and has thus been utilized to understand the long and dark legacy of colonialism, racism, capitalist exploitation, gender antagonisms, and class warfare. Along this vein of social-psychoanalytic thought comes the new magazine, *Parapraxis,* which seeks to "uncover the psychosocial dimension of our lives – investigating social, political, and personal issues in relation to violence and conflict, gender and sexuality, racism and diasporic experience, and care and welfare."[12] Psychologically ecumenical, and filled with articles penetrating into the deepest of social ills, conflicts, and social neuroses, which are of special interest

---

10 See Yannis Stavrakakis, ed. *Routledge Handbook of Psychoanalytic Political Theory* (New York: Routledge, 2020).

11 Nick Romeo, "When Philosophers Become Therapists: The Philosophical-Counseling Movement aims to apply Heady Logical Insights to Daily Life," *The New Yorker,* December 23, 2023, https://www.newyorker.com/culture/annals-of-inquiry/when-philosophers-become-therapists.

12 Parapraxis, "About," *Parapraxis Magazine,* https://www.parapraxismagazine.com/about.

to the socially conscious psychoanalytic Left, *Parapraxis* claims it is "hitching a ride to society's ongoing return to Sigmund Freud in the twenty-first century," a ride that is sure to be filled with pitfalls, setbacks, and extreme highs, as psychoanalytic thought ventures into the *kulturkampf* of the new and already extremely fractured age. No doubt *Parapraxis* will contribute to the "radicalization" of psychoanalysis, taking it out of the safe clinical space and into the political arena, wherein civil society attempts to hammers out its irreconcilable demands and imperatives.

An integral part of this radicalization of psychoanalysis is the "decolonization" movement, which seeks to identify, critique, and ultimately dissolve the residue of colonial logic and domination within a variety of academic fields, political structures, and societies at large. It has benefitted much from psychoanalytic insights into how mass psychology functions within subject populations. Amidst this turn to radical emancipatory politics, Lara and Stephen Sheehi's book, *Psychoanalysis under Occupation: Practicing Resistance in Palestine,* caused much controversy among those who objected to the application of Psychoanalysis – which is often understood to be intimately connected to Jewish life and culture – to the problems of Palestinians living under Israeli occupation.[13] Lara Sheehi, being influenced by left-wing anti-colonial thought, has challenged many of her psychoanalytic colleagues to see the need to "politicize" psychoanalysis, i.e., to let psychoanalytic thought apply its insights into the most vexing of socio-political problems: class, gender, race, and as always, capitalism and colonialism. Much like those who wish to interrogate Psychoanalysis' historic blindness on issues of race and racism, this "new model" of socially-conscious Psychoanalysis is not uniformly welcomed within the discipline.[14] For many more traditional psychoanalysts, especially those worried about the reputation of the discipline, such politicized thought could undermine Psychoanalysis' neutrality, its ability to remain "scientific," not to mention the possibility that it could lose its "impartiality" as the result of being saturated by partisan politics.

---

13   Oliver Conroy, "Inside the war tearing Psychoanalysis apart: 'The most hatred I've ever witnessed,'" *The Guardian,* June 16, 2023, https://www.theguardian.com/education/2023/jun/16/george-washington-university-professor-antisemitism-palestine-dc.

14   Conroy, "Inside the war tearing Psychoanalysis apart." Also see the documentary, *Black Psychoanalysts Speak* (Psychoanalytic Electronic Publishing, Inc., 2020) https://www.youtube.com/watch?v=N8-VIi7tb44. Also see the documentary, *Psychoanalysis in El Barrio,* produced by Christopher Christian, Richard Reichbart, and Michael Moskowitz, and directed by Basia Winograd (2016). https://pep-web.org/browse/document/pepgrantvs.001.0010a.

While Freud was known to ruffle the proverbial feathers of the Bourgeois Viennese society that he lived in, and later the entire West, the politicization of Psychoanalysis was simply too much for many conservative-minded psychoanalysts.[15] There continues to be a divide within the psychoanalytic community between those who are open to the "new model," wherein social ills, such as racism, gender inequality, class antagonisms, colonialization, etc., are interrogated by psychoanalytic means, and those who are comfortable keeping psychoanalysis safe within its self-imposed intellectual ghetto, where it can focus on the individual problem of the analysand, not the problems of society at large, which impinge on both analysands and the psychoanalytic community itself. While the prior seems new, in my opinion, it was not the method of Freud, as he, in his own time, applied psychoanalytic insights into the society around him. Thus, Psychoanalysis was not merely a means of psychotherapy, but a worldview that furnished conceptual tools through which the world could be interrogated. Therefore, it is not the socially conscious Psychoanalysis that transgresses the legacy of Freud, but rather those who have limited its application to individual therapy.

It is safe to say that not only is interest in Freud and Psychoanalysis growing, but it is also diversifying, both in terms of those seeking training as psychoanalysts and in the spheres of human life in which Psychoanalysis is utilized. Whether this is a fad that will eventually dissipate, or a trend that will fundamentally alter and cement the future of Psychoanalysis, its fate will most likely be determined within the first half of the 21st century, especially as artificial intelligence begins to make its way in human affairs.[16]

2 Anti-Freud Pathology

The problem with Sigmund Freud and Psychoanalysis goes beyond the divisions within the psychoanalytic community. Within that community, there is at least a tacit agreement on the importance of Freud as a founder of modern psychology, even if the community cannot agree on the engagements psychoanalysts should make regarding social problems. On the other hand, there are still many that simply deny the importance and validity of the work of Freud

---

15   Frank Tallis, *Mortal Secrets: Freud, Vienna, and the Discovery of the Modern Mind* (New York: St. Martin's Press, 2024).

16   For an excellent analysis of Artificial Intelligence from a psychoanalytic perspective, see Isabel Millar, *The Psychoanalysis of Artificial Intelligence* (London: Palgrave Macmillan, 2021).

and Psychoanalysis. While I was preparing the groundwork for this book, I spoke to many colleagues at a variety of institutions that were surprised I was working on Freud. I often heard reactions like, "we're still talking about Freud," or "what is there left to say about him," or "isn't he irrelevant?" As a Critical Theorist, their dismissive reactions puzzled me. Despite his faults, inconsistencies, and sometimes overly broad analyses, Freud remains an essential feature of the Frankfurt School's work, and my reading of Freud's corpus continues to spark psychoanalytically informed philosophical work. It seems to me that to toss out Freud at this point is to toss out a library of insights into the human condition exactly at the time when we are suffering from a poverty of understanding of the human condition within the 21st century. Thus, an abstract negation of Freud as opposed to a "determinate negation" (*Aufhaben*) appears to only further us from our existentialist goals.

This type of reflexive dismissiveness of Freud, what Frank Tallis calls "Freud-bashing," was on display at a conference I attended at the University of Oxford in 2023.[17] In one of our sessions, we were discussing the vexing issue of "working through the past" (*Vergangenheitsbewältigung*) as it relates to Germany's struggle to deal with its Nazi past. From a psychoanalytic perspective, I argued that there was an important difference between *understanding* the Shoah (Holocaust) and morally committing oneself to never allowing it to happen again to anyone, and the inculcation of an extreme form of pathological guilt within each generation of Germans, which I likened to "inter-generational tyranny" and "self-inflicted inter-generational trauma." A form of pathological guilt that is passed on to each generation doesn't help German society overcome (not forget) the crimes of their past, but rather locks the younger generations into a form of unwarranted ethnomasochism that will guarantee that German society today and in the future will view contemporary events in a morally distorted way, i.e., the fear of looking like Germany "invaded" the East again if the government helped Ukraine defend itself against Russian aggression (2022–2024); that Germany would unquestionably come to the moral defense of Israel (and the far-right Likud Prime Minister, Benjamin Netanyahu) regardless of Israel's brutality against Palestinians, even when Israel was credibly accused of engaging in genocide by South Africa and numerous other countries.[18] The distorted lenses in which much of German society and government saw the

---

17 Tallis, *Mortal Secrets*, 1.
18 Amnesty International, "Israel must comply with key ICJ ruling ordering it do all in its power to prevent genocide against Palestinians in Gaza," January 26, 2024, https://www.amnesty.org/en/latest/news/2024/01/israel-must-comply-with-key-icj-ruling-ordering-it-do-all-in-its-power-to-prevent-genocide-against-palestinians-in-gaza/.

moral component in these conflicts was partially due to the morally disfiguration that is the result of an inherited pathological guilt complex, as opposed to a rational and psychoanalytic "working through the past."[19]

After our discussion on German guilt, a young German scholar approached me in New College's front Quad and rebuked me for my "anti-German" critique. She said, "I was greatly offended by what you had to say about Germany and guilt. *We are not guilty enough.* Even those of us who were not alive during the Holocaust bear responsibility for the crimes against the Jews. *We too are guilty.*" At first, I was taken aback; the idea that young Germans born in the late 20th and/or early 21st century – some from immigrant families – must bear the guilt of their forefathers just seemed odd, misplaced, even grossly masochistic, like a form of psychological violence wielded upon the innocent for the mere sake of dispersing the particularities of historical guilt. The misguided adoption of *guilt* for what one *did not do* can easily turn into shame for *what one is*: *A German* – which no German (outside of immigrants) chose to be, but rather found themselves being by virtue of birth, parentage, etc. This moral masochism, in my estimation, is a dangerous space to inhabit for young adults just learning to navigate the world and finding their place in it. How psychologically damaging must it be to learn about the murderous rampage of your forefathers, only to be told that you are also *personally* responsible for their industrialized mass murder, even when you weren't alive to protest it – you, the innocent, simply inherited the guilt of the fathers. Unlike the actual perpetrators of the genocide, one today simply finds oneself condemned for history's bloody slaughterbench. It is certainly not the case that the Holocaust should be forgotten, buried safely under the sands of time. That too would be a misguided way of confronting Germany's ugly past. But it seems to me that intergenerational guilt, acting like a new "original sin" that distorts the German collective soul, is also the wrong approach when bearing responsibility for making the world free from such anti-Semitic hatred and violence (along with all other forms of prejudice, xenophobia, and bigotry). Those who were not Hitler's willing executioners should not be made to feel as if they were Hitler's willing executioners – let the guilty bear their own sins. As later generations, it is our task to learn from them, not to *be* them.

With deep respect to my German colleague, I retorted with the words, "You know, according to Freud," wherein I was promptly cut off. "You know what Freud said about women," she asked, "we do not have to listen to him." Again,

---

[19] See Theodor W. Adorno, "The Meaning of Working Through the Past," in *Can One Live After Auschwitz: A Philosophical Reader*, ed. Rolf Tiedemann. Trans. Rodney Livingstone and Others (Stanford, CA: Stanford University Press, 2003), 3–18.

I stood dumbfounded. It was not so much the discourse-avoidance tactics she took with me, but rather the arrogance of being able to silence Freud's entire corpus simply be *invoking* (not even arguing against) a context-dependent prejudice or an objectionable theory (possibly penis-envy), etc., that Freud may have held in his attempt to understand the complexities of the human psyche. Because of the shortcomings in one segment of his work, all his voluminous writings were thrown into the dustbin of history by her flippant statement: "we don't have to listen to him."[20] This wasn't the first time I heard someone feel that they had the authority to completely dismiss the work of another with nothing other than a simple remark. I remember an irate graduate student in my doctoral program at Michigan State University doing much the same with Georg W.F. Hegel. Halfway through the class, she protested having to read Hegel because of his misogynist statement that women were "not made for the higher sciences, for philosophy and certain artistic productions which require a universal element. Women may have insights, taste, and delicacy, but they do not possess the ideal."[21] Instead of arguing against Hegel utilizing Hegel's own philosophy, and proving him wrong (which he was), she simply chose to cancel him. At Oxford, it was happening again, but with Freud, and I was no more impressed than I was when I was in graduate school. It is a matter of historical fact that both Hegel and Freud modified their theories as they developed their theoretical systems of thought, but they too were subject to time and place. Had they been intellectuals in the 21st century, it is doubtful they would have maintained ideas more at home in the 18th and 19th centuries, just as the intellectuals of the 22nd century will find many of our ideas to be outdated and/or merely reflections of our own times. Historically contextualizing all theorists seems to be a rational practice, lest we fall into an irrational anachronistic critique.

As a Critical Theorist, political philosopher, steeped in psychoanalytic thought, I've been trained to think dialectically, through contradictions, and to engage in the logic of "determinate negation," wherein claims are taken seriously, evaluated for their ideological elements (in the Marxist sense of "ideology"), and transcended by preserving their truthfulness and negating their

---

20   Famously, Freud admitted to Marie Bonaparte that he didn't really understand women at all, saying, "The great question that has never been answered and which I have not yet been able to answer, despite my thirty years of research into the feminine soul, is 'What does a woman want?'" Sigmund Freud in Ernest Jones, *The Life and Work of Sigmund Freud: Years of Maturity 1901–1919* (New York: Basic Books, 1955), 421.

21   Georg W.F. Hegel, *Elements of the Philosophy of Right*, ed. Allen W. Wood (Cambridge: Cambridge University Press, 1991), 207.

falsity. What the young German scholar did, and many others I have spoken to regarding Freud continue to do, is engage in an "abstract negation" of Freud: the wholesale cancellation of his work, not because he is wrong in his entirety, but because some aspects of his thought prove to be offensive, mistaken, or outdated. In many ways, Freud is all those things: offensive, mistaken, and/or outdated, as nearly all thinkers of another age prove to be. Yet, as this collection of essays shows, Freud continues to be an invaluable source not only for psychotherapy, but also for psychoanalytic thought regarding socio-political and cultural issues. Freud's abundance of insights into the dynamics of the human psyche, both as individuals and collectives, not to mention the analytic tools, concepts, and ways in which his critiques of society undermine the dominant ideological narratives that we continue to perpetuate within the structures of neoliberalism, remain some of the most important reasons why we are still fascinated with him, and why philosophers, sociologists, and other academics continue to "return to Freud," as they are doing once again.

In 2022, I taught an undergraduate seminar on Sigmund Freud at The University of Olivet. The students and I focused on Freud's most famous four books regarding religion: *Totem and Taboo* (1913); The *Future of an Illusion* (1927); *Civilization and its Discontents* (1930), and *Moses and Monotheism* (1939). While many of the students were psychology majors, it was their first-time reading Freud in any systematic way. He was mentioned in their classes as the "father of psychology," the "man who started the discipline," etc., but no systematic attention to Freud or the work of neo-Freudians had ever been taught to the students. Like the German scholar, these students had absorbed what Freud got wrong (or assumed he got wrong), so he was easily dismissed as being passé in light of new positivistic forms of psychology and neurology, which in itself is the result of the very conservative trend to "medicalize" Psychoanalysis – a prospect that Freud himself wished to avoid.[22] Indeed, Freud was well aware of the scientific ambiguity of Psychoanalysis, stating, "I always envy the physicists and mathematicians who can stand on firm ground. I hover, so to speak, in the air. Mental events seem to be immeasurable and probably always will be so."[23]

---

22 See Sigmund Freud, *The Question of Lay Analysis*, in *The Standard Edition of the Complete Psychological Works of Sigmund Freud,* Vol 20, edited by James Strachey (London: The Hogarth Press, 1959). Freudian Psychoanalysis meets positivistic neuroscience in "neuropsychoanalysis," which is an interdisciplinary attempt to bring together materialistic studies of the brain and the thought/neuroses dynamics of the psyche. Freud was originally a neuroscientist but abandoned the discipline completely when he began to develop Psychoanalysis. We can only speculate as to what he would think to see the attempted reconciliation of these two trends in mental health studies.

23 Sigmund Freud in Ernest Jones, *The Life and work of Sigmund Freud*, 419.

In our Freud class, we spent a good deal discussing why such dismissiveness was pervasive among academic psychologists, why Psychoanalysis is often maligned by other mental health professionals, and why that it is such a loss to analysands, especially in an age of pharmacological "quick fixes," which address the individual's symptom but not their deeply embedded neuroses and detrimental character traits. While questions about the actual "historicity" of Freud's "primal horde" and the Egyptian identity of Moses certainly came up, we explored how to think psychoanalytically about the text, i.e., using Freud's methods to interrogate Freud and his work: what was Freud's latent message behind his manifest text? Do we read him literally, like the conservative Evangelicals do with the Bible, or do we look for more important latent, symbolic, and/or repressed meanings behind the words in Freud's text? Do we miss something important about Freud himself and the society he lived in when we read these four texts in a superficial way, or should we read such texts alongside an understanding of the historical context, pretext, and subtext in which they were written? Does Freud's critique of God, religion, religious institutions, the psychological exports of religion that address the psychological needs of man, and the illusionary/neurotic nature of religious beliefs, still hold water in our own post-secular age? What has been the psychological effect of desacralization and disenchantment on Western societies? Has it made us more just, more compassionate, more rational, as Freud would have thought? We've seen what man is capable of when he builds idols, either religious or secular. Not having religion saturate the Western world hasn't stopped Western man from being irrational, violent, and self-destructive, has it? Should we rethink Freud's critique of religion, as did many in the Frankfurt School, including the Neo-Freudian Erich Fromm, who saw core elements in religion as being worthy of preservation?[24] These and many other questions were contemplated, debated, and discussed in our seminar, and the students experienced firsthand the depth of thought that can be produced when engaging with Freud's texts. Out of this intensive intellectual labor came a new appreciation for Freud's psycho-philosophical works, one that their positivistic psychology instructors seemingly hoped to avoid.

---

24 Dustin J. Byrd, *The Frankfurt School and the Dialectics of Religion* (Kalamazoo: Ekpyrosis Press, 2020), 45–53.

3   The Persistence of Freud

This volume is a rebuke of the idea that we can simply assign Freud and Psychoanalysis to the dustbin of history. As the reader will see, the authors in this volume are varied in their disciplines and have utilized Freudian thought from a multitude of angles. As such, this book does not have a singular focus, such as Freud and religion, Freud and philosophy, Freud and sociology, etc. There are numerous books in print in a variety of languages that are readily available on these specific topics. Rather, reading Freud as a "critical social theorist" seeks to demonstrate the depth and diversity of analyses that Freud's work can inspire, through the utilization of Freudian concepts, through the expansion of Freudian concepts, and through the determinate negation of Freudian concepts. Freud's work speaks for itself. He remains a recalcitrant voice for enlightenment thought and modernity against the mythologization of reality, the mystification of the lifeworld, and the infantilization of humanity. Of course, he is not beyond reproach, and his work calls out to us to turn our critical lenses towards him, to criticize his unarticulated biases, his tendency to universalize the particular, etc. We are impelled to identify and criticize the cultural context that tacitly saturates his work, as well as to question his theoretical inflexibility, etc. Nevertheless, those who attempt to silence his thought through willful neglect or through the arrogant stance of "Freud was simply wrong" are of course still living within a Freudian Western world, wherein his thought on the psyche and its interplay with society determines much of how we live our lives today. As Frank Tallis says, 'Freud's ideas have been so thoroughly assimilated into our culture that even those who reject Freud still think, occasionally, like Freudians.'[25] Our openness about sexuality; our belief that we can – and should – express our inner-most emotions; our skepticism about the manifest and dogmatic claims of religion and cultural norms; the culture industry's bombardment of people with messages meant to stimulate and manipulate the libido; our therapy culture over the confessional; our demand for rational answers to humanity's dilemmas over answers derived from scripture, our attempt to cultivate personal autonomy as opposed to submitting to irrational heteronomic forces, all of these cultural facts testify to the continual influence of the Freudian Enlightenment on our society, and Freud's growing influence – and that of Psychoanalysis – outside of the West. In other words, all these determining factors of Western society point back to the influence of the

---

25   Frank Tallis, *Mortal Secrets*, 4.

Viennese doctor whose thoughts on the human condition disturbed not only his own society, but also global society in the 21st century.

Our appreciation of Freud's work does not make us into devoted automatons, blind to the limitations of Freudian thought. Rather, it is a testament to Freud's genius that we continue to take his psychoanalytic social theories and continue to develop them beyond what he could have imagined. Those who attempt to petrify Freud's work do not do him justice, for the internally driven dynamics of psychoanalytic thought must always overcome the tendency for stasis. While in some cases negation of disturbance (*Ataraxia*) and a state-of-being without suffering (*Apatheia*) may be the goals of some forms of psychotherapy, it cannot be the goal of psychoanalytic social theory, which is propelled into even greater analytic complexity by disturbance and suffering, especially as it relates to the psychodynamics of individual and society. It is in this light that we continue to take Freud and psychoanalytic social theory seriously, not only for what it has already done, but for the diversity and complexity of analyses it continues to produce. This richness of potential in Freudian thought is what keeps the "return to Freud" cycle perpetually in motion without any sign of its end.

Dustin J. Byrd, Ph.D.

•••

When I went to the Theology Department at the University of Gothenburg to study religions (*Religionsvetenskapen*), I came across Sigmund Freud. I remember courses we had on psychology of religion, wherein our professors taught us about Freud's theories on various aspects of religion, human nature, and civilization. However, I never got the chance to engage with Freud's work academically until I received a scholarship to study for one year at University of Bristol in England. There, I found great mentors, such as professors Gregor McLennan, James Ladyman, and Rohit Barot, in the departments of sociology and philosophy. There I started to do my Ph.D. studies under the supervisions of Gregor McLennan and Rohit Barot. My work was on inter-civilizational dialogue between East and West with a specific emphasis on respective intellectual traditions in relation to the works of Ali Shariati, Iqbal Lahouri, Anthony Giddens, and Irving Goffman. I focused on the concept of "religion" in the works of these social theorists. More specifically, I studied the concept of "religion" and how it has been conceptualized in different traditions, which has been one of my intellectual as well as existential concerns since then. I recall when I was writing on inter-civilizational dialogue, I was reading Freud's work on "civilization"

(*Kultur*) and religion, upon which I began to feel that there was something missing in his narrative, especially in his understanding of religion. In Bristol I was blessed to have the company of my lifelong friend Professor Michael J. Naughton, who was always open to discuss issues related to religion and inter-civilizational dialogue. We have been in dialogue for the past 30 years. Nevertheless, I could not formulate what I had in my "heart" until the arrival of the COVID-19 pandemic.

My family went for their annual visit to Orel in Russia, and I was in Tehran and all commuting routes were closed and life seemed to come to an apocalyptic suspension. I was alone in Tehran and my wife and sons stuck in Russia, when suddenly I received news that my in-laws and my wife and sons all contracted COVID-19. You may recall how horrible it was when one got infected. We watched as the death tolls grew higher, a human tragedy we witnessed every night on the news. My wife sent me a special invitation and I got a special visa to enter Russia. When I arrived at the Moscow airport, I was shocked to see that it was virtually empty. But when I stepped outside the airport, I realized in Russia the situation seems to be very different than Iran, as very few people wore masks and life seemed to be "normal" while everywhere else people were talking about the "new normal."

I arrived in January 2020 in Orel and spend few days at my in-laws. Orel is a very small city, and I had very few books with me, which made the situation boring. By accident, I talked to a good friend of mine in Saint-Petersburg, and he invited me over. I was planning to stay for a few days there, but my stay lasted for over six months. I got a beautiful flat through another good friend of mine, Sergey Kozin, who generously allowed my family and I to stay at his in-laws' residence in the center of Saint-Petersburg. These few months there was one of my most productive times in during the pandemic. In that time, I started many online classes and seminars on a variety of issues related to social and human sciences. One day, my wife and I went to a bookshop where you could purchase English books. I was thrilled and went through the shelves meticulously. Suddenly I came across a book entitled, *Civilization and its Discontents,* written by Sigmund Freud. I was deeply happy to find this book in Saint-Petersburg during the pandemic at a time wherein life was globally suspended, without any knowledge about when such a suspense would end. I came home and started reading the book, which I read in Swedish for the first time almost 33 years ago. I made notes in each page and wrote down my own arguments here and there. Subsequently, I talked to my dear brother Professor Dustin J. Byrd about a joint global project on "Freud and Critical Social Theory," and he as always opened his arms and encouraged me to go for it. Then we together contacted different colleagues from different parts of the world and various disciplines who joined us in this "intellectual adventure." In my view, Freud and his conception of religion is important and for that reason worthy of inspection in an inter-civilizational dialogue. In his view, religion is an "illusion," but this concept needs to be deconstructed and interpretated in a critical fashion. Because the framework he uses to conceptualize religion is theory-laden, i.e., affected by theoretical presuppositions. In other words, "illusion" is not simply equivalent to "misinterpreted perception of sensory experiences" in the lexical sense. On the contrary, the concept of "illusion" in the Freudian frame of reference could refer to an attempt to gain control over the external world. I think this is where we should engage with Freud and his conception of religion and that is where I have tried to dialogue with him in this work.

Seyed Javad Miri, Ph.D.

Bibliography

Adorno, Theodor W. "The Meaning of Working through the Past." In *Can One Live After Auschwitz: A Philosophical Reader,* edited by Rolf Tiedemann. Translated by Rodney Livingstone and Others, 3–18. Stanford, CA: Stanford University Press, 2003.

Amnesty International, "Israel must comply with key ICJ ruling ordering it do all in its power to prevent genocide against Palestinians in Gaza." January 26, 2024. https://www.amnesty.org/en/latest/news/2024/01/israel-must-comply-with-key-icj-ruling-ordering-it-do-all-in-its-power-to-prevent-genocide-against-palestinians-in-gaza/.

Byrd, Dustin J. *The Dark Charisma of Donald Trump: Political Psychology and the MAGA Movement.* Kalamazoo: Ekpyrosis Press, 2023.

Byrd, Dustin J. *The Frankfurt School and the Dialectics of Religion.* Kalamazoo: Ekpyrosis Press, 2020.

Conroy, Oliver. "Inside the war tearing Psychoanalysis apart: 'The most hatred I've ever witnessed.'" *The Guardian,* June 16, 2023. https://www.theguardian.com/education/2023/jun/16/george-washington-university-professor-antisemitism-palestine-dc.

Freud, Sigmund. Group Psychology and the Analysis of the Ego. In *The Standard Edition of the Complete Psychological Works of Sigmund Freud,* Vol. 18. Translated by James Strachey. London: The Hogarth Press, 1955.

Freud, Sigmund. The Question of Lay Analysis. In *The Standard Edition of the Complete Psychological Works of Sigmund Freud,* Vol 20. Translated by James Strachey. London: The Hogarth Press, 1959.

Freud, Sigmund. *The Standard Edition of the Complete Psychological Works of Sigmund Freud*. Translated by James Strachey. London: The Hogarth Press, 1961.

Fromm, Erich. "Freud and Jung." In *Psychoanalysis and Religion*. New Haven: Yale University Press, 1978.

Habermas, Jürgen, et al, *An Awareness that Something is Missing: Faith and Reason in a Post-Secular Age*. Translated by Ciaran Cronin. Cambridge: Polity Press, 2010.

Hegel, Georg W. F. *Elements of the Philosophy of Right,* edited by Allen W. Wood. Cambridge: Cambridge University Press, 1991.

Jones, Ernst. *The Life and Work of Sigmund Freud: Years of Maturity 1901–1919*. New York: Basic Books, 1955.

Millar, Isabel. *The Psychoanalysis of Artificial Intelligence*. London: Palgrave Macmillan, 2021.

Parapraxis, "About," *Parapraxis Magazine,* https://www.parapraxismagazine.com/about.

Romeo, Nick. "When Philosophers Become Therapists: The Philosophical-Counseling Movement aims to apply Heady Logical Insights to Daily Life." *The New Yorker,* December 23, 2023. https://www.newyorker.com/culture/annals-of-inquiry/when-philosophers-become-therapists.

Stavrakakis, Yannis. ed. *Routledge Handbook of Psychoanalytic Political Theory*. New York: Routledge, 2020.

Tallis, Frank. *Mortal Secrets: Freud, Vienna, and the Discovery of the Modern Mind*. New York: St. Martin's Press, 2024.

Zeavin, Hannah. "Psychoanalysis has Returned: Why 2023 brought a new Freud Revival." *The Guardian,* December 29, 2023. https://www.theguardian.com/us-news/2023/dec/29/freuds-last-session-sigmund-freud-film-psychoanalysis.

PART 1

Reviving Freud

CHAPTER 1

Exhuming the Freudian Corpus: On Freud as a Social and Cultural Theorist

Howard L. Kaye

"Surely there must be some mistake." Such, I imagine, might be the reaction of many 21st century readers, encountering a volume such as this, which seeks to resurrect Freud as a critical social theorist.[1] Yes, Freud was once thought to be a scientific genius and moral exemplar, whose ideas and interpretive practices were essential to understanding our inner and collective lives and thus were deemed essential to the humanities and social sciences as well, but those days are gone. In the realm of Sociological Theory, for example, from the 1920s through the 1970s, many leading writers considered Freud to be a seminal figure, joining Marx, Durkheim, and Weber to constitute the "Big Four."[2] Today, the memory of such a judgement stands as an embarrassment to the field, except as a reassuring sign of "progress."

Looking back on the decades of Freud's ascendancy, perhaps the best that sociological theorists and cultural historians can say about the man is that he was an ambitious, 19th century scientist and physician who got carried away with himself and began recklessly applying outdated psychological and biological ideas, along with the flawed insights that he claimed to have gained in treating individual patients, to social and cultural phenomena he knew little about.[3] At the worst, as Freud bashers have been telling the public for the last 40 years, he was a fraud, a charlatan, a cocaine addict, and a pervert, who

---

1   An earlier version of this paper was presented at the Institute for Advanced Studies in Culture on November 8, 2019. In addition, some passages were previously published in my book, *Freud as a Social and Cultural Theorist: On Human Nature and the Civilizing Process*. London: Routledge. © 2019 by Howard L. Kaye. Reproduced by permission of Taylor and Francis Group, LLC, a division of Informa plc.
2   Jeffrey Alexander, *Fin de Siècle Social Theory: Relativism, Reduction, and the Problem of Reason* (London: Verso, 1995), 5, 83; Charles Lemert, *Social Theory: The Multicultural, Global, and Classic Readings* (Boulder: Westview Press, 1993), 9; Lemert, Charles. *Sociology after the Crisis* (Boulder, CO: Westview Press, 1995), xi.
3   Randall Collins, *Four Sociological Traditions* (New York: Oxford University Press, 1994), 32–33; Alan Wolfe, "Professor of Desire," *The New Republic* (June 3, 1991): 29–35; Dennis H. Wrong, *Problem of Order: What Unites and Divides Society*. New York, NY: The Free Press, 1994.

conned both his patients and the intellectual elites with his so-called "discoveries," theories, and "cures."[4] Either way the contemporary consensus seems clear: Freud is irrelevant, except as the protagonist in a cautionary tale about intellectual gullibility and/or intellectual grifting. Thank goodness "real" scientific progress in recent decades has brought forth cognitive neuroscience, behavioral genetics, the fMRI, and a pharmacopeia of psychotropic drugs, so we can finally understand how our brains, and thus our behavior, really work and treat ourselves effectively – or so we are told.

But if this is true, why have I and others bothered to exhume the corpus of Freud's work? The simple answer, as I have argued in my recent book, is that both the idealization of Freud as a scientist, healer, and cultural hero and his condemnation as a charlatan and cultural villain are essentially in error, an error that stems, at least in part, from a fundamental misunderstanding of the nature and substance of his work, and of the concerns and questions that animated it.[5] Taking Freud to be the scientist he so often claimed to be, supporters and critics alike have tended to underplay the intellectual, social, political, cultural, and personal interests – and contexts – that helped to shape his efforts, because such things are usually seen as irrelevant to a proper understanding of any "scientific" work.

The distinguished cultural historian and Freud biographer, Peter Gay, for example, simply ignored Freud's repeated confessions that he had 'never been a doctor in the proper sense,' and that medicine and ultimately psychoanalysis were the long "detour" he was "compelled" to take before he 'found my way back to my earliest path,' namely "philosophy" and the riddles of our cultural existence.[6] Instead, Gay proclaimed him to be 'an ambitious neurologist ... [and]

---

4 See for example, Frederick Crews, *Memory Wars: Freud's Legacy in Dispute*. New York: New York Review Book, 1995; Frederick Crews, *Unauthorized Freud: Doubters Confront a Legend* (New York: Penguin Books, 1998); Frederick Crews, *Freud: Making an Illusion* (New York: Metropolitan Books, 2017); Malcolm MacMillan, "New Answers to Old Questions: What the Freud-Fliess Correspondence Tells Us," *Psychoanalytic Review* 77, no. 4 (1990): 555–572; Malcolm MacMillan, *Freud Evaluated: The Completed Arc* (Amsterdam: North-Holland, 1991); Malcolm MacMillan, "The Sources of Freud's Methods for Gathering and Evaluating Clinical Data," in *Freud and the History of Psychoanalysis*, edited by Toby Gelfand and John Kerr, 99–151 (Hillsdale, NJ: The Analytic Press, 1992).
5 Kaye, *Freud as Social Theorist*.
6 Sigmund Freud, *Autobiographical Study*, SE 20, edited and translated by James Strachey with Anna Freud, Alix Strachey, and Alan Tyson (London: The Hogarth Press and The Institute of Psycho-Analysis), 8; Sigmund Freud, "Postscript" to *Question of Lay Analysis*, SE 20, 253; Sigmund Freud, *The Complete Letters of Sigmund Freud to Wilhelm Fliess, 1887–1904*, edited and translated by Jeffrey Moussaieff Masson (Cambridge, MA: Belknap Press of Harvard University Press, 1985),159, 180; Ernest Jones, *The Life and Work of Sigmund Freud*. 3 vols. (New York: Basic Books, 1953–57), 3:41.

reputable physician who ... traveled, reluctantly, indeed painfully, far from his medical starting points.'[7] And despite Freud's frequent citations of poets and philosophers as authorities on the workings of the soul, Gay insisted, without argument, that 'when a historian must choose between a philosopher and a physician as an intellectual ancestor for Freud, the historian is well advised to take the physician.'[8] Gay even declared, without benefit of any evidence, that Freud's major work on mass psychology, *Group Psychology and the Analysis of the Ego* (1921), written in the wake of the Great War and the revolutions and counterrevolutions that followed, had nothing to do with the political realities of the day and was written for purely scientific reasons.[9]

Oddly enough, similar views prevail among Freud's bashers, although their evaluation of Freud's scientific merits obviously differs fundamentally from Gay's. For example, in his monumental and much acclaimed intellectual biography of Freud, the historian of science and Freud debunker, Frank Sulloway, argued that Freud is best understood, not as a humanistic, depth psychologist, but as a "biologist of the mind," whose theories are rooted in 'the faulty logic of outmoded nineteenth century biological assumptions' and are thus hopelessly obsolete.[10] As for Freud's late, cultural texts, Sulloway labeled them dismissively as "excursions" into other fields, motivated, not by an interest in the philosophical, religious, or social matters that they clearly address, but by a purely scientific determination 'to clarify his most basic unsolved problems in the theory of the psychoneuroses.'[11]

In opposition to such views, my work has endeavored to read Freud as the philosopher and social theorist he always aspired to be. Such a claim ought not to be surprising or controversial. Indeed, that Freud's "original interest" and "initial goal" was philosophy and social theory, not biology and medicine, has been known for decades, as his youthful letters to Eduard Silberstein, Martha Bernays, and Wilhelm Fliess make clear.[12] Nevertheless, this fact has rarely been allowed to count. Even Frederick Crews, in his latest pathography

---

7 Peter Gay, *Freud for Historians* (Oxford: Oxford University Press, 1985), 57.
8 Peter Gay, *The Bourgeois Experience: Victoria to Freud.* 5 vols. (New York: Oxford Univ. Press, Vols 1 & 2), (W. W. Norton, Vols 3–5, 1984–98), 2:88–89.
9 Peter Gay, *Freud: A Life for Our Time* (New York: W.W. Norton & Company, 1988), 405.
10 Sulloway, *Freud, Biologist of the Mind: Beyond the Psychoanalytic Legend* (Cambridge: Harvard University Press, 1979), 3, 5, 497–500.
11 Ibid., 364–367, 370.
12 See Sigmund Freud, *The Letters of Sigmund Freud to Eduard Silberstein, 1871–1881,* edited by Walter Boehlich. Translated by Arnold J. Pomerans (Cambridge: Harvard University Press, 1990), 70, 95–97, 109–112; Freud, *Letters to Fliess,* 159, 180, 398; Freud to Martha Bernays, August 16, 1882, in Jones, *Life and Work of Freud,* 3:41.

of Freud acknowledges that 'Philosophy ... was Freud's real intellectual passion in the first phase of his studies,' and yet he cannot allow it to have any significance for the body of psychoanalytic thought Freud went on to develop because doing so might undermine Crews' unremitting assault on the man's character and thereby his work.[13] In contrast, I have taken seriously Freud's various confessions from 1896 on, that the new psychology he was developing would enable him to fulfill, at last, the deepest longing of his intellectual life, namely for "philosophical knowledge" – particularly in regards to religious psychology, the nature of evil, and the course of our cultural development – and then trace the development of that "knowledge" throughout his work.[14]

Doing so, however, is not an easy or straightforward task. Particularly in his early years as a "psycho-analyst," it was essential that Freud portray himself as a scientist and physician in an effort to establish his career and legitimize his theory and therapy, while also lending authority and persuasive power to the cultural analyses and moral pronouncements that were often concealed in his work or were later passed off as merely "applied" science. In the "Preface" to the first edition of the *Interpretation of Dreams*, for example, Freud assured his readers that the strange book they were about to encounter did not go 'beyond the bounds of neuro-pathological interests.' Yet the book he actually wrote is stunning for the connections it makes to an extraordinary range of social, political, and cultural phenomena: the wellsprings of poetry, religion, myth, folklore, custom, and legend; the source of values and superstitions; the parental element in our relation to political authority; the power of phantasy in the life of the mind and its culture; and ultimately "the heart of our being" – our fundamental human nature – and how an understanding of that nature illuminates our inner lives and the dynamics of culture.[15]

The book's concluding remarks are equally misleading as Freud first denies that he will address the ethical significance of what his book has revealed about the unconscious wishes and mental processes that shape our lives, and then goes on to criticize what he terms "our superannuated morality," a morality that fails to appreciate the "complexity of human character" with its impossible demands and overly stark distinctions between virtue and vice.[16] Attentive readers, however, need not have waited to the book's end to grasp its moral thrust for it is announced in the Latin quotation from Vergil's *Aeneid*, which

---

13 Crews, *Freud: Making of an Illusion*, 27–28.
14 Freud, *Letters to Fliess*, 159; Kaye, *Freud as Social Theorist*.
15 Sigmund Freud, *The Interpretation of Dreams*. Translated by Joyce Crick (Oxford: Oxford University Press, 1999), 5, 398; Kaye, *Freud as Social Theorist*, 47–48.
16 Freud, *Interpretation*, 411.

Freud borrowed from a pamphlet by socialist, Ferdinand Lassalle, affixed to the title page, and then repeated in the book's concluding pages: 'If I cannot bend the Higher Powers, I will move the Infernal Regions.'[17]

This quote captures the moral agenda of Freud's early psychoanalytic works: to bend the Higher Powers of mind and culture, to moderate their excessive constraints and unrealistic moral demands, and raise the repressed wishes and unconscious desires of men – and particularly sexual ones – to the level of consciousness so that they might receive a fair hearing. For the early Freud, it was, of course, the unrealistically repressed sexual desires restlessly churning away in the Infernal Regions of the unconscious that were most in need of being raised, because he believed their excessive damming-up by the West's overly ascetic sexual morality was contributing to an epidemic of neuroses and producing considerable ethical and cultural harm.[18] Unfortunately, this first, simplistic theory of the neuroses, emphasizing sexual frustration, has too often been taken as the essence of Freud's cultural analysis.

One reason why it has been so difficult to get beyond this clichéd view and to gain a clearer grasp of Freud's more complex, more interesting, and more important social theory is that Freud, as he acknowledged repeatedly, was not a systematic writer on any subject. The twenty-three volumes of his collected works consist of fragments devoted to incomplete and often one-sided explorations of particular issues, occasionally taken up again at later dates and from other points of view, with no final synthesis. In terms of Freud's social and cultural thought, there simply is no single text that adequately expresses his views. Nor can these be pieced together by examining that small subset of Freud's writings that deal overtly with these matters, such as the so-called "cultural texts": *Totem and Taboo* (1912–13), *Group Psychology* (1921), *The Future of an Illusion* (1927), *Civilization and Its Discontents* (1930), and *Moses and Monotheism* (1939). Fragments of his social philosophy and cultural analysis are embedded throughout his writings – in his case histories; his "metapsychological" essays; his "applied" psychoanalysis; and his voluminous correspondence, etc. – all of which must be examined and weighed.

Such a task, which I undertook in my recent book, is a laborious one and is obviously beyond the scope of an essay. Here, I can merely offer up a few fragments for examination, drawn from various types of Freud's writings, which

---

17   Ibid., 1, 402.
18   Sigmund Freud, "Sexuality in the Aetiology of the Neuroses," *SE* 3:261–85; Sigmund Freud, "'Civilized' Sexual Morality and Modern Nervous Illness," *SE* 9:179–204; Freud, *Letters to Fliess*, 37–51, 57–66, 73–112.

I nevertheless hope will begin to sketch out a fuller account of at least some aspects of Freud's social and cultural thought.

1 The "Rat Man," Religion, and Neurosis

Freud's case histories have often been treated as pedagogic texts and recruiting documents designed to win over adherents and instruct analysts in the aetiology of, and psychoanalytic treatment of, the various neuroses.[19] Unfortunately, most readers, including analysts, are unaware that Freud considered such case studies to have another, and broader significance. As he explained to his Viennese followers at one of their so-called "scientific meetings" in November 1907, from case studies, 'we learn ... what is really going on in the world; we receive a genuine picture of the world. The analyses are cultural-historical documents of tremendous importance.'[20] This was particularly true of the case he was working on at the time – that of the unfortunate "Rat Man," Ernst Lanzer.[21] Despite this "tremendous importance," Freud kept what he saw as the cultural-historical meaning of this case largely concealed in its published version in order to maintain its purely scientific appearance. Fortunately, Freud left enough clues, particularly in his surviving case notes from the first few months of treatment, to reconstruct the "cultural-historical" aspect of the "Rat Man" case.

At the time he consulted Freud, Lanzer was a twenty-nine-year-old lawyer, crippled by his conflicting feelings of love and rage directed at both his cousin Gisela, who resisted his attentions, and at his deceased father (who had strongly opposed the match). In his misery, Lanzer was tormented by a bizarre collection of obsessional thoughts and compulsive actions, revenge fantasies and suicidal urges, perverse longings and devastating self-reproaches.

Although Lanzer had been born into an assimilated, middle-class Jewish family, he had still turned to prayer as his first line of defense against his inner demons. "Devoutly religious" until the age of fourteen or fifteen, when he gradually began to develop freethinking tendencies, Lanzer's ever-receding faith managed to keep his evil wishes and tormenting obsessions at bay until his early twenties. But with his problematic attachment to his cousin, and the long wished-for death of his father, which he could not bring himself to

---

19   Gay, *Freud: A Life for Our Time*, 245, 267.
20   Nunberg and Federn, eds. *Minutes of Vienna Psychoanalytic Society*, 4 vols. Translated by M. Nunberg (New York: International Universities Press, 1962–75), 1:251.
21   See Sigmund Freud, "Notes Upon a Case of Obsessional Neurosis," *SE* 10:155–318.

acknowledge, Lanzer's condition worsened. Desperately, he tried to revive the religious fears and feelings of piety that he had "outgrown," and to devise his own prayers to control his obsessional ideas and protect himself and his loved ones from the harm he secretly desired for them. But these efforts at defense repeatedly failed, as what he wished to repress inevitably leaked through his anxiously constructed prayers. No matter how long and fervently he prayed that "*God protect her* [Gisela]" from the harms he unconsciously wished to call down upon her, "a hostile '*not*'" would suddenly insert itself in the sentence, transforming his loving prayer into a vindictive curse.[22]

Next, Lanzer attempted to shorten his prayers or transform them into acronyms constructed out of the initial letters of his most powerful prayers in the hope of outwitting the evil within himself, but to no avail. These protective measures, too, were soon taken over by the very compulsions he was struggling to repress and transformed into means of expression. Finally, Lanzer even considered conversion to Christianity in the hope that intensified anxiety about life in the next world could help him combat his sacrilegious compulsions in this world. Although Lanzer rejected such a drastic step, he still tried to conjure up images of the "eternal" harm his obsessions might produce, in a desperate attempt to suppress them. Yet this strategy too, ultimately lost its effectiveness. With his residual Jewish piety nearly exhausted and his improvised religiosity a failure, Lanzer could no longer fend off his tormenting fantasies and crippling conviction of guilt and turned to Freud for help.

Freud's strategy was not simply to untangle the mystery of Lanzer's bizarre obsessions and terrifying compulsions, by tracing them to the repressed rage he felt towards both Gisela and his father, but, more fundamentally, to change Lanzer's understanding of "evil." In the hope of diminishing Lanzer's powerful feelings of guilt for the evil within him, Freud tried to persuade him that he was not really morally responsible for his shameful compulsions. All his 'reprehensible impulses originated from his infancy,' Freud told him, in the sexuality, "omnipotence," and "megalomania" of infancy, which continued to live on in his unconscious mind. In addition, as Freud explained, to counteract these so-called "evil impulses," Lanzer had developed ascetic, religious, and superstitious traits, which helped temporarily, but now only added to his torment. Together these warring personalities within him threatened to overwhelm the third personality he had still managed to develop: the rational, cheerful, and sensible young man whom Freud valued.[23]

---

22   Freud, "Notes Upon a Case of Obsessional Neurosis," SE 10:242, 260; Kaye, *Freud as Social Theorist*, 75–77.
23   Freud, "Notes on a Case of Obsessional Neurosis," 177, 185–186, 233–234, 248–249, 278.

By winning Lanzer over to such an account of the soul, Freud, like Plato, hoped to reintegrate the three personalities into which Lanzer had fragmented, and do so under the rule of reason, but Lanzer resisted conversion, at least initially, to Freud's comforting belief that 'all of his evil impulses had originated' out of his 'infantile predispositions.' Nevertheless, Freud managed to help Lanzer improve enough to resume an apparently normal life and even marry Gisella, only to die in the opening months of the Great War.

In addition to its pedagogic purposes, the case of the Rat Man has retained its significance among psychoanalysts because it contains the germ of several important concepts, which Freud developed in later years, such as, "narcissism," "the omnipotence of thought," and the tripartite model of the soul. What has often been overlooked, however, is its profound significance for Freud's emerging social philosophy and cultural analysis; for with this case history, Freud presents his *new* understanding of neurosis, not as the product of "strangulated" affects and especially "damned-up" sexual longings, but as a lack of unity among the warring parts of the soul, thereby echoing moral perspectives deeply rooted in the Western tradition, such as, Plato's understanding of "injustice" and Augustine's account of "sin." Of greater significance, Freud now argues that it was the *waning* of religion in terms of faith, institutions, and authority – *not* excessive repression – which was the historical cause of this dissolution of the soul: a theme he then returns to repeatedly in his subsequent work, including his "Leonardo" essay, the Schreber and "Wolf Man" cases, his correspondence with Pfister and Jung, *Totem and Taboo*, and *Group Psychology*.[24]

In the past, religious authority had more successfully sanctioned instinctual renunciation, while religious practices provided ready-made paths for sublimation, consolation, the control of ambivalence, and some degree of relief from feelings of helplessness and guilt. With the erosion of that authority, resistance to failing cultural forms, moral constraints, and moral ideals, and the resultant inner misery all intensified, forcing individuals like Lanzer to create what

---

24 Sigmund Freud, *Leonardo da Vinci and a Memory of His Childhood*, SE 11:63–137; Sigmund Freud, "Psycho-Analytic Notes on an Autobiographical Account of a Case of Paranoia (Dementia Paranoides)," SE 12:3–79; Sigmund Freud, "From the History of an Infantile Neurosis," SE 17:7–122; Heinrich Meng and Ernst L. Freud, eds., *Psychoanalysis and Faith: The Letters of Sigmund Freud & Oskar Pfister*. Translated by Eric Mosbacher (New York: Basic Books,1963); William McGuire, ed., *The Freud/Jung Letters: The Correspondence between Sigmund Freud and C.G. Jung*. Translated by Ralph Manheim and R.F.C. Hull (Princeton: Princeton University Press, 1974).

Freud called "caricatures of religion": desperate attempts 'to achieve by private means what is effected in society by collective effort.'[25]

With the failure of such efforts, troubled souls were left with a "craving for [an] authority" that would help reestablish order within their psyches and societies, a craving that Freud found even more disturbing because of its potential social and political consequences.[26] What then to do? Initially, Freud clung to the positivist belief that a peaceful transference of social authority could be accomplished from religion to science, and particularly to his "science" of psychoanalysis, but in January 1910, when he proposed a course of action to C.G. Jung in pursuit of this goal, the response was an antinomian and Dionysian outburst that horrified Freud.[27] "Religion," Jung insisted, "can be replaced only by religion" and doing so would require a new myth, one which could awaken, in Jung's words, an "infinite rapture and wantonness" and inspire a "drunken feast of joy" through the release of the "archaic-infantile" and "ecstatic instinctual forces" that have been lying dormant for 2000 years. 'Must we not love evil,' Jung effused, 'if we are to break away from the obsession with virtue that makes us sick and forbids us the joys of life?'[28] Twenty-four years later, Jung found an "evil" he could love and the culturally renewing myth for which he had long been wishing, in what he called the "explosive forces" emerging from the "Aryan unconscious," liberated by the Nazis.[29]

In opposition, Freud's response was to write *Totem and Taboo* to intensify his effort to pathologize religion by rendering it atavistic and to undermine "the craving for authority" that has sustained it by proposing his own countermyth, that of the "primal parricide." Such a myth, he hoped, might help break the cycle of rebellion, guilt, and deferred obedience that has fueled religious evolution. But the experience of the Great War and the social and political upheavals that followed both heightened, and *reoriented* Freud's anxieties. The massive loss of life; the shattering of cherished cultural ideals, the dissolution of social and political bonds throughout Europe had made "mourning and melancholia" a pervasive cultural condition, while the manic flare-up of collective violence, as socialist, nationalist, and ethnic groups confronted each

---

25   Freud, *Totem and Taboo*, SE 13:73.
26   Freud, *Leonardo*, SE 11:65, 122–23; Sigmund Freud, "Future Prospects of Psycho-Analytical Therapy," SE 11:146.
27   McGuire, *Freud/Jung Letters*, 288.
28   Ibid., 293–94.
29   C.G. Jung, "The State of Psychotherapy Today," as quoted in Yosef Hayim Yerushalmi, *Freud's Moses: Judaism Terminable and Interminable* (New Haven: Yale Univ. Press, 1991), 49.

other, foretold future slaughter, and compelled Freud to confront new and frightful realities. The war had obviously unleashed forces that had "bent" the "Higher Powers" and moved the "Infernal Regions" far beyond anything Freud could have imagined. In addition, the orgy of aggression and death made a mockery of Freud's early focus on sexuality in both his individual psychology and his cultural analysis.[30]

2 The Great War and the Transformation of Freudian Theory

With the end of the war, Freud began to develop his response in three disparate works upon which he was engaged simultaneously, early in 1919 – three works, that seem to have no connection with each other – but which should be read together to appreciate their full significance. First to be published, was a seemingly minor essay on what Freud passed off as a "remote" and neglected topic in aesthetics: "The Uncanny." Freud had started the essay while writing *Totem and Taboo* and then put it away in a drawer until something made him return to the essay at war's end, indeed, as he confessed, "impelled" him to do so.[31] That something was the haunting spectre of death hovering over Europe.

In this essay, Freud traces the peculiar feeling of eeriness, fear, dread, horror, and helplessness that constitutes the uncanny, back to what he claimed was its origin in the sudden reawakening of infantile and primitive wishes, fears, and modes of thought that we have foolishly believed we have overcome thanks to our subsequent mental development. Whether in literature or in life, the sudden reemergence of the wishes and anxieties of childhood, or the narcissism, animism, "omnipotence of thought," or "compulsion to repeat" of our infantile and primitive past can trigger the powerful feeling of the uncanny; a disturbing reminder that despite our vaunted rationality, we 'still think as [children and] savages do,' above all, when confronting death.[32]

Faced with the slaughter of millions and the mourning of their loved ones, this mass encounter with death generated a "great awakening" of the uncanny, thereby transforming a minor aesthetic problem into what was for Freud one of the central cultural problems of the day. It did so because the mass experience of the uncanny announced a revival of the 'old animistic conception of

---

30   Louise E. Hoffman, "War, Revolution, and Psychoanalysis: Freudian Thought begins to Grapple with Social Reality," *Journal of the History of the Behavioral Sciences* 17, no. 2 (1981): 251–269, 252; Kaye, *Freud as Social Theorist*, 116, 124.
31   Freud, "The Uncanny." SE 17:219.
32   Ibid., 242–243, 247, 249.

the universe' that Freud believed was the wellspring of superstition, religious faith, and charismatic authority. Quickened by the experience of the uncanny, gods and spirits, both old and new, might once again rise from the dead and the various persons and things associated with these uncanny forces might then be perceived as possessing extraordinary powers of "mana" or "charisma," which would release both them and their followers from "the manifest prohibitions of reality."[33]

Unbeknownst to Freud, his identification of the uncanny as the foundational experience out of which religious belief is born echoes that of theologian Rudolf Otto, whose *Idea of the Holy* was published two years earlier. For Otto, of course, this experience of the uncanny was primary, irreducible, and revelatory, leading us ultimately to grasp the real presence of the "holy" in the world.[34] For Freud, the reduction of the uncanny to the infantile and the primitive was thus essential to diminish the emotional intensity of such experiences and free us from its terrors and temptations, thereby preventing the rebirth of religious and/or political enthusiasms by driving a "scientific" stake through such phenomena. In 1919, Yeats may have wondered "what rough beast" was slouching towards Bethlehem to be born; but Freud refused to wait. Instead, he set off to slay that beast before it could reach its destination.

The second of these three pivotal works to be published was Freud's deeply problematic, even embarrassing "metapsychological" work: *Beyond the Pleasure Principle* (1920). In this allegedly "sober" scientific work, which even he acknowledged gave off a whiff of "mysticism and sham profundity," Freud reworked his instinct (or drive) theory by merging the formerly antagonistic sexual and self-preservative instincts into a newly incorporated life instinct or "eros," and by *inferring* the existence of an opposing "death instinct" to be its mythical and immortal combatant. Such an inference, Freud argued, was based on his recent "discovery" of a new principle of mental functioning that was prior to, and independent of, what he previously deemed foundational: the "pleasure principle." This new principle, derived from Freud's observation of a strange "compulsion to repeat" not only pleasurable experiences, but painful, even traumatic ones, suggested to Freud that all instincts are urges *'inherent in organic life to restore an earlier state of things* which the living entity has been obliged to abandon'; and since inorganic states preceded organic ones, the first

---

33   Ibid., 240.
34   Rudolf Otto, *The Idea of the Holy*. Translated by John W. Harvey (London: Oxford University Press, (1917) 1958), 7, 15, 125.

and most fundamental instinct must be a "death instinct" seeking a return to such a state.[35]

The "evidence" offered up by Freud to justify these wild speculations is so flimsy, and his reasoning, so flawed, that one cannot help but ask what he hoped to accomplish with such an embarrassing work. As has often been pointed out, positing a "death instinct" certainly enabled Freud to resolve several internal, theoretical problems.[36] It restored to his drive theory the fundamental dualism which his theory required, and which the concept of narcissism had called into question by blurring the distinction between his previous instinctual combatants, the sexual and self-preservative instincts. It also offered a pseudo-scientific explanation for the tendency of patients and others to compulsively repeat their same painful experiences over and over again, and even to regress psychologically. Finally, it offered a new account of aggression, destructiveness, and hatred, emphasizing their primary, instinctual basis, which the brutality of the war and the melancholia that followed made desirable.

What are often overlooked, however, are the moral and social theoretical ends that Freud's mythology of life and death instincts serves.[37] In the past, when Freud posited the fundamental conflict between sexual and self-preservative instincts, he was holding out hope for human moral and cultural progress by granting to prudence and reason an instinctual base from which it might counteract or tame the often, problematic demands of sexual desire. With the positing of a death instinct, that hope must be severely tempered, if not abandoned. Self-preservation may still have an instinctual basis, but it is now counterbalanced by an equally instinctual and equally powerful force oriented toward death and destruction. As Freud now declared, there simply are no biological or social forces 'tending towards change and progress,' 'no universal instinct towards higher development in the animal or plant world,' and no 'instinct towards perfection at work in human beings.'[38] On the contrary, the descent into destruction, self-destruction, and barbarism now has its own instinctual force and thus remains an ever-present threat against which all the resources that constitute a culture must be arrayed. Whatever tenuous progress humanity has achieved is due to the strenuous work of culture, through its repression of instinct and its provision of alternative, compensatory, and sublimated forms of expression.

---

35 Freud, *Beyond the Pleasure Principle*, SE 18:36–38.
36 Sulloway, *Freud, Biologist of the Mind*, 395, 408, 414–415, 497–498; Kaye, *Freud as Social Theorist*, 128.
37 Kaye, 129–130.
38 Freud, *Beyond the Pleasure Principle*, 41–42.

The last product of this creative outburst in the aftermath of the war is the overtly social theoretical work, *Group Psychology* (1921), a text that seems to have taken on renewed relevance in the age of Trump. Mass or crowd psychology was *a* central, if not *the* central political and sociological problem at the end of the 19th century and first decades of the 20th for obvious reasons.[39] This was the era of imperial and national disintegration and social revolution in which politics moved out into the streets.[40] Fearing the revolutionary, reactionary, ethnic, and anti-Semitic forces jostling for mass support by promising some sort of "salvation," but delivering brutality and bloodshed instead, Freud sought to inoculate his audience against such temptations, as he had done in "The Uncanny" and *Beyond the Pleasure Principle*. In this case by unmasking what he claimed were the erotic, infantile, and atavistic illusions behind our attraction to figures of authority, even in seemingly impersonal and highly organized groups like the Church and Army.

Of particular concern to Freud was the danger of narcissistic leaders who appealed to the narcissism of their audiences, offering them not only instinctual release, but what he called a "magnificent festival for the ego," in which the burdens of conscience, constraint, and cultural ideals could be tossed aside, relieving followers of guilt and consideration for others, and freeing them to once again feel a sense of "triumph and self-satisfaction."[41]

By identifying the fantasized father of childhood and of our primitive past behind the adored leader, Freud hoped to generate a kind of "Rumpelstiltskin" effect, breaking the erotic and uncanny tie to the leader and with it, the social bonds of identification with others similarly enthralled. But what then? Was not the dissolution of such bonds the cause of both political unrest and the psychological misery of neurosis? Why not follow the path of other social theorists of the age, like Marx and Durkheim, as well as Freud's psychoanalytic rivals, Jung and Adler, and offer some substitute form of salvation to bind together what modernity had torn asunder?

---

39   Christian Borch, *The Politics of Crowds: An Alternative History of Sociology* (Cambridge: Cambridge University Press, 2012).
40   Carl E. Schorske, "Politics in a New Key: An Austrian Trio," in Schorske, *Fin-de-Siècle Vienna* (New York: Vintage Books, 1981), 116–180.
41   Sigmund Freud, *Group Psychology and the Analysis of the Ego. SE* 18:131–133; Kaye, *Freud as Social Theorist*, 145–46.

3 Freud's Assault on Illusions and His Jewish Identity

Freud's answer is both revealing and deeply disturbing. Writing to novelist Romain Rolland in 1923, Freud confessed that 'A great part of my life's work … has been spent [trying to] destroy illusions of my own and those of mankind.'[42] And at the time of this confession, Freud had indeed left quite a path of destruction behind him, adding to the disillusionment and disenchantment associated with the Great War. In his theory and therapy, love was reduced to mere "sexual overvaluation"; respect for authority, to a child's guilty love, fear, and longing for parental protection; religion, to obsessional neurosis and the childish wish-fulfilling phantasies of the weak, the guilty, and the frightened; evil, to the infantile; patriotism, to the "narcissism of minor differences"; and morality, to the desperate attempt to restrain our impulses by the mental mechanism he termed "reaction formation."[43]

To account for this disenchanting goal, Freud pointed *not* to his scientific training but to his Jewish identity: 'I, of course, belong to a race which in the Middle Ages was held responsible for all epidemics and which today is blamed for the disintegration of the Austrian Empire and German defeat.'[44] Having experienced the barbarism and brutality unleashed by the fantasies of Judeophobes for over 2000 years, it was difficult for Jews to be sanguine about any illusions of the day – whether religious, racial, political, moral, or scientific – promising a "transformation of life." Ultimately, blood was going to be shed.

For Freud, the problem with all such illusions is not simply that they are rooted in wishes, not reality, and a delusional vision of our "human nature," but that all such illusions are actually "evil":[45] evil because of the discontent they nurture toward ourselves and the world as we both are; the brutality they justify in the name of some imagined good; and the misery and despair they cause with their inevitable failure. Faced with such "evils" was it not better to follow a liberal strategy, like that first pursued by Hobbes, and offer up a scientific myth designed to transform our understanding of our nature, thereby persuading us to lower our moral and political aspirations to nothing higher than the "desire of Ease, and sensual Delight," as Hobbes phrased it, and to the avoidance of chaos, pain, and discontent?[46] Inoculated against political

---

42 Sigmund Freud, *Letters of Sigmund Freud*, 341.
43 Kaye, *Freud as Social Theorist*, 156.
44 Sigmund Freud, *Letters*, 341.
45 Sigmund Freud, *New Introductory Lectures on Psycho-analysis*, SE 22:104.
46 Thomas Hobbes, *Leviathan,* edited by Richard Tuck (Cambridge: Cambridge University Press, (1651) 1991), 70.

and religious enthusiasms and thus less prone to indulge in the brutality these forces tend to release, a humanity educated by Freud, like the humanity educated by Hobbes, might be less heroic, virtuous, and pious, but they might become more prudent, rational, and orderly, and thus, less dangerous to themselves and others. Freud even thought they might be "better off psychologically" than those bound together by some political or religious faith. Despite a susceptibility to neurosis and what he later called the "psychological poverty of groups," they were less susceptible to intolerance and cruelty.[47]

In time, Freud believed, the strange hostility toward civilization so characteristic of the age and the resulting fantasies of renewal through rebarbarization would diminish due to the increased comfort, "ease and sensual delight," which the modern world could offer, and because of the "education to reality," "primacy of the intellect," and the love of all mankind, supposedly cultivated by the sciences and especially by his own.[48] Unfortunately, Freud lived long enough to see these hopes threatened, but he died before they would be utterly destroyed.

Nearing his own death, Freud clung desperately to one last illusion: a vision of the future in which our nature would be gradually transformed through what he believed was the continuing advancement of the "Intellectuality" and "Spirituality" (*Geistigkeit*) that had begun with the monotheism of Akhenaton, Moses, and the Hebrew prophets, and would be carried on by psychoanalysis.[49] But such a vision was wildly in error: a wish-fulfilling phantasy of the sort he had attacked throughout his life. Nevertheless, his diagnosis of his age and his social and cultural theory remain of value, and not simply because of their influence on how many people in the 20th century tried to make sense of their inner and outer lives and conduct them accordingly. Freud restored to social thought a focus on the much-maligned concept of "human nature," from which the social sciences in particular had diverged from the mid-18th century on. Beginning with Montesquieu's declaration that "man is a flexible being" shaped essentially by the social forces around us, and culminating with claims like that of Richard Rorty, that as natureless beings, we are free to 'make ourselves into whatever we are clever enough to imagine ourselves becoming,' the idea of a fixed human nature that tells us who we are and how we should live, has become highly suspect.[50]

---

47   Freud, *Group Psychology*, SE 18:98.
48   Sigmund Freud, *Future of an Illusion*, SE 21:49–50, 53; Sigmund Freud, *Civilization and Its Discontents*, SE 21:87.
49   Sigmund Freud, *Moses and Monotheism*, SE 23:111–118.
50   Charles de Secondat, Montesquieu, *The Spirit of the Laws*. Translated and edited by Anne E. Cohler, Basia Carolyn Miller, and Harold Samuel Stone (Cambridge: Cambridge

With Freud, the idea of a recalcitrant set of biologically-grounded, yet psychologically interpreted drives, impulses, wishes, and fantasies returns, along with the various mental principles and techniques by which such psychic phenomena are processed and our thoughts and actions are adjusted to the world around us, but does so, not in the mechanistic and reductionistic manner of much contemporary sociobiology and evolutionary psychology. Our ambivalent and problematic nature might set certain constraints on what sort of life and what sort of society are feasible, but it leaves room for some degree of cultural training, taming, modifying, redirecting, mastery, and even progress without which our lives would be even nastier, more brutish, and considerably shorter.

By imagining how nature works itself out in an "unconscious mind," Freud aligned himself with the similar efforts of other 19th German poets, philosophers, and scientists who hoped to preserve a belief in the soul and protect human inwardness and freedom from the threats of materialism and reductionism.[51] Writing to Georg Groddeck in 1917, Freud declared that the "unconscious" is the "right mediator" and "missing link" between the physical and the mental; and as he wrote in his 1921 essay on "Psychoanalysis and Telepathy," despite being 'incorrigible mechanists and materialists,' psychoanalysts 'seek to avoid robbing the mind and spirit' of its special characteristics, and do so by creating a sanctuary for them in the realm of the unconscious.[52] Humanists and the spiritually-minded might appreciate Freud's sanctuary for the soul, yet it is important to remember that this sanctuary also contains much that is deeply disturbing about ourselves – far more disturbing than even Hobbes's imaginings – requiring, Freud believed, both the acceptance of more limited hopes, and our constant cultural vigilance. The pursuit of life, liberty, happiness, order, perfection, and fulfillment may find a home in this sanctuary, but so too does a longing for death, chaos, punishment, regression, escape from the constraints of reason and conscience, and a desire for submission to a powerful and dangerous personality.

University Press, (1748) 1989), xliv; Richard Rorty, "Human Rights, Rationality, and Sentimentality," in *Truth and Progress: Philosophical Papers*, vol. 3, 167–185 (Cambridge: Cambridge University Press, 1998), 175.

51 Henri F. Ellenberger, *The Discovery of the Unconscious: The History and Evolution of Dynamic Psychiatry* (New York: Basic Books, 1970); Angus Nicholls, Martin Liebscher, eds. *Thinking the Unconscious: Nineteenth-Century German Thought* (Cambridge: Cambridge University Press, 2010).

52 Sigmund Freud., *Letters*, 318; Sigmund Freud, "Psycho-Analysis and Telepathy," SE 18:179.

With this dark and disenchanting vision, Freud may have wished to shatter the illusory hopes and deadly phantasies of Christians and Communists, mystics and positivists, humanitarians and Nazis, and do so without destroying those ideals to which he still clung, yet his mythology and doctrines may well have produced considerable collateral damage, replacing the comforting illusions of salvation, progress, and consolation, with the reality of fatalism and crippling despair, ironically, in a manner not unlike the Calvinist doctrine of predestination.

Bibliography

Alexander, Jeffrey. C. *Fin de Siècle Social Theory: Relativism, Reduction, and the Problem of Reason*. London: Verso, 1995.

Borch, Christian. *The Politics of Crowds: An Alternative History of Sociology*. Cambridge: Cambridge University Press, 2012.

Collins, Randall. *Four Sociological Traditions*. New York: Oxford University Press, 1994.

Crews, Frederick. *Freud: The Making of an Illusion*. New York: Metropolitan Books, 2017.

Crews, Frederick. *The Memory Wars: Freud's Legacy in Dispute*. New York: New York Review Book, 1995.

Crews, Frederick, ed. *Unauthorized Freud: Doubters Confront a Legend*. New York: Penguin Books, 1998.

Ellenberger, Henri. F. *The Discovery of the Unconscious: The History and Evolution of Dynamic Psychiatry*. New York: Basic Books, 1970.

Freud, Sigmund. *An Autobiographical Study. The Standard Edition of the Complete Psychological Works of Sigmund Freud*. 24 vols. Edited and translated by James Strachey with Anna Freud, Alix Strachey, and Alan Tyson. London: The Hogarth Press and The Institute of Psycho-Analysis, 1953–1974 (hereafter cited as SE followed by volume number). SE20:7–70.

Freud, Sigmund. *Beyond the Pleasure Principle*. SE18:7–64.

Freud, Sigmund. *Civilization and Its Discontents*. SE21:57–145.

Freud, Sigmund. "'Civilized' Sexual Morality and Modern Nervous Illness." SE9:179–204.

Freud, Sigmund. *The Complete Letters of Sigmund Freud to Wilhelm Fliess, 1887–1904*. Edited and translated by Jeffrey Moussaieff Masson. Cambridge, MA: Belknap Press of Harvard University Press, 1985.

Freud, Sigmund. "From the History of an Infantile Neurosis." SE17:7–122.

Freud, Sigmund. *The Future of an Illusion*. SE21:1–56.

Freud, Sigmund. "The Future Prospects of Psycho-Analytical Therapy." SE11:141–51.

Freud, Sigmund. *Group Psychology and the Analysis of the Ego*. SE18:65–143.

Freud, Sigmund. *The Interpretation of Dreams*. Translated by Joyce Crick. Oxford: Oxford University Press, (1900) 1999.

Freud, Sigmund. *Leonardo da Vinci and a Memory of His Childhood.* SE11:63–137.

Freud, Sigmund. *Letters of Sigmund Freud.* Edited by Ernst L. Freud. Translated by Tania Stern and James Stern. New York: Basic Books, 1960.

Freud, Sigmund. *The Letters of Sigmund Freud to Eduard Silberstein, 1871–1881.* Edited by Walter Boehlich. Translated by Arnold J. Pomerans. Cambridge: Harvard University Press, 1990.

Freud, Sigmund. *Moses and Monotheism.* SE23:7–137.

Freud, Sigmund. *New Introductory Lectures on Psycho-Analysis.* SE22:5–182.

Freud, Sigmund. "Notes upon a Case of Obsessional Neurosis." SE10:155–318.

Freud, Sigmund. "Postscript to *The Question of Lay Analysis.*" SE20:251–8.

Freud, Sigmund. "Psycho-Analysis and Telepathy." SE18:177–93.

Freud, Sigmund. "Psycho-Analytic Notes on an Autobiographical Account of a Case of Paranoia (Dementia Paranoides)." SE12:3–79.

Freud, Sigmund. "Sexuality in the Aetiology of the Neuroses." SE3:261–85.

Freud, Sigmund. *Totem and Taboo.* SE13:1–161.

Freud, Sigmund. "The Uncanny." SE17: 219–52.

Gay, Peter. *The Bourgeois Experience: Victoria to Freud.* 5 vols. New York: Oxford Univ. Press, Vols 1 & 2; W. W. Norton, Vols 3–5, 1984–98.

Gay, Peter. *Freud for Historians.* Oxford: Oxford University Press, 1985.

Gay, Peter. *Freud: A Life for Our Time.* New York: W.W. Norton & Company, 1988.

Hobbes, Thomas. *Leviathan.* Edited by Richard Tuck. Cambridge: Cambridge University Press, (1651) 1991.

Hoffman, Louise E. "War, Revolution, and Psychoanalysis: Freudian Thought begins to Grapple with Social Reality." *Journal of the History of the Behavioral Sciences* 17, no. 2 (1981): 251–69.

Jones, Ernest. *The Life and Work of Sigmund Freud.* 3 vols. New York: Basic Books, 1953–57.

Kaye, Howard L. *Freud as a Social and Cultural Theorist: On Human Nature and the Civilizing Process.* London: Routledge, 2019.

Lemert, Charles. *Social Theory: The Multicultural, Global, and Classic Readings.* Boulder: Westview Press, 1993.

Lemert, Charles. *Sociology after the Crisis.* Boulder, CO: Westview Press, 1995.

Macmillan, Malcolm. *Freud Evaluated: The Completed Arc.* Amsterdam: North-Holland, 1991.

Macmillan, Malcolm. "New Answers to Old Questions: What the Freud-Fliess Correspondence Tells Us." *Psychoanalytic Review* 77, no. 4 (1990): 555–72.

Macmillan, Malcolm. "The Sources of Freud's Methods for Gathering and Evaluating Clinical Data." In *Freud and the History of Psychoanalysis,* edited by Toby Gelfand and John Kerr, 99–151. Hillsdale, NJ: The Analytic Press, 1992.

McGuire, William, ed. *The Freud/Jung Letters: The Correspondence between Sigmund Freud and C.G. Jung.* Translated by Ralph Manheim and R.F.C. Hull. Princeton: Princeton University Press, 1974.

Meng, Heinrich and Ernst L. Freud, eds. 1963. *Psychoanalysis and Faith: The Letters of Sigmund Freud & Oskar Pfister.* Translated by Eric Mosbacher. New York: Basic Books, 1963.

Montesquieu, Charles de Secondat. *The Spirit of the Laws.* Translated and edited by Anne E. Cohler, Basia Carolyn Miller, and Harold Samuel Stone. Cambridge: Cambridge University Press, (1748) 1989.

Nicholls, Angus, and Martin Liebscher, eds. *Thinking the Unconscious: Nineteenth-Century German Thought.* Cambridge: Cambridge University Press, 2010.

Nunberg, Herman, and Ernst Federn, eds. *Minutes of the Vienna Psychoanalytic Society.* 4 vols. Translated by M. Nunberg. New York: International Universities Press, 1962–75.

Otto, Rudolf. *The Idea of the Holy.* Translated by John W. Harvey. London: Oxford University Press, (1917) 1958.

Rorty, Richard. "Human Rights, Rationality, and Sentimentality." In *Truth and Progress: Philosophical Papers,* vol. 3, 167–85. Cambridge: Cambridge University Press, 1998.

Schorske, Carl E. "Politics in a New Key: An Austrian Trio." In *Fin-de-Siècle Vienna,* 116–180. New York: Vintage Books, 1981.

Sulloway, Frank J. *Freud, Biologist of the Mind: Beyond the Psychoanalytic Legend.* Cambridge: Harvard University Press, 1979.

Wolfe, Alan. "The Professor of Desire." *The New Republic,* June 3, 1991: 29–35.

Wrong, Dennis H. *The Problem of Order: What Unites and Divides Society.* New York, NY: The Free Press, 1994.

Yerushalmi, Yosef Hayim. *Freud's Moses: Judaism Terminable and Interminable.* New Haven: Yale Univ. Press, 1991.

PART 2

Freud and the Frankfurt School

∴

CHAPTER 2

Freud's Psychology of Religion: The Frankfurt School, Determinate Negation, and Return to Religion

Dustin J. Byrd

Among the 19th and 20th century intellectuals who criticized religion in the name of emancipating humanity from its intellectual bondage, Sigmund Freud has stood out as being one of the fiercest voices, not because he harbored a pathological hatred for religion, but rather because he analyzed religion through the prism of his "new art and science," psychoanalysis, and found it to be all too human. Rooted in the secularizing and "scientific" zeitgeist of the 19th century, which also gave birth to the demystifying works of Ludwig Feuerbach, Karl Marx, and Friedrich Nietzsche, Freud's psychology of religion attempted to demonstrate that religion was merely an epiphenomenon of the human psyche reacting to the human condition, conditioned by time, place, material reality, culture, etc. In other words, religion was a product of humanity's attempt to understand reality and give itself a sense of meaning and purpose. With the four books most attuned to questions about religion, *Totem and Taboo* (1913), *The Future of an Illusion* (1927), *Civilization and its Discontents* (1930), and *Moses and Monotheism* (1939), Freud attempted to bring the gods down to earth and locate their realities within their true *fons et origo*: the psyche. However, in the process of negating religion through psychoanalysis, Freud utilized an analytical axe on a subject that called for the detailed work of an analytical scalpel. That scalpel, I claim, was developed by the Frankfurt School's psychoanalytic and philosophical reclamation of religion from Freud and his fellow materialists. While appropriating Freud's psychoanalysis as a means of "ideology critique," the Frankfurt School, especially Max Horkheimer, Theodor W. Adorno, Leo Löwenthal, Walter Benjamin, Erich Fromm, and later Jürgen Habermas, attempted to rescue certain semantic and semiotic elements from religion that had been discarded by Freud. What for believers was metaphysical truth, for Freud was an illusion, rooted in the Oedipus complex, psychological projection, wish fulfillment, and irrationality. For the Frankfurt School, partially rooted in Freud work, the whole of religion was not untrue; there were substantive truths hidden within religion's illusionary facade. Yet, despite the merits of the Frankfurt School's determinate negation of religion (and Freud's critique of religion), it is important today that we also re-engage with Freud's critical psychology of religion, as a psychoanalytical approach to understanding why religion in the West has become in many cases grossly pathological in the post-secular society.

In this essay, I will (1) briefly discuss Freud's relationship with, and analysis of, religion; (2) attempt to elucidate how and why the first generation of the Frankfurt School, who were deeply influenced by Freud, ultimately rejected Freud's *abstract negation* of a religion for a more nuanced *determinate negation* of religion, and (3), demonstrate why it is fruitful to return to Freud's original critiques of religion today, especially in light of the growing nihilistic conditions of modernity and religions' reactionary rebellion against those conditions.

1   Freud's Jewish Identity and Rejection of Religion

From a very early age, Sigmund Freud was concerned with religion, especially religions' role within the cultures of ancient societies, such as Greece and Rome. Although his parents, Jacob and Amalia, maintained a devoutly Jewish household, Sigmund could not bring himself to believe in the theological and cultural superstitions of Judaism, nor the Christian superstitions of his "ugly, elderly, but clever" Czech nanny – his *Kinderfrau* – Theresa "Resi" Wettik, who was a committed Catholic, and who "told [him] a great deal about God and hell."[1] Despite his aversion to religion, Sigmund never denied his "Jewishness," although he never clearly defined it either. For most of his life, it merely served as an ethnic identity, not a worldview.[2] Yet, by 1930, Freud's "Jewishness" seemed to be more than just a signifier of his ethnic origins.[3] In the preface to the Hebrew translation of *Totem and Taboo*, Freud claimed he was "ignorant of the language of holy writ," "completely estranged from the religion of his

---

1   Letter from Sigmund Freud to Wilhelm Fliess, in Sigmund Freud, *The Origins of Psychoanalysis, letters to Wilhelm Fliess, drafts and notes: 1887–1902*, ed. Maria Bonaparte, Anna Freud, and E. Kris, trans. E. Mosbacher and James Strachey (New York: Basic Books, 1954), 219–220; Harry T. Hardin, "On the vicissitudes of Freud's early mothering – I: Early Environment and Loss," *Psychoanalytic Quarterly* 56 (1988), 639. It is possible that Sigmund Freud was secretly baptized by his Czech nanny. See Paul C. Vitz, *Sigmund Freud's Christian Unconscious* (New York: The Guilford Press, 1988), 17–20.
2   Jerry Victor Diller, *Freud's Jewish Identity: A Case Study in the Impact of Ethnicity* (London: Associated University Presses, 1991), 90–146.
3   Sigmund Freud, "Preface to the Hebrew Translation," in *Totem and Taboo, Standard Edition Vol. 13* (London: The Hogarth Press, 1955), xv.

fathers – as well as from every other religion." Additionally, he claimed that he "cannot take a share in nationalist ideals" of the Jewish people via Zionism, yet nonetheless "never repudiated his people," and felt that he was "in his essential nature a Jew" and had "no desire to alter that nature."[4] When he posed the question about what is still Jewish about himself if he had abandoned such "common characteristics" of Jews, he replies: "a very great deal, and probably its very essence."[5] What precisely comprises the "essence" of Jewishness is a question for another study, but it is sufficient to point out here that Freud believed that he could thoroughly reject Judaism (and Zionism)[6] and remain in "essence" a Jew.[7] Unfortunately, the question of what constitutes the "essential Jew" is one that Freud uncomfortably shared with many Anti-Semites.[8] According to the Freud biographer, Louis Breger, 'Freud never hesitated to declare himself a Jew – he was proud to be a defiant member of a group of outsiders – yet he distanced himself from the religion … and enjoyed thinking about all the anger his new book [*Moses and Monotheism*] would stir up among [Jewish] believers.'[9] Throughout his life, Freud was a double-outsider: a *Jewish* outsider in Bourgeois-Christian Vienna, and an atheistic modern man-of-science within a believing Jewish community.

---

4 Ibid., XXXi.
5 Ibid.
6 In a February 26, 1930, letter to Dr. Chaim Koffler, who worked on behalf of the Zionist fundraising organization Keren HaYesod, Freud made his misgivings about the Zionist project in Palestine known. He wrote: "I do not think that Palestine could ever become a Jewish state, nor that the Christian and Islamic worlds would ever be prepared to have their holy places under Jewish care. It would have seemed more sensible to me to establish a Jewish homeland on a less historically-burdened land. But I know that such a rational viewpoint would never have gained the enthusiasm of the masses and the financial support of the wealthy." See Eran J. Rolnik, *Freud in Zion: Psychoanalysis and the Making of Modern Jewish Identity* (London: Karnac Books Ltd., 2012), 67–68.
7 I have attempted to give an answer to this question of what makes Freud "essentially Jewish" elsewhere. See Dustin J. Byrd, *The Frankfurt School and the Dialectics of Religion: Translating Critical Faith into Critical Theory* (Kalamazoo, MI: Ekpyrosis Press, 2020), 84–87.
8 A common trope among Anti-Semites, especially in the early 20th century, was that Jews remained Jews even when they assimilated European culture. Therefore, no matter how acculturated they were to their home countries, they always remained Jewish "in essence," i.e., there was something that made them non-identical to what they were living as. Thus, they may be living as a Dutchman, a German, an Italian, etc., but either through genetics or their inescapable *geist* (spirit), they remained Jewish, and such a recalcitrant element could never be assimilated away.
9 Louis Breger, *Freud: Darkness in the midst of Vision* (New York: John Wiley & Sons, Inc., 2000), 358.

Freud was also acutely aware that his lack of Jewish faith did not stop his critics from viewing psychoanalysis as a "Jewish science," one that undermined the ethics and morals of the Bourgeois-Christian society within which it was born.[10] This label disturbed Freud, who thought of psychoanalysis as a neutral science detached from his ethnic origins. The ability to break out of the intellectual ghetto of the Jews via an Aryan apostle was one of the core reasons why Freud was so heavily invested in Carl Gustav Jung; the Swiss psychiatrist would be the Aryan conduit that would give psychoanalysis the kind of social-scientific legitimacy it needed. Through Jung and other non-Jewish analysts, psychoanalysis would be liberated from the residue of Jewishness that Freud inevitably marked it with (or at least that society accused it of). That design went awry with Jung's defection from Freud's inner-circle, as well as with Jung's slide into "Aryan psychology," which he distinguished from "Jewish psychology," only later to lament his Nazi-inspired lapse in judgment.[11]

Beginning at the University of Vienna in 1873, through his time as a student and researcher, and with his later development of psychoanalysis, Freud's relationship to religion calcified. Having adopted a materialist *weltanschauung*, religion remained a subject of study, but never an object of emotional and/or spiritual investment. Although it is common for individuals to become more religious as death draws near, Freud resisted, having never felt the "oceanic feeling" that he discussed with the French dramatist and mystic, Romain Rolland.[12] However, he moved in a parallel fashion to such religious conversion; his attention to religious questions became acute in the later decades of his life, as religion became a core subject of psychoanalytic interrogation. It would be too much to say he had an intellectual *ersatz*-conversion to religion in his later years, but it is telling that religious questions appeared on his horizon as darkness closed in on his life, i.e., his jaw cancer became increasingly worse; the Nazis took power in Austria via the *Anschluss* in March of 1938; the fascist threat against his family (especially his daughter Anna), and his forced exile to London, where he would eventually die of an overdose of morphine (September 23, 1939). Even for the most devout atheist, which we can consider Freud, human suffering and the approach of death can provoke "religious-like"

---

10   Stephen Frosh, *Hate and the "Jewish Science": Anti-Semitism, Nazism and Psychoanalysis* (London: Palgrave Macmillan, 2005), 63–147.
11   Breger, *Freud,* 359.
12   Sigmund Freud, *Civilization and its Discontents, Standard Edition Vol. 21* (London: The Hogarth Press, 1961), 64. Freud believed that the "oceanic feeling" itself existed prior to religion, as it was a phenomenon common to the mind. Only later was it interpreted in a theological manner so that it became a "religious" phenomenon. Ibid., 72.

introspection, and it certainly did with Freud. However, he remains unconvinced of the essential truth claims of Judaism (and Christianity). He did not succumb to religious answers to such existential questions, and there is no evidence he ever entertained such religious answers. Rather, he continued to theorize about religion from the perspective of a psychoanalytic non-believer.

2   Freud's Main Critiques of Religion

For Freud, religion showed all the signs of being a very human phenomenon, one that played an important role in the development of civilization, especially as it contributed to the defense of humanity from nature.[13] Yet, despite its *historical* significance, religion within an age of enlightenment, science, and autonomous reason, only distorted mankind's metaphysical understanding of the world. Indeed, the residue of religion within modern Western man appeared to Freud to be akin to the neurotic: an old memory haunting and therefore distorting the existence of the present. In his 1927 book, *The Future of an Illusion,* Freud wrote,

> Our knowledge of the historical worth of certain religious doctrines increases our respect for them, but does not invalidate our proposal that they should cease to be put forward as the reason for the precepts of civilization. On the contrary! Those historical residues have helped us to view religious teachings, as it were, as neurotic relics, and we may now argue that the time has probably come, as it does in an analytic treatment, for replacing the effects of repression by the results of the rational operation of the intellectual.[14]

Much like his successors in the Frankfurt School, Freud believed that religion harbored certain humanistic truths, but religion disfigured them by presenting such truths within language that was appropriate for the pre-rational childhood of humanity. Freud writes, 'The truths contained in religious doctrines

---

13   Sigmund Freud, *The Future of an Illusion, Standard Edition 21* (London: The Hogarth Press, 1961), 15–20. Freud defines "civilization" in the following: "It includes on the one hand all the knowledge and capacity that men have acquired in order to control the forces of nature and extract its wealth for the satisfaction of human needs, and, on the other hand, all the regulations necessary in order to adjust the relations of men to one another and especially the distribution of the available wealth." Ibid., 6.
14   Ibid., 44.

are after all so distorted and systematically disguised that the mass of humanity cannot recognize them as truth.'[15] Freud's "appointed task," and therefore the task of psychoanalysis, was not necessarily to translate such "religious" truths into post-metaphysical language, as the philosopher Jürgen Habermas encourages religious people to do, but rather psychoanalysis' task is to forward the process of "reconciling men to civilization," and in that de-mystification and disenchanting process, *abstractly negate* religion.[16] Indeed, Freud argues that it is better to confront mankind with a picture of reality that bluntly shows it for what it is, as opposed to hiding reality behind religious semantic and semiotic materials. Even children ought not be spared a brutal image of the really-existing world: 'We have become convinced that it is better to avoid such symbolic disguising of the truth in what we tell children and not to withhold from them a knowledge of the true state of affairs commensurate with their intellectual level.'[17] Because religion was "the universal obsessional neurosis," arising out of the Oedipus complex, i.e., "out of the relation to the father," it was important that the "wishful-illusions" that it forwards be deflated by the reality principle.[18] Thus, it is the principle task of psychoanalysis to be the "sensible teacher," who seeks the betterment of their pupils by helping them ease into the "new development," i.e., reality beyond the wishful illusions, in such a way that it will "mitigate the violence of its irruption."[19]

For Freud, religion was an *illusion* – a neurotic attachment to the answers and ways-of-being of the past. While religion had its purpose within the childhood of human history, its continual anachronistic presence perpetuated the childishness of mankind's psychic life within modernity. Psychoanalysis, as being an element within the broader Enlightenment movement and its demythologization and disenchantment process, would contribute to the liberation of human beings from fear and help install them as masters of their own lives.[20] For Freud, emancipation meant to see the world for what it is, without the maternal/consoling function of religion, to see the rational within and beyond the given.

---

15 Ibid.
16 Ibid.
17 Ibid., 44–45.
18 Ibid., 43.
19 Ibid. 43.
20 For Theodor W. Adorno and Max Horkheimer, this was the core goal of the Enlightenment. See *Dialectic of Enlightenment: Philosophical Fragments,* ed. Gunzelin Schmid Noerr, trans. Edmund Jephcott (Stanford, CA: Stanford University Press, 2002), 1.

In *Civilization and its Discontents* (1930), published just three years after *The Future of an Illusion*, Freud returns to themes he already developed within his previous book, especially the psychic problems created by the heavy burden placed on the psyche by the normative demands of civilization. Referring to his previous book, Freud gives us a basic definition of what he thinks is religion:

> A system of doctrines and promises which on the one hand explains to him [the believer] the riddles of this world with enviable completeness, and, on the other, assures him that a careful Providence will watch over his life and will compensate him in a future existence for any frustrations he suffers here.[21]

For Freud, this "Providence" is merely a father-image projected into the cosmos; it is an ersatz-father that both replicates the individual's earthly father as well as constructs an idealized one.[22] If humans feel ambivalent towards their earthly father, so too do they feel ambivalent towards the "heavenly father," even though they often repress the animosity of such ambivalence in order to secure the protection and/or preferred status that only an all-powerful cosmic father can provide. Nevertheless, for Freud, the religious worldview, with its "completeness," soteriological assurances, and theological presuppositions, was infantile and delusional; it is a mental flight into a false reality, much like a psychosis. While it gave solace to the broken, hope to the hopeless, and psychological comfort for those in need, in the end it suppressed reason and directed the believer's priorities towards an afterlife at the expense of this life.[23] Ultimately, it was a coping mechanism for unfulfilled happiness, as it satiated the longing for something other than the brutality and alienation of the human condition. Religion was merely a means of sustaining oneself via delusions as one traverses the horror and terror of existence.[24]

---

21 Freud, *Civilization and its Discontents*, 74.
22 Sigmund Freud, *Totem and Taboo, Standard Edition Vol. 13* (London: The Hogarth Press, 1955), 1–162.
23 Freud, *Civilization and its Discontents*, 87.
24 Freud gives a variety of ways in which religion helps individuals cope with the suffering caused by unfulfilled happiness in chapter 2 of *Civilization and its Discontents*. Among these religious (and non-religious) coping mechanisms are: (1) the moderation of happiness, (2) cutting oneself off from unhappiness via monasticism or "happiness in quietness," (3) intoxicants to drown one's unhappiness away temporarily, (4) kill the instincts via religious praxis, especially in Buddhism and Yoga, (5) sublimation of unhappiness into other creative activities, (5) flight into illusions, i.e., a break from reality, (6) retreat into hermit status, which is a form of flight into illusion as it creates a new reality. Nevertheless, in agreement with Buddhism and Arthur Schopenhauer, Freud knows that the pleasure

Yet, humans are happiness-seeking creatures; we strive to maximize pleasure, fulfillment, eudaimonia, while simultaneously attempting to avoid pain, suffering, and hopelessness. Part of the maximization of pleasure is the fulfillment of instinctual needs, impulses, and drives that are endemic to the human condition. By being an all-encompassing and exclusivist system of thought and praxis, religion 'imposes equally on everyone its own path to the acquisition of happiness and protection from suffering,' writes Freud. He continues:

> Its technique consists in depressing the value of life and distorting the picture of the real world in a delusional manner – which presupposes an intimidation of the intelligence. At this price, by forcibly fixing them into a state of psychical infantilism and drawing them into a mass delusion, religions succeeds in sparing many people an individual neurosis. But hardly anything more.[25]

In the West, it is Christianity that is most at fault for the distortion of the psyche via the moral and ethical norms it imposes upon the population, which are always tied to its metaphysical claims. For Freud, such moral-ethical prohibitions stunt the obtainment of happiness, as it blocks the fulfillment of instincts, impulses, and drives. Freud states, 'what we call our [Christian] civilization is largely responsible for our misery, and that we should be much happier if we gave it up and returned to primitive conditions.'[26] Here, "primitive conditions" is a signifier for the "state of nature": existence without the instinct-repressing constraints of civilizations, especially religion's unnatural and/or irrational prohibitions absorbed and imposed by the super-ego. It is assumed that without such constraints, the neuroses caused by civilizational demands would be alleviated, as there would no longer be a psychological conflict between the demands of instincts and the equally powerful demands of the civilization. However, Freud admits that Thomas Hobbes' *bellum omnium contra omnes* (war of all against all) sits uneasily under the thin veneer of civilization, and therefore the weakening of civilizational norms and prohibitions could – and would – unleash mankind's instinctive aggressiveness, destructiveness, and inherent nihilism – a prospect he saw in both WWI and with the rise of the Nazis.

---

principle can never be fully satiated, and thus suffering will continue regardless of the coping mechanism deployed. Freud, *Civilization and its Discontents*, chapter 2.
25   Ibid., 84–85.
26   Ibid., 86.

Although the image of a society without restrictions appears momentarily as absolute freedom, upon reflection it becomes abundantly clear that freedom is elusive in such an anomic state. The desired autonomy of the individual in the anomic condition gives way to absolute heteronomy for the vast majority of individuals, while the few, the powerful, the Machiavellian, the most vicious and brutal, reign unencumbered by the restraints of empathy, compassion, and mercy. They flourish as the predators within the Aristocratic Law of Nature, while the many remain the prey, with no neutral higher authority – law or otherwise – to appeal to. Freedom is elusive amidst chaos; that much Thomas Hobbes, Freud, and others have assured us.

Freud argues that while religion's restrictions and prohibitions suppress instinctual fulfillment, it results in a well-ordered civilization, one that can regulate competing interests via rational means, as opposed to the unjust "law of the jungle," i.e., "might makes right." Substantive freedom, albeit eclipsed by cultural norms, is found only within the restrictions of civilization. Yet, this well-ordered civilization sacrifices the fulfillment of instincts that would run unencumbered within anomic conditions, thus stunting the happiness that would come about via the fulfillment of such instincts. Such a conflict between instinct-fulfillment and the necessity of civilization is the source of the ambivalence we feel towards civilization. On the one hand, we recognize its absolute necessary, while on the other hand, we resent the repression and suffering it demands of us. We live within perpetual ambivalence towards that which we need, which is also that which we hate, much like the father – another source of authority blunting our boundless happiness. Religion, as a civilizing force, is often a source of those restrictions and prohibitions, and thus shares in the blame for that which ails us. Indeed, for most of the West's history, it was the chief source such socially-induced neurotic ailments.

For Freud, mankind must escape its infantile attachments to religious thinking and religious ways-of-being-in-the-world if it is to maturate and realize the world for what it is. In other words, the reality principle must win over the illusion if mankind is to secure its future. However, in seeing religion in its totality as a "universal obsessional neurosis," worthy of the dustbin of history, did Freud inadvertently discard the humanistic "truths contained within religious doctrines" when in fact they were salvageable?[27] Admittedly, they were "distorted and systematically disguised" by their religious exterior, but they were obviously recognizable, even for Freud. How else would the truth be identifiable beyond their distorted form? Were these truths unworthy of rescue?[28]

---

27 Freud, *The Future of an Illusion*, 44.
28 Ibid.

Although Freud never fully articulates which truths he locates beyond their distorted religious form, it is clear that he saw something worthy of describing as "truths." The awareness that truths persisted within religion, despite its deleterious effect on society, impelled later Freudian theorists, especially the first generation of the Frankfurt School, to try to identify, translate, and therefore rescue such semantic and semiotic material. They will carry on the Freudian Enlightenment by retrieving that which Freud discarded: the demythologizing and enlightening aspects of religion that could still be translated into post-metaphysical language via autonomous reason – thus rescuing both religion *and* the enlightenment, which had become exhausted already by the mid-20th century.

3   The Frankfurt School's Determinate Negation of Religion Post-Freud

Max Horkheimer, the Freudian, Schopenhauerian, critical theorist, and long-time director of the Institute for Social Research (Frankfurt School), wrote the following on the dialectics of religion:

> In its symbols, religion places an apparatus at the disposal of tortured men through which they express their suffering and their hope. This is one of its most important functions. A respectable psychology of religion would have to distinguish between its positive and negative aspects, it would have to separate proper human feelings and ideas from an ideological form which falsifies them but which is also partly their product.[29]

In this passage, Horkheimer points to a very important aspect of religion that was overlooked by Freud's psychoanalytic approach to religion: religion is a *dialectical* phenomenon, one that has both progressive and regressive aspects, as well as authoritarian and emancipatory elements. Horkheimer's thinking echoes Marx's famous "opiate" definition of religion, which clearly identifies the dialectic of religion – both its truthful and ideological form. Yet, Marx chose to nevertheless follow Feuerbach's diminishment of God to anthropological projections – a reductionistic psychological theogony – and thus the whole of religion (within its religious form) was negated.[30] We can read

---

29 Max Horkheimer, *Dawn and Decline: Notes 1926–1931 & 1950–1969*, trans. Michael Shaw (New York: The Seabury Press, 1978), 58.
30 Marx writes in his *Contribution to the Critique of Hegel's Philosophy of Right: Introduction*, the often quoted but just as often misunderstood line: "Religious suffering is at the same

Horkheimer's comment about a "respectable psychology of religion" as being a subtle critique of the anti-religious dogmatism found in much of Freudian (and Feuerbachian) thought. Horkheimer points out that there are certain elements within religion that allow human suffering, misery, doubt, depression, etc., to be expressed, and such should be a priority for psychoanalysis. Indeed, for Theodor W. Adorno, 'The need to lend a voice to suffering is a condition of all truth.' This is true for theology, which is rooted in mankind's attempt to understand his suffering via theodicy, as well as in psychoanalysis, which is likewise an attempt to understand the psychological roots of mankind's mental ailments and torture.[31] Without the allowance of human suffering to speak, whether it be in prose, couched in theological language, or through the free association of an analysand, one can only have a distorted vision of what is true. In other words, if such suffering is repressed, it will emerge in neurotic form, a distorted outlet for the repressed. Theology and religious praxis, for Horkheimer, serves as an escape route for suffering via suffering's sublation, so that humanity can make sense of its misery, even if in a distorted and/or metaphysical form. To deny individuals religion as a vehicle of expression is to heighten the potential that the psychological conflicts that animate their suffering will be left unarticulated, i.e., repressed, and therefore more self-defeating.

Whether it's the psychoanalyst, interpreting the dreams, reflections, or memories of the analysand, or the psychoanalyst listening to the religious believer express their suffering, hopes, and desires through religious semantics, it is the task of the critical interlocutor to ascertain the latent truth within the manifest language. In other words, the truth-core of human suffering, which returns to the sufferer through their symbolic language and seemingly unexplainable actions, has to not only be recognized by the psychologist of religion, but also has to be understood as existing within the trauma caused by the brutal realities of human existence, thus giving birth to it. Max Horkheimer's "longing for the totally other," that which is other than the brutal realities of this world, is both a religious hope, as well as a deep-seated psychological desire conditioned by the damaged and damaging world.[32] It expresses the hopeless hope

---

time an expression of real suffering and protest against real suffering. Religion is the sigh of the oppressed creature, the sentiment of a heartless world, and the soul of soulless conditions. It is the opium of the people." Understanding religion to be both a protest as well as an opiate, Marx recognized the dialectical form of religion. Karl Marx, *The Marx-Engels Reader*, ed. by Robert C. Tucker (New York: W.W. Norton & Co., Inc, 1978), 54.

31   Theodor W. Adorno, *Negative Dialectics,* trans. E.B. Ashton (New York: Continuum, 1999), 17–18.

32   Max Horkheimer, *Die Sehnsucht nach dem ganz Anderen: Ein Interview mit Kommentar von Helmut Gumnior* (Hamburg: Furche-Verlag, 1970).

that the *not-yet* but *ought-to-be* may still be brought into existence; it expresses the hope that the tyranny of the phenomenal world is not all that exists, but that the promised grace of the noumena is not merely a wish-fulfilling idea, but a possible reality; and finally it expresses the life-sustaining hope that the murderer shall ultimately not triumph over the innocent victim, but that the victim will have their day in court, if not in this life than in the next.[33] For Horkheimer, it is the "respectable psychology of religion" that understands the human truth within theological language and religious praxis. An *abstract negation* of religion, which sees religion merely as ideology and/or the result of a neurosis, leaves the psychoanalyst blind to the reality of the dialectic of religion: that it is comprised of both "proper human feelings and ideas" as well as the "ideological form which falsifies them,"[34] and that it is the "catalogue" of humanity's attempt to make sense of its suffering.[35] In other words, religion is the storehouse of humanity's collective psyche objectified into theistic thought. As such, nothing could be richer for psychoanalytic investigation than the history of religious thought and praxis.

In ages past, Horkheimer contends, religion played a much more critical function within the West. It was not merely a "crude transfiguration of existing conditions," an ideological force that sanctified the status quo, but rather a force that undermined such dehumanizing conditions.[36] Horkheimer writes,

> Historically, the religious machinery did not always serve to distract from earthly practice; in part, it itself developed the energies which today unmask these distractions. The idea of justice which is absolutely impartial toward the things of this world is contained in the belief in the resurrection of the dead and the last judgment. If those ideas were to be discarded along with the myth, mankind would be deprived of a *propulsive concept* which, though certainly not as a belief, might today be applied as a criterion to judge the powers that be, and the church in particular.[37]

For Horkheimer, *abstract negation* of religion is a mistake, as it fails to "separate proper human feelings and ideas from an ideological form" and discards the *propulsive elements* along with the *regressive elements* of religion. The

---

33 Ibid.
34 Horkheimer, *Dawn and Decline*, 58.
35 Erich Fromm, *Beyond the Chains of Illusion: My Encounter with Marx and Freud* (New York: Continuum, 2001), 174.
36 Horkheimer, *Dawn and Decline*, 59.
37 Ibid., 58. Emphasis added.

simultaneous abstract negation of the propulsive potentials latent within religion in conjunction with its regressive and disfigured ideological forms, takes revolutionary religion out of the game within emancipatory struggles, such as struggles for class, racial, and gender equality, as well as struggles against colonialism, imperialism, etc.

Horkheimer well understood that religion has long serviced the powerful within societies, acting as their legitimation and sanctification force, but it is also the case that religion has historically acted as a means to overcome unjust status-quos, propelling much of mankind to struggle for an existence worthy of mankind in this world.[38] If religion is abstractly negated, as Freud thought it ought to be, by consequence, all forms of social transformation would have to come from the realm of the secular, as *all* forms of religion would be considered illusionary, infantile, or as ideological falsity distorting its kernel of truth. This severance of religion from emancipatory struggle weakens the attempt to transcend authoritarian regimes and other systems of domination, as not all who struggle against such have adopted an agnostic or atheistic worldview. For Horkheimer, Freud's simplistic *reductio ad neurosis* of religion renders psychoanalysis – at least as it pertains to religion – to the "non-respectable," for it failed to adequately differentiate the dialectical reality of religion and therefore the human suffering animating the religious form.[39]

While it is the case that Freud clearly identified the importance of religion as an element within culture, especially as it relates to civilization building, the question of whether religion ought to persist within the modern world is a separate question. While the psychoanalytic enlightenment contributed to the continual de-Christianization of the West (some have even accused it of being a rival religion), and Freud would have approved of such, it is less clear as to whether the first generation of critical theorist believed religion *should* have a continual role within Western modernity. The question of "should it" as opposed to "will it" have a future in the West are two very different questions.

---

38   Horkheimer writes, 'Whether noted by a bourgeois or a proletarian revolutionary, the alliance between the church and the ruling clique, for example, is a fact, and that fact is all the more revolting because it is directed against the one element which might serve the church as an excuse: suffering men.' Ibid., 60.

39   Erich Fromm famously tried to deflate the idea that Freud was explicitly anti-religious, especially in his essay, "Freud and Jung," wherein he tried to show that Freud 'opposes religion in the name of ethics – an attitude which can be termed "religious."' In my opinion, Fromm did not succeed in his argument on the face of it, although his points are well taken. In his search for truth, Freud takes on a charge that religion set for itself, and truth is located somewhere beyond the given. See Erich Fromm, *Psychoanalysis and Religion* (New Haven, CT: Yale University Press, 1978), 10–20, 20.

The question of "should it" have a future is subjective, and a matter argued for-or-against via subjective critique and conviction. The question of "will it" have a future is a matter of social dynamics, out of the hands of the subjective wish-fulfillments. Secularizing trends are observable, quantifiable, and objective. While Freud believed religion *should not* have a future, he was not confident that it *would not* have a future, thus was his pessimism about humanity's inability to relinquish its infantile condition. Horkheimer and Adorno on the other hand, were confident that traditional religion and religious ways-of-being were on their way out, that the Enlightenment as a secularizing force in the West would eventually engulf the religious worldview and render it a neurotic, irrational, and an obsolete relic of the past. Such a conviction about the overwhelming power of secular modernity led Adorno, in his essay, "Reason and Revelation," to write, 'Nothing of theological content will persist without being transformed; every content will have to put itself to the test of migrating into the realm of the secular, the profane.'[40] For Adorno, nothing of the theological, and thus religious, tradition will survive modernity unless it is translated into autonomous reason, i.e., post-metaphysical language. In other words, if certain semantic and semiotic materials rooted within the depth of the religious mythos and way-of-being are to survive within the secular Enlightenment, especially the Bourgeois, Freudian, and Marxist variants, they will have to migrate into the "realm of the secular," where it can be transformed into positive legislation, social norms, and democratic ideals, values, and principles, leaving behind the legitimation of divinity (*Theos*) it is currently afforded within its closed semantic universe, and satisfying itself with the legitimation of humanity (*Humanitas*).

One may ask if religious and theological concepts can escape their "translation" (determinate negation) into post-metaphysical reasoning by offering a defense of their validity through rational arguments, thus matching their critics' accusations with rational defenses of their own. Adorno argues in the negative, citing those in the 18th century who already attempted to do so. He writes,

> such a defense against *ratio* had to be carried out with rational means and was in this respect, as Hegel pronounced in the *Phenomenology*, hopeless from the very start: with the means of argumentation it used, the very defense already assumed the principle that belonged to its adversary.[41]

---

40 Theodor W. Adorno, "Reason and Revelation," in *Critical Models: Interventions and Catchwords,* trans. Henry W. Pickford (New York: Columbia University Press, 2005), 136.
41 Ibid., 136.

For Adorno, there is no secret exit from the inevitable: the preservation of religion via secular translation into post-metaphysical reasoning is the only way (at least in the West) to rescue religious semantics and semiotics. The Bourgeois, Freudian, and Marxist Enlightenments have gone too far down the Western *Sonderweg* (deviant path) for religion to comfortably live within a fundamentally non-religious Western world. It reveals itself as a relic of the past, painfully alienated in the current demythologized *Zeitgeist* and *Lebenswelt*. As such, religion can no longer depend upon the "authority of society," i.e., the consensus it enjoyed in a more homogeneously religious age.[42] No longer is the sacred afforded a privileged and therefore "unquestionable" position. Now, all claims have to go through the democratic process through which a consensus is formed; all is up for debate and subjected to autonomous reason's inquisition, even the most sacred of ideals. Although many still resist such a process, the age of *argumentum ad antiquitatem* is finished in the West, and it cannot be resurrected anachronistically without collapsing into absurdity and/or authoritarian. It would appear that Freud's wish for a Western world without religion is swiftly materializing. The question is: can religion be preserved within secular form within the secular world?

Horkheimer and Adorno's sociology, philosophy, and psychology of religion reveal two important aspects: (1) they think that the secularization process within the West is ongoing and inevitable, and (2) unlike Freud, there are certain elements within religion and theology that *ought* to be translated into post-metaphysical thought, lest they fall victim to the abstract negation of religion, as advocated by modern nominalists and dogmatic materialists. The most profound example of the first generation of critical theorists' determinate negation of religion can be found in the attention paid to one of Judaism's foundational beliefs: the *Bilderverbot*, i.e., or "image ban," the 2nd Commandment of the Jewish Decalogue. This monotheistic commandment establishes the absolute prohibition on the construction of any image purporting to be the Divine. It states, "Thou shalt not make unto thee any graven image."[43] This "anti-idolatry" commandment, which prohibits the association of the created with the creator; the imperfect with the perfect; the contingent with the absolute; the finite with the infinite; the untruth with the truth, was appropriated by the first generation of the Frankfurt School and translated into political philosophy. The *apophatic theology* (negative theology) of Judaism, which can only articulate what "God is not," stands in contrast to *cataphatic theology*, which

---

42   Ibid.
43   Exodus 20:4. New International Version.

discusses in positive language endemic to our species what "God is," was dialectically transformed into critical theory's *apophatic philosophy*, which helps to explain the inherent and abiding "negativity" of the Frankfurt School – in contrast to Freud's epiphenomenal explanations of God and religion.

While for some it may be strange to think of the neo-Marxist and Freudian Frankfurt School as being philosophically rooted in Judaism's most central theological commandments, such a reality can be attested to by the words of many of the Frankfurt School's first generation. For example, on the occasion of Theodor W. Adorno's death in 1969, Horkheimer wrote a letter to Otto O. Herz, who had inquired about Adorno's religious affiliations.[44] Horkheimer wrote,

> I tell you this in order to make Adorno's complicated relationship to religion, to religious allegiance, comprehensible. On the other hand, may I say that the critical theory that we both had a hand in developing has its roots in Judaism. It arises from the idea: *Thou shalt not make any graven images of God.*[45]

Here, Horkheimer attests to the Jewish religious concept of Bilderverbot as being at the root of Critical Theory. Leo Löwenthal, another of the Frankfurt School's first-generation scholars, also attested to the centrality of Judaism's apophatic monotheism within Critical Theory. In an interview with Helmut Dubiel, Löwenthal stated, 'However much I once tried to convince Martin Jay that there were no Jewish motifs among us at the Institute, now, years later and after mature consideration, I must admit to a certain influence of Jewish tradition, which was *co-determinative*.'[46] While Löwenthal does not divulge which particular "Jewish motifs" were "co-determinative" within the Frankfurt School, Adorno gives us a stronger indication in his "Reason and Revelation" essay. In discussing the fate of religion within modern society, he writes, 'I see no other possibility than an extreme ascesis toward any type of revealed faith, an extreme loyalty to the prohibition of images, far beyond what this once originally meant.'[47]

---

44 Adorno was born of a Jewish father and a Corsican Catholic mother, but he was baptized a Protestant. He subsequently became an atheist, albeit not a conventional atheist.
45 Max Horkheimer, *A Life in Letters: Selected Correspondence*, ed. and trans., Manfred R. Jacobson and Evelyn M. Jacobson (Lincoln, NB: The University of Lincoln Press, 2007), 361.
46 Leo Löwenthal, *An Unmastered Past: An Autobiographical Reflection of Leo Lowenthal* (Berkeley: The University of California Press, 1987), 112. Emphasis added.
47 Adorno, "Reason and Revelation," 142.

In Adorno's *Negative Dialectics*, he expressed the counter-intuitive convergence of materialism, especially historical materialism, with the negative theology of the Bilderverbot. He writes,

> The materialist longing to grasp the thing aims at the opposite: it is only in the absence of images that the full object could be conceived. Such absence concurs [*konvergiert*] with the theological ban on images. Materialism brought that ban into secular form by not permitting Utopia to be positively pictured; this is the substance of its negativity. At its most materialistic, materialism comes to agree with theology.[48]

Having taken over the Bilderverbot by translating it into the negativity of apophatic philosophy, the Frankfurt School refused to produce any positive image of what a future wholly-reconciled society would look like. They produced no blueprint for the future world they wished to see. In other words, they exercised an "extreme loyalty to the prohibition of images," that once was a theological ban but became a ban against creating images of utopia (which are all false by definition) that were prevalent within the Cold War. Through the translation of apophatic theology into apophatic philosophy, they stood ready to critique all false images of utopia, all false images of truth, and all false images of the omniscient and powerful leaders, while offering up no positive articulations as alternatives. What was once a ban on false gods, i.e., a ban on theological idolatry, became a ban political idolatry, i.e., the false gods of politics, economics, and society.

This form of "rescue" of certain negative elements within religion via "translation," i.e., a Hegelian "determinate negation," was precisely what Horkheimer and Adorno believed Freud failed to comprehend. His *abstract negation* of religion, wherein those socially emancipatory and psychologically propulsive elements of religion were left in the dustbin of history, only contributed to the present distorted conditions that continue to cause the psychological traumas of today, often because Western man has succumbed to nihilism through its disconnect with reality and metaphysical meaning. Nevertheless, the Frankfurt School did not wholly abandon Freud's critique of religion. Indeed, as religion became more ideological in the post-secular world, i.e., more of a crude transfiguration of already existing conditions, the more Freud's critique of religion became relevant, as the psychological nature of religion was functionalized by those pushing particular ideologies. To explore this, we return to

---

48   Adorno, *Negative Dialectics*, 207.

Freud's critique of religion as it relates to religions' continual existence within the domain of non-religion.

4 After Religion: Subjectivity, Conscience, and the Problem of Meaninglessness

The Austrian psychiatrist and Holocaust survivor, Viktor E. Frankl, believed that the central crisis of humanity in the 20th century was the absence of meaning.[49] Life in the West, despite all of its progress, abundance, education, and prosperity, was suffering from an existential void; life seemed to be purposeless, rudderless, and without inherent value. The traditional religious answers to the question, "what is the point of it all," were no longer sufficient to calm the troubled consciousness of an increasingly secularized civilization. Everything seemed subjectively relative, and outside of scientific "facts" the very validity of the notion of "truth" seemed to be diminishing with each passing day. Something had gone horribly wrong with the Enlightenment, and it was having a deleterious effect on the mental health of Westerners. In response to this existential disaster, Frankl developed his own psychiatric form of therapy, *Logotherapy*, which sought to address the meaning void head on. He would help people find meaning in their lives through their work, their love relations, and through courage in challenging times. But Logotherapy was itself highly subjective, a creature of the very conditions it sought to remedy. Logotherapy helped the *individual* find their *subjective* sense of meaning in life, but subjectivity lacks the very objectivity that was sought by the longing subject. Within the secular society, "meaning" was what individuals believed to be meaningful, and therefore relative to the subject that devised such particular meaning. Beyond one's own subjectivity, individual truths/meaning were not very comforting, as they were no more valid than anyone else's individual truths and meaning, which logically could cancel each other out. While the soul of the *individual* benefited from Frankl's subjective Logotherapy, the *collective* soul of the West continued to be plagued with thoughts and feelings of nihilism. Objective truth, and therefore objective meaning, remained elusive. Frankl was right in thinking therapy was needed, but how does one put a whole civilization on the Logotherapist's couch?

The problem of meaninglessness is nothing new to Western civilization. The subjectivity of individuals expresses itself through the notion of

---

49 Viktor E. Frankl, *Man's Search for Meaning* (Boston: Beacon Press, 2006).

individual conscience. Socrates introduced such conscience through his recalcitrant philosophy in ancient Athens, and Jesus of Nazareth introduced much the same in his version of messianic Judaism in Jerusalem. The Scholastic, St. Thomas Aquinas, taught of the importance of forming the individual conscience in accordance with the teachings of the *Ekklēsia* (Church), demonstrating how conscience ought to be reconciled to tradition. It was Martin Luther who elevated subjectivity above tradition, with his *"hier stehe Ich, Ich kann nicht anders,"* at the Diet of Worms in AD 1521, as well as his "Priesthood of all Believers," which ushered in a de-Hellenized and highly individualistic form of Christianity.[50] Deism, the theology of the Bourgeois Enlightenment, attempted to reconcile man's free will with the concept of God through their own "rational" version of *Deus Otiosus* (Absent God). Later, the German idealists attempted to wrestle with the growing ascent of autonomous subjectivity with the still-lingering objectivity of God. Yet, it was Friedrich Nietzsche who foresaw the inevitable results of subjectivity disassociated from established tradition. He saw nihilism as the ailment that plagued the West, as nihilism was the radical repudiation of objective, universal meaning.[51] Nietzsche claimed that the modern West was experiencing a 'disintegration – that is to say, uncertainty – [which is] peculiar to this age: nothing stands on solid ground or on a sound faith.'[52] The crisis of meaning, i.e., the nightside of autonomous subjectivity, was expressed in Nietzsche's parable of the "madman," who proclaimed the reality of the impossible: the "death of God."

> I mean to tell you! We have killed him – you and I! We are all his murderers! But how have we done it? How were we able to drink up the sea? Who gave us the sponge to wipe away the whole horizon? What did we do when we loosened this earth from its sun? Whither does it now move? Whither do we move? Away from all suns? Do we not dash on unceasingly? Backwards, sideways, forwards, in all directions? Is there still an above and below? Do we not stray, as through infinite nothingness?[53]

The full impact of the disorienting and alienating nature of the liquidation of the Divine was not lost on Nietzsche, but according to Carl Gustav Jung,

---

50   'Here I stand, I can do no others.'
51   Friedrich Nietzsche, *The Will to Power,* trans. Anthony M. Ludovici (New York: Barnes & Nobles, 2006), 5–32.
52   Ibid., 33.
53   Friedrich Nietzsche, *The Gay Science,* trans. Thomas Common (New York: Barnes & Noble, 2008), 103.

who drew on Nietzsche as much as Freud did, moderns have compounded the problem of meaninglessness by not understanding its magnitude.[54] He wrote, 'the lack of meaning in life is a soul-sickness whose full extent and import our age has not yet begun to comprehend.'[55] Modernity's *deicide* left Western man untethered, free from religious restrictions but also fundamentally alone in the world. While some flourished, able to meet the challenge of this ontological isolation, others retreated into non-religious ideologies that provided meaning. In Erich Fromm's words, they "escaped" the horror of their subjective freedom by submitting to the comforting confines of ideologies and leaders, thus providing them with prefabricated meaning, purpose, and community.[56] Many others found themselves stumbling through existence without the former theological *summun bonum* to guide their way through life. Without a sense of objective truth, they were set adrift in a sea of uncertainty with nothing certain above him to appeal to, which led to an inescapable sense of aloneness and insignificance, confusion and despair. Without meaningful ceremonies, rituals, rites of passage, cosmologies, cosmogonies, answers to the theodicy question, etc., even death lost its meaning. Through the materialist's eyes, death was simply the cessation of life. Thus, the dead are gone forever, only symbolically "alive" as long as they're remembered. There is no eternal existence outside of history; the world-as-it-is, is all there is. Because no substantive answers can be given to death in our nihilistic period, death too becomes the subject to ad hoc subjectivity. Thus, to the embarrassment of the modern age, we no longer know how to die. Yet, the meaningless death is merely a symptom of the fact that we are missing something that is "irretrievably lost": authentic religiosity.[57]

Following the Bourgeois and Marxist enlightenments, Freudian psychoanalysis served as one of the pallbearers of existentialist objectivity, that is, of course, after it helped seal the coffin. Freud's anthropomorphic theogony of the Divine tore down the last remains of God's objectivity; it became a mere epiphenomenon of the human mind: a chimera of the longful psyche. Yet, Freud's psychoanalysis, literally the "analysis of the soul (*psyche*)," itself seemed irreconcilable with materialistic, mechanistic, and reductionistic

---

54 Ronald Lehrer, *Nietzsche's Presence in Freud's Life and Thought: On the Origins of a Psychology of Dynamic Unconscious Mental Functioning* (Albany, NY: State University of New York, 1995).
55 Carl Gustav Jung, "The Structure and Dynamics of the Psyche," in *Collected Work Vol. 8* (Princeton, NJ: Princeton University Press, 1970), 815.
56 Erich Fromm, *Escape from Freedom* (New York: Henry Holt & Co., 1994), 23–38.
57 Jürgen Habermas, *An Awareness of What is Missing: Faith and Reason in a Post-Secular Age*, trans. Ciaran Cronin (Malden, MA: Polity Press, 2011), 15.

worldviews, which found no convincing evidence that humans were animated by anything that could be termed a "soul/psyche." The concept of the soul/psyche itself was a relic of the religious past. As a result of this materialization of psychology, various forms of behavioral analysis supplanted psychoanalysis as the "objective" and "scientific" way to study human activity and motivation. It appeared to the behaviorist that psychoanalysis itself was still in the realm of the "mystical," that it retained a little religious residue within its core tenets. Thus, it too must be discarded for scientific materialist and its promise of strict objectivity.

The unintended consequences of secularization via the Enlightenment, scientific materialism, reductionist thought, and extreme rationalism, not only vacated a religious sense of "otherness" within Western society, but it also colonized the very social structure of the West. In other words, the all-encompassing nature of religion was replaced by the all-encompassing nature of non-religion, or in some cases anti-religion, or even theomachism in the case of the Soviet Union. This did not end religion *per se*, but rather transformed the religious individual's belief attitude: *how* they believed their pre-modern beliefs was altered irretrievably.

Those who on the surface remained religious, secretly questioned, or even unconsciously discarded, much of what their religious traditions taught them. The religiosity that once inhabited every aspect of life in the European Middle Ages evaporated under the weight of secular Modernity, autonomous reason, and science. Society had moved from mythos to logos. Heaven and Hell became psychologized: mere wish-fulfillments invoked when confronted with friend of foe. Sacred texts, such as the Bible, were demoted to "self-help" books, i.e., repositories of good advice for attaining high self-esteem, self-assurance, self-righteousness, and moral certitude. Prayer was self-directed meditation, not actual communication with the "totally other." Angels too were wish-fulfillments; they were not real beings among us, but were enchanting figments of the Axial Age imagination, that served merely to anesthetize our painful sense of aloneness. In this theologically-deflated condition, public piety served to mask inner-doubts and garnish bourgeois respectability.

For other "believers," stunted by the oppressiveness of life, the "return to religion" served as subjective – and sometimes familial – therapy. Their motivation to retreat into a religious identity (and community) was based on the psychological and social *needs* of the individual, not the result of the individual being *convinced* of the religion's truth claims, but a search for something – anything – that could assuage the psychological distress caused by the meaning void, as well as to find some form of solidarity in an antagonistically atomized society. The greater the strife, the greater the retreat.

Additionally, religion ceased to be a realm from which the status quo could be questioned. Neutered of his prophetic nature, which in the case of Christianity began in the 4th century with Emperor Constantine (c. 272–337 AD), it was most often recruited into the reproduction of the status quo, not its interrogation. As Max Horkheimer wrote in the mid-20th century, 'These days, Christianity is not primarily used as a religion but as a crude transfiguration of existing conditions.'[58] With only a few exceptions, Christianity no longer challenged the systematic injustices of the world, but rather sanctified that which caused and sustained such injustices.

With the modern deflation into a mere facet of the psyche, religion was no longer the all-encompassing and meaning-giving force it used to be within the whole of the Western society; it had become a mere shadow of its former self, the product of the human mind, not the reality outside of the mind. Autonomous subjectivity was all that was left for the individual in the modern West, and that subjectivity often devolved into pathological individualism and malignant narcissism, often as means to defend against the horror of an all-encompassing subjectivity. Nevertheless, just because religion was now all-but-dead, it did not mean that Western man no longer desired a sense of meaning, connectedness, or purpose. Rather, the need remained, but the traditional giver was gone. What would replace it?

5 An Awareness that Something is Missing: Can we Return to Freud?

The "return to religion" reveals that there is a growing awareness that "something is missing" in the modern West.[59] While religion was demoted, that which was promoted has failed to satisfy a deep-seated "oceanic feeling" within us. As Habermas writes, 'the enlightened modern age has failed to find a suitable replacement for [religion].'[60] Like Nietzsche, Freud understood that the void left by the "Death of God" could be filled by other human endeavors, some individual in nature, while others more collectivist. He saw first-hand the madness that could be brought about by the unifying force of nationalism, hatred of the "other," and the ersatz religion of racist neo-paganism, when he witnessed World War I and the subsequent rise of the Nazis, both of which were forces that brought meaning to populations that were once deeply religious, and in many cases still claimed to be. Subjectivity, that which should

---

58 Horkheimer, *Dawn and Decline*, 59.
59 Habermas, *An Awareness of What is Missing*, 15–23.
60 Ibid., 15.

strengthen the Ego so it would not fall victim to the mass psychogenic delusions purposely conjured up by political ideologies, demagogues, and agitators, was no match for the power of mass movements, which, in the void of authentically critical religion, temporarily brought meaning to the lives of the meaning-devoid masses. The 20th century's descent into genocidal madness teaches us two things: (1) meaning is still important to Western man, and even more so now since the cancer of nihilism has so thoroughly metastasized in his civilization, and (2) there is a distinction between "truth" and "meaning" that must be considered, as it has a massive bearing on the psychological health and wellbeing of Western civilization. Political ideologies may not be true, they may be rooted in irrationality, but they are meaningful, and thus is the power they have over the consciouses of the masses.

Psychoanalysis postulates that the analysand must be confronted with the uncomfortable truths of their biography in order to overcome the neuroses that are impacting their lives. That which is unconscious must be brought to consciousness, so it can be worked through in partnership with the psychoanalyst. Indeed, the greater the repression of the traumatic experience, the more likely it is a contributing factor to the neuroses the analysand struggles with in their daily lives. Therefore, "truth" is both traumatic, being the cause of psychological repression (unless it's a delusion), and also liberating, as confronting it successfully can relieve the analysand of the neurotic symptoms they suffer from. Thus, there is no doubt that truth matters, and that truth is beyond mere subjectivity: it is something concrete, even when it's not in materialist form.[61] However, we must also be prepared to go where Freud wouldn't and distinguish between truth and meaningfulness.

Freud, throughout his whole career, was a seeker of truth. Admirably, truth is what had meaning for him, and that led him to some very uncomfortable situations in conservative Bourgeois Vienna: the Oedipus complex, the sexuality of children, the existence of the death drive (*Todestrieb/Thanatos*), are just a few "truths" that Freud discovered, theorized, and presented to the world, despite such truths being highly controversial, challenging, and discomforting. In articulating these truths within a society that did not want to accept them, let alone simply hear them, he found meaning in them. In fact, the more social resistance such concepts invoked, the more truthful they had to be, for only the most uncomfortable truths engendered such staunch resistance. Yet, for the

---

61 I do not accept post-modernist claims that there is no truth, for even in proclaiming that metaphysical position they *assume* it to be true. Thus, a self-defeating and irreconcilable contradiction lies at the heart of their claims: their claim can only be true if truth exists, but since they postulate that truth does not exist, their claims cannot be true.

sake of argument, let's for a moment claim that such psychological realities are not true. Would they still have been meaningful for Freud if he believed them to be true? I think they would. Why? Because that which is not always true can still be meaningful to those who find meaning in it. Even if much of Freud's psychoanalysis can be found "not to be true" in the strictest scientific/materialist sense, psychoanalysts still find meaning in Freudian thought, because Freud's "truths" about the human condition were not always strict scientific claims. We find philosophical, sociological, and therapeutic truth in his discoveries, arguments, and theories, and that is meaningful to us as academics and therapists, and often are more meaningful to those whom we affect by articulating such Freudian material: our students and analysands.

The historian Diarmaid MacCulloch, in his book, *Christianity: The First Three Thousand Years,* argues for the conceptual difference between "truth" and "meaning" in regard to religion and the Christian tradition in particular. He writes that as a "candid friend of Christianity,"

> I still appreciate the seriousness which a religious mentality brings to the mystery and misery of human existence, and I appreciate the solemnity of religious liturgy as a way of confronting these problems ... I make no pronouncement as to whether Christianity, or indeed any religious belief, is 'true.' This is a necessary self-denying ordinance. Is Shakespeare's *Hamlet* 'true'? It never happened, but it seems to me to be much more 'true,' full of meaning and significance for human beings, than the reality of the breakfast I ate this morning, which was certainly 'true' in a banal sense.[62]

For MacCulloch, the incarnation of God into man may not be a truth that can be verified by any "objective" and/or materialist standards, but it is an objective fact that millions of believers find that religious belief to be meaningful, and because it is meaningful, it is truth in a substantive sense. Just as we can find existential meaning in Ancient Greek tragedies, even though the content of such tragedies most likely never occurred historically, we can find meaning in religious claims that may not be scientifically "true." Did Jonah really spend days within the stomach of a "big fish," only to emerge anew afterwards? Of course not. But the meaning of the story is separate from the objective possibility of a man named Jonah being the delicious breakfast of an unusually large sea-dwelling creature. While stories like that of Jonah and his sea-fairing

---

62 Diarmaid MacCulloch, *Christianity: The First Three Thousand Years* (New York: Viking, 2009), 11.

travails are trivial for some, they are imbued with meaning for others. And as C.G. Jung, has written: 'the least of things with a meaning is always worth more in life than the greatest of things without it.'[63] One is hard pressed to find a more apt sense of existential truth in our post-secular societies than that.

Can we return to a comprehensive state of religiosity within the Western world as we had before? In my opinion, no. That age is irretrievable, and thus is its religious character.[64] No peripeteic-dialectics can de-negate that which the *Sonderweg* has already negated.[65] Can we return to religion through determinate negation, as did the Frankfurt School, and retrieve meaningful elements that are beyond scientific fact? I believe we must. Does that mean that Freud's critique of religion was wrong? No. Freud saw religion from a limited conception of "truth," one that is absolutely necessary to preserve, as it reminds us of the psychological reality of humanity – its hopes, longings, and suffering – which resides in the heart of religion. It also reminds us that religion can be distorted, especially when it gets involved with political ideologies, often contributing to the mass psychoses of civilizational narcissism. Yet, in an age of constant crises – global climate change, pandemics, wars, economic collapses, as well as the crisis of nihilism, which have caused a dramatic rise in anxiety disorders, depression, and a myriad of new neuroses – we must be prepared to let humanity find meaning in the good, even if the good is not technically "true." The "awareness of something missing," as Jürgen Habermas describes our post-modern condition, is a condition that yearns for substantive meaning, in fact requires it.[66] However, if substantive meaning is not provided by the good, it will be provided by the bad. That bad can come in the form of bad religion, which either justifies the unjust status quo, or fights for an anachronistic return to the *status quo ante*, in an attempt to erase the progress achieved by modernity (universal equality, human rights, international law, etc.) in the name of soteriological security. Or the bad can come in the form of destructive political ideologies and demagogues, which, often via populism, temporarily

---

63   Carl Gustav Jung, *The Practice of Psychotherapy, Collected Works 16* (Princeton, NJ: Princeton University Press, 1954), Para 96.
64   My position is not universally accepted. Many religious individuals and communities will attempt to recreate anachronistically the religiosity of a bygone ages. Indeed, Nicholas Berdyaev, the Russian philosopher and Orthodox theologian, believed such a return was not only possible, but was desirable. See Nicolas Berdyaev, "The New Middle Ages," in *The End of our Time,* trans. Donald Attwater (San Rafael, CA: Semantron Press, 2009), 67–120.
65   Dustin J. Byrd, "Palingenetic Ultra-Nationalist Christianity: History, Identity, and the Falsity of Peripeteic Dialectics," *Praktyka Teoretyczna* 42, no. 4 (2021): 7–37.
66   Habermas, *An Awareness of What is Missing,* 15–23.

assuage the meaning-void by giving the masses a political project, one that usually ends with their own disillusionment and demise.[67]

The turn towards nihilism in the West was unintended. In many ways, it too was an epiphenomenon of the dialectics of the Enlightenment. However, we now live within it, and we have very few effective ways of addressing the meaning void it creates. A religiously sensitive form of psychoanalysis/psychotherapy, one that is open to the religiosity of the analysand (or longing for transcendence), is needed as to strengthen the Ego by way of the good and the beautiful, and in many cases, the true, so it does not succumb to the nihilism it encounters in the secularized, meaningless, and alienating lifeworld. As the first generation of the Frankfurt School showed through their determinate negation of religion, the true (*Verum*), the good (*Bonum*), and the beautiful (*Pulchrum*), i.e., that which allows us to transcend the ugliness, brokenness, and deforming character of the real, can be translated into subjective meaningfulness. If the very possibility of the "other" is crushed under the foot of the real, what is left is only this meaningless world-as-it-is, which, in the words of Herbert Marcuse, 'is becoming ever more terrible, beyond our capacity of imagination.'[68] That is crushing for many in search of existential healing, wholeness, and connectedness. If only a mere semblance of the Divine can be translated and brought into the individual constitution of the analysand, then it ought to be done if it will contribute to the reclamation of a sense of eudaimonia. For many, the accursed alienation felt while living in a fully-secularized capitalist society is as oppressive as it would be for fully-secularized citizens to live in a wholly theocratic society, wherein religion saturates all aspects of life. Wherein the latter attempt to imbue religious meaning into everything, the former makes sure it cannot be found in anything. A "respectable psychology of religion," as one would find in a religiously-sensitive and religiously-open form of psychoanalysis, would understand this reality. And thus, we have to determinately negate both Freud *and* religion.

---

67   See Dustin J. Byrd, *The Dark Charisma of Donald Trump: Political Psychology and the MAGA Movement* (Kalamazoo, MI: Ekpyrosis Press, 2023).

68   Herbert Marcuse, "Letter of Max Horkheimer – January 1973," in *Max Horkheimer: A Life in Letters – Selected Correspondence*, ed. and trans. Manfred R. Jacobson and Evelyn M. Jacobson (Lincoln, NB: University of Nebraska Press, 2007), 374.

Bibliography

Adorno, Theodor W. *Negative Dialectics.* Translated by E.B. Ashton. New York: Continuum, 1999.

Adorno, Theodor W. "Reason and Revelation." In *Critical Models: Interventions and Catchwords.* Translated by Henry W. Pickford. New York: Columbia University Press, 2005.

Adorno, Theodor W., and Max Horkheimer. *Dialectic of Enlightenment: Philosophical Fragments,* edited by Gunzelin Schmid Noerr. Translated by Edmund Jephcott. Stanford, CA: Stanford University Press, 2002.

Berdyaev, Nicolas. "The New Middle Ages." In *The End of Our Time.* Translated by Donald Attwater. San Rafael, CA: Semantron Press, 2009.

Breger, Louis. *Freud: Darkness in the Midst of Vision.* New York: John Wiley & Sons, Inc., 2000.

Byrd, Dustin J. *The Dark Charisma of Donald Trump: Political Psychology and the MAGA Movement.* Kalamazoo, MI: Ekpyrosis Press, 2023.

Byrd, Dustin J. *The Frankfurt School and the Dialectics of Religion: Translating Critical Faith into Critical Theory.* Kalamazoo, MI: Ekpyrosis Press, 2020.

Byrd, Dustin J. "Palingenetic Ultra-Nationalist Christianity: History, Identity, and the Falsity of Peripeteic Dialectics." *Praktyka Teoretyczna* 42, no. 4 (2021): 7–37.

Diller, Jerry Victor. *Freud's Jewish Identity: A Case Study in the Impact of Ethnicity.* London: Associated University Presses, 1991.

Frankl, Viktor E. *Man's Search for Meaning.* Boston: Beacon Press, 2006.

Freud, Sigmund. *Civilization and its Discontents, Standard Edition Vol. 21.* London: The Hogarth Press, 1961.

Freud, Sigmund. *The Future of an Illusion, Standard Edition Vol. 21.* London: The Hogarth Press, 1961.

Freud, Sigmund. *The Origins of Psycho-analysis, Letters to Wilhelm Fliess, Drafts and Notes: 1887–1902,* edited by Maria Bonaparte, Anna Freud, and E. Kris. Translated by E. Mosbacher and James Strachey. New York: Basic Books, 1954.

Freud, Sigmund. *Totem and Taboo, Standard Edition Vol. 13.* London: The Hogarth Press, 1955.

Freud, Sigmund. "Preface to the Hebrew Translation." In *Totem and Taboo, Standard Edition Vol. 13.* London: The Hogarth Press, 1955.

Fromm, Erich. *Beyond the Chains of Illusion: My Encounter with Marx and Freud.* New York: Continuum, 2001.

Fromm, Erich. *Escape from Freedom.* New York: Henry Holt & Co., 1994.

Fromm, Erich. *Psychoanalysis and Religion.* New Haven, CT: Yale University Press, 1978.

Frosh, Stephen. *Hate and the "Jewish Science": Anti-Semitism, Nazism and Psychoanalysis.* London: Palgrave Macmillan, 2005.

Habermas, Jürgen. *An Awareness of What Is Missing: Faith and Reason in a Post-secular Age.* Translated by Ciaran Cronin. Malden, MA: Polity Press, 2011.

Hardin, Harry T. "On the vicissitudes of Freud's early mothering – I: Early Environment and Loss," *Psychoanalytic Quarterly* 56 (1988): 628–644.

Horkheimer, Max. *A Life in Letters: Selected Correspondence,* edited and translated by Manfred R. Jacobson and Evelyn M. Jacobson. Lincoln, NB: The University of Lincoln Press, 2007.

Horkheimer, Max. *Dawn and Decline: Notes 1926–1931 & 1950–1969.* Translated by Michael Shaw. New York: The Seabury Press, 1978.

Horkheimer, Max. *Die Sehnsucht nach dem ganz Anderen: Ein Interview mit Kommentar von Helmut Gumnior.* Hamburg: Furche-Verlag, 1970.

Jung, Carl Gustav. *The Practice of Psychotherapy. In Collected Works 16.* Princeton, NJ: Princeton University Press, 1954.

Jung, Carl Gustav. "The Structure and Dynamics of the Psyche." In *Collected Work Vol. 8.* Princeton, NJ: Princeton University Press, 1970.

Lehrer, Ronald. *Nietzsche's Presence in Freud's Life and Thought: On the Origins of a Psychology of Dynamic Unconscious Mental Functioning.* Albany, NY: State University of New York, 1995.

Löwenthal, Leo. *An Unmastered Past: An Autobiographical Reflection of Leo Lowenthal.* Berkeley: The University of California Press, 1987.

MacCulloch, Diarmaid. *Christianity: The First Three Thousand Years.* New York: Viking, 2009.

Marx, Karl. *The Marx-Engels Reader,* edited by Robert C. Tucker. New York: W.W. Norton & Co., Inc, 1978.

Nietzsche, Friedrich. *The Gay Science.* Translated by Thomas Common. New York: Barnes & Noble, 2008.

Nietzsche, Friedrich. *The Will to Power.* Translated by Anthony M. Ludovici. New York: Barnes & Nobles, 2006.

Rolnik, Eran J. *Freud in Zion: Psychoanalysis and the Making of Modern Jewish Identity.* London: Karnac Books Ltd., 2012.

Vitz, Paul C. *Sigmund Freud's Christian Unconscious.* New York: The Guilford Press, 1988.

CHAPTER 3

Adorno, Freud, and the Dialectic of the Individual and the Social

Gregory Joseph Menillo

Lecturing at the University of Frankfurt toward the end of his life, Adorno identifies psychoanalysis as sociology's extreme opposite – a discipline most intensely focused on the individual, furthest from societal questions.[1] And yet, he remarks, 'through its purely internal connections, it is constantly coming up against social concepts.'[2] For example, what Adorno calls "vital need," or Freud's drive toward self-preservation.[3] For Adorno, this psychoanalytic concept suggests that bourgeois society, in both Freud's time and his, does *not* meet people's vital needs: 'what objectively underlies the term, regardless of whether Freud fully realized it or not, is the following circumstance: society, as arranged up to now, has not produced sufficient provisions [*Lebensmittel*] – in the broadest sense of "means of life" – for all its members.'[4] Essentially, in addition to the internal conflict between the ego-instinct and the libido, the individual is also confronted externally by a commodity society in which use is always secondary to exchange; the satisfaction of people's "vital needs" is always subordinated to the necessity of the productive apparatus of society to reproduce itself. As he elaborates elsewhere:

> The commodity is characterized by its exchange-value. It is precisely not need that constitutes the commodity. Commodity value is not derived from need but from objective conditions of production of which need is

---

1 Theodor W. Adorno, *Introduction to Sociology* (Stanford: Stanford University Press, 2000), 108–16.
2 Ibid., 110.
3 Adorno was conversant with the entirety of Freud's thought and the more prominent interpretations and extensions of Freud's theories by his acolytes. However, Adorno found Freud's middle period, through the first *Introductory Lectures* (1916–17), most relevant, although his appreciation of later developments – particularly the ego-ideal in *Group Psychology and the Analysis of the Ego* (1921), and of course the late-period topography introduced in *The Ego and the Id* (1923) – is apparent throughout his work. As we will see, Adorno found Freud's theory of drives to be a bulwark against the reifying tendencies of postwar ego psychology.
4 Adorno, *Introduction to Sociology*, 111.

an element but only in the last instance, that is, mediated by the interest to "get rid of the stuff." ... the world does not turn according to our needs. The latter are only an epiphenomenon. What is decisive is the primacy of the apparatus of production over needs.[5]

For Adorno, the "primacy of production," over the satisfaction of human need is one of the core antagonisms of capitalist society. Adorno's theoretical idea, as it concerns psychoanalysis, is that the objective contradiction between use-value and exchange-value underlies Freud's reality principle, the ego-instinct responsible for ensuring self-preservation. Or, more generally speaking, that psychoanalytic concepts, seemingly focused on the individual at the expense of all other considerations, nonetheless "come up against" socio-economic issues, despite psychoanalysis not recognizing this as such. For example, when outlining his genetic psychology, Freud does not extend speculation beyond the psyche; he does not ask why it is that the "real circumstances in the external world" impose restrictions upon the subject with the effect of creating the reality principle, or why it is that bourgeois society demands the "renunciation" and "dissatisfaction" of the pleasure principle.[6] Freud's paper is concerned solely with individual psychology. Yet, his theoretical formulation, unilaterally committed to understanding the psychodynamics of the individual, nonetheless points to its apparent opposite. This insight is crucial for Adorno, who endeavors to emphasize the dialectical relationship between the individual

---

5 Theodor W. Adorno, "Marx and the Basic Concepts of Sociological Theory," in *Adorno and Marx*, ed. by Werner Bonefeld and Chris O'Kane (London: Bloomsbury Academic, 2022), 246–47.

6 'It was only the non-occurrence of the expected satisfaction, the disappointment experienced, that led to the abandonment of this attempt at satisfaction by means of [infantile] hallucination. Instead of it, the psychical apparatus had to decide to form a conception of the real circumstances in the external world and to endeavor to make a real alteration in them. A new principle of mental functioning was thus introduced; what was presented in the mind was no longer what was agreeable but what was real, even if it happened to be disagreeable.' Sigmund Freud, "Formulations on the Two Principles of Mental Functioning," in *The Standard Edition of the Complete Psychological Works of Sigmund Freud*, Volume XII, ed. by James Strachey (London: Hogarth Press, 1995), 219. And later: 'An artist is originally a man who turns away from reality because he cannot come to terms with the renunciation of the instinctual satisfaction which it at first demands, and who allows his erotic and ambitious wishes full play in the life of phantasy. He finds his way back to reality, however, from this world of phantasy by making use of special gifts to mold his phantasies into truths of a new kind, which are valued by men as precious reflections of reality ... But he can only achieve this because other men feel the same dissatisfaction as he does with the renunciation demanded by reality, and because that dissatisfaction, which results from the replacement of the pleasure principle by the reality principle, is itself a part of reality.' Ibid., 224.

and the social. For Adorno, Freud's "so-called psychological processes" contain a "social moment at their core" – this "social moment" is the "origin" of psychoanalytic concepts, without which 'the psychological processes could not be understood at all.'[7] As we will see, it is "exchange society" that has 'imposed all those renunciations of the erotic drive the dynamic theory of which forms the essential content of the Freudian doctrine.'[8] In other words, the objective structure of commodity society, particularly the relations of production under capitalism, is what underlies the psychological antagonisms Freud analyzes within the bourgeois subject. Adorno unfortunately does not pursue this insight further in either lecture. His point is to underscore what is ignored by empirical sociology (and, to a large extent, also modern psychology), but what a careful reading of Freud reveals: the dialectical nature of the individual and the social. 'Both,' Adorno cautions elsewhere, 'need to be recognized as internally bound up with each other if the analysis of either is to yield any rigorous meaning.'[9] This chapter will first trace these "complimentary concepts" in Adorno's thought through his concept of reification under capitalism, before turning to his critique of Neo-Freudian Revisionism, with the purpose of showing that Adorno's dialectical analysis is critical in revealing the significance of the alleged "inner" psychoanalytic categories and their relation to the seemingly "external" social world.

1   Individual and Society: Complementary Concepts

The demand that we recognize that the seemingly opposed are nonetheless "internally bound up" with one another brings us to the heart of both his method and his observation, the dialectic of the particular and the universal, or the individual and the social. Adorno stresses their internal relation bluntly: 'the particular *is* the universal and the universal the particular.'[10] He explains this "dialectical motif" as follows: 'the more deeply one explores the phenomena of human individuation, the more unreservedly one grasps the individual as self-contained and dynamic entity, the closer one draws to that

---

7   Adorno, "Marx and the Basic Concepts of Sociological Theory," 111–12.
8   Ibid., 111.
9   Theodor W. Adorno, *Philosophy and Sociology* (Cambridge: Polity Press, 2022), 73.
10 Adorno, *Introduction to Sociology*, 115. Translation modified. Adorno's term for "the universal" is Hegel's *das Allgemein*, which is often improperly translated as "the general." For consistency's sake, I will make this modification throughout the following discussion where necessary.

in the individual which is really no longer individual.'[11] Freud is significant because this is "rediscovered" in his work. In Adorno's reading, 'the individual person with whom psychoanalysis concerns itself is an abstraction *vis-à-vis* the social context in which individuals find themselves.'[12] In other words, outside of the formative and constitutive network of human relations, the individual does not signify anything specific and concrete; it is rather a moment of the social totality, a product of social mediation. In his chapter on "The Individual" in *Aspects of Sociology*, published by the Frankfurt Institute for Social Research in 1956, Adorno illuminates the socially mediated nature of individuality as follows:

> The specification of the human being as a person implies that he always finds himself in specific interpersonal roles within the social relations in which he lives before he is even aware of this. Because of this, he is what he is in relation to others: child of a mother, student of a teacher, member of a tribe or of a profession; this relation then is not external to him, but one within which and in terms of which he defines himself as specifically this or that. If one sought to disregard this functional character, and sought to look instead for the singular, absolute meaning or significance of each human being, one still would not arrive at the pure individual in his ineffable singularity, but rather at a wholly abstract point of reference.[13]

Understood in this way, the individual as such is meaningless, "abstract," if imagined as distinct from the social totality. Adorno's observation about "vital

---

11   Ibid., 113.
12   Ibid., 112.
13   Frankfurt Institute for Social Research, *Aspects of Sociology* (Boston: Beacon Press, 1973), 40–41. This volume does not bear Adorno's name in authorship, although it includes an introduction signed by both him and Max Horkheimer. Much of the book was undoubtedly written by Adorno (most chapters bear his unmistakable style throughout), and the passages I quote in this paper are nonetheless consistent with his writings elsewhere. Müller-Doohm has noted that this "textbook like anthology" was intended to serve as an introduction to fundamental concepts of sociology: 'In his teaching Adorno constantly resisted the canonization of the twelve thematic fields of sociology contained in the book ... but the chapters in this slim volume soon came to be regarded as, if not a sufficient foundation for an understanding of what students began to identify as the "Frankfurt School," then at least a necessary one. For whole generations of Frankfurt sociology students, [*Aspects of Sociology*] came to be the first point of access to the way of thinking that incorporated the "spirit of the house."' See Stefan Müller-Doohm, *Adorno: A Biography* (Cambridge: Polity Press, 2005), 369–70.

need" above intends to show precisely that the psyche, which appears as internal to the subject, is determined first by the objective conditions of society, which are constitutive in the development of the individual: 'those specific factors which form individuality must be interpreted as internalizations of social compulsions, needs, and demands.'[14] This is why through intense analysis of the individual isolated from larger questions of context and milieu, psychoanalysis is nonetheless able to reveal the social content at the depths of his psychological categories, which become apparent if read "against the grain."[15]

The more general point necessary to first pursue is Adorno's notion that the individual as such is a social category, a product of a particular form of social (re)productive relations that are both concrete and historical; specifically, that the individual is itself a category of bourgeois capitalist society. Such a thing must be "rediscovered" because liberalism projects a very different picture: the substantive individual as both prior to social relations and external to society (which only enters into society via contract, as we will see below). For Adorno, Leibnitz's concept of a monad offers a model of this liberal subject. The individual monad is a distinct entity differentiated from every other monad; yet, at the same time, it is also an abstraction of a universal principle that is common to each, represented internally in each – individual monads are therefore complete, discrete, and equivalent.[16] Instead of the picture suggested above, wherein the individual is shown to be socially determined by a complex of intersubjective relations mediated by societal institutions, 'under the influence of liberalism, of its doctrine of free competition, we have become fully accustomed to thinking of the Monad [sic] as an absolute, existing for and by itself.'[17]

---

14   Adorno, *Introduction to Sociology*, 112.
15   The phrase comes from Benjamin; see Walter Benjamin, *Illuminations* (New York: Schocken Books, 2007), 256–257.
16   This universal principle, in Adorno's mind, is the principal of exchange. I will discuss this in the following section.
17   Frankfurt Institute, *Aspects of Sociology*, 39. Consider Adorno's fuller commentary on Leibnitz (his quotations are from the latter): 'The doctrine of the Monads contains the model for the individualistic conception of the concrete human being in bourgeois society [*bürgerliche Gesellschaft*]: that a particular substance never acts upon another particular substance, nor is it acted upon by it; namely if one takes into consideration, that all which happens to each one is only the consequence of its complete idea or concept, since this idea already includes all the predicates and expresses the whole universe.' 'The Monads have no windows through which something can come in or go out'; the changes which take place within them are not externally caused but can be traced back to an "inner principle." Finally, every single Monad is differentiated from every other Monad. Society consequently becomes the sum of single individuals: 'The essence of a being by aggregation consists solely in the mode of being of its component elements; for example,

We have not only become accustomed to thinking of the individual as a monad under liberal society but have also been accustomed to understanding liberal society as a mere aggregate of atomized monads. As I will show in the next section, this inadequate picture is the "socially necessary illusion" of capitalism that must be critiqued in order for us to gain purchase on both the individual, the social, and their (inadequate) mediation. But first it is important to remember that capitalism is a form of *social* production, that its "doctrine of free competition" can only (but must necessarily) *assume* the individual as monad. This is not to say that the individual as monad is false; the appearance of the alienated individual is also a feature of bourgeois society, but it is intended to undermine its ideological force: what is presupposed by society – atomized individuals as monads – is actually engendered by it.

> The faith in the radical independence of the individual from the whole is indeed mere illusion. The form of the individual itself is one proper to a society which maintains its life by means of the free market, where free and independent economic subjects come together ... The two, individual and society, are [actually] *complementary concepts* ... The interaction and tension between the individual and society to a great measure govern the entire dynamics of the whole.[18]

It is here where the 'untiring effort to attain the unity of the universal and particular' is necessary to see beyond the one-sided, monadic picture of liberal society in order to reveal the tension – and apparent contradiction – between the individual and the social.[19] It is the means through which we may understand that the individual (as monad) is both false and true: individuals are both social entities but also *appear* as atomized monads distinct from liberal capitalist society. Indeed, the opposition between psychology and sociology is a result of this apparent bifurcation between the objects of their inquiry: 'both of these very one-sided approaches ... derive from a reified opposition between the domain of society and that of the individual, between the "domain of the many" and the "domain of the individual"' – two "domains" which must be understood as aspects of the same antagonistic whole.[20]

---

what constitutes the essence of an army is simply the mode of being of the men who compose it.' 'Under the influence of liberalism, of its doctrine of free competition, we have become fully accustomed to thinking of the Monad as an absolute, existing for and by itself.' Ibid.

18 Ibid., 45. My emphasis.
19 Ibid., 26. Translation modified as above (see footnote ten).
20 Adorno, *Philosophy and Sociology*, 72–73.

2 Reification, Exchange, and the False Totality

Adorno argues that this "reified opposition" is a product of the exchange principle that governs the way in which capitalist relations of production are defined and therefore the manner in which social reproduction under capitalism is determined. As mentioned above, the apparent separation of the individual and the social is an illusion, albeit one that is "socially necessary." Adorno explains this as follows:

> The socially necessary illusion needs to be derived from the exchange relation ... Marxian theory analyses the way that exchange, which is actually a relation between human beings, necessarily appears to us as a quality of things, as their value, and derives this from the fact that the comparable element between the goods which are exchanged, namely their value, is something abstract, i.e. socially necessary labor time. It claims that this abstract equivalent of exchange can no longer easily be recognized in terms of its actual relationship to living human beings and living labor. Thus, once it has been abstracted and become independent in this way, it ceases to appear as a direct relation between human beings and therefore becomes reified.[21]

Lukács' concept of "reification" here is key, an extension of Marx's "commodity-fetish," the phenomenon in which 'the definite [productive] social relation between men ... assumes, for them, the fantastic form of a relation between things.'[22] Essentially, when commodity exchange becomes the dominant law governing social metabolism, what is human and social, i.e., labor, the products of labor, etc., appears to people as "thing-like," not as a result of their own collective making. Through this, and concomitant specializations and divisions of labor, individuals themselves likewise appear distinct, separate from the social world they engender.[23] As Lukács concludes, 'the atomization of the

---

21 Ibid., 100.
22 Karl Marx, *Capital: A Critique of Political Economy*, Volume I (London: Penguin Classics, 1990), 165. For the concept of reification, see Georg Lukács, *History and Class Consciousness: Studies in Marxist Dialectics* (Cambridge: MIT Press, 1972), 83–110.
23 Adorno derives the bifurcation between society and mind (*Geist*) as stemming from the separation between intellectual and manual labor was required for the organization of social production under capitalism: 'if this separation between physical and mental labor had not come about, and if so-called mental labor had not already involved the planning or organization of social production and thus also control over the labor of others, then society, at least in its earlier stages, would probably not have been able to reproduce itself

individual is, then, only the reflex of consciousness of the fact that the "natural laws" of capitalist production have been extended to cover every manifestation of life in society.'[24]

Adorno echoes Lukács in suggesting that reification is not only a "mere illusion," subjectively speaking, but again is also an illusion that is "socially necessary" in the objective sense. Capitalist society must assume atomized, discrete individuals as freely entering into labor contracts in order for it to reproduce itself – that is, assume a society of monads. And yet, the picture is not so unidirectional; as Adorno also notes, 'from the dialectical relationship of labor and property results not only the "universal" society, but also the existence of the individual as a human being, as a person.'[25] In other words, the individual historically comes into its own under bourgeois relations of production.[26] This is another example of the contradiction within the concept of the individual, which is only solved with recourse to the whole as a dialectical process: while the individual is realized historically through bourgeois society, the capitalist exchange relation also determines it in a particular form. The individual both appears as a product of bourgeois society but is also prevented by capitalism from fulfilling its ideal. As Adorno notes in *Negative Dialectics*, this picture of "the individual in individualist society" thus turns out to be both adequate and inadequate:

> It is adequate because the principle of the exchange society realized itself only by means the individuation of the specific contracting parties; because the *principium individuationis* was thus literally its principle, its [universality]. It is inadequate because in the total functional context,

---

in the first place.' Only at later stage did this separation assume an ideological character necessary for social reproduction: 'the absolute independence of mind or spirit is itself a socially necessary illusion, for, in fact, mental labor has come to be separated from physical labor only over the course of history, and only now finds itself subject to a distinctive law of its own.' Adorno, *Philosophy and Sociology*, 98.

24 Lukács, *History and Class Consciousness*, 91–92.
25 Frankfurt Institute for Social Research, *Aspects of Sociology*, 24.
26 The dialectical nature of "free" labor under capitalism was also observed by Lukács: commodity society both 'depends on the emergence of the "free" worker who is freely able to take his labor-power to market and offer it for sale as a commodity "belonging" to him, a thing that he "possesses"'; yet 'only when the whole life of society is thus fragmented into the isolated acts of commodity exchange can the "free" worker come into being.' Lukács, *History and Class Consciousness*, 91.

which requires the form of individuation, individuals are relegated to mere executive organs of the [universal].[27]

So, while the principle of exchange, the "universal" governing the metabolism of society, is fully realized through a society of individual contracting parties, the social realization of the individual, in a robust sense, is not. After all, the exchange relation is not performed by "free and equal" monads, but by people belonging to a hierarchy of classes compelled by the market to reproduce the objective inequality that relegates them to their respective class positions. Reification, or the subjective appearance of a "formal equality of human labor in the abstract,"[28] masks the non-identity at the heart of these productive relations; the apparent exchange of equivalates under capitalism hides the non-identical, the "more" [*das Mehr*] appropriated by capital: surplus value. The equivalence contractually drawn between capital and labor masks their inequality.[29] The "ideal of free and fair exchange" is therefore a "mere pretext" under liberalism, not actual.[30] Likewise, the individual: as a mere executor of exchange, the individual engendered by capitalism is also denied by it. From the standpoint of the whole, the unequal control of productive means, the private accumulation of wealth, and the institutions that serve these structural imperatives (which all fall under Adorno's heading of the "administered society") constitute a social system that is structurally inegalitarian, despite claiming otherwise. Thus, as an anti-egalitarian totality, it negates its own principle, its own "universal"; it depends on the idea of free and equal

---

27   Theodor W. Adorno, *Negative Dialectics,* translated by Dennis Redmond (Morrisville: Lulu Press, 2022) 309–10. Translation modified as above (see footnote ten). Redmond's translation is the most accurate available in English; all citations will refer to Redmond's translation unless otherwise noted.
28   Lukács, *History and Class Consciousness,* 87.
29   'But it is only critical reflection that can reveal that this relation of equivalent exchange cannot possibly be equivalent, can show in other words that the labor time the worker provides is greater than the labor time that is required for the reproduction of his own life. Thus, the worker necessarily gives more than he or she receives, and the entire gigantic process of capitalism, of the accumulation of capital, actually rests on this "more" which has thus specifically been defined as surplus value.' Adorno, *Philosophy and Sociology,* 101.
30   'For the exchange of equivalents was based since time immemorial exactly on this, that something unequal was exchanged in its name, that the surplus-value of labor was appropriated ... What the critique of the exchange-principle as the identifying one of thought wishes, is that the ideal of free and fair exchange, until today only a mere pretext, would be realized.' Adorno, *Negative Dialectics,* 138.

individuals – liberalism's social necessity – who, as social actors, as executors of capitalist exchange relations, are socially realized as neither equal nor free.[31]

This is where the dialectic of the individual and the social as a paradigmatic method of analysis, the "reciprocal critique of the universal and the particular" bears fruit.[32] Adorno shows that 'critical insight into the construction of society as a whole, critical insight into the totality of society and into the relationship between this totality and its individual aspects or moments,' reveals 'that the whole in question does not live up to its own concept.'[33] Or, put more pointedly, bourgeois society 'conforms to its own concept, and by conforming to it also contradicts its own concept.'[34] Indeed, Adorno submits that '[i]f no human being was deprived of their share of their living labor, then rational identity would be achieved, and society would be beyond identifying thought,' – will have sublated its principle of exchange.[35] Reification, along with contemporary relations of production, would cease to exist, and the individual would finally "fulfill its own concept" (although, dialectically speaking, the concept would also be transcended as its social basis is transformed).

However, instead of an adequate mediation between whole and part, society and the individual, the inequality at the heart of capitalist exchange ensures that society is irrational; for Adorno, existing society is therefore a fundamentally *false totality*.[36] Adorno is generally taken to be nihilistic on this point, but I understand it as the unavoidable conclusion of his analysis and a particularly crucial insight for understanding his critique of ego-psychology outlined

---

31 Both capital and labor are compelled by the "coercive laws of competition," albeit in different ways. Labor is obviously compelled to sell its labor power as a commodity in a competitive labor market. Capital is compelled to compete with capital. As Marx reminds us, '[u]nder free competition, the immanent laws of capitalist production confront the individual capitalist as a coercive force external to him.' Marx, *Capital,* 381.

32 Adorno, *Negative Dialectics,* 137. Translation modified as above.

33 Adorno, *Philosophy and Sociology,* 103.

34 Adorno, "Marx and the Basic Concepts of Sociological Theory," 245.

35 Adorno, *Negative Dialectics,* 138.

36 Summed up as "the whole is the false" in Theodor W. Adorno, *Minima Moralia: Reflections from Damaged Life* (London: Verso, 2005), 50. It is Adorno's reversal of Hegel's "The true is the whole," G.W.F. Hegel, *Phenomenology of Spirit* (Oxford: Oxford University Press, 1977), 11. Accepting Hegel's teleology means accepting not only the notion that the historical arc of humanity tends toward greater progress, emancipation, and the like, but also that the current state of humanity is, by definition, a greater actualization of Spirit than hitherto before – in other words, a more "rational totality." For Adorno, in light of the cataclysmic events of the early 20th century, this is unacceptable. See the section entitled "Universal History" in Adorno, *Negative Dialectics,* 388–89.

below.[37] The logical argument aside, this false totality is antagonistic toward the individual. His diagnosis of the condition of the latter under the former provides an adequate summation of the foregoing discussion:

> Bourgeois society has evolved a dynamic which forces the individual economic subject to pursue his financial interests ruthlessly and without consideration for the welfare of the generality ... The antifeudal ideal of autonomy, the intended aim of which originally was political self-determination, became transformed within the context of the economic structure into that ideology which was required for the maintenance of the social order and for the growth of the "output." So, for the totally internalized [monadic] individual, reality becomes appearance and appearance reality. In asserting his existence, which in fact is isolated and dependent on society ... as absolute, the individual makes himself into an absolute cliché. ... And society, which produced the development of the individual, now is developing by alienating and fragmenting this individual. At the same time, the individual, for his part, misconstrues the world, on which he is dependent down to his innermost being, mistaking it for his own.[38]

In truth, the individual's divergence from the social is both of social origin and is socially reproduced. The "individualist society," a contradiction in terms masked only by the reality to which it refers, stands against the individual, which is no longer a social being but instead must behave as an "economic subject" pursuing its own allegedly individual interests. Of course, these interests actually serve capital, serve the reproduction of the entire "productive apparatus," which the individual "misconstrues" as being identical to its own. The more the individual must take itself to be absolute, the more it must see itself as a monad, the more it both misrecognizes itself as being independent from society and is unable to grasp the whole as antagonistic, as responsible for its own alienation and depravation. Society 'no longer accomplishes precisely

---

37   For some uncharacteristic hopefulness, consider the following quote from a 1965 lecture: 'I believe ... that a possible starting-point for a correct practice is to rethink how to put a society on the right path when, on the one hand, it threatens to stagnate owing to the ossified relations of production and the attitudes resulting from that situation, while, on the other hand, it ceaselessly produces the forces that initially promote destruction *but* that tomorrow or the day after, if I may put it crassly, *could actually make possible a paradise on earth*.' Theodor W. Adorno, *Lectures on Negative Dialectics* (Cambridge: Polity Press, 2008), 48. Emphasis mine.
38   Frankfurt School for Social Research, *Aspects of Sociology*, 48.

what it was supposed to accomplish' – i.e., providing for the general welfare, ensuring that peoples "vital needs" are met, and forming a basis for the actualization of true human subjects – 'for the human beings who are exposed and subjected to this interconnected whole are also mortally and fatefully threatened by the very society to which they owe their life.'[39] In sum, modern society, which has historically engendered the individual, also stands against its flourishing.[40] This fundamental, central idea animates Adorno's critique of postwar ego-psychology, particularly Karen Horney, the foremost representative of Neo-Freudian revisionism.[41]

3   Reification of the Ego: Revisionism as a Psychology of the False Totality

Neo-Freudian revisionists sought to broaden psychoanalytic theory to account for the impact of "direct" social and cultural "interventions" in the determination of the ego, thereby de-emphasizing its unconscious instinctual foundation.[42] This grew out of a dissatisfaction with classical psychoanalytic theory, deemed closed off from social considerations beyond the familial, Oedipal dynamic – too cloistered from the question of greater society, which revisionists identified as being damaging to the subject. Freud's instinct theory and the

---

39   Adorno, *Philosophy and Sociology*, 103.
40   While Adorno's point of reference was postwar "embedded" liberalism, what he referred to as "late capitalism," his analysis and insights are still relevant (perhaps more so) under its present neoliberal form. For an excellent historical analysis of the transformation from "embedded" to "disembedded" liberalism in the United Sates (and Sweden) see Mark Blyth, *Great Transformations: Economic Ideas and Institutional Change in the Twentieth Century* (Cambridge: Cambridge University Press, 2002). For a recent volume that assesses the relevance of Adorno thought specifically to neoliberalism, see Charles Andrew Prusik, *Adorno and Neoliberalism: The Critique of Exchange Society* (London: Bloomsbury Academic, 2020).
41   My commentary will be limited to Theodor W. Adorno, "The Revisionist Psychoanalysis," translated by Nan-Nan Lee in *Philosophy and Social Criticism* 40, no. 3 (New York: Sage Publishing, 2014), 326–339, within which Adorno focuses on the work of Horney. Adorno's earlier critique of both Horney and Erich Fromm is in an unpublished essay from 1946 entitled "Social Science and Sociological Tendencies in Psychoanalysis," which contains many of the same points. For a brief overview, see Martin Jay, *The Dialectical Imagination: A History of the Frankfurt School and the Institute of Social Research, 1923–1950* (Berkeley: University of California Press, 1973), 103–106.
42   For a discussion of Adorno's critique, see Verlain Freitas, "Theodor Adorno and the Freudian Revisionism" in *Veritas* 63, no. 2, *maio-ago* (Porto Alegre: EDIPUCRS, 2018): 780–800.

dynamic of the pleasure principle, which Adorno finds revolutionary, are therefore downplayed by psychoanalysts like Karen Horney, who emphasize the ego instead, wishing to strengthen the totality of an individual's "character structure" against the repressive forces of the world. While seemingly progressive on first glance, Adorno argues that Horney is misled by the reified appearance of the individual as separate from society; in short, she ignores the dialectical nature of the two. For Adorno, Horney's "ideal self," the presupposed normative ego, is a theoretical mistake rooted in the appearance of the individual as distinct from society. By beginning with the individual *a priori*, Horney tacitly absolutizes it, falsely "attribute[s] to the ego a being-in-itself"; this "ideal" ego, imagined in some hypothetical "harmonious" society, is supposedly damaged upon entering into antagonistic society as it actually exists.[43] This theoretical "blunder" obscures the degree to which the individual's "system of scars" are "the form which the society asserts itself in the individual experience."[44]

Adorno's main issue is with the alleged "unity of character" that Horney believes can be "integrated" with society through therapy. Adorno's first point is that "the totality of the so-called 'character'" that revisionists presuppose "is fictitious."[45] As with modern society, the bourgeois individual is likewise fractured. Theorizing and treating the individual as a unified (or unifiable) subject seeks to harmonize what psychoanalysis has already shown to be a constitutive conflict. Freud's groundbreaking "discovery," after all, is that there is an irreconcilable rift at the core of the human psyche, that the subject is torn between their conscious thoughts and their unconscious drives, bifurcated between ego and id.[46] The true import of Freudian psychoanalysis is this fundamental schism, the very fact that, as Freud so eloquently stated, the ego "is not even master in its own house."[47] This point is rejected by Horney.[48] Adorno suggests, in not so many words, that the reason is more ideological than theoretical.

---

43 Adorno, "Revisionist Psychoanalysis," 327.
44 Ibid., 328.
45 Ibid.
46 While Adorno uses these latter concepts, he is generally wary of Freud's system outlined in *The Ego and the Id* (1923). As his critique of revisionism suggests, the topographical system tends toward the reification of the ego, rather than the more dynamic interaction of drives theorized in Freud's earlier work.
47 Freud's famous line from Part III of the *Introductory Lectures on Psychoanalysis*: 'But human megalomania will have suffered its third and most wounding blow from the psychological research of the present time which seeks to prove to the ego that is not even master in its own house but must content itself with scanty information of what is going on unconsciously in its mind.' Freud, *Standard Edition*, XVI, 285.
48 Fromm also, who ultimately admits to "giving up" the libido theory. See Jay, *Dialectical Imagination*, 88–100.

> The insistence on the totality, as the antithesis to the unique, fragmentary impulse, implies a harmonious belief in the unity of a person, which is impossible in the [sic] existing society ... The sedimented totality of the character, which the revisionists push into the foreground, is in truth the result of a reification of real experiences. If one absolutizes this totality, it might easily enough become an ideological hiding place for the psychological status quo of the individual.[49]

Adorno's second point is that the theoretical mistake of "absolutizing" the ego not only mistakes fragmentation for unity, but in effect also reinforces social reification that is already "sedimented" in the individual. Abandoning the instincts, or "fragmentary impulses," which can resist reification, Horney's psychology reifies the ego instead, models it off of the very reified totality which stands against the individual. In this regard, Horney's psychology actually sanctions the antagonisms of society, while her therapy ultimately seeks to adapt individuals to the status quo. For Adorno, this makes psychoanalysis into 'a part of the [sic] industrialized mass culture ... which traps the individual completely in [its] seamless organization'.[50]

Adorno's abiding concern, both here and throughout his work, is over the coercive societal powers that seek to integrate the individual into a false and antagonistic totality. What he refers to as the "decline of the individual" under modern society is achieved in part by the "culture industry."[51] As discussed above, when social production is organized to maximize private profit, satisfying peoples' "vital needs" only indirectly, and when alienating and exploitative relations of production deny people the possibility of collective self-determination, the bourgeois notion of the autonomous individual exists only in an illusory, fetishistic form. As Adorno argues in "Freudian Theory and the Pattern of Fascist Propaganda," the individual is therefore faced with 'the

---

49   Adorno, "Revisionist Psychoanalysis," 329.
50   Ibid., 337. Adorno often polemically characterizes such issues in extreme terms. As he labors to show elsewhere, the "trap" is not so seamless and complete. Consider Part III of Theodor W. Adorno, *History and Freedom: Lectures 1964–1965* (Cambridge: Polity Press, 2006), 177–266, in which he addresses the issue of human freedom and autonomy over the course of ten lectures. These lectures can be read as a prolegomenon to his section on freedom in Adorno, *Negative Dialectics*, 192–270.
51   The seminal essay on the "culture industry" can be found in Max Horkheimer and Theodor W. Adorno, *Dialectic of Enlightenment: Philosophical Fragments* (Stanford: Stanford University Press, 2002). See also the compact and helpful "Culture Industry Revisited," in Theodor W. Adorno, *The Culture Industry: Selected Essays on Mass Culture*, edited by Jay Bernstein (London: Routledge Classics, 2001), 98–106.

characteristic modern conflict between a strongly developed rational, self-preserving ego agency' on the one hand – especially if revisionism would have its way – 'and the continuous failure to satisfy their own needs' on the other.[52] This results in a 'new type of psychological affliction so characteristic of the era that, for socio-economic reasons, witness[es] the decline of the individual and his subsequent weakness.'[53] He elaborates:

> while psychology always denotes some bondage of the individual, it also presupposes freedom in the sense of a certain self-sufficiency and autonomy of the individual ... In a thoroughly reified society, [however,] in which there are virtually no direct relationships between men, and in which each person has been reduced to a social atom ... the psychological processes, though they still persist in each individual, have ceased to appear as the determining forces of the social process.[54]

In essence, to take the individual ego as the subject of society, as autonomous agent, would be to ignore the degree to which its potential for realization is restricted by the reified and repressive totality. And yet, as Adorno is wont to point out, the "psychological processes" still persist: 'self-alienated subjects remain human beings, nevertheless.'[55] The fact that people cannot wholly be dominated by the totality therefore requires a continual means of societal adjustment. Therefore, while barred from recognizing and fulfilling their true needs as self-actualized subjects, people are instead mediated by mass consumer culture, which forces them to 'experience themselves through their needs only as eternal consumers, as the culture industry's object.'[56] Cultural commodities offer a substitute gratification, in purchasable form, for the space, foreclosed by modern society, to develop true subjective autonomy; at the same time, the culture industry reinforces a "psychic bondage," keeping people dependent on its products and therefore the larger network of economic institutions that constitute the antagonistic whole.[57] In short, what can

---

52 Theodor W. Adorno, "Freudian Theory and the Pattern of Fascist Propaganda," in *The Culture Industry: Selected Essays on Mass Culture*, edited by Jay Bernstein (London: Routledge Classics, 2001), 140.
53 Ibid., 134.
54 Ibid., 151–52.
55 Theodor W. Adorno, "Sociology and Psychology (Part I)," in *New Left Review*, I/46, November-December (London: New Left Review Ltd., 1967), 77.
56 Horkheimer and Adorno, *Dialectic of Enlightenment*, 113.
57 Leo Löwenthal, Adorno's lifelong friend and colleague, insightfully characterized mass consumer culture as "psychoanalysis in reverse": 'that is, as more or less constantly

be called the "phantasmagoria" of consumer society masks the truth of the economically frustrated, politically impotent, de-individualized subject.[58]

For this reason, the ego-psychology of Horney is not only problematic from a psychoanalytic standpoint, but also regressive from a political one. By seeking to strengthen the ego, revisionists throw their lot in with the antagonistic whole; their therapy becomes "part of mass culture," which likewise seeks to incorporate individuals, instead of enlightening them: 'In their hands, Freudian theory turns into another means which assimilates psychological movements to the status quo.'[59] In fact, as I will suggest below, revisionists seek to strengthen the ego at the peril of sublimating the only aspect of the subject that actually resists reification, may perhaps be the last preserve of a truly uncoerced subjectivity: the "unique, fragmentary impulse," or unconscious drives.[60] Contra Horney, Adorno does not advocate for an unchecked irrationalism, a "psychology of the id," for lack of a better locution, but a return to Freud at his most "revolutionary" moment, wherein he is most unconcerned with society. Indeed, a psychology truly concerned with society must turn away from "social theoretical" formulations of it; it must instead seek society's "mechanisms" in the inner depths of the individual psyche.

---

manipulated devices to keep people in permanent psychic bondage, to increase and reinforce neurotic and even psychotic behavior culminating in perpetual dependency on a "leader" or on institutions or products.' Leo Löwenthal, *An Unmastered Past: The Autobiographical Reflections of Leo Löwenthal* (Berkeley: University of California Press, 1987), 186.

58 I am here paraphrasing myself. 'In essence, the phantasmagoria of consumer society similarly hides the truth of the economically frustrated, politically impotent, de-individualized subject. Under fascism, what *takes the form of* theater, sport, and spectacle in order to gratify the follower, *is* theater, sport, and spectacle in the culture industry. The latter offers the same substitute gratification – except in purchasable form – for the space to truly develop the subjective autonomy that is simultaneously promised and denied by modern society. Consumers become individuals insofar as they submit to the mechanisms of the system, buying their culture instead of developing it themselves. This purchase of identity, as opposed to the development of true autonomy, is in essence the *pseudo-individuality* of the otherwise dependent and coerced masses – individualism only as another "*ideological veil*" that hides the truth of submission behind the illusion of participation in the culture industry's spectacle.' Gregory Joseph Menillo, "'Variation Within a Single Paradigm': The Latent Authoritarian Dynamics of the Culture Industry," in *How to Critique Authoritarian Populism: Methodologies of the Frankfurt School*, edited by Jeremiah Morelock (Lieden: Brill Publishers, 2021), 259.

59 Adorno, "Revisionist Psychoanalysis," 337.
60 Ibid., 329.

> The deeper that psychology probes the critical areas within the individual, the more adequately it can become aware of the social mechanisms that produced the individuality; and the more the interaction between internal and external world is displaced on to the surface, the more apparent the explication is against the social theoretical consideration of psychology.[61]

Here we again see the force of Adorno's dialectical thinking: only through in-depth analysis of the individual does the truth of social mediation become apparent. Against the revisionists, *Adorno champions Freud not in spite of his general exclusion of society, but because of it*: 'More than [revisionists'] nimble sidelong glance at social conditions, Freud adheres to the nature of socialization by staying just with the individual's atomistic existence persistently.'[62] Freud does better justice to truth because his thought expresses the fundamental rift at the core of individual psychology, and therefore between the individual and society, despite its alleged blinders to the social world. Therefore, Freud's "psychology of atomism" is a more "adequate expression" of a 'reality in which people are in fact atomized and are separated from one another by an insurmountable divide.'[63] Despite their alleged pragmatism, revisionists actually domesticate Freud's theory, when it is the very contradictions themselves that express the truth of the whole.

> Revisionists want to isolate only the practical realistic side of the Freudian doctrine and to put the psychoanalytic method in service of adaptation without any reservation, in order to feel themselves executors of the Freudian intentions and at the same time to break the intentions' backbone. It is not so very much about heretical deviations of Freud's doctrine as about a convenient smoothing-over of its contradictions. In their hands, Freudian theory turns into another means which assimilates psychological movements to the status quo.[64]

For Adorno, the "greatness" of Freud is due to the fact that he leaves the contradiction between the individual and the social "unresolved" and therefore 'makes the antagonistic character of social reality apparent.'[65] After all, the

---

61 Ibid., 330.
62 Ibid., 328.
63 Ibid., 334.
64 Ibid., 337.
65 Ibid.

antagonistic character of social reality is also the truth of the individual psyche. Where revisionists imagine a possible harmony, Freud faithfully pursues the unreconciled tension between individual and social, part and whole. In his hands, psychoanalysis is both an "indictment of civilization" and an "instrument of Enlightenment."[66] Only a dialectical standpoint could reveal this.

4 Addendum/Additional Factor

In this final section I would like to briefly discuss an important Adornian concept that has deep ties to Freud: the "unique, fragmentary impulse" mentioned above, which forms the basis for the possibility of a critical subjectivity that could potentially stand against the reifying forces of society. Adorno's term is *das Hinzutretende*, which has been translated as "addendum" or the "additional factor."[67] In *Negative Dialectics*, Adorno says it is the crucial moment in the "vague experience" of deciding, which occurs like a "jolt."[68] In his lectures on freedom from the same time, Adorno adds to the non-causal, jolt-like quality of *das Hinzutretende*, saying it goes "beyond intellectualization," having the character of a physical, somatic impulse:

> When we speak of acts of will, we experience a sort of jolt ... some kind of impulse, I would almost say a physical impulse, a somatic impulse that goes beyond the pure intellectualization of what is supposed ... alone to constitute the will.[69]

It is an aspect of "taking action that goes beyond rationality," an "additional spontaneous factor," even an "irrational element" that "forces its way to the surface."[70] Adorno is here theorizing an element of human spontaneity that

---

66 Ibid.
67 The former is E.B. Ashton's in Theodor W. Adorno, *Negative Dialectics* (New York: Continuum, 2007), the latter R. Livingstone's in Adorno, *History and Freedom*. Denis Redmond chooses "the supplementary"; another possibility would be "the added." For an interpretation of the concept see Martin Shuster, *Autonomy After Auschwitz: Adorno, German Idealism, and Modernity* (Chicago: Chicago University Press, 2014), 71–99. See also Joel Whitebook, "Weighty Objects: On Adorno's Kant-Freud Interpretation," in *The Cambridge Companion to Adorno* (Cambridge: Cambridge University Press, 2004), 51–78.
68 'The decisions of the subject do not roll off as in a causal chain but occur as a jolt.' Adorno, *Negative Dialectics*, 206. (Redmon's translation).
69 Adorno, *History and Freedom*, 228.
70 Ibid., 234.

must lie outside rational, reflective reason. Against Kant, who places human freedom within practical reason, Adorno argues that in order for an act, and therefore a subject, to be considered truly free, it cannot be wholly legislated by the "causal laws" of rationality.[71] To put this in terms consistent with the above discussion, a free act cannot be wholly determined by the ego. It is clear why Adorno resists the psychology of Horney, who would leave no room for this spontaneous, instinctual element in her reified conception of the latter.

For Adorno, the "impulsive action" is not only the precondition for all human freedom, but it generally enables our corporal engagement with the world: 'with this impulsiveness, freedom extends into the realm of experience ... this impulse enables us to enter, to take a leap ... into the realm of objects that is normally barred to us by our own rationality.'[72] In this moment, 'the sense of being divided, of being between inner and outer, is overcome as in a flash.'[73] For Adorno, the two poles of this divide – inner and outer, reason and impulse – are *both* necessary for a "willed act" or any human practice considered spontaneous and free: both elements "are needed if freedom is to make its appearance," both "are mutually interdependent."[74] While reason, seated squarely in the rigidified ego, is resistant to the notion of a seemingly alien and regressive impulsive element, Adorno's point is that such an element is both necessary for reason to gain purchase on the world as it is genetically internal to the ego itself. This is a very complex issue at the core of Adorno's philosophy; for our purposes, it is where the traces of Freud's instinct theory can be most clearly seen:

---

71   In Kant, one has a "duty" to act in accordance with moral law, which inspires "free submission" to the law's "will" – see Immanuel Kant, *Critique of Practical Reason* (Indianapolis: Hackett Publishing Company, 2002), 104. This is an unsatisfying account for Adorno, who argues that freedom of the will cannot be formalized. For Adorno, the moral conscience described here is none other than Freud's super-ego: 'the psychological counterpart of that Kantian concept, namely the super-ego, in fact exerts a kind of coercive psychological force that corresponds entirely to the effect that Kant ascribes to the moral law.' Theodor W. Adorno, *Kant's Critique of Pure Reason* (Stanford: Stanford University Press, 2001), 190. See also "Reason, Ego, Super-Ego," in Adorno, *Negative Dialectics*, 245–248.

72   Adorno, *History and Freedom*, 237.

73   Ibid.

74   Ibid., 239. He continues: 'On the one hand, there is intellect, reason, about which I would say that, if you take the notion of practice very seriously, it contains or presupposes the idea of the unrestricted, highly progressive theoretical consciousness. On the other hand, there is what I have labelled the additional factor, the bodily impulse that cannot be reduced to reason.' Ibid.

> For we know today that the ego principle – that is to say, the rationality that scrutinizes reality – is actually a form of energy that has been diverted from the reservoir of drives in our possession in the interests of self-preservation. This instinctual element, which underlies every act of cognition in one way or another, as everyone can observe in himself as a knowing subject, is denied and resisted. This denial involves an act of repression, such as is found in the glorification of self-control [*Haltung*], a particular kind of demeanor that allegedly arises from the direct passage of metaphysical experiences into one's everyday mode of experience – while the psychological study of how this process is supposed to work is dispensed with.[75]

In this a crucial dialectic comes into view. On the one hand, the instinctual element, originally operant "in the interest of self-preservation" (serving "vital need"), is internally related to the ego, is that from which the ego derives. It is not only genetically prior, but is also implicated in every willed act, which has a non-rational, somatic element: 'a bodily impulse that cannot be reduced to reason.'[76] The mature ego, on the other hand, in an effort to remain "in control" – via reflective reason – turns against the instinctual element, which nonetheless still underscores every action of rational consciousness. Rationality by its very nature attempts to subsume all experience under its conceptual laws, so must deny its instinctual foundation – both genetically and functionally – and therefore must repress its own nature. Concomitantly, the reifying forces of bourgeois society reinforce this repression in everyday experience.

Revisionist psychoanalysis, instead of pursuing the dialectic of reason and impulse, ego and id, doubles down on the side of reification. An adequate psychology, like Freud's, would endeavor to develop a greater understanding of it, seek to make people "conscious of their unconscious" through a dialectical embrace of what is unique and fragmentary in the subject.[77] For Adorno, this "addendum" or "additional factor" is the spark of uncoerced subjectivity; it is the kernel of the spontaneous will, the flash of individual freedom. Any psychoanalytic theory that ignores (or resists) this runs the risk of denying what is potentially revolutionary in its "object" of study: the possibility of a truly critical subject under an otherwise fully administered, antagonistic world.

---

75   Adorno, *Kant's Critique of Pure Reason*, 193.
76   Adorno, *History and Freedom*, 239.
77   Adorno, "Freudian Theory," 151.

Bibliography

Adorno, Theodor W. "Culture Industry Revisited." In *The Culture Industry: Selected Essays on Mass Culture*, edited by Jay Bernstein, 98–106. London: Routledge Classics, 2001.

Adorno, Theodor W. "Freudian Theory and the Pattern of Fascist Propaganda." In *The Culture Industry: Selected Essays on Mass Culture*, edited by Jay Bernstein, 132–157. London: Routledge Classics, 2001.

Adorno, Theodor W. *Introduction to Sociology*. Stanford: Stanford University Press, 2000.

Adorno, Theodor W. *Kant's Critique of Pure Reason*. Stanford: Stanford University Press, 2001.

Adorno, Theodor W. *Lectures on Negative Dialectics*. Cambridge: Polity Press, 2008.

Adorno, Theodor W. "Marx and the Basic Concepts of Sociological Theory." In *Adorno and Marx*, edited by Werner Bonefeld and Chris O'Kane, 241–51. London: Bloomsbury Academic, 2022.

Adorno, Theodor W. *Minima Moralia: Reflections from Damaged Life*. London: Verso, 2005.

Adorno, Theodor W. *Negative Dialectics*. Translated by E.B. Ashton. New York: Continuum, 2007.

Adorno, Theodor W. *Negative Dialectics*. Translated by Dennis Redmond. Morrisville: Lulu Press, 2022.

Adorno, Theodor W. *Philosophy and Sociology*. Cambridge: Polity Press, 2022.

Adorno, Theodor W. "The Revisionist Psychoanalysis." Translated by Nan-Nan Lee. In *Philosophy and Social Criticism* 40, no. 3. (2014): 326–39.

Adorno, Theodor W. "Sociology and Psychology (Part I)." In *New Left Review*, I/46, Nov/Dec. London: New Left Review Ltd., 1967.

Benjamin, Walter. *Illuminations*. New York: Schocken Books, 2007.

Blyth, Mark. *Great Transformations: Economic Ideas and Institutional Change in the Twentieth Century*. Cambridge: Cambridge University Press, 2002.

Frankfurt Institute for Social Research. *Aspects of Sociology*. Boston: Beacon Press, 1973.

Freitas, Verlain. "Theodor Adorno and the Freudian Revisionism." In *Veritas* 63, no. 2, maio-ago, 780–800. Porto Alegre: EDIPUCRS, 2018.

Freud, Sigmund. "Formulations on the Two Principles of Mental Functioning." In *The Standard Edition of the Complete Psychological Works of Sigmund Freud*, edited by James Strachey, Volume XII, 213–26. London: Hogarth Press, 1995.

Freud, Sigmund. "Introductory Lectures on Psychoanalysis, Part III". In *The Standard Edition of the Complete Psychological Works of Sigmund Freud*, edited by James Strachey, Volume XVI. London: Hogarth Press, 1995.

Hegel, G.W.F. *Phenomenology of Spirit*. Oxford: Oxford University Press, 1977.

Horkheimer, Max, and Theodor W. Adorno. *Dialectic of Enlightenment: Philosophical Fragments*. Stanford: Stanford University Press, 2002.

Jay, Martin. *The Dialectical Imagination: A History of the Frankfurt School and the Institute of Social Research, 1923–1950*. Berkeley: University of California Press, 1973.

Kant, Immanuel. *Critique of Practical Reason*. Indianapolis: Hackett Publishing Company, 2002.

Löwenthal, Leo. *An Unmastered Past: The Autobiographical Reflections of Leo Löwenthal*. Berkeley: University of California Press, 1987.

Lukács, Georg. *History and Class Consciousness: Studies in Marxist Dialectics*. Cambridge: MIT Press, 1972.

Marx, Karl. *Capital: A Critique of Political Economy*, Volume I. London: Penguin Classics, 1990.

Menillo, Gregory Joseph. "'Variation Within a Single Paradigm': The Latent Authoritarian Dynamics of the Culture Industry." In *How to Critique Authoritarian Populism: Methodologies of the Frankfurt School*, edited by Jeremiah Morelock, 239–66. Lieden: Brill Publishers, 2021.

Müller-Doohm, Stefan. *Adorno: A Biography*. Cambridge: Polity Press, 2005.

Prusik, Charles Andrew. *Adorno and Neoliberalism: The Critique of Exchange Society*. London: Bloomsbury Academic, 2020.

Shuster, Martin. *Autonomy After Auschwitz: Adorno, German Idealism, and Modernity*. Chicago: Chicago University Press, 2014.

Whitebook, Joel. "Weighty Objects: On Adorno's Kant-Freud Interpretation." In *The Cambridge Companion to Adorno*, edited by Tom Huhn, 51–78. Cambridge: Cambridge University Press, 2004.

CHAPTER 4

Marx and Freud, Horkheimer and Adorno: Beyond the Historical Gender Struggle

Rudolf J. Siebert

Early on, Max Horkheimer, the founder of the Critical Theory of Society and the Frankfurt School, informed by Immanuel Kant, Georg W.F. Hegel, Karl Marx, and Sigmund Freud, had personal contact with Freudian psychoanalysis when he visited as a patient the psychoanalyst and later friend, Karl Landauer, who was to help him to speak freely and without notes in the lecture halls of the Johann Wolfgang von Goethe Universität, in Frankfurt a.M., Germany.[1] The analysis was short, because Horkheimer and his beloved wife Maidon were such happy people, and thus were no longer in need of treatment by Landauer. A few years later, the Jewish psychoanalyst Landauer was starved to death in the Nazi concentration camp Bergen Belsen.

1   Freud and Marx

Max Horkheimer was the Director of the Institute of Social Research, popularly called "Caffe Marx" on the campus of the Frankfurt University, which was in continual contact with the nearby Freudian Psychoanalytical Institute, and the psychoanalysts Erich Fromm and Karl Landauer.[2] Later, both institutes merged in one building, and Fromm became a member of the Institute of Social Research, and Landauer became the director of its psychological department. The building was confiscated by the National Socialist cultural minister in 1933 and was bombed out by the Americans in 1944/1945, and rebuilt after the end of World War II, with the financial support of the City of Frankfurt and of the Military Government of the American Occupational Zone of Germany. Horkheimer and Fromm combined, like Herbert Marcuse, Theodor W. Adorno, Wilhelm Reich, Alexander and Margaret Mitscherlich, and much later Slavoj

---

1   Rolf Wiggershaus, *The Frankfurt School: Its History, Theories, and Political Significance*, trans. Michael Robertson (Cambridge, MA: The MIT Press, 1994); Karl Landauer. *Theory der Affekte und andere Schriften zur Ich – Organisation*. Frankfurt a. M.: Fischer Verlag, 1999.
2   Wiggershaus, *The Frankfurt School*, 9–105.

Žižek, Sigmund Freud and Karl Marx, psychoanalysis and political economics, as well as sociology. Marx, who had no psychology, was supplemented by Freud's psychoanalysis, and Freud, who had no sociology, was complemented by Marx's historical materialism. Horkheimer's Institute of Social Research combined individual and society, personal autonomy and universal solidarity.[3] The same was true of the Critical Theory of Religion and Society, or "Dialectical Religiology," which we derived from Horkheimer's Critical Theory of Society since the end of World War II.[4] For several years a deep friendship bound together Erich Fromm not only with the existentialist and socialist theologian Paul Tillich, but also with Horkheimer.[5] When Fromm left the Institute of Social Research, which had migrated to Columbia University in New York from fascist Germany, because of his financial and other reasons, e.g., his revisionism concerning Marx and Freud, meant for Horkheimer and the Institute of Social Research the greatest loss in comparison to other scholars who had departed.[6] While Horkheimer was mainly concerned with class and distribution of wealth, he was also interested in issues of cultural recognition or respect, like race issues (especially Anti-Semitism), generational issues, and gender issues, like the "battle of the sexes" through the centuries.[7] Throughout history, men and women were located in different classes: nobility, bourgeoisie, proletariat in civil society. Men may be related closer to women in their own class than to men in a different class. Women may be related closer to men in their own class than to women in a different class. Thus, class struggle and gender struggle are interconnected. Men and women did not only need recognition and respect, but also an income in civil society, one equal to that of men.[8] According to Dialectical Religiology, while Hegel built his gigantic philosophical system on the Idea, as well as on all five human potentials – language and memory, work and tool, sexual love, struggle for recognition, and community – his anti-systematic disciple Marx, after giving up his teacher's Idea, grounded his dialectical materialism in the evolutionary universal of work and tool. Freud based his psychoanalysis on the human potential of sexual

---

3 Ibid.
4 Rudolf J. Siebert, *The Critical Theory of Religion: Personal Autonomy and Universal Autonomy* (New York: Peter Lang Publishing, 2002).
5 Wiggershaus, *The Frankfurt School*, 34, 37, 52–60.
6 Ibid., 149–260.
7 Max Horkheimer, "Geschichte und Psychologie," *Zeitschrift für Sozialforschung* 1, no. 1/2 (1932): 125–144.
8 Axel Honneth, *Kritik der Macht. Reflexionsstufen einer kritischen Gesellschaftstheorie* (Frankfurt a.M.: Suhrkamp Verlag. 1985).

love.⁹ While Hegel was the greatest idealist, Marx and Freud were materialists. While Friedrich Engels, the friend of Marx, considered all religions to be idealistic, Hegel showed that Christianity was not only idealistic, but also materialistic through the incarnation of the Logos in Jesus of Nazareth.¹⁰ That was true of all positive religions in so far as they all had some kind of an incarnation: e.g., Hinduism, the *Religion of Imagination,* in the Bhagavad Gita; Judaism, the *Religion of Sublimity*, in the Torah; Islam, the *Religion of Law*, in the Holy Qur'ān. Thus, in the 21st century, there existed in American and European civil society a bourgeois, Marxian, and Freudian, as well as a legitimate, religious, e.g., Hindu, Jewish, Islamic, or Christian materialism. Like the Abrahamic Religions and German Idealism, the anti-systematic Horkheimer united the sense for reality with the imperturbable holding on to the Idea, the very opposite of the reality, and to the insight into the impossibility to imagine or name the Absolute, or the Unconditional.¹¹ While Freud looked with interest towards the Marxist/Leninist revolution going on in Russia in the 1920s, his biological determinism prevented him from becoming a Marxist, because of man's aggressive or death instinct (*Thanatos*). Even if the class struggle would end victoriously with the proletariat, other forms of conflict would continue, including the antagonisms between races, genders, and generations.¹² The Critical Theory of Religion and Society, which was also, like Horkheimer's critical theory of society, based on Kant and Hegel, Marx and Freud, traced the historical development from the original relative union of the genders under the primitive communism of hunters, fishermen, and food gatherers, through their antagonism in terms of matriarchy and patriarchy, to their possible reunion in terms of not only a formal, but rather a material, egalitarian, social democracy of brothers and sisters, not only in civil society and political state and history, but also in family and religion.¹³ Freud based his psychoanalysis and psychotherapy on organism, including form, assimilation, and species process, and on the connected psychic apparatus, including Id, Ego, and Super-

---

9 Sigmund Freud, *Three Essays on the Theory of Sexuality,* in *The Basic Writings of Sigmund Freud,* trans. A.A. Brill (New York: Modern Library, 1995), 521–600.

10 Georg W.F. Hegel, *Vorlesungen über die Philosophie der Religion, Vol. I–IV* (Frankfurt a.M.: Suhrkamp Verlag, 1986).

11 Max Horkheimer, *Critique of Instrumental Reason* (New York: The Seabury Press, 1974); Max Horkheimer, *Dawn and Decline. Notes 1926–1931 and 1950–1969* (New York: The Seabury Press, 1978); Max Horkheimer, *Gesellschaft im Übergang. Aufsätze. Reden und Vortrage 1942–1970* (Frankfurt a. M.: Fischer Verlag, 1981).

12 Sigmund Freud, *Civilization and its Discontents* (New York: W.W. Norton and Company, 1962).

13 Siebert, *The Critical Theory of Religion.*

Ego, and on the family, including marriage, familial property, and education of children, as the source of the gender conflict between parents and children, father and son, son and father, wife and husband, son and mother, daughter and mother, etc.[14] The class struggle for equal distribution of the surplus value included the gender conflict, as well as the race struggle, and the generational battle for equal, cultural recognition, and respect, as well as the environmental fight for species survival on this planet, but not *vice versa*. Not only women, but also LGBTQ+ communities participated in the historical gender struggle and fought more and more successfully for gender identity, equality, and justice, while secular as well as religious, exclusive rightwing authoritarian and totalitarian populists continued to consider them to be perverse and decadent expressions of a declining culture and civilization, and to resist them with violent identity policies and politics as the fascists had done in the first half of the 20th century. Not only Jews, Romani, and communists, men and women were murdered in the fascist concentration camps in Eastern Europe in the 20th century, but also homosexuals. Simon Wiesenthal was one of the first to discuss what happened to homosexuals before and during the Holocaust, and about the anti-gay edict that the Catholic Heinrich Himmler, the architect of the Jewish Shoah, enacted in 1937 in Nazi Berlin. The Simon Wiesenthal Center, usually devoted to the fight against Anti-Semitism, remembered during Gay Pride Month (June 2021) those gay men who were persecuted and murdered together with Jews during the Holocaust. The gender struggle was most closely connected not only with the class struggle, but also with the fight of the LGBTQ+ communities as a whole for equality and justice. The gender struggle took place most passionately not only in the secular, but also in the religious sphere. Jesuit Father Mitch Pacwa mentioned in a public discourse with a Hungarian priest in June 2021, in preparation of the Eucharistic Congress in Budapest in August 2021, the terror of communism in Catholic Hungary, and even the dangers of recent neo-liberalism for the faith, but forgot completely that Catholic Hungary, like Catholic Spain, and Catholic Portugal, and Catholic Croatia, and Catholic Italy, and half-Catholic Germany, had also been patriarchal, fascist, and anti-Semitic, and thus allies of Nazi Germany in the Second World War. I personally witnessed 300 Hungarian officers fighting most fanatically with German troops against General Patton's tank army in the Battle of Aschaffenburg, on Easter 1945, and that they only deserted when the battle was finally lost. Even though there existed an all too late Papal Encyclical Letter, which condemned fascism as pagan, no fascist leader was ever

---

14 Sigmund Freud, *Beyond the Pleasure Principle* (New York: W.W. Norton & Company, 1990).

excommunicated or deprived of receiving communion. Not only was Adolf Hitler never excommunicated, but a mass was celebrated for him in all German Catholic parishes after he had ordered people to be executed up to his last day, and after he and his wife Eva Braun had committed suicide, both having been educated by Catholic priests and nuns in Austria. On the other hand, all socialists and communists were automatically excommunicated. While the Vatican had concordats with all fascist states, there was no agreement with the Soviet Union. While Catholic communities helped innocent Jews during World War II, the Vatican also helped criminal Nazi leaders flee to South America after the War. When in 2020 the Vatican reached an agreement with the Communist Government in China, in order to make good what had been done wrong through one-sided policies in the 20th century, Fox News and the conservative Catholic news station, Eternal Word Television Network (EWTN), and the whole Catholic Right in the USA and in Europe were outraged and protested wildly. The patriarchal gender struggle continued most recently in the religious sphere in the USA, while the Republican Party seemed to have turned fascist, and socialism was gaining popularity in the polls. The latter was resisted most fanatically by the secular, exclusive, rightwing, populist Fox News, and the likewise exclusive, rightwing, populist Catholic EWTN, both of which shared even the same contributor and anchorman, Raymond Arroyo. Women could still not yet be ordained to the priesthood in the patriarchal, authoritarian Roman Catholic Church as late as 2024, as Jews had already modified their patriarchal attitude and had ordained female rabbis for quite some time, and Protestant Churches had given up their patriarchy to a large extent and had ordained female ministers for even much longer.

2 Athens

According to Max Horkheimer, the initiator of the psychoanalysis, Sigmund Freud, explained in his theory about the Oedipus complex the identification of the boy with the father out of their love for the mother.[15] Freud based his psychoanalysis on the tragedies of Aeschylus and Sophocles in Athens: a chain of gender crimes.[16] The tragedies reflected on the level of the absolute

---

15 Joel Whitebook, "The Urgeschichte of Subjectivity Reconsidered," *New German Critique* 81 (Autumn 2000): 125–141.
16 Aeschylus, *The Complete Aeschylus: Volume 1: The Oresteia* (Oxford: Oxford University Press, 2011); Sophocles, *The Theban Plays* (Baltimore, MD: Penguin Books, 1964).

spirit, of culture, of art and of religion, namely the Greek *Religion of Fate and Beauty*, the real struggle of the genders on the level of the objective spirit, of the Athenian family, civil society, city state and history.[17] According to Aeschylus's *Agamemnon*, Thyestes seduced Atreus' wife.[18] Atreus killed Thyestes' young children and gave him them as meat. Helen forsook her husband and went to Troy with Paris. Agamemnon, in order to promote the Trojan war, sacrificed his daughter Iphigeneia. Aigisthos and Clytemnestra murdered Agamemnon after his return from Troy. Orestes killed Aigisthos and his mother Clytemnestra with the support of his sister Electra. However, for his matricide, Orestes was pursued throughout Greece in revenge by the female spirits, the Erinyes (Furies), until he came to Athens, where Athena, who had, according to Greek patriarchal imagination come out of the head of Zeus, as Eve had come, according to Jewish patriarchal imagination, from the rib of Adam, atoned for and reconciled Orestes for the price of a patriarchy, in which man protected woman and child, and woman served man. Agamemnon represented the arrival of patriarchy, Clytemnestra return of matriarchy, and Orestes the reestablishment of patriarchy. According to Sophocles, after *Oedipus* had returned from his exile, into which he had been sent as a boy by his parents, because of an ominous oracle, and after he had solved the riddle of the Sphinx on the marketplace of Thebes, and thus had redeemed the city, he killed unconsciously and unintentionally his father, when he blocked his way to the city, and then married unconsciously and unintentionally his mother, Jocasta, retaking the patriarchal power position of his late father.[19] Teiresias, a blind prophet, revealed the gender tragedy. The Chorus of Theban elders commented on it. At least since the Axial age, the battle of the sexes raged on under the patriarchy, interrupted admittedly by the armistice of marriage, family, partnership, and friendship. This armistice, however, broke down in the West more and more, in higher and higher rates of different expressions and forms of the *battle of the sexes*, like divorce, adultery, abortion, birth control, homosexuality, LGBTQ+ communities, which continued to be discriminated against heavily by rightwing Catholics and Southern Baptists, etc., until they reached in the 20th and 21st centuries a level never seen before since the late Roman Empire.

---

17   Hegel, *Vorlesungen über die Philosophie der Religion*.
18   Aeschylus, *The Complete Aeschylus*, 44–105.
19   Ibid.

3 Jerusalem

In the view of Dialectical Religiology, not only Athens was aware of the historical gender struggle, but also Jerusalem. In Jewish history the struggle of the genders reached its climax with two courageous women. The Book of Judith tells the story of the defeat of Nebuchadnezzar's armies through a woman's single-handed assassination of their commander. The book was written about 100 B.C. The theme of the Book of Esther was similarly the deliverance of the Jewish nation by the actions of a woman. The Hebrew version was probably written about 300 B.C. The Hebrew Prophet Micah stated concerning the gender conflict in the neighborhood and in the family:

> Put no trust in a neighbor,
> have no confidence in a friend;
> to the woman who shares your bed
> do not open your mouth,
> for son insults father,
> daughter defies mother,
> daughter-in-law defies mother-in-law;
> a man's enemies are those of his own household
> among them, the best is like a briar,
> the most honest a hedge of thorn.
> Today will come their ordeal from the North,
> now is the time of their confusion.[20]

Rabbi Jesus spoke of the dissention in the family, following the Prophet Micah:

> Do not suppose that I have come to bring peace to the earth: it is not peace I have come to bring, but a sword. For I have come to set a man against his father, a daughter against her mother, a daughter-in-law against her mother-in-law. A man's enemies will be those of his own household.[21]
>
> Do you suppose that I am here to bring peace on earth? No, I tell you, but rather division. For from now on a household of five will be divided: three against two and two against three; the father divided against the son, son against father, mother against daughter, daughter

---

20 Micah 7:5–8.
21 Matthew 10:34–36.

against mother, mother-in-law against daughter-in-law, daughter in law against mother-in-law.[22]

According to Jesus, there were men who were castrated, eunuchs, in the contemporary Jewish and Roman culture: 'There are eunuchs born that way from their mother's womb, there are eunuchs made by men and there are eunuchs who have made themselves that way for the sake of the kingdom of heaven.'[23]

According to the Critical Theory of Religion and Society, only Essenes made themselves into eunuchs for the sake of the kingdom of God. According to the context, Jesus used the Essene statement not in order to establish a celibate priesthood, but rather in order to tell divorced people not to get married again. Jesus did this after he had criticized Moses's permission of divorce, because the Israelites had not been teachable, despite of the fact that in the beginning it was not so: according to the will of the Creator God in the Genesis. While according to the book Genesis, Sodom was destroyed because of homosexuality, and while according to the book Leviticus homosexuals had to be sentenced to death and executed, despite of the fact that according to the Prophet Isaiah, Sodom had been destroyed because its rich women did not share their wealth with the poor, and according to Jesus's teaching, Sodom had been destroyed because of a lack of hospitality toward strangers. In Jesus's view, the men of Sodom could repent and be forgiven easier than the men of Sidon, who did not repent after he had preached to them.[24] Also Jesus taught: 'You have learned how it was said: you must love your neighbor and hate your enemy.'[25]

According to Dialectical Religiology, the quotation was from Leviticus 19:18. The hated enemy could be inside, as well as outside the family. However, the second part of this commandment was not in the written Hebrew Law. It was an Aramaic, Essene, way of saying: *'You do not have to love your enemy.'*

Also, this rule was valid inside as well as outside the family. The Greek tragedies found their climax and their final resolution in the ultimate Christian tragedy, in which the son, born without the original sin of patricide, redeemed through his own self-sacrifice the world from its sins.[26] When Jesus was executed, his mother and his disciple John were present, but the rest of his family, his father Joseph, and his four brothers and his sisters, as well as most of his disciples were missing: Judas having betrayed him; Peter having denied him

---

22   Luke 12:51–53.
23   Matthew 19:12.
24   Genesis 19; Matthew 10:15.
25   Matthew 5:43.
26   Matthew 26–28; Mark 14–16; Luke 22–24; John 18–20.

three times; and all the other disciples having fled, after three years of intense teaching.²⁷

4   Animus, Anima, and Self

Sigmund Freud's student, Carl Gustav Jung, who as an Aryan and was supposed to spread psychoanalysis beyond Jewish circles, based his individuation psychology on mythology, not only from Athens and Jerusalem, but also from Africa, Asia, and the Near East, insofar as it reflected the gender struggle, and developed a psychic apparatus that contained the trinitarian structure of *Animus*, representing the male element, *Anima*, representing the female element, and of *Self*, representing the absolute component, in which the *Animus* and the *Anima* were united and reconciled in a sacred marriage, in which each individual had to achieve his or her own individuation and integration.²⁸ Man and woman had both archetypes: Animus and Anima. In man the Animus was dominant, and the Anima was recessive. In woman the Anima was dominant, and the Animus was recessive. Each element of the psychic trinity in both genders had its positive and negative side. The *Animus* was symbolized by the good king and the bad dwarf. The *Anima* was symbolized by the good Queen and the bad witch. The good Self had its bright side, symbolized by the Buddha or the Christ, and its dark side, the shadow, symbolized by Lucifer or Satan. During the male, or *Animus*-dominated fascist period, the fascist, Swiss citizen, Jung, taught that the German people had symbolized the good Self through their great leader, Adolf Hitler. After the fascist period, Jung taught that the German people had projected the shadow of the Self on the Jewish people and had thus produced Auschwitz (Shoah).²⁹ While Martin Heidegger, Carl Schmitt, and Mircea Eliade died as fascists, Jung converted and left fascism behind. He later hired a Jewish secretary who wrote his biography in which she described him as a very religious person.³⁰ But Jung's so-called "Aryan" psychoanalysis remained opposed to Freud's so-called "Semitic" psychoanalysis. The critical theory of society as well as the Critical Theory of Religion and Society, followed

---

27   John 18–20.
28   Tony Judt and Timothy Snyder, *Nachdenken über das 20. Jahrhundert* (München: Carl Hanser Verlag, 2012); Carl G. Jung, *Modern Man in Search of a Soul* (New York: Harcourt, Brace, Jovanovich, 2017).
29   Richard Noll, *The Aryan Christ: The Secret Life of Carl Jung* (New York: Random House, 1997).
30   C.G. Jung and Aniela Jaffé, *Memories, Dreams, Reflections,* trans. Richard and Clara Winston (New York: Vintage Books, 1989).

Freud rather than Jung since the archetypes in the individuation psychology were ahistorical.

5 Thinking

While for the dialectical philosopher and theologian, Georg F.W. Hegel, the Greek tragedies, art, and Christianity, religion, still belonged together with philosophy into the sphere of the absolute spirit, they moved after the secularization of the collective consciousness of the Unconditional for Marx and Freud, and for Horkheimer, Adorno, Marcuse, and Fromm, and the other critical theorists, into the dimension of the subjective spirit, including the anthropological, phenomenological and psychological level, and of the objective spirit, including abstract right, personal morality, family, civil society, state, and history. According to Horkheimer's psychological, as well as sociological interpretation of Freud's Oedipus theory, the mother belonged to the father, the grown up, and strong, and powerful man. Therefore, the boy must make himself *equal* and *identical* with the father.[31] The father could defend himself against the competitor, the child, the son, the boy.[32] The boy had to be like the father in order to possess the mother. But there was for Horkheimer a much simpler, and clearer explanation than the one given by Freud: what one *thinks* of, that one turns into. The father, i.e., the reality principle, demanded, forbid, and taught the child, the boy, the son. The unchangeable, refusing realty was what people, particularly young people, wanted to change, according to their own youthful utopia. However, this reality principle forced on its part people to identify themselves with it, in order to be able to endure it. That precisely was the principle of *thinking*. Perhaps *thinking* was the principle of all cultures and civilizations in general. I taught my seven children in Europe and America that if they would be *thinking*, then they would have to suffer less in life, and that what they did not learn through thinking, they would have to learn through suffering: and so, it happened.

For Horkheimer, out of this *principle of thinking*, functional thinking, instrumental rationality, rooted in the human potential of work and tool, rather than the evolutionary universal of language and memory, sexual love, struggle for recognition, social union, this *identification* in order to endure, resulted then

---

31 Horkheimer, *Dawn and Decline*; Sigmund Freud, *Das Ich Und Das Es* (Frankfurt a.M.: Fischer Taschenbuch Verlag 1992), 193–251.
32 Ibid.

also the rule, control, and mastery of nature.[33] *Identification* was the presupposition of power and domination. My uncle, the physicist Albin Kehl, started as a boy to observe the doves and their flight patterns from a little house in his backyard in Frankfurt, Eckenheim. He was later employed by the Max Plank Institute and developed new forms of wings for modern airplanes, and finally new types of airplanes, which improved substantially air travel, and thus control over nature. Horkheimer was fully aware that as soon as thinking and identification had succeeded, identification disappeared: that which was controlled turned into a thing, and it became nothing else than only the controlled thing.

6   Reification

For Horkheimer, it was terminologically confusing that Karl Marx, the founder of dialectical (or historical) materialism, called the lack of regulation according to the economical relationships under capitalism, as the "private appropriation of collective surplus labor," *reification* of the human relationships.[34] The Aristotelian, Spinozian, Kantian, and Hegelian Marx developed his dialectical materialistic theory of surplus value out of and against Hegel's dialectical idealistic *Phenomenology of Spirit*, *Science of Logic*, *Philosophy of Law*, and *Philosophy of History* in continual discourse with and against the political economists Adam Smith, Ricardo, Sais, and Malthus: the notion of human work, or production, out of the evolutionary universal of what Hegel had called *work and tool*. Marx traced the notion of human work to the goal of production as the satisfaction of human, material, and spiritual needs, through the means of production as accumulation of capital as dead labor of yesterday, the productive forces, the division of labor, the commodities, the productive relations as social system, and the course of production from primitive communism, through slavery, feudalism, private capitalism, socialism, to mature communism, as collective appropriation by *all* of the collective surplus labor, produced by *all*, the freedom of *all*, on the basis of the necessity of nature, and beyond – and ultimately to the kingdom of heaven, grounded since the beginning of creation, without stealing, murdering, lying, adultery, revenge, death, tears and mourning, and determined by the love of God and man.[35] After the bourgeoisie had developed in the most advanced capitalistic country, in England, the new science of political economics as an instrument

---

33   Horkheimer, "Geschichte und Psychologie".
34   Karl Marx, *Zur Kritik der politischen Ökonomie* (Berlin: Dietz Verlag, 1951).
35   Genesis 1–13; Exodus 20; Isaiah 11:65–66; Matthew 5–7; Acts 17; Revelation 21–22.

for understanding and reinforcing the private appropriation of collective surplus labor, the proletariat could transform it into an instrument of its own emancipation and liberation, and its own collective appropriation of its own collective surplus value. The bourgeois or liberal enlightenment and revolutions were followed by the proletarian or socialist enlightenment and revolutions, which continue, resisted most forcefully and powerfully by American and European capital, and the American military all around the globe. The economic contradiction of modernity was nevertheless in the process of being resolved into a new social macro-paradigm, post-modern, alternative Future III: the more reconciled, free and egalitarian society. The new science of Freudian psychoanalysis supported in the sphere of the subjective spirit the new science of political economics in the sphere of the objective spirit as instrument of emancipation and liberation. According to Horkheimer, in contrast to psychoanalysis, "reification" was regressively a mythologization, an elevation of human productive relationships into the rank of natural deities, of idols: idolatry. Reification meant a shift from what Hegel had called the subjective spirit, or the objective spirit, to the absolute spirit, from civil society to religion, which collective consciousness of the Unconditional had since the bourgeois, Marxist, and Freudian materialistic enlightenment been inverted through secularization: religion, art, and philosophy had become part of the objective and the subjective spirit, as the absolute spirit disintegrated.[36] For Horkheimer, the laws of the market were not merely the day and night and thunder of the Victorian age, what Hegel had called the "zeitgeist," the spirit of the times, but "moira," the fate as such, in terms of the Greek *Religion of Fate and Beauty*, or *Fortuna*, in terms of the *Roman Religion of Utility*.[37] Only in the 20th and 21st centuries were the laws of the market – as the consequence of that identification – controllable things, and objects of manipulation, e.g., in terms of Lord Keynes, or of Friedmann. Adolf Hitler did Keynesian economics better than Keynes himself.[38] President Reagan shifted from Keynes to Friedmann in the belief that capitalism would no longer have any crises.[39] President Biden shifted back from Friedmann to Keynes, because it had become obvious during the financial crisis of 2008, and during the pandemic of 2020–2021, that private capitalism could still have crises, and would

---

36 Horkheimer, *Dawn and Decline*.
37 Hegel, *Vorlesungen über die Philosophie der Religion I–IV*.
38 Ian Kershaw, *Hitler: Hubris. 1989–1934* (New York: W. W. Norton and Company, 1999).
39 Thomas Piketty, *Capital in the Twenty-First Century* (Cambridge, MA: The Belknap Press of Harvard University Press, 2014).

have them increasingly up to its very end, despite of all manipulation of the laws of the market, simply because of its internal contradiction between private appropriation by the Few, men as well as women, of the surplus labor, produced by the Many, men as well as women, which drove beyond private capitalism, toward a new socio-cultural macro-paradigm.

7   Fear, Love, Power

In Horkheimer's triplicate, or trinitarian, dialectical view, informed and inspired by Immanuel Kant, Georg F.W, Hegel, Karl Marx, and Sigmund Freud, out of the angst, anxiety, or fear, followed the love, and out of the love followed the power, the rule, and the master and servant relationship between slave and slave holder, serf and feudal lord, capitalist and so-called *free* worker. According to Horkheimer's triplicity of fear, love, and power, only from what people were afraid of do they learned to love, and only from what they loved did they learn: the powerful. However, people knew they ceased to love and to fear. That, precisely, was the history of culture and civilization as such. Each of the termini, *fear, love,* and *power,* contained the others, and the whole. The middle term, the loving, was the *identification*, the *thinking*. It was posted and located between the extremes of angst and power. Despite of the closeness between critical theory and evangelical-reformatory faith idea, there was also a difference; unlike Kant and Hegel, Horkheimer could, like Marx and Freud, no longer comprehend the trinitarian idea in the sphere of the absolute spirit, in Christianity as the *Religion of Becoming, Freedom and Complete Manifestation*, or in any other trinitarian religion.[40] But Horkheimer was still able to recognize with Kant and Hegel, Marx and Freud, the principle of triplicity in the spheres of the subjective spirit, through Freudian psychoanalysis and in the dimension of the objective spirit, through the Marxist dialectical materialism. For Horkheimer, the trinity had the social function to reconcile Jewish monotheism with the Christian notion of the Divinity of Christ, or the ethical monotheism of Judaism, Christianity and Islam with the African, Asian, and Near Eastern, as well as Greek and Roman polytheism.[41]

---

40 Hegel, *Vorlesungen über die Philosophie der Religion I–IV*.
41 Horkheimer, *Dawn and Decline*; Max Horkheimer, *Die Sehnsucht nach dem ganz Anderen. Ein Interview mit Kommentar von Helmut Gumnior* (Hamburg: Furche Verlag, 1970).

8 Patriarchal Religion

The derivation of a need for patriarchal religion from the child's feeling of helplessness and the longing it evoked for a father, seemed to Freud incontrovertible, especially since this feeling was not simply carried on from childhood days, but was kept alive perpetually by the angst, anxiety, or fear, or of what the superior power of Fate will bring, as it appeared in the Greek *Religion of Fate and Beauty*.[42] For Freud, patriarchal religion was an attempt to get control over the sensory world, in which people were placed, by means of the wish-world, which they had developed inside themselves as a result of biological and psychological necessities. But patriarchal religion could not achieve its end. The religious doctrines carried within themselves the stamp of the times, in which they originated: the ignorant childhood days of humanity. Freud did not trust the consolations of patriarchal religion. If Freud attempted to assign to religion its place in man's evolution, it seemed not so much to be a lasting acquisition, as a parallel to the neurosis, which the civilized individual had to pass through on his or her way from childhood to maturity. Freud understood patriarchal, or matriarchal, religious phenomena only on the model of the neurotic symptoms of the individual, which were so familiar to him as a return of long forgotten, important, happenings in the primeval history of the human family, e.g., patricide as original sin; that they owed their obsessive character to that very origin, and therefore derived their effect on humanity from the historical truth they contained. Freud ventured to regard the obsessional neurosis as a pathological counterpart to the formation of a patriarchal religion. Freud described this neurosis as a private, religious system, and patriarchal religion as a "universal, obsessive neurosis." It was easy for Freud to see wherein lay the resemblance between neurotic ceremonial, on one hand, and religious rites, cult or liturgy, on the other. It was in the fear of pangs of conscience after their omission, in the complete isolation of them from all other activities, the feeling that one must not be disturbed, and in the conscientiousness with which the details were carried out. Freud was mainly concerned with patriarchal religions like Judaism, the *Religion of Sublimity*, and Christianity, the *Religion of Becoming, Freedom and Full Manifestation*. He did not recognize clearly enough the strong matriarchal element in Eastern and Western Catholicism, their Mariology. The strong, general, one-sidedly, patriarchal orientation of Freud's psychoanalysis was its greatest weakness. It shared this weakness with its surrounding Jewish and Austrian culture. It became visible particularly after

---

42   Hegel, *Vorlesungen über die Philosophie der Religion I–IV*.

strong anti-patriarchal tendencies asserted themselves in Europe and America after World War I, and then again after World War II in the second half of the 20th century, and still in the beginning of the 21st century.

9 Identification

According to Horkheimer, informed by Freud, the Swiss, antiquarian, jurist, philologist, cultural anthropologist, sociologist, philosopher of history, and professor of Roman Law, Johann Jakob Bachofen, author of the book *Mother Right and Primordial Religion*, and the teacher of both inclusive Leftwing populists, as well as of exclusive rightwing populists of the 20th and 21st centuries, who were interested in matriarchy, reported on the basis of a quotation by the Roman poet Plutarch, that the Lycian men in the case of death or bereavement had to put on women clothing.[43] Bachofen interpreted the Lycian custom as "identification" with the mother, who had born the deceased, and had received him again. Only the mother concerned the whole process and participated in it. Therefore, to think of dying meant to think of the mother, and to think of the mother meant to make oneself into the mother. The boy identified with the father. According to Horkheimer, this process was more primitive than Sigmund Freud described.[44] It was not so understandable, and not so clear and lucid. It did not need Freud's detour and roundabout way over the sexual desire and passion for the mother, which he had opened up and developed out of the analogy with the genital relationship of adults, in order to explain the boy's adjustment to, or identification with the father. For Freud the identification meant first of all the original form of an emotional tie with an object. Secondly, it meant that in a regressive way it became a substitute for a libidinal objective, as it were by means of the introjection of the object into the Ego. Thirdly, it meant that it may arise with every new perception of a common quality shared with some other person, who was not an object of the sexual instinct. In the identification, one Ego became like another. One Ego resulted in the first Ego behaving itself in certain respects in the same way as the second one. It imitated it, and as it were, took it into itself. Freud compared this identification not inappropriately with the oral cannibalistic incorporation of another person. Nevertheless, such archaic identification was radically superseded and sublimated in the Christian Eucharist. Freud showed that he was

---

43 Jakob Bachofen, *Das Mutterrecht. In Der Mythos von Orient und Occident: Eine Metaphysik der alten Welt*. (München: Verlag C.H. Beck, 1926).
44 Horkheimer, *Dawn and Decline*.

not prejudiced against women when he discovered that not only women could be hysterical, but also men, even though they did not have uteri. According to Freud, in the hysteria of women and men identification was most frequently employed to express a sexual community. The hysterical woman identified herself by her symptoms most readily – though not exclusively – with persons, with whom she had sexual relations, or who have had sexual intercourse with the same persons as herself. Language took cognizance of this tendency; two lovers were said to be *one*. In hysterical fantasy, as well as in dreams, identification may ensure, if one simply thinks of sexual relations. They need not necessarily become actual. For Freud, identification was a very important kind of relationship with another person, probably the most primitive one. It was not to be confused with object-choice. Thus, Erich Fromm pointed out in his revision of Freud, that Oedipus, in his identification with his father and marriage to his mother, did not sexually desire her, but that she was given to him by the citizens of Thebes as a gift for his redemption and liberation of the city from the mortal danger of the Sphinx, who ate a victim every morning for breakfast.[45] Freud could express the difference between identification and object choice in this way: when a boy identified himself with his father he wanted to be *like* his father. When he made him the object of his choice, he wanted to *have* him, to possess him. In the first case, Ego was altered on the model of the boy's father, in the second case that was not necessary. Identification and object-choice were, broadly speaking, independent of each other. But one could identify oneself with a person and alter one's Ego accordingly and take the same person as one's sexual object. Freud heard it said that this influencing of the Ego by the sexual object took place very often with women and was characteristic for femininity. According to Freud, if one had lost a love-object, or had to give it up, one often compensated oneself by identifying oneself with it. One set it up again inside one's own Ego, so that in this case object-choice regressed, as it were, to identification.

10   Primordial Powers

According to Horkheimer, informed by Freud and Fromm, the *fear* of the father was the primordial cause not only of religion, but of culture and civilization in general.[46] In Freud's view, fear required a definite object, of which one was

---

45   Sophocles, *The Theben Plays*.
46   Max Horkheimer, *Critical Theory: Selected Essays* (New York: The Seabury Press, 1972).

afraid: e.g. zoophobia. The father was the intruder in the relationship of mother and child: the external, the coldness of the reality principle. Here, Horkheimer had still to agree with Freud. Freud had also correctly seen the belonging together of the triplicity of mother, home, and death. In Horkheimer's critical view, Freud's prejudice, particularly in his earlier periods, lay in his dogmatic start, to develop the male and female as separate primitive, "primordial powers," while the sexual love of the male child for the mother was probably only first of all a consequence of the adjustment to, or identification of the boy with the father as intruder. Freud suspected this relationship since he wrote his book *Beyond the Pleasure Principle*.[47] According to Freud, the Ego's activities were governed by consideration of the tensions produced by stimuli present within the Ego, or introduced into it. The raising of these tensions was in general felt as displeasure, and their lowering as pleasure. In his psychoanalytical theory of the mind, Freud took for granted that the course of mental processes was automatically regulated by the pleasure-pain principle. Freud believed that any given process originated in an unpleasant state of tension and there upon determined for itself such a path, that its ultimate issue coincided with a relaxation of this tension, i.e., with avoidance of *pain*, or with the production of pleasure. The pleasure principle was a tendency that subserved a certain function: namely, that of rendering the psychic apparatus as a whole free from any excitation, or to keep the amount of excitation constant, or as low as possible. The pleasure-pain principle was brought into action in response to the danger signal and played a part in repression. This principle had unrestricted sway over the processes in the Id, rather than in the Ego, or the Super-Ego, in the trinitarian structure and dynamic of the psychic apparatus.

11   Longing

In the view of Horkheimer, Freud's title, *Beyond the Pleasure Principle*, should be *Beyond the Gender Principle*.[48] In this case, in that classical Oedipus myth of the origin of love, out of the division of the One, contained the truth about the extra-libidinous *longing*: the death drive. This longing could fulfill itself only in the power of the libidinous desire, as was shown in Shakespeare's *Romeo and*

---

47   Freud wrote *Beyond the Pleasure Principle* in 1920, wherein he introduced the idea of "death drives," or *Thanatos,* a Greek name that personifies death. This *Thanatos* alludes to human beings' tendencies towards destructiveness, against themselves, others, and society.
48   Horkheimer, *Dawn and Decline*.

Juliette, and in Arthur Schopenhauer's philosophy.[49] According to Horkheimer, in contrast to the original Freudian opposition of self-preservation and male *Eros,* these two together formed the unity of the creating principle. Freud precisely indicated as such in his book, *Civilization and its Discontent*.[50] In the power of this creating principle the "utopia" of the reconciliation was to fulfill itself. That was, of course, excluded precisely through the immediate antagonism of *Eros* and *Thanatos*.[51] Freud decided to assume the existence of only two basic instincts in the Id: *Eros* and *Thanatos* – the destructive, or the "death drive."[52] For Freud, the contrast between the instincts of self-preservation and of the preservation of the species, as well as the contrast between Ego-love and object love, fell within the bounds of the *Eros:* 'You must love your neighbor, because he is you.'[53]

The translation of this Hebrew text came from the dissertation of one of Horkheimer's female doctoral students in the Philosophy Department of the Johann Wolfgang von Goethe Universität in Frankfurt. According to Freud, the aim of the first of these basic instincts, *Eros,* was to establish ever greater unities, and to preserve them by binding them together. Freud supposed that the final aim of the destructive instinct was to reduce living things to an inorganic state.[54] For this reason, Freud also called it the "death instinct" (Thanatos) with some hesitation. The fear of death was alien to the child. Being dead meant, for the child, who had been spared the sight of the suffering that preceded death, much the same as *being gone,* and ceasing to annoy the survivors. The child did not distinguish the means by which this absence was brought about, whether by distance, or estrangement, or death. According to Freud, the fear of death was to be regarded as an analogue of the fear of castration, and that the situation to which the Ego reacted was the state of being forsaken, or deserted by the protecting Super-Ego, by the powers of Destiny, which put an end to security against every danger: 'My God, my God, why have you deserted me.'[55] Again, Freud supposed that the final aim of the destructive instinct was to

---

49 William Shakespeare, *The Complete Works* (Albany, NY: James B. Lyon Publisher, 1878); Arthur Schopenhauer, *Aphorismen zur Lebensweischeit* (Wiesbaden: Brockhaus Verlag, 1946).
50 Sigmund Freud, *Civilization and its Discontents.*
51 Ibid.
52 Freud, *Beyond the Pleasure Principle,* 46–49, 53, 55–56, 58–69, 72.
53 Ibid.
54 Ibid.
55 Rudolf J. Siebert, *Manifesto of the Critical Theory of Society and Religion: The Wholly Other, Liberation, Happiness and the Rescue of the Hopeless, Vol I–III* (Leiden: Brill, 2010).

reduce living things to an inorganic state.⁵⁶ Thus, Freud called it "Thanatos." For Freud, as for the dialectical materialist Bertolt Brecht, and as in contrast to the Christians Immanuel Kant and Georg W. F. Hegel, Hans Küng, Johannes Baptist Metz, and Gregory Baum, human beings, men and women alike, died like the animals.⁵⁷

12   Harmonization

According to Horkheimer, people had to guard themselves from the optimistic harmonization of the subjective striving for self-preservation with the objective satisfaction or gratification, as against the all too quick identification of the *Eros* with the male and fatherly principle, and of the home coming, the Thanatos, with the female and motherly principle.⁵⁸ In the view of the Schopenhauerian Horkheimer, the death, into which the active life of the civilization lead people, was precisely not the homeland, but the abandonment, not the peace, but the decay and disintegration, not the rest, quiet, and calm, but the nothing.⁵⁹ Michelangelo's famous *Pieta*, the sculpture of Mary holding her crucified son Jesus on her lap, portrayed him as having returned in death to the mother who had birthed him, despite the fact that there was no such report in the Gospels. The Schopenhauerian Adolf Hitler went from his office in the Führer Bunker, in defeated Berlin, where the picture stood on the desk of his beloved mother, who shared with him her blue eyes, and whom he had taken care of when he was 18 years old, when she was dying from breast cancer, with the help and support of a Jewish doctor. This picture stood in the room in which he would commit suicide with his wife Eva Braun, ordering the SS to burn their bodies outside in the backyard: the final rest without a grave.⁶⁰

13   Ego, Super-Ego, Id

While for the greatest idealistic philosopher, G. W.F. Hegel, the traditional family had consisted of the triplicity of marriage, familial property, and the education of children, for the materialist physician and psychoanalyst, Sigmund

---

56   Freud, *Beyond the Pleasure Principle*.
57   Ibid.
58   Horkheimer, *Critique of Instrumental Reason*.
59   Ibid.
60   Ian Kershaw, *Hitler: Nemesis. 1936–1945* (New York: W.W. Norton and Company, 2001).

Freud, it consisted of the duality of parents, i.e., father and mother, and boys and girls. According to Freud, the parents produced in their children the Super-Ego.[61] In Freud's view, in the course of the individual development a part of the inhibiting forces in the outer world became internalized. A standard was created in the Ego, which opposed the other faculties by observation, criticism, and prohibition. Freud called this new standard the Super-Ego. The Super-Ego was the successor and representative of the parents in the family and the educators, who superintended the actions of the individual in the first years of life. It perpetuated their functions almost without a change. When Freud established the trinitarian structure of the psychical apparatus, and when he set out the relationship of Ego and Id, he kept back an important part of his theory of this apparatus. Freud was forced to assume that in the Ego itself a special agency had become differentiated, which he named the Super-Ego. The Super-Ego held a special position between the Ego and the Id. It belonged to the Ego. It shared the Ego's high psychological organization. But it stood in an especially intimate connection with the Id, the instincts. It borrowed its aggressive energy from the Id. It was to precipitate of the Ego's first attachments to objects. It was the heir of the Oedipus complex, when that had been vacated.[62] This Super-Ego could set itself up against the Ego. It could treat the Ego as an object. It often reprimanded the Ego very harshly. It was just as important for the Ego to live in concord and harmony with the Super-Ego, the internalized culture values, as with the Id. Discords between the Ego and the Id, as well as between the Ego and the Super-Ego, had great significance for the psychical life. The Super-Ego was the vehicle for the phenomenon, which Hegel had still called conscience in his dialectical *Philosophy of Right*, under personal morality.[63] According to Freud, it was very important for mental health that the Super-Ego should develop normally, i.e., that it should become sufficiently depersonalized. It was precisely that which did not happen in the case of a neurotic, because his Oedipus complex did not undergo the right transformation. His Super-Ego dealt with his Ego like a strict father with a child, and his idea of morality displaced itself in primitive ways by making the Ego submit to punishment by the Super-Ego. Illness was employed as a means for this *self-punishment,* with an aggression borrowed from the Id, and the death instinct. The neurotic had to behave as though he were mastered by guilt, which the illness served to punish, and so to relieve him. According to Freud, the Super-Ego

---

61 Sigmund Freud, *Beyond the Pleasure Principle*.
62 Ibid.
63 Georg W.F. Hegel, *Grundlinien der Philosophie des Rechts oder Naturrecht und Staatswissenschaft im Grundriss*. (Frankfurt a.M.: Suhrkamp Verlag, 1986).

may bring fresh needs to the fore, but its chief function remained the limitation of satisfaction.

14 Parents

According to Freud, the first love-object of the boy was his mother, and she remained as such in the formation of his Oedipus complex, and, ultimately, throughout his whole life.[64] For the little girl, too, her mother had to be her first object, together with figures of nurses, and other attendants, that merge into hers. The first object-cathexis, indeed, followed the lines of the satisfaction of the great and simple needs of life, and the circumstances in which the child was nursed were the same for both sexes. In the Oedipus situation, however, the father became the little girl's love-object. It was from him that in the normal course of development the girl should find her way to her ultimate object-choice. The girl had, then, in the course of time to change both the erotogenic zone and her object, while the boy kept both of them unchanged. But no fact had more claim to Freud's attention than this: that a small child's sexual wishes were regularly directed towards those who stood in the closest relationship to it, in the first place, its father and mother, and beyond them, its brothers and sisters. For a boy, the mother was the first love-object; for a girl the father, so far, as a bisexual his position did not call for the reverse attitude at the same time. The other parent was felt to be a disturbing rival, and was not seldom regarded with acute enmity, which played a role in the battle of the sexes.

15 Father

Freud could not point to any need in childhood so strong as that for a father's protection.[65] The idea of being eaten by the father belonged to the typical primal stock of childhood ideas: analogies from mythology, like e.g. the Greek God *Chronos*, the God of Time, and from animal life were generally familiar.[66] Freud made the most surprising discoveries about women, who displayed intense and prolonged father-fixations. He knew, of course, that there had been an early stage in which women were attached to their mother. But Freud did not yet

---

64 Sigmund Freud, *The Interpretation of Dreams: The Complete and Definitive Text* (New York: Basic Books, 2010).
65 Ibid.
66 Ibid.

know that it was so rich in content, that it persisted so long, and that it could leave behind so many occasions for fixations, and predispositions. During this early time, their father was for young girls as for young boys no more than an irksome rival. For girls in many cases the attachment to the mother lasted beyond the fourth year. Almost everything that Freud found later in the father-relation was already present in that attachment and had been subsequently transferred on to the father. In short, Freud gained the conviction that one could not understand women unless one estimated this pre-Oedipal attachment to the mother at its proper value.

16 Mother

According to Freud, a child's first erotic object was the mother's breast that fed him.[67] Love in its beginning attached itself to the satisfaction of the need for food. To start with, the child certainly made no distinction between object and subject, the mother's breast and his own body. When the mother's breast had to be separated from the child's body and shifted to the outside, because he so often found it absent, carrying with it, now that it was an object, part of the original narcistic cathexis.[68] This first object of the child, the mother's breast, subsequently became completed into the whole person of the mother, who not only fed him, but also looked after him, and thus aroused in him many other physical sensations, pleasant and unpleasant. By the mother's care of the child's body, she became his first seducer. In Freud's view, in these two relations lay the root of a mother's importance; being unique and without parallel, it laid down unalterably for a whole lifetime the first and strongest love-object, and as the prototype of all later love relations. The phylogenetic foundation had the upper hand over accidental personal experiences that it made no difference whether a child was really sucked at the breast or had been brought up on the bottle and never enjoyed the tenderness of a mother's care. The child's development took the same path in both cases. It may be that in the latter event the boys later longing was all the greater. For however long a child was fed at his mother's breast, the boy would always be left with a conviction, after he had been weaned, that his feeding was too short and too little. Important biological analogies had taught Freud that the psychic development of the individual was a short repetition of the course of development of humanity as a whole,

---

67 Ibid.
68 Ibid.

including the gender struggle. Therefore, Freud did not find improbable what the psychoanalytic investigation of the child's psyche asserted concerning the infantile estimation of the genitals. The infantile assumption of the maternal penis was thus the common source of origin for the androgynous formation of the maternal deities, e.g., the Goddess Mut in the trinitarian Egyptian *Religion of Riddle*.[69] For Freud, the strong pre-Oedipal attachment of the girl to the mother was fated to give way to an attachment to her father. This development was not merely a question of a change of object; the girl's turning away from the mother occurred in an atmosphere of antagonism, enmity, and struggle. The girl's attachment to the mother ended in hate. Such a hatred may persist throughout an entire lifetime. It may later be carefully overcompensated. As a rule, one part of it was overcome while another part persisted. The outcome was naturally influenced by the actual events of later years. The girl's love had as its object the phallic mother. With the discovery that the mother was castrated, it became possible to drop her as a love-object, so that the incentives to hostility, which had been so long accumulating, got the upper hand. This antagonism, hatred, enmity, and hostility constituted an element in the historical gender conflict and struggle. Freud could see the mother-identification of the woman to have two levels, the pre-Oedipal level, which was based on the tender attachment to the mother, and which took her as a model, and the later level, derived from the Oedipus complex, which tried to get rid of the mother and to replace her in her relationship with the father. Much of both levels remained over for the future.[70]

17 Cunning of Reason

According to the Freudian psychologist, Max Horkheimer, Freud's mere opposition between the "male" and the "fatherly" element, on one hand, and the "female" and the "motherly" element, on the other, did not contain any mediation.[71] Bachofen had seen already clearly that the fatherly element, on one hand, and the motherly element, on the other, were no genuine alternating notions.[72] In Horkheimer's view, in contrast to Freud, in the *Philosophy of History* of G.W.F. Hegel, who compared in a paternalistic way men with animals

---

69   Ibid.
70   Ibid.
71   Horkheimer, *Critique of Instrumental Reason*, 5–8, 15, 27, 41, 98–99, 177–178, 181, 346–347.
72   Bachofen, *Das Mutterrecht*; Jakob Bachofen, *Mutterrecht und Urreligion* (Stuttgart: Alfred Kröner Verlag, 1954).

and women with flowers, the subjective element, the drives, the instincts, the passions, appeared essentially as "cunning of reason," or of Providence, i.e., as means or manufacturers of identity, as mediators of the Absolute in the sense of regained immediacy.[73] Hegel's *Philosophy of History* included the rule of Reason, or Providence, toward the goal of the realm of rational freedom, through the means of agents of change, motivated by their own instincts and passions, in the material of the structures of individual personality, family, civil society, political state, history as international relations, culture as art, religion and philosophy, in the course of the freedom of the One, of the Few, and of All. Nothing happened in society and history without human passions. When in the face of the negative in human history produced by human passions, the theodicy problem arose concerning God's benevolence, man's freedom, and the origin of evil, Hegel directed the consciousness of the reader, following the Greek historians Herodotus or Thucydides, and the Hebrew prophets, Ezekiel or Daniel, from the *a posteriori* experience to the *a priori* principle, that Reason, or Providence, governed the world, and thus transformed even the man made tragedies to serve as means toward the goal of education and liberation of humanity. Hegel's *Philosophy of History* skipped, in what Horkheimer's teacher Arthur Schopenhauer had called a cursed, phantastic, theological optimism, the possibility of failures; it experienced itself as part of the absolute spirit, that had success already in its pocked.[74] According to the Critical Theory of Religion and Society, Horkheimer and the critical theorists cancelled, like Freud, the sphere of the absolute spirit, and retained only the dimensions of the natural, subjective, and objective spirit.[75] Now not only history, but also the *Philosophy of History*, belonged into the sphere of the objective spirit. It seemed to Horkheimer, in contrast to the Hegelian *Philosophy* of *History*, that the possibility of global failure was rooted in the nature of the spiritual process particularly in the 1950s, and out of the perspective of America and Europe: the antagonism between the capitalistic and the communistic block, and the new atomic weapons on both sides. Fortunately, this world-historical failure has not yet occurred, not even through the global COVID-19 pandemic. Not Schopenhauer's, Freud's, or Horkheimer's philosophical and scientific pessimism, but Hegel's theological optimism prevailed so far, so that the American World and the Slavic World would supersede the European World, as once before Greece determinately negated Persia, or Rome determinately

---

73   Max Horkheimer, *Zur Kritik der instrumentellen Vernunft* (Frankfurt a.M.: Fischer Verlag, 1967), 248–269, 302–317.
74   Hegel, *Vorlesungen über die Philosophie der Geschichte*.
75   Siebert, *Manifesto of the Critical Theory of Society and Religion*.

negated Greece, or Germanic Europe determinately negated Rome, and that they would determine the future toward a universal world federation with one army. However, we must admit that during Russia's war on Ukraine, beginning in 2022, the tensions between the American World and the Slavic World were still great. We hoped that Hegel's theological optimism would prevail also in the future, and not the antagonism of the past. Still in 1944/1945, I was trained in the officers' school in Büdingen, Germany, to march to the Eastern front and destroy Russian tanks, kill communists, and colonize up to the Volga. But in reality, I was then sent to fight against the tanks of General Patton, crossing the Rhine and the Main, who dreamed similar dreams, to be accomplished even with liberated German prisoners of war.

18 Prohibitions

According to Horkheimer, Freudian psychoanalysis was the cause of its own necessity.[76] The therapy of Freudian psychoanalysis consisted in the attempt to give to *jammed affects* the possibility of expression. Psychoanalytical therapy wanted to remove the threat, which constituted the door behind which the affects, the matriarchal as well as the patriarchal ones, made a noise. Freudian psychoanalytic therapy meant to create pure air. But according to the revisionist-Freudian Horkheimer, the door only had its compressing effect in the psychic *apparatus* of men and women because it was manufactured out of false material: namely out of matriarchal, or patriarchal *prohibitions*, e.g., patriarchal ones against LGBTQ+ communities, in which people no longer believe.[77] While psychoanalysis no longer considered the LGBTQ+ lifestyles to be pathological, they were nevertheless all somewhat alienated from the fundamental biological species process like cohabitation, fornication, masturbation, *coitus interruptus*, artificial birth control, abortion, stem cell research, celibacy, divorce, etc. To be sure, the psychological and sociological consequences of LGBTQ+ lives could often be rather negative and require psychotherapy. While Christianity relaxed in the late Roman Empire and in the following Germanic civilization, the cultural compulsion for all people to get married and to have a family, and praised virginity, could not change the structure of the human organism, including form, assimilation, and species process, and the connected psychic apparatus, including Id, Ego, and Super-Ego, and

---

76 Horkheimer, *Critique of Instrumental Reason*, 15.
77 Ibid.

continued to emphasize the importance of marriage and family and enforced strict moral norms concerning not only marital love and faithfulness, but also the significance of the species reproduction process. The recently introduced Pride Month in American civil society reminded people not to repeat the brutal treatment of LGBTQ+ people by fascists, and to prevent any further prejudices and discrimination concerning occupations, professions, housing, schools, etc. It should be remembered that the exclusive, authoritarian, totalitarian populists, the German, national socialists of the 20th century, did not only hold prejudices and discriminated against homosexuals, but even put them into concentration camps.[78] For Horkheimer, the unsuspecting security with which the Freudian therapist felt to be called to the removal of obstacles, proved not just exactly the meaninglessness of the ban, or the moral prohibition, which like its power caused the neurosis. According to Horkheimer, force and meaninglessness had been in the last analysis one and the same in the long history of the gender conflict and struggle. At present, we observed right-wing Catholics, like EWTN, trying daily to recriminalize abortion and preserve the death penalty despite of the fact that neither of them ever stopped or prevented abortion, or murder. The recriminalization of abortion would create the same situation that existed before Roe v. Wade: the rich people would get their abortions outside of the U.S. and the poor people in the slums would use cloth hangers to kill the embryo and endanger the mother's life at the same time. While Rabbi Jesus never spoke about abortion, EWTN preached against it every day, from the morning to the night, using it politically, and weaponizing it against Leftwing populism, the Democratic Party, and the Biden administration, who refuse to criminalizing it. It would be much better to explore the causes for the high abortion rate and remove them, if possible: irrational freedom, individualism, selfishness, lack of living wages, not to speak of family wages for millions of workers, lack of adequate housing, health reasons, lack of health insurance, etc. For Horkheimer, rationality was not a formal, but a material category. While the Freudian psychoanalyst and therapist posited the rapture of the painful love of children, or of husband and wife, during the analysis into the arbitrary wishes of the subjects involved, he negated the taboo, which was already eaten up to a large extend through the progressing decay and disintegration of the bourgeois culture, and particularly of the bourgeois enlightenment, which in the process of secularization replaced the sacrificial love of the founder of Christianity with a love without all pain. One should

---

78   Richard Plant, *The Pink Triangle: The Nazi War against Homosexual* (New York: Henry Holt and Company, 1986).

remember that numerous Cardinals and Bishops were very upset because of Pope Benedict XVI's resignation from the papacy, criticizing him for "climbing down from the cross" of painful, sacrificial love, after years telling married people to stay on the cross and avoid divorce.[79] According to Horkheimer, the Freudian psychoanalyst only pushed, like a little Friedrich Nietzsche, the last bourgeoise enlightener, what was already falling.[80] During analysis, the psychotherapist pushed the dagger into the heart of the partner of his patient, or client. The psychoanalyst called healing his encouragement to the unscrupulousness, on that side of the gender and family conflict, to which he could and would present the bill. Horkheimer observed in the 1950s that the most solid *taboo*, the still undiminished incest and perversion prohibition, remained still in existence. But the psychotherapists analyzed lust in order to break through this moral ban. The Critical Theory of Religion and Society observed in the 2020s that this desire had already progressed further in the past 50 years and had started to break through this primordial moral prohibition of incest and perversions in innumerable child abuse cases in the religious as well as in the secular sphere.

19 Reason

According to the Marxist and Freudian Max Horkheimer, the "reason" of the Freudian psychoanalyst reflected the capitalistic power and rule relationships and conditions, based on the private appropriation of the collective surplus labor in the liberal, bourgeois, civil society. This psychoanalytical "reason" negated abstractly, as superstition, everything that the working class holds against the ruling bourgeois class, with the exception of the censure: the bourgeois "bad conscience" concerning their private appropriation and exploitation of the collective surplus value, because they have not yet all been healed by psychoanalysis: their Super-Ego still malfunctioned on the basis of their still surviving religious and moral superstitions.[81] According to Horkheimer, the "reason" of the psychoanalysts left those beaten by life (the poor, the proletariat, the precariat) in civil society even without the hope that the bad

---

79 Daniel Miller, "'You don't get down from the cross'": Polish cardinal provokes fury by suggesting Pope should have died in office.'" *Daily Mail.* February 13, 2013. https://www.dailymail.co.uk/news/article-2277980/You-dont-cross-Polish-cardinal-provokes-fury-comments-comparing-Popes-resignation-crucifixion.html.
80 Walter Kaufmann, *The Portable Nietzsche* (New York: Viking Press, 1986).
81 Horkheimer, *Critique of Instrumental Reason,* 346–347.

conscience would not be the highest judge, because the life was for the psychoanalytical "reason" the highest judge. The "reason" of psychoanalysis knew nothing else to say to the dying person in his or her pain and torment, then that he or she did not seek psychoanalysis in time.

20   Judge

For Horkheimer, psychoanalysis appeared as judge.[82] Psychoanalysis was the continuation of the psychological novel, drama, and movie, if it was still a work of art. They all put the emphasis, or better the *guilt*, on the internal drives of the treated person. They made the foreign, also one's own subject, into their main object, not the objective "constellation" once present as "ideality," like person, family, civil society, state, history and culture, in Sophocles and Aeschylus, Plato and Aristotle, Herodotus and Thucydides, Isaiah, Ezekiel and Daniel, and more recently in Kant, Fichte, Schelling and Hegel. In Horkheimer's view, within psychoanalysis the subject may justify themselves as much as they wanted to, they were, nevertheless, condemned from the start: their justification was always considered to be a "rationalization." For the Jewish Horkheimer, this appeared as an inheritance of Christian psychology, which was supported by the bourgeois, Marxist, and Freudian enlightenment: from Augustine through Meister Eckhart, and Pascal to Vauvenargues, and not to forget to the Fathers of the Holy Inquisition, the unredeemed, uneducated, unknowing man was in the words of the mystical theologian Eckhart harshly called an animal man, an ape, a fool, already long before Darwin.[83] The modern exploration of the soul was only more forsaken by hope in comparison with the Christian psychology. With every step of this internal exploration of an other-worldly salvation – for the sake of which the Christian psychology had once been started – became unholier and more terrible and was confounded with the abstract process through which it was to be reached. That happened until the goal of redemption and salvation was completely forgotten, and the process, psychoanalysis, was worshipped for itself alone. The last phase, anticipated in the farce play of the self-analysis of the psychoanalyst Karen Horney, was then the *self-criticism* in the former Stalinist Soviet Union. Here in the Stalinist show trials of the 1920s, like in the case of Freud, the powerless subject was interrogated by the examining magistrate and finally, anticipating him and introjecting him, by

---

82   Ibid., 15, 27–28, 346–347.
83   Ibid.

one's own Ego, the supposedly immanent consequence of the thought, which the subject had performed naively once more. Whatever the subject may say against the objection, it was always considered as "rationalization" of the condemned intention, or with Stalin – more coarse and gross than with Freud – as excuse and lie. But for both, Freud and Stalin, the facts of the case were certain before the procedure even started, which was to be proven by it, be it the Oedipus or Electra Complex and the patricide and matricide, or the betrayal of the proletariat. In both cases, the subject was already condemned, sentenced, and convicted from the start. However, Stalin, the former seminarian in the Orthodox Church, still recognized the existence of the *soul,* unlike the Russian dog behaviorist Ivan Pavlov and the American rat behaviorist B.F. Skinner, in the moral phraseology as well as in the insistence, with which was demanded the confession of guilt in the show trials. The "Father Peccavi" or "Father I have sinned" of the Orthodox and Roman Catholic confessional had to be spoken at least in those cases, in which the gallows entered action in the face of the world. Obedience, self-degradation, remorse, regret, atonement, and penance had once been the old venerable pieces of jewelry of Christian psychology. After the Crusades, the torture and burning of witches, Jews, and heretics, by the state, authorized by the Holy Inquisition, the 20th and 21st centuries experienced a renaissance of the old psychological practices with concentration camps, gas chambers, saturation bombing, waterboarding, drone assassinations, etc. The terror of the external powers transformed itself, or better supplemented and completed itself, into voluntary discipline. Friedrich Nietzsche, the disciple of Schopenhauer, knew only too well how it stood with this "internalization," as the rightwing, external, authoritarian, and totalitarian populists, along with the fascists of the 20th and 21st centuries learned from him.[84] The critical psychologist Horkheimer posited a pertinent question: was the self-criticism of the Freudian and the red-fascist Stalinism the dreadful beginning, or the terrible end?

21   Suspicion

In the view of Freudian psychoanalysis, sexual love was already *suspect*, because it, as being sublimated, could regress and change back into destructive instinct, and even into aggression: again, *Eros* into *Thanatos.*[85] The

---

84   Kaufmann, *The Portable Nietzsche.*
85   Freud, *Civilization and its Discontents.*

psychoanalyst could not only observe the origin and possible future of sexual love, but with the transformation of one instinct into the other, which changed not only the object, but the essence of the impulse itself. What counted was not only the moment, but also the genesis toward the truth.

22 Freud and Heidegger

According to Horkheimer and Adorno, the concepts of Sigmund Freud's psychoanalysis may, despite of all empirical confessions, be no less speculative than the notions of Martin Heidegger's existential analysis, which lived from the fact that Freud did not deliver empirical proof.[86] The difference between Freud and Heidegger consisted in that the miserable outcomes from Heideggerian ontology, the existential anxiety, the preliminary being-towards-death (*Sein-zum-Tode*), and Heidegger's notion of authenticity (*Eigentlichkeit*), lead toward the coldness against the individual, and toward Adolf Hitler's dictatorship in family, civil society, state, history, and culture, while those of the Freudian psychoanalysis lead toward the understanding of human illness and health, toward a humane education, and toward humanity beyond the battle of the sexes, generations, races, and classes. Freud's psychoanalysis threatened the conventional lie, which constituted the mask of the penal code and of the general cruelty. That, of course, was reason enough to try at least to remove not only Freud, but also Marx, and Horkheimer, *coute que coute*, from the collective consciousness, the subjective, objective, and absolute spirit of the 20th and 21st centuries.

23 Transference

According to Horkheimer, Freudian psychoanalysis possessed as theory a questionable power.[87] Its most significant effect was to deliver to theory new experiences, particularly concerning the age-old battle of the sexes. Beyond that, its effect rested essentially on "transference." In psychoanalysis, the patient gained significant relationship to the analyst that mirrored the relationship between an adult and a child. Mimetic behavior took place in all decisive issues. For Freud, in transference the patient saw in their analyst the

---

86 Horkheimer, *Critique of Instrumental Reason*, 15, 27–28, 41, 98–99, 177–178, 346–347.
87 Ibid.

return, a so-called reincarnation, of some important figure out of their childhood, and consequently transferred onto the psychoanalyst their feelings.[88] It soon became evident to Freud that transference was a factor of importance. On one hand, transference was an instrument of irreplaceable value. On the other hand, it was a source of serious danger. Transference was as ambivalent as the whole conflict of the genders. It comprised positive, and affectionate, as well as negative and hostile attitudes toward the analyst: toxic-positive. The psychoanalyst, as a rule, was put in the place of one of the patient's parents. So long as the transference was positive, it served the client admirably. It altered the whole analytical situation and sidetracked the patient's rational aim of becoming well. However, there emerged the tendency to please the analyst, of winning their applause and their love. This became the true motivating force for the patient's collaboration with the analyst. Through transference, the weak Ego became strong. Under the influence of the pleased analyst, the patient achieved things that would otherwise have been beyond his or her power. The client's symptoms disappeared. They seemed to have recovered. All of this simply happened out of love for their analyst. In Freud's view, therapeutic successes that took place under the sway of the positive transference were under the suspicion of being of a suggestive nature. If the negative transference gained the upper hand, the therapeutic successes were blown away like spray before the wind. Analyst and analysand themselves became once more part of the historical gender struggle or battle of the sexes and its toxic negativity or positivity.

24   Mimesis

According to Horkheimer, transference as *mimetic* behavior served the establishment of childhood history, state and condition, and moment in the gender conflict.[89] The doubtful, dangerous, and risky element in such *mimetic* transference was only that the analyst was not able to make himself, or herself, really equal, or identical, with the true father, and even less so with the loving mother. There existed the so-called countertransference, or *mimesis*. That meant the analyst's own inclination toward the patient. But that was a wretched substitute for the real love of the father, not to speak of the mother. The psyche of the analyst used to be enlightened, natural science-like, positivistic,

---

88   Sigmund Freud, *Das Ich und das Es*.
89   Horkheimer, *Critique of Instrumental Reason*, 15, 27–28, 41, 98–99, 178, 346–347.

pragmatistic, and rationalistic in the doubtful, dangerous, and risky sense.[90] Precisely because in the transference this positivistic nuance, intonation and gestures of thinking and feeling were taken over mimetically, it was the dryness of positivism, which went usually over to the healed patient, despite the recommendation of liberation and freedom. With the father confessor in Eastern and Western Catholicism it happened sometimes *mimetically* in a similar way, insofar as Catholics still went to confession in the post-secular civil society.

25   Sacrament of Love

According to the Jungian psychoanalyst and Roman Catholic priest and theologian, Eugen Drewermann, toward the end of the 20th century, occidental Christendom had come so far with its connection of sexual repression, patriarchal hostility toward women, moral sadism and masochism, psychic oppression, cultural violence, and holy wars, that even the benevolent profession of priests, this likewise great and splendid heritage of paganism, as such determined and destined to bless the existence of man, and to show ways back to the lost paradise of the world, was since centuries directed and trained as a kind of administration and management officials, to strangle the sexual and erotic love.[91] Jesus had opposed the hypocritical and vain Pharisees and scribes of his time by saying to the people and his disciples:

> The scribes and the Pharisees occupy the chair of Moses. You must therefore do what they tell you and listen to what they say, but do not be guided by what they do; since they do not practice what they preach. They tie up heavy burdens and lay them on men's shoulders, but will they lift a finger to move them? Not they! Everything they do is done to attract attention, like wearing broader phylacteries and longer tassels, like wanting to take the place of honor at banquets and the front seats in the synagogues, being greeted obsequiously in the market squares and having people call them Rabbi.
>
> You, however, must not allow yourselves to be called Rabbi, since you have only one Master, and you are all brothers. You must call no one on earth your father, since you have only one Father, and he is in heaven. Nor must you allow yourselves to be called teachers, for you have only

---

90   Ibid.
91   Matthew 5–7; Jung, *Modern Man in Search of a Soul*.

one Teacher, the Christ. The greatest among you must be your servant. Anyone who exalts himself will be humbled, and anyone who humbles himself will be exalted.[92]

Phylacteries were containers for short texts taken from the Law: e.g., the *Shema Israel* concerning the love of God and of neighbor. They were worn on the arm or the forehead in obedience to Exodus 13:9–16, and Deuteronomy 6:8. The tassels were sewn to the corners of the cloak. The Pharisees and scribes interpreted the Law so strictly that nobody could obey all of it. It seemed to Drewermann as if the profession of clerics in the Church wanted to relate the reproach of Jesus deliberately to themselves. That was so because alone through this sacrament of love, which God concluded through the mediation of no profession, but only through the immediacy of the heart, alone into this mysterious realm, of which the clerics themselves could, since the connection of priesthood and celibacy in the Latin Church around the year AD 1000, only have meagre experiences. This patriarchal, clerical profession, from which women were excluded, had to govern and direct the laity through unending directives, orders, and regulations, concerning divorce, birth control, abortion, *in vitro* fertilization, masturbation, premarital and extramarital sex, stem cell research, etc. The fairytales and myths of nations knew of no danger that could overcome man more terribly than this energy toward love, which would out of anxiety and fear of men, harden into stone. Again and again, these fairytales and myths told about the gender struggles, which had been necessary to leave behind the all-to-strong bond to the will of the parents, and to find the freedom of love. Drewermann remembered that already late Judaism itself had portrayed in the legend of the little Tobit book the threat that came from an aged piety, which out of fear and anxiety had become legalized and dogmatic.[93] According to the legend, such neurotic piety made even the just Tobit heartless and loveless. It also prevented in the far away Ekbatana a young girl not only to find a way to love, but it also let her appear as a complete, perfect, men-murdering witch. Drewermann thought that Christ may have come precisely in order to refute this truest portrait of Israel from its most terrible danger, and to give validity and reality to the figure of the Angel Raphael. According to Drewermann's interpretation of the book Tobit, God healed man as companion of his way of

---

92 Matthew 23:2–38.
93 Eugen Drewermann, *Der Krieg und das Christentum: Von der Ohn-macht und Notwendigkeit des Religiösen* (Regensburg: Friedrich Pustet, 1984); Eugen Drewermann, *Psychoanalyse und Moral Theologie.2. Wege und Umwege der Liebe* (Mainz: Matthias Gruunewald Verlag, 1992), 13–14.

life, and showed him the wealth of his heart, as he taught him the love, and dissolved for him the darkness of his eyes. Drewermann asked, how differently the Church would have to look in the light of the well interpreted and comprehended book Tobit?[94]

26   Love of the Mother

According to the Critical Theory of Religion and Society, even after matriarchy – the rule of the mothers, and patriarchy – the rule of the fathers, and the struggle of the genders have been concretely superseded in post-modern alternative Future III – the reconciled society, i.e., formal and material democracy, the rule of the brothers and the sisters: the *love of the mother* may still prevail.[95] According to the critical theorist Horkheimer, Freud's theory that the mother was the young boy's and girl's first love, and that at least the man was still inclined to see his mother in every woman, sounded easily like a denunciation. Horkheimer thought, however, that Freud was at that point righter than he himself suspected. Horkheimer may have thought of his own mother, who under Nazi persecution in fascist Germany prayed Psalm 91 for God's protection:

> If you live in the shelter of Elyon
> and make your home in the shadow of Shaddai,
> you can say to Jahweh, My refuge, my fortress,
> my God in whom I trust![96]

The Mother's prayer of Psalm 91 was heard. Horkheimer's parents were driven by a Catholic taxi driver from Stuttgart to Switzerland, where they were saved from the Nazis. The Freudian and Marxist Horkheimer put in contrast to his atheistic or pantheistic Jewish teachers, the first verse of Psalm 91 on his parents' grave in the Jewish cemetery of Zürich, Switzerland. He put the second verse on his own and his wife Maidon's grave. According to Horkheimer, a man's highest love still for the youngest woman, could in itself, determinately negated, be the highest account, repetition, performance, and reproduction of the gift, which once the child received from the loving mother. The mother's visual contact with the just born son radiated back in the man's longing for

---

94   Ibid.
95   Horkheimer, *Critique of Instrumental Reason*, 15, 181, 346–347.
96   Psalm 91.

the loved woman, his mother. The loving man meant only the loved woman alone, for whom he conquered every hindrance. Self-forgotten in dreams, in the unstained word, appeared the mother as soul at the same time and as goal in the man's love. Where this was not the case, and where the mother was not present, and unsuspectingly longed for at the same time, love remained weak, powerless, invalid, and empty. Here Freud was righter than the loving man or woman could possibly have a presentiment of.

27   In Touch with Reality

The Marxist and Freudian Horkheimer had difficulties with the psychoanalytical notion of being in touch with reality as criterion for mental health. According to Horkheimer, if a revolutionary, be it in matters of class, gender, race, generation, or environment, had lived in touch with reality or not, he is depended on the status of the class struggle in a particular moment of the historical process. If the revolutionary's life constituted a sequence of excessive suffering, failures, difficult internal and external crises, prison or penitentiary, with pain, agony, and anguish of any kind, then he could have been likewise clever and sensible, and consequential, sober, brave as in the stroke of luck of the final victory: alternative Future III – the reconciled society on the basis of class, gender, race, generational equality, and social justice. Were the revolutionary's politics in touch with reality? In Horkheimer's view, for the life of the working class, this question was decided by the historical future. But, so Horkheimer asked, which instance decided this question for the revolutionary: for the fighter for class, gender, race, generation equality and justice, or for the rescue of the environment? The Freudian psychoanalyst could perhaps respond that the question was not so important. What in any case mattered was not the objective suffering of the revolutionary, but rather their internal psychological health. However, Horkheimer had doubts if the revolutionary would be able to decide about themselves to what extend they were healthy, neurotic, one with themselves, or torn apart and disintegrated in themselves. For Horkheimer, those bourgeois categories corresponded to their own bourgeois world, not to the class, gender, race, generation, or environmental struggles, which were supposed to turn upside down in a gigantic post-modern paradigm change.

Bibliography

Aeschylus, *The Complete Aeschylus: Volume 1: The Oresteia.* Oxford: Oxford University Press, 2011.

Bachofen, Jakob. *Das Mutterrecht. In Der Mythos von Orient und Occident: Eine Metaphysik der alten Welt.* München: Verlag C.H. Beck, 1926.

Bachofen, Jakob. *Mutterrecht und Urreligion.* Stuttgart: Alfred Kröner Verlag, 1954.

Drewermann, Eugen. *Der Krieg und das Christentum: Von der Ohn-macht und Notwendigkeit des Religiösen.* Regensburg: Friedrich Pustet, 1984.

Drewermann, Eugen. *Psychoanalyse und Moral Theologie 2. Wege und Umwege der Liebe.* Mainz: Matthias Gruunewald Verlag, 1992.

Freud, Sigmund. *Beyond the Pleasure Principle.* New York: W.W. Norton & Company, 1990.

Freud, Sigmund. *Civilization and its Discontents.* New York: W.W. Norton and Company, 1962.

Freud, Sigmund. *Das Ich und das Es.* Frankfurt a.M.: Fischer Taschenbuch Verlag 1992.

Freud, Sigmund. *The Interpretation of Dreams: The Complete and Definitive Text.* New York: Basic Books, 2010.

Freud, Sigmund. *Three Essays on the Theory of Sexuality,* in *The Basic Writings of Sigmund Freud.* Translated by A.A. Brill. New York: Modern Library, 1995.

Hegel, Georg W.F. *Grundlinien der Philosophie des Rechts oder Naturrecht und Staatswissenschaft im Grundriss.* Frankfurt a.M.: Suhrkamp Verlag, 1986.

Hegel, Georg W.F. *Vorlesungen über die Philosophie der Religion, Vol. I–IV.* Frankfurt a.M.: Suhrkamp Verlag, 1986.

Honneth, Axel. *Kritik der Macht. Reflexionsstufen einer kritischen Gesellschaftstheorie.* Frankfurt a.M.: Suhrkamp Verlag. 1985.

Horkheimer, Max. *Critical Theory: Selected Essays.* New York: The Seabury Press, 1972.

Horkheimer, Max. *Critique of Instrumental Reason.* New York: The Seabury Press, 1974.

Horkheimer, Max. *Dawn and Decline. Notes 1926–1931 and 1950–1969.* New York: The Seabury Press, 1978.

Horkheimer, Max. *Die Sehnsucht nach dem ganz Anderen. Ein Interview mit Kommentar von Helmut Gumnior* Hamburg: Furche Verlag, 1970.

Horkheimer, Max. "Geschichte und Psychologie." *Zeitschrift für Sozialforschung* 1 no. 1/2 (1932): 125–144.

Horkheimer, Max. *Gesellschaft im Übergang. Aufsätze. Reden und Vortrage 1942–1970.* Frankfurt a. M.: Fischer Verlag, 1981.

Horkheimer, Max. *Zur Kritik der instrumentellen Vernunft.* Frankfurt a.M.: Fischer Verlag, 1967.

Judt, Tony, and Timothy Snyder. *Nachdenken über das 20. Jahrhundert.* München: Carl Hanser Verlag, 2012.

Jung, Carl G. *Modern man in Search of a Soul.* New York: Harcourt, Brace, & Jovanovich, 2017.
Jung, Carl G., and Aniela Jaffé. *Memories, Dreams, Reflections.* Translated by Richard and Clara Winston. New York: Vintage Books, 1989.
Kaufmann, Walter. *The Portable Nietzsche.* New York: Viking Press, 1986.
Kershaw, Ian. *Hitler: Hubris. 1989–1934.* New York: W. W. Norton and Company, 1999.
Kershaw, Ian. *Hitler: Nemesis. 1936–1945.* New York: W.W. Norton and Company, 2001.
Landauer, Karl. *Theory der Affekte und andere Schriften zur Ich – Organisation.* Frankfurt a. M.: Fischer Verlag, 1999.
Marx, Karl. *Zur Kritik der politischen Ökonomie.* Berlin: Dietz Verlag, 1951.
Miller, Daniel. "'You don't get down from the cross'": Polish cardinal provokes fury by suggesting Pope should have died in office." *Daily Mail.* February 13, 2013. https://www.dailymail.co.uk/news/article-2277980/You-dont-cross-Polish-cardinal-provokes-fury-comments-comparing-Popes-resignation-crucifixion.html.
Noll, Richard. *The Aryan Christ: The Secret Life of Carl Jung.* New York: Random House, 1997.
Piketty, Thomas. *Capital in the Twenty-First Century.* Cambridge, MA: The Belknap Press of Harvard University Press, 2014.
Plant, Richard. *The Pink Triangle: The Nazi War against Homosexual.* New York: Henry Holt and Company, 1986.
Schopenhauer, Arthur. *Aphorismen zur Lebensweischeit.* Wiesbaden: Brockhaus Verlag, 1946.
Shakespeare, William. *The Complete Works.* Albany, NY: James B. Lyon Publisher, 1878.
Siebert, Rudolf J. *The Critical Theory of Religion: Personal Autonomy and Universal Autonomy.* New York: Peter Lang Publishing, 2002.
Siebert, Rudolf J. *Manifesto of the Critical Theory of Society and Religion: The Wholly Other, Liberation, Happiness and the Rescue of the Hopeless, Vol I–III.* Leiden: Brill, 2010.
Wiggershaus, Rolf. *The Frankfurt School: Its History, Theories, and Political Significance.* Translated by Michael Robertson. Cambridge, MA: The MIT Press, 1994.
Sophocles, *The Theban Plays.* Baltimore, MD: Penguin Books, 1964.
Whitebook, Joel. "The Urgeschichte of Subjectivity Reconsidered." *New German Critique* 81 (Autumn 2000): 125–141.

PART 3

Freud and Religion

∴

CHAPTER 5

Critical Social Theory and Religion: Revisiting Sigmund Freud's Discourse on Religion

Seyed Javad Miri

1   Introduction

In this chapter, my main concern is to engage with Freud's conception of "religion." But before entering this thorny terrain of analysis, we need to clarify a few issues as far as "critical social theory" is concerned. What does this branch of social theory consist of? How do we conceptualize "critical social theory" and in what sense is this related to Sigmund Freud's theoretical endeavors? These questions are of critical significance as many scholars may not consider Freud as a social theorist or let alone a *critical* social theorist. However, we are of the opinion that Freud is indeed a great social theorist who approaches vital questions of humanity from a *critical* point of departure. In other words, his psychoanalytic approach is rooted in the soil of society and preoccupied with ways in which we can improve the "social conditions" of the human species. Thus, it would be wrong to fathom his psychoanalytic concerns as a form of *disciplinary engagements* with individual psyche alone. This is to argue that Freud's psychoanalytic approach is an *analytical tool* to unearth deep civilizational/cultural habits of humanity that have reshaped the contours of the "human condition" in the widest sense of the term.

In this way, we are not faced with a psychoanalyst in the *ordinary* fashion but rather with a social theorist in the true sense of the term, i.e., a grand theorist who is equipped with a comprehensive vision of human reality. However, we need to dwell upon the very adjective of *critical* as far as Freud's social theory is concerned by posing the question: in what sense is Freud a critical thinker? Of course, the concept of "critical" has been employed in different fashions by distinct scholars and theorists around the globe but we can conceptualize criticality in the same fashion that Horkheimer eloquently conceptualizes it: in contrast to the *positive* form of analysis where scholars attempt to *describe* rather than critically interpret issues and problems of existential significance. As such, we can assert that Freud is not solely concerned with describing the "human condition." On the contrary, Freud attempts to appraise the state of the human species as a distinct type of terrestrial being without succumbing to the normative frames of the *received traditions*. When we state that Freud is a "critical social theorist" it means that he has a *normative frame of analysis* that enables him to exercise careful and judicious evaluation of forms of life, cultural habits, social habitus, worldviews, types of civilizational trends, i.e., all that makes up the parameters of "human existence." He is *critical* in this grand sense of the definition. In other words, Sigmund Freud is a critical social thinker who has approached one of the most enduring modes of human existence that has fundamentally shaped the parameters of civilization for more than hundred millennia, i.e., *religion*. It could be argued that the specter of religion haunted Freud during his entire intellectual life. Freud's earliest published work on the problem of religion was in the paper entitled, "Obsessive Actions and Religious Practices," which was published in 1907. In this paper, Freud speaks of the correlation between neurosis and religion by arguing that:

> one might venture to regard obsessional neurosis as the pathological counterpart of the formation of a religion, and to describe that neurosis as an individual religiosity and religion as a universal obsessional neurosis.[1]

Then in 1913, his book, *Totem and Taboo*, continued his engagements with the question of religion in a more detailed fashion by arguing that all modern forms of socialization are formed by the primitive culture of origin, wherein he deployed a model of primitivity based on Aborigines of Australia. In this study, Freud argues that these simplistic societies would basically have had no way of knowing the physiological effects of incest. Instead, Freud contends that these primitive societies are driven by something else. Thus, Freud instigated an inquiry into these groups and devised conclusions regarding the origin of religions and how they emerged. Finally, in this work, Freud argues that all societies, no matter how advanced, originate from the Oedipus complex.[2] He also suggests that it is the basis for all religion. Although he never saw it occur, he envisaged that an end to religion would also see a dramatic reduction in all forms of conflict. While much progress seems to be made in various societies around the globe, there still exist many hurdles in seeing his vision to be realized. After this work, Freud published *Die Zukunft Einer Illusion*

---

1 Sigmund Freud, "Obsessive actions and religious practices," in *The Standard Edition of the Complete Psychological Works of Sigmund Freud, Vol. 9*, ed. and trans. by James Strachey (London: Hogarth Press, 1907), 126–127.
2 Sigmund Freud, *Totem and Taboo*, in *The Standard Edition of the Complete Psychological Works of Sigmund Freud, Vol. 13*, ed. and trans. James Strachey. London: Hogarth Press, 1913.

in 1927, which was translated into English as *The Future of an Illusion* in 1928. In this work, Freud comes back to *cultural problems* that had fascinated him since he embarked upon his academic path. After this seminal work, Freud wrote *Civilization and its Discontents* in 1930, which is the direct successor to *The Future of an Illusion* in that it is also on religions "as examples of mass delusion."[3]

Freud considered religion as an "illusion." Yet, this concept in the Freudian discourse is far from the colloquial understanding of this term. In everyday language, the term is used to refer to an instance of a wrong or misinterpreted perception of a sensory experience or a deceptive appearance or impression. By comparing illusion as a term with its synonyms in English, we may understand its connotations much better. For instance, words like "mirage," "hallucination," "phantasm," "phantom," "fantasy," or "specter" are considered similar to the term "illusion." By studying their lexical and linguistic usages we could readily understand that "illusion" is a word that attempts to give us this idea that we are faced with a "false idea" or "false belief." For example, when we talk about a *mirage,* we know that it is an optical illusion caused by atmospheric conditions, especially the appearance of a sheet of water in a desert or on a hot road caused by the refraction of light from the sky by the heated air. In other words, where there is no "real" water and the weather is extremely hot, there we get the wrong/false vision of a mirage that is literally equivalent to the absence of water. Thus, the term illusion refers to a *condition* that denotes an absence of reality. But the question is how does Freud conceptualize this term and in what sense is it related to religion, and why did Freud utilize this concept in relation to civilization?

2   Individual and Civilization

Before replying to these questions, we need to dwell upon the Freudian conception of "civilization," as he does not recognize the theoretical distinction between *civilization* and *culture*. In his view, the concept of human civilization refers to:

> all those respects in which human life has raised itself above its animal status and differs from the life of beasts [and it] presents, as we know, two

---

3 Sigmund Freud, *Civilization and its Discontents,* trans. David McLintock (London: Penguin Books, 2002), 19.

aspects to the observer. It includes on the one hand all the knowledge and capacity that men have acquired in order to control the forces of nature and extract its wealth for the satisfaction of human needs, and, on the other hand, all the regulations necessary in order to adjust the relations of men to one another and especially the distribution of the available wealth.[4]

In other words, in the Freudian discourse there is no theoretical distinction between the "the realm of culture" and the "realm of civilization," as what he conceptualizes as *human civilization* is constructed in opposition to the "human realm of animality." Freud asserts very clearly that he scorns "to distinguish between culture and civilization" as what he conceptualizes as "two trends of civilization" are the fundamentals of what underpins the "social order" as a uniquely human phenomenon.[5] In order to clarify what he means by the trends of civilization, he argues that these two trends of civilization,

are not independent of each other: firstly, because the mutual relations of men are profoundly influenced by the amount of instinctual satisfaction which the existing wealth makes possible; secondly, because an individual man can himself come to function as wealth in relation to another one, in so far as the other person makes use of his capacity for work, or chooses him as a sexual object, and thirdly, moreover, because every individual is virtually an enemy of civilization, though civilization is supposed to be an object of universal human interest. It is remarkable that, little as men are able to exist in isolation, they should nevertheless feel as a heavy burden the sacrifices which civilization expects of them in order to make a communal life possible.[6]

Here we see one of the most fundamental assumptions of Freud as far as the relation between an individual and a civilization is concerned; it is what he conceptualizes as "virtual enmity" that exists in human individuals against civilization. Based on this assumption, Freud contends that 'civilization has to be defended against the individual, and its regulations, institutions, and commands are directed to that task.' This is to argue that human beings need a "tool" in order to bear the heavy burden of "order" that makes the communal

---

4　Sigmund Freud, *The Future of an Illusion*, ed. and trans. by James Strachey (New York: W.W. Norton & Co., 1961), 5–6.
5　Ibid., 6.
6　Ibid.

life possible. But the question is what kind of tool can make this gigantic project occur? In other words, if we believe that the individual is the enemy of order, yet he cannot live without that order, how then could we make him accept this *hostile condition*? Is it possible to achieve this seemingly unattainable goal? From my perspective, it is possible, and humanity has already achieved this goal. Nevertheless, the question is how has humanity achieved this goal in accordance with the Freudian discourse?

3 Possibility of the "Social Order"

Allow me to take a detour here by bringing up a very important point about Sigmund Freud and the question of critical social theory. The reason that this question should be brought up at this juncture is to make a point that he should not be understood solely in psychological terms, as his concerns are deeply related to the broad problem of the "human condition," which is not limited to any singular discipline as such. On the contrary, we need to have an integral/inclusive approach to understand the polylectic nature of *order* and *chaos* in relation to the *individual* and *society*. As such, the main problem of Freud is what all philosophers, sociologists, and theologians have interrogated: how is society (i.e., the social order) possible. For instance, when Freud inquires upon the sources of human suffering, his approach cannot exclusively be considered "psychological" or "psychoanalytic." We cannot classify Freud as a pure psychologist-cum-psychoanalyst. In my reading, he cannot be limited to the parameters of disciplinary thought and categorized solely as a psychoanalyst. Rather, due to the style of his encounter with the "human condition" in its broadest sense, he is a critical social theorist *par excellence*.

By looking at the expansiveness of the "human condition," Freud breaks up the boundaries of disciplinary rationality and demonstrates the depth of his critique within the parameters of social theory where general concepts and broad concerns of humanity are the *raison d'être* of contemplation. In *Unbehagen der Kultur*, translated into English as *Civilization and its Discontents*, Freud contends that the suffering of humanity has three sources, i.e., 'the superior power of nature, the frailty of our bodies, and the inadequacy of the institutions that regulate people's relations with one another in the family, the state, and society.'[7]

---

7 Freud, *Civilization and its Discontents*, 24.

Here we can discern that Freud is not reducing the sources of human suffering and the impact of it on the "human condition" into mental dimensions of psyche, but, on the contrary, he is taking an integral approach to the question of the human condition in a comprehensive fashion. In other words, the Freudian discourse is focused on the inadequacy of the institutions that regulate human beings' relations with one another at different institutional levels of the family, state, and social reality. We cannot reduce Freud into a simple psychologist or psychoanalyst who approaches the human condition without any authentic reference to the complex institutional dimensions of the societal realities. The decisive question for Freud is whether 'and to what extent it is possible to lessen the burden of the instinctual sacrifices imposed on men, to reconcile men to those which must necessarily remain and to provide a compensation for them.'[8] This is to argue that Freud is focused on the possibility and sustainment of society, or to put it in a more accurate fashion, the social order. His inquiry is directed at the fundamental elements that have made human society a historic concrete possibility. Because the social order is based on the shoulders of the masses and they

> are lazy and unintelligent: they have not love for instinctual renunciation, and they are not to be convinced by argument of its inevitability; and the individuals composing them support one another in giving free rein to their indiscipline. It is only through the influence of individuals who can set an example and how masses recognize as their leaders that they can be induced to perform the work and undergo the renunciations on which the existence of civilization depends.[9]

Here one can discern that Freud is of the opinion that the social order is possible if the instinctual drives of the masses are harnessed and redirected towards work that could continually reproduce society (i.e., civilization). But the question is what kind of system could achieve such an efficient impact? In other words, the task of renunciation is a *traumatic* issue, and human beings cannot reach to that level of abstraction. Because Freud argues that masses are not equipped intellectually enough to grasp the necessity of the social order, and since the masses lack sufficient depth of intelligence, it does not understand the significance of *reasoning, demonstration,* or *argument*. When they cannot fathom the importance of arguments then it is impossible to convince the

---

8   Freud, *The Future of an Illusion*, 7.
9   Ibid., 7–8.

masses through reasoning to renounce their instinctual desires. Thus, order cannot determine society, and chaos would be the supreme rule among the masses. This lack of order would mean the end of civilization as we know it. Therefore, *intelligent* human beings have "invented" something that could coerce individuals into renouncing their love for instinctual pursuits without employing arguments that are incomprehensible for the masses. But this coercive system should not be enforced upon them in a naked fashion, as this would backfire and not last for long. Why? For Freud, men are psychological beings, and this dimension of the human being should not be neglected; suffering and pain, which humanity would inevitably endure due to its instinctual renunciations, needs to be compensated in a meaningful fashion. We know that societies cannot compensate for the instinctual renunciations the masses endured, as the ruling classes should always dominate, and the masses must constantly obey them. Thus, when Freud speaks of the "compensatory system," this should not be understood in a material sense, as the origin of civilization in the dawn of history of humankind could not have been able to afford such luxuries for the masses. This is to remember that the Freudian discourse is attentive both to historical analysis and evolutionary logic.

4 Seminal Personalities and the "Invented Narrative"

The question for Freud is what did the "great leaders" of humanity *invent* in order to master the masses in pre-industrial eras? Social order or civilization is only possible if the masses are inwardly convinced that they should renounce their Dionysian inclinations and instead follow the Apollonian principles by performing works that the very existence of civilization depends on. But Freud has already stated that the masses lack the adequate intelligence for realizing that fact. In that case, how could the masses be convinced, and not only coerced, to follow "order," and not fall into chaos, which itself is based on "rational thinking" (which appeals to logic)?

Here it seems there is a paradox in the Freudian discourse, as on the one hand he argues that the masses are unintelligent, and on the other hand he states that they should voluntarily renounce their Dionysian inclinations. We know that *order* is an abstract concept that the masses would not intellectually fathom, nor would they understand. Being the case, the result would be that they would not willingly submit themselves to such order. If this argument is valid, then how could the masses be subdued in a fashion that would not be felt as submission? How would they submit themselves based on their own inner-conviction? Here we need to introduce the concept of "indoctrination" in order to conceptualize what Freud is describing as the *seminal invention* of superior leaders of humanity at the dawn of the axial ages. What does the concept of indoctrination mean?

Indoctrination is the process of teaching an individual or group to accept a set of beliefs uncritically, as critique would upset the norms of submissions that civilization depends on. But now the question is who are these great leaders or superior persons that can set examples for the masses? Freud answers this question in the following terms: 'these leaders are persons who possess superior insight into the necessities of life and who have risen to the height of mastering their own instinctual wishes.'[10] In other words, they have understood the importance of the "social order" and have realized that the sustenance of this order is linked to the mastering of the complex system of instinctual drives. If these sets of beliefs are sufficiently adequate, have functioned historically, and have sustained the process of civilization, then what is Freud's objections to these doctrinal systems? Why is he trying to free the masses from the yoke that has so far kept intact the civilizational parameters of humanity?

In his book, *The Future of an Illusion*, Freud alludes to a problem with the historical belief-system of indoctrination that he considers as a "danger" as far as the current (and future) maintenance of civilization is concerned. He states that there is 'a danger that in order not to lose their influence, they [i.e., superior leaders] may give way to the mass more than it gives way to them.'[11] By way of explanation, it seems that Freud is of the opinion that we are now faced with the "danger" that he thought "may give way to the mass," the results of which would prove disastrous for the preservation of civilization.[12] This is a theme that needs to be studied and discussed in more detail. Nevertheless, allow us to focus here on the very conception of "civilization" in Freud's writings and see what he thinks of civilization as a category. He holds that civilization 'began to detach man from his primordial animal condition. We have found to our surprise that these privations are still operative and still form the kernel of hostility to civilization.'[13]

When Freud speaks of the detachment from man's primordial condition, he is tacitly referring to the power of the unique *invention* of humanity that he conceptualizes as an "illusion." Although Freud considers this invention as an illusion, he accepts that this *illusive system* has coerced man into submission and also forced human beings to renounce their instinctual wishes, including

---

10   Ibid., 8.
11   Ibid.
12   Ibid.
13   Ibid., 11.

incest, cannibalism, and lust for killing. On the one hand, Freud argues that civilization puts a great burden on the shoulders of humanity, as men are forced to detach themselves from their primordial animal condition, and, on the other hand, he contends that humanity needs to be compensated for this gigantic detachment from his true essence, i.e., the natural condition of animality. In addition, Freud seems to rate this "illusive invention" as a great step forward, yet nobody knows when it was invented. Nevertheless, the invention's fundamental prohibitions gave rise to "societal cosmos," "social order," and/or "civilization."

Freud asserts that this detachment from the primordial animal condition puts an extreme burden on human beings, but this illusive system that was invented at the dawn of history in one way or another lessens the burden of the instinctual sacrifices imposed on men, and this in turn opens up the path towards civilization, i.e., the regulation of human behaviors in all forms and shapes, both inwardly and outwardly. Strictly speaking, this illusive invention has an important place in the Freudian discourse on human existence. He considers this invention as the 'most important item in the psychical inventory of a civilization.'[14] If we ask Freud about the concept of the "psychical inventory" of a civilization, what would be his brief answer? He would without any hesitation reply that any civilization's psychical inventory is its "religious ideals." However, it would be a strategic mistake to read Freud's answer in a simplistic fashion. Because, in the Freudian discourse, religion is for the masses; it is an "invention" to protect civilization from the masses. This is to argue that religion as an invention is a complex inventory, i.e., it is both a "device" and also part of the "creative ability" of humanity.

5   Religion as an "Illusion"

When we consider religion as a "device" (even a creative apparatus) it seems we are suggesting that it is a method or trick with a particular aim and adopted for a specific purpose. Defining religion as a *creative device* entails that it has no truthfulness whatsoever. As a device, it is only a thing made for a specific design, i.e., the renunciation of instincts.

In the last paragraph of *The Future of an Illusion*, Freud talks about religion in a very complex fashion, arguing that perhaps 'the most important item in the psychical inventory of a civilization consists in its religious ideals in the

---

14   Ibid., 14.

widest sense, in other words, in its illusions.'[15] From one perspective, it appears that Freud holds religion in a great esteem, but at the same time he rejects the truth-claim of religion by conceptualizing it as an "illusion." What should be done? How should we interpret the Freudian approach towards religion? All religions claim to be the truest interpretation of "the real." If we refute the truth-claim of religions, then what would be left of religious ideas? If we conceptualize religion as an illusion, then it could be reduced merely to a *device* that has been invented as a means to adapt humanity for a purpose that is only known by "superior leaders." But let us not jump into conclusions so fast. Allow us to ponder upon the concept of "illusion" in a Freudian frame of analysis and then make a judgment. In other words, what does the concept of *illusion* mean in this approach? We know that he considers religion as the "psychical inventory of a civilization." In this capacity religion cannot be underrated as a redundant issue in the constitution of self and society. On the contrary, Freud considers religion as a significant tool for the development of man's psychological maturity and also an important invention for the creation of the "social order." Thus, we cannot simplify Freud's views on religion without taking into consideration the theoretical complexities of his theory on religion as a form of illusion. It seems we need to delve into the concept of "illusion" both as a general concept in social theory and also in the Freudian social theory of religion. In other words, we need to research the concept of "illusion," which makes up the contours of religious ideas in the widest sense, and at the same time, is argued by Freud to be the foundation of human civilization. How is this paradoxical position justified?

We are faced with a very complex type of social theory of religion that is (1) "critical" in the most critical sense of the term, and (2) a form of analysis that is simultaneously trying to negate religion as well as attempting to de-negate its own negation. Although Freud does not refer to Hegel in his critical analysis on religion, it is undeniable that there is a Hegelian moment in the Freudian approach to religion. Hegel's concept of *Aufhebung* looms large in Freud's conception of religion. *Aufhebung* has been defined as *abolish, preserve,* and finally *transcend*. In Hegel's philosophy, the dialectical interplay is realized through the process of *Aufhebung*. Freud does not refer to this metaphysical dimension of Hegel's thought in his analysis of religion. Nevertheless, *sublation* is the motor by which his dialectical analysis of religion seems to function. This is to assume that in Freud we are faced with a dialectical approach to religion that is negating the historical position of religion as a sacred canopy but at the same

---

15   Ibid.

time is attempting to preserve aspects of that renunciative power both for the growth of man and the sustenance of the "social order," i.e., the civilizational regulations of communal life. Thus, the crucial step forward is to focus on the concept of "illusion" as defined by Sigmund Freud. Freud used the concept of "illusion" in the German text that was translated by James Strachey as "illusion" in English. In the German language, we could employ eight words that could be used as equivalent for *illusion*: *Täuschung; Trügerische; Hoffnung; Trug; Schein; Sinnestäuschung; Wahn*; and *Illusion*. These words in different fashions may express one aspect of illusion, which in essence means an entity that is likely to be wrongly perceived or wrongly interpreted by the senses. In other words, Freud seems to address a fundamental problem of human cognition as far as religion is concerned. He is not rejecting religion as a human phenomenon, but rather seems to be refuting the way(s) it has been perceived in various human societies along the course of history.

Here, one can raise another question about Freud's conception of religion as an *illusion* in the context of civilization. He argues that the 'principal task of civilization, its actual raison d'être, is to defend us against nature.'[16] What does Freud mean by this? Nature is a threat for man as a species, argues Freud. Civilization, Freud argues, relieves him of this threat. But how does civilization accomplish this task? It seems here we can find the kernel of Freud's conception of religion as an "illusion." Because if we can find out how civilization accomplishes such a task then we may figure out his analytical logic in a more complex fashion. In the Freudian discourse, civilization relieves the individual against the superior powers of nature, of the untamed nature (i.e., Fate), and all other anxieties of life. But the question is how does civilization perform such a gigantic task? It, argues Freud, performs:

> in the same way for all alike, and it is noteworthy that in this almost all civilizations act alike. Civilization does not call a halt in the task of defending man against nature; it merely pursues it by other means. The task is a manifold one. Man's self-regard, seriously menaced, calls for consolation; life and the universe must be robbed of their terrors, moreover his curiosity, moved, it is true, by the strongest practical interest, demands an answer.[17]

---

16   Ibid., 15.
17   Ibid., 16.

Strictly speaking, animization of impersonal forces and destinies sets in by human beings who attempt to humanize nature and its daunting forces of terror. Here we can discern that Freud is attempting to give us a genealogical explanation of the origins of religion as a "consolative reservoir of power" at the infantile stage of human evolution. In the Freudian parlance, religion could achieve its supreme goal of regulating people's relations with one another in the family, state, and society. He even argues that religion at the infantile stage of human evolution could console humanity in front of the cruelties of nature and provide a meaningful explanation for the frailty of our bodies and even death. But what Freud is trying to interrogate is the role of religion today. He is of the opinion that civilization needed religion at its infancy stage to support the institutions that regulated people's relations with one another in the family, state, and in their larger communal life. However, religion cannot play that great role in the era of science and modern epoch.

6   Psychoanalyst as the Messiah?

In *The Future of an Illusion*, Freud argues that religion is "a store of ideas" that is created to credit the "precepts of civilization" with a divine origin.[18] Freud states that religion is "born from man's need to make his helplessness tolerable," but the question is from where does humanity conjure these ideas? If we look at this problem through a Freudian lens, the answer is that man creates these ideas 'from the material memories of the helplessness of his own childhood and the childhood of the human race.'[19] Although Freud concedes that these ideas protect man against the dangers of Nature and Fate, as well as console him against the injuries that threaten him from human society itself, he nevertheless considers religion as an "infantile model" for emancipation from life's sufferings. Based on this assumption, he tries to replace religion with something more suitable for man in his "adulthood era": psychoanalysis.

Psychoanalysis (as regarded by Sigmund Freud) is not only a method of analyzing neurotic patients in strict clinical sense, but it should also be considered as a model for liberating them from illusions born of their infantile state of mind, thus moving them towards a state of psychological maturity. Just as Moses liberated the Hebrews from the darkness of Pharaoh by leading them across the Nile, Freud is attempting to deliver modern man from the shackles

---

18   Ibid., 18.
19   Ibid.

of nonage by giving him psychoanalysis. It seems that Freud's psychoanalysis is rooted within the Judaic archetype of Messiah. We can discern messianic nuances in the Freudian type of psychoanalysis as well as his approach to religion as a healing source for humanity. Because, in his view, the sources of human suffering are 'the superior power of nature, the frailty of our bodies, and the inadequacy of the institutions that regulate people's relations with one another in the family, the state, and society.'[20] Freud further argues that regarding the

> first two, our judgment cannot vacillate for long: it obliges us to acknowledge these sources of suffering and submit to the inevitable. We shall never wholly control nature; our constitution, itself part of this nature, will always remain a transient structure, with a limited capacity for adaptation and achievement. Recognition of this fact does not have a paralyzing effect on us; on the contrary, it gives direction to our activity. Even if we cannot put an end to all suffering, we can remove or alleviate some of it, the experience of thousands of years has convinced us of this. Our attitude to the third source of suffering, the social source, is different. We refuse to recognize it at all; we cannot see why institutions that we ourselves have created should not protect and benefit us all.[21]

First, we can discern that Freud is not addressing fundamental questions of being in an ordinary psychological/psychiatric fashion, i.e., as a disciplinary thinker who is concerned with mental problems of human beings. On the contrary, he is a critical social theorist who is concerned with "big questions," which have preoccupied sages, philosophers, theologians, Gnostics, and social theorists, all of whom have searched for the sources of human suffering. Freud belongs to this class of thinkers and should be studied as one of the great classics of humanity. Having said that, now we need to inquire upon his original contribution as far as religion as a critical issue is concerned.

7   Religion as an Infantile Neurosis

Religion, Freud argues, is an expression of underlying psychological neuroses and distress. He explains this distress by referring to the state of "helplessness"

---

20   Freud, *Civilization and its Discontents*, 24.
21   Ibid.

that defines the human condition, which he thinks plays 'the chief role in the formation of religion.'[22] This is to emphasize that Freud seems to suggest that religion is an attempt to control the Oedipal Complex, i.e., a means of giving structure to social groups, wish fulfillment and an attempt to control the outside world. This means that religion in the Freudian discourse is conceptualized as an "infantile delusion." If religion is an "infantile delusion," then why is it conceptualized as an "illusion" by Freud? An answer to this question is of grave importance. When humanity was at its early stages of evolution, it could be considered as a misperception, but now that humanity has reached its adulthood stage (as understood by Freud), it is no longer a delusion. In other words, when man did not have any real access to the structures of reality, he could be excused in having misconceived the constitutions of reality. However, we are now in the age of science; this means that we have other means of knowledge that the primitive man was deprived of. As such, religion is an illusion, and it derives its strength from its readiness to fit in with our instinctual wishful impulses.

In the Freudian parlance, religion is comparable to a childhood neurosis. This is to contend that Freud considered human beings to be ill at their core, i.e., that mental illness is an inevitable byproduct of human psychological processes. This is to state that man as a being needs to feel secure and thus the search for safety activates his unconscious mind to create a powerful "father-figure," which is constructed as God. From here we can discern that religion has no truth-value for Freud and that is why he conceptualizes it as an "illusion," i.e., religion as it cannot interpret reality adequately. In other words, when Freud argues that religion is an illusion he is referring to religion as an instance of misinterpreted perception of a sensory experience. He does not argue that founders of religions or religious leaders lie about the constitutions of self and reality or being, but he instead contends that they have misunderstood their sensory experiences due to the fact that they did not have sufficient intellectual tools to decode the complexities of reality. This is to assert that religion does not have any "cognitive significance" for humanity today. If it does not have any cognitive importance, then what is it good for?

Here, it appears that Freud presents himself as a social theorist rather than a clinical psychiatrist or psychologist by arguing that religion plays an important role for the "maintenance of human society."[23] At this juncture we are faced with a paradox as far as religion is concerned. On the one hand, Freud

---

22   Freud, *The Future of an Illusion*, 22.
23   Ibid., 28–29.

argues that religion has no "cognitive significance," but, on the other hand, he reminds us that religion has an incomparable importance for the maintenance of human civilization. How is that possible? If something is completely of fictitious nature, then how could it have preoccupied humanity for thousands of years, as well as be the fundamental ground of human civilization? Freud contends that the religious doctrines:

> are called fictions, but for a variety of practical reasons we have to behave as if we believed in these fictions. [Why should we do that?] ... because of their incomparable importance for the maintenance of human civilization.[24]

8   The Freudian Social Theory of Religion

In the Freudian social theory of religion, we are faced with two key concepts of "illusion" and "fiction," which are seemingly not constructed and interpreted in the usual sense we employ them respectively in the English language. Strictly speaking, when Freud is arguing that religious doctrines are "fictions," it seems he is not talking about "non-facts," as it is clear that these fictions are parts of social facts, and as a matter of fact they constitute the fundamentals of our social reality. Thus, we need to ask Freud what he means by the concept of "fiction." Does he employ this concept as Dostoevsky uses it in his literary novels? When Freud argues that the religious doctrines are fictions, is he referring to them as "imaginary" events and people? If this is the fashion that he conceptualizes the terms "fiction," then why not speak of religious doctrines as products of *human imagination*? Because, if the religious doctrines are fictions in the sense that they are products of the human imagination, then there is no need to talk about religion and its future as an "illusion." But it seems the concept of "fiction" in the Freudian discourse is not employed in this fashion. On the contrary, when we realize that these fictions are categorized under the key concept of *illusion,* then it becomes clear that Freud is not viewing religions as inspirational sparks of human imagination. It seems the concept of fiction is conceptualized in the sense that these religious doctrines are *somethings* "invented," and therefore "untrue." For instance, when Ibn ʿArabī speaks of religion and its relation to the resourceful ability of imagination, he does not reduce reality in terms of rationalism. On the contrary, in Ibn ʿArabī's ontology, *imagination*

---

24   Ibid.

plays an essential role. It is seen as the creative source of manifestation, the very cause of human existence, and the powerful intermediary that enables us to remain in constant contact with the infinite and the Absolute.[25]

Said differently, the concept of "fiction" in the Freudian critical social theory of religion refers to ideas that are practically useful but theoretically untrue.[26] Here we should realize that Freud is functioning through the parameters of the ideology of rationalism, and it is also wrong to assume that rationalism (as a school of thought) is equivalent to either "reason" or "intellect." On the contrary, the rationalist discourse is a historicized aspect of reason that interprets the scope of human reason within the parameters of rational thinking. This is to assert that rationalism cannot express any significant verdict upon the human ability that emanates from the faculty of intellect or trans-rational/discursive possibilities of human intellect.

In Freud we are faced with a Eurocentric vision of thinking that limits the abilities of human contemplation in terms of the Cartesian Cogito and the Kantian conception of phenomenon, which is unable to grasp the realms of Noumenon. This is to argue that in the Freudian frame of reference we are faced with a *particular* philosophy of being or metaphysics that is agnostic about the transcendent possibilities of human contemplation. But when Freud argues that religion's claim for truth is false and of illusory nature, he is not only *describing* but *proscribing* as well. We are here faced with a normative social theory that seems to be uncritical about its critical position, which needs to be discussed in detail. Once Freud establishes the claim that the cognitive dimension of religion is false, then it is not difficult to claim that its teaching regarding "moral precepts" of civilization have no intellectual value but are only significant for "practical reasons." Now that we are in the "Age of Reason," then those practical reasons have no value either. Why?

Religious precepts were supposed to regulate human life at institutional levels of family, state, and society, apart from its consolitative functions. Now, religion, argues Freud, performs these functions independently, as religion (as a system) belongs to the infantile age of humanity. Thus, for the institutional regulations in society we need to turn to science and its various forms of disciplines, i.e., natural sciences and natural social sciences. As far as the daunting power of nature is concerned, we have advanced technology at our disposal, which has somehow decreased the violence of nature against humanity. Then there is only one existential dimension left for religion: how to bear the burden

---

25 Henry Corbin, *Creative Imagination in the Sufism of Ibn Arabi*, trans. Ralph Manheim. Princeton University Press, 1969.
26 Freud, *The Future of an Illusion*, 29.

of life and encounter death. On this, Freud seems to provide an alternative for religion and that is psychoanalysis. But it would be a mistake to view it solely as a "scientific method," i.e., an empirical method of inquiry.

In Freud's discourse, the psychoanalytic method is a comprehensive system of life that aims to replace religion (or religious modes of life). In other words, if we agree with Freud that religions are based on fictions that, prior to the *Age of Science* (i.e., the age of maturity of humankind), could function as "practical fictions," it is now high time to replace them with "theoretical truths" that are derived from the science of psychoanalysis. Thanks to science, we know that these religious fictions lack "theoretical truths" and their significance as "practical fictions" do not function as they did in the past. Thus, Freud attempts to replace these religious doctrines by scientific doctrines that have both practical significance and theoretical truthfulness. This is a new-age religion with an "atheistic theology," where there is no God but the psychoanalyst, who is playing the scientific act of Divinity.

9 Religion: Illusion or Imagination?

Earlier we touched upon the idea of religion as an "illusion," and we developed some remarks regarding this concept in Freudian thought. We have also mentioned the fictitious nature of illusions that have made human civilization historically possible. But we have not referred to Freud's own definition of religion as an "illusion." In other words, if we agree that there is a theoretical distinction in relation to the concept of religion as an aspect of *fiction*, then we could realize that we should transcend the linguistic definitions as far as religion is concerned. This is to contend that we are faced with different intellectual/metaphysical traditions where words/terms have been conceptualized differently based on distinct axioms or "background assumptions." In the Ibn 'Arabīan ontology, religion is an expression of *imagination* and hence a source of knowledge (i.e., a kind of knowledge that enriches human existence), while in the Freudian ontology, religion is an expression of *illusion* and therefore is devoid of "theoretical truths." This is to assert that we should not minimize the significance of paradigms in appraising views expressed by classical thinkers.

When Freud is talking about religion as an "illusion" – and Ibn 'Arabī reads religion as an expression of "imagination," and this concept is not viewed in terms of fiction (i.e., untruthful statements) – we should be reminded that concepts could be understood as "paradigm-bound" rather than "lexically." This is to suggest that the paradigm of Freudian thought should not be understood in a universal sense without any reference to the historicity of science and the axiomatic frame of reference in the scientific worldview. Science as a historical manifestation of the human capacity to create knowledge should not be treated as the sole form of knowledge, as it may result in nullifying all other possible historical manifestations of "episteme." Plato distinguishes between three forms of knowledge, i.e., *episteme, doxa,* and *techne*. He argues that episteme refers to a principled system of understanding that is different from doxa, which is based on "belief" or "opinion." He distinguishes also between episteme and techne by contending that techne refers to a craft or applied practice. Nevertheless, the interesting point in Freud is that he rejects all forms of knowledge that do not share the principles of empiricism-cum-rationalism although episteme is only the scientific form of analysis, while other forms are rated as opinion or doxa. That is why religion is practically significant but theoretically false in the Freudian frame of thought. In order to understand the Freudian approach to religion, we need to comprehend the paradigm that his conceptual framework is constructed upon. Otherwise, we would run the risk of reconstructing other forms of epistemes as "doxa" and rate his frame of knowledge as the only true form of "episteme" in the sense Plato conceptualized knowledge.

> The grand idea of Freud in regard to religion is that religion is an *infantile* expression about the fundamentals of reality while the Freudian psychoanalytic method is based on *science,* which is a *mature* conception of reality in the broadest sense of this term. The irony is that on this account Freud has simultaneously been critiqued both by scientists and philosophers. Criticism from science and philosophy is not so easily deflected by appeals to technicalities, precisely because what they question is the very basis of the theory. Karl Popper, Fredrick Crews, and Adolf Grünbaum figure largely in this critique. Among other things, they charge that the empirical basis of psychoanalysis is inadequate, that its key concepts are untestable, and that its aim, which is to give a comprehensive theory of human nature, is overambitious. Based on their respective critiques, its methodology is inadequate, because it rests on speculation and subjective insights, not on an objective examination of public and repeatable phenomena. It depends on generalizations from single cases or very small samples, and its reasoning relies on analogies, subjective associations, memories real or supposed, puns, and mistakes and coincidences. It is interesting to note that Freud in *The Future of an Illusion* argues that religion as a source of knowledge cannot be taken seriously due to the fact that its doctrine may be based on "ecstasy," which could give someone 'an unshakable conviction of the true reality of religious doctrines

from a state of ecstasy which has deeply moved him.'[27] But this cannot have any significance for others. Why? Because, Freud argues, ecstasy is a subjective inner feeling and cannot have significance for others. In order to be binding on others we need to have a "scientific approach," and Freud seems to suggest that his psychoanalysis is a scientific form of engagement with religion. However, it is exactly on this account, i.e., his claim upon truth, that the judgment of philosophers and scientists stand against him. In other words, Freud argues that religion is an illusion, whereas psychoanalysis is a form of science that is not an illusion. However, a pertinent question must follow: what is an illusion in the Freudian frame of reference? Although it seems that many philosophers and scientists deny the *scientificity* of Freud's psychoanalysis, we need to read the text and see how Freud himself defined the concept of "illusion," then we can argue with him about the illusory nature of religion.

In *The Future of an Illusion*, Freud states that the concept of "illusion" needs to be defined lest we misunderstand him. He argues that religious doctrines,

> are illusion. An illusion is not the same thing as an error; nor is it necessarily an error. Aristotle's belief that vermin are developed out of dung (a belief to which ignorant people still cling) was an error; so was the belief of a former generation of doctors that tabes dorsalis is the result of sexual excess. It would be incorrect to call these errors illusions. On the other hand, it was an illusion of Columbus's that he had discovered a new sea-route to the Indies. The part played by his wish in this error is very clear. One may describe as an illusion the assertion made by certain nationalists that the Indo-Germanic race is the only one capable of civilization; or the belief, which was only destroyed by psycho-analysis, that children are creatures without sexuality.[28]

10 Freud's Metaphysical Position

Freud distinguishes between *erroneous* belief and *illusionary* belief by arguing that what is 'characteristic of illusions is that they are derived from human wishes.'[29] This is to contend that illusions are erroneous beliefs too but

---

27   Ibid., 28.
28   Ibid., 30–31.
29   Ibid., 31.

their structures are different from erroneous beliefs. In order to investigate the Freudian conception of an "illusion," we need to distinguish between three distinct concepts of "illusion," "delusion," and "wish." Freud states that illusions are derived from "wishes," and in this sense illusions are coming closer to "delusions" in the psychiatric sense of the term. Delusional disorder is a type of serious mental illness – conceptualized as psychosis – in which a person cannot tell what is *real* from what is *unreal*. The main feature of this disorder is the presence of delusions, which are unshakable beliefs in something untrue. Thus, Freud is of the view that religion is an illusion in the sense that people who believe in it are unable to distinguish between the boundaries of *real* and *fictional*, or to put it bluntly, those who believe in religion have unshakable beliefs in something untrue. However, he asserts that there are some differences between delusions and illusions in the sense that 'they differ from [each other while illusions come near to delusions] ... [as delusions have a] more complicated structure [in comparison to illusions].'[30]

Freud is attempting to distinguish between an "illusion" and a "delusion" by contending that a delusional person is someone who is unable to distinguish between realms of reality and fictionality, while an illusional person is somebody who is motivated by "wish-fulfillment." However, it seems the examples he provides are not really supportive of his stance on religion as an illusion. In *The Future of an Illusion*, he states that:

> a middle-class girl [for instance] may have the illusion that a prince will come and marry her. This is possible; and a few such cases have occurred. That the Messiah will come and found a golden age is much less likely. Whether one classifies this belief as an illusion or something analogues to a delusion will depend on one's personal attitude. Examples of illusions which have proved true are not easy to find, but the illusion of the alchemists that all metals can be turned into gold might be one of them.[31]

Illusion as defined by Freud is equivalent a "wish" and a wish by definition is part of the "emotive dimension" of the human psyche that could be conceptualized as a strong hope for something that cannot or probably will not happen. Thus, Freud considers a belief as an 'illusion when a wish-fulfillment is a prominent factor in its motivation, and in doing so we disregard its relation to reality, just as the illusion itself sets no store by verification.'[32]

---

30   Ibid.
31   Ibid.
32   Ibid.

Here we can see that the three concepts of "illusion," "delusion," and "wish" (or hope) are conceptualized in terms of their respective relations to reality. But the irony is that Freud does not provide any metaphysical foundation for his conception of reality. He presents this concept in a very rudimentary fashion as though it is an innocent (and not highly pregnant) term. It seems his philosophy of "realness" is based on a crude form of positivism that is predicated on verification. One might ask what is wrong with the verification principle. If we assume that religion is an illusion in the sense that Freud conceptualizes it and therefore its claims cannot be verified, then one could ask the same question of Freud and his psychoanalysis ideology, i.e., could its claims be verified or are they similar to the claims of the religious doctrines?

Of course, Freud seems to be anti-philosophical or even anti-metaphysical, but this does not necessarily rule out the fact that his philosophical/metaphysical position is based on the correspondence theory. It is not a secret that philosophical controversies concerning the nature of truth began to play an important part in psychoanalytic theorizing and the Freudian discourse is deeply interwoven in these theoretical debates. The two major philosophical notions of the *coherence* and the *correspondence* theories and their use in psychoanalytic theory making were debated by the participants for a long time. It was argued that although coherence is part of the criteria of truth, correspondence is the more essential and fundamental criterion. It was in this way that Freud used these concepts in creating psychoanalysis. Psychoanalytic discoveries concerning the psychogenesis of objectivity in perception and thought support the correspondence theory of truth. Strictly speaking, the correspondence theory as a basic attitude of mind is a necessary element in the respect for the patient upon which psychoanalytic therapy depends. In this type of theory, which underlies the Freudian conception of reality, the adherents of this theory attempt to posit a relationship between thoughts and statements on one hand, and things or facts on the other hand. Although Freud distinguishes between delusion and illusion, and also argues laboriously that religion is not of delusional nature, he nevertheless cannot help but to 'compare religious doctrines to delusions.'[33] This is to assert that it seems there is no essential difference between illusion and delusion in the Freudian frame of analysis as both produce mental impairments in the forms of "neurosis" and "psychosis." It is interesting to note that while psychosis is conceptualized as a severe mental disorder in which thought and emotions are so impaired that contact is lost with "external reality," neurosis is also conceptualized as a

---

33 Ibid.

mental illness, but the difference in Freud's eyes is that a religious man has not radically lost his touch with reality yet. In other words, the difference is not in "quality" but in "intensity" of the *impairment*. This is to contend that religion is an impairment that has disordered the mental capacity of humanity. Here we need to ask Freud what is real and unreal as far as the human existence is concerned?

The language of religion is surely different from the language of science, and it seems Freud has made a "metaphysical choice" in terms of what language should be the criterion for judging between real and unreal. In the language of science, the boundaries of real and unreal are decoded by the concept of "concreteness," but this is not the criterion for assessing real from unreal in religion, art, literature, metaphysics, sculpture, philosophy, and poetry. In Freud's view, the path towards *redemption* goes through the work of science. He argues that:

> scientific work is the only road which can lead us to a knowledge of reality outside ourselves. It is merely an illusion to expect anything from intuition and introspection; they can give us nothing but particulars about our own mental life, which are hard to interpret.[34]

Freud seems to be confused about the order of reality and consequently reduces reality into "concreteness," and ironically it should be remarked that the term "concrete" refers to material/physical realm and also to a building material made from a mixture of broken stone, cement, and water. Said differently, when reality as a complex concept is reduced to the simple concept of concreteness, then human potentials are all disregarded as illusions/delusions. A question that needs to be raised – but Freud has ignored – is the question on humanity's "sources of knowledge." In other words, what are the sources of knowledge? When Freud limits the sources of knowledge to empirical/rational tools, it seems we are faced with a particular (not universal) interpretation of "epistemic source," which is not explicitly elaborated but implicitly agreed upon. This is to argue that Freud's emphasis on science as the sole path to human liberation is part of the ideology of scientism that is the fountainhead of Eurocentrism.

Although he does not talk about these issues, it is clear that his vision of human civilization is deeply Eurocentric and faithfully evolutionary in the sense that all human cultures prior to the rise of science (empirical form of knowledge and rationalistic fashion of perception and formulation of reality)

---

34   Ibid., 31–32.

were at the stage of *infancy* and now the road towards *maturity* has just been paved. These are the articles of Eurocentric faith that have been radically critiqued. Science as a form of knowledge is fundamentally significant but we need to accommodate it with a more comprehensive theory of knowledge, and more importantly, we must distinguish between "religious knowledge" and other forms of knowledge.

11   The Freudian Caricature of Religion

The way Freud talks about religious knowledge seems to be rather a caricature of religion, which has been critiqued by non-Eurocentric philosophers. For instance, we can refer to the contemporary Iranian philosopher, Allama Mohammad Taghi Jafari, who conceptualizes "religious episteme" in a very radical fashion that cannot be categorized as either illusion or delusion. In my book, *Beyond Eurocentrism: Probing into Epistemological Endeavors of Allama Jafari*, I wrote about the "Heptafold Realms of Knowledge," which in its totality makes up the foundations of "religious episteme."[35] This argues that it is erroneous to conceptualize religious episteme in terms of the so-called "sacred scriptures" of respective religious traditions, or even talk about religious sciences versus secular sciences. On the contrary, in accordance with Allama Jafari, knowledge cannot be categorized as "religious" versus "secular," or "profane" versus "sacred." The religious episteme is constituted by seven realms of knowledge: the philosophical knowledge (i.e., the form of knowledge that is derived from demonstration); the scientific knowledge (i.e., the form of knowledge that is based on empirical ground); the intuitional knowledge (i.e., the form of knowledge that is based on illumination/inspiration); the ethical knowledge (i.e., the form of knowledge that is acquired through praxis); the theosophical knowledge (i.e., the form of knowledge that is based on knowledge by presence); the gnostical knowledge (i.e., the form of knowledge that is acquired through ascetic practice); the revelational knowledge (i.e., the form of knowledge that is composed in sacral texts in different sacrosanct traditions). Once knowledge based on these seven realms are systematically integrated into a coherent whole, the result is conceptualized as the "religious episteme," (*Ma'refat Dini*). This is what Allama Jafari considers as "religious," which is completely different than what Freud construes as "religious." In

---

35   Seyed Javad Miri, *Beyond Eurocentrism: Probing into Epistemological Endeavors of Allama Jafari* (London: London Academy of Iranian Studies Press, 2014), 32.

Freudian thought, the concepts of religion and the religious are conceptualized in a rudimentary fashion as though the "religious" is tantamount to a "fairy-tale." Although Freud is a critical social theorist, he is not *critical* enough when it comes to his Eurocentrism, i.e., his "received tradition."

If religion is an illusion (false conception of reality) then how could it have sustained the civilization during such a long journey? This is a question that we need to reflect upon. Time and again, Freud states that religion 'has clearly performed great services for human civilization,' but he does not touch upon this question regarding the falsity of religion.[36] In other words, he does not problematize the question of how can religion perform such an enduring service for human civilization while being simultaneously epistemologically false? It seems here we need to pose certain questions regarding the "nature" of humanity and the constitutive dimensions of human existence. In the Swedish language (and philosophical debates), a particular concept emerges when one attempts to conceptualize an intellectual's or a philosopher's views on human being: *Människosyn*. This refers to the views one may have on fundamentals of humanity or the concept of mankind. This is to contend that the concept of *Människosyn* refers to a philosopher's understanding of human being as a species. Based on this interpretation, one needs to inquire upon Freud's Människosyn.

If religion could perform great services for human civilization and it has also 'contributed much towards the taming of the asocial instincts,' then there must be existentially a better or feasible *Människosyn* embedded in the soil of religions, as opposed to the worldview of psychoanalysis.[37] Freud emphasizes that religion suffers from the lack of credibility vis-à-vis the scientific spirit. In other words, the "scientific critique" of religion, Freud argues, whittled away the evidential significance of religion. He believes that the

> scientific spirit brings about a particular attitude towards worldly matters; before religious matters it pauses for a little, hesitates, and finally there too crosses the threshold. In this process there is no stopping; the greater the number of men to whom the treasures of knowledge become accessible, the more widespread is the falling-away from religious belief – at first only from its obsolete and objectionable trappings, but later from its fundamental postulates as well.[38]

---

36   Freud, *The Future of an Illusion*, 37.
37   Ibid.
38   Ibid., 38.

12 The Scientific Spirit or Scientism?

It seems Freud conceptualizes secularization theory in a very rudimentary fashion. However, this is not an adequate formulation of the "scientific spirit," but rather Freud is conceptualizing the "spirit of scientism." These two are not synonymous, yet many great intellectuals have sadly employed them as such. The spirit of science refers to a method and temper of study, which is also based on "humility." Scientism, on the other hand, is a "radical ideology" that considers religion (and in particular the ecclesiastical forms of religious organization) as its archenemy, and more importantly it is a "belief-system" in the strict sociological sense of the term. While the scientific spirit is based on "humility," i.e., the quality of having a modest view of one's position in the order of life, scientism as a combative ideology based on "excessive belief" in the power of scientific knowledge and techniques. Freud is under the spell of the latter and based on this ideology he attempts to debunk religion.

We are faced with two "meaning-systems," religion and scientism, and it is impossible to adjudicate between these two incommensurable paradigms. Freud strives to demonstrate that he is approaching religion from a neutral position of science and that his pronouncements are value-free. However, he has made a "metaphysical choice" between the "scientistic belief" and the "religious quest." In *The Monk and the Philosopher* (1999), Jean-Francois Revel and Matthieu Ricard eloquently alluded to the problem of "metaphysical choice," which we make between the "scientific pursuit" and "spiritual quest." Freud does not reflect upon his own "metaphysical choice" and takes that for granted due the *discursive hegemony of science* in the 19th and 20th century.[39] In other words, the idea of science is what Freud refers to time and again as

> a matter of fact, it is the basis of his metaphysical agnosticism. It seems that [Freud] defines science as an act of knowing about the mechanism of life, but calls religion [an infantile way of] being in life. To say the least, this categorical distinction between knowing and being (and referring the former to the cognitive aspect of man and the latter to the emotional) is more of a recent [Eurocentric] ethos than a universal and absolute category.[40]

---

39 Seyed Javad Miri, "The Monk and the Philosopher: East Meets West in a Father-Son Dialogue." *Journal of Buddhist Ethics* 10 (2003): 58–61.
40 Ibid., 60.

Another problem in Freud's critique of religion is his "crude evidentialism." Evidentialism is a thesis in epistemology that states that one is justified to believe something if and only if that individual has evidence that endorses said belief. Evidentialism is simply a thesis about which beliefs are justified and which are unjustified. But the question which Freud does not pose regarding religion is whether we can rule out religion (even in its limited form of conceptualization of religious knowledge) based on an evidentialist approach. To put it succinctly, evidentialism cannot account for religious beliefs that are properly basic (i.e., touch the base of human existence as a species in life and world), just as it cannot rule out requisite preliminary faith in the case of *friendship*. For all its merits as a philosophical approach, it cannot be considered as a viable philosophical theory of justification for reaching justified true beliefs. Here we need to dig even more as it seems the Freudian conception of evidence (and hence his unstudied theory of evidentialism) is deeply flawed and inconsequential.

13 Freud and "To Leave God Out"

In *The Future of an Illusion*, Freud is deeply preoccupied with the idea of morality as the basis of human civilization. He is of the opinion that religion was able to sanction moral precepts that regulated 'people's relation with one another,' and based on this notion of "divine origin" of communal commandments, social order became a historical possibility.[41] However, religions in the "Age of Reason" do not function as before and since that time many people 'find them less credible.'[42] This loss of credibility puts dual pressure on humanity: on the one hand, it makes the burden of civilization more unbearable and on the other hand, by the loss of credibility in religions, civilization loses its moral appeal on humanity, which is a real danger. What then is Freud's strategy for these fundamental problems in the "Age of Reason"? He contends that:

> either these dangerous masses must be held down most severely and kept most carefully away from any chance of intellectual awakening, or else the relationship between civilization and religion must undergo a fundamental revision.[43]

---

41 Freud, *The Future of an Illusion*, 24.
42 Ibid. 38.
43 Ibid. 39.

If we want to reconceptualize the revisionist approach of Freud on the relationship between religion and civilization, then that would appear as an *atheistic theology*, where God is absent from the constitution of self and society. Once we agree that prohibitions in any social order have not been issued by God, then 'it would be an undoubted advantage if we were to leave God out altogether and honestly admit the purely human origin of all the regulations and precepts of civilization.'[44] Yet, it seems Freud has forgotten *Dostoevsky's objection* in this regard: Following Dostoevsky argument, if we forward the position that God does not exist, then everything is permitted, then we must admit that there is no inherent distinction between right and wrong, and thus no inherently true morality. This is to argue that Freud does not see why the moral virtue of honesty should be preferrable to simple utility. Freud argues that if people understand that morality has no divine origin, they will then realize that moral precepts are made simply to serve their interests. However, he does not consider that when someone is faced with a decision concerning honesty (without having any interest) and utility (with high financial interests) – in the absence of God – why then should that person choose honesty without any interest and loss of status/position in society?[45] This requires a form of idealism that is not congruent with Freudian realism (embedded in ideology of scientism). It seems we need to counter Freud's daunting questions with the Dostoevskian awesome answers.

Freud's conception of science is worth reflecting upon as it appears his notion of science is like a Hegelian *Geist* that gradually gains consciousness about its abilities. He says, 'Our God, Logos, will fulfill whichever wishes nature outside of us allows, but he will do it very gradually, only in the unforeseeable future.'[46] The God of religion, Freud argues, is an illusion, but he is worried that the God of science will be accused of the same, so he is hasty to contend that 'science has given us evidence by its numerous and important successes that it is no illusion.'[47] It is interesting that Freud attempts to deny the reliability of religious belief by relying on the "scientific belief" (i.e., the meaning system constructed on the basis of scientism) by contending that 'we believe that it is possible for scientific work to gain some knowledge by means of which we can arrange our life.'[48] What does the arrangement of life by science mean? It means that life should be organized based on *Logos* without the presence of

---

44 Ibid., 41.
45 Ibid., 41.
46 Ibid., 54.
47 Ibid., 55.
48 Ibid.

religion, i.e., *Mythos*. This Freudian position is a very problematic position, one that tells us something fundamental about the Euro-Atlantic-centric conception of civilization and/or Social Order.

14   Instead of Conclusion: Freud or Dostoevsky on Religion?

In sum, religion for Freud is a category that belongs to the realm of Mythos and by the rise of science it cannot stay at the center of the demythologized order. The God of religion springs out of Mythos, while the God of science is the product of Logos. Freud knows that man cannot bear the burdens of reason, thus the *religion of psychoanalysis* (in the form conceptualized by Freud) induces in the logical order of "modernity" the principle of Eros, which does not have the illusory dimensions of Mythos, and in addition it gives pleasure to man here and now (unlike the God of religion that postpones all the pleasures to the Hereafter). Instead of Grace, Freud gives the common man orgasm. This is how Freud solves the riddles of humanity and emancipates the masses from the yoke of the morality that scared them for ages. And since religion has lost its grip on them, secularization destroyed the basis of the social order, which was Freud's supreme concern. As such, Eros and Logos together make up the Ethos of the Brave New Age of Reason. But is life without Mythos possible? How to conceptualize the polylectic of *Mythos, Logos*, and *Eros*? This is a question that Freud never gave an answer to. It is exactly at this juncture that we should leave Freud behind and walk the rest of the path with Dostoevsky. In other words, Freud paves the way for the Dostoevskian approach towards religion, which has not been conceptualized within the context of critical theory yet.

Bibliography

Corbin, Henry. *Creative Imagination in the Sufism of Ibn Arabi*. Translated by Ralph Manheim. Princeton: Princeton University Press, 1969.

Freud, Sigmund. "Obsessive Actions and Religious Practices." In *The Standard Edition of the Complete Psychological Works of Sigmund Freud, Vol. 9*, edited and translated by James Strachey. London: Hogarth Press, 1907.

Freud, Sigmund. "Totem and Taboo". In *The Standard Edition of the Complete Psychological Works of Sigmund Freud, Vol 13*, edited and translated by James Strachey. London: Hogarth Press, 1913.

Freud, Sigmund. *The Future of an Illusion*, edited and translated James Strachey. New York: W.W. Norton & Company, 1961.

Freud, Sigmund. *Civilization and its Discontents*, Translated by David McLintock. London: Penguin Books, 2002.

Miri, Seyed Javad. "The Monk and the Philosopher: East Meets West in a Father-Son Dialogue." *Journal of Buddhist Ethics* 10 (2003): 58–61.

Miri, Seyed Javad. *Beyond Eurocentrism: Probing into Epistemological Endeavors of Allama Jafari*, London: London Academy of Iranian Studies Press, 2014.

Revel, Jean-Francois & Ricard Matthieu. *The Monk and the Philosopher: East Meets West in a Father-Son Dialogue*, Translated by John Canti. London: Harper Collins, 1999.

CHAPTER 6

Black Power's Deification of the Son: A Freudian Reading of the Reverse Oedipal Relationship between Malcolm X and Elijah Muhammad

Jimmy Butts

1 Introduction

It is fascinating to recount the stories of the initial interaction of religious movements with their deity. In the Abrahamic traditions, this first exposure typically begins with the deity revealing himself to the primary carriers of his message (usually through an angel). In the Hebrew Bible, the deity's encounter with Moses inaugurates his special relationship with the Children of Israel as the God who delivers them from bondage. During this initial encounter, the deity spoke to Moses from a burning bush calling him to proclaim to his people that he has come to rescue them and give them their own land. Moses was initially ambivalent about whether he should follow the instructions of the deity because his instructions seemed too implausible. Nevertheless, Moses eventually was convinced that it was wise to follow the deity (Exodus 3:1–14, 4:18). Similarly, in the Christian scriptures Jesus' earliest encounters with those who would spread his message was met with some ambivalence. One example is when his prospective disciple Nathanael first heard Jesus was from Nazareth; he did not believe that could be the place where the savior of Israel would be found (John 1:45–46). However, after meeting Jesus, Nathanael declared, "Rabbi, you are the Son of God; You are the King of Israel" (John 1:49). Once again, there is a pattern of initial doubt, and then fierce commitment. Likewise, on one occasion during his normal practice of going to the cave of Hira to worship, Muhammad ibn 'Abdullah encountered an angel that asked him to read. Muhammad's response was that he did not know how to read. The angel grabbed him and pressed very hard and then asked him once more to read, but he received the same response. Finally, after the third time being pressed, Muhammad would recite the first verses of the Qur'ān and eventually accept that it was an angel from the deity that had spoken to him.[1] Thus, the

---

1 Sahih Al-Bukhari, *The Translation of the Meanings of Sahih Al-Bukhari* vol. 1, trans., Muhammad Muhsin Khan (Riyadh: Darussalam Publishers, 1997), 46–48.

pattern continues that the first contact with the deity results in a feeling of ambivalence, but then a subsequent commitment to follow him.

Comparably, if one was to view the Black Power Movement as a "religion," the first encounter with its deity follows a similar trajectory of ambivalence.[2] Associating this movement with religion is not novel. As one of the earliest scholars to articulate this perspective, James Cone declared that Black Power was the central message of Christianity and the gospel of Jesus itself.[3] Similarly, Terrence Johnson has recently argued that Black Power was infused with resources from Black religion.[4] Moreover, he described the ethical turn in Black politics expressed in the Black Power Movement as the "religion of Black Power."[5] While Cone seemed to be asserting that Black Power was a praxis of the Christian gospel, Johnson contended that religion provided the foundational infrastructure and platform from which Black Power built upon and expanded.[6] What distinguishes this study, however, is that by using Sigmund Freud's conception of the Oedipus complex, the author goes beyond the claim that it was the practical manifestation of a religious message, or that it was infused and founded on religion. Rather, the argument here is that the Black Power Movement can be understood as an actual religion with a deity and religious devotion.

During the 1960s and early 1970s, there was a shift among some African Americans away from the goal of integration to the pursuit of Black self-determination. This ideology of self-determination was central to the Black Power Movement and was expressed in the pursuit of institutional, economic, community, educational, and social control.[7] The source of this movement trace back to Malcolm X. In fact, Peniel Joseph asserts that "Malcolm X, perhaps more than any single individual figure, reflects the 'roots' of Black Power."[8] Moreover, the leaders of the Black Power Movement, according to

---

2 Explained in more detail below, my use of the word religion here is consistent with Freud's notion of religion as the deification of the father in response to the guilty feeling for killing him.
3 James Cone, *Black Theology and Black Power* (New York: Orbis Books, 2011), 1, 37, 38, 48.
4 Terrence Johnson, *We Testify with Our Lives: How Religion Transformed Radical Thought from Black Power to Black Lives Matter* (New York: Columbia University Press, 2021), 115.
5 Ibid., 244.
6 Ibid., 218.
7 Peniel Joseph, "Introduction: Community Organizing, Grassroots Politics, and Neighborhood Rebels: Local Struggles for Black Power in America," in *Neighborhood Rebels: Black Power at the Local Level*, ed. Peniel Joseph (New York: Palgrave Macmillan, 2010), 5, 7, 11.
8 Peniel Joseph, "Introduction: Toward a Historiography of the Black Power Movement," in *The Black Power Movement: Rethinking the Civil Rights-Black Power Era*, ed. Peniel Joseph (New York: Routledge, 2006), 6–7.

Komozi Woodard, saw themselves as sons and daughters of Malcolm X and as carrying on his legacy.[9] While Joseph places the beginning of Black Power in 1966, Kimberly Springer suggests that the movement began in 1965 and ended in 1975.[10] For Joseph, the Meredith March on June 16, 1966 was the point that Black Power emerged. During this march, Willie Ricks spread the Black Power slogan, but it was Stokely Carmichael who popularized the phrase.[11] Woodard asserts that despite the differences, there were various Black Power groups that shared certain fundamental beliefs such as being the heirs of Malcolm X, supporting African liberation movements, conceiving of African Americans as being an internal colony of the United States, and demanding Black self-determination.[12] With the help of Freud, the author will demonstrate that this movement fits within the paradigm of a religion. The first indication of this can be seen in the fact that, similar to the Abrahamic religions mentioned above, Black Power's origin story follows the same motif.

2 The "Prophet" of Black Power Encounters the Deity

One of the earliest encounters the deity had with those who would eventually be the main propagators of his message was during a debate held at Howard University on October 30, 1961. Students at Howard (which included Stokely Carmichael) had established something called Project Awareness that would bring people in for debate. This debate between Malcolm X and Bayard Rustin was the first debate and caused a lot of tension between the students and the administration. Howard's administration was hesitant to have Malcolm X speak to the students but because of the attention it had garnered they did not want to interfere with it. Prior to the debate, Malcolm X attended a dinner organized by the students for their guests. When he arrived, all conversations stopped immediately, and everyone was staring at him. After he took his seat he politely answered questions students presented to him.

---

9   Komozi Woodard and Amiri Baraka, "The Congress of African People, and Black Power Politics from the 1961 United Nations Protest to the 1972 Gary Convention," in *The Black Power Movement: Rethinking the Civil Rights-Black Power Era*, ed. Peniel Joseph (New York: Routledge, 2006), 65.

10 Joseph, *Toward a Historiography of the Black Power Movement*, 2; Kimberly Springer, "Black Feminists Respond to Black Power Masculinism," in *The Black Power Movement: Rethinking the Civil Rights-Black Power Era*, ed. Peniel Joseph (New York: Routledge, 2006), 107.

11 Joseph, *Toward a Historiography of the Black Power Movement*, 2.

12 Woodard and Baraka, *The Congress of African People, and Black Power Politics*, 69.

About fifteen hundred people were inside the Cramton Auditorium, with five hundred outside. The debate was about approaches to Black advancement. It reflected some of the divisions that were present in the activist group, the Student Nonviolent Coordinating Committee (SNCC), at that time. Rustin represented the nonviolent approach with the aim to integrate into the American system. Malcolm X represented a rejection of nonviolence as a philosophy, almost even denouncing it as a tactic; rather, he called for a violent clash of arms against the American system and separation from it. Malcolm X did concede that while the tactics of those who use nonviolence was different than his, he believed that they shared the goal of obtaining complete freedom for Black people.[13] At the close of the debate nearly the whole room was on their feet. SNCC activist, Stokely Carmichael, attended the debate and stated that although many students thought that Rustin would win because they shared his views, the overwhelming majority of the audience agreed that Malcolm won the debate.[14]

The debate had a profound effect on SNCC, as Malcolm X's ideas began to gain traction in the organization. It clarified and drove a line between those who were nationalists and those who were not, within the organization.[15] Carmichael provides some important details: "He [Malcolm X] gave us all the intellectual arguments and opened up the way for us to show clearly an intellectual basis for a nationalism and an ability to smash all ideas that were in contradiction to it. Malcolm opened up the way and more importantly, he opened up the way for ... violence as a legitimate weapon in a struggle for human rights."[16] Continuing to describe Malcolm's influence, Carmichael argues that in dormitories at Howard, and likely other Black colleges, were students who were shaped by Malcolm X's example; they would never tire of watching him. As the Civil Rights Movement would advance, Malcolm X gained more attention,

---

13   Stokely Carmichael [Kwame Ture] with Ekwueme Michael Thelwell, *Ready For Revolution: The Life and Struggles of Stokely Carmichael [Kwame Ture]* (New York: Scribner, 2003), 256–257, 260–261; Stokely Carmichael, *Stokely Speaks: From Black Power to Pan-Africanism* (Chicago: Lawrence Hill Books, 2007), 190; Manning Marable and Garrett Felber, *The Portable Malcolm X Reader* (New York: Penguin Books, 2013), 185.
14   Carmichael, *Revolution*, 258–261.
15   Stokely Carmichael, *Interview with Stokely Carmichael*, Interviewed by Judy Richardson on November 7, 1988, for *Eyes on the Prize II Interviews*, Washington University Digital Gateway Texts. Also see Akiniyele K. Umoja, "From Malcolm X to Omowale Malik Shabazz: The Transformation and Its Impact on the Black Liberation Struggle" in *Malcolm X: A Historical Reader*, eds. James L. Conyers and Andrew P. Smallwood (North Carolina: Carolina Academic Press, 2008), 48–49.
16   Carmichael, *Interview with Judy Richardson*.

particularly among Black youth. The Rustin debate planted seeds that would turn many who were in the audience to become ardent Black nationalists, Pan-Africanists, and political radicals over time.[17] In particular, Carmichael states that Malcolm X's critique of nonviolence as unmanly, especially when women are being brutalized, had a powerful effect on him. Outside of his speeches, (the deity) Malcolm X spoke with the one who would popularize (the religion of) Black Power, Carmichael, on numerous occasions. Carmichael notes that Malcolm X meant a lot to his generation of Black people because of his bold representation.[18] Peniel Joseph describes it this way: "For Stokely's generation, Malcolm X became the avatar of a new movement for black liberation, one anchored in the quest for self-determination epitomized by Garveyism and its many variations that would come to be known as Black Power."[19] This initial encounter with the deity of Black Power gained some immediate excitement, but at this stage in the movement most ambivalently still kept their distance from Malcolm X.

This essay aims to interpret the rise of Black Power as a religion utilizing Freudian theory. Through the symbolic castration of Elijah Muhammad (the father), the symbolic (and literal) killing and postmortem deification of Malcolm X (the son), Freud's Oedipus theory applied in reverse suggests that the guilt of the younger Civil Rights Movement generation explains the postmortem exaltation of Malcolm X and the development of the religion of Black Power. At the center of this analysis is the relationship between Elijah Muhammad and Malcolm X. Claude Clegg argues that there has not been a time when two men's public relationship took on so many varieties and had such consequences for Black thought and politics as Muhammad and Malcolm's did.[20]

---

17   Carmichael, *Revolution*, 255; Umoja, *From Malcolm X to Omowale*, 36; Peniel Joseph, *Stokely: A Life* (New York: Basic Civitas, 2014), 42.
18   Carmichael, *Stokely Speaks*, 204; Carmichael, *Revolution*, 100, 255, 260.
19   Joseph, *Stokely*, 40. Ricks contends that Black Power comes from Malcolm. Mukasa [Willie] Ricks in Zayid Muhammad, "Malcolm X and His Impact SNCC." facebook.com/mxcc519/videos/2765673517086613/.
20   Claude Clegg, "Malcolm X and Elijah Muhammad," in *The Cambridge Companion to Malcolm X*, ed. Robert E. Terrill (New York: Cambridge University Press, 2010), 22.

3 Meeting the Father and the Son

Elijah Poole was born in Georgia in 1897 to a Baptist preacher. When he got older, he became a Baptist preacher as well, and in 1923 he migrated north to Detroit looking for work. Initially, Poole did not do well, but in 1931, he met a man named W.D. Fard, which dramatically changed his life. Although Fard was a mysterious figure, Poole claimed to have learned about Islam from him.[21] Fard disappeared a few years later and Poole, who would eventually be known as Elijah Muhammad, subsequently became the sole authority on matters of ideology, theology, and policy within the religious movement Fard had begun: the Nation of Islam (NOI).[22]

Malcolm Little, later known as Malcolm X, was born May 19, 1925, in Omaha, Nebraska. He was Earl Little's seventh child. Malcolm lost both his father and mother, Louise Little, at a young age and eventually gave up on school when he was told by one of his teachers that he should temper his aspirations to the limits of his race.[23] As an adolescent, Malcolm lived in a juvenile detention home in Mason, Michigan, but when he was fifteen he moved to Boston to live with his older half-sister Ella Little. Malcolm began living a criminal lifestyle and landed in prison where he would encounter the teachings of Elijah Muhammad from his siblings who had converted to the NOI. When Malcolm was released from prison he soon after became a minister of the NOI and played a pivotal role in expanding the NOI across the United States.[24]

Although Malcolm X was a well-known figure during the Civil Rights Movement, the acceptance he has received after his death far exceeds his reception during his lifetime. This paper will provide an interpretation of this occurrence using the psychoanalytic thought of Sigmund Freud, specifically his discussion of the Oedipus complex. As will be shown below, Freud saw guilt as motivating religious devotion. After giving a description of this theoretical framework, I will then examine the unique relationship between the father (Elijah Muhammad) and the son (Malcolm X). Following this I will discuss Malcolm X's relationship with the larger Civil Rights Movement and

---

21   E.U. Essien-Udom, *Black Nationalism: The Rise of the Black Muslims in the U.S.A.* (Great Britain: Pelican Books, 1966), 77; Edward E. Curtis IV, *Islam in Black America: Identity, Liberation, and Difference in African American Islamic Thought* (New York: State University of New York Press, 2002), 72–74.
22   Essien-Udom, *Black Nationalism*, 133.
23   Malcolm X and Alex Haley, *The Autobiography of Malcolm X* (New York: Ballantine Books, 1999), 2, 10, 38; Manning Marable, *Malcolm X: A Life of Reinvention* (New York: Penguin Books, 2011), 35.
24   Malcolm X, *Autobiography*, 161–163, 296; Marable, *Malcolm X*, 36, 38, 397.

the circumstances surrounding his eventual split from the NOI. Finally, the author will describe the killing of the son (Malcolm X) and the subsequent guilt motivated response of many. Ultimately, this format will show that the belated praise Malcolm X received after his death stems from the guilt many had for not supporting him while he was alive.

4   Freudian Theory

Freud traces religion to a feeling of guilt, and the consequent deification of the father and prohibition against incest, based on a primal killing of the father and desire to have sex with the mother. The connection between religion and guilt in Freud's view comes from his observation that obsessive actions resemble religious life. One who is under compulsion is similar to one under prohibitions in that they both behave like someone who is dominated by a consciousness of guilt.[25] For example, ceremonies exaggerate orderly procedure and produce guilt if they are not performed. Freud states, "neurotic ceremonies consist in making small adjustments to particular everyday actions, small additions or restrictions or arrangements, which have always to be carried out in the same, or in a methodically varied, manner."[26] Thus, for him, religion is an "obsessional neurosis" based on the sense of guilt.[27] As support for these claims, Freud used data gathered from religious life of Aboriginals in Australia.

Totemism among the native Australians reflects religion in its most basic form and shows its origins with the deification of a murdered father. As both a religious and a social system, Totemism refers to the reverence given to a totem by a group of people who consider themselves to be of one blood and descendants of a common ancestor. Moreover, these people are bound together by common obligations and a common faith in the totem.[28]

A central component of totemism is the taboo prohibitions. The term "taboo" can be defined in two divergent ways: sacred/consecrated and unclean/ forbidden. Going further, according to Freud, taboo is a prohibition against something that people are strongly inclined to do in their unconscious mind. This is an important insight for Freud's model because if one can locate the

---

25 Sigmund Freud, "Obsessive Actions and Religious Practices," in *The Freud Reader*, ed. Peter Gay (New York: W.W. Norton and Company, 1995), 429, 433.
26 Ibid., 430.
27 Sigmund Freud, *Totem and Taboo* (New York: W.W. Norton & Company, 1950), 146; Freud, *Obsessive Actions and Religious Practices*, 435.
28 Freud, *Totem and Taboo*, 2, 103–104.

earliest taboos one could discover the origins of religion. According to Freud, the most ancient taboos are the totemic prohibition from killing the totem animal and having sexual intercourse with a member of the totem clan.[29] The presence of these two urges can be seen even in the Greek mythological story about Oedipus. Oedipus' father, Laius, learned from a dream that his son would kill him and so he tried to kill Oedipus by abandoning him on a mountain. However, Oedipus was rescued, and when he got older, he was warned that one day he would kill his father and marry his mother. Even with this warning, Oedipus unknowingly killed his father in an argument. Furthermore, he also married his mother, his father's widow. When a seer revealed Oedipus's identity, thus realizing she was sleeping with her son, his mother committed suicide and Oedipus blinded himself (substitution for castration; see below).[30] Mythology like this, according to Freud, ultimately expresses desires that cannot be revealed openly. Thus, this Oedipus story supports Freud's contention that there is a drive in male children to kill their father and have sex with their mother. These twin urges led to the two taboos mentioned above. For the purposes of this essay it is important to look more closely at these prohibitions.

The prohibition against killing the totem animal reflects the unique identity of the totem. Freud argues that the taboo against killing and eating the totem animal constitutes the nucleus of Totemism. Pointing to the research of Robertson Smith, Freud focuses on the relevance of festivals in Totemism. These celebrations allow people to do things that are usually prohibited apart from the events. One example of this Freud highlights is the centrality of the sacrificial meal. When the meal is consumed, it is thought that the participants partake of the life of the sacrificial animal. What is unique about this practice is that the sacrificial animal was the totem animal.[31] For the indigenous Australians, the totem animal was seen as a common ancestor to the whole clan; it is their guardian spirit and helper. This common ancestor represented by the totem animal is the murdered father of the clan. The father is said to have been killed by his sons, and the totem meal is a repetition of that killing. Freud argues that the guilt for killing their father reflects the ambivalence of their feelings for him and is the basis for the first attempt at religion: Totemism. In this way, Totemism was a covenant with their father in which he promised them protection and care while they would refrain from killing the totem animal (symbolically represented in the totem) like they killed their father. Thus,

---

29 Ibid., 18, 32, 144.
30 The Free Library. S.v. "Oedipus." Retrieved Jul 05, 2021. from https://www.thefreelibrary.com/Oedipus.-a018424210.
31 Freud, *Totem and Taboo*, 23, 136–7, 140.

the totem animal represented a surrogate father and the primitive god himself.[32] Or, as Freud contends, "God is nothing other than an exalted father."[33]

This notion of an "exalted father" is also connected to Freud's conception of a "great man." According to Freud, the vast majority of people have a need for an authority figure they can admire, submit to, and who dominates them. Great men typically come and fulfill this need amongst people. Freud saw Moses as an example of a great man. The correlation between the totem animal and the great man is the fact that Freud identifies the origin of them both as stemming from a longing for the father that is in humans from the time of their childhood.[34] In other words, humans will fulfill their longing for their father with a substitute that could take the form of a god (totem animal) or a man (great man).

The taboo against incest points back to the exclusive sexual rights of the primal father over his community. After the strong father was dead, the brothers had to find a peaceful solution to the question: who would gain access to the dead father's sexual partners now? They did this by forbidding sexual desires for their mother first, and eventually requiring members of the community to marry and have sex with people outside their community.[35]

Freud argued that this phenomenon traces back to the earliest humans. Based on the scholarship of Charles Darwin, Freud claims that the habits of the higher apes indicated that men also lived in hordes within which the male leader had as many wives as he could support. He jealously prevented other males' access to those women in his horde. Lack of access to the women established exogamy. Being driven out, the males would establish their own similar hordes and would have the same prohibition from sex with their women and would guard it jealously. Freud argues that one way this prohibition was enforced was through the threat of castration (or blinding, as its substitute mentioned in the Oedipus myth articulated above). As time went on this would eventually produce a conscious law against sex with those in one's own home. Upon the arrival of Totemism, the prohibition would be against sex within the totem group.[36] What becomes obvious then is that the totemic (and thus, religious) prohibitions surrounding sexual intercourse and marriage

---

32 Ibid., 2, 138, 141–142, 144, 149.
33 Ibid., 147.
34 Sigmund Freud, *Moses and Monotheism*, trans. Katherine Jones (New York: Vintage Books, 1967), 139–140.
35 Freud, *Totem and Taboo*, 4–6, 143.
36 Ibid., 125–126, 130.

derive from a jealous male leader fighting for exclusive access to the women in his community.

As seen above, Freud provides a useful model for analyzing the relationship between Elijah Muhammad and Malcolm X, as well as the rise of the religion of Black Power. It was argued that religion, according to Freud, is based on a deep-seated feeling of guilt. Going further, an analysis of Totemism reveals that the earliest form of religion was based on a murdered father who was subsequently deified out of the ambivalent feelings of his sons towards their father. Readers were also introduced to the Freudian notion that religious prohibitions around sex are meant to eliminate all rivals of the leader for sexual access to the women of the community. This theory will now be applied to the relationship between Elijah Muhammad and Malcolm X and the rise of the religion of Black Power.

5   Muhammad, Malcolm X, and their Reverse Oedipus Relationship

Although Elijah Muhammad and Malcolm X's relationship began with a loving father/son dynamic, it ended with the father killing the son, a reverse of the Oedipus myth. Clegg, Muhammad's biographer, agrees when he asserts that the relationship between the two men could be described as mentor and protégé, a father and son. Having lost his father at an early age, Malcolm and many others "engaged a paternal dimension of Muhammad's personality."[37] However, Clegg continues, this relationship was not a unidirectional one, but rather went both ways. At times Malcolm advised Muhammad, thus reversing the stereotypical relations between father and son. For example, in 1959, Malcolm counseled Muhammad to learn Arabic before he took his trip to the Middle East and North Africa. The next year Muhammad renamed the NOI temples to mosques and instituted Arabic instruction.[38] In this way, anticipations of the reverse Oedipus relationship (father acting like the son, and the son acting as the father) between the two men were present before Malcolm's death.

Beginning after his release from prison, the interactions between Malcolm X and Elijah Muhammad became regular and familial in nature. Clegg states that Muhammad favored Malcolm above all his other ministers and publicly designated him as the NOI's spokesman.[39] Similarly, Malcolm believed in the

---

37 Clegg, *Malcolm X and Elijah Muhammad*, 11.
38 Marable and Felber, *The Portable Malcolm X Reader*, 134–135; Clegg, *Malcolm X and Elijah Muhammad*, 11.
39 Clegg, *Malcolm X and Elijah Muhammad*, 15, 17.

divinity of Muhammad. Along with other members of the group, Malcolm believed that the NOI *was* Muhammad.[40] Malcolm thought so highly of Muhammad that he honored him by naming his third daughter "Ilyasah," a "feminized Arabic version of Elijah."[41] Thus, at this point Muhammad loved his (spiritual) son, and Malcolm loved his (spiritual) father.

However, this relationship was marked by ambivalence even at this early stage, with both figures displaying hostility toward the other. There is some indication that Muhammad may have been jealous of the invitations Malcolm was receiving to speak on college campuses. Muhammad even kept Malcolm from speaking at certain places.[42] Therefore, it is apparent that there was both love and hostility directed toward Malcolm by Muhammad.

Malcolm X showed his hostility to Elijah Muhammad while in the NOI through insubordination. There were multiple instances where Malcolm got involved with the Civil Rights Movement which Muhammad had forbidden. Even his famous "chickens coming home to roost" statement was in direct violation of Muhammad's instructions not to comment on the assassination of President John F. Kennedy.[43] Furthermore, Malcolm resented Muhammad's order not to retaliate for the murder of Ronald (X) Stokes, an NOI member who was killed by police in Temple No. 27 in Los Angeles.[44] These examples show that although Malcolm revered Muhammad, he still harbored some internal hostility toward him.

By contrast, the leaders of the much larger Civil Rights Movement were generally hostile toward Malcolm X, even though some would gradually embrace him. The urban working poor, unemployed youth hustlers, and "street" people were under-represented in the Civil Rights Movement. In the early 1960s, Elijah Muhammad started to allow Malcolm to participate in debates with significant figures in the Civil Rights Movement. Malcolm often described the mainstream leaders as "sell-outs" and "Uncle Toms."[45]

---

40   Malcolm X, *Malcolm X Speaks: Selected Speeches and Statements*, ed. George Breitman (New York: Merit Publishers, 1965), 177; Malcolm X, *Autobiography*, 294.
41   Clegg, *Malcolm X and Elijah Muhammad*, 18.
42   Malcolm X, *Autobiography*, 290–296; Les Payne and Tamara Payne, *The Dead Are Arising: The Life of Malcolm X* (New York: Liveright Publishing Corporation, 2020), 274.
43   Malcolm X, *Autobiography*, 307–308; Clayborne Carson, *Malcolm X: The FBI File*, ed. David Gallen (New York: Carroll and Graf Publishers), 245–246; Marable, *Malcolm X: A Life of Reinvention*, 215–217, 269, 274.
44   Payne, *The Dead are Arising*, 427.
45   William Sales, *From Civil Rights to Black Liberation: Malcolm X and the Organization of Afro-American Unity* (Boston: South End Press, 1994), 74; Marable, *Portable Malcolm X*, 184; Robin D.G. Kelley, "House Negroes on the Loose: Malcolm X and the Black Bourgeoisie," *Callaloo* 21, no. 2 (Spring 1998), 430.

When Malcolm X eventually attempted to reach out to these leaders, they largely ignored him. In August of 1963, he wrote to Martin Luther King Jr. and other Civil Rights leaders inviting them to attend a rally in Harlem. However, similar to the others, King avoided the multiple attempts to connect with Malcolm. Peter Goldman explains that as much as Malcolm wanted to connect with the mainstream Civil Rights leadership, Malcolm's militancy, his negative public image, and other fundamental disagreements kept them separate.[46] Even prominent Black organizations such as the National Association for the Advancement of Colored People (NAACP) denounced the NOI by saying they preached hatred.[47]

Beyond ignoring and denouncing him, on other occasions leaders tried to restrict his speaking opportunities and influence. In 1961, when Malcolm was invited to speak by the students at Howard University, as mentioned above, the event was changed to a debate because leaders did not want Malcolm to give an unchallenged lecture. This rejection was mirrored by Black Christian leaders who did not want Malcolm to be a part of a set of meetings meant for Black leaders.[48] Furthermore, when leaders of the Southern Christian Leadership Council (SCLC) realized Malcolm would be speaking in Selma, Alabama, they took numerous precautions, including trying to encourage him not to incite the audience and having Coretta Scott King speak after him to undue any critiques of nonviolence.[49] Thus, Malcolm continually found himself ostracized from the mainstream movement and was viewed as a leader that no one wanted to be affiliated with.

Nevertheless, just like there were ambivalent feelings between Elijah Muhammad and Malcolm X, there was a similar dynamic within the mainstream Civil Rights Movement, precisely because some began to accept

---

46 Carson, *FBI File*, 34; Lewis V. Baldwin, "Malcolm and Martin Luther King Jr.: What They Thought About Each Other" in *Islamic Studies* 25, no. 4 (Winter 1986), 395; Peniel Joseph, *The Sword and the Shield: The Revolutionary Lives of Malcolm X and Martin Luther King Jr.* (New York: Basic Books, 2020), 155; Peter Goldman, *The Death and Life of Malcolm X* (Chicago: University of Illinois Press, 1979), 229; George Breitman, *The Last Year of Malcolm X: The Evolution of a Revolutionary* (New York: Pathfinder, 1967), 76.
47 Baldwin, *Malcolm and Martin Luther King Jr.*, 396; Kelley, *House Negroes*, 429.
48 Bayrand Rustin, "Reminiscences of Bayard Rustin: Oral History, 1987, Columbia University Oral History Research Office, 217–219" in *Portable Malcolm X*, ed. Manning Marable, 190; Marable, *Portable Malcolm X*, 184–185.
49 Alvin Adams, "Malcolm X Seemed Sincere About Helping Cause: Mrs. King," *Jet* 27, no. 22 (March 11, 1965): 28–30; Coretta Scott King, "Interview with Coretta Scott King, Conducted by Blackside, Inc. on December 20, 1985," for *Eyes on the Prize: America's Civil Rights Years (1954–1965)*. Washington University Libraries, Film and Media Archive, Henry Hampton Collection, 25.

Malcolm's more militant vision for change over Dr. King's Christian nonviolence. Goldman explains that SNCC was initially put off by Malcolm's image until the extremely violent summer of 1964 that included numerous beatings, bombings, arrests, and harassment. After such beatings, students became more willing to look towards Malcolm. Whitney Young was even willing to meet with Malcolm one Saturday off-the-record.[50] Also, the FBI was able to find evidence that Malcolm had possibly established a connection with King for collaboration.[51] These examples show that while Malcolm was largely rejected by the mainstream movement, ambivalent feelings are displayed on some occasions.

5.1 *The Son Castrates the Father*

When Malcolm X (the son) finds out the father (Elijah Muhammad) was utilizing his sexual access to the females in the NOI (the horde) while forbidding this access to the other males, he eventually exposed (castrated) him to eliminate this sexual access. Malcolm explained that members of the NOI saw themselves as moral examples for other Black Americans due to their numerous taboos[52] against things like lying, gambling, smoking, fornication and adultery. Muhammad (the father) would personally mete out sentences, such as isolation and expulsion, as punishment for those infractions. One of Malcolm's own brothers was even expelled from the NOI for having sex with a female member of the NOI (horde).[53]

Yet, Malcolm had heard numerous rumors out of Chicago since 1955 about the extramarital affairs Muhammad had with his secretaries but did not find those accusations convincing. However, after a religious event in 1963, Malcolm consulted with one of the sons of Muhammad, Warith Deen Muhammad, and three of Muhammad's former secretaries and they all confirmed that the rumors were true and that some of the secretaries had become pregnant and were sentenced to isolation, receiving little support from Muhammad.[54] Malcolm's initial inclination was to try to prevent further damage in preparation for the possibility that this immorality would be revealed. Thus, as he sought to prepare other ministers with this news before they heard it from anyone else, it was told to Muhammad that Malcolm was aiming to tarnish his

---

50 Goldman, *The Death and Life of Malcolm X*, 228–230.
51 Karl Evanzz, *The Judas Factor: The Plot to Kill Malcolm X* (New York: Thunder's Mouth Press, 1992), 229.
52 Malcolm did not use this terminology here. My use of it here conforms to the notion of prohibition.
53 Malcolm X, *Autobiography*, 294–5; Marable, *Malcolm X*, 92–93.
54 Payne, *The Dead are Arising*, 278; Marable, *Malcolm X*, 233.

name and character. Muhammad was able to use Malcolm's defiant comment on JFK's assassination to indefinitely suspend him from public speaking. As time went on and Malcolm realized he would not be reinstated, he formally left the NOI, publicly announcing such on March 8th, 1964.[55]

Having been pushed out of the NOI (horde), Malcolm (the son) castrates Muhammad (the father) by exposing his sexual infidelities. In June of 1964, Malcolm announced detailed information about Muhammad's sexual misconduct. One of the women Muhammad impregnated, Evelyn Williams, was supposed to have been Malcolm's ex-fiancé. Despite having been threatened with death for exposing Muhammad, Williams and another woman filed paternity suits against him.[56] It is important to emphasize that Muhammad (the father) had sexual intercourse with one of Malcolm's (the son's) former love interest. This encroachment on Malcolm's (the son's) former sexual interest likely played a role in his castration of Muhammad (the father).

6   The Killing of the Son

The castrated Muhammad (father) conspired with his other "sons" to have (his son) Malcolm X killed. While there is considerable evidence that the government instigated and created the atmosphere for Malcolm to be successfully killed, members of the NOI are the ones who murdered him.[57] Many in the group wanted him dead and numerous attempts were made on his life. Elijah Muhammad Jr., the leader's son, publicly encouraged NOI members to harm Malcolm and applied pressure on some to kill him. Followers of Muhammad were told how well the person who killed Malcolm would be cared for.[58] Members of Temple Number Seven, under the direction of Captain Joseph, threw Molotov Cocktails through the windows of Malcolm's home on February 14, 1965, catching it on fire and forcing Malcolm and his family to evacuate their home in the middle of the night.[59] The NOI members attempting to murder Malcolm, however, were working under the direct orders of Muhammad

---

55   Goldman, *The Death and Life of Malcolm X*, 125; Marable, *Malcolm X*, 266, 269, 278–9, 293; Malcolm X, *Two Speeches by Malcolm X* (New York: Pathfinder Press, 1990), 4; Carson, *The FBI File*, 247–8.
56   Marable, *Malcolm X*, 340–1; "Ex-sweetheart of Malcolm X Accuses Elijah: Denies Paternity Charges, *Amsterdam News*, July 11, 1964," in Marable, *Portable Malcolm X*, 355–6.
57   Marable, *Malcolm X*, 231; Payne, *The Dead are Arising*, 467, 481–3, 486–7, 493, 505.
58   Evanzz, *The Judas Factor*, 282; Payne, *The Dead are Arising*, 496, 508–9.
59   Ibid., 458, 465.

(the father). In a deathbed confession, NOI member Jeremiah X confirmed that Muhammad himself gave the order to kill Malcolm.[60] Therefore, on February 21, 1965, while beginning a speech at the Audubon Ballroom in Harlem, Malcolm was shot multiple times by members of the NOI, and subsequently died.[61] However, although Muhammad (the father) was able to have Malcolm (the son) killed, Malcolm (the son) would obtain more importance in death than he had in life.

7 The Deification of the Son

While many were hesitant to embrace Malcolm X in life, their guilt for rejecting him caused them to deify him in death. Michael Eric Dyson states that the life and thought of Malcolm has gained a high level of Black cultural authority since his assassination; many characterize him as a hero and even saint.[62] Goldman argues that Malcolm's death allowed people to claim devotion to him without cost.[63] Going further, he states:

> There are traces of guilt in some of the breast-beating over Malcolm; some of the cult are children who were too young to have known him alive, but some are grownups for whom he was a discomfort in life, like an unhappy memory or an unquiet conscience.[64]

Thus, Goldman gives further support to my contention that the deification of Malcolm X after his death stems from the guilt for not being fully committed to him in life. Joseph interprets this phenomenon as planted seeds finally bearing fruit among Malcolm's listeners. Among young people in the 1960s, Malcolm became the avatar of the Black Power Movement.[65] For example, the "prophet" Carmichael, who popularized the phrase "Black Power," saw Malcolm as a hero that should be followed; he treated Malcolm's words as authoritative.[66] However, while Joseph attributes the late positive responses of some toward

---

60   Ibid., 459, 465.
61   Ibid., 477.
62   Michael Eric Dyson, *Making Malcolm: The Myth and Meaning of Malcolm X* (Oxford: Oxford University Press, 1995), 21, 24.
63   Goldman, *The Death and Life of Malcolm X*, 380.
64   Ibid., 396–397.
65   Peniel Joseph, *Stokely: A Life* (New York: Basic Civitas, 2014), 40, 42.
66   Stokely Carmichael [Kwame Ture], *Stokely Speaks: From Black Power to Pan-Africanism* (Chicago: Lawrence Hill Books, 2007), 178, 198; Stokely Carmichael [Kwame Ture] with

Malcolm to the natural process of growth, I think that Freud's psychoanalytic theory supports Goldman's assertion that this delayed exaltation arises from guilt.

This deification can be most clearly seen in the literary expression of Black Power, the Black Arts Movement (BAM), and from authors who sought to honor Malcolm X after his death.[67] BAM's founder, Leroi Jones (Amiri Baraka), stated that it was Malcolm's death that caused the explosive transformation among Black intellectuals in New York and led to the inauguration of this new development.[68] Carolyn Gerald explains that Malcolm X was the most important hero for BAM and that their work was filled with photographs and drawings of him along with poetry about him.[69] Hinting at the deification of Malcolm, Gerald contends that "Malcolm is the epic hero of our struggle, of our journey toward new consciousness, toward a new nation. His significance, far more than historical, is mythological."[70] Similarly, Audre Lorde defined herself as an inheritor of Malcolm's tradition and asserted that the ghost of Malcolm's voice speaks through her mouth. Moreover, she argued that Malcolm lives in the energy of Black people struggling for justice.[71]

It is BAM poetry, however, that seems to solidify the construction of Malcolm X as a deity. For example, Jones explicitly refers to Malcolm as a "black god" and the "prince of the earth."[72] Similarly, Robert Price called Malcolm the "people's prophet" and a "phoenix aflame." He even referred to the day of Malcolm's death, February 21st, as a holy day.[73] In his Eulogy for Malcolm, Ossie Davis described Malcolm as a "gallant young champion" and "our own shining Prince!—who didn't hesitate to die, because he loved us so."[74] Another example is when Etheridge Knight compared the ability of Malcolm's words to those of the words of God given to Moses on Mount Sinai.[75] Describing Malcolm as

---

Ekwueme Michael Thelwell, *Ready For Revolution: The Life and Struggles of Stokely Carmichael [Kwame Ture]* (New York: Scribner, 2003), 254–255, 464.

67   Joseph, *Toward a Historiography of the Black Power Movement*, 4–5.
68   Amiri Baraka, "The Black Arts Movement," in *SOS – Calling all Black People: A Black Arts Movement Reader*, eds. John Bracey Jr., Sonia Sanchez, and James Smethurst (Amherst: University of Massachusetts Press, 2014), 12–13.
69   Carolyn Gerald, "Symposium: The Measure and Meaning of the Sixties" in Bracey, *SOS*, 49.
70   Ibid.
71   Audre Lorde, "Learning from the 60s" in Bracey, *SOS*, 656, 662.
72   Leroi Jones, "Poem for Black Hearts," in *For Malcolm: Poems on the Life and Death of Malcolm X*, eds. Dudley Randall and Margaret Burroughs (Detroit: Broadside Press, 1969), 62.
73   Robert Price, "Elegy for the Seventh Son," in Randall, *For Malcolm*, 40–41, 43.
74   Ossie Davis, "Eulogy of Malcolm X," in Bracey, *SOS*, 309–310.
75   Etheridge Knight, "Portriat of Malcolm X," in Bracey, *SOS*, 313.

a "cosmic spirit," Quincy Troupe states: "He had been coming a very long time, had been here many times before in the flesh of other persons, in the spirit of other gods."[76] These authors display explicit language deifying Malcolm (black god, cosmic spirit, etc.), implicit language deifying him (prince of the earth, shining Prince), and honorific language (phoenix, champion, etc.) praising Malcolm. These attributions of deity ascribed to Malcolm all came subsequent to his death, just as the father is deified after his death in the Oedipus myth.

8 Conclusion

This essay has set forth the argument that a reversal of the roles in Freud's Oedipus theory in the lives of Elijah Muhammad and Malcolm X suggests that young African Americans of the late 1960s deified Malcolm out of guilt for not wholly embracing him when he was alive. I began with the notion that religion is based on a feeling of guilt and that this guilt derives from the successful killing of the primal father. Moreover, humans sometimes satisfy their longing for their father by replacing him with great men as a substitute. It was also argued that religion was used to guard the exclusive sexual right of the father over the females in his horde. These claims provided a lens to interpret the relationship of Elijah Muhammad and Malcolm X and the latter's postmortem deification in the religion of Black Power.

It is clear that the early association between Elijah Muhammad and Malcolm X was one that could be described as resembling a father/son relationship. However, rather than the son being castrated, the father was castrated in this historical scenario: When Malcolm became aware that the taboo against sex in the NOI is only meant to protect Muhammad's access to NOI women, he castrated him by exposing his immorality. Further, in this relationship, the son is killed rather than the father: When Malcolm castrates Muhammad, Muhammad responds by giving the order to have him killed. Finally, in this context after his death, the son, rather than the father, is deified: Following his assassination, many people felt more comfortable associating themselves with Malcolm and his teachings. Moreover, many people both literally and symbolically used deifying language to refer to Malcolm X after his assassination.

This research provides an explanation for the origin of the Black Power Movement as a religion. As discussed above, Malcolm was viewed as establishing the theoretical foundation of the Black Power Movement and its main

---

76 Quincy Troupe, "For Malcolm Who Walks in the Eyes of Our Children" in Bracey, *SOS*, 319.

figure of inspiration. This current paper lends support for the suggestion that the Black Power Movement could be viewed as a religion and Malcolm X as its deity. Just as Freud argued, that the murdered father became the deity of the totemic religion, Malcolm became the deity of the Black Power Movement. Thus, the Black Power Movement could be conceived as a religion, a religion based on the guilt for not supporting its murdered deity while he was still living.

Bibliography

Adams, Alvin. "Malcolm X Seemed Sincere About Helping Cause: Mrs. King." *Jet* 27, no. 22. ((March 11, 1965)).

Baldwin, Lewis V. "Malcolm X and Martin Luther King Jr.: What They Thought About Each Other." In *Islamic Studies* 25, no. 4 (Winter, 1986): 395–416.

John, Bracey Jr., Sonia Sanchez, and James Smethurst, eds. *SOS – Calling all Black People: A Black Arts Movement Reader*. Amherst: University of Massachusetts Press, 2014.

Breitman, George. *The Last Year of Malcolm X: The Evolution of a Revolutionary*. New York: Pathfinder, 1967.

Bukhari, Sahih al-. *The Translation of the Meanings of Sahih Al-Bukhari: Vol.1*. Translated by Muhammad Muhsin Khan. Riyadh-Saudi Arabia: Darussalam Publishers, 1997.

Carmichael, Stokely. "Interview with Stokely Carmichael, Interviewed by Judy Richardson on November 7, 1988." In *Eyes on the Prize II Interviews*. Washington University Digital Gateway Texts. digital.wustl.edu/e/eii/eiiweb/car5427.0967.029stokelycarmichael.html.

Carmichael, Stokely [Kwame Ture], with Ekwueme Michael Thelwell. *Ready for Revolution: The Life and Struggles of Stokely Carmichael [Kwame Ture]*. New York: Scribner, 2003.

Carmichael, Stokely [Kwame Ture]. *Stokely Speaks: From Black Power to Pan-Africanism*. Chicago: Lawrence Hill Books, 2007.

Carson, Clayborne. *Malcolm X: The FBI File*, edited by David Gallen. New York: Carrol and Graf Publishers Inc., 1991.

Cone, James. *Black Theology and Black Power*. New York: Orbis Books, 2011.

Conyers, James L. and Andrew P. Smallwood. eds. *Malcolm X: A Historical Reader*. North Carolina: Carolina Academic Press, 2008.

Curtis IV, Edward E. *Islam in Black America: Identity, Liberation, and Difference in African American Islamic Thought*. New York: State University of New York Press, 2002.

Dyson, Michael Eric. *Making Malcolm: The Myth and Meaning of Malcolm X*. Oxford: Oxford University Press, 1995.

Essien-Udom, E.U. *Black Nationalism: The Rise of the Black Muslims in the U.S.A.* Great Britain: Pelican Books, 1966.

Evanzz, Karl. *The Judas Factor: The Plot to Kill Malcolm X.* New York: Thunder's Mouth Press, 1992.

Freud, Sigmund. *Moses and Monotheism*, Translated by Katherine Jones. New York: Vintage Books, 1967.

Freud, Sigmund. *Totem and Taboo.* New York: W.W. Norton & Company, 1950.

Gay, Peter., ed. *The Freud Reader.* New York: W.W. Norton and Company, 1995.

Goldman, Peter. *The Death and Life of Malcolm X.* Chicago: University of Illinois Press, 1979.

Johnson, Terrence. *We Testify with Our Lives: How Religion Transformed Radical Thought from Black Power to Black Lives Matter.* New York: Columbia University Press, 2021.

Joseph, Peniel, ed. *Neighborhood Rebels: Black Power at the Local Level.* New York: Palgrave Macmillan, 2010.

Joseph, Peniel. *Stokely: A Life.* New York: Basic Civitas, 2014.

Joseph, Peniel, ed. *The Black Power Movement: Rethinking the Civil Rights—Black Power Era.* New York: Routledge, 2006.

Joseph, Peniel. *The Sword and the Shield: The Revolutionary Lives of Malcolm X and Martin Luther King Jr.* New York: Basic Books, 2020.

Kelley, Robin D.G. "House Negroes on the Loose: Malcolm X and the Black Bourgeoisie." In *Callaloo* 21, no. 2 (Spring 1998): 419–435.

King, Coretta Scott. "Interview with Coretta Scott King, Conducted by Blackside, Inc. on December 20, 1985." In *Eyes on the Prize: America's Civil Rights Years (1954–1965).* Washington University Libraries, Film and Media Archive, Henry Hampton Collection. Retrieved from: http://digital.wustl.edu/cgi/t/text/text-idx?c=eop;cc=eop;rgn=main;view=text;idno=kin0015.0223.057.

Malcolm X. *Malcolm X Speaks: Selected Speeches and Statements*, edited by George Breitman. New York: Merit Publishers: NY, 1965.

Malcolm X and Alex Haley. *The Autobiography of Malcolm X.* New York: Ballantine Books, 1999.

Malcolm X. *Two Speeches by Malcolm X.* New York: Pathfinder Press, 1990.

Marable, Manning, and Garrett Felber. *The Portable Malcolm X Reader.* New York: Penguin Books, 2013.

Marable, Manning. *Malcolm X: A Life of Reinvention.* New York: Penguin Books, 2011.

Muhammad, Zayid, "Malcolm X and His Impact SNCC." Retrieved from facebook.com/mxcc519/videos/2765673517086613/.

Payne, Les, and Tamara Payne. *The Dead Are Arising: The Life of Malcolm X.* New York: Liveright Publishing Corporation, 2020.

Randall, Dudley, and Margaret Burroughs, eds. *For Malcolm: Poems on the Life and Death of Malcolm X.* Detroit: Broadside Press, 1969.

Sales, William. *From Civil Rights to Black Liberation: Malcolm X and the Organization of Afro-American Unity*. Boston: South End Press, 1994.

Terrill, Robert E., ed. *The Cambridge Companion to Malcolm X*. New York: Cambridge University Press, 2010.

The Free Library. S.v. "Oedipus." Retrieved Jul 05, 2021, from https://www.thefreelibrary.com/Oedipus.-a018424210.

PART 4

Freud and the Political

∴

CHAPTER 7

Freud's Mass Psychology Today: Psychoanalysis, Politics, and Populism in the Age of Post-truth

Yannis Stavrakakis

1   Introduction[1]

2021 marks one century from the first publication of *Mass Psychology and the Analysis of the Ego* by Sigmund Freud.[2] What has been the importance of this text for social and political inquiry diachronically? What is its relevance today? It is to these two questions I will be devoting this text. In particular, I will be developing three main arguments: one related to the first question and two more pertaining to the second: First, this text signifies an explicit passage from the clinic, narrowly viewed, to the broader psychosocial domain where subjectivity and sociality are seen as thoroughly interpenetrating each other. It thus triggers a long theoretico-political trajectory (encompassing the so-called Freudian Left – and, by extension, the Lacanian Left as well), which has especially benefited critical inquiry and the left. Second, this is particularly evident in contemporary theorizations of populism, notably in the one advanced by Ernesto Laclau, which is premised on a close reading of Freud's aforementioned text. Third, a similar angle (both the psychoanalytic perspective and the link with populism research) could also illuminate another crucial issue that currently dominates the public terrain, that of "post-truth." Let me discuss in some more detail these three claims one by one.

2   Freud, Psychoanalysis and the Emergence of Psychoanalytic Political Theory

Arguably this text represents Freud's gradual shift of interest towards a sustained analysis of social and political phenomena. Significantly, the latter are

---

1   Sigmund Freud, *Group Psychology and the Analysis of the Ego* (London: The Hogarth Press and the Institute of Psycho-Analysis, 1949).
2   First published as Yannis Stavrakakis, "Freud's Mass Psychology Today: Psychoanalysis, Politics and Populism in the Age of Post-Truth," *Psychoanalytische Perspectieven* 39, no. 3 (2021): 555–576. Reprinted with permission.

not seen as external to the psychical apparatus – and vice-versa. We have, perhaps, an instance of what Lacan will later call *extimité*. At any rate, as Freud observes already in the opening sentence of the text, 'the contrast between Individual psychology and Social or Group psychology, which at a first glance may seem to be full of significance, loses a great deal of its sharpness when it is examined more closely.[3] And then he adds:

> only rarely and under certain exceptional conditions is Individual Psychology in a position to disregard the relations of this individual to others. In the individual's mental life someone else is invariably involved, as a model, as an object, as a helper, as an opponent, and so from the very first Individual Psychology is at the same time Social Psychology as well – in this extended but entirely justifiable sense of the words.[4]

Many years later, someone greatly influenced by Freud, sociologist Norbert Elias, will put it like that: categories like 'individual' and 'society' do not refer to *a priori* different objects "existing separately," but rather to "different yet inseparable" sides of the same object.[5] It is here we should, perhaps, locate the implicit origins of psychosocial studies, which will flourish from the 1990s onwards.

Well before that, Freudian metapsychology will start to impact considerably on socio-political theorization leading to the formation of an intellectual wave to which Paul Robinson will apply the name: "Freudian Left."[6] The category "left" here indicates both a progressive political orientation as well as a clear focus on the critical impetus of theoretical work. But why the left? Arguably, both the political and the intellectual left had to benefit significantly from the confluence at stake: they had previously endorsed a rather simplistic understanding of subjectivity and agency akin to the rationalism that will lead to the formation of "rational choice" theories with their mainstream economism. Especially after World War I it turned out that such a simplistic account could neither capture the complexity of human behavior nor effectively guide political strategy (last but not least, it could only facilitate rather poor critical scholarship).

---

3   Ibid., 1.
4   Ibid., 1–2.
5   Norbert Elias, "Appendix I: Introduction to the 1968 edition," in *The Civilizing Process, vol. I: The History of Manners* (Oxford: Blackwell, 1983): 228–229.
6   Paul A. Robinson, *The Freudian Left* (New York: Harper and Row, 1967).

These limitations were amply revealed by the frustration of internationalist expectations during the War and beyond. Indeed, whether in 1914 or 1933, 'socialist consciousness [...] had been consistently undermined by the proletariat's sense of national belonging.'[7] As Eric Hobsbawm later argued, in most cases, class consciousness was trumped by national affiliation when the two came into a conflictual relation.[8] In other words,

> class identity, in the sense of an objective sense of classness, did not prevent other forms of identity emerging within any particular working class, especially not national identity; and objective class consciousness, far from guaranteeing the rise of a socialist consciousness, most often succumbed to other forms of identity when they came into conflict.[9]

No doubt, the conditions of possibility for the formation and the sticking of "class consciousness" as an object of (political) identification had been grossly overestimated and parallel (largely) unconscious operations obstructing this result had been underestimated. For example, with few notable exceptions, 'according to one commentator [Anderson], Marxists have not just got nationalism wrong, they have systematically evaded it.'[10] No wonder that the 'serious underestimation of the power of nationalism' is very often seen as one of the major limitations of Marxism.[11] Although one should not neglect the significant efforts by Lenin and Stalin, Otto Bauer and others – even by French *fin de siècle* Marxism – to come to terms with the challenge of national identification one way or the other, the fact remains that:

> The workers of the world have not united into the universal "genre humain" promised by the *Internationale*. The nineteenth century gave way, not to the radiant socialist world order anticipated by Marx, but to a 'world of nations' imperiously commanded by nationalists, and sometimes brutally ruled by national socialists.[12]

---

7   Wade Matthews, "Class, Nation, and Capitalist Globalization: Eric Hobsbawm and the National Question," *International Review of Social History* 53, no. 1 (2008): 85–86.
8   Ibid., 85.
9   Ibid., 84.
10 Ibid., 98.
11 Leslie Holmes, *Communism: A Very Short Introduction* (Oxford: Oxford University Press, 2009), 138.
12 Robert Stuart, *Marxism and National Identity* (Albany: SUNY Press, 2006), 1.

It is within such a context that major left-wing theorists and philosophers will turn to psychoanalysis. Thus, when Theodor Adorno and his collaborators plan their major study of the so-called "authoritarian personality" to explain the popular endorsement of political projects like the one put forward by the Nazis, it is to Freud they will turn: 'What are the forces of personality and what are the processes by which they are organized? For theory as to the structure of personality we have leaned most heavily upon Freud.'[13]

On the one hand, *contra* economic reductionism (left and right), economic interest cannot possibly be the sole or even the *a priori* main determinant at play in such psychosocial and political processes: 'economic motives in the individual may not have the dominant and crucial role that is often ascribed to them.'[14] On the other, it may even be the case that rationality itself is not enough to resolve the issue:

> it is becoming increasingly plain that people very frequently do not behave in such a way as to further their material interests, even when it is clear to them what these interests are. The resistance of white-collar workers to organization is not due to a belief that the union will not help them economically; the tendency of the small businessman to side with big business in most economic and political matters cannot be due entirely to a belief that this is the way to guarantee his economic independence. In instances such as these [one could certainly add the choice of "the working class" and many of its organizations to mobilize and go to war during WWI instead of sticking to prior internationalist or cosmopolitan declarations and conscious commitments] the individual seems not only not to consider his material interests, but even to go against them. [...] Indeed, it is with a sense of relief today that one is assured that a group conflict is merely a clash of economic interests – that each side is merely out to "do" the other and not a struggle in which deep-lying emotional drives have been let loose. When it comes to the ways in which people appraise the social world, irrational trends stand out glaringly.[15]

And where can we find the key to unlock such "irrationalities"? How can we introduce some partial order into the chaos? Here is where Freud and

---

13   Adorno, Theodor W., Frenkel-Brunswik, E., Levinson, D. & Sanford, R. N. *The Authoritarian Personality* (New York: Harper and Brothers, 1950), 5.
14   Ibid., 8. Alternatively, one could argue that psychical (libidinal, for example) economies are equally potent with economy traditionally viewed.
15   Ibid.

unconscious processes become relevant: 'rather we should seek where psychology has already found the sources of dreams, fantasies, and misinterpretations of the world – that is, in the deep-lying needs of the personality.'[16] It is debatable whether Adorno fully realizes that, but what also seems to emerge here is death drive at its purest: a repetitive impetus to experience again and again an originary traumatic and constitutive loss.[17] At any rate, another drive, the one to register and systematically account for such processes, has facilitated the slow emergence of *psychoanalytic political theory* in its many forms.[18] Indeed, although the ensuing psychoanalytic political terrain shares with Marxism certain sensibilities, 'it represents a genuine alternative that has the virtue of explaining the latter's failures.'[19]

It is not only subjective choices, desires and behavior which are thus illuminated; it is also collective subjectivity and group formation – in addition, what is greatly illuminated together with them is the ground zero of an axial dimension of political inquiry as well as political strategy: agency and collective action in its broader sense. What is thus gradually sidelined, with relation to the left, is (a) on a first level: the simplistic idea that, within a symbolically and libidinally sedimented world of nation-states (often manipulating enjoyment through the staging of phantasmatic nostalgia and the paranoiac production of a "symptomatic" enemy),[20] nationalist identifications will be miraculously abandoned in favor of a rationalistic, internationalist class consciousness; and (b) on a second level: the underlying – and similarly idealist – intuition that workers are bound to, more or less, automatically develop a salient realization of their (objective) class consciousness. Indeed, they were also supposed to develop a passionate (unmediated) attachment to it and collectively act on the basis of automatically and rationally identifying with their true, objective interests as captured by the superior jargon of political economy and revealed

---

16   Ibid., 9.
17   What if masochism functions here as one of the paradigmatic forms of subjectivity within the social bond? See Todd McGowan, *Enjoying What We Don't Have: The Political Project of Psychoanalysis* (Lincoln: University of Nebraska Press, 2013), 13–14.
18   Yannis Stavrakakis, "On Laclau's Alleged Monism." *POPULISMUS working papers* 11 (2020) http://www.populismus.gr/wp-content/uploads/2020/11/Stavrakakis-monism-wp111.pdf.
19   McGowan, *Enjoying What We Don't Have*, 1.
20   Slavoj Žižek, *Tarrying with the Negative* (Durham: Duke University Press, 1993); Yannis Stavrakakis and Nikos Chrysoloras, "'(I Can't Get No) Enjoyment: Lacanian Theory and the Analysis of Nationalism," *Psychoanalysis, Culture & Society* 11, no. 2 (August 2006): 144–163; McGowen, *Enjoying What We Don't Have*, 39–49; Amanda Machin, "Nationalism," in *The Routledge Handbook of Psychoanalytic Political Theory*, ed. Yannis Stavrakakis (New York: Routledge, 2020): 285–295.

by a superior (party) avant-garde. Fortunately, on the ground, where such elitist and rationalistic operations were met with rather limited success, antagonism was often embraced in a way accepting contingency and the political and gradually giving the attention they deserve to libidinal dynamics and negativity. This operation progressed through the increasing relevance of "hegemony."[21] At the same time, strategy followed a *de facto* impure, "populist" course, prioritizing articulations between different struggles – and thus registering the inherent limitations of all of them taken individually – and addressing plebeian sectors in a language they not only understood but were also willing to identify with because they recognized in its texture a negotiation of their own challenges, frustrations and demands.

3   Freud, Lacan and Laclau: What Populism?

This alternative (pragmatic) populist logic acquires importance already from Marx's final years. Indeed, today, we have numerous elaborate accounts of the engagement of Marx himself with the (Russian) populists, which needs to be thoroughly highlighted.[22] In the words of Marcello Musto, one of the contemporary biographers of late Marx:

> Marx [...] highly regarded the down-to-earth character of the political activity of Russian populism – which at the time was a left-wing, anti-capitalist movement – particularly because it did not resort to senseless ultrarevolutionary flourishes or to counterproductive generalizations. Marx assessed the relevance of the socialist organizations existing in Russia by their pragmatic character, not by declaration of loyalty to his own theories. In fact, he observed that it was often those who claimed to be 'Marxists' who were the most doctrinaire. His exposure to the theories and the political activity of Russian Populists – as with the Paris Communards a decade earlier – helped him to be more flexible in

---

21   Ernesto Laclau and Chantal Mouffe, *Towards a Radical Democratic Politics* (New York: Verso, 1985), chapters 1 & 2.
22   Teodor Shanin, ed. *Late Marx and the Russian Road: Marx and "the Peripheries of Capitalism"* (New York: Monthly Review Press, 1983); Ettore Cinnella, *L'altro Marx* (Roma: Della Porta, Editori, 2019).

analyzing the irruption of revolutionary events and the subjective forces that shaped them.[23]

Even before that, a certain "populist" logic had influenced the emergence of important popular movements like the Chartists in the UK during the first half of the 19th century. In fact, the Chartists, a nation-wide mass movement demanding universal suffrage and other democratic rights (comprising the so-called Charter) for working and plebeian sectors, have been often misrepresented on the basis of an ultimately reductionist, retroactive socio-economic (often "class") determination. What was thus lost was the proto-populist character of the movement. Such retroactive re-significations are reproduced today when the *de facto* populist strategy embraced by figures like, for example, Bernie Sanders (his hegemonic intervention involving a critical mass related to prior movements like Occupy, his naming of the adversary and his articulation of an alternative collective subjectivity) is misrecognized and presented as an example of relatively successful class-based politics.[24] The political strategy developed by "Popular Fronts" in the 1930s in many European countries offers another suitable example of the *de facto* populist logic present in the genealogy of the radical tradition in the West within the last two centuries. Commenting on the French experience, David Broder will argue about this *impure* politics: 'The Popular Front wasn't all smiles and sunshine [...] Nonetheless, Blum's policy had major effects [...] This ray of light would long be remembered.'[25]

In that sense, Laclau (and Mouffe) may have been the ones to systematize – in a thoroughly sophisticated manner partly inspired by psychoanalysis – contemporary political struggles and the populist waves and moment(s) marking them, but, clearly, they were not the ones that formulated populist strategy or even initiated its theorization in the first place.[26] Strong opposition to the system and real change cannot ensue automatically from an objective class positionality, but requires political mediation: the creation of alliances ("chains of

---

23 Marcello Musto, "On His Birthday, Let's Celebrate the Old Man Karl Marx," interview given to Nicolas Allen. *Jacobin*, May 5, 2021. https://www.jacobinmag.com/2021/05/birthday-old-man-karl-marx-later-years.

24 Curt Ries, "Our Path Forward After Bernie Must Include Rank-and-File Unionism and Class-Struggle Elections," *Jacobin*, September 8 2020. https://www.jacobinmag.com/2020/08/bernie-sanders-campaign-unions-class-struggle.

25 David Broder "Socialists Invented the Summer Holiday." *Jacobin*, August 7, 2019. https://jacobin.com/2019/08/socialists-invented-summer-vacation-popular-front-france.

26 See, on this particular question, Laclau (2021), a text originally published in French in 1981 on Popular Fronts strategy as debated during the seventh congress of the Comintern in 1935.

equivalence" in Laclau's terminology) between different struggles, sectors and (frustrated, traumatized) subjectivities. Only thus can salient points of identification ("the people" in modern political grammar) emerge out of dispersed multitudes. Often, the ensuing collectivities gain the ability to challenge the *status quo* without reproducing ultra-phantasmatic (and ultimately elitist) patterns of interpellation and identification. At the discursive level, such projects prioritize (1) people-centrism and (2) anti-elitism.[27] Yet, once more, no comprehensive account of populist mobilization(s) can be formulated without reference to psychoanalysis, without reference to the dynamics of the drives and *jouissance*. Why is that and how is Freud's *Mass Psychology* relevant here?

The sophisticated understanding of "populism" put forward by Ernesto Laclau is very much premised on a close reading of Freud's aforementioned text.[28] This becomes evident in his last major work, *On Populist Reason*.[29] Interestingly enough, the first part of the book includes a section characteristically entitled 'The Freudian Breakthrough' in which attention is directed to Freud's *Mass Psychology*: 'Freud's *Group Psychology* (1921) was, no doubt, the most radical breakthrough which had so far been accomplished in mass psychology,' Laclau comments.[30] Laclau highlights Freud's insights on the operations of identification at both the *horizontal* and *vertical* planes of libidinal attachment (love): A description ensues of the libidinal ties operating in the Church and in the Army, which, on the one hand, link the members of these institutions to one another and, on the other, link all of them to their leaders.'[31]

He also stresses the significant implications of Freud's argument on the way we can conceptualize the populist understanding of leadership as negotiating between the two aforementioned planes:

---

27 Yannis Stavrakakis, "Discourse Theory in Populism Research: Three Challenges and a Dilemma," *Journal of Language and Politics* 16, no. 4 (June 2017): 523–534.
28 For a first yet comprehensive take on Laclau's theorization of populism from a psychoanalytic point of view, see Paul Biglieri Gloria Perelló, "Populism," in *The Routledge Handbook of Psychoanalytic Political Theory*, ed. Yannis Stavrakakis, 330–340 (New York: Routledge, 2020). The text starts with an account of the anti-populist mainstream before accounting for Laclau's distinct contribution and the sustained debates it has created within psychoanalytic political theory. See (in Spanish) Nora Merlin, "El populismo como construcción política distinta a la masa," *Revista Universitaria de Psicoanálisis* 11 (2011): 275–84; Nora Merlin, *Populismo y Psicoanálisis* (Buenos Aires: Letra Viva, 2014).
29 Ernesto Laclau, *On Populist Reason* (London: Verso, 2005).
30 Ibid., 52, 56.
31 Ibid., 53.

The need for leadership could still be there – for structural reasons that Freud does not really explore, but to which we shall return in a moment – but it is a far more democratic leadership than the one involved in the notion of the narcissistic despot. We are, in fact, not far away from that peculiar combination of consensus and coercion that Gramsci called hegemony.³²

This is not only important for envisaging a *progressive populism* as something articulating the two, something Laclau had also highlighted elsewhere:

> The horizontal dimension of autonomy will be incapable, left to itself, of bringing about long-term historical change if it is not complemented by the vertical dimension of 'hegemony' [...] But hegemony not accompanied by mass action at the level of civil society leads to a bureaucratism that will be easily colonized by the corporative power of the forces of the status quo. To advance both in the directions of autonomy and hegemony is the real challenge to those who aim for a democratic future [...] ³³

It is also crucial in thinking populism against its stereotypical identification with personalistic leadership. The populist reason (logic) does not directly legitimize or produce a despotic leader; so much so is now also accepted even by mainstream empirical accounts: 'In fact, only a minority of strongmen are populists and only a minority of populists is a strongman.'³⁴

Nevertheless, the danger of despotism is always present in politics, whether populist or not. Arguably a progressive populist leader who is committed to democratic transformation must facilitate a transition from social dispersion to collective coordination and step aside once they have fulfilled their role of facilitator and initiator, instead of continuously concentrating power in their own hands and claiming any mystical "direct representation" of the (national) essence of the people.³⁵ The leader – like the analyst, who knows s/he will be discarded at the end of analysis – must be ready to accept his dis-investment

---

32   Ibid., 60.
33   Ernesto Laclau, *The Rhetorical Foundations of Society* (London: Verso, 2014), 9.
34   Cas Mudde and Cristóbal Rovira Kaltwasser, *Populism: A Very Short Introduction* (London: Oxford University Press, 2017), 63.
35   Yannis Stavrakakis, "Laclau and Psychoanalysis: An Appraisal," *Contemporary Political Theory* 15, no. 3 (2016): 304–335.

at a certain point(s) as a sign of reflexive popular empowerment.[36] Machiavelli offers a concrete example of such civic leadership:

> Camillus, Rome's frequently appointed supreme magistrate, gained unprecedented trust and authority from the Roman people by accepting their decision to exile him, by faithfully returning to the city during a dire crisis when they summoned him back, and, on numerous subsequent occasions, by eagerly relinquishing command once he'd fulfilled his designated assignments.[37]

Nor does the populist reason produce and/or imagine a homogeneous and docile "people." Why?

> As Laclau and I have repeatedly stressed, a relation of equivalence is not one in which all differences collapse into identity but in which differences are still active. If such differences were eliminated, that would not be equivalence but a simple identity.[38]

In that sense, the process of the construction of "the people," the way populist discourse establishes a hegemonic relation, is neither holistic nor monist; it never results in establishing homogeneity and unity. In fact, this would be impossible within the negative ontology of hegemony theory as it is re-signified by a discursive (psychoanalytically inspired) perspective. Why?

Well, simply because hegemony as a process is enabled because hegemony as a final state is ultimately impossible. Indeed, in the subsequent parts of *On Populist Reason*, Laclau clarifies further his take on populism by staging a sustained dialogue with psychoanalysis, mostly Lacanian theory. Here, it becomes clear that the impure politics of populism negotiate a delicate balancing act between the *impossible* and the *necessary*.[39] They can only be understood through an elaboration of political desire and (repetitive) *jouissance* within

---

36 For a full elaboration of this point, see Yannis Stavrakakis, "The (Discursive) Limits of (Left) Populism," *Journal of Language and Politics* 20, no. 1 (2021): 162–177. Needless to say, what is also required here is a process (a working-through) through which democratic popular empowerment will be prepared to advance further at the socio-political level without the leader, something which can never be never taken for granted.

37 John P. McCormick, "Machiavelli's Camillus and the Tension Between Leadership and Democracy," in *The Oxford Handbook of Law and Humanities*, ed. Simon Stern, Maksymillian Del Mar, and Bernadette Meyler (Oxford: Oxford University Press, 2019), 410.

38 Chantal Mouffe, *For a Left Populism* (New York: Verso, 2018), 63.

39 Laclau, *On Populist Reason*, 70.

an ontological terrain of impossibility. Within this context, "demand" – with its many psychoanalytic connotations – becomes the starting point of analysis.[40] Only a performative articulation of frustrated demands that enter a hegemonic relation of equivalence can lead to the emergence and affective investment of "the people" as a collective subject. And yet, the production of populism merely involves a process of naming and its ensuing political results: 'the construction of "the people" will be the attempt to give a name to that absent fullness of the community.'[41] This naming also involves a process of affective investment[42] that channels *jouissance*.[43] The confluence created thus between psychoanalysis and political theory indicates, for Laclau, a significant proximity: 'The logic of the *objet petit a* and the hegemonic logic are not just similar: they are simply identical.'[44]

The revolt of the elites and the post-democratic turn that currently threatens our democratic future cannot be resolved at the normative level in line with rationalist principles: a passionate endorsement of radical democracy would require the cultivation and hegemony of a different type of ethical relation to negativity and enjoyment. Such an alternative relation to negativity can only be attractive if it manages to offer access to some kind of (alternative) enjoyment. What is needed, in other words, is an enjoyable democratic ethics of the political.[45] What is at stake here is, once more, the issue of agency and

---

40   Thomás Zicman de Barros has highlighted certain ambiguities in Laclau's notion of "demands" that seem to potentially contradict his theory. Although passing from a given "people" as a taken for granted (unitary) sociological category or from identities as fully developed entities to the "demand" as the main unit of analysis helps Laclau avoid essentialism and reductionism, it may reproduce a small-scale 'unintended essentialism of demands.' See Thomás Zicman de Barros, "Desire and Collective Identities: Decomposing Ernesto Laclau's Notion of Demand," *Constellations* 28, no. 4 (December 2021), 1–11, 3. This can be resolved by the adoption of a fully-fledged Lacanian conceptualization of demand, desire and the drive beyond the deceptive "metonymy of desire": 'highlighting the importance of desire permits a new interpretation of Laclau through the distinction between the dynamic of desire in idealization and the dynamic of the drive in sublimation. It is productive for the understanding of democracy as a political ethic that accepts the constitutive lack of ground of social practices and embraces it as an openness to constant questioning of the identity of the "people."' (Ibid., 9). For his part, Sebastian Ronderos has linked this operation of populist desire with the discourse of hysteria. See Sebastián Ronderos, "Hysteria in the squares: Approaching populism from a perspective of desire," *Psychoanalysis, Culture and Society* 26 (2021): 46–64.
41   Laclau, *On Populist Reason*, 85.
42   Ibid., 110.
43   Ibid., 113.
44   Ibid., 116.
45   Yannis Stavrakakis, *The Lacanian Left* (Albany: SUNY Press, 2007), 268–269.

collective subjectivity; their re-negotiation in a way rigorously registering but also transforming the social bond and group psychology. As Laclau has put it, 'it is necessary to transfer the notion of emptiness from the place of power in a democratic regime – as proposed by Lefort – to the very subjects occupying that place.' We need to pass from the formal aspects of democracy to a consideration of a "community's whole political way of life."[46] Emptiness here has to be a "political construction," passionately embodied in our own political identifications.[47] The contemporary democratic citizen needs to be re-conceptualized not only as enduring but as enjoying social lack and emptiness.[48] This requires a process of productive mourning able to inscribe lack within the formation of the new.[49] It also requires the formulation of a democratic *jouissance*: this would be a *jouissance* beyond accumulation, domination and fantasy, an enjoyment of the not-all or not-whole.[50] A challenging predicament and, certainly, not a risk-free one.

Many modalities of such an orientation have been put forward over the years inspired by Lacanian theorization: identification with the symptom, sublimation and *suppléance*, to name but a few.[51] Indeed Tomas Zicman de Barros has recently argued that the use of certain psychoanalytic metaphors ("symptom" and "sublimation") can prove quite fruitful here, facilitating the consistent formulation of a typology of populist discourses: 'While the metaphor of symptom may describe non-democratic expressions of populism, sublimation would be an adequate metaphor for democratic populism.'[52] Although it is impossible to disentangle completely the one from the other – and although (social and political) symptoms, as localized projections of a certain blockage, can be useful in highlighting the limits of a certain social order – by focusing on sublimation we can perhaps mitigate the morbid character of certain symptomatic formations and the paranoiac scapegoating involved in their potential reliance on illusory fantasies of nostalgic fullness and wholeness (typical of so-called far-right populism): 'Populism as sublimation would involve the

---

46 Laclau, *On Populist Reason*, 169.
47 Ibid., 170.
48 Stavrakakis, *The Lacanian Left*, 273.
49 Ibid., 276.
50 Further elaboration of this point can be found in Stavrakakis, *The Lacanian Left*, 279–280.
51 Stavrakakis, *The Lacanian Left*; Yannis Stavrakakis, *Lacan and the Political* (London: Routledge, 1999).
52 Thomás Zicman de Barros, "Populism: Symptom or Sublimation? Reassessing the Use of Psychoanalytic Metaphors," *Psychoanalysis, Culture and Society* 27, no. 3 (April 2022): 1–17.

construction of a "people" with an open identity which accepts its own contingency and institutes a non-saturated symbolic space.'[53]

At any rate, we need to highlight that Laclau's and Mouffe's focus on the generative and enabling operation of (populist) discursive articulation(s) relies on a horizon of negativity: 'It is because hegemony supposes the incomplete and open character of the social, that it can take place only in a field dominated by articulatory practices.'[54] What they designate as "hegemony" comprises an irreducible Sisyphean struggle to negotiate the dislocations, failures and crises that political projects encounter from within (from their inherent inability to fully capture and reshape the real and to represent their constituencies in a definitive way), and from without (from the challenges put forward by other representations within political antagonism). No closure is achievable here:

> The requirements of 'hegemony' as a central category of political analysis are essentially three. The first is that something constitutively heterogeneous to the social system or structure has to be present in the latter from the very beginning, preventing it from constituting itself as a closed or representable totality. If such a closure were achievable, no hegemonic event would be possible, and the political, far from being an ontological dimension of the social – an 'existential' of the social – would be just an ontic dimension of the latter. Secondly, however, the hegemonic suture has to produce a re-totalizing effect, without which no hegemonic articulation would be possible either. But, thirdly, this re-totalization must not have the character of a dialectical reintegration. It has, on the contrary, to maintain alive and visible the original and constitutive heterogeneity from which the hegemonic articulation started.[55]

Accordingly, what is at stake in politics is never the end of history or some sort of definitive resolution of all contradictions and antagonisms. On the contrary, it is rather a temporary crystallization, a partial fixation of the balance of forces and representations, which may retroactively and temporarily be accepted as the "common sense" of a community, as what it "takes for granted" gradually effecting a shift of position.[56]

---

53 Ibid.
54 Ernesto Laclau and Chantal Mouffe, *Hegemony and Social Strategy* (New York: Verso, 2001), 134.
55 Laclau, *The Rhetorical Foundations of Society,* 80–81.
56 Also see, in this respect, Stavrakakis, "On Laclau's Alleged Monism," on which I am drawing here.

This constitutive character of negativity and heterogeneity, of limits and impossibilities,[57] was part and parcel of Laclau's theory from very early on: 'For me [...] "populism" is the permanent expression of the fact that in the final instance, a society always fails in its efforts to constitute itself as an objective order.'[58] It is against such an impossibility that hegemony and populism operate.[59] Furthermore, it is an impossibility they cannot eliminate and are bound to reproduce; yet, in negotiating this failure they may also facilitate a populist unification process potentially increasing the chances of popular empowerment: 'If the fullness of society is unachievable, the attempts at reaching it will necessarily fail – although they will be able, in the search for that impossible object, to solve a variety of partial problems.'[60] Laclau – and his theorization of populism – seems to be touching here on something recently highlighted by McGowan: 'The key of the politics of the death drive is grasping [...] the nothingness of the object and thereby finding satisfaction in the drive itself,' and in the partial accomplishments and shifts of position resulting from an ultimately impossible yet necessary political choreography.[61]

"The people" emerges, of course, within particular contexts, as a single signifying unit and only thus (through its affective valuation) can it facilitate the strategic unification still necessary – but surely not enough – for (partial) popular empowerment. However, this single signifier can only operate, within Laclau's Lacanian ontology, as a signifier of the lack in the Other, as a vanishing mediator. As what temporarily and repetitively registers trauma by making sense of social antagonism and polarization in a way allowing identification with the (often obscene) accursed share of the social order (Peron's *descamisados*), the subject on whose exclusion such an order is established. Flirting with the terrain of fantasy only in order to traverse it, that is to say, in order to facilitate a potentially post-phantasmatic sublimation encircling the movement of the drive, this populist reason points to and renders visible a constitutive split; its partial meaning is never transparent and holistic, it is always subject to anomalies and displacements, within a horizon of ultimate failure

---

57 Paula Biglieri and Gloria Perelló, "Populism," in *The Routledge Handbook of Psychoanalytic Political Theory*, ed. Yannis Stavrakakis (New York: Routledge, 2020): 330–340.

58 Ernesto Laclau, *New Reflections on the Revolution of our Time* (London: Routledge, 1990), 201.

59 Francisco Panizza and Yannis Stavrakakis, "Populism, Hegemony, and the Political Construction of 'The People,'" in *Populism in Global Perspective: A Performative and Discursive Approach*, ed. Pierre Ostiguy, Francisco Panizza, and Benjamin Moffitt (New York: Routledge, 2020).

60 Laclau, *The Rhetorical Foundations of Society*, 93.

61 McCowan, *Enjoying What We Don't Have*, 31.

and negativity. Such a progressive populist sensibility could be seen then as a properly psychoanalytic politics that transforms the "obstacle" into a point of identification and thus could potentially energize an "emancipatory politics of the limit."[62]

4 Truth or Trust? Deconstructing "Post-truth"

From the point of view of psychoanalytic political theory (drawing on Freud's *Mass Psychology* and the Freudian and Lacanian Left(s) it has inspired) as well as of the orientation in populism research it has helped formulate, one could also illuminate another crucial issue that currently seems to shape the public terrain, that of "post-truth."

As is well-known, and the relevant *Wikipedia* entry amply demonstrates that, "post-truth" has been at the forefront of global public spheres following the 2015 Trump election in the US and the BREXIT referendum in the UK. No wonder that it emerged as the Word of the Year for 2016 for the *Oxford Dictionary*. As Illing, who is given a prominent place by *Wikipedia*, argues: post-truth signifies the lack of "shared objective standards for truth"; according to the aforementioned *Dictionary*, it has the following meaning: 'Relating to or denoting circumstances in which objective facts are less influential in shaping public opinion than appeals to emotion and personal belief.'[63] This is how post-truth has commonly been defined – which immediately raises certain questions at the intersection of subjectivity, knowledge and politics.[64]

Let me start with a personal note by saying that references to post-truth always made me feel a bit uncomfortable, instinctively uncomfortable, and I have tried a lot to determine how exactly this affect was produced, because in a classical Freudian take on repression, what is repressed is meaning, a representation that makes us feel that we have thought about something forbidden,

---

62 Ibid., 263, 264.
63 Oxford University Press, *Word of the year 2016*. 2017. https://languages.oup.com/word-of-the-year/2016/.
64 See, in this respect, Galanopoulos & Stavrakakis from where these introductory remarks are taken. Antonis Galanopoulos and Yannis Stavrakakis, "Populism, Anti-populism and Post-truth," in *The Palgrave Handbook of Populism*, ed. Michael Oswald (London: Palgrave, 2021).

something inadmissible and improper, and thus the affect, the feeling, remains as something largely unexplained and troubling.[65]

So, what was this idea that made me feel that I should not have thought about it in the first place and, as a result, had to be repressed? I think it was something that had to do with the value of truth itself. Because, obviously, it is such an over-valuation of "truth" that the utilization of "post-truth" as a tool of political criticism presupposes.

Obviously, if asked in a survey, people might say that "truth" is extremely important, perhaps the most precious value or ideal. This would be especially true for academics who are bound to over-value and over-invest truth and knowledge, because they are the contemporary practitioners of truth, the soldiers of a particular (late) modern "regime of truth" (a concept used by Foucault who helped us to bracket this self-idealization), the agents of the "Discourse of the University" in Lacan's terms, which reveals a lot about the operation of power in our societies. But this political over-determination of truth and knowledge (highlighted by Foucault and Lacan) is not easily acknowledged in practice; it makes us feel uncomfortable because it is seen as damaging our credibility, our supposedly privileged access to an unmediated, objective truth, a fantasy that resurfaces in all references to "post-truth."[66]

Already this Freudian, Foucauldian and Lacanian take starts framing truth (as a construction of reality) in a particular – very modest – light stressing the constitutivity of repression, the relevance of the power-knowledge nexus and the *extimate* relationship between power and our psychosocial construction of (all) reality. It also indicates certain problems with regards to the concept of "post-truth":

(1) The old, very strong, dichotomy "truth vs. falsity" returns with a vengeance through references to post-truth. A distinction that has to be premised on some kind of transcendental guarantee, theological, scientific, political etc.; on our *trust* towards one of these big Others. This may be a symptom of our inability to accept, to come to terms with the "Death of God," and the problems around the so-called "legitimacy of modernity" in Hans Blumenberg's conceptualization (shouldn't modern reflexivity

---

[65] In the next few paragraphs, I will be drawing on the text of a talk presented at the "Psychoanalysis 'Post-truth': US Election Special" interdisciplinary online conference (Freud Museum, London, 1 & 8 November 2020).

[66] We have already criticized a (left-wing) version of this arrogance in the first section of this chapter.

make us abandon the quest for an ultimate truth, after all?), with the lack in the big Other.[67]

(2) Yet this trust towards a late modern (fully consistent, objective) big Other (for example, science) is ultimately impossible to sustain today.

(a) Such an objective truth cannot be mastered practically today; and it cannot be *represented faithfully* – as Lacan has put it, "the words are lacking," it is thus materially impossible to claim such a representational privilege.[68]

(b) In addition, it cannot be presented as conquered, at the *ethical* level, to the extent that – as the history and philosophy of science reveal – science can only thrive on critical openness, on registering the lack in the big Other, otherwise reflexive science morphs into some sort of simplified theology. However, very often, by disavowing the subject (Lacan) it creates the illusion that it can provide some sort of objective, purely cognitive foundation – but this is a slippery, self-defeating path.[69] Inter-subjectivity and the political are always involved. It is not a coincidence that in Thomas Kuhn's understanding of the operations of science, what is enlisted and utilized is a series of thoroughly political concepts and group dynamics.[70]

At any rate, the ensuing fantasy in "post-truth" is that political frictions and antagonisms can be resolved once and for all by recourse to some sort of unmediated scientific objectivity and certainty; without, that is to say, considering the dynamics of debate, controversy, argument and persuasion. Yet no simplistic false-true dichotomy can provide a tenable solution here; Aristotle already knew that, and this is amply demonstrated in his *Rhetoric*.[71]

(c) Most important, on a broader level, this may be not only impossible and unethical, but also *undesirable*. I don't want to sound very provocative here but let us say that "truth" is of limited value

---

67 For a critique of such representationalism, which has conditioned diachronically the critique of ideology, see Yanni Stavrakakis, "Ambiguous Ideology and the Lacanian Twist," *Journal of the Centre of Freudian Analysis and Research*, 8 (January 1997).
68 Jacques Lacan, *Television, A Challenge to the Psychoanalytic Establishment* (New York: Norton, 1990), 7.
69 Jacques Lacan, "Science and Truth," in *Écrits* (New York: Norton, 2006), 726–745.
70 Thomas Kuhn, *The Structure of Scientific Revolutions* (Chicago: Chicago University Press, 1996).
71 Aristotle, *The Art of Rhetoric* (London: Penguin, 1992).

anyway; desire and enjoyment seem to take precedence on many occasions. If you think about it, very often we prefer not to know the "truth" – or to forget it. Could we continue living without the gift to forget and repress? What would an inability to disavow or ignore *the* truth entail?

But also: what would an inability to encounter and encircle a truth beyond our social constructions of reality mean? We can and should be able to invoke such a truth. This is what Lacan explicitly does – although he simultaneously registers the ultimate impossibility, the limitations involved in this operation: 'I always speak the truth. Not the whole truth, because there's no way to say it all. Saying it all is literally [materially] impossible: words fail. Yet it's through this very impossibility that the truth holds onto the real.'[72] Arguably this is very different from the "truth" as objective fantasy on which discursive uses of "post-truth" are premised. This psychoanalytic truth is a partial *savoir* encircling impossibility as an encounter with a real beyond reality (the truth as *cause*, as traumatic encounter).[73] Obviously, such a psychoanalytically-inspired truth is never defined on the basis of the *adequation* of language (and politics) to reality. It aims at orienting action.[74]

So, to conclude, for a variety of reasons, "truth" – conceived in an absolute representationalist, epistemic manner – cannot function today as the foundation of our societies and our politics. And inter-subjective *trust*, which is what is at stake here, has to be articulated – always in a partial way – on something else, which will always be partly political, on particular structures of shared patterns of desire and enjoyment encircling our repetitive traumatic encounter with the real. How to try to make these structures more democratic,

---

72   Lacan, *Television*, 7.
73   It is here that Foucault and Lacan seem to part company. For Foucault, all truth is post-truth. Truth and knowledge production are always overdetermined by processes of articulation that cannot operate in isolation from power. Always alert to the intricacies of the power/knowledge nexus, Foucault coins the paradoxical term "regimes of Truth," meaning the frameworks that regulate public discourse by controlling what can be said and what has to remain implicit, what is from what is not assigned with truth value. See Michel Foucault, "'Truth and Power,' interview given to Alessandro Fontana and Pasquale Pasquino," in *The Foucault Reader*, ed. Paul Rabinow (London: Penguin, 1991), 51–75. Also see Galanopoulos and Stavrakakis, "Populism, Anti-Populism, and Post-Truth." Although, on one level, he seems to agree with Foucault, Lacan will also add that beyond the realm of such politically overdetermined truths (knowledge/reality constructions) there is also a real that operates on a level, which is extimate to the symbolic: it entails a realm that, although clearly beyond direct representation, also interacts in various ways with our symbolic realities and may also inform their negative ontology.
74   Stavrakakis, *The Lacanian Left*, 12.

inclusive and egalitarian seems to be the foremost challenge of our age. It is here that progressive populism could perhaps operate as a vehicle for such an enrichment of the democratic not-all. Like the Lacanian truth process we have described, populism could potentially operate – as we have seen in the previous section – as a paradoxical attempt to negotiate a (partial and temporary) solution to a *strategic* problem, that of unifying split subjects not in order to produce a phantasmatic homogeneity but in order to register the inherent social division that hegemonic orders foreclose, and advance their ability to push forward recognition/incorporation and influence decision-making (producing as a secondary gain certain social advances in terms of equality and democracy in a way similar to the psychoanalytic cure that may also produce therapeutic effects as by-products that should not be seen as its exclusive goals).[75]

And this is why "post-truth" has ended up being utilized by *anti-populist* discourses. Indeed, a Laclau-inspired approach to populism must register the importance of studying *anti-populism* as a priority. Already from Saussure, we know that identity is premised on difference and thus the nexus populism/anti-populism needs to be analyzed in its mutual constitutivity. Our everyday political experience also indicates that, especially within a Eurocentric setting (where populism conveys a predominantly pejorative meaning), "populism" is very often introduced by mainstream forces themselves in order to delegitimize alternatives no matter where they emanate from and what type of sensibility (desire) they articulate (and vice-versa).

For example, within the context of the Greek crisis (post-2010), we have witnessed mainstream discourses praising systemic continuity and "normality" engage in a very aggressive demonization of populism projected on anyone proposing any type of alternative. Populism thus emerged as the synecdoche of everything pathological in Greek politics: irresponsibility, demagogy, corruption, destruction, irrationalism. Not only was it to blame for the crisis itself, but it was also what obstructed the implementation of the required rational solutions, namely austerity.[76] Such anti-populist political claims attempted to camouflage their partisanship as epistemic authority and thus demand a total extra-political acceptance silencing the opposition. They claimed, in other

---

75 Stavrakakis, *Lacan and the Political*, 149, n. 26.
76 Antonis Galanopoulos and Yannis Stavrakakis, "Discursive Uses of 'Abnormality' in the Greek Crisis," in *Discourse Analysis and Austerity: Critical Studies from Economics and Linguistics*, ed. Kate Power, Tanweer Ali, and Eva Lebdušková, (New York: Routledge, 2019): 177–195.

words, that they possess the (single) truth and that they incarnate a supreme rationality.[77] This claim also implied the condemnation of the irrationalism and the reliance on "post-truth" by their opponents (populism), who were seen as objectively wrong, often irrespective of their concrete ideological profile (inclusionary vs. exclusionary) and concrete proposals.[78]

5 Conclusion

In the 100 years since the first publication of Freud's *Mass Psychology and the Analysis of the Ego*, the text has proved much more influential than anybody could predict. And in thoroughly unpredictable ways. Not only did it facilitate the confluence between psychoanalysis and politics later on crystallized in theoretico-political movements like the Freudian and the Lacanian Left. Furthermore, it keeps on inspiring innovative understandings of contemporary phenomena; we have seen how it helped formulate Ernesto Laclau's take on populism. We have also seen how the ensuing psychoanalytic political theory can illuminate debates such as the one on "post-truth" and thus enhance critical theoretical and analytical perspectives.

In all these fronts, what is also at stake is a potential re-positioning – a shift – in (political) subjectivity and a novel understanding of agency. If the present is dominated by the new challenges the pandemic has introduced on a variety of levels, only the future can tell whether the orientation sketched in these pages will be able to partially inspire a democratic reframing of the social bond.

---

[77] Needless to say, such a production of populist "abnormality" must be interpreted within the understanding of the normal/abnormal nexus initiated by Canguilhem (also see Michel Foucault, *Abnormal: Lectures at the Collège de France, 1974–1975* (New York: Picador, 2003)) debunking claims about epistemic superiority. Indeed, in his celebrated study, *The Normal and the Pathological*, Canguilhem concludes that 'the normal is not a static or peaceful, but a dynamic and polemical concept.' (Georges Canguilhem, *The Normal and the Pathological* (New York: Zone Books, 1991), 239). It legitimizes a decision (Canguilhem, *The Normal and the Pathological*, 245) and, most importantly, it does so on the basis of an inverted causality that, crucially, relies on the production of "abnormality." See, for a more sustained elaboration, Galanopoulos & Stavrakakis, "Populism, Anti-Populism, and Post-Truth in Crisis-ridden Greece."

[78] For a typology allowing the differential identification of different and even antithetical forms of populism, something that is of paramount importance, see Benjamin De Cleen and Yannis Stavrakakis, "Distinctions and Articulations: A Discourse Theoretical Framework for the Study of Populism and Nationalism," *Javnost/The Public* 24, no. 4 (2017): 301–319.

Bibliography

Adorno, Theodor W., Frenkel-Brunswik, E., Levinson, D. & Sanford, R. N. *The Authoritarian Personality*. New York: Harper and Brothers, 1950.

Aristotle, *The Art of Rhetoric*. London: Penguin, 1992.

Biglieri, Paula, and Gloria Perelló G. "Populism." In *The Routledge Handbook of Psychoanalytic Political Theory*, edited by Yannis Stavrakakis, 330–340. New York: Routledge, 2020.

Broder, David. "Socialists Invented the Summer Holiday." *Jacobin*, August 7, 2019. https://jacobin.com/2019/08/socialists-invented-summer-vacation-popular-front-france.

Canguilhem, Georges. *The Normal and the Pathological*. New York: Zone Books, 1991.

Cinnella, Ettore. *L'altro Marx*. Roma: Della Porta, Editori, 2019.

De Cleen, Benjamin, and Yannis Stavrakakis. "Distinctions and Articulations: A Discourse Theoretical Framework for the Study of Populism and Nationalism." *Javnost/The Public* 24, no. 4 (2017): 301–319.

Elias, Norbert. "Appendix I: Introduction to the 1968 edition." In *The Civilizing Process, vol. I: The History of Manners*. Oxford: Blackwell, 1983.

Foucault, Michel. *Abnormal: Lectures at the Collège de France, 1974–1975*. New York: Picador, 2003.

Foucault, Michel. "'Truth and Power,' interview given to Alessandro Fontana and Pasquale Pasquino." In *The Foucault Reader*, edited by Paul Rabinow, 51–75. London: Penguin, 1991.

Freud, Sigmund. *Group Psychology and the Analysis of the Ego*. London: The Hogarth Press and the Institute of Psycho-Analysis, 1949.

Galanopoulos, Antonis, and Yannis Stavrakakis. "Discursive Uses of 'Abnormality' in the Greek Crisis." In *Discourse Analysis and Austerity: Critical Studies from Economics and Linguistics*, edited by Kate Power, Tanweer Ali, and Eva Lebdušková, 177–195. New York: Routledge, 2019.

Galanopoulos, Antonis, and Yannis Stavrakakis. "Populism, Anti-populism and Post-truth." In *The Palgrave Handbook of Populism*, edited by Michael Oswald. London: Palgrave, 2021.

Holmes, Leslie. *Communism: A Very Short Introduction*. Oxford: Oxford University Press, 2009.

Kuhn, Thomas. *The Structure of Scientific Revolutions*. Chicago: Chicago University Press, 1996.

Lacan, Jacques. "Science and Truth." In *Écrits*, 726–745. New York: Norton, 2006.

Lacan, Jacques. *Television, A Challenge to the Psychoanalytic Establishment*. New York: Norton, 1990.

Laclau, Ernesto. *New Reflections on the Revolution of our Time*. London: Routledge, 1990.

Laclau, Ernesto. *On Populist Reason*. London: Verso, 2005.
Laclau, Ernesto. *The Rhetorical Foundations of Society*. London: Verso, 2014.
Laclau, Ernesto, and Chantal Mouffe. *Hegemony and Social Strategy*. New York: Verso, 2001.
Laclau, Ernesto, and Chantal Mouffe. *Towards a Radical Democratic Politics*. New York: Verso, 1985.
Machin, Amanda. "Nationalism." In *The Routledge Handbook of Psychoanalytic Political Theory*, edited by Yannis Stavrakakis, 285–295. New York: Routledge, 2020.
Matthews, Wade. "Class, Nation, and Capitalist Globalization: Eric Hobsbawm and the National Question." *International Review of Social History* 53, no. 1 (2008): 85–86.
McCormick, John P. "Machiavelli's Camillus and the Tension Between Leadership and Democracy." In *The Oxford Handbook of Law and Humanities*, edited by Simon Stern, Maksymillian Del Mar, and Bernadette Meyler. Oxford: Oxford University Press, 2019.
McGowan, Todd. *Enjoying What We Don't Have: The Political Project of Psychoanalysis*. Lincoln: University of Nebraska Press, 2013.
Merlin, Nora. "El populismo como construcción política distinta a la masa." *Revista Universitaria de Psicoanálisis* 11 (2011): 275–84.
Merlin, Nora. *Populismo y Psicoanálisis*, Buenos Aires: Letra Viva, 2014.
Mouffe, Chantal. *For a Left Populism*. New York: Verso, 2018.
Mudde, Cas, and Cristóbal Rovira Kaltwasser. *Populism: A Very Short Introduction*. London: Oxford University Press, 2017.
Musto, Marcello. "On His Birthday, Let's Celebrate the Old Man Karl Marx," interview given to Nicolas Allen. *Jacobin*, May 5, 2021. https://www.jacobinmag.com/2021/05/birthday-old-man-karl-marx-later-years.
Oxford University Press. *Word of the year 2016*. 2017. https://languages.oup.com/word-of-the-year/2016/.
Panizza, Francisco, and Yannis Stavrakakis. "Populism, Hegemony, and the Political Construction of 'The People.'" In *Populism in Global Perspective: A Performative and Discursive Approach*, edited by Pierre Ostiguy, Francisco Panizza, and Benjamin Moffitt. New York: Routledge, 2020.
Ries, Curt. "Our Path Forward After Bernie Must Include Rank-and-File Unionism and Class-Struggle Elections." *Jacobin*, September 8 2020. https://www.jacobinmag.com/2020/08/bernie-sanders-campaign-unions-class-struggle.
Robinson, Paul A. *The Freudian Left*. New York: Harper and Row, 1967.
Ronderos, Sebastián. "Hysteria in the squares: Approaching populism from a perspective of desire." *Psychoanalysis, Culture and Society* 26 (2021): 46–64.
Shanin, Teodor, ed. *Late Marx and the Russian Road: Marx and "the Peripheries of Capitalism."* New York: Monthly Review Press, 1983.

Stavrakakis, Yannis. "Ambiguous Ideology and the Lacanian Twist." *Journal of the Centre of Freudian Analysis and Research,* 8 (January 1997).

Stavrakakis, Yannis. "Discourse Theory in Populism Research: Three Challenges and a Dilemma." *Journal of Language and Politics* 16, no. 4 (June 2017): 523–534.

Stavrakakis, Yannis. "The (Discursive) Limits of (Left) Populism." *Journal of Language and Politics* 20, no. 1 (2021): 162–177.

Stavrakakis, Yannis. *Lacan and the Political.* London: Routledge, 1999.

Stavrakakis, Yannis. *The Lacanian Left.* Albany: SUNY Press, 2007.

Stavrakakis, Yannis. "Laclau and Psychoanalysis: An Appraisal." *Contemporary Political Theory* 15, no. 3 (2016): 304–335.

Stavrakakis, Yannis. "On Laclau's Alleged Monism." POPULISMUS working papers 11 (2020) http://www.populismus.gr/wp-content/uploads/2020/11/Stavrakakis-monism-wp111.pdf.

Stavrakakis, Yannis. "Populism, Anti-populism and Post-truth." In *The Palgrave Handbook of Populism,* edited by Michael Oswald. London: Palgrave, 2021.

Stavrakakis, Yannis, and Nikos Chrysoloras. "(I Can't Get No) Enjoyment: Lacanian Theory and the Analysis of Nationalism." *Psychoanalysis, Culture & Society* 11, no. 2 (August 2006): 144–163.

Stuart, Robert. *Marxism and National Identity.* Albany: SUNY Press, 2006.

Zicman de Barros, Thomás. "Desire and Collective Identities: Decomposing Ernesto Laclau's Notion of Demand." *Constellations* 28, no. 4 (December 2021): 1–11.

Zicman de Barros, Thomás. "Populism: Symptom or Sublimation? Reassessing the Use of Psychoanalytic Metaphors." *Psychoanalysis, Culture and Society* 27, no. 3 (April 2022): 1–17.

Žižek, Slavoj. *Tarrying with the Negative.* Durham: Duke University Press, 1993.

CHAPTER 8

Freud, Marx, and the Structure of Freedom

Michael J. Thompson

1 Introduction

Psychoanalysis has receded as one of the core projects of contemporary critical theory. My central thesis in this chapter is that a different axis can be constructed between the ideas of Freud and Marx: namely that there is a phylogenetic capacity of human beings for both purposive activity, that is, to posit themselves in the world, as well as for forming and living within relations with others. Both of these phylogenetic capacities in human beings take on different forms in different social contexts and can lead either to the fulfillment or suffering of individuals. That both share, although on different levels of analysis, a conception of human being that emphasizes the creative, world-producing capacity of human beings. For Freud, this took the form of drives, of certain psychic needs and desires that could be either realizes in the world or frustrated leading to neuroses or other forms of psychic pathology. For Marx, this capacity is also, in a certain sense, psychic, but also social-ontological in that our mental ideas become realized in the world via praxis, or the manipulation of the brute facts of physical nature.

What this points to is a conception of freedom that considers both our inherently subjective and social dimensions; a conception of freedom that hinges on a self-consciousness of our creative and relational dynamics. To be free is not simply to be free from the interference of another agent, it is, more essentially and more fruitfully, to be seen as the capacity to be a *self-authorizing agent*, that is, to a conception of human autonomy not merely as free agency but, more richly, as *a form of human freedom where the purposes and ends that we posit are authentically our own and not dominated or structured by the projects of others*. What both Freud and Marx point to is the possibility for a radical idea of self-consciousness: one that considers the subject's capacity to know oneself as a font or co-creator of one's world. The concept of autonomy in this sense can be seen to be the capacity for judging, for critically relating to the internalized norms and values that underwrite our practical and institutional lives. But to achieve this state of critical autonomy, the capacity for critical judgment requires that we (1) de-reify consciousness as well as (2) achieve self-consciousness of our ontology as socio-practical beings. Only then will we be able to realize freedom in a concrete sense, that is, as actual ways of living, relating and acting in the world. Freud and Marx have much to teach us in the construction of such a theory of autonomy, one I will explore in what follows.

Taking my own cue from the essential insights of Hegelian-Marxism, I want to argue that access to a critical form of self-consciousness can only be achieved via the capacity for de-reifying consciousness. From a Freudian perspective, this entails the breaking up of the sedimented layers of the unconscious and pre-conscious substrates that shape character as well as the mental processes and affective states that articulate one's selfhood. The self's capacity for self-consciousness (in a philosophical sense) is itself constrained by its actual determinativeness by dynamic interpersonal configurations that are internalized and become dimensions of selfhood. To be free in this sense is to be able to achieve a self-consciousness of oneself as a relational and ontoformative being, as a self that is capable of generating a form of life with others that is at once self-determining as well as one that serves universal, common ends. To be able to judge those forms of praxis and categories of knowing that are no longer rooted in, or are compromise formations against, the prevailing nexus of normative reality; to develop a capacity of critical judgment about what norms, desires, and institutions are worthy of our obligation and participation, and those that are not, is in this sense the cynosure of what I will refer to here as a *critical psychoanalysis,* or one that is able to cultivate a kind of thinking that achieves critical autonomy as a first step toward the positing of a more concrete form of freedom.

2   Freud, Autonomy, and Freedom

A core idea that Freud's work asks us to reconsider is the concept of autonomy, which was at the heart of the cultural, ethical, and political project of modernity. Freedom was seen as a capacity for individuals to manage and organize their own lives, to achieve a state of self-determination by resolving those neurotic conflicts that interfered with a generative life project. For Freud, it was not only the postulating of an unconscious that places this structure of thought into question, but also the ways that primitive, archaic drives actively worked against the otherwise rational capacity for self-reflection and self-legislation. How could one be autonomous – in either Spinoza's, Locke's, or Kant's terms – if we were unable to achieve some pure form of practical reason? Was freedom, in this sense, even possible if repression and the contents of the unconscious were to remain active on consciousness but nevertheless out of our awareness? It seems clear that what early modern Enlightenment thinkers had in mind was a capacity to achieve just such a domination of the effects that would permit a freedom of the will.

What classical Enlightenment thinkers such as Spinoza, Locke, and Kant point to is the possibility of *free agency*: the capacity to act according to a will that is itself determined by reason rather than some external other or some irrational dimension of one's personality or some external norm that has been non-reflectively internalized. The idea of free agency essentially captures the concept of autonomy as a model and expression of human freedom. A free agent was one who acted not as a reaction to an emotion – from fear to avarice or cupidity – but from a standpoint of pure reflection for its own sake. Spinoza's idea of "human bondage," therefore entailed that 'he who is led by fear and does what is good in order that he may avoid what is evil is not led by reason.'[1] Such a person, Spinoza contends, is not free, and thinkers such as Locke and Kant, central thinkers in the creation of the modern liberal self, continue along this line of thinking. For Locke, to act as a free agent is to perform an act that is the result of the reflection on natural law just as for Kant, it was the subject's reflection on the "categorial imperative" that articulated the form for an act of free agency.

To rest with this model of autonomy is problematic, however. One reason for this is the rise of instrumental reason and its effect on the nature of social relations and self-constitution. With the crumbling of traditional forms of authority came the rise of what Weber termed "rational authority" or domination.[2] The displacement of the former by the latter entailed not only a transformation in the external world of dependency, from traditional and religious doctrines of authority to modern, post-metaphysical conceptions of authority. It also, and perhaps more importantly, entailed a shift in the internal world of the subject. Tradition wants to diminish the fecundity of agency; it seeks to desiccate the subject's self-reflective will and chain it to a system of external rituals and beliefs. Such value-orientations are externally rooted, but they also require a thinner conception of subjectivity than more modern forms of life. In rational forms of authority, agency is encouraged. It is the means by which modern forms of coordination are conducted and enacted. What both share, however, is a control over the ends and purposes of the subject, of agency itself. Both traditional and rational structures of authority are precisely that: forms of authorizing the scope of agency, the very ends and purposes toward which we direct our lives.

---

1 Benedict Spinoza, *Ethica Ordine Geometrico Demonstrata. Opera*, vol. 2 (Darmstadt: Wissenschaftliche Buchgesellschaft, 1989), 402.
2 Max Weber, *Wirtschaft und Gesellschaft* (Tübingen: J.C.B. Mohr, 1972), 122–130.

As technological change has increased and instrumental reason has expanded, so too does the self increasingly become the agent not for one's own ends and purposes, but for those of the powerful, of the systems and logics of the social order we inhabit. Today, to accommodate reality, to internalize its norms, values and practices is, to quote James Block, 'an internalization of authoritative mandates, no longer as subservience to traditional rules, but as a way to order one's internal processes in correspondence with collective processes and parameters.'[3] We can see reification in a similar light; with the inculcation of rationalized values, norms and practices, the self and its agency becomes an extension of external social systems. The internal world becomes corrupted and one's self-conscious agency reflects not the ends and purposes of an authentically self-authorizing agent, but a reified self that acts on projects and from values that are not its own, but are taken up from the outside.

This *reification problem*, as I have called it elsewhere,[4] severely impacts the idea of autonomy and freedom that early-modern philosophers were constructing. Freud's power, in this respect, is to be able to shatter the ways that these values and norms have been rooted in our psyche in such a way so as to account for a normative psychic structure. These values and norms not only find themselves deposited in the super-ego but also the very structure of the ego as well. Freud's analytic procedure and its project of unearthing the deeper recesses of the mind holds out for us the capacity to strip away the sedimented layers of non-reflective mentation that corrupt and stand in the way of critical self-consciousness, and it is precisely these sedimented layers of non-reflective aspects of mental life that constitute the heteronomic power of reification. Crucial, in this regard, is the repudiation, the repression, or even the outright dissociation on the part of the individual subject of its own self-consciousness, which can be used as a fulcrum against the reality principle. As Freud points out describing the founding of psychoanalysis:

> The theory of repression became the corner-stone of our understanding of neuroses. A different view had now to be taken of the task of therapy. Its aim was no longer to "abreact" an affect which had got onto the wrong lines, but to uncover repressions and replace them by acts of judgment

---

3 James Block, *A Nation of Agents: The American Path to a Modern Self and Society* (Cambridge, MA: Harvard University Press, 2002), 540.
4 See Michael J. Thompson, "Reification as an Ontological Concept," *Metodo: International Studies in Phenomenology and Philosophy* 9, no. 2 (2021): 417–445.

which might result either in the accepting or the condemning of what had previously been repudiated.[5]

Here Freud points us toward a central and, I believe, very rich thesis about the purpose of psychoanalysis. Not only are we to be concerned with the resolution of conflict, but also to be able to achieve a capacity for *judgment*, or a critical attitude toward what one thinks and feels, toward one's ideas and affects. Judgment is here viewed as a form of self-knowing, an orientation toward oneself that means strengthening ego functioning. As Freud puts it: 'The method by which we strengthen the patient's weakened ego has as its starting point an increase in the ego's self-knowledge.'[6] It is not the suppression of feeling or emotion that should concern us, but their deconstruction: an understanding of how one's mind is shaped and how this enables or frustrates his or her capacity for self-authorization; in other words, to live a life according to forms of meaning and purposes *that are one's own*.

Such a conception of freedom involves deeper, more exploratory journey of the self. The problem of the reification of consciousness shapes the very symbolic and phenomenological nexus we share with others to such an extent that only by a process of de-reification can we hope to achieve a level of self-consciousness that can capture the spontaneous level of human thought and activity. Freud's emphasis on the need to replace repressions with "acts of judgment" itself requires an objective, ontological conception of human life as defined by socio-relational praxis. It involves, as Paul Ricoeur has argued in his interpretation of Freud, a "dialectic of archeology and teleology."[7] As Ricoeur argues:

> It seems to me that the concept of an archeology of the subject remains very abstract so long as it has not been set in a relationship of dialectical opposition to the complementary concept of teleology. In order to have an *archê* a subject must have a *telos*. ... But if the subject is to attain to its true being, it is not enough for it to discover the inadequacy of its self-awareness, or even to discover the power of desire that posits it in existence. The subject must also discover that the process of "becoming

---

5 Sigmund Freud, "Autobiographical Study," *Standard Edition*, Vol. 20 (London: The Hogarth Press, 1973), 30.
6 Sigmund Freud, "An Outline of Psycho-Analysis," *Standard Edition*, Vol. 23 (London: The Hogarth Press, 1973), 70.
7 Paul Ricoeur, *Freud and Philosophy: An Essay on Interpretation*, trans. Denis Savage (New Haven, CT: Yale University Press, 1970), 460.

conscious," through which it *appropriates* the meaning of its existence as desire and effort, does not belong to it, but belongs to the *meaning* that is formed in it. The subject must mediate self-consciousness through spirit or mind, that it, through the figures that give a telos to this "becoming conscious."[8]

The idea that archeology and teleology fit together to form a higher understanding of the self is a central idea I would like to pursue, but in a different way than Ricoeur. As I see it, a richer understanding of human autonomy and freedom must be grasped from the point of view that sees human beings as essentially praxis-oriented beings. By this I mean that human activity is essentially teleological in that it seeks to posit some end or purpose in the world. This is not to be construed narrowly, as instrumental labor but ontologically as an essential, determining feature of human life. It is not only the manipulation of nature that encapsulates the capacity for realizing oneself in the world; the entire system of social facts and social ontology is a production of our inner worlds.

To this end, to refer back to Ricoeur for a moment, Freud's salience for a critical social theory lies in his capacity to peel back the layers of sedimented, internalized relational configurations that have shaped our intrapsychic world; the very mental processes, value-orientations, normative configurations, and so on, that bind us to the prevailing social order or shape our neurotic responses to it. The archeological process of analysis leads us to the realization that we are teleological beings, that we posit ends in the world. To know this leads to a capacity for critical autonomy: for the capacity of the ego to shatter the encrusted layers of reification and ideology larded onto it by socialization and internalization processes. These sedimented layers of prior experience and the mind's adaptation to as well as repression or accommodation to them is the point of contact between self and world. It is the way the mind is shaped by the structural and functional dynamics of the social world, of any given phase of history.

The method therefore entails exploding the distorted forms of self-understanding that result from the processes of repression and the contents of the unconscious. As Yirmiyahu Yovel argues: 'Freud maintains that self-knowledge can have a solid basis in science as objective truth. Freud also sees lucidity – a demystified consciousness in various modes – as an end in itself

---

8   Ricoeur, *Freud and Philosophy*, 459.

and as a leading cultural value.'[9] But I want to suggest that it is precisely here where Freud's theoretical approach cedes its critical power. In Ricoeur's parlance, an archeology without a teleology in Freud means that we can achieve some lucidity, but nevertheless not have a ground for judging; we may be able to gain some degree of self-understanding given certain genetic interpretations of how our intrapsychic world has been shaped. But we will nevertheless lack a critical form of self-consciousness in an ontological sense – that is, we will lack the capacity to judge in a critical, transformative sense. As Yovel remarks, comparing Freud's project to that of Spinoza's: 'the goal of Freudian therapy is to produce a normal person; the goal of Spinoza's ethics is to produce a non-normal person – a rare human being of uncommon inner excellence.'[10]

I think that it is precisely here that a synthesis of Freud and Marx finds it philosophical as well as practical point of departure. Since Freud's therapeutic, as opposed to his meta-psychological, project is to cure the individual of the suffering of neuroses, there is no space for further self-consciousness and self-knowledge. Marx's philosophical anthropology, or what I think we should understand as his critical social ontology of the human species captures this deeper structure of human self-consciousness and self-understanding. It does this by grasping not the dynamics of the mind, but of the practical, teleological nature of human activity and social being. A comprehensive form of critical judgment opens up for us when Freud and Marx are brought into critical contact, that is, when they are seen as complimenting one another – a materialist, praxis-oriented twist on Ricoeur's plea to merge archeology and teleology.

3   Ontogeny and Phylogeny in Freud and Marx

Both Freud and Marx work with a dialectical relation between phylogeny and ontogeny or, to put it a different way, with the inherent capacities of human beings as members of a distinct species and the particular forms that these capacities take given the particular dynamics that have produced the individual. Freud elucidates his ideas on this question in the 1914 preface to his *Three Essays on the Theory of Sexuality*:

> The relation between ontogenesis and phylogenesis is a similar one. Ontogenesis may be regarded as a recapitulation of phylogenesis, in so

---

9   Yirmiyahu Yovel, *Spinoza and Other Heretics: The Adventures of Immanence* (Princeton: Princeton University Press, 1989), 154.
10 Yovel, *Spinoza and Other Heretics*, 155.

far as the latter has not been modified by more recent experience. The phylogenetic disposition can be seen at work behind the ontogenetic process. But disposition is ultimately the precipitate of earlier experience of the species to which more recent experience of the individual, as the sum of the accidental factors, is super-added.[11]

The distinction between the phylogenetic and the ontogenetic means a distinction between capacities and drives that we have as a member of the species (phylogeny) that take on particular patterns and forms based on the specific developmental history of any given individual (ontogeny). The divergence between these two dimensions of human life points to the possibility of grasping a non-biological dimension to human beings. In this sense, the ontogenetic supervenes upon the phylogenetic; there exist certain capacities inherent in the species that can be shaped and find distinctive expression in any specific individual. This is not reducible to biology but is a property of a distinctive psychological realm that the biological makes possible. Freud goes on to that: 'I must, however, emphasize that the present work is characterized not only by being completely based on psychological research, but also by being deliberately independent of the findings of biology.'[12]

For Freud, our ontogenesis seems to be constituted by two core phylogenetic capacities we all share. First, there is what we can call the *synthetic* or *creative-organizational capacity of the mind*. For Freud, our experience of the world is not directly empirical; we are not mirrors of the external world. Rather, we interact with it based on our drives and associations with other people (external objects). It is therefore filtered through the net of drives and specific ways that these drives have been shaped by the relational matrices with others during our development. The synthetic capacity of the mind therefore refers to the activity of the subject in re-organizing experience in such a way so as to enable them to possess some degree of freedom to satisfy their drives, particularly sexual or erotic drives. A drive (*Trieb*) is not instinctual as it is in non-human animals. Rather, Freud emphasizes that although it has its origin in our biological makeup, the satisfaction of that drive can take on a number of different forms, or to use Freud's language, the aim is to achieve satisfaction with a variety of objects. As Freud says: 'It has been brought to our notice that we have been in the habit of regarding the connection between the sexual instinct and the sexual object as more intimate than it in fact is ... We are thus

---

11 Sigmund Freud, *Three Essays on the Theory of Sexuality*, Standard Edition, Vol. 7 (London: The Hogarth Press, 1973), 131.
12 Freud, *Three Essays on Sexuality*, 131.

warned to loosen the bond that exists in our thoughts between instinct and object.'[13]

The loosening of this bond is a crucial point of departure for Freud's understanding of the mind. More than a mechanical relation between instinct or drive and its satisfaction, sexuality is a sensual satisfaction via the capacity for reorganizing our experience of the world. Eros now can be seen as a force that binds things together, a force that impels cohesion and unity. The function of Eros, Freud notes, 'is to establish ever greater unities and to preserve them thus – in short, to bind them together.'[14] He sees this as akin to the basic processes of cellular life wherein,

> the union of a number of cells into a vital association – the multicellular character of organisms – has become a means of prolonging their life … The germ-cells require their libido, the activity of their life instincts, for themselves, as a reserve against their later momentous constructive activity … In this way the libido of our sexual instincts would coincide with the Eros of the poets and philosophers which holds all living things together'.[15]

The erotic is therefore more than mere sexual desire or drive; it connotes the capacity for the self to seek out creative ways for the satisfaction of desires and urges within the self by means of the outside world. The erotic, in this sense, transcends the sexual. In Jonathan Lear's words, human beings "reach beyond themselves" through Eros.

> There are primal gratifications in this urge, to be sure; but there is embedded in this an elemental desire for understanding and for orientation. This is why the "sexual" drives should ultimately be understood as erotic drives. What Freud had been calling sexuality, he now tells us, isn't just an urge towards procreation, nor towards pleasurable bodily satisfaction: rather it has 'far more resemblance to the all-inclusive and all-embracing Eros of Plato's *Symposium*.'[16]

---

13 Freud, *Three Essays on Sexuality*, 147–148.
14 Freud, "An Outline of Psycho-Analysis," 148.
15 Sigmund Freud, *Beyond the Pleasure Principle. Standard Edition*, Vol. 18 (London: The Hogarth Press, 1973), 50.
16 Jonathan Lear, *Freud* (London: Routledge, 2005), 86–87.

Indeed, the discharge of this tension is the very substance of sexual pleasure, but the core idea Freud is after here is that, unlike a raw instinct that admits to no possible variation of the object as in non-human animals, human beings can satisfy the drive through a variety of objects:

> a light is thrown on the nature of the sexual instinct by the fact that it permits of so much variation in its objects and such a cheapening of them – which hunger with its far more energetic retention of its objects, would only permit in the most extreme instances.[17]

These diversions of drive and object are not to be construed as pathologies, but as perversions. The capacity of the mind to create substitute objects (fetishes) that stand in for the object as a whole, or any other set of associations of sexual pleasure with pain or aggression, are present in all "normal" forms of sexuality for Freud. It constitutes the essence of the creative capacity of the mind to deviate from any inherently rooted instinctual pattern.[18]

In the sexual act and drive, we see this creative capacity of the mind in one of its fullest and most robust expressions. But it is also a drive toward *action*, toward a unity with others and with the express purpose of holding life together. Here we can see the second phylogenetic capacity that Freud points to in his psychoanalytic theory: a capacity for associating, for forming relations with others what we can call a *conjunctive capacity* for individuals to seek out others and to form relations with them. The key idea here is that the erotic is not only a drive toward life, but also, as Freud lays it out, a drive toward unity with others, toward relating with others. Narcissism, in this sense, is counter-productive to the proliferation of life. Eros seeks out others just as it seeks out pleasure. It is an energic force for life and unity whereas narcissism is a turn inward, a move toward disintegration. We see now that Freud is pointing toward not only the first capacity of the mind, that of the creative-organizational capacity,

---

17   Freud, *Three Essays on Sexuality*, 148. Later in the same section, Freud further remarks that: 'The most general conclusion that follows from all these discussions seems, however, to be this. Under a great number of conditions and in surprisingly numerous individuals, the nature and importance of the sexual object recedes into the background.' Ibid., 149.

18   Throughout the various editions of the *Three Essays on Sexuality*, Freud is consistent in his emphasis that perversions are not necessarily by any means pathological: 'If a perversion, instead of appearing merely *alongside* the normal sexual aim and object, and only when circumstances are unfavorable to *them* and favorable to *it* – if, instead of this, it ousts them completely and takes their place in *all* circumstances – if, in short, a perversion has the characteristics of exclusiveness and fixation – then we shall usually be justified in regarding it as a pathological symptom.' Ibid., 161.

but also toward a drive toward relatedness, toward associating with others for the purposes of life. "Sexual instincts," Freud emphasizes, are to be "equated with life instincts."[19] Again, Freud stresses that we have a phylogenetic need for satisfaction defined as the discharge of tension, but this is mingled with the capacity for fantasy, for the capacity for imagination, for the mind's capacity to create and organize its energies in ways that satisfy the drive.

But as we can see, the core idea in Eros is a kind of living vitality to connect with the world, to creatively organize the world spontaneously rather than merely chart it empirically, as if the psyche were some kind of AI device. It is also a drive toward unification with others – not only via the unification of the genitals, but also in broader terms for the purposes of expanding life. Freud's concept of Eros therefore points toward two core phylogenetic capacities of human beings: to creatively organize the experience of their world and to form relations with others for the vital purposes of life. Both are part of the same force, as Joel Whitebook argues:

> At the same time as the child binds itself to its mother, developing a relationship with her, she binds – organizes and articulates – the infant's disorganized unarticulated inner experience by containing and mirroring it back to him/her. In addition to synthetic tendencies that arise from the hardwiring of the human mind, the erotic striving for unification – for reunification – derives from the memory of that undifferentiated matrix.[20]

The erotic is a longing for satisfaction, but not through some instrumental use of the object domain. Rather, it is constitutive of a kind of template for relatedness and association. Eros therefore encapsulates both the synthetic as well as the conjunctive phylogenetic capacities of human beings: we are spontaneously creative in the organization of our experience and prone toward relatedness with others for the very promulgation of life. The opposite – narcissism – Freud sees as constitutive of the disintegrative force of the death drive.[21]

---

19 Freud, *Beyond the Pleasure Principle*, 53. Joel Whitebook emphasizes the way that eros functions not only as a force for the individual alone, but also as a force that integrates the ego with others: "Put in simple economic terms, the increase in energy that results from the union counteracts the disintegrative forces of the death instinct. This suggests another intrinsic connection, between narcissism and death. When an organism operates alone *narcissistically* – it succumbs to death; when it invests in objects and unites with other organisms, its vitality is enhanced." Joel Whitebook, *Freud: An Intellectual Biography* (New York: Cambridge University Press, 2017), 372.

20 Whitebook, *Freud: An Intellectual Biography*, 374.

21 Freud, *Beyond the Pleasure Principle*, 44ff.

Freud's understanding of the human mind as possessing the phylogenetic capacities for *spontaneous creative-organizational mental activity* as well as forming unifying relations with others points toward two core elemental aspects of human life. What I want to highlight in the capacity for the erotic emerging out of his theory of sexuality is this capacity to create and organize, to point beyond itself, as Lear describes it, but also to conjoin with others, to form relations of unity for the purposes of life. In this way, Freud adds a psychological twist to similar ideas of Aristotle, who saw in his *Politics* the desire for the good life as an impulse for individuals to form higher forms of association. For Aristotle, the core idea was that of a desire (*Orexis*) for the good life, for a kind of self-sufficiency defined as a life ensconced in mutual relations where self-development could reach its maximum.[22] Indeed, Freud's ideas point in the direction of a psychic need for relatedness just as it does a mental capacity for creativity and self-organization. It is not simply an instinctual need, however: it takes the form of desire, of a kind of drive that is different from non-human forms of instinct. In this sense, Freud is able to blend together affect and idea, feeling and thought.

Marx's ideas about human life are distinct form Freud's, but also share in the same dynamics. I want to suggest that there is a similar theory about the phylogenetic capacities of human life that both Freud and Marx share. Marx, emerging out of the post-Hegelian world of the "Young" or "Left Hegelians" saw human praxis as the center of his social ontology. In the reaction to Idealism, post-Hegelian philosophy sought to understand the human capacity to posit themselves in the world as a central feature of human life. Unlike Fichte's radical subjectivist account of the constitution of the object domain by the subject, thinkers such as Ludwig Feuerbach, August von Ciezskowski, and Bruno Bauer saw human praxis as a means of shaping and manipulating the object domain in accordance with consciousness.[23] The opposition between subject and object that was a defining feature of Kant's philosophical ideas was seen as frustrating the human capacity to realize freedom concretely in the world, in one's practices, structure of self, and culture.[24]

---

22   For Aristotle, "desire" (*Orexis*) is to be differentiated from an "appetite" (*Epithumia*) for eating or sexual activity, for instance. See the important discussion by Jonathan Lear, *Aristotle: The Desire to Understand* (Cambridge: Cambridge University Press, 1988), 141ff.

23   See August von Cieszkowski, *Prolegomena zur Historiosophie* (Hamburg: Felix Meiner Verlag, 1981); Ludwig Feuerbach, *Die Philosophie der Zukunft* (Stuttgart, 1922); and Bruno Bauer, *Die Posaune des jüngsten Gerichts über Hegel, den Atheisten und Antichristen* (Leipzig, 1841).

24   For a discussion see Frederick Beiser, *German Idealism: The Struggle against Subjectivism, 1781–1801* (Cambridge, MA: Harvard University Press, 2002).

Marx takes this idea to a new level. He argues that human beings are both practical and social, that we possess a teleological capacity to realize ends in the world and that these practical capacities emerge within matrices of relations with others. These are phylogenetic in the sense that they are essential capacities, i.e., capacities that are definitive of the species but also take on different ontogenetic forms depending on how social forms are organized. Marx's basic idea is that we are *socio-practical beings*; that is to say, we are beings that are essentially relational as well as in possession of a capacity of mind that can externalize itself in the world, make itself objective, real. To say that we are practical is to say that we are a special kind of teleological being: one who is able to, as with Freud, use our minds and interactivity with the external world to point beyond our instinctual patterns. Our freedom, in this sense, is to be found in our capacity for realizing ends in the world; rather than objects of our internal natures, we are subjects of the world.

At the same time, we are *relational*, social beings. Marx builds his ontology of human beings as both practical as well as relational, gradually mapping out what he sees as the "essence" of human being. As he says in the *Theses on Feuerbach*: 'the essence of man is no abstraction inhering in each single individual. In its actuality it is the ensemble of human relationships.'[25] By failing to see this, Feuerbach must 'view the essence of man merely as "species," as the inner, dumb generality which unites many individuals *naturally*.'[26] Here, like Freud, Marx is positing that to fail to grasp our essence as social entails failing to see that we are capable of richer forms of human life not dictated by the instincts of the species. Our phylogenetic capacities are precisely that: capacities and potentialities that can take on innumerable forms in concrete life. As argues, 'circumstances are changes by men,' and '[t]he coincidence of the change of circumstances and of human activity or self-change can be comprehended and rationally understood only as *revolutionary practice*.'[27]

So praxis is, like relationality, a phylogenetic capacity or potentiality distinctive of the human species: it is the genetic capacity to create and to transform what exists not according to a natural plan, but according to our practical activity, that is, the synthesis of our ideas and our poetic capacity to create in the world. 'All social life,' Marx contends, 'is essentially *practical*,' which means that the social is unlike a heard or some other form of collective animal life.[28]

---

25   Karl Marx, "Theses on Feuerbach," in *Writings of the Young Marx on Philosophy and Society*, eds. Lloyd D. Easton and Kurt H. Guddat (New York: Doubleday, 1967), 402.
26   Ibid., 402.
27   Ibid., 401.
28   Ibid., 402.

To be sure, we are, as human beings, unlike other social animals in that we have a core capacity to choose the ends we desire to realize; we essentially can change our activity from instinctual, naturally pre-patterned forms of activity to *praxis*, to involve choice and decision to enter into what and how we realize things in the world. In this sense, Marx's idea touches on Freud's emphasis on the creative-organizational capacity of human mental life; it, too, is not defined by instinct, but varies according to a capacity for creation. Marx's thesis, unlike Freud's, does not contain the idea of the unconscious and it therefore has a more rationalistic tone, but it nevertheless points to a common phylogenetic capacity that can inform a distinctive and rich idea of human freedom.

One reason for this is that freedom consists not in a negative sense, or with the removal of interferences for our activities, but rather is conceived as a capacity to deviate from an instinctual pattern of activity. Praxis is organized by ideas and activated via our participation in the world of others as well as nature. The *poietic* dimension of praxis is therefore the very nucleus of human freedom in that it grounds our capacity for a human life beyond the mere satisfaction of human needs. "Labor," for Marx,

> is an exclusively human characteristic ... [W]hat distinguishes the worst architect from the best of bees is that the architect builds the cell in his mind before he constructs it in wax. At the end of every labor process, a result emerges which had already been conceived by the worker at the beginning, hence already existing ideally.[29]

This not only applies to the creation of external objects, the refashioning of nature, and so on. By being self-consciously aware of one's creative capacity for praxis, we have ourselves as an end, we essentially make ourselves and our world ontologically richer in the process.[30]

---

29   Karl Marx, *Capital*, Vol. 1 (New York: Vintage, 1977), 284. Karel Kosík emphasizes this important point when he writes: 'In its essence and generality, praxis is the exposure of the mystery of man as an onto-formative being, as a being that *forms* the (socio-human) reality and *therefore* also grasps and interprets it (i.e., reality both human and extra-human, reality in its totality). Man's praxis is not practical activity as opposed to theorizing; it is the determination of human being as the process of *forming* reality.' Karl Kosík, *Dialectics of the Concrete: A Study on Problems of Man and World* (Dordrecht: D. Reidel Publishing, 1976), 137.

30   Mihailo Marković insightfully notes that: 'das Motiv seiner Tätigkeit nicht nur die Herstellung nützlicher Gegenstände ist, die ein unmittelbares Bedürfnis befriedigen oder die menschliche Macht vergrößern, sondern auch die Produktion solcher Eigenschaften von Gegenständen, die *sich selbst Ziel sind*, die den Gegenstand *verschönern*.' ['The motive of his activity is not only the production of useful objects, which satisfy an

This capacity is rooted in each of us as particular members of the species but is activated and developed in relation to others. 'The more deeply we go back into history, the more does the individual, and hence also the producing individual, appear as dependent, as belonging to a greater whole.'[31] Hence, we are socio-practical beings which is, as Marx argues:

> [T]he *social* character is the universal character of the whole movement; as society itself produces *man* as *man*, so it is produced by him. Activity and mind are social in their content as well as in their *origin*; they are social activity and social mind ... [C]ommunal activity and mind, i.e., activity and mind which express and confirm themselves directly in a *real association* with other men, occur everywhere where this *direct* expression of sociability arises from the content of the activity or corresponds to the nature of mind.[32]

Here, Marx's relation of phylogeny and ontology can be more firmly grasped. The human mind is naturally prone toward sociability; each of us possesses the potentiality for social relatedness as well as the capacity for praxis, for realizing some purpose or end in the world. Like Freud's concept of Eros, which posits both a creative-organizational capacity of the mind as well as a conjunctive impulse toward unity with others, Marx sees our needs as interdependent and our social, productive activities as essentially for one another:

> Suppose we had produced as human beings: in his production each of us would have *twice affirmed* himself and the other ... In my individual life I would have directly created your life; in my individual activity I would have immediately *confirmed* and *realized* my true *human* and *social* nature."[33]

Marx's language over and over again emphasizes the idea that we realize a true nature, we become fully human, etc., when we are able to realize for one

---

immediate need or increase human power, but also the production of those properties of objects *which are ends in themselves*, which *embellish* the object.'] Mihailo Marković, "Entfremdung und Selbstverwaltung," in *Folgen einer Theorie. Essays über Das Kapital von Marx* (Frankfurt: Suhrkamp Verlag, 1967): 178–204, 178.

31 Karl Marx, *Grundrisse* (London: Penguin, 1973), 84.
32 Karl Marx, *Economic and Philosophical Manuscripts*, trans. Tom Bottomore (New York: Frederick Ungar, 1964), 129–130.
33 Karl Marx, "Excerpt Notes from 1844," in *Writings of the Young Marx on Philosophy and Society*, 281.

another our capacity to produce, to make things in the world, to render that which is subjective, objective – or what Marx emphasizes as the capacity for the objectification (*Vergegenständlichkeit*) of oneself in the world, that is, to move from a state of being abstracted in thought to one realized concretely in the world. The reason is that when we realize ourselves as socio-practical beings, we are also realizing in our ontology the highest plenitude of our capacities, the ontological realization of the full development of our phylogenetic capacities.

In this way, we can see that Marx's concept of human life is one that embraces the idea of the species as teleological: that is, as beings that are able to posit ends and projects in the world that we realize through our interaction with the physical (natural) and intersubjective (social) world.[34] This results in a kind of freedom that is quite unlike the classical Enlightenment conception of Spinoza and Kant. The synthesis of Freud and Marx informs a concept of autonomous individuality (of freedom, in other words), which is able to put us in touch with the active, life-enhancing dimensions of our being. This being is relational and in need of others, but not merely for instrumental purposes. Freud may see libido as a drive toward satisfaction of one's aims in another object, but he also sees that the erotic is an impulse toward unity, toward higher forms of living and being just as Marx is insistent that history is a human creation that is above the structure of nature. The positing of meaning beyond ourselves, for Freud in the sense of phantasy and departing from natural instinctual patterns, as well as Marx's idea of human praxis as realizing an idea in the world, holds the key to a kind of freedom that is more robust than that of the modern liberal idea of freedom.

4 The Psychopathologies of Capitalism

In Freud's view, the real heart of psychoanalysis was that of repression. As he puts it: 'The theory of repression is the corner-stone on which the whole structure of psycho-analysis rests.'[35] Repression entails the existence of the

---

34 Marx Wartofsky notes that, for Marx, 'The activity of production, as a teleological activity embodied in a means of production, and in the generation of relations of production which are involved in the utilization of such means, may be characterized as *praxis*, i.e., as the distinctively human mode of self-reproduction.' Marx Wartofsky, "Consciousness, Praxis, and Reality: Marxism vs. Phenomenology," in *Interdisciplinary Phenomenology*, eds. D. Ihde and Richard M. Zaner (Dordrecht: Springer, 1977): 133–151, 138.

35 Sigmund Freud, "On the History of the Psycho-Analytic Movement," in *Standard Edition*, Vol. 14 (London: The Hogarth Press, 1973), 16.

distinction between conscious and unconscious processes, a distinction that is at the center of Freud's contribution to understanding the nature of psychic pathology. The capacity of the mind to repress, to place into unconsciousness aspects of experience and knowledge is essential to understanding the dynamics of not only the neuroses, but also of social pathologies as well. The fundamental idea to grasp here is that social power becomes a kind of domination once we live lives according to the normative and systemic logics of projects that are not our own, or which can be ratified by us in accordance with reasons rooted in our cooperative, self-developing ontology.[36] It is not only repression that is central here, but also the capacity to invest in the particular shape of mind that one has developed or which has been shaped by one's experiences of the object domain. This means looking at the mechanisms of transference as well as that of resistance. As Freud continues to argue:

> It may thus be said that the theory of psycho-analysis is an attempt to account for two striking and unexpected facts of observation which emerge whenever an attempt is made to trace the symptoms of a neurotic back to their sources in his past life: the facts of transference and of resistance.[37]

What can this mean in trying to unpack the relation between the psychic and the social? For one thing, it indicates a capacity of the mind to be shaped and configured according to external events and relational dynamics. Freud is clear that repression into the unconscious results in a kind of deformation of our agency in that the repressed contents of the unconscious shape our conscious processes. In this sense, it shapes our secondary processes of cognition, the social epistemology that we use to navigate our world becomes warped by the dynamics of transference: a kind of template within the mind, constructed from early developmental experience, that organizes on-going experiences in the world. Freud warns us not to look at our epistemology, our conscious processes of perceiving and "knowing" reality as not being warped by the contents of the repressed unconscious:

> Just as Kant warned us not to overlook the fact that our perceptions are subjectively conditioned and must not be regarded as identical with what is perceived though unknowable, so psycho-analysis warns us not

---

36   I have elaborated this at length in my study, *The Specter of Babel: A Reconstruction of Political Judgment* (Albany, NY: SUNY Press, 2020).
37   Freud, "On the History of the Psycho-Analytic Movement," 16.

to equate perceptions by means of consciousness with the unconscious mental processes which are their object.[38]

Repression therefore becomes a kind of not-knowing, but a not-knowing that nevertheless holds out the possibility of being known.

This adds something important to the Marxian account of consciousness and alienation. Marx's view was that social processes directly shape conscious subjective processes; he believed that this was what ideology essentially consisted of. But Freud is adding the unconscious as a crucial new dimension to this process. Capitalism affects us at the unconscious level just as it does at the conscious level. At the unconscious level, it organizes our phylogenetic capacities for spontaneous mental organization as well as our motivations for object relations: in short, for Eros. Repression acts in a Marxian way via the process of *fetishism*: or the repression of the social and praxis-laden content of reality.[39] The commodity form establishes fetishism as a central mechanism for the deformation of consciousness. Human exploitation, both of other human beings as well as non-human animals and of nature, is hidden beneath the veneer of the commodity form. It acts to repress, to push into unconsciousness the reality of human and non-human suffering. What the commodity form and exchange value obscure is the teleological and cooperative essence of human life; this becomes the content of a repressed social unconscious that needs to be formulated via a process analytically breaking down the reified structure of consciousness.

But it is also the case that, in addition to the repression that is affected by fetishization, there is also an active organization of desire – of the motivational and cathectic elements of self that are rooted in unconscious processes. Freud emphasizes that repression not only acts upon the consciousness of things, of phenomenal events, facts and objects, but also of emotions: 'repression results not only in withholding things from consciousness, but also in preventing the development of affect.'[40] The process of repression entails a structurization of mental organization, a kind of reification in the mind of certain thoughts, ideas, and affects that would seem to be intolerable or in some other way, taboo. This means that, as normative patterns are internalized by the developing self, there is a repression of those aspects of reality that do not conform to those

---

38 Sigmund Freud, "The Unconscious," in *Standard Edition*, Vol. 14 (London: The Hogarth Press, 1973), 171.
39 For a discussion, see Richard Lichtman, *The Production of Desire: The Integration of Psychoanalysis into Marxian Theory* (New York: The Free Press, 1982), 256ff.
40 Freud, "The Unconscious," 179.

patterns. This sets up a self-reinforcing process as the ego develops in light of those repressed contents: 'Since these impulses are not *ego-syntonic*, the ego has *repressed* them: that is to say, it has withdrawn its interest from them and has shut them off from becoming conscious as well as from obtaining satisfaction.'[41] Reification and repression can now be seen as two dimensions of the same socio-psychological process of cutting off parts of experience and cognition that are dystonic with the conformist bond between self and world established by socialization.

Returning once again to Ricoeur's thesis of the synthesis of archeology and teleology, a first step toward understanding the power of Freud's analytic is that it is a processes of stripping away the defective and pathological dynamics of the individual mind. Capitalist modernity affects the shape of the mind in specific ways – perhaps most emphatically by its capacity to organize the normative patterns that govern the social world. By doing this, it must also shape the value-orientations and norms that are internalized by consciousness, subsuming the self into the matrix of external social dynamics and normative pattern maintenance. For Marx, the ontogenesis of human beings change according to their historical and social matrix just as for Freud, the ontogenesis of the self is a function of how one's drives are frustrated, how repression functions, and how we internalize other people (objects) during our psychic development. In this sense, we can synthesize Freud and Marx to understand not only a theoretical phylogeny of human beings, but also a critical theory of the ontogenesis of human beings with an eye toward diagnostic criticism.

The core of the psychopathology that capitalism creates is the isolation of the individual, not only in a structural sense, but also in an ontological as well as epistemic sense. As inequality between classes expands, so too does the vertical integrational patterns and dynamics of society. But we also become psychically unfree: unable to achieve a self-consciousness of ourselves as social and practical beings. Most importantly, we lose the capacity for critical judgment, we lose grip of our autonomy as it become invaded by heteronomous norms, concepts, and values, the very building blocks of our ability to know the world and act within it. We become less able to call pathological relations and norms into question as we lose touch with our self-consciousness as relational-practical beings. This has an effect on the structure of desire itself, on the capacity of the individual to experience and to express Eros. Instead, the commodity form – both of that which is consumed as well as what the individual becomes

---

41   Sigmund Freud, "Two Encyclopedia Articles," in *Standard Edition*, vol. 18 (London: Hogarth, 1973), 246.

ontologically as a producer – degrade the drives promoting conformity as well as a degradation of culture. As Alexander Mitscherlich explains:

> The propaganda of the pleasure providers is based with apparent *naivete* on the promise that they will relieve our burden of unpleasure, but the concealed dynamics that makes them so successful is of quite different origin. It arises from the anxiety produced by the frustrations of mass living … The morbid plunge into surrogate pleasures can be explained only as a reaction-formation against an anxiety with which the ego cannot cope. Obedience to instinct and anxiety reactions fuse in patterns of behavior the only common factor in the multiplicity of which is that they are to a large extent inaccessible to the critical ego. They are produced by social processes and promote conformity, but they also bring about a state of pathological obedience to the instincts and a chronic pathogenous state of anxiety.[42]

As a result, *desire is coopted by the system*: the reservoir of pent-up energies that have been created by the processes of sublimation become channeled into the narrow forms of material and physical pleasure and satisfaction that derail rather than engage authentic forms of creative-erotic activity.

Capitalism should therefore be seen as a *total form of life* in that its logics gradually penetrate into every form of non-economic life, culture, and the self.[43] Crucial to the process of commodity production is the subsumption of labor and the exploitation of labor into the process of production. By absorbing the praxis of human life into the system of production, capitalism is able to excise the capacity for poietic praxis and utilize it for its own projects. The repression that occurs as a result of the fetishization of commodities results in the reification of consciousness: that is, in the repression of the crucial self-consciousness of our world-generating powers (*Praxis*) as human beings. There is something akin here to what Freud points to in the split between the reality principle and pleasure principle into two different forms of mental functioning:

---

[42] Alexander Mitscherlich, *Society without the Father: A Contribution to Social Psychology* (New York: Harcourt, Brace and World, 1969), 170.

[43] I have explored this thesis with more detail in my *Twilight of the Self: The Decline of the Individual in Late Capitalism* (Stanford: Stanford University Press, 2022). Also see the important discussion by Samir Gandesha, "Totality and Technological Form," in *The Sage Handbook of Critical Theory*, ed. Beverly Best, Werner Bonefeld, and Chris O'Kane (London: Sage, 2017): 642–660.

> With the introduction of the reality principle one species of thought-activity was split off; it was kept free from reality-testing and remained subordinated to the pleasure principle alone. This activity is *phantasying*, which begins already in children's play, and later, continued as *daydreaming*, abandons dependence on real objects.[44]

Both Marx and Freud see that the mind can be split off and turned against itself. For Marx, capitalist social relations entail an alienation of our capacities as poietic beings, as beings who create and shape the world for the mutual development and satisfaction of needs of others and oneself. For Freud, the reality principle comes to dominate secondary mental processes, consigning the pleasure principle to the unconscious and to non-reality, to *phantasy*.

But taken together, we can see that capitalism can be viewed as a distortion of our social relations, our creative, practical capacities, and our drives for satisfying desire. It recodes and subsumes the self into its patterned logics. Heteronomy is, in this sense, not merely a defect of practical reason, it becomes the very substance, the very ontology of life under capitalism. Such defects of consciousness force the individual into ideological spheres of thinking that conflict with his real needs and authentic capacities for living. This is perhaps why Freud notes that 'every neurosis has as its result, and probably therefore as its purpose, a forcing of the patient out of real life, an alienating him from reality.'[45] Capitalist society, through its processes of reification, of commodification, technical mediation, and shredding of social relations, can be seen as such an alienating force. We live in the structured phantasy that such a commodified world creates: one that shapes our desire and, in the process, shapes the very intrapsychic structures and processes that produce our inner world of thought, feeling and motivation.

5   De-reification as Psycho-ontological Process

The capacity to shape the inner life of individuals, to form and organize the inner psychic life of the minds of people is a crucial dimension of social power and the particular shapes that our social ontology take. As Bruce Brown has put it, for Freud,

---

44 Sigmund Freud, "Formulations on the Two Principles of Mental Functioning," in *Standard Edition*, Vol. 12 (London: The Hogarth Press, 1973), 222.

45 Freud, "Formulations on the Two Principles of Mental Functioning," 218.

unlocking the reified structures of the patient's consciousness, elicits feedback in the form of new data regarding the patient's experience which must be decoded with the analyst's help in such a way as to unmask the patient's increasingly artful rationalizations.[46]

Under capitalism, the artful rationalizations of the individual serve to prop up the system of domination in a distinctively modern sense. That is, heteronomy becomes realized as a concrete mode of thinking, acting, and living. We become ensconced in the normative matrices of power relations and absorb; we are socialized into, and therefore internalize, the value-orientations that will organize the self.

As I have been trying to show, however, this Freudian step, as centrally crucial as it certainly is, is nevertheless only a first step toward a broader means of understanding self-transformation. Since reification is more than a merely cognitive or epistemic defect of consciousness, but also a deformation of our socio-ontological, praxic activity as well, it needs to be seen as the sedimentation of layers of developmental interpersonal configurations and the ways that these have been introjected and internalized into the matrix of the self. Freud demonstrates how our drives can be subverted by the internalized values of external objects and object configurations. The core idea here is that the ego operates – thinks, feels, acts – according to motives rooted in tendencies that are not authentically its own. As Richard Lichtman puts it discussing the idea of a "Marxist unconscious":

> Social structures are sustained not merely by the rules of the social system, however estranged and autonomous, but by the tendencies, hidden to the agents themselves, which reproduce the deepest aspects of character necessary to the continued maintenance of the social system.[47]

Reification operates not only through the commodification of consciousness, it also operates by patterning the most fundamental and spontaneous dynamics of the mind in accordance with heteronomous value-orientations and normative patterns. These values and norms are not only restricted to maintaining the tacit legitimacy of the social system but so too, it stands to reason, as Freud would no doubt suggest, are the system of drives, of desire and the affects more broadly. Cathexis now becomes invested more and more in what

---

46 Bruce Brown, *Marx, Freud, and the Critique of Everyday Life: Toward a Permanent Revolution* (New York: Monthly Review Press, 1973), 39–40.
47 Lichtman, *The Production of Desire*, 252.

the commodified world can produce (think of the craze induced by the "stars" of popular culture or other such sensational products of the culture industry). The ego becomes increasingly subsumed by the imperatives of the system. Psychoanalytic method and praxis must therefore take as a fundamental imperative the dissolving of these conflicts between the ego and the impinging values of the social world.[48]

Once the self is able to achieve a genuine, rational, and emotionally enriching form of self-consciousness, then the path to a genuine freedom can begin to take shape. Autonomy, in this sense, means being more than a mere agent whose will is deduced from an immutable sphere of reason, as the classical Enlightenment thinkers believed. It means understanding oneself as a purposive, meaning-making, and teleologically positing being; it means understanding one's own capacity for self-directedness, as a self-reflective, critical being that can judge the defective structures of relatedness and social praxis that do not contribute to common goods and individual self-development but rather for external goods such as productivity, profit, efficiency, and so on. Freud's own conception of psychoanalysis points us in a direction that is deeply dialectical. Through the process of analyzing our distinctive mental processes, we begin to raise to objective, rational awareness our non-reflective modes of experience. When this occurs, we are able to differentiate these states from our normal mode of thinking and feeling. This process of differentiation can then be re-integrated back into the conscious self and psychic growth results. It is this process of self-objectification, differentiation, and re-integration of psychic material that leads to an expansion of consciousness and a de-reification of internalized psychic structures. It is, in this sense, a central mechanism for self-transformation.

The de-reification of consciousness begins with this capacity for evolved self-understanding. Since our psychic structure is altered and shaped by external forces and the dynamics of our object relations, the self's capacity to break from those early introjects and form new psychic structures and dynamics opens up the possibility of shattering the concretized mental states

---

48 As Paul Ricoeur insightfully notes: 'The object of psychoanalysis is not human desire as such – by which we mean wishes, libido, instinct, and eros (all these words having a specific signification in their specific contexts) – but human desire as understood in a more or less conflictual relation with a cultural world, whether this world is represented by parents – especially by the father – or by authorities, by anonymous external and internal prohibitions, whether articulated in discourse or incorporated in works of art or social, political, and religious institutions. In one way or another, the object of psychoanalysis is always *desires plus culture*.' Paul Ricoeur, *On Psychoanalysis: Writings and Lectures*, Vol. 1 (Cambridge: Polity Press, 2012), 121.

that penetrate outward from those more primary relational object ties. Georg Lukács, in his statement of the problem of reification under capitalism, notes that it is the commodity form that essentially comes to structure our consciousness. This occurs because as the commodity form takes on an increasingly omnipresent role in social life, so too does it shape our relation to self and world: consciousness becomes embedded within the dominant external logics of the system as they increasingly also become constitutive of psychic life. As Karel Kosík, expanding the implications of Lukács' idea, writes:

> The everyday utilitarian praxis gives rise to "routine thinking" – which voices both familiarity with things and with their superficial appearance ... But the world that exposes itself to man in his fetishized praxis, in procuring and manipulation, it not a real world, though it does have a real world's "firmness" and its "effectiveness"; rather, it is a "world of appearances."[49]

The problems of neurosis seem to grow from a similar relation of mind and world. The self's inner conflicts appear in ways that are divergent from their origins. The genetic structure of the conflict needs to be brought to conscious awareness, but even then, there is a need for any genetic interpretation to be re-integrated by the patient in order for new psychic functioning and change to occur. Reification acts in a similar way: by concealing the origins of world that actively dehumanizes and degrades the self, it confers our pathologies of the self on to others. Shattering the reified structure of consciousness, however, can take place in a similar way to the patient's resolution of neurotic conflicts in that what gets revealed via a critical form of psychoanalysis is one's gradual realization of their onto-formative capacities. To become aware of oneself as a being that is constituted by practical relations with others is also to reveal the damaged nature of reality. This opens the possibility for critique, for the possibility of the self-consciousness of oneself as an interdependent being who can find self-realization only in the context of mutual relations where each has intrinsic value as ends in themselves.[50] As Kosík rightly notes: 'The

---

49   Kosík, *Dialectics of the Concrete*, 5.
50   Michael Quante insightfully notes that, for Marx, 'Der Mensch kann sich bzw. Sein Wesen nur als leibliches Wesen realisieren. Unter der Prämisse, dass die Wesensverwirklichung nicht nur eine metaphysisch-ontologische Struktur ist, sondern auch eine evaluative Dimension aufweist, bietet die Marxsche Konzeption damit die Möglichkeit, der Leiblichkeit und Bedürftigkeit des Menschen nicht nur den Status einer kausalen Ermöglichungsbedingung und eines instrumentellen Vehikels für autonomes Handeln zuzuerkennen, sondern sie als integralen Bestandteil menschlicher Autonomie miteinem

onto-formative process of human praxis is the basis for the possibility of ontology, i.e., for understanding being. The process of forming a (socio-human) reality is a prerequisite for disclosing and comprehending reality.'[51]

6   Freud, Marx, and the Structure of Freedom

It may be correct to say that Freud and Marx can help us understand the nature of what a less repressive, non-dominating form of life can look like. Both Freud and Marx did make room for the realm of necessity, or *Ananke*, in their own respective ways. Neither, in their full mature theories, are romantics. But each did see that human freedom resides in the capacity for human beings to rework and reshape the structures of necessity that form the parameters of life. Putting consciousness into contact with the erotic, life-giving, creative essence that lies at the heart of human existence paves the way to a richer project of critical theory and freedom. The emancipation of the self is therefore a crucial pre-requisite to the transformation of the social. In this sense, the formulation of autonomy put forth by Castoriadis takes us closer to what I think a Freud-Marx synthesis can achieve:

> Autonomy does not consist in acting according to a law discovered in an immutable Reason and given once and for all. It is the unlimited self-questioning about the law and its foundations as well as the capacity, in light of this interrogation, *to make, to do* and *to institute* (therefore, *to say*). Autonomy is the reflective activity of a reason creating itself in an endless movement, both as individual and social reason.[52]

---

 intrinsischen Wert auszustatten.' ['Man can only realize himself or his being as a physical being. Under the premise that the realization of essence is not only a metaphysical-ontological structure, but also has an evaluative dimension, Marx's conception thus offers the possibility of giving the corporeality and neediness of humans not only the status of a causal enabling condition and an instrumental vehicle for autonomous acknowledging action, but endowing it with intrinsic value as an integral part of human autonomy.'] Michael Quante, "Das gegenständliche Gattungswesen: Bemerkungen zum intrinsischen Wert menschlicher Dependenz," in *Nach Marx. Philosophy, Kritik, Praxis*, eds. R. Jaeggi and D. Loick (Frankfurt: Suhrkamp Verlag, 2013): 69–86, 79.

51 Kosík, *Dialectics of the Concrete*, 139.
52 Cornelius Castoriadis, "Power, Politics, Autonomy," in his *Philosophy, Politics, Autonomy: Essays in Political Philosophy*, ed. David Ames Curtis (New York: Oxford University Press, 1991): 143–174, 164.

Marx, however, notes that this is not a sufficient account: 'The human being is in the most literal sense a ζῷον πολίτικον (political animal), not merely a gregarious animal, but an animal which can individuate itself only in the midst of society.'[53] In this passage, Marx is pointing toward the Aristotelian category of *Autarky* or "self-sufficiency," which Aristotle tells us is a status of being ensconced in relations that provide for each member of the community the resources needed for their full individual development. But a critical sense of *autonomy*, as I have been trying to show, is itself *the product of a kind of reflection that is able to take this ontology of the species as the ground for its practical reasoning*. A critical autonomy is an achieved status that is reached only when the psychic process of de-reification has been sufficiently accomplished. It paves the way for a critical theory of judgment that can enable the concrete form of freedom that Marx has in view to emerge; a more dialectical comprehension of the relation between self and society where true freedom is both the reception of what others give and your own willingness to produce for others.[54] Such a relational dynamic takes each member of the community as an intrinsic end in itself, not from some deduction of practical reason, but because of the concrete needs that are shared universally among all.

Marx therefore sees human freedom not in narrow liberal terms, as an absence of interference or constraint, but in terms of a kind of relational autonomy where reciprocal praxis is the very substance of what it means to be free. Freedom is an *ontological state*: it is not merely a state of being non-dominated, it is the achieved status of being where one inhabits a social context of mutual, reciprocal relations, where each produces and orients their projects toward the needs and satisfactions of others. This is not to be construed in utilitarian or productivist terms. When Marx talks about "producing for others," he means organizing our onto-formative practices toward ends that are beneficial for all rather than in egoistic terms. Freedom is a property of a practical relation; to be autonomous, in this sense, is to be able to work within

---

53   Marx, *Grundrisse*, 84.
54   Iring Fetscher summarizes Marx's position nicely when he writes: 'Marx looked ahead to a cooperative civilization in which each man would take satisfaction in his own accomplishments because they contributed to the gratification of others and would accept the work of others as contributing to his own gratification. Instead of dissolving the mutual relations which corresponded to the ideal of the city-state, Marx preferred their universalization, and a radical transformation of their character.' Iring Fetscher, "Marx's Concretization of the Concept of Freedom," in *Socialist Humanism: An International Symposium*, ed. Erich Fromm (New York: Doubleday, 1965): 238–249, 239. Also see Fetscher's discussion of this theme in his *Marx and Marxism* (New York: Herder and Herder, 1971), 26ff.

such a structure, to organize one's desires and activities within the mutuality of a cooperative practical life. Capital distorts this relational reciprocity by rendering us dependent on others rather than interdependent; we produce not with others as ends in themselves, but with an eye toward exchange value.[55]

Autonomy now takes on a different register from the liberal and Kantian paradigm in that it is aware that freedom consists in the capacity to live in relation to others; that it is a capacity to think and act outside of the framework of narrow self-interest. Autonomy is not the achievement of freedom, that needs to be a social achievement. It is, however, an achievement of self-consciousness: it entails the capacity to think in authentic terms, to move in a space of reasons that is rooted in our social ontology and to slough off the reified structures of thought that impel us to reproduce a world of unfreedom. To be free in Marx's sense is to orient oneself toward a relational dynamic with others that is mutual as well as reciprocal. To be free is to live, in Hegelian parlance, an individual life: one where particularity does not dominate, but a *dialectical mediation between the universal and the particular producing the individual.* A critical form of autonomy is one that seeks out and invests one's capacities in the mutual production of ends for the satisfaction and development of others knowing that, in turn, these mutual, reciprocal interactions nourish one's individuality as well. In this sense, Marx follows the line of thought first explored by Plato in his *Republic,* where the common interest manifests itself in the individual life projects of each member of the community, a kind of sociality, as Iring Fetscher observes, 'in which individuals would not be barriers to each other's freedom but would supplement and enrich one another's being.'[56]

Autonomy, in this sense, does not imply the subject's reflection on a formal or abstract form of reason (or, in its more contemporary formulation, an

---

[55] This is why Marx sees capital's logic of the production of exchange values as distorting the true, free substance of human social life: 'But in production based on capital, consumption is mediated at all points by exchange, and labor never has a *direct* use value for those who are working. Its entire basis is labor as exchange value and as the creation of exchange value.' Marx, *Grundrisse*, 419. The emphasis Marx places on the word "*direct*" in this passage seems to be key since he is contrasting this to what is potential within free cooperative production: each reciprocally producing use values for each other. For a discussion, see Daniel Brudney, "Producing for Others," in *The Philosophy of Recognition: Historical and Contemporary Perspectives*, ed. Hans-Christoph Schmidt am Busch and Christopher Zurn (Lanham, MD: Lexington Books, 2009). Also see, Andrew Chitty, "Recognition and Property in Hegel and the Early Marx," *Ethical Theory and Moral Practice* 16, no. 4 (2013): 685–697.

[56] Fetscher, *Marx and Marxism*, 36.

intersubjective form of communal agreement), but the capacity to know oneself as a self-directing being whose formative capacities and relational dynamics are substantively at the heart of a concrete expression of life. As Marx puts it: 'Universally developed individuals, whose social relations, as their own communal (*Gemeinschaftlich*) relations, are hence also subordinated to their own communal control, are no product of nature, but of history.'[57] Capital is the defective perversion of this capacity for true sociality; it inverts our cooperative and creative capacities for egoistic, not common, universal ends. Judgment, critique, is only possible in its socially transformative sense once autonomy has been achieved, once we are able to gain a self-reflection free of the repressive modes of consciousness that squeezes us into the patterned external world.

Freud, too, sees that our own suffering comes from an inability to achieve a psychic, generative orientation. But he also sees that to achieve this orientation, we must be able to uncover the ways that desire has been perverted away from a creative orientation via the refractions within the mind rooted in repressed, unconscious contents. The capacity to love an other in a truly erotic sense is what promotes our health. It is our self-involvement that brings on illness: 'A strong egoism is a protection against falling ill, but in the last resort we must begin to love in order not to fall ill, and we are bound to fall ill if, in consequence of frustration, we are unable to love.'[58] Erotic love and mutually productive praxis are two facets of the same fundamental human capacity for relations and creation; they both inform a richer expression of human life that is capable of generating ends and relations that correspond to universal human need and not merely the egoistic interests of the atomized self.[59] Love exists within a structure of reciprocal mutuality; it can only become real, existent in the world between two people who orient themselves toward one another in a loving way. As Marx says: 'If you love without evoking love in return, if you are unable, by the *manifestation* of yourself as a loving person, to make yourself

---

57 Marx, *Grundrisse*, 162.
58 Sigmund Freud, "On Narcissism: An Introduction," in *Standard Edition*, Vol. 14 (London: The Hogarth Press, 1973), 85.
59 Freud often notes the conflict and duality between the need to satisfy one's internal drives and the need to relate to others. As he makes clear: 'The individual does actually carry on a twofold existence: one to serve his own purposes and the other as a link in a chain, which he serves against his will, or at least involuntarily. The individual himself regards sexuality as one of his own ends; whereas from another point of view he is an appendage to his germplasm, at whose disposal he puts his energies in return for a bonus of pleasure.' Freud, "On Narcissism," 78.

a *beloved person*, then your love is impotent, a misfortune.'[60] Although Freud contrasts this erotic energy with the destructiveness of *Thanatos*, he nevertheless associates the capacity for psychic health with the achievement of a status of being able to love and to create.

Emphasis on the transformation of the self, on the need for fostering autonomy in a critical sense, is what makes the connection between Freud and Marx so crucial. One reason for this is that it places the dialectic between the individual and society, between subject and object, and between consciousness and reality into more detailed context. It is only when the self begins to judge, to shift perspective, to create new forms of knowing and seeing that the social can become an object of change and transformation. De-reifying consciousness, as I argued above, means a self-consciousness of oneself as an onto-formative being; but this leads to seeing society itself as a dimension of the self, as forming the field of possibility for one's own self-development and freedom. The Freudian archeology is therefore a prerequisite to the discovery of ourselves as teleological beings: as beings that seek to create and make our world. Unlike orthodox version of Marxism that see social change as resulting from the architectonics of class conflict, a more nuanced synthesis of Freud and Marx highlights the importance of consciousness, or self-consciousness, as the nucleus for an immanent critique of the social world. For only when we uncover ourselves as socio-creative beings can we begin to experience the ontic world as one that hampers freedom. Here true critique begins: judgment that entails transformative (radical) praxis.

We now approach more directly the synthesis of Freud and Marx: both share the project of liberating human life from the confines of self-mystification, from the irrational and disfigured modes of experience and self-understanding that shape our agency. As beings with the capacity for relational and spontaneous activity, we are prone to be shaped by modes of power that can render us unfree – that is, create for us a state where our purposive activities are not our own, but somehow imprisoned by others. In Marx's case, such imprisonment takes the shape of class power, the capacity of some segment of the community to shape the productive, onto-formative powers of each of us according to their projects and ends. We live in a world created *by us* but *for others*. For Freud, the imprisonment takes on a different shape: that of an intrapsychic world that has been organized by our relations to the object configurations during our psychic development. We live with the particular shape of mind that we do because of the ways that the dynamics of repression and other mental dynamics derived

---

60   Marx, *Economic and Philosophical Manuscripts*, 168.

from our developmental experiences have formed into psychic patterns that continue to organize our internal psychic world; and these developmental experiences are themselves shaped by the kind of social and economic forces that form the particular world we inhabit and which socializes us.

This is why the process of de-reification is at its base a *psychic process*: that is, it is a process of recovering a form of self-consciousness of oneself as an onto-formative, social being. Just as it is important in the analysis of the self to uncover the ways that external objects have been introjected, how forms of anxiety and insecurity have been fostered by certain interpersonal dynamics and familial influences in one's development, so too it is crucial for a critical psychoanalysis to reclaim one's sense of self as a generative being, capable of generating new relations and worlds of meaning. It is wrong to see the intimate world of familial development as a separate domain from the external social world and its structures and processes – both are intertwined in a broader totality and give shape to psychic structure.[61] To exorcise the internalized structures of consciousness and affect that have been pressed into the self requires a breaking up of the reified forms of thought that have been produced by socialization into a society dominated by the commodity form and exchange value. It entails a migration from a heteronomic sphere of experience toward an authentic form of self-reflection and self-determination.

Bibliography

Bauer, Bruno. *Die Posaune des jüngsten Gerichts über Hegel, den Atheisten und Antichristen*. Leipzig, 1841.

Beiser, Frederick. *German Idealism: The Struggle against Subjectivism, 1781–1801*. Cambridge, MA: Harvard University Press, 2002.

Block, James. *A Nation of Agents: The American Path to a Modern Self and Society*. Cambridge, MA: Harvard University Press, 2002.

Brown, Bruce. *Marx, Freud, and the Critique of Everyday Life: Toward a Permanent Revolution*. New York: Monthly Review Press, 1973.

---

61   Freud does see a separation between these two aspects of the individual's relation to the external world. In his comments on Marx's theory of ideology and the "superstructural" theory consciousness, he notes: 'Mankind never lives entirely in the present. The past, the tradition of the race and of the people, lives on in the ideologies of the super-ego, and yields only slowly to the influences of the present and to new changes; and so long as it operates through the super-ego it plays a powerful part in human life, independently of economic conditions.' Sigmund Freud, *New Introductory Lectures on Psycho-Analysis*, in *Standard Edition*, Vol. 22 (London: The Hogarth Press, 1973), 67 as well as 176ff.

Brudney, Daniel. "Producing for Others." In *The Philosophy of Recognition: Historical and Contemporary Perspectives*, edited by Hans-Christoph Schmidt am Busch and Christopher Zurn. Lanham, MD: Lexington Books, 2009.

Castoriadis, Cornelius. "Power, Politics, Autonomy." In *Philosophy, Politics, Autonomy: Essays in Political Philosophy*, edited by David Ames Curtis. New York: Oxford University Press, 1991.

Chitty, Andrew. "Recognition and Property in Hegel and the Early Marx." *Ethical Theory and Moral Practice* 16, no. 4 (2013): 685–697.

Cieszkowski, August von. *Prolegomena zur Historiosophie*. Hamburg: Felix Meiner Verlag, 1981.

Fetscher, Iring. *Marx and Marxism*. New York: Herder and Herder, 1971.

Fetscher, Iring. "Marx's Concretization of the Concept of Freedom." In *Socialist Humanism: An International Symposium*, edited by Erich Fromm, 238–249. New York: Doubleday, 1965.

Feuerbach, Ludwig. *Die Philosophie der Zukunft*. Stuttgart, 1922.

Freud, Sigmund. "An Outline of Psycho-Analysis." In *Standard Edition*, Vol. 23. London: The Hogarth Press, 1973.

Freud, Sigmund. "Autobiographical Study." In *Standard Edition*, Vol. 20. London: The Hogarth Press, 1973.

Freud, Sigmund. "Beyond the Pleasure Principle". In *Standard Edition*, Vol. 18. London: The Hogarth Press, 1973.

Freud, Sigmund. "Formulations on the Two Principles of Mental Functioning." In *Standard Edition*, Vol. 12. London: The Hogarth Press, 1973.

Freud, Sigmund. "New Introductory Lectures on Psycho-Analysis". In *Standard Edition*, Vol. 22. London: The Hogarth Press, 1973.

Freud, Sigmund. "On Narcissism: An Introduction." In *Standard Edition*, Vol. 14. London: The Hogarth Press, 1973.

Freud, Sigmund. "On the History of the Psycho-Analytic Movement." In *Standard Edition*, Vol. 14. London: The Hogarth Press, 1973.

Freud, Sigmund. "Three Essays on the Theory of Sexuality". In *Standard Edition*, Vol. 7. London: The Hogarth Press, 1973.

Freud, Sigmund. "Two Encyclopedia Articles." In *Standard Edition*, vol. 18. London: Hogarth, 1973.

Freud, Sigmund. "The Unconscious." In *Standard Edition*, Vol. 14. London: The Hogarth Press, 1973.

Gandesha, Samir. "Totality and Technological Form." In *The Sage Handbook of Critical Theory*, edited by Beverly Best, Werner Bonefeld, and Chris O'Kane. London: Sage, 2017.

Kosík, Karel. *Dialectics of the Concrete: A Study on Problems of Man and World*. Dordrecht: D. Reidel Publishing, 1976.

Lear, Jonathan. *Freud.* London: Routledge, 2005.
Lear, Jonathan. *Aristotle: The Desire to Understand.* Cambridge: Cambridge University Press, 1988.
Lichtman, Richard. *The Production of Desire: The Integration of Psychoanalysis into Marxian Theory.* New York: The Free Press, 1982.
Marković, Mihailo. "Entfremdung und Selbstverwaltung." In *Folgen einer Theorie. Essays über Das Kapital von Marx.* Frankfurt: Suhrkamp Verlag, 1967.
Marx, Karl. *Capital,* Vol. 1. New York: Vintage, 1977.
Marx, Karl. *Economic and Philosophical Manuscripts.* Translated by Tom Bottomore. New York: Frederick Ungar, 1964.
Marx, Karl. "Excerpt Notes from 1844." In *Writings of the Young Marx on Philosophy and Society,* edited by Lloyd D. Easton and Kurt H. Guddat. New York: Doubleday, 1967.
Marx, Karl. *Grundrisse.* London: Penguin, 1973.
Marx, Karl. "Theses on Feuerbach." In *Writings of the Young Marx on Philosophy and Society,* edited by Lloyd D. Easton and Kurt H. Guddat. New York: Doubleday, 1967.
Mitscherlich, Alexander. *Society without the Father: A Contribution to Social Psychology.* New York: Harcourt, Brace and World, 1969.
Michael Quante, "Das gegenständliche Gattungswesen: Bemerkungen zum intrinsischen Wert menschlicher Dependenz." In *Nach Marx. Philosophy, Kritik, Praxis,* edited by R. Jaeggi and D. Loick, 69–86. Frankfurt: Suhrkamp Verlag, 2013.
Ricoeur, Paul. *Freud and Philosophy: An Essay on Interpretation.* Translated by Denis Savage. New Haven, CT: Yale University Press, 1970.
Ricoeur, Paul. *On Psychoanalysis: Writings and Lectures,* Vol. 1. Cambridge: Polity Press, 2012.
Spinoza, Benedict. *Ethica Ordine Geometrico Demonstrata. Opera,* vol. 2. Darmstadt: Wissenschaftliche Buchgeselleschaft, 1989.
Thompson, Michael J. "Reification as an Ontological Concept." *Metodo: International Studies in Phenomenology and Philosophy* 9, no. 2 (2021): 417–445.
Thompson, Michael J. *The Specter of Babel: A Reconstruction of Political Judgment.* Albany, NY: SUNY Press, 2020.
Thompson, Michael J. *Twilight of the Self: The Decline of the Individual in Late Capitalism.* Stanford: Stanford University Press, 2022.
Wartofsky, Marx. "Consciousness, Praxis, and Reality: Marxism vs. Phenomenology." In *Interdisciplinary Phenomenology,* edited by D. Ihde and Richard M. Zaner. Dordrecht: Springer, 1977.
Weber, Max. *Wirtschaft und Gesellschaft.* Tübingen: J.C.B. Mohr, 1972.
Whitebook, Joel. *Freud: An Intellectual Biography.* New York: Cambridge University Press, 2017.
Yovel, Yirmiyahu. *Spinoza and Other Heretics: The Adventures of Immanence.* Princeton: Princeton University Press, 1989.

CHAPTER 9

How to Conceive of the Unconscious and its Political Significance

Fabio Molinari

1   A (Failed) Attempt at an Epistemology of Psychoanalysis

On the 2nd of October 1927, the *Privatdozent* Max Horkheimer replied to Theodor Adorno's concerns about a manuscript he had written.[1] The manuscript they discussed is Adorno's first attempt at obtaining the habilitation necessary to teach in German universities, *Der Begriff des Unbewußten in der transzendentalen Seelenlehre*. According to the periodization performed by Carlo Pettazzi, one of the pioneers in Adornian studies, this epistolary exchange occurred at the end of Adorno's so-called transcendental phase (which was mainly academic) and at the dawn of his career as the dialectical philosopher we all know him to be.[2] Before the text on Kierkegaard, which led the philosopher to obtain his habilitation, there was another project he strongly believed in. This manuscript was delivered to Hans Cornelius, a professor at the University of Frankfurt, who had developed an eccentric form of neo-Kantianism, and whose assistant was Horkheimer.[3] We could say that Adorno fell prey to the opposite problem Walter Benjamin experienced, whose *Trauerspiel* had been rejected two years earlier by Cornelius and Horkheimer because it was considered too eccentric.[4] In Adorno's case, instead, the work was judged to be a repetition, or at best, an expansion on his professor's theses,

---

1   From Horkheimer's reply, it would appear that Adorno is particularly concerned about the final pages of the manuscript. Theodor W. Adorno and Max Horkheimer, *Briefwechsel 1927–1969. Band I: 1927–1937* (Frankfurt a.M.: Suhrkamp Verlag, 2003), 9.
2   Carlo Pettazzi, "La fase trascendentale del pensiero di Adorno: Hans Cornelius," *Rivista Critica di Storia della Filosofia* 32, no.4 (1977): 436–449.
3   Hans Cornelius, trained in chemistry but later becoming devoted to philosophy, is mainly remembered for being Horkheimer and Adorno's teacher and for being criticized by both Lenin and Husserl. With the latter, he engaged in an epistolary exchange for over a decade. On his life and doctrine, see Hans Cornelius, "Leben und Lehre," in *Die deutsche Philosophie der Gegenwart in Selbstdarstellungen*, ed. R. Schmidt, vol. II (Leipzig: Felix Meiner Verlag, 1921).
4   Rolf Wiggershaus, *The Frankfurt School: Its History, Theories, and Political Significance*, trans. Michael Robertson (Cambridge, MA: MIT Press, 1995), 81.

except for the third part, which consisted in an interpretation of Freudian psychoanalysis. Even though this part was deemed original, Cornelius claimed it wouldn't be enough for a habilitation thesis.[5]

But what specifically was the topic of this *Habilitationschrifft*? In this work, the young Frankfurtian brought forward a critique of a set of popular philosophies that he baptized "doctrines of the unconscious." Under this label, Adorno gathered all those thinkers who contributed to reifying the concept of the unconscious as a substance unrelated to experience, which could be investigated only by means of intuitive and mystical knowledge that defied symbolic and discursive rationality. No stranger to this reification, according to the philosopher, was the hunger for wholeness that raged in the German interregnum between the two world wars. This desire manifested itself through a call to the pre-symbolic, the Origin, and the mythical and irrational forces of man and society, which the concept of the unconscious seemed to include.

Adorno opposed this call with the disruptive power of psychoanalytical rationality, which contrasted such irrational forces through the strength of rational knowledge of the unconscious. By means of a philosophically enlightened reading of psychoanalysis, the young Frankfurtian found – long before his future colleagues at the *Institüt für Sozialforschung* – a powerful ally against the identitarian and immediate organicism of conservative forces. What Adorno wanted to fight with this text was an anthropological conception that the Swiss psychiatrist Ludwig Binswanger saw in the "*homo natura* of Nietzsche and Klages";[6] namely, a "biopsychological idea" of man, 'a natural-scientific construct like the biophysiological idea of the organism [...], [where] the reality of the phenomenal, its uniqueness and independence, is absorbed by the hypothesized forces, drives and the laws that govern them.'[7] In the few concluding pages, Adorno's work shows its Janus-faced character, torn between the prehistory and the origin of critical theory. The purely epistemological considerations conducted up to the point of the conclusion are abruptly transformed into materialistic considerations, aiming to unmask the ideological function of a certain notion of the "unconscious."

---

5   Cornelius' comment is expressed in a written note to another member of the commission. Theodor W. Adorno Archiv, *Adorno. Eine Bildmonographie*, (Frankfurt am Main: Suhrkamp Verlag, 2003), 102.
6   Ludwig Binswanger, "Freud's Conception of Man in the Light of Anthropology," in *Being-in-the-World. Selected Papers of Ludwig Binswanger*, trans. Jacob Needleman (New York: Harper & Row, 1968), 159.
7   Binswanger, "Freud's Conception," 157.

2 The Unconscious in the Weimar Republic

Beyond the personal idiosyncrasies and suggestions that influenced the young Frankfurtian, this type of thesis in the context of the Weimar Republic comes as no surprise. When Adorno developed his dissertation, twenty-seven years had gone by since Freud published *The Interpretation of Dreams*, the inaugural step of psychoanalysis and depth psychology. In 1929, Alf Nyman introduced his article *"Über das "Unbewußte""* as follows: 'few philosophical and psychological concepts are today so central to scientific interest as the concept of the "unconscious" (*unbewußt*), the life of the "unconscious" soul (*unbewutßes Seelenleben*), and the "subliminal"; [and] yet, at the same time, few terms are more controversial and subject to various and ever-changing interpretations and evaluations.'[8] With the term "doctrines of the unconscious," Adorno referred to what he considered the most controversial application and evaluation of the "unconscious," and decided to clarify how this term can be conceived both in terms of its scientific meaning and its illegitimate metaphysical use.

Despite the author's scant use of precise references, it is quite clear who Adorno is referring to. Amongst those 'varied, mutually (and sometimes internally contradictory), unanalyzed and often unanalyzable'[9] ideas that spread during the Weimar era involving a true "hunger for wholeness," in a world dismembered and torn apart by the progressive rationalization of the market, there was no shortage of philosophies displaying the limits of rationality and intellect. These "worldviews" sought a sense of community and common roots by celebrating feelings, the irrational and death, popularized by 'a great regression stemming from a great fear: the fear of modernity.'[10] Among those who promoted these ideas besides Martin Heidegger, Ernst Jünger, and Carl Schmitt, were the most popular representatives of the *Lebensphilosophie*. The latter, along with characterology and its psychoanalytical "sisters" (Jung and Adler) are Adorno's targets.[11]

---

8   Alf Nyman, "Über das "Unbewußte"," *Kant-Studien* 34, no. 1–4 (1929): 151. (My translation).
9   Peter Gay, *Weimar Culture. The Outsider as Insider* (New York: W.W. Norton & Company, 2001), 95.
10 Gay, *Weimar Culture*, 110.
11 In Adorno's eyes, 'Freud's works and those of his close colleagues' are closer to transcendental philosophy and further 'from metaphysical arbitrariness compared to, for example, Jung's and Adler's theories, which can hardly come into our epistemological interpretation, considering their closeness to characterology and our general doubts on the latter.' Theodor W. Adorno, "Der Begriff des Unbewußten in der transzendentalen Seelenlehre," in *Gesammelte Schriften I. Philosophische Frühschriften*, ed. Rolf Tiedemann (Frankfurt a. M: Suhrkamp, 1973), 240. (All translations of Adorno's text are mine).

Among those who made use of the concept of the "unconscious," particularly as a metaphor for the "unconscious" soul, was Ludwig Klages.[12] Klages inherited an interest in psychology from his teacher Theodor Lipps, developing a philosophy of character and an in-depth study of handwriting as an expression of the struggle between the soul – the unity of the unconscious instinctive forces – and the spirit – the unity of the conscious-rational activities of man. As a successor of Nietzsche and Bergson's philosophies, and as a critic of industrialization and modernity, Klages embodied the pinnacle of the *Lebensphilosophie* in Weimarian Germany, a philosophy which saw the spirit or intellect (*Geist*) as a destructive force, guilty of reifying nature and alienating human beings from their lived lives.[13] During the 1920s, these philosophies elevated "life" to an all-encompassing principle, creating a popular and widespread worldview. What distinguishes their metaphysics from any other conception that, to simplify somewhat abruptly, regards the "irrational" or "a-rational" as foundational and prior to rationality and reason – as psychoanalysis itself – is an ethical evaluation that understands the origin (in this case, life) as true, good, and healthy. If the irrational comes first, it is foundational, what comes after becomes mathematically false, negative, insane, deadly, and decadent. This dichotomy lies at the heart of Klages's metaphysics of life, which aims to show 'that body and soul are inseparable *poles* of the vital cell, into which the spirit, like a wedge, inserts itself from the *outside*, trying to divide them from one another; that is, to de-animate the body and disembody the soul, and in this way finally kill all the life it can reach.'[14] According to Klages and several of his followers, all critics of psychoanalysis,[15] Freud made himself

---

12   Anthony D. Kauders, '"Psychoanalysis is good, synthesis is better": the German reception of Freud, 1930 and 1956,' *Journal of the History of the Behavioural Sciences* 47, no. 4 (2011): 383.

13   The origins of the philosophy of life can be traced all the way back to the anti-enlightenment Romanticism of Hamann, Herder, Novalis, Schlegel and Jacobi's philosophy of intuition. In these philosophies, the concept of "life" stood for everything that was dynamic, living, organic, perception and experience, against that which was static, dead, mechanical and abstractions of the intellect. *Lebensphilosophie* developed further and then gained a prominent position in German cultural life from 1880 to 1930, alongside and against positivism. Thus, the concept of life is not to be understood in its medical or sheer biological sense, but rather within the framework of a cultural conflict. 'The banner of life led the attack on all that was dead and congealed, on a civilization which had become intellectualistic and anti-life.' Herbert Schnädelbach, *Philosophy in Germany. 1831–1933*, trans. Eric Matthews (Cambridge: Cambridge University Press, 1984), 139.

14   Ludwig Klages, *Der Geist als Widersacher der Seele* (Bonn: Bouvier Verlag, 1981), 7.

15   Klages's followers included Werner Deubel, a representative of the Frankfurt Press Association and a direct student of Klages; Hanz Prinzhorn, a neurologist and characterologist who as early as 1926 had published writings against psychoanalysis and

a spokesman for the intellectual colonization of life and nature.[16] After years of experimental and soulless psychology, it was time to grasp human complexity in its entirety and embrace (or rather, reintegrate) a psychology of the soul.[17]

Another effective worldview in Weimar Germany was Oswald Spengler's peculiar philosophy of history. This time, the "unconscious" is deployed as a stand-in for the soul of entire cultures and civilizations, within a philosophy of history in opposition to the optimistic nineteenth-century model of unlimited progress. Spengler's philosophy of history relied on a circular, biological model inspired by the natural sciences, representing every culture's cycle of birth, growth and decline. This model shaped a dichotomy between *Kultur* – the young and rising phase – and *Zivilisation* – the decline and death – of entire socio-historical communities, nations and empires.

> What is Civilization, understood as the organic-logical sequel, fulfillment and finale of a culture? ... [Civilizations] are a conclusion, the thing-become succeeding the thing-becoming, death following life, rigidity following expansion, intellectual age and the stone-built, petrifying world-city following mother-earth and the spiritual childhood of Doric and Gothic. They are an end, irrevocable, yet by inward necessity reached again and again.[18]

On the other hand, the vitalistic reaction to mechanicism brought to life a revival of Lamarckism in an anti-Darwinian fashion in the world of biology. This found its greatest expression in Hans Driesch. Despite the persistence of mechanistic categories in physiology, the impact of Blumenbach and Kant's philosophies on biology undermined the mechanical explanation of the growth of organisms; the apparent intentionality beyond their orderly growth

---

its "rationalist limitations" as opposed to the fundamental dignity of "life" reestablished by the legacy of Carus, Nietzsche, and Klages; Carl Haeberlin, a medical doctor from Bad Nauheim who argued that, unlike the holistic views of Klages, Carus, and Nietzsche, Freud failed to appreciate the nature of the Id and its potential to expand and strengthen life forces. Anthony D. Kauders, "The Crisis of the Psyche and the Future of Germany: The Encounter with Freud in the Weimar Republic," *Central European History* 46 (2013): 335–336.

16 Kauders, "The Crisis of the Psyche," 334.
17 Ibid., 326. Starting from the second half of the nineteenth-century, German institutional psychology tried to free itself from the concept of the "soul," conceived as a metaphysical residual of old philosophies.
18 Oswald Spengler, *The Decline of the West. Form and Actuality*, trans. Charles F. Atkinson (New York: Alfred A Knopf Publishers, 1945), 31.

seemed to be explainable only by assuming an internal teleological principle.[19] Several experiments on cells led Driesch to consider the existence of a dynamic teleology in nature, a thesis he would later expand outside biology with *Die Seele als elementarer Naturfaktor* in 1903. These ideas would become a full-fledged philosophy in the *Philosophie des Organischen* in 1909, where the term "soul" is replaced by the Aristotelian "entelechy." According to Driesch, this immaterial power gives form to the organism, but it manifests itself only in its effects, and therefore we cannot experience it.[20] Furthermore, if this principle presides over humans and animals' instinctual or motor behavior[21] – which is also unexplainable from a mechanical point of view – it is called "psychoid" (*Das Psychoid*), a principle that is neither physical nor psychic, but rules over both and allows them to interact.[22]

It is hardly surprising, then, that the followers of these philosophies and "worldviews" made opposite criticisms of psychoanalysis to those made in 1900: if psychoanalysis was previously branded as unscientific and subjectivist, in the cultural conflict of pre-Nazi Germany it was accused of rationalism, mechanicism, and scientism, accused of being oblivious to the power of intuition and charisma, authoritarian towards the irrational and a depressive force on vital momentum. Even in the psychoanalytic field itself, traces of such an atmosphere can be observed. In 1923, Otto Fenichel – a socialist psychoanalyst close to Freud – warned his readers against a possible metaphysical reading of Freudian psychoanalysis. The analogy between the concept of the unconscious and the concept of the thing-in-itself – formulated by Freud himself at the end

---

19 On this *impasse* in mechanicism in biology, see Ernst Cassirer, *The Problem of Knowledge: Philosophy, Science, and History since Hegel*, trans. William H. Woglom and Charles W. Hendel (New Haven: Yale University Press, 1950), 187–216.

20 Mitchell G. Ash, *Gestalt psychology in German culture, 1890–1967* (Cambridge: Cambridge University Press, 1995), 79–83.

21 Driesch makes a distinction between primary and secondary actions, respectively "without experience" and "with experience." The first is an instinctual, automatic action that is nonetheless teleological, which can be understood as an unconscious form of knowledge and will. Hans Driesch, *The Science and Philosophy of the Organism: The Gifford Lectures delivered before the University of Aberdeen in the year 1908, Vol. II* (London: Adam and Charles Black, 1908), 143.

22 Considering Adorno's idea of the close relationship existing between vitalism and some psychoanalytic theories, it is interesting to point out that the term "Psychoid" used by Carl Gustav Jung comes from Driesch. In the pursuit of a vital force that could explain the purposeful and organizational activity of the soul, Jung was naturally pushed towards Driesch's works and adopted the term *Psychoid*. Ann Addison, "Jung's Psychoid Concept: An Hermeneutic Understanding," *International Journal of Jungian Studies* 9, no. 1 (2016): 1–3.

of his metapsychological essay, *The Unconscious*[23] – could lead many analysts to understand psychoanalysis as a gateway to the noumenon and the unconscious as a metaphysical entity.[24] If this were the case, psychoanalysis would be subject to the same critique Kant launched at all metaphysics; namely, the idea that the nature of things is inaccessible to human beings since all experience is co-determined by the percipient subject. Thus, 'attempting to evade this logically compelling train of thought, [some psychoanalysts] make appeal to Bergson, whose philosophy has much – some of it actual and some apparent – in common with psychoanalytic knowledge. ... Intuition, he thinks, does better than reason.'[25] In 1930, the renowned psychoanalyst (who was also a socialist) Siegfried Bernfeld claimed that encouragement, significant values for life and affirmation of their culture were what the German public demanded at that time.[26] Instead, Freud embodied the nineteenth-century culture that promoted rational self-control of emotions, far too much optimism about the power of reason, and pessimism about the individual's ability to alter the destiny of his own people or race. Briefly, at the end of the Weimar Republic, Freud appeared to some as a spokesperson of an out-of-date, decadent, liberal-bourgeois Victorian world, as a standard-bearer of mechanistic positivism and the most vulgar and abstract rationalism.[27]

Adorno brought forward a critique of the "doctrines of the unconscious" and their attempt to appropriate the concept of the unconscious in a vitalistic and anti-Freudian sense. This attempt thus reflected the need to counter this irrationalist movement, which, in light of its later absorption into the national-socialist rhetoric, also entailed taking a position against the politics of the time.

---

23   Sigmund Freud, "Papers on Metapsychology," in *The Standard Edition of the Complete Psychological Works of Sigmund Freud*, trans. James Strachey, vol. XIV (London: The Hogarth Press, 1957), 171.
24   Fenichel refers to Paul Ferdinand Schilder, Sabina Spielrein and Oskar Pfister. Otto Fenichel, "Psychoanalysis and Metaphysics. A Critical Inquiry," in *The Collected Papers of Otto Fenichel. First series*, ed. Hanna Fenichel and David Rapaport (New York: W.W. Norton & Co., 2014), 25–26.
25   Fenichel, "Psychoanalysis and Metaphysics," 26.
26   Siegfried Bernfeld, "'Neuer Geist" contra "Nihilismus": Die Psychologie und ihr Publikum," *Die psychoanalytische Bewegung* 2, no. 2 (March-April 1930): 117.
27   On 10th January 1933, Freud's works were burned in the public square. Opponents of psychoanalysis, who attacked it as a Jewish science, affirmed that 'Freud had perverted the ideas of the creators of depth psychology, such as Novalis, Goethe, and Nietzsche, turning psychology into a business aimed at rich hysterics.' Eli Zaretsky, *Secrets of the Soul: A Social and Cultural History of Psychoanalysis* (New York: Alfred A. Knopf Publishers, 2004), 225.

3   Transcendentalism versus Transcendence

Adorno's habilitation thesis could be summarized, in one sentence, as the attempt to construct a transcendental theory of the unconscious. This goal is developed in three steps: the critique, purely epistemological, of the so-called "doctrines of the unconscious" and related metaphysics of the soul; the construction of a positive transcendental theory of the unconscious in accordance with Hans Cornelius's neo-Kantianism; and the philosophical legitimization of the empirical concept of the unconscious – namely, the unconscious as understood in clinical and empirical research, i.e., psychoanalysis.

First, it is necessary to clarify what is meant by transcendental philosophy – or, rather, which version is made use of – and what is meant by philosophies of the unconscious, the latter being defined in opposition to the former. With the term transcendental philosophy, Adorno refers to his teacher Cornelius's philosophy, a blend of the leading schools of thought at the time, including empiriocriticism, neo-Kantianism, and elements of Gestalt psychology.[28] Cornelius's philosophy strives to be anti-metaphysical, without any "naturalistic" assumptions. The strong empiricist approach, which comes from the need to base all knowledge on past experience, diverges from classical empiricism in considering this knowledge as universally valid for all future experiences. In this way, Cornelius fits into the neo-Kantian tradition, while distancing himself from Marburg Kantianism and its radicalization of the *a priori*. Likewise, the phenomenological description of psychic mechanics, which is neither causal nor descriptive in the Brentanian fashion, leaves no room for any atomistic psychology, criticized at length in his works.[29] One could claim that the professor's entire philosophical production results in a balanced system of mutual corrections, where Gestalt elements correct associationist psychology and mechanicism, empiricism corrects idealism and dogmatic presuppositions, and Kantianism corrects empiricism. We could define Cornelius's philosophy as an attempt to construct a theory of knowledge starting from a radical

---

28   In the thesis preface, this framework is explicitly expressed as "the epistemological point of view" that laid the foundations for the entire work: the philosophy of Hans Cornelius and "especially the analysis of the constant factors of the I through the appeal of unnoticed recollection (Erinnerung)" carried out in the "*Transcendentale Systematik.*" Adorno, *Der Begriff*, 81.

29   For Cornelius's critique of associationist psychology and his endorsement – and contribution – to Gestalt psychology, see Hans Cornelius, *Einleitung in die Philosophie*, 2 ed. (Leipzig-Berlin: B.G. Teubner Verlag, 1919), 195.

monistic immanentism, making use of an anthropological-psychological revision of the Kantian framework.

Transcendental philosophy, Adorno states, has its main purpose in the quest for the possibility of synthetic a priori judgments. This knowledge is gained through an analysis of experience – which manifests itself in one's nexus of consciousness (*Bewußtseinszusammenhang*) – and of so-called transcendental factors, which, in turn, are the conditions for the possibility of that nexus and experience. The only legitimate source of every conceptual form investigated by transcendental philosophy is always exclusively the so-called "immediately given"; namely, what appears in the immediate conscious experience. The quest is, for Adorno, to create a valid concept of the "unconscious" starting from a philosophy that accepts as non-dogmatic only what, ultimately, can be founded in conscious experience and in the immediately given. In order to do this, Adorno recalls how his teacher understood the concept of the "thing" (*Ding*): if consciousness is the only certain foundation of any concept that purports to be transcendent – i.e., to have an existence beyond our immediate experience, such as that of 'I' and 'thing' – these must be understood only as lawful connections (*gesetzmäßige Zusammenhänge*) of the phenomenal experience.[30]

Let us clarify this point, for it is fundamental for the construction of a transcendental concept of the unconscious. According to Cornelius, the concept of "thing" is a naturalistic concept,[31] only apparently self-evident.[32] This concept is used to refer to something that is meant to have a real and objective existence – that is, independent of our perception – in the physical world. The concept of a "coin" as a "thing" implies a whole series of assumptions that are not given to us in the present perception of the coin: what I actually see is just the appearance, in my current perception, of a definite shape and (a) certain color(s) in my field of vision. What, on the other hand, is not given in this single momentary perception is all the other properties of the coin, such as its shape in space (through the overall perception of all its faces), its weight, its chemical

---

30 Adorno, *Der Begriff*, 87.

31 By "naturalistic" Cornelius means those concepts used in common sense or dogmatic philosophy that are taken for granted and whose foundation and premises are unanalyzed. Cornelius argued against what Richard Avenarius called the "natural image of the world" (*natürliches Weltbild*).

32 'One sought primarily the obvious conceptual forms – *the concept of genus and species*, on which the designation and division into classes of things are based; … but one did not look for where the *concept of thing itself* originated, what elements enter into this concept, and in what way these elements are related to each other.' Cornelius, *Einleitung in die Philosophie*, 139 (My translation).

properties, etc. Nonetheless, I believe that these other features of "the coin" are there even if I do not perceive them, and that they are there before and after my perception of them. All these perceptions of the same object (*Gegenstand*) are what I call the "coin," but none of them individually are the coin.[33] These single and current perceptions are what Cornelius calls "immediately given" (*unmittelbar Gegebenes*): a minimal definition of what is immediately given is what we know without the need to know anything else (neither concepts nor other perceptions).[34] The immediately given, however, does not appear as a mere empirical-atomistic fact to be recorded passively, but as a complex connection (*Zusammenhang*) made up of sensible and intellectual elements (Kantian categories that in turn will be reformulated, within a broader project of freeing Kant from his own dogmas).[35] The idea of the classical empiricism of sense data as amorphous material – on which the subject should impress the form – is refused in favor of an internal structure immanent in the data itself.

The minimal condition for having connections between experiences is for there to be a unity in which these related objects appear, for 'only by possessing the given objects immediately as parts in a nexus of personal consciousness (*persönliche Bewußtseinszusammenhang*) do relations concretely exist between them.'[36] This unity of consciousness is possible, in turn, by means of what Cornelius calls the transcendental factors of experience, an anthropological version of Kantian categories. These factors are always and only inferred from experience – they are not logically deduced, either before or beyond experience – but, at the same time, constitute its form and possibility. These

---

33 Cornelius uses "object" (*Gegenstand*) to denote perceptual units that occur in our immediate lived experience and present perception, to be distinguished from "thing" (*Ding*) as a *concept*, i.e., not an immediate experience.

34 Cornelius gives a few examples to make this point: knowing another person's state of mind is a kind of knowledge mediated by their words, while that person has immediate knowledge of it; when I see my house and I know that when I enter there will be a red floor, this knowledge is mediated by the recollection of my past experiences; while when I see a piece of "iron," I do not need any other experience to know that in my field of vision there is a spot of a certain color (e.g., an iron-gray spot), whereas to know that there is a "piece of iron" I must have the previous perception first, *and* a certain signification that allows me to distinguish my knowledge of this iron from any other gray spots. Hans Cornelius, *Grundlagen der Erkenntnistheorie. Transzendentale Systematik*, 2 ed. (München: Ernst Reinhardt Verlag, 1926), 19–20.

35 The entire third section of the introduction to the *Transzendentale Systematik* is devoted to introducing seven dogmatic assumptions of the Critique of pure reason. This, according to Cornelius, is the unpurified legacy of the dogmatic and pre-critical rationalism which still lived inside Kant's philosophy. Cornelius, *Grundlagen*, 29–41.

36 Ibid., 25. (My translation).

factors are the distinction between the whole and its parts,[37] memory (or better, recollection (*die Erinnerung*)),[38] and the recognition of similarity and identity.[39] Thus, in this "nexus of consciousness" made possible by transcendental factors, the immediately given is called the "phenomenal," while what appears to be mediated by past experience and anticipation of the future, is called "thingly" (*dinglich*). Thus, from the pure immanence of consciousness it is possible to derive a non-naturalistic concept of the "thing." The thing is a mediated given and, more specifically, phenomena considered in their connections according to a law (*gesetzmäßiger Zusammenhang*). The thing is not a sum of perceptions, but the lawful succession of determined perceptions, which we define as a particular thing and that exists beyond our present perception. Thus, the "coin" is an objectively existing "thing" because given a phenomenon P (the sense data corresponding to the "head" of the coin) and a condition C (my action of turning it by 180 degrees) a certain phenomenon T must necessarily follow (the sense data corresponding to the "tail" of the coin). If this anticipated phenomenon does not occur, it means that a change has occurred (the thing has changed) and the previous law of succession must be corrected with – or better, subsumed in – a superior law that can explain the occurrence of the new phenomenon. Every phenomenon is part of "things" – part of a law of succession – and, in turn, every "thing" is given only as the combination of a series of phenomena. Thus, a thing, i.e., a law of succession, exists beyond our perception but must always be confirmed, or changed, by it.

In contrast to this, philosophies of the unconscious are 'all doctrines that claim independence from consciousness for the validity of their assertions, and claim to possess a way of knowing that is independent from consciousness – which is usually in relation to the transcendent foundation of the "thing-in-itself" – which would allow them to support statements that are in principle absolute, and superior to those based on consciousness.'[40] The philosophies of the unconscious are defined negatively in comparison to transcendental philosophy, and specifically to the dignity that the latter assigns to consciousness and the conditions for possibility of experience. According to Adorno, 'the pivotal reason for the construction of all philosophies of the unconscious is resistance against the first coherent philosophy of consciousness: against the Kantian doctrine.'[41] What Adorno means in this passage is

---

37   Cornelius, *Einleitung*, 213–215.
38   Ibid., 215–216.
39   Cornelius, *Grundlagen*, 79.
40   Adorno, *Der Begriff*, 88.
41   Ibid., 90.

that these philosophies are a refuge for old theology and all those dogmatic philosophies that intend to lay the foundation for a renewed ontology of Being. To do this, the concept of the unconscious is employed to make space for pre-critical theological elements in post-Kantian philosophy; what all these philosophies have in common is a certain "ontological will" expressed by the search for immutable and permanent essences, free from codependency with phenomena. The necessity is therefore to maintain an ontological foundation, and simultaneously to avoid determining it as an external object that should affect consciousness. Through a metaphysical concept of the unconscious, the foundation of Being is first transferred into consciousness itself, and then, in order to eliminate any relation to experience and what is given, translated into the unconscious as something beneath and prior to consciousness. The pivotal function of the "unconscious" quality of this new foundation of being and consciousness is to release it from the world and interrupt any exchange or relation with it.[42] The "essence" of the object is no longer naively realistic, as an external thing-in-itself beyond our perception, and nor is it purely immanent, as consciousness: it is an internal thing-in-itself – it is (the) unconscious.

4 Adorno's Critique

Adorno's target is thus a conception of the unconscious as what internally evades consciousness and which, nonetheless, determines its nature and the ways in which it relates to the external world. In this manner, these philosophies become "philosophies of the absolute," which, 'insofar as they presume to possess absolute grounding (*Grund*) of their propositions in the concept of the unconscious,' are able to evade the limits of knowledge imposed by the link to experience (as required by Kant).[43] Adorno's immanent critique attempts to show how these doctrines develop some ambiguous concepts present in the Kantian system – spontaneity, thing-in-itself, and teleology – in a transcendent and positive manner, and how, by doing so, they contradict themselves. While Cornelius helped to clarify these concepts and transformed them into their real critical versions, the doctrines of the unconscious decline all of them into

---

42   Although Adorno conducts a purely gnoseological critique, some historical references are given: Fichte's concept of *Tathandlung*, Schelling's concept of absolute spirit, Schopenhauer and Nietzsche's concepts of will and – of course – Bergson's concept of "life" or *"élan vital"* are all concepts that stand for an internal-trascendental essence which determines reality and consciousness. See Adorno, *Der Begriff*, 93–96.

43   Ibid., 305.

a variation of the unconscious phenomenon as "invisible cause," intelligible character, the internal organizational principle of external multiplicity, soul forces, etc. Every variation of this kind results in a fundamental contradiction; namely, in considering the unconscious to be simultaneously immanent and transcendent.

After creating a logical opposition between the unconscious and consciousness, the "unconscious facts" (*unbewußte Tatbestände*) enter the field of consciousness anyway. They cannot undergo rational analysis, but they are nonetheless psychic objects. They can be investigated, but only with special knowledge. Within the metaphysical framework, unconscious facts are a blunt violation of basic logical-terminological principles: because 'every claim about an object presupposed as unknowable is *a priori* contradictory.'[44] This elementary contradiction covers up a basic aporia of the unconscious: if it is thought of as "absolute otherness," we cannot know anything about it; if it can become conscious, it is no longer unconscious. The unconscious seems to be characterized by an original and derivative duality; unveiled through its ramification into the consciousness, while fleeing from it at the same time. About twenty years later, Adorno would also launch the same criticism at the occultists.[45] In the young Adorno's eyes, this contradiction remains unresolvable, starting from a dualistic way of thinking, which attributes *ex post facto* an unconscious origin or foundation for a conscious phenomenon. This is why these philosophies summon intuition as a special "way of knowing," which bypasses symbolic knowledge and gives them access to unconscious facts.

Moreover, the metaphysical unconscious is justified through two of the main transcendental illusions that Kant had described in his first critique. As a renewed version of the concept of "soul," the unconscious is conceived as the unconditioned unity of the psychic reality, and suffers from the same problems brought forward in Kant's transcendental dialectic. The critique of the doctrines of the unconscious is a critique addressed to every metaphysics of the soul, which 'starting from Leibniz … needs to dogmatically assume some type of unconsciousness, a psychic entity that persists independently of and without any relation to experience, in order to affirm its so-called independence and its transcending of the stream of consciousness.'[46] As the ultimate origin

---

44 Ibid., 129.
45 'They inveigh against materialism. But they want to weigh the astral body. The objects of their interest are supposed at once to transcend the possibility of experience, and be experienced.' Theodor W. Adorno, *Minima Moralia: Reflections on a Damaged Life*, trans. E.F.N. Jephcott (New York: Verso, 2005), 243.
46 Adorno, *Der Begriff*, 306.

of reality or consciousness, the unconscious is an absolutely unconditioned entity, which is considered to be 'a part of the series, to which the remaining members of the series are subordinated but that itself stands under no other condition.'[47] The doctrines of the unconscious reintroduce both the paralogisms of reason and cosmological antinomies when they make use of the concept of an actual infinity. The joint presence of finite and infinite entities, of simple parts and infinite divisibility of the whole, can justify the impossibility of knowing every psychic object.[48] In the end, the philosophies of the unconscious attempt to circumvent the conditions of possibility of experience, conceiving them as posited by the unconscious instead. For Adorno, the problem is that we cannot say anything (without contradicting ourselves) about the unconscious unless we make use of those same conditions that the unconscious should determine. The hypostasis of the soul, of life or character as unconscious elements has the same systematic meaning as the transcendental conditions in transcendental philosophies: they claim to be the ultimate and irreducible basis of experience. However, unlike Cornelius' transcendental factors, which have no genesis other than abstraction from experience itself, the vitalistic unconscious is supposed to be beyond and beneath experience.

After Adorno's critique, we could say that Driesch's entelechy, Klages' individual soul and Spengler's collective soul are nothing other than different variants of Bergson's concept of "life," a concept which, despite what it aims to signify, becomes more static the more it frees itself from fundamental structures of knowledge. The same concepts that aim to define movement, dynamism, and subtraction from the mortifying influence of symbolic thought and civilization are, in actual fact, unthinkable without those fixed structures of knowledge. The more they detach themselves from such structures, the more they require mystical images and transcendent essences. Thus, the unconscious – as an internal and extra-cognitive essence – becomes its own opposite: an image that is both mythical and fixed, to be grasped by means of one's (mythical) intuition.[49] First in their general form, then as theories of

---

47   Immanuel Kant, *Critique of Pure Reason*, trans. Paul Guyer and Allen W. Wood (Cambridge: Cambridge University Press, 1999), 465.

48   The acceptance of infinity as a completely given wholeness, rather than negatively, as unlimited progress of experience (as Cornelius claims), implies an antinomy: 'every fact of my consciousness is knowable, as part of my consciousness. But since, in the progress of my experience, I can never be sure of the totality of the connections to my consciousness, not every fact of it can be known.' Adorno, *Der Begriff*, 139.

49   Here we find the fundamental structure of a recurrent critique in Adorno's thought for the first time. In the *Negative Dialectic*: 'Every cognition including Bergson's own needs rationality he scorns, and needs it precisely at the moment of concretion. Absolutized

character, the doctrines of the unconscious are opposed each time (as dualistic, static and transcendent) through their critical dissolution within a monistic, dynamic, and immanent framework.

5   Towards an Immanent Concept of the Unconscious

The critique results in four fundamental impossibilities: considering the unconscious as separate from and opposed to consciousness; avoiding analytical and symbolic knowledge; evading the transcendental conditions of experience; and considering the unconscious as actual infinity. Only an immanent version of the concept of the unconscious could overcome these contradictions. Adorno finds the right place to start in the Kantian critique of paralogisms of reason and the rational doctrine of the soul; he agrees with the destructive role of Kant's critique, but he tries to go beyond the concept of the "I" as a mere logical concept. Within Kantian philosophy the "I" remains merely a formal unity, thus excluding not only psychology from the realm of sciences, but also the concept of an empirical "I" from philosophy.[50] The empirical (and not merely logical) "I" can be conceived as the highest lawful connection of all our psychic experiences. If the totality of my current psychic experiences is connected to my phenomenal "I," the empirical "I" is the highest unity of past, present, and future psychic experiences and the relations between them. As phenomena of the external world are subsumed under lawful connections, so are my psychological experiences; they are not unrelated phenomena, but things that can be subsumed under that lawful connection which is called the "I."[51] This concept is the condition of possibility for an empirical concept of the unconscious.[52]

Let us clarify this point. It is possible to briefly summarize Adorno's operation as one single movement: he does nothing but transfer the concept of thing "internally" and translate it into the concept of psychic unconscious. This operation is parallel and symmetrical to what he criticizes: if the philosophies of the unconscious revitalize a transcendent and pre-critical concept

---

duration, pure becoming, the pure act – these would recoil into the same timelessness which Bergson chides in metaphysics since Plato and Aristotle.' Theodor W. Adorno, *Negative Dialectics*, trans. E. B. Ashton (New York: Continuum, 2007), 9.

50   Adorno, *Der Begriff*, 158–178.
51   Defining the empirical I is possible only after the definition of "psychic experience" within a purely immanent philosophy. The psychic dominion is obtained by subtraction of the purely physical relations among things, i.e., external permanent relations among objects, from the immanent field of experience.
52   Adorno, *Der Begriff*, 179–199.

of psychic-thing, Adorno replaces it with an immanent version. The concept of "thing" as lawful connections to external phenomena becomes the concept of the unconscious as lawful connections of psychic phenomena. In this manner, the concept of the empirical "I" is tantamount to the concept of the unconscious in general, because the empirical "I" is nothing but the individual totality of every lawful connection of psychic phenomena, and as such is a "thing," a law that persists beyond my present perception. As the unconscious can never be given immediately, so the empirical subject can never be given in its entirety. On the other hand, it is necessary to presuppose an "I," which even if built upon experiences, is at the same time independent from each single one of them. If this were not the case, there would not be the chance to link this "I" to other psychic states of affairs beyond present perception, i.e., it would not be possible to speak of unconscious facts.[53] Although this is the essential determination of the unconscious, it is not the only one. With this concept Adorno also refers to the Gestalt relations between the parts and the whole; namely, the unnoticed effects of past events on present experience.[54] In this last instance, the concept of the unconscious is the foundation for the concept of the empirical "I," for if the phenomenal "I" is the highest Gestalt psychic relation (which includes all the others) *hic et nunc*, the empirical "I" implies the feeling of unity that ties all previous experiences to the present in a single totality.

Through the strict definition of what we can conceive as "being aware of something" within a philosophy of immanence, Adorno puts forward four meanings of the word "unconscious": as unnoticed recollection (i.e., unnoticed effect of the past on the present); as an unconscious *phenomenon* (i.e., a single rudimentary recollection of something not present at the moment, namely, something latent); as an unconscious *thing* (i.e., as lawful connection of

---

53   According to Adorno, unconscious means, within the psychic realm, what we refer to as "unknown" (*unbekannt*) in the physical-spatial realm; namely, the unknown rule that describes some connections among physical phenomena. However, unconscious also means something that exists beyond our present perception, i.e., something that objectively exists. Therefore, the unconscious is an unknown psychic thing that does not stop being a thing even if it is known. Thus, if the empirical "I" is tantamount to the concept of the unconscious, the unconscious is tantamount to the core of psychic reality.

54   Cornelius's favorite example used to illustrate Gestalt relations among experiences is the relation between musical notes: the sound of note A is different if it comes after note B or C; the alteration of A based on the previous note is the unnoticed Gestalt effect in the present moment; i.e., the unnoticed modification that B or C induce in A. Regarding the unconscious, this can be easily translated into the idea that every past experience contributes to modifying our present experience, and thus in every present experience the unnoticed effects of past experiences are present.

psychic phenomena as yet unknown and/or beyond our present perception); and as empirical "I" (i.e., the highest connection of all other psychic connections).[55] In any case, the unconscious is something not given immediately but, nonetheless, it is grounded in the immediate given experience. It either has to do with what Adorno calls "real unconscious" – something experienced long ago and resurfacing in the present with rudimentary recollections – or with the "ideal unconscious" – something which was never experienced, because it is a *relation* among events. In both cases, it is possible to describe something as unconscious only through its conscious phenomena, which, in turn, can be given only within an "unconscious" lawful connection. Only in this manner can the concept of the unconscious be rewritten within the limits and impossibilities shown throughout this critique of irrationalist philosophies.

As something "as-yet-unknown," and as a name for the link between conscious phenomena, the unconscious is thus co-opted into an immanent monism. There is no clear separation or logical contradiction between consciousness and the unconscious, and there is no metaphysical inference or logical deduction that could lead to a radical "otherness" of consciousness. Firstly, the unconscious is transformed into a functional concept as a law that describes a concatenation of conscious phenomena under certain given conditions. As such, for Adorno too, the unconscious is simultaneously present and not-present in consciousness: it is present as a law of *conscious* phenomena, and it is not present as the as-yet-*unknown* and/or existent *beyond* our perception of it. In any case, it is not something that flees consciousness; instead, 'every unconscious is, without exception, necessarily related to consciousness.'[56] Secondly, the unconscious does not gain its legitimation through intuition, but through (even if poor and rudimentary) recollections of what constitutes the subject's psychic things (i.e., his or her dispositions, qualities, emotional tonalities, complexes). The existence of some unconscious law can be predicated only through conscious phenomena and recollections, and only with this method is it possible to avoid any metaphysics of the unconscious. Within this framework, the transcendental conditions of experience are not violated. Instead, the distinction between the whole and its parts, recollection and recognition of similarity are the very tools through which we can identify some unconscious object. Finally, the problem of actual infinity is translated into its critical version, as the impossibility of limiting the discovery of the connections that we can call unconscious.

---

55 Adorno, *Der Begriff*, 200–215.
56 Ibid., 203.

In the third part of the thesis, the young scholar claims that psychoanalysis is the only empirical psychology capable of conceiving such an unconscious, and for this reason, of providing an empirical confirmation of the aforementioned philosophical inquiry. Despite some naturalistic remnants,[57] Freudian psychoanalysis is 'the only psychological discipline which performs an analysis of the nexus of consciousness in its temporal development,'[58] namely, in that dynamic structure – rather than merely descriptive – which presupposes the transition from phenomena to things. To properly conceive of the unconscious is to consider that everything psychic has meaning, and to create significant connections between psychic facts that seem unrelated to one another. The interpretations of parapraxes, dreams, and neurosis in the 1915 edition of the *Introductory lectures on Psycho-Analysis* provide Adorno the opportunity to show how the aforementioned philosophical inquiry is confirmed by the empirical research on the unconscious. We could reasonably summarize what Adorno looks for in psychoanalysis by reporting the words of Freud; indeed, it is surprising that the following quote is not mentioned in the young scholar's thesis. Freud describes his interpretation of a subtle obsessive act his patients performed: whenever they found the waiting room empty, they left the study door open as a gesture of disrespect to Freud himself.

> The analysis of this small symptomatic action tells you nothing you did not know before: the thesis that it was not a matter of chance but had a motive, a *sense* and an intention, that it had a *place* in an assignable *mental context* (*seelische Zusammenhang*) and that it provided information, by a small indication, of a *more important* mental process. But, more than anything else, it tells you that the process thus indicated was *unknown* (*unbekannt*) to the consciousness of the person who carried the action ... Some of them would probably have been aware of a sense of disappointment when they entered the empty waiting-room; but the *connection* between this impression and the symptomatic action which followed certainly remained unknown (*unerkannt*) to their consciousness.[59]

---

57 These naturalistic aspects of Freudian theory are: the ontologization of the Oedipus complex as a universal explicative principle, to be found in the phylogenetic history of humanity; resorting to so-called objective (universal) dream symbols to explain dreams; and the transition from a dynamic point of view to an economic standpoint, as vague inheritance of Fechner's theory, which 'was critically resolved a long time before.' Ibid., 266.
58 Ibid., 314.
59 Sigmund Freud, "Introductory Lectures on Psycho-Analysis," in *The Standard Edition of the Complete Psychological Works of Sigmund Freud*, trans. James Strachey, vol. XVI (London: The Hogarth Press, 1963), 248. (Emphasis added).

This short quote sufficiently summarizes why there is a non-metaphysical concept of the unconscious at work in psychoanalysis: the discovery of the meaning of a phenomenon through its connection within the same nexus of consciousness (i.e., without referring to something non-psychic); the affirmation of the existence of a more important psychic process (which Adorno would call a "thing"), which unifies the seemingly separate phenomena; the definition of this process as unconscious because it is unknown to the subject; and its description as a connection between two phenomena (in this case between an impression and an action), i.e., as a law that subsumes two experiences, which by themselves, are part of phenomenal-conscious experience. Freudian psychoanalysis presupposes the unity of personal consciousness beyond the immediately given data to account for psychic phenomena and establishes lawful connections among different experiences. Moreover, Freud discovered an empirical law that he called "repression," which produces unconscious things as *unknown* lawful connections: drives, complexes, and censorship, are all concepts that explain why these lawful connections remain unknown.[60] Besides, for psychoanalysis there is no way to investigate these connections other than through symbolic analysis; namely, through the reading of a symptom as something that refers to something else. Psycho-analytic practice, i.e., the breakdown into parts of the patient's material and the creation of connections among experiences not present at that moment, is thus the inevitable rational method for any science of the unconscious. A science which, far from avoiding transcendental factors, uses them to create connections and awareness about the meaning of phenomena, aiming to alleviate repression and to dissolve problematic complexes. To do this, however, it can only recur to connections between phenomena that are themselves conscious, and their occurrence alone can determine whether they exist or not.

In the end, what forms the scientific character of the Freudian unconscious is the ability to establish a psychic dynamic able to account for changes. To do this, the unity and lawfulness of consciousness must be assumed, which can be investigated through an analytical method (proceeding from whole to parts) and the exclusive use of memory and experience. Finally, Adorno argues against the deterministic reading of Freudian psychoanalysis. In his eyes, Freud's own words on the illusion of psychic freedom are not a negation of the possibility of free actions, but simply the negation of their randomness, namely, of their

---

60   For Adorno's attempt to translate the analysis of Freudian slips, dreams and neurosis into transcendental-philosophical language, see Adorno, *Der Begriff*, 268–302. Repression, on the other hand, is an empirical law that only empirical (and not transcendental) science can discover.

unrelatedness to the rest of lived experiences. Free actions constitute immediately given data and as such are unanalyzable; but precisely because they are immediately given, as with any other phenomenon, they must be part of lawful connections; they cannot be conceived of as non-existent because of their compliance with a law, precisely because it is *their* compliance. This argument reveals itself to be essential as we move on to an ideological critique, in which supposedly unconscious laws are used to justify violence and exploitation.

6   The Politics of the Unconscious

The final pages of the thesis retrospectively lay the foundation for the whole theoretical challenge, as the theoretical clarification of the notion of the unconscious comes after 'the popularity of and confusion around this concept, which we believe arises from a deep necessity of this age.'[61] The social function of a theory is neither in the author's psychology nor in the structure of the theory isolated from its context, but in the current existing social relations. If this is the case, how can the critique of *Zivilisation*, which to a greater or lesser extent is consubstantial with Bergson, Spengler, and Klage's philosophies, be so popular in the age of rational-economic supremacy? In Adorno's eyes, they play a crucial symbolic role within the crisis of the latter, as they perform two important ideological functions: 'integrating what is lacking in reality and, at the same time, transfiguring reality's shortcomings.'[62] The popularity of these philosophies is thus to be found in their ancillary role in relation to the status quo.

First, as a compensatory tool, the vitalistic concept of the unconscious is in clear contradiction with the rationality of the dominant order. Thus,

> these doctrines try to divert the focus from the dominant mode of production and from the predominance of the economy altogether. In showing that outside economic powers there are other forms of power, the latter are subtracted from the economic tendency towards rationalization.[63]

These claims add a new meaning to the aforementioned theoretical inquiry. If the latter can be summarized as an attempt to tie the unconscious to consciousness and demonstrate the theoretical impossibility of a psychic entity

---

61   Adorno, *Der Begriff*, 316.
62   Ibid., 318.
63   Ibid.

independent from it, we can now see that this intellectual challenge was not only a theoretical and formal tantrum, as if the author wanted to lash out at his enemy's logical fallacies, but that it also finds its deeper meaning in contrasting the ideological function of these philosophies. The requirements needed to incorporate the unconscious into Cornelius' philosophy – to create an inseparable bond between consciousness and the unconscious – is at the same time the creation of a bond between the social order and unconscious facts. The philosophers that make the unconscious an oasis in the middle of the economic rationalization desert forget that, as general law of the empirical "I," the unconscious subsumes conscious life in its entirety; the latter, however, is also strictly bound to the economic order. That which has a strictly epistemological function in Cornelius – the concept of the nexus of consciousness with its prohibition of imagining any transcendence beyond it – gains in Adorno's thesis the broader sense of "reality." This reality is not a hypostasis of a given order, but rather something generated from the infinite mutual exchange between subjects and objects, where there cannot be any definitive distinction between social and psychic facts. It is possible to avoid the necessary consequence of a metaphysical unconscious (the introversion 'of the individual into themselves and their distraction from social relations') only in this way.[64] If the unconscious becomes something private, prior to and more important than the external world, individual energies are going to be directed towards that detached world rather than towards changing social relations.

However, the metaphysical unconscious has a second, even more dangerous ideological effect. When the unconscious is understood as a receptacle of drives and vital forces that 'despise any justified legitimization within consciousness,' the unconscious is needed to 'defend society when economic businesses go beyond what can be reasonably legitimized and are blindly motivated by power and drive.'[65] The exaltation of unconscious forces not only distracts from reality, but also justifies it when the economic order runs up against its own contradictions, i.e., overproduction and sales crises, and the dominant reasoning is unable to legitimize or comprehend them within their immanent logic. The catastrophic consequences of these crises are viewed as unconscious necessities; namely, as an immanent and transcendent destiny.

> To evade once and for all any rational critique, imperialist tendencies – the ideology of fascism in the most blatant manner – are traced back to

---

64 Ibid., 319.
65 Ibid., 319.

ontological entities, independent from consciousness and, to a certain extent, sacred. The blind self-dissolution of the existent mode of production appears as if willed by God, and to be necessary in this way ... The origin of the doctrines of the unconscious in Nietzsche's philosophy of power is here confirmed by facts. The strict bond between the metaphysics of the unconscious, philosophy of power and destiny, the critical situation of society, and current political affairs, reaches its most exemplary expression in Spengler's philosophy.[66]

Thus, the *social* necessity of imperialism and fascism as results of liberal crises becomes a *vital* necessity as the explosion of the blind powers of nature and the revelation of ontological essences of nations or individuals. When reason cannot explain the contradictions of capitalism within its own logic, it must base them on something else. If we were to say that fascism was 'a tribal nationalism based on biological determinism [and] a philosophy of action based on intuition, élan, and heroism,' we could understand why Adorno saw, in the vulgarization of the concept of the unconscious, the prelude to the ideology that would outclass the German liberal order.[67]

This second ideological function of the metaphysical unconscious makes Adorno's strong defense of the possibility of free (but not random) actions clear. For if it is possible to deduce actions as necessary products of unconscious laws, it is also possible to see imperialism as the necessary consequence of the vital expression of the social order. The real aim of the whole "disenchantment of the unconscious (*Entzauberung des Unbewußten*)" is to neutralize any possible discourse on the so-called unconscious powers of the soul.[68] For this reason, psychoanalysis has a fundamental role, not only because it understands the unconscious in empirical terms, but also because it promises rational knowledge of it. The latter is an essential feature to eliminate any shadowy planes on which metaphysical fantasies can be projected.

However, psychoanalysis itself could be used for ideological purposes, too. As we have seen, even Freud postulates some dogmatic concepts, for example, when he thinks of the Oedipus complex as some universal principle to trace back to the phylogenesis of human history. In Adorno's eyes, these dogmatic residuals are not caused by Freudian positivism, but rather because 'the unraveling of much crucial unconscious content has its own presupposition in changes in actual social conditions, and, in any case, mere knowledge

---

66   Ibid., 319–320.
67   Zaretsky, *Secrets of the Soul*, 218.
68   Adorno, *Der Begriff*, 320.

of unconscious facts leads to nothing as long as the social reality remains unchanged.'[69] This idea is confirmed by Freud himself, when he discusses his crucial concept of repression, affirming that society itself incites that repression to channel vital energies into work-force.[70] Likewise, we could claim that all psychoanalysis that conceives some entities as absolutely detached from social reality has a potentially regressive character, as these entities gain some kind of privilege in regard to external reality, and cannot enter into a dialectical relationship with it.[71] As we have seen, the primary goal of metaphysical claims on the unconscious is ontological, the nullification of becoming. Their irresolvable contradictions are thus intertwined with the necessity of obliterating the relationship between the unconscious and time: while becoming becomes an eternal recurrence of identical, meaningless, and superficial occurrences, the fixed and permanent essence is detached from every possible real mutation and remains unchanged.

We can still hear the echo of this conviction thirty-five years later, in a Frankfurt University course titled *Philosophical Terminology* (1962). In the fifteenth lecture, it is claimed that the more the unconscious is detached from its phenomenal manifestations, the more it becomes something 'undifferentiated, devoid of plasticity, ahistorical, and, strictly speaking, that cannot be said to be different at all between single individuals.'[72] This conceptual framework is symmetrical to the one of the pure "I" in the first Kantian critique, where a

---

69 Ibid., 321.
70 'The motive of human society is in the last resort an economic one; since it does not possess enough provisions to keep its members alive unless they work, it must restrict the number of its members and divert their energies from sexual activity to work. It is faced, in short, by the eternal, primaeval exigencies of life, which are with us to this day.' Freud, *Introductory lectures*, 312.
71 This claim is valid beyond the intentions of individual authors, and thus also for sociopsychoanalytical theories that aim to be avowedly revolutionary, such as that of Wilhelm Reich. Despite the great value of Reich's insights and their underestimated influence on the Frankfurt school's theories on authoritarian personality, his biologism and orgone theory lead to an undialectical relationship between the socio-historical realm and the psyche. After the "discovery of the orgone," Reich considers unconscious drives and sexuality as primary and original principles able to self-regulate and give order to the entire life of human beings (work life and mode of production included), obliterating as such every supra-individual law of economic development. Unsurprisingly, in this way, Reich comes to reject the very concept of politics and conceives of any possible revolutionary praxis in the sole terms of eliminating all obstacles to the proliferation of vital forces. See Wilhelm Reich, *The Mass Psychology of Fascism*, trans. Theodore P. Wolfe (New York: Orgone Institute Press, 1946), 310–341.
72 Theodor W. Adorno, *Philosophische Terminologie. Band 1*, ed. Rudolf zur Lippe (Frankfurt am Main: Suhrkamp, 1973), 180. (My translation).

mere logical unity lies at the core of the subject. In psychoanalysis, when 'in the end, at the concrete pole of individual consciousness there is nothing but the amorphous, unspecified libido, then in this concrete pole there is nothing but the same abstractness of the subject's determination that has resulted in the opposite pole, the transcendental one – namely, in the constitutive principle of a consciousness in general.'[73] This lecture is not intended as a rejection of libido theory, just as it is not a rejection of the transcendental conditions of consciousness. Rather, these two poles must be interpreted as moments; that is to say, as necessary parts of a greater process aimed at the most concrete and rational definition of "human being," where becoming and what-is-become have greater importance than the "abstract and mythical identity" from which they arise. The lecture closes with two relevant warnings: first, Adorno warns his pupils against what is being called "depth psychology" instead of psychoanalysis in Germany; while the former perpetuates the ideological notion of depth, psychoanalysis 'becomes deeper, the more it renounces the illusion of a metaphysical depth at the origin of the subject.'[74] Secondly, if the concept of something as an absolute first – as could be the case for "pure I" or "absolute unconscious" – reveals itself to be an absolutely empty concept, we can search for truth and philosophy in 'mutual mediation, in the reciprocal penetration of moments, in the process.'[75]

Bibliography

Addison, Ann. "Jung's Psychoid Concept: An Hermeneutic Understanding." *International Journal of Jungian Studies* 9, no. 1 (2016): 1–16.

Adorno, Theodor W. "Der Begriff des Unbewußten in der transzendentalen Seelenlehre." In *Gesammelte Schriften I. Philosophische Frühschriften*, edited by Rolf Tiedemann, 79–322. Frankfurt a. M: Suhrkamp Verlag, 1973.

Adorno, Theodor W. *Minima Moralia: Reflections on a Damaged Life*. Translated by E.F.N. Jephcott. London-New York: Verso, 2005.

Adorno, Theodor W. *Negative Dialectics*. Translated by E. B. Ashton. New York-London: Continuum, 2007.

Adorno, Theodor W. *Philosophische Terminologie. Band I*, edited by Rudolf zur Lippe, Frankfurt a.M.: Suhrkamp Verlag, 1973.

---

73   Adorno, *Philosophische Terminologie*, 181.
74   Ibid., 183.
75   Ibid., 184.

Adorno, Theodor. W. and Max Horkheimer. *Briefwechsel 1927–1969. Band I: 1927–1937*. Frankfurt a.M.: Suhrkamp Verlag, 2003.

Ash, Mitchell G. *Gestalt Psychology in German Culture, 1890–1967*. Cambridge: Cambridge University Press, 1995.

Bernfeld, Siegfried. "'Neuer Geist" contra "Nihilismus": Die Psychologie und ihr Publikum." *Die Psychoanalytische Bewegung* 2, no. 2, (March-April 1930): 105–122.

Binswanger, Ludwig. "Freud's Conception of Man in the Light of Anthropology." In *Being-in-the-World. Selected Papers of Ludwig Binswanger*. Translated by Jacob Needleman, 149–181. New York: Harper & Row Publishers, 1968.

Cassirer, Ernst. *The Problem of Knowledge: Philosophy, Science, and History since Hegel*. Translated by William H. Woglom and Charles W. Hendel. New Haven: Yale University Press, 1950.

Cornelius, Hans. *Einleitung in die Philosophie*, 2nd Edition. Leipzig-Berlin: B.G. Teubner Verlag, 1919.

Cornelius, Hans. *Grundlagen der Erkenntnistheorie. Transzendentale Systematik*, 2nd Edition. München: Ernst Reinhardt Verlag, 1926.

Cornelius, Hans. "Leben und Lehre." In *Die deutsche Philosophie der Gegenwart in Selbstdarstellungen*, edited by Raymund Schmidt, 81–99, Vol. II. Leipzig: Felix Meiner Verlag, 1921.

Driesch, Hans. *The Science and Philosophy of the Organism. The Gifford Lectures delivered before the University of Aberdeen in the year 1908, Vol. II*. London: Adam and Charles Black Publishers, 1908.

Fenichel, Otto. "Psychoanalysis and Metaphysics: A Critical Inquiry." In *The Collected Papers of Otto Fenichel. First series*, edited by Hanna Fenichel and David Rapaport, 25–42. New York: W.W. Norton & Co., 2014.

Freud, Sigmund. "Introductory Lectures on Psycho-Analysis." In *The Standard Edition of the Complete Psychological Works of Sigmund Freud*. Translated by James Strachey, Vol. XVI, London: The Hogarth Press, 1963.

Freud, Sigmund. "Papers on metapsychology." In *The Standard Edition of the Complete Psychological Works of Sigmund Freud*. Translated by James Strachey. Vol. XIV, London: The Hogarth Press, 1957.

Gay, Peter. *Weimar Culture: The Outsider as Insider*. New York: W.W. Norton & Co., 2001.

Kant, Immanuel. *Critique of Pure Reason*. Translated by Paul Guyer and Allen W. Wood. Cambridge: Cambridge University Press, 1999.

Kauders, Anthony D. "'Psychoanalysis is good, Synthesis is better": the German reception of Freud, 1930 and 1956." *Journal of the History of the Behavioural Sciences* 47, no. 4 (2011): 383.

Kauders, Anthony D. "The Crisis of the Psyche and the Future of Germany: The Encounter with Freud in the Weimar Republic." *Central European History* 46 (2013): 335–336.

Klages, Ludwig. *Der Geist als Widersacher der Seele*. Bonn: Bouvier Verlag, 1981.

Lebovic, Nitzan. *The Philosophy of Life and Death: Ludwig Klages and the Rise of Nazi Biopolitics*. New York: Palgrave MacMillan, 2013.
Müller-Doohm, Stefan. *Adorno: A Biography*. Translated by Rodney Livingston, Cambridge, MA: Polity Press, 2005.
Nyman, Alf. "Über das "Unbewußte"." *Kant-Studien* 34, no. 1–4 (1929): 151–166.
Pettazzi, Carlo. "La fase trascendentale del pensiero di Adorno: Hans Cornelius." *Rivista Critica di Storia della Filosofia* 32, no. 4 (1977): 436–449.
Reich, Wilhelm. *The Mass Psychology of Fascism*. Translated by Theodore P. Wolfe. New York: Orgone Institute Press, 1946.
Schnädelbach, Herbert. *Philosophy in Germany. 1831–1933*. Translated by Eric Matthews. Cambridge: Cambridge University Press, 1984.
Spengler, Oswald. *The Decline of the West. Form and Actuality*. Translated by Charles F. Atkinson. New York: Alfred A. Knopf Publishers, 1945.
Theodor W. Adorno Archiv. *Adorno. Eine Bildmonographie*. Frankfurt a.M.: Suhrkamp Verlag, 2003.
Wiggershaus, Rolf. *The Frankfurt School: Its History, Theories, and Political Significance*. Translated by Michael Robertson. Cambridge, MA: MIT Press, 1995.
Zaretsky, Eli. *Secrets of the Soul: A Social and Cultural History of Psychoanalysis*. New York: Alfred A. Knopf Publishers, 2004.

PART 5

Freud, Morality, and the Death Drive

CHAPTER 10

Beyond the Death-Drive: Psychoanalysis and Social Critique

Delia Popa and Iaan Reynolds

The belief in an endemic human tendency towards aggression is often understood to spell out a threshold for the hopes of liberatory politics. If humans are inherently violent regardless of their historical circumstances, there seems to be limited use in transforming these circumstances. Not only in philosophical literature, but in popular discourse as well, it is common to draw on *Civilization and Its Discontents'* Hobbesian assertion that *Homo homini lupus* (man is a wolf to man), and to follow the anti-utopian political implications Sigmund Freud draws from this 'indestructible feature of human nature.'[1] As Jean Laplanche notes in a commentary on this tendency: 'In the general thought of cultured people, the death-drive becomes a useful ideological theme.'[2] If the death-drive serves an ideological function, it partially involves the way such a drive blocks or limits thought aiming to fundamentally change society.

However, the anti-utopian use of the death-drive is not limited to popular social and political thought, nor to a more general belief in an innate human proclivity for aggression. As we will see, the roots of such an ideological function are also at play in metapsychological attempts to separate the psychoanalysis of the drive from social and political history. In coming to terms with this separation, our aim is to explore the relationship between the metapsychological concept of the drive and the disavowal of utopia in social and political analysis. While bringing together these two areas of concern is not an easy endeavor, it is our conviction that reading the drive theory in the light of socio-political critique allows for a deeper understanding of its philosophical meaning.[3] Accordingly, this paper focuses on an investigation of the

---

1 Sigmund Freud, *Civilization and Its Discontents*, trans. James Strachey (New York: W.W. Norton, 2010 [1930]), 98.
2 Jean Laplanche, "The So-Called 'Death Drive': A Sexual Drive," *British Journal of Psychotherapy* 20, no. 4 (2004): 455–471, 462.
3 We understand critique as a process of unfolding and clarifying the conditions of possibility and the finalities at stake in a given experience. As Jean Laplanche notices, a critical investigation cannot fail to pose problems of genesis. See: Jean Laplanche, *Life and Death*

drive theory that makes room for a critical function of utopia, understood not as a straightforward "fulfillment" of the drives, but rather as a possibility of their maturation, even in adverse socio-political and cultural conditions. In our view, the differentiation that ultimately produces the opposition between *Eros* and *Thanatos* in Freud is a site of philosophical reflection not only on the problematic function of the death-drive, but also on the – socially conditioned – possibility of human life as such. Consequently, the ambivalences and tensions found within Freud's shifting articulations of the drive theory provide resources for rethinking human sociality beyond the bounds of Freud's own social and political pessimism.

Following the development of Freud's drive theory, the first two sections will show how the drive's status as a 'concept on the borderline between the mental and the physical' generates a conceptual ambiguity that becomes, through the course of its elaboration, a timeless metaphysical opposition of *Eros* and *Thanatos*.[4] The third section will argue that Adrian Johnston's transcendental strategy for accommodating the ambiguity of the drive repeats the Freudian gesture of closing metapsychology off from historical change. Our next section will explore alternative ways to historicize the drive, focusing on Theodor W. Adorno's dialectical understanding of the drive conflict, in which the separation between *psyche* and society is understood as an ideology masking society's nonidentity with itself. The final section will explore the relationship between the drives and social emancipation through a further investigation of Freud's theory of repression and sublimation. In sublimation, which we interpret as the social maturation of partial drives, the utopian desire for a livable life is expressed as a critical project.

1   The Life of the Drives

In his 1915 essay, "The Unconscious," Freud describes metapsychology as an all-encompassing project in which the various ways of understanding psychic phenomena developed through years of clinical work are brought together. Each psychic act, according to Freud, can be grasped in terms of its dynamic, topographic, and economic dimensions. The first aspect understands psychic phenomena as stages in a process of historical development, the second

---

  in *Psychoanalysis*, trans. Jeffrey Mehlman (Baltimore and London: The Johns Hopkins University Press, 1976), 129.
4 Sigmund Freud, "Drives and Their Fates," in *The Unconscious*, ed. Adam Phillips, and trans. Graham Frankland (New York: Penguin, 2005 [1915]): 13–31, 16.

understands them as interactions happening among the mind's different systems, and the third sees them as attempts to regulate variable quantities of psychic energy. Grasping a phenomenon simultaneously in dynamic, topographic, and economic terms produces its own perspective: "the culmination of all psychological investigation," which is proper to metapsychology.[5] However, since the metapsychological perspective incorporates various theorizations and empirical investigations, Freud describes it as an unfinished project.[6]

Freud describes the same project from the standpoint of the production of its concepts in "Drives and Their Fates." Even when a field is well-established and seems capable of providing certain knowledge of its domain of study, as well as a progressively broader applicability of its concepts, he writes, the advance of knowledge will brook no rigidity here. As the example of physics strikingly demonstrates, even those "basic concepts" firmly established in the form of definitions are constantly being substantially revised.[7] The fact that basic phenomena in psychology can be understood according to their dynamic, topographic, or economic aspects, attests to psychoanalysis' flexible strategy for accommodating this ambiguity. The metapsychological attempt to unite these various aspects will always be open to revision, as an inflexible definition of its basic terms would render it unable to incorporate new discoveries.

In "Drives and Their Fates," the drive is introduced as a liminal concept between the biological organism and the psyche. More precisely, the drive is 'the psychic representative of stimuli flowing into the psyche from inside the body, or the degree of workload imposed on the psyche as a result of its relation to the body.'[8] Initially differentiating the drive from a physiological stimulus or instinct, Freud notes that drive excitations (*Triebreize*) originate within the living organism, being transmitted to the psyche through the mediation of a "representative."[9] The drive is not manifested through a momentary impact, but rather exerts a constant pressure on the organism. In other words, drives ought to be understood as forces constantly pushing towards change and development. These factors combine to complicate the biological assumption of purposiveness provisionally adopted to understand the organism's

---

5 Sigmund Freud, "The Unconscious," in *The Unconscious,* ed. Adam Phillips, and trans. Graham Frankland (New York: Penguin, 2005 [1915]): 47–85, 64.
6 'Given the present state of our knowledge, we can safely say that [a metapsychological account] will prove possible only in a few isolated areas.' Freud, "The Unconscious," 64.
7 Freud, "Drives and Their Fates," 13–14.
8 Ibid., 16.
9 'First, a drive stimulus emanates not from the outside world, but from inside the organism itself. For this reason, it affects the psyche differently and different actions are needed to remove it.' *Ibid.,* 14.

relationship to stimuli or excitations. If we view the organism's function as the mastery of stimuli, and we further recognize the presence of drive excitations exerting a constant pressure from within the organism, then the psychological concept of the drive introduces great variability into the merely physiological or biological understanding of the organism itself:

> External stimuli set the organism a single task, evasion; this is accomplished by muscle movements, one of which eventually achieves the aim and, being the most expedient, goes on to become an hereditary disposition. Drive stimuli, emanating from the organism, cannot be dealt with by this mechanism. They therefore make much greater demands on the nervous system, causing it to undertake intricate, convoluted activities that alter the outside world sufficiently for it to provide satisfaction to the inner source of stimulation; above all, they force the nervous system to renounce its ideal intention of avoiding stimuli because they supply a constant, inescapable flow of stimulation.[10]

While the drive originates in the biological functioning of the organism, the demands it places on the nervous system are here understood to interrupt this functioning.[11] In one way, this ambiguity opposes the ontogenetic temporality pertaining to the life of the individual, through which we can articulate changes in the drives throughout each individual's life, to the phylogenetic temporality relating to the evolution of the species, through which we can trace the biological sources of the drive impulse. The drive itself, falling between these two levels, seems to combine elements from the life of the individual organism with those emanating from the development of the species. But we can also consider this ambiguity as pertaining to the introduction of a new dimension within the system of our biological needs, which opens them up to a distinct temporality of sexual fantasy understood as a sort of inner bodily reflexivity

---

10   Ibid., 15–16.
11   This aligns with the way Freud would characterize psychoanalysis' relationship to biology in the 1914 Preface to the Third Edition of the *Three Essays on the Theory of Sexuality*. In this Preface, Freud considers drives to be related to the life of the human as a biological organism, but nevertheless aims to keep the nature of this relation open, by refraining from bringing biological assumptions into the analysis. Rather than understanding psychological reality in terms of biological findings, he writes in his 1914 Preface to the Third Edition that his aim is to 'discover how far psychological investigation can throw light upon the biology of the sexual life of man.' Sigmund Freud, *Three Essays on the Theory of Sexuality*, in *The Standard Edition of the Works of Sigmund Freud, Vol. VII (1901–1905)*, ed. and trans. James Strachey (London: The Hogarth Press, 1953 [1905]): 125–243, 130.

that is discovered in relationship with another human being (the parent or the caregiver). Here, a pole of otherness has to be highlighted as a distinctive feature of the drive, which also clearly determines its social orientation.[12]

Derived from Freud's clinical work, the four drive fates listed in "Drives and Their Fates" include: (1) reversal into its opposite; (2) turning back on the self; (3) repression; and (4) sublimation.[13] Freud treats the first two fates that correspond, respectively, to changes in the drive's aims and objects, illustrated by a discussion on the ambivalent pairings sadism-masochism and voyeurism-exhibitionism.[14] We can see a case of the drive's reversion to its opposite through the transformation from voyeurism to exhibitionism, or from sadism to masochism, through which the aim of the drive – a desire to look, the desire to hurt – is reversed into a desire to be looked at, or to be hurt. When drives turn in on themselves, to contrast, they apply the same aim (to hurt, to look) to a different direction – in this case, turning from an external object to the self. These two fates thus seem to be complementary, with the latter highlighting a reflexivity of the drive that we will examine further below.

The highly variable nature of the drives appears here as a holdover from Freud's earlier explorations of the drive theory in the *Three Essays on the Theory of Sexuality*, where drives are presented as forces exerting pressure on psychic life, but which transform in time, adopting new aims and attachments.[15] This variability introduces the possibility of sexual deviance and perversion, but is also what allows for sexual development over time. The "normal" genital organization of sexuality is understood as the limited end-result of a broader process of development leading through earlier "pregenital" stages, involving oscillations and regressions.[16] According to the later metapsychological perspective, drives have both a highly variable aspect and a relatively invariable one. From the way Freud characterizes the source and pressure exerted by the drive, it seems that the part resisting variation pertains to the bodily elements of the drive inherited through the development of the species. Nevertheless, we can speak of a "life of the drives" because these forces in psychic life have a strong developmental component – whether we understand this in terms of the four possible drive fates listed in the 1915 essay, or in terms of the stages of development outlined in the *Three Essays*. When later stages are reached, or

---

12 See, Jean Laplanche, "The Drive and its Source-Object: Its Fate in the Transference," in *Essays on Otherness* (London: Routledge, 1999 [1992]): 120–135.
13 Freud, "Drives and Their Fates," 20.
14 Ibid., 21.
15 Freud, *Three Essays*, 135–136.
16 Ibid., 197–198.

when the sexual drives are resolved to new fates, parts of the previous stages or moments inevitably remain, which, as we will see, is an important aspect of the problem we tackle in the following sections.

2 The Drive Fates between Eros and Thanatos

Since the first metapsychological sketches of the drive theory, Freud is not as concerned with drives *as such*, as he is with their *fates* (*Triebschicksale*), in which the differentiation between progressive and regressive drives should be sought. With the publication of *Beyond the Pleasure Principle* in 1920, a stronger division is introduced between the drives oriented towards life and those oriented towards death. What had been presented in the 1914 essay, "On the Introduction of Narcissism," as a division between conservative ego-drives and progressive sexual- or object-drives is here radicalized into an antagonism between *Thanatos* and *Eros*.[17] Let us note from the beginning that this opposition is a twisted one, as the opposites of *Eros* are discord, hunger or hatred, and the opposite of *Thanatos* is life. We would like to complicate this conceptual twist in the direction of a psychoanalysis of human life that is challenged by the regressive tendency of the death-drive.

The main problem, noticed by several commentators,[18] with the new terminological distinction adopted in *Beyond the Pleasure Principle* is related to the ambiguous nature of the death-drive, which is understood both as a "Nirvana principle" of a total reduction of tension and as a homeostatic constancy; as a peaceful absence of excitation and as an arousal of aggression; as an irrepressible tendency to unpleasure and self-destructiveness, and as the pleasure of repetition. While clarifying these contradictions is a challenging task, it appears that the death-drive is not a different kind of drive that simply disobeys the pleasure principle, but rather a tendency present in the life of all drives,[19] each time they engage in regressive/conservative movements and compulsive repetitions, whether they seek for self-disintegration, for restaging former stages of their history, or for cultivating homeostatic constancies that

---

17 Sigmund Freud, "On the Introduction of Narcissism," in *The Penguin Freud Reader*, ed. Adam Phillips, and trans. John Reddick (New York: Penguin, 2006 [1914]): 358–390, 362ff.
18 Daniel Lagache, "Situation de l'agressivité," *Bulletin de Psychologie* (1961): 99–112. See also Jean Laplanche, *Life and Death in Psychoanalysis*, 108 ff.; Stéphane Haber, *Freud et la théorie sociale* (Paris: La Dispute, 2012), 50 ff.
19 'The death drive is the soul of every drive, the most driving aspect of the drive.' Jean Laplanche, *Problématiques III: La sublimation* (Paris: PUF, 2008 [1980]), 215.

allow for a different take on former traumatic events. Indeed, in Freud's own words, the compulsion to repeat initially associated with the death-drive is 'a universal attribute of drives' related to 'a powerful tendency inherent in every living organism to restore a prior state,' and 'a kind of organic elasticity.'[20]

However, this universality becomes problematic as soon as we consider the variety of ends pursued by the compulsion to repeat: if its goal is mere self-disintegration, it conflicts with the attempt to revisit past traumatic episodes in order to make available a more accurate representation of the danger to which one is exposed; and if the goal of such a regression is to restage former moments of development, it means that it can no longer be associated with a mere self-dissolution. Moreover, the pleasure principle itself is displaced from its initial function when it is engaged in compulsory repetition. While Freud defines pleasure as a discharge of free-flowing energy that comes "from the inner depths of the body,"[21] he also relates it to an "annexing process" of this energy as it aligns with the reality principle.[22] Hence, on one side, we have an energy that is untamed and unbound, looking for release through primary processes such as dreams and unconscious fantasies, while on the other side, we have an energy that is bound to objects through secondary conscious processes.[23] However, at a strictly economic level of analysis, it is not easy to understand how these energies pass into one another and relate to each other over time.

Jean Laplanche describes this relationship with the help of the concept of "leaning-on" (or propping), which translates the French term "*étayage*" and the German term "*Anlehnung*": the free-flowing energy "leans on" the energy that is initially bound through vital functions of the body, bringing forth an "erotic body" out of the biological body, and a temporality that cannot be superimposed on the biological one. This process, in which the vital functions detach themselves from their object and return to themselves by introjecting an "original phantasm (*ursprüngliche Phantasie*)," is for Laplanche none other than the genesis of the drive as such.[24] Interestingly, this return to oneself that begins

---

20 Sigmund Freud, *Beyond the Pleasure Principle*, in *The Penguin Freud Reader*, ed. Adam Phillips, trans. John Reddick (New York: Penguin, 2006 [1920]): 132–195, 64–65.
21 Ibid., 155.
22 Ibid., 163.
23 From Freud's own account, this economic distinction is a reworking of Breuer's neurological distinction between quiescent energy and kinetic energy. However, as Jean Laplanche has shown, Freud is not merely inheriting Breuer's perspective, but rather modifying it, with a view on Helmholz's theory of free-flowing energy and bound energy. See Jean Laplanche, *Life and Death in Psychoanalysis*, 117ff.
24 Ibid., 88ff.

in auto-eroticism is also related to a reflexive return of hetero-aggressivity (sadism) into auto-aggression (masochism), grounding both in an original masochism.[25] The eroticization of one's body is thus understood as a process not restricted to genital sexuality, encompassing a complex expressivity of our humanity that is forever risky and unsettled.[26] At the same time, "leaning-on" does refer to sexuality as a dimension of our psychic life that emerges from biologic needs; it is an original bodily reflexivity that allows for new sources of gratification and attachment. Therefore, the homeostatic goal of pleasure has to be understood in light of the risk and the indetermination entailed by this "phantasmatic" origin of the drive.

From this perspective, pleasure is nothing else than the phantasmatic expression of bodily vital necessities, which are "translated" and continuously transformed throughout one's life-history. Yet this transformation also entails moments of tension and mutual inhibition between the "erotic body" and the "animal body," as they challenge each other. At stake in the process of leaning-on is a certain human freedom from vital necessity, which is at the same time a source of danger posed to the constancy of the living organism. At an economic level, pleasure is a source of stability only inasmuch as it allows for transitional inscriptions of the free-flowing energy into the already existing relations in which psychic energy is invested (bound energy). The normative system that regulates psychic energy is thus necessarily disturbed by inputs of "demonic" free-flowing energy, without which it is probably destined to diminish and die. However, if this free-flowing energy exceeds the organism's ability to bind it, it puts the body itself at risk by compromising its stability. A subtle dialectic seems to be responsible for keeping us alive, then, as an interaction between excessive and destructive free-flowing energy and annexed energy that cannot maintain itself as such over time.

This economic problem is reflected in the metapsychological differentiation of the drives, which also takes its dynamic and topographic aspects into account. However, each time the differentiation of the drives is rearticulated by Freud, a slight displacement seems to be at work, pushing *Eros* to the side of *Thanatos*, and *Thanatos* into the heart of *Eros*. The relationship between the two sequences connecting sexual drives with disruptive discharges of free-flowing energy manifested mainly in primary unconscious processes, on the one hand, and connecting ego-drives with bound energy in secondary conscious processes, on the other hand, is thus inverted in such a way that we

---

25   Ibid., chapter 5.
26   Also see, Christophe Dejours, *Le corps, d'abord* (Paris: Payot, 2001); *Les dissidences du corps* (Paris: Payot, 2017).

ultimately find *Eros* as a binding force that is related to the ego, and *Thanatos* as a disruptive drive.[27] While this new alignment is incompatible with the argument of Freud's earlier texts, it is only under its reign that death can be considered as "the motor of sexual life" and the death-drive as a tendency in all drives.[28] The ambiguity of leaning-on complicates the role of life as related to both sexual drives and deadly attachments, or to disruption and unification.

In *Beyond the Pleasure Principle*, Freud attempts to clarify the double dimension of pleasure – destructive discharge and homeostasis – through a speculative consideration of the compulsion to repeat as older than the pleasure principle, and as rooted in the life of every organism. From the example of 'living organisms in their simplest possible form as an undifferentiated vesicle of irritable matter,'[29] Freud describes the differentiation that must develop between the organism's inner and outer layers, with the latter forming a shield protecting the inside from stimulation.[30] Since excitations arising from within the inside of the organism do not have to pass through such a protective layer, however, the organism would have to bind this inner energy, investing it with libido in order to keep the intrusion from overwhelming or destroying it. In order for the pleasure principle to work, the organism must have enough of a structure to bind the energy flowing from within and without. But in order to attain such a structure, it seems that another principle must be relied on, one based not on maintaining a balance of pleasure and pain, but on an attempt to return to an earlier state. In this self-preserving function, Freud sees a task that goes on 'independently of [the pleasure principle] and to some extent quite heedless of it.'[31]

The regressive tendency of the drive in *Beyond the Pleasure Principle* is expanded to a metaphysical opposition in later works that see the violence associated with "instincts" as an immediate feature of human nature. While in *Beyond the Pleasure Principle*, Freud still seems to have faith in the drives' ability to find new aims and objects, the later works find Freud downplaying their capacity for development. This is clearest in *Civilization and Its Discontents*. While the *Eros-Thanatos* opposition had been tentatively conjectured in *Beyond the Pleasure Principle*, as a modification of the earlier distinction

---

27   Jean Laplanche refers to a *chiasm* in order to describe this awkward intertwinement of the drives. Laplanche, *Life and Death in Psychoanalysis*, 124.
28   Patricia Gherovici, *Transgender Psychoanalysis: A Lacanian Perspective on Sexual Difference* (London: Routledge, 2017), 165.
29   Freud, *Beyond the Pleasure Principle*, 153.
30   Ibid., 154.
31   Ibid., 163.

between the sexual drives and the ego drives,[32] here it is expressed as a metaphysical difference underlying the "common knowledge" and "self-evident" fact of the predominance of human aggression.[33] *Eros* is now a civilizational principle 'combining single human individuals, and after that families, then races, peoples, and nations, into one great unity, the unity of mankind.'[34] The death-drive, too, is at once 'an original, self-subsisting, instinctual disposition in man' and an irreducible social and political reality opposing the historical aims of *Eros*.[35] The Hobbesian war of all against all is here elevated to a metaphysical principle whose struggle with *Eros* describes the evolution of civilization itself.

One result of this rigidified opposition is that aggression becomes 'an indestructible feature of human nature,' working on ontogenetic and phylogenetic timescales.[36] This is significant, from one side, because it appears to make the "life of the drives" more expansive, encompassing all of human history. At the same time, however, the conjecture of an inborn aggressive drive also greatly limits the developmental picture of Freud's earlier drive theory. Freud rejects any substantive hope in the transformation of psychic life through social and political means since human civilization is integrated through the work of a decadent repressive apparatus. Since the tendency for aggression is inborn and "indestructible," the reorganization of society will 'have in no way altered the differences in power and influence which are misused by aggressiveness, nor have ... altered anything in its nature.'[37] Most striking here is the way that such a reflection eliminates the historical character of the drives. The highly variable nature of the drive fates exhibited in the early metapsychology is displaced in favor of a metaphysical opposition between *Eros* and *Thanatos*. In this sense, the chain of speculations begun in *Beyond the Pleasure Principle* and leading to *Civilization and Its Discontents* introduces a fatalism into the drive theory at odds with the earlier, more robust conception of the *Triebschicksale*.

---

32   Ibid., 191–92, n. 28; see also: Sigmund Freud, *Civilization and Its Discontents*, chap. 6.
33   Freud, *Civilization and Its Discontents*, 103.
34   Ibid., 111.
35   '[M]an's natural aggressive drive, the hostility of each against all and of all against each, opposes this programme of civilization.' Ibid., 110–111.
36   Ibid., 98.
37   Ibid.

3   Fatalism Repeated: A Metapsychology of Split Drives

We find a radicalization of this problem in Adrian Johnston's interpretation of Freud's drive theory, which outlines a conflict between two different paradigms of temporality found in Freud's work: a deterministic paradigm according to which the past overdetermines the present, and an emancipatory paradigm that allows for transformation. The belief that the symptoms of present mental life have their origins in earlier conflicts and stages of development makes use of the first temporal model. In other parts of his work, however, Freud recognizes that individuals can transform their relationship to the past, as for example when he reflects on deferred action, on sublimation and afterwardness (*Nachträglichkeit*), in the light of which new orientations and attachments can retroactively rewrite old conflicts or cast them anew. Neither of these paradigms alone can provide a satisfying guide to metapsychology. Adopting a linear and deterministic idea of time threatens to erase analysis' capacity to liberate analysands from past traumas, while an exclusively retroactive and hermeneutic understanding of time would eliminate the importance of the basic concepts of psychoanalysis: 'the unconscious, repetition, transference, and the drive.'[38]

Johnston's answer to this difficulty is to understand the apparently opposed conceptions of time as conflicting moments found within every drive. Accordingly, each drive has an "axis of iteration" that strives insatiably to return to past states. This axis pertains to the inner source of the drive and the pressure it exerts on the mental system.[39] But in dealing with the continuous pressure exerted by the drive, the psyche supplies libidinal investments that are necessarily incompatible with the original state the drive strives to restore. Johnston sees this process as the work of a temporally distinct "axis of alteration."[40] Drives themselves are thus temporally complex entities, rather than 'some internal biological reality welling up from the chaotic depths of the id.'[41]

---

38   Adrian Johnston, *Time Driven: Metapsychology and the Splitting of the Drive* (Evanston, IL: Northwestern University Press, 2005), 141.

39   'The axis of iteration consists of the indefinitely iterated "demand for work" impinging upon the representational level of the psychical apparatus. Freud portrays the drive-source as a quasi-somatic force, whereas the drive-pressure is identified as the negative affect (anxiety and/or various states of discomfort) accompanying the source.' Ibid., 150. Johnston quotes Freud's characterization of drive pressure in: Freud, "Drives and Their Fates," 16.

40   See Johnston, *Time Driven*, §25, as well as Chapters 9 and 10 for further discussions on these two drive axes.

41   Ibid., 143.

Johnston writes: '*Trieb* is the conceptual, metapsychological embodiment of an unsuccessful mediation between a nonhistoricized, quasi-somatic source ... and a temporalized realm of both objectival representations and historically alterable aims.'[42] The generic ambivalence of the drive we noticed in the first section is thus turned into a fundamental feature of each drive, with the variable aspect pertaining to the axis of alteration, and the invariable aspect pertaining to the aspect of iteration. The frustration that arises from the inability to fulfill the demands of the drive stems from the fact that this entity's atemporal striving for an "eternal return" must realize itself in concrete historical conditions, adopting real objects and aims that necessarily fall short of the demand issuing from the axis of iteration.[43]

In his transcendental radicalization of Freud's dualism of *Eros* and *Thanatos*,[44] Johnston likens the atemporal axis of iteration and the temporal axis of alteration to the antinomy of the noumenon and phenomenon in Kant's critical philosophy.[45] Unlike Kant, however, who conceived of antinomies as incompatible *theoretical positions* with equal logical justification, Johnston argues – with Hegel – that the antinomy between iteration and alteration designates *a division within reality itself*.[46] He writes: 'The unthematized

---

42 Ibid., 167.
43 'Since the representational components of the axis of alteration are subject to modification by temporal factors, a pure, undiluted repetition of the initial satisfaction sought by the axis of iteration is, strictly speaking, impossible.' Ibid., 151.
44 This transcendental focus means that the question of the number and type of drives has limited relevance for Johnston's project: 'If metapsychology contains the conceptual possibility conditions for the psychoanalytic field, then an investigation into the inherent structural organization of *Trieb* has procedural priority over proclamations about specific traits and subdivisions of this fundamental concept.' Ibid., 154.
45 'These two axes are rightly analogous to the Kantian distinction between the noumenal and the phenomenological as utilized in his exposition of why self-consciousness is shaped by its own internal conditions of (im)possibility: Fully transparent self-consciousness is impossible, in Kant's view, because the timeless subject, as the set of transcendental conditions making all determinate acts of consciousness possible, only ever recovers itself through the necessary distortion imposed upon it by a spatio-temporal medium, namely, phenomenal inner sense as the medium of reflective consciousness.' Ibid., 150.
46 'Kant stopped short at the merely negative result of the unknowability of the in-itself of things and did not press on to the true and positive significance of the antinomies. The true and positive significance of the antinomies consists in general in this: that everything actual contains with itself opposite determinations, and that therefore knowing and, more specifically, comprehending an object means nothing more or less than becoming conscious of it as a unity of oppositions.' G.W.F. Hegel, *Encyclopedia of the Philosophical Sciences in Basic Outline, Part I: Science of Logic*, trans. Klaus Brinkmann and Daniel O. Dahlstrom (Cambridge: Cambridge University Press, 2010), 94–95, §48.

antinomies arising from Freud's various presentations of drive theory are not mere contradictions within the conceptual-discursive fabric of psychoanalytic reason, but are reflective of the primordial antagonism of *Trieb an sich*.'[47] While Johnston's initial intervention is metaphysically deflationary, in the sense that it does away with the idea of drives as permanently opposed forces playing out on all levels of human life, he still posits the internal division of the drive as a truth outstripping the bounds of all possible experience.

If the introduction of temporal heterogeneity into the structure of the drive productively questions Freud's attempts to base the drive theory on a relatively invariant biological basis in his later work, a metaphysical remainder seems to lead to the repetition of the socio-historical fatalism that we observed at the close of the last section. This is clearest when the antagonism of the drives is presented as the source of a continuous frustration: 'Drive is nothing other than an intrinsic dysfunctionality, a perpetual margin of dissatisfaction, generated by an irresolvable difference between the axis of iteration's repetitious (a)temporality and the axis of alteration's dialectical temporality.'[48] Conceived as the site of interaction between time and eternity, or life and death, the drive becomes a "locus of permanent incompatibility."[49] Furthermore, the conflict within the drive – as a "primordial antagonism of *Trieb an sich*" – is an ineliminable part of human nature. While this temporal structure of drives introduces an opposition between an ahistorical axis and a temporally variable axis – in this sense "temporalizing the drive" – the conflict between these axes also involves an equal and opposite "detemporalizing" movement. Psychic life is bound to be eternally frustrating, and this fact no longer expresses a productive limitation of our theoretical capacities, but an unassailable truth that must henceforth condition all theories.

This repetition of Freud's historical fatalism has its most directly political consequences in Johnston's reading of the "Freudo-Marxist" tradition, and particularly of Herbert Marcuse's idealization of the possibility of a non-repressive condition outside of the confines of contemporary civilization. Marcuse introduces a utopian element into psychological theorizing since he holds that the drives can be fulfilled in principle. But this latter assumption is unwarranted: 'Satisfaction of the drives is impossible, since it is always-already prohibited by the inherent structuration of each and every drive.'[50] The hope for a form of social and political organization substantially decreasing the

---

47   Johnston, *Time Driven*, 230–31.
48   Ibid., 231.
49   Ibid.
50   Ibid., 248.

share of psychological suffering borne by its members is therefore a naïve wish.[51] The ineradicable and ahistorical tension between the two sides of every drive means that attempts such as Marcuse's deny reality, rather than working within its well-established bounds. For this reason, Johnston describes Freudo-Marxism as 'utopianism licensed by an ignorance of the nonhistoricized, self-defeating nature of *Trieb*,' continuing that, 'Even if prohibitions specific to a particular social arrangement like capitalism are lifted, the achievement of a full satisfaction through a messianically anticipated "living out of the drives" in an alternative social system yet-to-come is a fantasy veiling the eternally necessary failure of the drives.'[52] While Marcuse is here grouped with Freud, Johnston clearly shares something of Freud's later resignation in the face of an eternal conflict of the drives. Whether this conflict takes place between metaphysically distinct principles or within each drive seems less important than the way in which its eternal nature renders it invulnerable to social and political change.

Here we face the paradox of a transcendental metapsychology that introduces temporal heterogeneity as an inner quality of psychological concepts, but simultaneously seals these concepts themselves off from temporal change. The dialectic in this case has a stopping point, at the dividing line between metapsychology and history. The attempt to mix Kant and Hegel – utilizing Kant's critical prohibition on constitutive ideas of pure reason on the one hand but purporting to speak about the things themselves on the other; adopting Hegel's critique of Kantian formalism but rejecting the fundamental dynamism of his dialectic – serves ultimately to establish metapsychology as an independent undertaking capable of describing things in themselves. While it is true that Johnston locates the possibility of freedom in his thesis of an eternally frustrated drive, since its negativity implies that nature has no eternally binding plans for humanity,[53] it also seems true that this account encloses frustration and psychic suffering within an individualistic shell invulnerable to the movement of history.

---

51 'If "external" constraints are a residual by-product of the antagonism within all drives, then some form of Freudian "civilization," as a prohibitory *Umwelt* in whatever particular forms, will always be necessary so as to sustain the fantasy of full satisfaction, regardless of whether this fantasy is of a Freudian past that is always-already lost or of a Marxist future endlessly *à venir*.' Ibid., 254.

52 Ibid., 154–155.

53 'Since drives are essentially dysfunctional, subjects are able to act otherwise than as would be dictated by instinctually compelled pursuits of gratification, satisfaction, and pleasure. In fact, subjects are forced to be free, since, for such beings, the mandate of nature is forever missing.' Ibid., 340.

4   The Dialectic of Nature and History

The historical fatalism we outlined at the end of the second section reaches its most developed expression in Johnston's division between the quasi-somatic compulsion to repeat found in the axis of iteration and the historically variable and symbolically mediated play of aims and objects found in the axis of alteration. Whereas this account sees the drive as a mixture of the ancient and the contemporary, the conflict internal to it is not only an ancient remnant of evolutionary history, but eternal and ahistorical. This is another way to say that the tension between human connection and aggression, between life and death, is not historically mediated, as Freud's early, open-ended conception of the drive fates is collapsed into a single fate: eternal conflict and frustration. While understanding the life of the drives must take account of their complicated temporal character, it is unclear why their inner temporality should be divorced from social and political history. We can begin to see the possibility of a different approach to the drive theory by critiquing this ahistorical reduction.

Such an approach is the focus of Theodor W. Adorno's reflections on metapsychology. Adorno draws on the dialectic of nature and history outlined in his early essay titled "The Idea of Natural-History," in which he levels a critique of any attempts to one-sidedly understand nature on the basis of history, or historical change on the basis of nature, arguing instead in favor of a dialectical account 'pushing these concepts to a point where they are mediated in their apparent difference.'[54] For Adorno, neither the apparent permanence of nature nor the apparent flux of history are primordial realities capable of grounding the other. Each is, rather, a source of access to a perspective from which the other may be dissolved through critique. The drives are implicated in such a dialectic by their "borderline" status between biology and psychological reality, as we can see from the "Theses on Need," where Adorno writes: 'Every drive is socially mediated in such a way that its natural side never appears directly, but only as something socially produced. The appeal to nature in relation to need of any kind is always a mere mask for denial and domination.'[55] Here,

---

54 Theodor W. Adorno, "The Idea of Natural-History," in *Things Beyond Resemblance: Collected Essays on Theodor W. Adorno*, ed. and trans. Robert Hullot-Kentor (New York: Columbia University Press, 2008 [1932]): 252–304, 252–53.

55 Theodor W. Adorno, "Theses on Need," trans. David Fernbach, *New Left Review* 128 (2021 [1942]): 79–82, 79. While Johnston criticizes Marcuse's conflation of needs and drives, Adorno is less wary of asserting a fundamental relationship between these two categories: 'Need is a social category. Nature, as "drive," is included in it.' See, Johnston, *Time Driven*, 244.

the recognition of a natural moment and a social moment within each drive is combined with that of the impossibility of any pronouncements about the *Trieb an sich*. Whether we might try to locate it in a biological substratum, or in a constitutive conflict within an ambiguously biological-psychological entity, the drive *in itself* can never appear, since it is always socially mediated. While Freud had suggested that the "silent" death-drive is only visible in its admixtures with the sexual drives,[56] Adorno puts this distinction between essence and appearance – and the profound limitation it implies for our knowledge – at the center of his interpretation of the drive.

Adorno's recognition of irreducibly social and natural moments in each drive (and each need, which he significantly sees as a more general category) has important ramifications for his view on the interaction of psychoanalysis and social theory. While sociologists and psychologists who consider these fields together do so under an assumption of the fundamental coherence of society and the sciences that study it,[57] this assumption is unwarranted, as capitalist society is not a unified and logically consistent whole: 'An ideal of conceptual unification taken from the natural sciences cannot ... be indiscriminately applied to a society whose unity resides in its not being unified.'[58] Underlying this critique is a conception of society as a non-identical totality. While the shaping of social experience under capitalism works toward ends that can be discerned through dialectical analysis – the production of surplus value and all its subsidiary ends – the society reproduced by the actions of individuals is incapable of conceptual unification. This also means that capitalist society bears un-subsumable particularities within itself. Forms of conceptuality that halt before this nonidentity, attempting to render society self-identical, are *ideological* in the sense that they mask the fundamentally contradictory nature of capitalist society. In this sense, Adorno describes both the separation of metapsychology from sociology, and their facile combination, as socially produced illusions.

However, even if the division between psychology and sociology giving each field validity over a limited domain of human life is "false consciousness" or ideology, it cannot be eliminated through merely methodological injunctions.

---

56   Freud, *Civilization and Its Discontents*, 106.
57   'Where any thought at all has been devoted to the relation between social theory and psychology, it has not gone beyond merely assigning the two disciplines their place within the total scheme of the sciences; the difficulties their relation involves have been treated as a matter of employing the right conceptual model.' Theodor W. Adorno, "Sociology and Psychology – I," trans. Irving Wohlfarth, *New Left Review* 46 (1967): 67–80, 68.
58   Ibid., 69.

Ideology here, and in Adorno's work more generally, is a *socially necessary* delusion; it is necessary, since it accurately expresses the alienation felt by humans in society. From this side, the hope for a metapsychology separated from social and political change has its moment of validity: its alienation of *psyche* from society expresses the objective conditions of socialization in capitalist society. On the other hand, however, this validity is illusory, since alienation is not an eternal feature of human life, but one that is historically produced. Adorno writes:

> People are incapable of recognizing themselves in society and society in themselves because they are alienated from each other and the totality. Their reified social relations necessarily appear to them as an "in itself." What compartmentalized disciplines project on to reality merely reflects back what has taken place in reality.[59]

While any apparent access to an "in itself" within alienated society is illusory, Adorno also recognizes that the power of this illusion stems from the real relationship between society and the individuals comprising it.

It is important to note that Adorno is not here suggesting the need for a "hybrid" discipline of sociology and psychology, capable of resolving the tensions between these fields into a unified whole. This is clearest in his critique of neo-Freudians such as Karen Horney and Erich Fromm, who attempted to introduce a conception of society into Freudian psychoanalysis. As Adorno puts it, 'Freud was right where he was wrong. The authority of his theory lives off his blindness in the face of the separation of sociology and psychology, which ... is ... the result of those social processes some revisionists call ... the self-alienation of the human being.'[60] Since the truth of society lies in its falsity, or its inability to be seen as a unified whole without contradiction, the limitations adopted by compartmentalized fields are the condition for their ability to say anything about society at all. Adorno thus holds that:

> a psychology that turns its back on society and idiosyncratically concentrates on the individual and his archaic heritage says more about the hapless state of society than one which seeks by its "wholistic approach" or

---

59 Ibid.
60 Theodor W. Adorno, "Revisionist Psychoanalysis," trans. Nan-Nan Lee. *Philosophy and Social Criticism* 40, no. 3 (2014 [1952]): 309–338, 334.

an inclusion of social "factors" to join the ranks of a no longer existent *universitas literarum*.[61]

Rather than stretching the concepts of these fields to align with one another, Adorno seeks to articulate their irreducible differences. Similar to his conception of natural-history, the aim here is less to reduce *psyche* to society or society to *psyche*, and more to see each one as providing a perspective from which the other can be critiqued.

The issue revealed through a development of metapsychology's contradiction with dialectical social theory is that the former is always, in a sense, "too late" or obsolete, as it can only articulate the psychical side of social structures that have already been formed:

> The social power-structure hardly needs the mediating agencies of ego and individuality any longer. An outward sign of this is, precisely, the spread of so-called ego-psychology, whereas in reality the individual psychological dynamic is replaced by the partly conscious and partly regressive adjustment of the individual to society.[62]

In a society that no longer depends on the internalization of its rules by individuals but impresses these rules, as it were, directly as reflexes, psychology holding on to the task of helping the ego to acknowledge the conflicts working within it can become false.[63] The implication here is that the dehistoricization of psychic conflict will set up metapsychology as a field unable to accept its own increasing irrelevance. By recognizing a dialectical relationship between *psyche* and society, there remains a chance that the domination of the individual by society can be reflectively comprehended, and thus seen as a product of historical development, rather than an ineradicable truth.

---

61   Adorno, "Sociology and Psychology – I," 70.
62   Ibid.
63   Adorno writes: 'A brutal, total, standardizing society arrests all differentiation, and to this end it exploits the primitive core of the unconscious. Both conspire to annihilate the mediating ego; the triumphant archaic impulses, the victory of id over ego, harmonize with the triumph of society over the individual.' Adorno, "Sociology and Psychology – II," 95. The withering of the ego in the functioning of the social structure is also expressed in: Herbert Marcuse, *One-Dimensional Man: Studies in the Ideology of Advanced Industrial Society* (Boston: Beacon Press, 1964), 10. For a look at the history of this idea in the Frankfurt School theorists, as well as its limitations, see: Jessica Benjamin, "The End of Internalization: Adorno's Social Psychology," *Telos* 32 (1977): 42–64.

We have seen how a metapsychological theory that remains unaffected by social and political change entails a rejection of utopia, viewing the desire for wholly transformed social relations as a denial of reality. When we recognize metapsychology's independence as a socially necessary illusion, we can further grasp the apparently coincidental agreement between anti-utopian admonitions and prevalent social and political conditions. It is notable in this regard that Johnston's transcendental metapsychology departs from the scheme of Kant's Transcendental Dialectic, in which the conflict of transcendental ideas is seen as a "natural and unavoidable illusion."[64] From this Kantian perspective, the idea of nature as a system of law-like regularity has an opposed idea, corresponding to an opposed interest, in the idea of freedom.[65] While Kant's philosophy is centrally concerned with a self-comprehension of reason's limitations, it never rejects the ideal of a society in which individuals are capable of recognizing the universal moral law. If he proscribes positing this conception of autonomy as an object of experience, Kant also recognizes that reason needs such ideals, since they allow for the cultivation of a reciprocity in freedom.

It is in a similar sense that Adorno defends the utopian moment in philosophy. As he writes in the well-known final aphorism of *Minima Moralia*:

> The only philosophy which can be responsibly practiced in face of despair is the attempt to contemplate all things as they would present themselves from the standpoint of redemption ... Perspectives must be fashioned that displace and estrange the world, reveal it to be, with its rifts and crevices, as indigent and distorted as it will appear one day in the messianic light.[66]

The standpoint of redemption yields a view of the "rifts and crevices," the indigency and distortion of the world as it appears. Far from supporting a naïve belief in the fulfillment of all drives, the retention of utopia utilizes this possibility as a perspective from which established truths can be critiqued. The

---

64   Immanuel Kant, *Critique of Pure Reason*, trans. Paul Guyer and Allen Wood (Cambridge: Cambridge University Press: 1998 [1781/1787]), A 297/B 354.
65   Kant, *Critique of Pure Reason*, A 444–451/B 472–479.
66   Theodor W. Adorno, *Minima Moralia: Reflections on Damaged Life*, trans. E.N.F. Jephcott (London: Verso, 2005 [1951]), 247. Adorno's conception of messianic redemption is drawn from the works of Walter Benjamin. See, for example: Walter Benjamin, "On the Concept of History," in *Selected Writings: Volume 4: 1938–1940*, ed. Howard Eiland and Michael W. Jennings, trans. Harry Zohn (Cambridge, MA: Harvard University Press, 2003 [1940]): 389–40, Thesis 17.

risk remains, in doing away with utopia, that we also do away with such a form of critique – a form whose possibility must be carefully cultivated in order to prevent the world from becoming an eternal repetition of capital accumulation in which real people are mutilated. The negative-utopian hope animating Adorno's critical theory thus recognizes that: 'Whether there will be further want and oppression – which are the same thing – will be decided solely by the avoidance of catastrophe through the rational establishment of the whole society as humanity.'[67] While he avoids making positive prescriptions for political change, Adorno recognizes a society meeting human needs would fundamentally alter the conflict of the drives, offering a guiding thread for social and political reflection.[68] Retaining utopia as a negative, critical concept allows us to recognize the necessity of the hope for a life free of alienation.

5   Leaning-on: Repression and Sublimation

We can get a better idea of the critical utopian perspective in psychoanalysis by exploring two other drive fates not discussed in detail in "Drives and Their Fates," namely repression and sublimation. From Freud's essay on "Repression," we would like to focus on the hypothesis of a primal repression intrinsic to our psychic apparatus, and from the sketches of his theory of sublimation, we are interested in the way in which sublimation can transform the historical development of drives by detaching them from their initial limitation to an object. In our view, these two dimensions of repression and sublimation are related, and they have a direct impact on the interpretation of the late drive theory. Interestingly, when Freud describes primal repression as a fixation of a particular drive-representative that continues to exist unchanged, it is in order to stress the 'attraction that the primally repressed material exerts on everything with which it can associate itself.'[69] However, the modality of this primal unconscious attraction cannot be understood without recognizing it as part of a broader antagonism that also opens the psyche to new discoveries and further associations.

---

67   Theodor W. Adorno, "Progress," in *Critical Models: Interventions and Catchwords*, trans. Henry W. Pickford (New York: Columbia University Press, 2005 [1962]): 143–160, 144.
68   'If want disappears, the relation between need and satisfaction changes.' Adorno, "Theses on Need," 82.
69   Sigmund Freud, "Repression," in *The Unconscious*, ed. Adam Phillips, trans. Graham Frankland (New York: Penguin, 2005 [1915]): 35–45, 37.

Discussing the hypothesis of the "primal repression," Laplanche distinguishes a passive phase of seduction understood as the reception of an enigmatic message from the other and a phase of internal reactivation borne by an "endeavor to bind,"[70] which leads to the unconscious organization of repressed sexual fantasies. Yet, this primal repression also seems to be at the origin of the split of the drive itself, understood as *'the impact on the individual and on the ego of the constant stimulation exerted from the inside by the repressed thing-presentations* [représentations des choses], *which can be described as the source-objects of the drive.'*[71] There seems to be a pact between primal repression and the phantasmatic representative, through which the quantum of affect carried by the drive is suspended. This view is supported by Freud's own theory of unconscious feelings[72] understood as a 'potential onset that has been prevented from developing,'[73] and thus removed from proper existence. While phantasmatic representations continue to develop within the unconscious and to attract investments of psychic energy, emotional formations have a frailer fate, hovering ambiguously at the frontier between conscious and unconscious.[74]

We would like to establish a connection between this strange fate of the affective aspect of the drive in general and later reflections on the development of the life of the drives. Indeed, as Freud notes in *Beyond the Pleasure Principle*, not all the drive-impulses (*Triebregungen*) are granted access to later phases of development. Some are called to change and mature, while others are separated from the former and remain forever immature. A contradiction is created in the psychic apparatus between individualized drives or elements of individualized drives that remain partially "unfulfilled" and others, when the aim and the demands of the former prove to be incompatible with 'all those others that are capable of joining together to yield the all-embracing unity of the ego.'[75] This division cuts through the entire psychic apparatus, setting up the unity of the ego on one side and partial drives that continue to look for gratification on the other, in such a way that no direct mingling is possible between them. The cohesion of the ego is thus obtained at the price of a division between a

---

70   Laplanche, "The Drive and its Source-Object," 132.
71   Ibid. Original emphasis.
72   Freud, "The Unconscious," 59–61.
73   Ibid., 60.
74   Freud's explanation for this difference of fate between drive-representatives and drive-affects is that the latter correspond to processes of discharge, while the former are "investments of energy." See Freud, "The Unconscious," 59–61.
75   Freud, *Beyond the Pleasure Principle*, 135.

pacified zone belonging to its unity and a more undetermined zone of struggle where immature drive-elements continue to strive for gratification.

This division inscribed in the history of the drives can be understood topographically as a translation of the economic difference between free-flowing and bound energy that we pointed out when we described the ambiguity of the pleasure principle. It is now time for us to understand the metapsychological consequences of the "leaning-on" process that accounts, generally speaking, for the transformation of the self-conservative tendencies of our drives into sexual ones. When we analyzed this process earlier, in economic terms, we noted that it can only succeed because it can also fail. Shouldn't then sublimation be considered as a possible trajectory taken by this potential failure, when the process of leaning-on is reversed in such a way that drives are desexualized? In support of such an interpretation we could advance that, while as a general tendency, sublimation diverts the trajectory of the drives from their initial sexual aim,[76] Freud's grounding work on narcissism allows for further elaborations of this diversion that highlight the importance of a withdrawal of the sexual drives within the sphere of the ego.[77] Diversion can thus be understood as a reversion, following the second self-directed fate of the drives. Therefore, in *The Ego and the Id*, the energy of the ego will be described as desexualized *and* sublimated.[78]

However, concluding that the only aim of sublimation is to work in service of the newly established conservative unity of the ego is in tension with its social component, participating in "cultural achievements."[79] In regard to its social function, sublimation seems to serve a deeper purpose related to new object-investments, but also to the lost fate of the drives that cannot join the sphere of the ego and thus be recognized as part of it. We would like to suggest that the real drive-material for sublimation is not provided by the ego-drives, but by the partial drives that remain unfulfilled because they are incompatible with the cohesion of the ego, and particularly by their affective charge that hovers at the frontier between the conscious and the unconscious. These partial drives that are, so to speak, left aside, form a dark zone of struggle for

---

76 Freud, *Three Essays*, 178.
77 Freud, "On the Introduction of Narcissism," 386 ff.
78 'If this displaceable energy is desexualised libido, it may also be described as sublimated energy; for it would still retain the main purpose of *Eros* – that of uniting and binding – in so far as it helps towards establishing the unity, or tendency to unity, which is particularly characteristic of the ego.' Sigmund Freud, *The Ego and the Id*, trans. Joan Rivere (New York, W.W. Norton, 1960 [1923]), 44.
79 Freud, *Three Essays*, 178.

gratification that sublimation can liberate by providing new aims and supporting new transfers of energy. This point can be complicated if we consider the hypothesis that the gap between the partial drives and ego-drives is crystallized through the tension between the ego and the super-ego, which invites us to consider that sublimation also works on our aggressive tendencies, possibly redirecting their fate.

What are the consequences of these topographic moves for the metapsychological understanding of the relationship between *Eros* and *Thanatos* as opposed tendencies of our psychic life? If *Eros* is the demonic free-flowing energy that conscious processes seek to repress, *Thanatos* can only appear as a force of conservation and fixation of this energy that ends up shutting down its free-flow. But if the energy that circulates unbound is destructive, *Eros* can be opposed to its thanatic-demonic flow as a binding force that supports the unity of the ego. At the heart of this chiasm, the possibility of sublimation as a distinct fate of our drives introduces a third option between demonic progress and conservative fixation, between destructive phantasmatic desire and binding unity. This option is the chance that is given to the immature part of us that still needs to grow and attain its realization, in conditions that are often unfavorable to their transformation. But instead of simply tracing a third path as an additional option, sublimation could be understood as the *zone* where a dialectic between progression and conservation becomes possible anew, in such a way that death and life tendencies constantly disrupt and disorient each other in order to find new sources and new objects. In the same way in which repression intervenes between flight and disapproval,[80] sublimation allows for redirections in the life of our drives that liberate them from regression without forcing them on the path of a demonic progression. Moreover, these redirections also disrupt the cohesion of the ego in such a way that its unity is experienced intermittently and not as a substantial basis of self-conservation.

While this latter thesis deserves a separate analysis, it is clear that the emphasis on regressive tendencies in *Beyond the Pleasure Principle* stems from complications of Freud's theory of repression. Here, every progression is made at the expense of a repression and every repression creates opportunities for other forms of pleasure. The repressed drives never give up their search for fulfillment, which is another way to say that the life of our drives continues to develop beyond (or rather beneath) their momentary suspension from our consciousness. In regard to the ongoing struggle for pleasure borne by the primary processes, Freud writes that 'the gulf between the level of gratificatory

---

80   Freud, "Repression," 35.

pleasure *demanded* and the level actually *achieved* produces the driving force that prevents the individual from resting content with any situation he ever contrives.'[81] Yet, far from confirming the existence of a universal drive for perfection, this disconnection between the pleasure that is expected and the pleasure that is realized problematizes the role of *Eros* as a force responsible for unity and co-existence.[82] When Freud quotes from Goethe's *Faust* ("he presses ever onward unbridled, untamed"), it is clear that *Eros* is nothing else than a demonic free-flowing energy that conscious processes constantly seek to repress, a sort of mysterious inner force stemming from the body for which we have no appropriate defense.[83]

While it is an excess of life that seems to be responsible here for self-destruction, is it hard to understand how this excess can be encapsulated by an outgoing "aggressive tendency" that would define our humanity. Isn't humanity's fate to *resist* aggressivity in order to perpetuate bonds and expand connections that would otherwise be doomed to disappear? In other words, isn't our humanity dependent on a cultivation of social relations – a retranslation of the untranslatable message of the other – rather than being destined to turn against them? Analyzing the trans-individual and historical reproduction of life, Freud describes the sexual drives as conservative in two senses: (1) because 'they reincorporate previous states of the relevant living matter to a more marked degree only inasmuch as they show themselves to be particularly resistant to external influences,' and (2) because 'they preserve life itself for longer periods.' He continues:

> They constitute the true life-drives; and the fact that they act against the intent of the other drives, an intent that by its very nature conduces to death, points to a conflict between them and the rest (…). It amounts to a kind of fluctuating rhythm within the life of organisms: one group of drives goes storming ahead in order to attain the ultimate goal of life at the earliest possible moment, another goes rushing back to a certain point along the way in order to do part of it all over again and thus prolong the journey [84]

---

81 Freud, *Beyond the Pleasure Principle*, 170.
82 Freud defines *Eros* as 'the force that seeks to push the various parts of living matter into direct association with each other and then keep them together.' Ibid., 191, n. 28.
83 Ibid., 170.
84 Ibid., 169.

As a goal, life seems to belong to the drives that go "storming ahead," but as a process, life is also the consequence of resisting their pressure for early extinction. The regressive drives thus contribute to "prolonging the journey," allowing for a span of life that can transform itself without necessarily being destroyed. It is following from this analysis that Freud questions the schema of a biological evolution driven exclusively by 'a universal drive favoring higher development,'[85] and the very sense of a hierarchy in nature.[86] We would like to see this intertwinement of regression and progression as an opportunity to understand the splitting of the drives as an internal division through which a new chance is given to the repressed to overcome its immature condition. Sublimation as a dialectical zone allows for a reconsideration of what has remained in the dark, not in order to simply disclose new demonic forces, but rather to offer them an unforeseen possibility of maturation and cultivation. This perspective's utopian moment is its recognition that a livable life is possible even when it appears impossible. But this possibility can become real only if the social component of the life of the drives is itself seen as both a resource and a horizon of actualization.

Bibliography

Adorno, Theodor W. "The Idea of Natural-History." In *Things Beyond Resemblance: Collected Essays on Theodor W. Adorno*, edited and translated by Robert Hullot-Kentor, 252–304. New York: Columbia University Press, 2008 [1932].

Adorno, Theodor W. *Minima Moralia: Reflections on Damaged Life*. Translated by E.N.F. Jephcott. London: Verso, 2005 [1951].

Adorno, Theodor W. "Progress." In *Critical Models: Interventions and Catchwords*. Translated by Henry W. Pickford, 143–160. New York: Columbia University Press, 2005 [1962].

---

85   Ibid.
86   'for one thing, it is in many cases merely a matter of subjective judgement when we declare one level of development to be "higher" than some other; and for another thing, biology shows us that higher development in one particular respect is very often paid for or balanced out by regression in another. Moreover, there are plenty of animal forms whose early stages clearly reveal that they have developed regressively rather than progressively. Higher development and regression might both be the result of the pressure to adapt exerted by external forces, and the role of the drives might be limited in both cases to the task of assimilating the imposed change as an inner source of pleasure.' Ibid., 169–170.

Adorno, Theodor W. "Revisionist Psychoanalysis." Translated by Nan-Nan Lee. *Philosophy and Social Criticism* 40, no. 3 (2014 [1952]): 309–338.

Adorno, Theodor W. "Sociology and Psychology – I." Translated by Irving Wohlfarth. *New Left Review* 46 (1967): 67–80.

Adorno, Theodor W. "Sociology and Psychology – II." Translated by Irving Wohlfarth. *New Left Review* 47 (1968): 79–97.

Adorno, Theodor W. "Theses on Need." Translated by David Fernbach. *New Left Review* 128 (2021 [1942]): 79–82.

Benjamin, Jessica. "The End of Internalization: Adorno's Social Psychology." *Telos* 32 (1977): 42–64.

Benjamin, Walter. "On the Concept of History." In *Selected Writings: Volume 4: 1938–1940*, edited by Howard Eiland and Michael W. Jennings. Translated by Harry Zohn, 389–40. Cambridge, MA: Harvard University Press, 2003 [1940].

Dejours, Christophe. *Le corps, d'abord*. Paris: Payot, 2001.

Dejours, Christophe. *Les dissidences du corps*. Paris: Payot, 2017.

François, Arnaud. "La division de la vie: creation, conservation et pulsion de mort chez Bergson et Freud." In *Bergson et Freud*, edited by Brigitte Sibbon, 121–139. Paris: PUF, 2014.

Freud, Sigmund. "Beyond the Pleasure Principle". In *The Penguin Freud Reader*, edited by Adam Phillips. Translated by John Reddick, 132–195. New York: Penguin, 2006 [1920].

Freud, Sigmund. *Civilization and Its Discontents*. Translated by James Strachey. New York: W.W. Norton, 2010 [1930].

Freud, Sigmund. "On the Introduction of Narcissism." In *The Penguin Freud Reader*, edited by Adam Phillips. Translated by John Reddick, 358–390, New York: Penguin, 2006 [1914].

Freud, Sigmund. "Drives and Their Fates." In *The Unconscious*, edited by Adam Phillips. Translated by Graham Frankland, 13–31. New York: Penguin, 2005 [1915].

Freud, Sigmund. *The Ego and the Id*. Translated by Joan Rivere. New York: W.W. Norton, 1960 [1923].

Freud, Sigmund. "Repression." In *The Unconscious*, edited by Adam Phillips. Translated by Graham Frankland, 35–45. New York: Penguin, 2005 [1915].

Freud, Sigmund. "Three Essays on the Theory of Sexuality". In *The Standard Edition of the Works of Sigmund Freud, Vol. VII (1901–1905)*, edited and translated by James Strachey, 125–243. London: The Hogarth Press, 1953 [1905].

Freud, Sigmund. "The Unconscious." In *The Unconscious*, edited by Adam Phillips. Translated by Graham Frankland, 47–85. New York: Penguin, 2005 [1915].

Gherovici, Patricia. *Transgender Psychoanalysis: A Lacanian Perspective on Sexual Difference*. London: Routledge, 2017.

Haber, Stéphane. *Freud et la théorie sociale*. Paris: La Dispute, 2012.

Hegel, G.W.F. *Encyclopedia of the Philosophical Sciences in Basic Outline, Part I: Science of Logic*. Translated by Klaus Brinkmann and Daniel O. Dahlstrom. Cambridge: Cambridge University Press, 2010.

Johnston, Adrian. *Time Driven: Metapsychology and the Splitting of the Drive*. Evanston, IL: Northwestern University Press, 2005.

Lagache, Daniel. "Situation de l'agressivité." *Bulletin de Psychologie* (1961): 99–112.

Kant, Immanuel. *Critique of Pure Reason*. Translated by Paul Guyer and Allen Wood. Cambridge: Cambridge University Press: 1998 [1781/1787].

Laplanche, Jean. *Life and Death in Psychoanalysis*. Translated by Jeffrey Mehlman. Baltimore and London: The Johns Hopkins University Press, 1976.

Laplanche, Jean. *Problématiques III: La sublimation*. Paris: PUF, 2008 [1980].

Laplanche, Jean. "The So-Called 'Death Drive': A Sexual Drive." *British Journal of Psychotherapy* 20, no. 4 (2004): 455–471.

Marcuse, Herbert. *One-Dimensional Man: Studies in the Ideology of Advanced Industrial Society*. Boston: Beacon Press, 1964.

CHAPTER 11

"I Know Very Well, but Nevertheless": Moral Immaturity of the 21st Century Humanitarian Witness

Mlado Ivanovic

In one of the central paragraphs from "A Plea for Solidarity," Eugene V. Debs ponders the human condition's significance determined by the capitalist age's insensitivity and coldness. Reflecting on a world amid the imminent horrors of the twentieth century that seems to lack a central aspect of moral and political meaning, he writes the following about the nature of solidarity:

> Solidarity is not a matter of sentiment but a fact, cold and impassive as the granite foundations of a skyscraper. If the basic elements, identity of interest, clarity of vision, honesty of intent, and oneness of purpose, or any of these is lacking, all sentimental pleas for solidarity, and all other efforts to achieve it will be barren of results.[1]

While it is fascinating how Debs recounts the necessities of a moral compass through this poetic portrayal of the requirements of social justice, a subtler yet poignant lesson can be learned here focusing on moral and political errors of today's world. As we grapple with ongoing humanitarian crises across the globe, Debs' words force us to confront the question that seems natural and almost unavoidable in the face of towering global inequalities and ongoing human deprivation: How to mobilize solidarity with people who are culturally and geographically distant from the general Western public?

When attending to this task in the face of widespread and ongoing deprivation experienced by millions of people worldwide, it is crucial to analyze not only the interplay between historical conditions and dominant power structures that perpetuate inequality, but also the internalized attitudes and beliefs that shape individuals' agency and contribute to the maintenance of such a state of affairs. This is where Freudian psychoanalysis and the Frankfurt

---

1 Eugene V. Debs. "A Plea for Solidarity," *The International Socialist Review* 14, no. 9 (March 1914), 534.

School's critical work converge. Both sought to expose the ways in which social norms, ideologies, and cultural values shape the behavior of individuals and the ways in which their choices (or omissions) perpetuate dominant power structures. By examining the role of unconscious dimensions of human behavior, Freud and the Frankfurt School aimed to uncover the hidden motivations and repressed desires that fuel social structures and simultaneously hinder solidarity towards oppressed social groups. Although Freud's ideas have been subject to debate and critique, his analysis of the role of unconscious drives in shaping our beliefs and behavior provides a useful framework for understanding how individuals internalize and perpetuate often pathological social relations. When combined with the broader social and historical perspective of critical theory, which analyzes the ways in which different social formations of power (i.e., economy, media, technology, etc.) shape society as a whole, Freud's insights can offer a deeper understanding of the complex interplay between individual psychology and dominant social forces. This, in turn, can provide new insights and pathways for resistance and liberation in the face of ongoing global inequalities and human deprivation.

In what follows, this chapter draws on this task and focuses on three different, yet interrelated points. First, it analyzes the critical potential of psychoanalysis in terms of its presence in the work of traditional critical theory. Namely, the early Frankfurt School thinkers tried to bring Marxism and psychoanalysis together to offer a more nuanced picture of modern society. I explore their developments by focusing on three aspects that I find relevant for today's social critique: (a) articulation of a realistic conception of the person; (b) understanding critical theory's conception of the aims and methods of critique by avoiding excessive rationalism and idealism, and (c) articulation of a set of normative and ethical principles that can guide the overall critical project. Second, I turn to the Freudian notion of the "pleasure principle" – more specifically its negative expression: the attempt to avoid displeasure as much as possible – in order to draw political and moral contours of an account of moral and political insensitivity in the face of human suffering and injustice in general. I accompany this analysis with Theodor W. Adorno's reflections on the same topic and refer to his concept of "bourgeois coldness" to illustrate the overall aspects of moral atrophy that he was so adamant about. To say that one is insensitive towards the lives and experiences of others is not to say that in the eyes of bystanders the exploited and suffering multitudes are rendered completely invisible. Instead, it stresses that aspects of these insensitive spectators' lives and personal experiences inevitably become subject to public narratives wherein there is a reductive simplification and abstraction of the exploited and violence done to them. Finally, the last portion of the chapter takes these points further by focusing on urgent social challenges tied to current failures of humanitarian management and the inclusion of Non-Western others in "developed" Western societies. More precisely, it explores some of the downfalls of the present moral tendencies and dispositions by focusing on the insufficiency of humanitarian discourses (and practices) to foster longstanding solidarity with vulnerable strangers and the difficult conditions they endure. Ultimately, I argue that the political, moral, and epistemic problems of the current state of humanitarianism are all closely related to the psychological dispositions of social actors, and an awareness of their intertwinement may help us to understand the ambivalent nature of current humanism and why it fails so often.

1 The Critical Potential of Psychoanalysis in Critical Theory

> We welcome illusions because they spare us unpleasurable feelings, and enable us to enjoy satisfactions instead. We must not complain, then, if now and again they come into collision with some portion of reality, and are shattered against it.[2]

Retrospectively, the relationship between classic psychoanalysis and Critical Theory, which to some extent defines most of the work of the first-generation Frankfurt School, is fundamentally concerned with showing how the traditional borders between psychology on the one side, and political and social philosophy on the other, have been made obsolete. Taking into account how psychological processes are being determined (and absorbed) by the development of the individual within the social nexus of present cultural, political, and economic circumstances, psychoanalysis teaches us that whatever values and ideals societies adopt, they are always mediated through unconscious psychological processes that condition the collective in terms of its moral identity and its commitments in terms of social justice.

Centering its emancipatory potential in this intertwinement between the disenchantment of the relation between the individual and society, critical theory ultimately requires psychoanalysis in order to develop a realistic conception of the social critique and chart possible venues of emancipation. This approach not only allows them to understand the manifold ways in which moral and political conditions, individual agency, and social pathologies are

---

2 Sigmund Freud, *On the History of the Psycho-Analytic Movement: Papers on Metapsychology and Other Works* (London: The Hogarth Press, 1957), 280.

correlated and co-constitutive, but also to develop a more nuanced perspective on the social and psychological factors that can potentially help a difficult task of shaping emancipatory collective action. While much of mainstream political theory operates on the notion of *rational and free persons concerned with their own interests*,[3] critical social thought has to deal with the reality of irrational, suppressed, and repressed subjectivity often acting against their own interests. Hence, taking into consideration how psychoanalysis has historically offered the best accounts of irrationality, suffering, apathy, and guilt, Freud's discoveries have allowed Frankfurt School thinkers to have a more nuanced understanding of modern society and the ways in which individuals are shaped by social forces.

Overall, the attempt of early Frankfurt School thinkers to combine Marxism and psychoanalysis was an important contribution to critical capacities of philosophy amidst the fallout of the Second World War and life within advanced capitalist societies. Such a theoretical unity between these two intellectual projects was deemed necessary as these thinkers believed that individual cognitive dispositions and the social structures of society are interdependent and mutually constitutive, which in turn requires that an analysis of one must also include an analysis of the other. Exactly this interdependency and co-constitutive nature of 20th century subject identified psychoanalysis as the main source of several distinct and yet interrelated valuable insights and tools that were instrumental to Frankfurt School's critical project. First, the articulation of a realistic conception of personhood with its emphasis on the unconscious and the importance of the irrational and emotional dimensions of human experience. Second, the understanding of the Frankfurt School's conception of the aims and methods of social critique by avoiding excessive rationalism and idealism while simultaneously emphasizing the need for a more nuanced and historically grounded analysis of power relations and the development of social structures.[4] Third, the reliance on psychoanalysis has provided Adorno, Horkheimer, and Marcuse with a set of normative and ethical principles that offered nuanced humanistic undertones to their overall critical project. These included a commitment to empathy, solidarity, and

---

3   John Rawls, *A Theory of Justice* (Cambridge, MA: Belknap Press, 1971).
4   Psychoanalysis provided the Frankfurt School with a set of tools for analyzing the deep-seated psychic structures and mechanisms that underlie individual behavior and social phenomena. These tools helped critical theory to develop a more nuanced and critical understanding of the social and psychological dimensions of power, ideology, domination, and resistance.

critical self-reflection, as well as a belief in the importance of social and political emancipation and the realization of human potential.

2   The Search for a Realistic Conception of a Person

In terms of articulating a realistic conception of the person, the Frankfurt School's approach was fundamentally different from the idealistic and rationalistic views that had dominated Western philosophy. Rather than seeing individuals as rational, autonomous agents, the early Frankfurt School thinkers believed that individuals are not self-contained entities that can be understood independently of their social contexts and historical conditions. Instead, they argued that our desires, needs, beliefs, and other epistemic, moral, and political dispositions are largely shaped by external social factors. This insight allowed them to challenge the dominant rationalist and positivist paradigms in social theory that had a tendency either to reduce individuals to abstract and universal categories or to posit them as merely rational or self-interested actors. In their attempt to combine Marxism and psychoanalysis, the Frankfurt School not only rejected the notion of self-determining agents independent of historical contexts, but also argued that individual psychological dispositions were not entirely conscious, and that unconscious desires, anxieties, and conflicts played a crucial role in how social and symbolic factors are internalized (while simultaneously shaping the individual's beliefs, choices, and behaviors further).

While acknowledging the usefulness of psychological frameworks in understanding the complex ways in which social structures and individual mental dispositions interact, Freud's theory of the unconscious was particularly appealing to the Frankfurt School because it provided a way to understand subtle ways in which individuals are shaped by social forces and how they, in turn, sustain or influence social conditions. By exploring the ways in which our desires and needs influence our beliefs and behavior, psychoanalysis offered a valuable framework for understanding the ways in which individuals are embedded in the social fabric and how they can potentially resist or transform their immediate circumstances. For example, Theodor Adorno saw the unconscious as a repository of repressed desires and needs that were shaped by larger social and cultural forces, and that understanding the unconscious is crucial to understanding the darker aspects of modernity. As he wrote in his "Introduction to Sociology:"

> According to Freudian theory, it appears that, on the surface, certain recurrent, similar, relatively abstract situations predominate, being standardized by the reality principle to which all human beings have to adapt, but that a differentiation emerges if one immerses oneself in the so-called psychical dynamic, in the unconscious mechanisms, and above all in the interplay between the unconscious and the individual ego; and then – at a still deeper level, as if at the core of individuation – one becomes aware of the collective.[5]

In other words, Adorno believed that by exploring the unconscious, individuals could gain important insight into the ways in which societal forces shape their lives, which would subsequently result in a capacity to resist them.

Furthermore, Adorno thought that Freud's insights were important for understanding the dynamics of social domination and oppression. By uncovering the unconscious motivations of individuals, psychoanalysis could reveal the ways in which oppressive social structures are internalized and reproduced in individual behavior. This understanding of the role of the unconscious in shaping individuals' agency was central to Adorno's own work, which sought to expose the ways in which domination and oppression are embedded in social structures and cultural practices. As he writes, '[T]he fact that the innermost core on which the psychology of the single individual rests is itself something general: namely certain very general – though admittedly archaic – structures of the social context in which individuals are contained.'[6] This illusion of autonomy, according to Adorno, is perpetuated by the dominant culture and ideology in modern society, which presents the image of the free, self-determining individual as a central value and ideal, while in reality, the same social conditions safeguard a person's enthrallment through dominating values and interests of the ruling elite. The strong reinforcement of this illusion of autonomy among social actors can be attributed to the sociogenesis of subjectivity, which is shaped by mechanisms of domination and control that often operate in ways that are hidden or obscured, thereby preventing individuals from recognizing them.[7]

---

5 Theodor W. Adorno, *Introduction to Sociology* (Stanford: Stanford University Press, 2000), 114.
6 Ibid., 115.
7 It is worth noting that the idea of repression and conflict, which Freud argued were key mechanisms for dealing with traumatic experiences and unacceptable impulses, was also very important for Adorno's early analysis. Namely, he saw repression as a way in which individuals internalized societal norms and values, leading to an ideological surrender that concealed the true nature of social and economic relations. In addition, both Freud and the Frankfurt School emphasized the role of conflict in shaping human behavior. Freud saw the

While acknowledging the important impact of Freud on the specific nature and aims of critical theory, Adorno also remains aware of the distinctive differences between classical psychoanalysis and the overall critical paradigm that the Frankfurt School is committed to. In Adorno's reading of Freud, his focus on the individual psyche and narrow understanding of society as a source of repression and constraints missed the broader contexts in which individuals are shaped by social, economic, and cultural forces. By neglecting larger social and economic structures, Freud's view of the individual remains somewhat limited. Additionally, Freud's emphasis on the role of the unconscious and past experiences and trauma in shaping present behavior has been criticized for limiting the capacity of individuals to actively change their lives and society. Adorno's statement in "Minima Moralia" that, 'in psycho-analysis, nothing is true except exaggerations,' further highlights the concerns surrounding the deterministic nature of Freud's theories.[8]

3 Psychoanalytic Critique of Rationalism, Idealism, and Positivism in Critical Theory

Psychoanalysis did not only provide critical theory with a realistic conception of personhood, but it also helped to rethink its commitment to historically grounded analysis of power relations and setting the aims of its critique. Namely, at the heart of the Frankfurt School's critical work was a rejection of abstract, universalizing concepts and models that failed to account for the complexity and historical contingency of social reality and human experience. Instead, Horkheimer, Adorno, and Marcuse emphasized the importance of a more nuanced and historically grounded analysis that could account for the specificities of different social contexts and the ways in which power operates within them. In their own response to the devastating experiences of the 20th Century, the Frankfurt School was marked by a deep concern with the ways in which power and domination operate in contemporary society. Starting in the late 1930s, they were critical of the goal-oriented rationality and bureaucratic structures of modern society, which they saw as an inevitable path to

---

conflict as arising from the tension between an individual's unconscious desires and the demands of society, while the Frankfurt School focused on the conflict between individual needs and the demands of a capitalist economic system. In both cases, the result was a view of human behavior as being driven by competing forces that could lead to alienation, indifference, political atrophy, and other negative individual dispositions.

8   Theodor W. Adorno, *Minima Moralia* (London: Verso, 2005), 29.

the domination and exploitation of individuals and historically marginalized social groups. They also emphasized the importance of culture and ideology in shaping social reality, arguing that symbolic forms of power such as mass media and popular culture played a crucial role in shaping perceptions and attitudes of social actors.

Insofar as their critique was aimed at excessive rationalism and idealism, psychoanalysis played a significant conceptual role in informing their inquiry in the face of the main conceptual modes of dominant philosophies and social theory. Regarding rationalism and reductionism, the Frankfurt School, and especially Adorno, were critical of ongoing tendencies to reduce complex phenomena to simpler or more abstract forms. Adorno argued that rationalism had become too narrow in its focus and that it failed to account for the complexities and contradictions of human experience. In the beginning pages of his nominal work *Negative Dialectics*, Adorno argues that the "positivity" of rationalism leads to an oversimplified and static understanding of reality. The emphasis on clear distinctions and certainty, he suggests, fails to capture the complexities of the world, including the ways in which different aspects of reality (either in their social or natural form) are constantly changing and contradicting each other. The problem with this positivity, Adorno believes, is that it leads to an "ideology of the 'idea'" that prioritizes the idea of totality over the fragmentary and the different. In other words, rationalism and the Enlightenment project have tended to view the world as a static and unchanging object of knowledge that can be fully grasped and controlled through the application of reason. For Adorno, the "non-identical" is the key to understanding the dialectical nature of reality. The non-identical refers to aspects of our knowledge about epistemic objects that cannot be fully subsumed under a concept or category, as they resist and challenge attempts to impose order and coherence on the world.[9]

In confronting the problem of reductionism, Adorno saw Freud's work as an avenue to grasp the subjective and irrational facets of human experience that rationalism tended to neglect. He posited that the rise of fascism and totalitarianism in Europe during the first half of the 20th century was an indication of the limitations of the prevalent form of reason. Adorno saw these forms of social organization as a result of a public ethos that had become overly rationalized, while simultaneously suppressing and navigating the irrational and emotional aspects of the human experience. This resulted in moral decay, paving the way for the support of immoral actions and injustices. Adorno's initial response to this problem was taking under critical scrutiny philosophical

---

9   Theodor W. Adorno, *Negative Dialectics* (London: Routledge, 2004), 3–18.

emphasis on clear distinctions and certainty while at the same time disclosing the innate contradictions and ambiguities implicit in human knowledge and experience.[10] Indeed, rationalism's focus on objective knowledge, logic, and rationality overlooked the subjective and emotional aspects of human life. This tendency resulted in a social reality that nurtured a limited and misleading understanding of the world and human agency, often disregarding the dehumanizing power structures and social hierarchies it reinforces.

In this context, the Frankfurt School, and Adorno in particular, were also critical of universalism, which refers to the tendency to apply general theories or concepts to all social phenomena, regardless of their historical or cultural contingency and context. In a nutshell, this process awards social phenomena a certain ahistorical nature that makes them more palatable for ideological forms of social control and manipulation of the general public. By doing so, universalism has the potential to reify and naturalize social structures and hierarchies, such as race, gender, and class, which are in fact historically and culturally constructed. Accordingly, critical theorists argued that applying universalism to social phenomena tends to strip them of their specificity and uniqueness, forcing them into pre-existing categories and concepts that are often limiting and reductionist. Instead, they advocated for a critical project that recognizes the historical and cultural contingency and context of social phenomena and aims to uncover the underlying power structures and social hierarchies that shape them. This critical approach allows for a more nuanced and complex understanding of social phenomena, which can help to challenge and transform oppressive power relations. As Adorno writes in several of his works, any philosophical consideration that claims to be universally valid is in danger of forgetting the specificity of historical conditions. By ignoring the historical and cultural contingency and context of social phenomena, we run the risk of distorting their nature and perpetuating ideological forms of social control and manipulation. To truly understand social and cultural phenomena, we must approach them dialectically and recognize their specific historical and cultural contexts. This means acknowledging the unique and specific aspects of individual human experience and considering the historical and cultural genesis of these experiences. Only then can we have a more nuanced and accurate understanding of the world around us.

Finally, The Frankfurt School thinkers were also highly critical of positivism, which is the belief that social reality can be comprehended through objective,

---

10   He saw this tendency of dominant forms of philosophy to act as a pervasive force that operates at all levels of society, shaping how people think, feel, act, and interact with one another while also defining what is considered "normal" or "acceptable".

empirical methods. Adorno was of the view that positivism reduces knowledge to a collection of objective and empirical facts, disregarding the subjective and interpretive aspects of human experience. Furthermore, he believed that positivism is not merely an epistemological inclination with an ideological bias, but has significant moral and political ramifications, as it serves to fortify the status quo and sustain social inequity. Positivism not only limits reality to a set of measurable and quantifiable data but also becomes 'the subjection of all existing things to logical formalism' wherein 'knowledge confines itself to repeating it, thought makes itself mere tautology.'[11] Ultimately, Adorno believed that a more historically nuanced and critical approach to knowledge and understanding was necessary to capture the intricacy of human experience and challenge the dominant power structures of modern societies.

4 The Ethical Principles Guiding the Frankfurt School's Critical Project

Although the early Frankfurt School is often known for its uncompromising critique of modernity and its cultural and social forms, their inquiry into the dysfunctions of the modern world was rooted in a series of normative and ethical principles that offer a sophisticated and compassionate view of the possibilities for social and political liberation. For instance, Adorno's work emphasizes the importance of solidarity, and critical self-reflection, all in service of achieving social justice. While Adorno's ethical commitments are not a systematic set of claims, they were central to his work and contributed to a nuanced and humanistic vision of social and political emancipation. To better understand the significance of these principles and the reliance on psychoanalysis by Adorno and his colleagues, one must consider the historical context in which they were writing. Witnessing the horrors of World War II and grappling with the devastation it wrought on the Western intellectual ethos deeply influenced Adorno's thinking and contributed to his ethical and normative commitments. In response to the atrocities of the war and the rise of totalitarianism, Adorno sought to articulate a humanistic vision grounded in recognizing the value and dignity of human life. This vision emphasized social

---

11 Theodor W. Adorno and Max Horkheimer, *Dialectic of Enlightenment: Philosophical Fragments* (Stanford: Stanford University Press, 2002), 20.

and political emancipation that rejected the complacency and increasing indifference of the dominant culture.

To begin illustrating such commitment, one has to start with the Frankfurt School's focus on intellectual autonomy, which they saw as essential to maintaining a critical distance from dominant ideologies and power structures that they sustain. This connection between critical epistemology and ethics is most evident in Adorno's work, for whom the project of social emancipation relied on unearthing the hidden dimensions of domination and oppression perpetuated by modern society. Adorno's emphasis on the non-identical and his critique of modern epistemologies was rooted in his belief that the task of critical theory was not only to expose the limitations and contradictions of dominant thought, but also to develop a new understanding of alterity that could challenge and transform the existing order. By fostering intellectual autonomy, critical theory could open up new avenues of thought and action, promoting solidarity and empathy, and providing a foundation for a more just and humane society. When epistemology adheres to the primacy of the object, refusing to identify it with the subject or its social determination; when it imprints the object's resistance and weakness in cognition; and when it accepts the ensuing non-identity with oneself, epistemology becomes ethical. Such a persistent emphasis of critical theory on subordinating theory to praxis is based on the preservation of negativity and non-identity within the existing social order. As Adorno writes:

> Contradiction is non-identity under the aspect of identity; the dialectical primary of the principle of contradiction makes the thought of unity the measure of heterogeneity. As the heterogeneous collides with its limit it exceeds itself. Dialectics is the consistent sense of non-identity. It does not begin by taking a standpoint. My thought is driven to it by its own inevitable insufficiency, by my guilt of what I am thinking.[12]

Along these lines, for Adorno, ethical and epistemological commitments were inseparable. His critique of dominant culture and rationality was informed by his belief in the significance of solidarity with marginalized others. At the same time, however, Adorno recognized that this critical project was not merely an intellectual exercise, but also a moral imperative that demanded a deep and sustained commitment to justice. Therefore, intellectual autonomy

---

12   Theodor W. Adorno, *Negative Dialectics*, trans. by E. B. Ashton (New York: Continuum, 1973), 5.

and critical distance were not merely intellectual endeavors but also ethical obligations that demanded a profound awareness of the historical and social contexts in which they were embedded. By nurturing a critical and empathetic outlook, Adorno argued that individuals could transcend the constraints and limitations of a dominant political culture characterized by indifference and apathy towards the vulnerability and suffering of others. Consequently, they could acquire a more comprehensive and compassionate understanding of the world that recognized the value and dignity of human life.[13]

Indeed, Adorno's emphasis on compassion and solidarity was a direct response to what he saw as the callousness and indifference of modern capitalist societies and fascist regimes towards human suffering. He referred to this as "indifference to the fate of others" or "bourgeois coldness," a condition in which people become desensitized to the suffering of others and lose touch with their own capacity for empathy and compassion.[14] For Adorno, this phenomenon was not only a product of economic and political structures but was also perpetuated by dominant cultural and intellectual discourses that reduced individuals to mere objects of instrumental reason and efficiency. As a result, Adorno saw the development of a critical and empathetic perspective as crucial for challenging and transforming the dominant culture and political order. By emphasizing their importance, Adorno sought to offer a counterpoint to the indifference and callousness that he saw as pervasive in modern societies. In his view, compassion was not simply a matter of individual feeling or psychological disposition, but a social and political practice that required a critical awareness of the historical and cultural contexts that shape our perceptions and actions. Otherwise, this moral disposition fails to encourage change or action to address the underlying causes of suffering, but instead suggests that these circumstances are unavoidable and cannot be altered. Hence, Adorno's indirect emphasis on empathy was an integral part of his larger project of critique and social transformation, which sought to challenge the dominant forms of thought and behavior that perpetuated the conditions of domination and oppression in modern societies. Adorno saw empathy as a necessary antidote to increasing moral indifference, a means of rehumanizing society by cultivating a sense of solidarity and shared humanity.

---

13   In this way, Adorno's normative and ethical principles were not abstract ideals, but rather practical tools for achieving social and political emancipation and realizing the full potential of human existence.

14   Theodor W. Adorno, "Education after Auschwitz," in *Critical Models: Interventions and Catchwords*, eds. Theodor W. Adorno and Henry W. Pickford (New York: Columbia University Press, 1998), 201.

Furthermore, Adorno's understanding of social transformation relied on a multifaceted approach that involved the intersections between moral sentiments and psychoanalysis. Although he had reservations about certain aspects of traditional Freudian psychoanalysis, he believed that it was an essential tool for uncovering the underlying social and cultural factors that shape individual subjectivity and behavior. Specifically, Adorno found value in the concept of "projection," which refers to the displacement of one's anxieties and desires onto others, perpetuating oppressive power structures and leading to the scapegoating of marginalized groups. By examining projection within individuals and society, Adorno believed it was possible to gain insights into the mechanisms of domination and oppression. His emphasis on solidarity and moral sentiments further strengthened his critique and social transformation project, which aimed to challenge the dominant forms of thought and behavior that perpetuated these conditions in modern societies.

5 The Pleasure Principle and Humanitarian Insensitivity

> In the depths of my heart I can't help being convinced that my dear fellow-men, with a few exceptions, are worthless.[15]

We live in a world that is surrounded by an overwhelming amount of humanitarian imagery that depicts instances of human deprivation and suffering. While exposure to such information can have positive effects, such as raising awareness and inspiring empathy and action, it can also result in negative consequences. The constant bombardment of graphic images can lead to "compassion fatigue," a sense of helplessness, and even withdrawal from the pressing issues altogether. This is especially problematic in a culture that seems to prioritize individual pleasure and comfort over ethical responsibilities toward those in need. As a result, it can be difficult to predict when and how the Western public will acknowledge and act upon their obligations to those in vulnerable situations. The fact that people have an innate drive for self-gratification, even if it only means avoiding the discomfort that comes with encountering atrocities, raises an important question about increasing moral selectivism and

---

15   Sigmund Freud, "Letter from Sigmund Freud to Lou Andreas-Salone, July 28th, 1929," in *Letters of Sigmund Freud 1873–1939*, ed. Ernst L. Freud (New York: Dover Publication, Inc., 1992), 390.

insensitivity towards pressing humanitarian issues.¹⁶ As individuals become more particular in expressing their solidarity towards those who suffer, it creates a co-dependence between these two concepts that represents one of the most significant moral dilemmas of our political and humanitarian culture. The pursuit of pleasure and avoidance of discomfort often clashes with the moral imperative to alleviate the suffering of those in need. To understand this intricate relationship better, we need to delve deeper into the complexities and implications of how the Freudian pleasure principle hinders our humanitarian and moral responsibilities, resulting in a lack of empathy and compassion toward those who are suffering.

To shed light on this relationship, Adorno's concept of "bourgeois coldness" can be helpful in understanding the dispositions of a society where material comfort and personal indulgence often supersede moral obligations. Adorno contends that the incessant pursuit of pleasure and convenience, especially among the privileged layers of society, can result in detachment and apathy towards pressing social issues and the suffering of others. The phenomenon of *bourgeois coldness,* hence, reflects a societal tendency where individuals consumed by their own comforts and luxuries become insensitive to the plight of marginalized and oppressed groups. Of course, Adorno's critique of this phenomenon is more complex than my basic reiteration here, however, one crucial aspect of this critique is its recognition of the role of psychoanalysis, and specifically Freud's insights about the pleasure principle, in understanding the root causes of moral atrophy and indifference towards precarity of others. By highlighting the dangers of the relentless pursuit of pleasure and personal gratification at the expense of ethical and social obligations, Adorno's critique points to the importance of incorporating psychoanalytic perspectives into broader discussions of morality and social justice. In this way, Adorno's work underscores the ongoing relevance of psychoanalysis as a tool for critically examining the complex interplay between individual desire and social responsibility. Consequently, Adorno's hope is that these insights may prompt us to reconsider our values and actions in light of our ethical responsibilities towards those in need, recognizing that the pursuit of pleasure should not come at the cost of disregarding the welfare of others.[17]

---

16   This selectivism can lead to a form of moral hierarchy, where individuals prioritize the suffering of those who are perceived as more deserving of compassion, while ignoring or minimizing the suffering of those who are not. This tendency is particularly evident in the media coverage of humanitarian crises, where certain issues and populations receive more attention than others, often based on geopolitical, cultural, or economic factors.

17   Adorno's criticism of bourgeois coldness reflects how the capitalist system, which prioritizes consumerism and individualism, can promote a culture of self-gratification and

6   The Pleasure Principle and Moral Insensitivity

Although Adorno did not explicitly reference Freud's Pleasure Principle in his critique of Western society's moral decay, we can draw a parallel between Freud's insights and Adorno's concept of moral insensitivity and indifference, as both expose the egoistic pursuit of personal pleasure and avoidance of discomfort at the expense of others. The pleasure principle plays a significant role in shaping human behavior and it is one of the key concepts in Freudian psychoanalysis as it refers to the innate human drive to seek pleasure and avoid discomfort or pain.[18] According to Freud, the pleasure principle is a logical necessity, and the *id* functions according to it as human beings inevitably want fulfillment and strive to avoid pain, both of which are essential human desires. One can find reference to this psychological disposition throughout several of Freud's writings, and yet his analysis in *Beyond the Pleasure Principle* (1920) offers the most compelling rendition of the concept. There he emphasized that the pleasure principle involves an urge to reduce all tensions and that the fundamental motivation for human behavior is driven by the avoidance of any form of discomfort or pain, leading individuals to seek ways to alleviate tension and achieve a state of relief.[19]

Obviously, the relevance of this concept for the critical project of the Frankfurt School becomes particularly pronounced when examining Adorno's claims about the atrophied moral dispositions of modern individuals. The pleasure principle, then, can be seen as a contributing factor to this phenomenon, as individuals prioritize their own immediate gratification and comfort over moral considerations (i.e., solidarity, responsibility, compassion, etc.). The pursuit of pleasure and avoidance of discomfort can lead to an absence of active engagement in addressing pressing aspects of looming humanitarian crises. Therefore, understanding the various influences of unconscious drives

---

ethical neglect, which resonates well with Freud's concept. By establishing this link, we can highlight the influence of Freud's ideas on Adorno's understanding of human behavior and how Adorno's critique of bourgeois coldness reveals the implications of moral insensitivity and indifference towards the suffering of others in a capitalist society.

18   In the context of moral decision-making, the pleasure principle, can manifest in individuals prioritizing their own pleasure, comfort, or self-interest over moral considerations, such as the welfare of others or adherence to ethical principles. For example, individuals may exhibit moral indifference by ignoring moral dilemmas or ethical responsibilities that require effort, sacrifice, or discomfort to address. They may choose to turn a blind eye to injustices, engage in unethical behaviors for personal gain, or rationalize morally questionable actions to avoid feelings of guilt or discomfort.

19   Sigmund Freud, *Beyond the Pleasure Principle* (London: The Hogarth Press, 1955), 7–8.

and dispositions on human behavior can provide valuable insights into the deeper mechanisms that contribute to moral apathy in society. This underscores the importance of critical self-reflection, cultivating ethical awareness, and making intentional moral decisions that go beyond immediate gratification. Acknowledging and transcending the instinctual pursuit of pleasure and comfort seems to be crucial in prioritizing moral considerations and empathic responses toward those in need.

When we reflect on pressing issues in our society and the world at large, it becomes evident that selective moral response towards humanitarian crises highlights a complex phenomenon that encompasses a range of behaviors and attitudes. Moral insensitivity can manifest in various ways, such as indifference to the plight of marginalized groups, apathy towards social injustices, disregard for human rights violations, or a failure to recognize and address systemic issues that perpetuate inequality and suffering. Moral and humanitarian apathy can arise from a myriad of factors, including psychological defenses such as denial or repression, self-interest and self-preservation, societal norms and values that prioritize individualism or profit-seeking over collective well-being, and desensitization to human suffering due to information overload and emotional numbing.[20] Moreover, moral and humanitarian insensitivity can also be perpetuated by structural and systemic factors, such as economic disparities, political ideologies, cultural biases, and historical injustices that shape social structures and institutions. All these factors can contribute to the normalization of moral callousness, indifference, or even cruelty toward those who are marginalized, vulnerable, or perceived as different. Hence, the erosion of empathy, compassion, and moral responsibility, can have profound consequences for individuals, communities, and societies, leading to a breakdown of social cohesion, diminished ethical engagement, and a disregard for fundamental human values.[21]

---

20   Paul Slovic, "'If I look at the mass I will never act': Psychic numbing and genocide," *Judgment and Decision Making* 2, no. 2 (April 2007): 79–95.

21   In my understanding, empathy and compassion are related concepts, but they have subtle differences in their meanings and applications. Empathy refers to the ability to understand and share the feelings and emotions of others. It involves putting oneself in another's shoes, experiencing their emotions, and being able to understand their perspective and emotions from within. Empathy allows individuals to connect with others on an emotional level and recognize their emotions, whether it be joy, sorrow, pain, or fear, without necessarily taking any action. Compassion, on the other hand, goes beyond empathy. It involves not only understanding and sharing the emotions of others but also feeling a deep concern and genuine care for their well-being. Compassion often motivates individuals to take action to alleviate the suffering of others, to offer support or

Facing the historical reality of the Holocaust, and the accelerated pace of development of communication technologies, Adorno believed that moral atrophy is an inevitable consequence of modern capitalist societies plagued by fascism, excessive nationalism, and other forms of cultural, and sociopolitical extremism. Even if one may take offense with the grim nature of such a claim and hold Adorno accountable for an exacerbated form of pessimism, decades of human conflict, genocide, towering inequalities, and waves of forceful migration that define our humanitarian present show how pathological aspects of our globalized world foster a culture of individualism, selfishness, and moral atrophy towards others.[22] Furthermore, Adorno's critique of fascism highlights how authoritarian ideologies and structures can manipulate and distort individuals' moral sensibilities. Faced with ongoing brutal conflicts in Europe and the rest of the world, Adorno's focus on pathological social ideologies (such as fascism, nationalism, etc.) promotes a hierarchical and authoritarian worldview that prioritizes the interests of a specific social group (or nation) while dehumanizing and devaluing those deemed outside of that group. These divisive and exclusionary ideologies can foster a sense of moral superiority and entitlement among their adherents, leading to indifference, or even hostility, towards those perceived as different or inferior. In such societies, moral and humanitarian concerns may be subverted or suppressed in favor of loyalty to the authoritarian regime or group identity. What is worse, Adorno saw these systemic influences, combined with individual psychological factors, as the main aspects that contribute to the phenomenon of moral insensitivity and neglect of humanitarian responsibilities in modern societies. The dehumanizing effects of capitalism and the manipulative tactics of authoritarian ideologies can erode individuals' capacity for solidarity and moral responsibility towards others. This can result in a lack of concern or indifference towards humanitarian issues, and even facilitate or justify acts of cruelty or violence against marginalized groups.

In contemporary political culture, individuals are encouraged to continuously seek out novel products, experiences, and sensations in the perpetual pursuit of pleasure, fostering a culture of hedonism and superficiality. Adorno draws on Freud's notion of the id, which represents the impulsive

---

assistance, and to engage in acts of kindness and empathy in response to the suffering of others.

22   Some of the pathological aspects of capitalism are its emphasis on the pursuit of economic success and material wealth, the commodification of human relationships, the objectification of individuals as mere consumers, and dominant mindset wherein individuals prioritize their own interests and gains over the needs and welfare of others.

and instinctual aspects of the human psyche, to argue that consumer culture and media capitalize on these primal desires and instincts, exploiting them for profit and promoting impulsive and hedonistic behaviors. According to Adorno, this constant pursuit of instant gratification, fueled by consumer culture and media, leads to a shallow and superficial way of life, where individuals prioritize immediate pleasures over deeper aspects of human existence, such as different contexts of moral, and social responsibilities. Furthermore, Adorno contends that consumer culture and media perpetuate a culture of commodification and consumption, where individuals are encouraged to continually consume and indulge in material possessions and sensational experiences in the pursuit of pleasure. This capitalist logic of commodification and consumption reinforces the societal emphasis on instant gratification, as individuals are bombarded with messages that their happiness and fulfillment can be found in the consumption of products and experiences. As a result, Adorno argues, this creates a culture of superficiality and emptiness, where genuine fulfillment and meaningful engagement with the world are sacrificed in pursuit of transient pleasures.[23]

Although Freud's insights about unconscious drives have clearly influenced Adorno's thinking about personal dispositions and needs, Adorno's perspective departs from Freud's in that he does not view the individual as an autonomous entity. Rather, in order to understand individuals, both their subjective psychological dispositions and the ways in which social and historical structures shape them must be taken into account. Adorno's rejection of the individualistic and hedonistic assumptions underlying Freud's account of the pleasure principle can be seen as part of his broader critique of individualism. Despite the significance of Freud's work, Adorno believed that his emphasis

---

23   Adorno, drawing on Freudian ideas, provides a thought-provoking critique of the societal emphasis on instant gratification and pleasure-seeking behaviors promoted by consumer culture and media. Adorno argues that this emphasis on immediate gratification and pleasure-seeking is symptomatic of a broader cultural trend that prioritizes superficial and short-term pleasures over deeper, more meaningful pursuits. He sees this trend as being perpetuated and amplified by consumer culture and mass media, which bombard individuals with messages that promote instant gratification, hedonism, and materialistic desires. Adorno contends that this cultural fixation on immediate gratification and pleasure-seeking not only reinforces capitalist ideologies, but also leads to a range of negative consequences for individuals and society as a whole. Adorno's work consistently intertwines these sentiments, and while they permeate most of his writings, some specific instances where these insights are prominently evident include: "Dialectic of Enlightenment," particularly in the section titled "The Culture Industry: The Enlightenment as Mass Deception," as well as in "The Culture Industry Revisited" and *Introduction to Sociology*, among others.

on individual desires and drives obscured the ways in which these desires and drives are shaped by social conditions and relationships of power. As he writes in his *Introduction to Sociology*:

> (T)he category of the individual ... is a social category in the fullest sense. It is not social only in that simply everything which is individual and takes place within the realm of individual psychology can be directly ascribed to society, but rather in that the category of individuation itself, and the specific factors which form individuality, must be interpreted as internalizations of social compulsions, needs and demands.[24]

Building on this critique, Adorno explored the role of the individual in society, particularly the individual's relationship to power and domination. Adorno believed that the increasing rationalization and bureaucratization of modern society had led to a distancing from emotions and a prioritization of efficiency over moral sentiments and solidarity. This was particularly evident in the context of humanitarian crises where the suffering of others is often ignored or downplayed in the name of maintaining the status quo. He believed that the ruling system encouraged a narcissistic and solipsistic attitude among individuals, who were encouraged to focus on their own narrow, self-centered worldviews that prioritize individual comfort and security at the expense of engagement with broader social issues and collective well-being. Adorno saw this attitude as a fundamental obstacle to any kind of meaningful social change or progress, as he believed that it was essential to challenge the dominant values and assumptions of capitalist society and to create new forms of social solidarity and collective action that could counteract the atomization and isolation of modern life. This not only required a fundamental rethinking of the relationship between the individual and society, but also a rejection of the narrow, abstract, and individualistic understanding of morality.

Therefore, both the pleasure principle and the concept of bourgeois coldness are relevant in contemporary analyses of humanitarian dispositions, as they provide insights into two different aspects of individual moral agency. One is the unconscious influence of psychological drives, while the other emphasizes the sociogenic nature of these dispositions. Together, they help us comprehend the bystander apathy that often accompanies human deprivation, by revealing how the avoidance of discomfort or pain can drive human behavior and prevent individuals from recognizing their moral responsibilities. This has

---

24   Adorno, *Introduction to Sociology*, 112.

significant implications for addressing humanitarian crises and human rights abuses, as it suggests that appealing to people's moral instincts alone may not be sufficient to motivate them to act. Instead, addressing the issue of moral insensitivity and selectivism requires a more profound understanding of the cultural and structural factors that contribute to apathy and indifference. This may require challenging the dominant values and assumptions of society and fostering new forms of social solidarity and collective action that prioritize the needs and well-being of all people, not just those who are closest to us.

7 Beyond Superficiality: Adorno's Critique of Humanitarianism and Moral Insensitivity

Moving onto the topic of humanitarianism, it is important to recognize that the issues discussed thus far have direct implications for the way we approach humanitarian crises and human rights abuses. As we have seen, the pleasure principle and the concept of bourgeois coldness shed light on the various factors that contribute to moral apathy and indifference in society. However, to truly understand the root causes of these issues and how to address them, we must consider the specific challenges that arise in the discursive and material contexts of humanitarianism. In this section, we will explore some of these challenges and discuss potential solutions for fostering greater empathy and moral responsibility toward those in need.

Traditionally, the concept of humanitarianism in the contemporary conventional liberal context is a definite set of ideas and practices that can be located materially in their institutional and discursive form. As Didier Fassin argues, humanitarianism is a system of governance that designates 'the deployment of moral sentiments in contemporary politics.'[25] Humanitarianism has been exposed in recent decades to increased critical scrutiny due to the failure of humanitarian practices and discourses to successfully address

---

25 Didier Fassin, *Humanitarian Reason: A Moral History of the Present* (Berkeley: University of California Press, 2011), 2. Governance here should be understood in a broad sense, as a set of procedures established and actions conducted in order to manage, regulate, and support the existence of human beings and an economy of harm that they are exposed to. On the other hand, "moral sentiments" refer to emotions that direct our attention to the suffering of others and make us want to remedy that suffering. Similarly, "humanitarian" should be understood in meaning, "as connoting both dimensions encompassed by the concept of humanity: on the one hand the generality of human beings who share a similar condition (mankind), and on the other an affective movement drawing humans toward their fellows (humaneness)."

increasing inequalities, harm, and deprivation that billions of people endure. Considering that humanitarianism ultimately deals with conditions that are a product of human choices, institutional settings, and policies, such state of affairs raise important questions of justice and responsibility in the face of suffering that the humanitarian system not only fails to prevent but often further perpetuates. The result is a harmful international system of governance whose impact can be measured by the exclusion and disenfranchisement that it creates. Reinvigorating the relevance of Critical Theory and psychoanalysis for evaluating principles and commitments of our humanitarian present allows us to address the moral threshold of humanitarian commitments, practices, and consequences confronted with the evidence of harm that they do. In simple terms, behind the veneer of compassion and solidarity in modern societies lies a deeper issue that points to historical and structural causes of present inequalities whose persistence vehemently continues to fuel human deprivation worldwide. These structures, in fact, are a subtle, invisible state of affairs, that due to their normalization in social relations and institutions serve as a norm of behavior and as such are rarely challenged (especially by social groups that benefit from such state of affairs). In terms of their relevance for analyzing the humanitarian conditions of people affected by these policies and discourses (e.g., refugees, asylum seekers, victims of war and famine, etc.) it helps us understand the hazardous nature of humanitarian practices and policies that the international community is currently enforcing. The result is a harmful international system of governance whose impact can be measured by the exclusion and disenfranchisement that it creates. Exactly here, a return to Adorno allows us to understand the intersection of both symbolic and structural causes of humanitarian failures.[26]

Adorno's incisive analysis of the moral apathy of 20th century humanitarian witness sheds light on the complex interplay of social, psychological, and cultural factors that shape our moral sensibilities in the modern world. The central argument of Adorno's critique of humanitarianism and moral insensitivity is that superficial and selective acts of charity or philanthropy, often driven by capitalist interests (and influenced by the pursuit of immediate gratification and pleasure-seeking behaviors), can perpetuate systemic issues and contribute to a lack of genuine solidarity and denial of moral responsibilities towards others. Adorno believed that true compassion requires recognizing

---

26   Namely, throughout his reflections on moral insensitivity, Adorno unveils the superficiality of collective responses to suffering, revealing the systemic issues and underlying psychological factors that contribute to a selective and shallow approach towards humanitarian concerns.

and addressing the root causes of suffering and inequality. Selective acts of charity or philanthropy that do not challenge the underlying social, economic, and political structures that perpetuate suffering are insufficient and may even reinforce oppressive systems. As I wrote elsewhere, unable to go beyond a neoliberal-capitalist social determinism of human agency grounded in pursuit of self-interest, Adorno's major line of criticism is centered on the view that an ethics of compassion sets out only to mitigate injustice, and not actually change the conditions that create and reproduce it. Rather than challenge the social contexts that give rise to human suffering, compassionate behavior takes such contexts as a starting point, and at least implicitly resigns itself to them. As he elaborates on this theme in one of his lectures:

> This is because the concept of compassion tacitly maintains and gives its sanction to the negative condition of powerlessness in which the object of our pity finds itself. The idea of compassion contains nothing about changing the circumstances that give rise to the need for it, but instead, as in Schopenhauer, these circumstances are absorbed into the moral doctrine and interpreted as its main foundation. In short, they are hypostatized and treated as if they were immutable. We may conclude from this that pity you express for someone always contains an element of injustice towards that person; he experiences not just our pity but also impotence and the specious character of the compassionate act.[27]

Adorno's criticism seems to rest on two distinct, though related, considerations. First, compassion does not entail address of the cultural, economic, legal or political context of the victims' suffering. The benefactor responds exclusively to the bare fact of the victim's deprivation, while for social criticism (and Adorno himself) it is of crucial importance to track and address its systematic causes. Such a depoliticized understanding of compassion, Adorno argues, occludes the political dimensions of suffering which leaves victims without proper means to invoke questions of justice and responsibility of individuals and collectives accountable for their misfortune.

Adorno critiques the superficial and selective nature of humanitarianism, highlighting the limitations of relying solely on moral sentiments as a response to social and moral issues. He argues that such efforts can be co-opted by capitalist interests, resulting in superficial and ineffective solutions that fail to

---

27 Theodor W. Adorno, *Problems of Moral Philosophy* (Stanford: Stanford University Press, 2001), 173.

address the root causes of social problems. Adorno contends that such gestures can serve as a form of social pacification, allowing the privileged class to assuage their guilt or maintain a sense of moral superiority without addressing the deeper social, economic, and political structures that contribute to the very problems they claim to alleviate. Given these complexities, it is crucial to critically examine the underlying assumptions and practices of the international community and diverse humanitarian organizations. One of the key challenges is the tension between the humanitarian imperative to alleviate suffering and the political interests and power dynamics that shape the distribution of resources and aid. In many cases, humanitarian interventions are motivated not solely by a desire to alleviate suffering, but also by geopolitical and economic interests, which can exacerbate existing inequalities and conflicts. Moreover, the uneven distribution of power between Western humanitarian actors and local communities can result in paternalistic and top-down approaches that undermine local agency and self-determination. These issues underscore the importance of taking a critical approach to humanitarianism that considers the political and economic contexts in which interventions occur, and that seeks to empower and center the voices and needs of local communities.

As we have observed in earlier sections, Western humanitarian actors often exhibit selective moral dispositions by prioritizing certain issues or groups over others. This tendency is compounded by the increasing use of communication technologies and online social platforms, which can turn solidarity and compassion into performative acts that serve more to satisfy the individual's need for moral recognition than to address the underlying issues at hand.[28] In light of these challenges, Adorno's critical insights urge us to question the efficacy of humanitarianism in tackling the complex problems of our times and compel us to explore more fundamental and transformative approaches that aim to address the root causes of social and moral issues. For Adorno, such a process cannot be merely a sentimental or superficial response to the suffering of others, but a profound commitment to understanding and challenging the systemic factors that contribute to their plight. To grasp Adorno's viewpoint, it is essential to acknowledge that genuine humanitarianism necessitates individuals to confront the uneasy truths of the social, economic, and political systems that sustain their privilege on one end, and exploitation and oppression on the other. This involves critically examining and challenging the dominant ideologies, power dynamics, and economic systems that contribute

---

28   Lilie Chouliaraki, *The Ironic Spectator* (Cambridge: Polity, 2013).

to the suffering of marginalized and oppressed groups. It is not surprising that Adorno emphasized how moral responsibility goes beyond personal acts of charity or philanthropy but rather involves active engagement in social and political action to challenge and transform the systemic causes of suffering.[29]

In the end, Adorno's insights remain highly relevant for the critical evaluation of humanitarianism in today's globalized epoch, wherein global social inequality, suffering, and moral insensitivity stubbornly persist. His ideas not only reveal how media, consumer culture, and capitalist interests shape individual perceptions, values, and behaviors, but also stress the need to move beyond superficial gestures and address the root causes of social issues, which aligns well with contemporary calls for systemic change and social justice movements that recognize the interconnectedness of various forms of oppression and inequality. Adorno's ideas on the limitations of humanitarianism and the need for critical engagement with social, economic, and political structures also resonate with contemporary debates on the efficacy of charity, philanthropy, and token gestures in addressing social inequality and systemic issues. He emphasizes critical reflection and transformative action, all which are necessary for structural change, advocacy for marginalized communities, and addressing the root causes of social problems. Furthermore, the intersection of psychological and societal impulses that shape individual dispositions and behavioral tendencies, marked by instant gratification, discomfort-avoiding behaviors, and the impact of consumer culture on moral dispositions, highlights the relevance of bringing Adorno together with Freud. Adorno's synthesis of psychoanalysis with his structural and epistemological critique

---

29   Adorno, *Problems of Moral Philosophy*, 175. Another important aspect of Adorno's overall work that could serve as a potent reevaluation of humanitarian practices is the role of media as a powerful tool that shapes individual perceptions, values, and behaviors. I wrote on this theme in several other writings, but it is important here to note that Adorno argued how media, particularly in a capitalist society, is driven by profit-oriented motives that prioritize sensationalism, superficiality, and desensitization over meaningful and nuanced representations of injustices. According to Adorno, media tends to package suffering into sensationalized and superficial narratives that prioritize entertainment value and marketability, rather than addressing the complex systemic issues that underlie the suffering. This superficial portrayal of suffering, Adorno believed, can desensitize individuals to the reality of others' pain, leading to moral insensitivity and a lack of genuine compassion and solidarity. Furthermore, as a product of capitalist interests, media is inherently shaped by the dominant ideologies and values of the ruling class, which can perpetuate oppressive systems and promote a false consciousness among individuals. In other words, media can create an illusion of reality that distorts individuals' perception of social issues, contributing to moral insensitivity by promoting shallow and biased representations of suffering that align with the interests of the powerful.

underscores the need for a holistic understanding of societal dynamics and subject formation. This approach remains crucial for addressing contemporary challenges of social inequality and troubling moral dispositions of the 21st century humanitarian witness. It simultaneously promotes a more equitable, just, and compassionate society that values the well-being and dignity of all individuals, especially those who have historically faced marginalization and oppression.

Bibliography

Adorno, Theodor W. "Education after Auschwitz." In *Critical Models: Interventions and Catchwords*, edited by Theodor W. Adorno and Henry W. Pickford, 191–204. New York: Columbia University Press, 1998.

Adorno, Theodor W. *Introduction to Sociology*. Stanford: Stanford University Press, 2000.

Adorno, Theodor W. *Minima Moralia*. London: Verso, 2005.

Adorno, Theodor W. *Negative Dialectics*. Translated by E. B. Ashton. New York: Continuum, 1973.

Adorno, Theodor W. *Negative Dialectics*. London: Routledge, 2004.

Adorno, Theodor W. *Problems of Moral Philosophy*. Stanford: Stanford University Press, 2001.

Adorno, Theodor W., and Max Horkheimer. *Dialectic of Enlightenment: Philosophical Fragments*. Stanford: Stanford University Press, 2002.

Chouliaraki, Lilie. *The Ironic Spectator*. Cambridge: Polity, 2013.

Debs, Eugene V. "A Plea for Solidarity." *The International Socialist Review* 14, no. 9 (March 1914): 534–538.

Fassin, Didier. *Humanitarian Reason: A Moral History of the Present*. Berkeley: University of California Press, 2011.

Freud, Sigmund. *Beyond the Pleasure Principle*. London: The Hogarth Press, 1955.

Freud, Sigmund. "Letter from Sigmund Freud to Lou Andreas-Salone, July 28th, 1929." In *Letters of Sigmund Freud 1873–1939*, edited by Ernst L. Freud, 389–391. New York: Dover Publication, Inc., 1992.

Freud, Sigmund. *On the History of the Psycho-Analytic Movement: Papers on Metapsychology and Other Works*. London: The Hogarth Press, 1957.

Rawls, John. *A Theory of Justice*. Cambridge, MA: Belknap Press, 1971.

Slovic, Paul. "'If I look at the mass I will never act': Psychic numbing and genocide." *Judgment and Decision Making* 2, no. 2 (April 2007): 79–95.

CHAPTER 12

Freud and the Problem of Moral Agency

Alfred I. Tauber

During Freud's only visit to the United States in 1909, he took a short walk with William James to the railway station in Worcester, Massachusetts. They had a private discussion, whose subject is not known. James, already suffering heart disease, returned to Cambridge and in the cursory comments we have about their meeting, he seemingly harbored doubts about the Viennese venture.[1] Given their divergent psychologies, a common theme might have been difficult to achieve, so the dismissal, while not generous, is well within expectations. However, beneath their obvious different cultural, philosophical, and scientific attitudes, they walked upon a shared humane ground. Indeed, their encounter, at least symbolically, captures two titanic thinkers pondering how to forge ethics for a new century. Let us imagine an exchange in which the infra-structure of their thought is exposed. It would center on the trials of the modernist subject, who had already been targeted by Nietzsche and later would suffer debilitating postmodern attacks. In several respects, Freud and James fought a rear-guard action. Discerning their positions, divergent yet closely aligned in a larger cause, illumines the identity conundrum of our own era in which moral agency has seemingly lost its footing and uncertainty has raised its hoary head.

1 A Synoptic History of the "Self"

In the early modern period, Descartes had asserted the incontrovertible solidity of his own ego as the foundation of knowledge. He thought that construction followed a reasoned, logical deduction from the certainty of his own self-awareness. However, that notion of identity has been challenged from its first presentation, and today many would say that the ego has not only been defrocked but finally torn asunder. In this latter regard, the rationalities bequeathed by Descartes, Locke, and Kant have been assaulted from every side and the reach of these critiques has altered the ways in which to think of the

---

1 Saul Rosenzweig, *The Historic Expedition to America (1909): Freud, Jung, and Hall the Kingmaker* (St. Louis: Rana House, 1994), 171–74; Alfred I. Tauber, *William James and Sigmund Freud on the Mind. Saving Subjectivity* (London: Routledge, 2025), Introduction.

subject as autonomous and individuated. The philosophical conclusion (as extended by Hume, Kierkegaard, Nietzsche, Heidegger, and Wittgenstein) is that the self does not exist as an entity. Persons, agents, subjects appear and function within social contexts and assume identities as derivative of those behaviors, but the *self* is an abstraction of a third-person viewpoint; there is no *object* as such and thus no objectification of personal identity in terms applicable to an apple or a description of the mechanics of its falling to the ground. Simply, the self is a product of faulty grammar and mis-aligned metaphysics.

While the Cartesian *ego* connotes an entity, a *something*, it was already clear with John Locke that selfhood comprised a moving target, and no core *it* could be identified. Not only did Locke fail to provide a means by which identity cohered beyond the continuity of memory (and what held the past together, exactly?), he made no attempt to offer a philosophical basis for the self as such. Despite the elegance of Locke's construction, by the mid-18th century, the cracks in the statue began to appear. David Hume simply observed his own self-consciousness and noted that the self is but a "bundle ... of different perceptions," and because the fleeting perceptions of his consciousness could not coalesce around a "self," he concluded, that 'all the nice and subtle questions concerning personal identity can never possibly be decided.'[2] Because states of consciousness are fleeting and passing, no substantive identity may be located or defined, 'for when one is here the other is irrevocably dead and gone.'[3] In other words, Hume sought an *epistemological* basis for identifying the self and noted that because his self-consciousness was comprised of fleeting perceptions or thoughts, he 'never can catch' *himself* 'at any time without a perception, and never can observe any thing but the perception.'[4] Kant and Wittgenstein made the same point: *the I* is a referent, a locus of thought which can be characterized no better than through its ephemeral states of self-consciousness. Such a subject has *relational* continuity of various sorts, but no *substantive* basis.

---

2 David Hume, *Treatise of Human Nature*, ed. L. A. Selby-Bigge and P. H. Nidditch (Oxford: Oxford University Press, 1978 [1739]), 262. Hume went on to write, 'and are to be regarded rather as grammatical than as philosophical difficulties.' Beyond asserting that the self "has no clothes," i.e., no basis in fact, Hume laid the corner stone for Wittgenstein's later faulty grammar argument that became a central theme of twentieth century philosophy. See Alfred I. Tauber, *Requiem for the Ego: Freud and the Origins of Postmodernism* (Stanford: Stanford University Press, 2013), 166–190.

3 William James, *Psychology: The Briefer Course* (Mineola, NY: Dover Publications, [1892], 2001), 69.

4 Hume, *Treatise*, 252.

And as he dismissed any such entity as the self, Hume also introduced the so-called "hard problem" of consciousness,[5] the piecemeal aggregate of perceptions – fragmentary, often incoherent, frequently rationally disordered, and powerfully driven by the "passions."[6] Notwithstanding Descartes's certainty of an ego as some basic organizing principle for me-ness, no one has satisfactorily offered a definition of what self-reflection *is*. How is a subjective mental state *explained* as arising from physical processes? What is the circuitry that provides self-reflection, I-ness, reasoning, etc.? Freud, the neurologist might have had confidence that a future "science of the mind" would bridge the so-called explanatory gap of the mind/body problem, but this promissory note cannot be assured of payment. There seems to be an irreconcilable difference of the first- and third-person perspectives: Consciousness, the subjective experience of being, is inaccessible to objective studies. We can correlate physical traces of some conscious processes, but there is no translation of the physicality to the subjective experience.[7] In other words, subjectivity cannot be reduced to physical terms, and the argument in philosophical circles is whether this is an ontological or epistemological problem. This issue in many respects has nagged modernity from its very origins, namely the basis for understanding

---

5 David Chalmers, "Facing up to the Problem of Consciousness," *Journal of Consciousness Studies* 2, no. 3 (1995): 200–219. And closely following, if consciousness is the "hard problem," then finding meaning in a material world is the "really hard problem:" Owen Flanagan, *The Really Hard Problem: Meaning in a Material World* (Cambridge, MA: MIT Press, 2007).

6 Hume, *Treatise of Human Nature*, 252. For overview, see Udo Thiel, *The Early Modern Subject: Self-consciousness and Personal Identity from Descartes to Hume* (Oxford: Oxford University Press, 2011).

7 The literature on introspection melds into questions revolving around self-knowledge, and then slips into the vast studies of consciousness (represented by pockets of scholarship based on phenomenological approaches, analytical philosophy, cognitive psychology, neuroscience, etc.). Reviewing self-knowledge/self-deception, see Peter Carruthers, *The Opacity of Mind. An Integrative Theory of Self-knowledge* (Oxford: Oxford University Press, 2011); Quassim Cassam, ed., *Self-knowledge* (Oxford: Oxford University Press, 1994); David A. Jopling, *Self-Knowledge and the Self* (New York: Routledge, 2000); Brie Gertler, *Self-Knowledge* (London: Routledge, 2011); Brian P. McLaughlin and Amélie Oksenberg Rorty, eds., *Perspectives on Self-Deception* (Berkeley: University of California Press, 1988); Roger T. Ames and Wimal Dissanayake, *Self and Deception: A Cross-cultural Philosophical Inquiry*, (Albany: State University of New York Press, 1996); Herbert Fingarette, *Self-Deception* (Berkeley: University of California Press, 2000); Alfred R. Mele, *Self-Deception Unmasked* (Princeton: Princeton University Press, 2001). Interesting recent philosophically oriented essays on introspection per se: Declan Smithies and Dabuek Stoljar, eds., *Introspection and Consciousness* (Oxford: Oxford University Press, 2012); Uriah Kriegel, *Subjective Consciousness: A Self-Representational Theory* (Oxford: Oxford University Press, 2009).

selfhood in terms of self-consciousness. Indeed, what is such experience and what function might it serve?

Immanuel Kant essentially gave up the quest altogether and contented himself with defining the conditions for knowing. He concurred with Hume that the self cannot be construed as an entity and further agreed that the sense of a unitary self is the inevitable consequence of the mind's structure. However, their respective interpretations differed. Hume thought the notion of selfhood is based on the activity of the imagination working on experiential material, while Kant argued that self-consciousness is a *necessity* of thought, a psychological construct that constitutes the necessary conditions for cognition.[8]

Accordingly, the self is not an observable *thing*, but rather belongs to the *noumenal* domain – a "something" that is not part of the describable natural world. So beyond positing the requirements of an epistemological agent, Kant left in abeyance any other criteria for designating the ego's "what-ness" and was content with accounting for self-awareness as a necessary condition of thought itself. For Kant, "I think" does not lead to the Cartesian ego, to some object, or to a soul. It means simply, and exactly what it says: "I think" expresses 'our consciousness of being engaged in a mental activity we take to be our own.'[9] No further claims are made, or, according to Kant, can be made other than self-consciousness is a constitutive condition of experience.[10]

Kant thus fulfilled the epistemological requirements of a knowing "self," but more, the ability to self-reflect is demanded for his understanding of human autonomy. This construction became the foundation of selfhood construed

---

8 'Now no cognitions can occur in us, no connection and unity among them, without that unity of consciousness that precedes all data of the intuitions, and in relation to which all representation of objects is alone possible. This pure, original unchanging consciousness I will now name transcendental apperception.' Immanuel Kant, *Critique of Pure Reason*, ed. Paul Guyer and Allen W. Wood. Trans. Allen W. Wood (Cambridge: Cambridge University Press, 1998), 232. "Apperception" refers to a necessary condition of experience, i.e., the mental process by which an idea is assimilated to the body of previously derived ideas. See Robert B. Pippin, *Hegel's Idealism: The Satisfactions of Self-Consciousness* (Cambridge: Cambridge University Press, 1989), 19.

9 Béatrice Longuenesse, *I, Me, Mine: Back to Kant, and Back Again* (New York: Oxford University Press, 2017), 1.

10 There are three claims (or features) for this faculty: identity, unity, and self-consciousness. The subject must be identical through time, for without such identity, the ability to recall and maintain continuity would fail. The basis of unity refers to the requirement of an active subject to unify its experience. This ability in turn rests upon the third feature, that of self-consciousness, which refers to the capacity to reflect on its own unity and identity, a constitutive condition of experience. H.J. Paton, *In Defense of Reason* (New York: Hutchinson's University Library, 1951), 102–105.

as a moral category: For Kant, to be moral requires reasoned autonomy. Note, *das Ich*, "the I," has shifted from an epistemological construct to a moral one. So, instead of searching for a *something*, Kant posited the requirements of an epistemological agent, employed that schema for his ethical project, and left in abeyance any other criteria for designating the ego's "what-ness." He narrowed the inquiry to an account of self-awareness as a condition of thought itself. He provided a cogent model for the epistemological requirements of a knowing "agent," but more, the ability to self-reflect is demanded for his understanding of human autonomy, the true telos of his presentation, i.e., selfhood construed as a moral category. For Kant, to be moral requires reasoned autonomy, a mind functioning self-reflexively, rationally, and independently. Simply, for Kant, the "ego" enterprise was architected to create an autonomous individual capable of exercising autonomous judgment. This became, and remains, the modernist tenet of personal identity. Freud, despite major misgivings (and denial) followed Kant.[11]

2   The Freudian "Ego"

The debate about personal identity effectively focuses the larger cultural and philosophical divisions that have placed identity politics at the center of postmodernity. The central theme is that the self, a definable ego, like the rest of the world, has no reference point and must be regarded as having melted away. Twentieth-century postmodernists (more specifically, poststructuralists) highlighted the contingency of such a construction.[12] Since no transcendental significance to limit meanings existed, they spoke of the self's "indeterminacy" – a decentered subject, no longer an origin or a source, but rather the product of multiple historical, social, and psychological forces. From this perspective, no claims might be held regarding the natural state of cultural structures (e.g., language, kinship systems, social and economic hierarchies, sexual norms, religious beliefs) that would define identity. This rich anthropological literature effectively revealed the idiosyncratic character of the prevailing notions of Western personhood.[13]

---

11   Alfred I. Tauber, *Freud, the Reluctant Philosopher* (Princeton: Princeton University Press, 2010).
12   Feminist critiques have been at the forefront of this re-assessment. See for example, Judith Butler, *Gender Trouble: Feminism and the Subversion of Identity* (New York: Routledge, 1990).
13   For example, Brian Morris, *Anthropology of the Self: The Individual in Cultural Perspective* (London: Pluto Press, 1994); Alan Roland, *In Search of Self in India and Japan: Toward a Cross-cultural Psychology* (Princeton: Princeton University Press, 1988); Marcel Mauss,

Central to the Enlightenment view of the autonomous individual is the faculty of Reason. Instead of accepting the expectations of the rational mind to know the world, govern the social, and attain self-knowledge, judicious circumspection has taken hold, where a cautious, aspirational certitude had once resided. Recognizing the limits of thought and the extent of faulty reasoning; the influence of unrecognized emotion; the determinism of unconscious motivation, assembled to generate a sense of personal identity clouded by a "hermeneutics of suspicion."[14] Freud is the key architect of that sense of *me*, a construct in which uncertainty rules the most intimate notion of human being. Yet he is also the last modernist in his persistent attempts to rescue moral agency from psychoanalytic insights that deprive the subject of autonomy. Freud drew from the elemental tenet of Western philosophy, the divine Delphic command – *gnothi seauton* ("Know thyself"), a dictum originating in philosophy's earliest Socratic stirrings.[15] What that means today differs from the expectations of the ancient Greeks, but across the millennia, the imperative of self-inquiry remains intact as an ethical dictate. How Freud could maintain this moral stance in light of his deep skepticism about autonomous choices may have been the subject of his chat with James. And in that imagined exchange, perhaps the Freudian paradox – we are determined yet free – finds a tentative resolution.

Students of Freudian theory have long acknowledged that he had focused his efforts on the unconscious at the expense of the conscious ego, and only

---

"A Category of the Person: Anthropology, Philosophy, History, the Notion of Self," in *The Category of the Person: Anthropology, Philosophy, History*, eds. Michael Carrithers, Steven Collins and Steven Lukes (Cambridge: Cambridge University Press. 1985), 1–25.

14   Paul Ricoeur, *Freud and Philosophy: An Essay on Interpretation* (New Haven: Yale University Press, 1970); Alison Scott-Bauman, *Ricoeur and the Hermeneutics of Suspicion* (London: Continuum, 2009).

15   *Gnothi seauton*, literally translates to "know thy soul or psyche." Although there is a Greek pronoun for self in Plato, it is not used as a substantive; *psyche* functions as the noun corresponding to our self. See Charles L. Griswold, *Self-Knowledge in Plato's Phaedrus* (New Haven: Yale University Press, 1986). To know oneself is to know the psyche, which is best declared in its virtue and wisdom, *sophia*, upon which Socrates's entire ethic is erected. *Psyche's* complex and laden meanings may be simplified as that which is capable of attaining wisdom or, in Socratic terms, as the true self: 'The living man *is* the *psyche*, and the body ... is only the set of tools or instruments of which he makes use in order to live ... [L]ife can only be lived well if the *psyche* is in command of the body. It meant purely and simply the intelligence, which in a properly ordered life is in complete control of the senses and emotions.' See W.K.C. Guthrie, *Socrates* (Cambridge: Cambridge University Press, 1971), 149–50. The roots of such an ethos may be discerned in Ionian scientific thought and in Pythagoreanism. See R.B. Onians, *The Origins of European Thought About the Body, the Mind, the Soul, the World, Time and Fate* (Cambridge University Press, 1951).

later theorists made the ego the center of their versions of revised Freudianism. Indeed, Freud explicitly defined psychoanalysis as the "science of the unconscious." The ego, as such was not his concern. He assumed a commonsensical understanding of the ego, namely the seat of consciousness that mediates between the deeper drives and external reality. Accordingly, the ego examines and attempts to control the unconscious forces that remain hidden from normal scrutiny. Functioning within a sector of the mind, the ego has the unique property of following "rational" and "logical" rules. That faculty, of course, is only part of a more general functional apparatus that serves to mediate the demands of the unconscious and the social reality of the exterior world. This formulation gives the ego topographical characteristics and thus it is situated in a "location" of the mind. And locality implies "borders."[16]

However, there is a fundamental problem with this mental structure: The ego as an entity *does not exist*. Drawing from the Kantian understanding, (1) agency is not defined, only the conditions of knowing; (2) the reasoning faculty has dubious autonomy and is left uncharacterized other than being constitutive to ego-function; and (3) consciousness serves as an observing function that processes inputs from the unconscious forces into meaningful understanding through the means of psychoanalysis.[17] The nexus of those mental transactions ultimately depend on ego functions. So, *what* is the Freudian ego?

Psychoanalysis' underlying premise holds that emotional recognition and rational insight leads to personal freedom. Accordingly, self-consciousness becomes the therapeutic means towards psychological and existential health. Yet, Freud does not explicitly consider the character of self-consciousness – the "relation of oneself to oneself" – and leaves the ego (ironically) uncharacterized. Moreover, what is the relationship of reason to the general category of consciousness, and more specifically, how is self-consciousness conceived? Freud provided scanty consideration to these questions, as he explained in his *New Introductory Lectures*, 'There is no need to discuss what is to be called conscious: it is removed from all doubt.'[18] Further discernment apparently was

---

16   In Freud's mature work, *The Ego and the Id* (1923), the ego stretches from conscious deliberation and memory gatherer to unconscious regions as well. Thus, the architecture of the mind assumed a more complex configuration than in his earlier formulations. And from a historical point of view, this work heralds the beginning of a major shift in psychoanalysis to what became "ego psychology." See Sigmund Freud, *The Ego and the Id*, in *The Complete Psychological Works of Sigmund Freud, Vol XIX* (London: The Hogarth Press, 1961), 12–66.
17   Longuenesse, *I, Me, Mine*; Tauber, *Freud*.
18   Sigmund Freud, *New Introductory Lectures on Psycho-analysis*, in *The Complete Psychological Works of Sigmund Freud, Vol XXII* (London: The Hogarth Press, 1964), 70.

not necessary for his theoretical purposes, and, in regard to reason, Freud was satisfied with its instrumental use.

Furthermore, personal identity finds no philosophical home in Freud's thought. Indeed, he never gave "the self" a passing nod. *Das Ich (the I)* in the Freudian context, has a specific *psychological* structural and economic character; its functions are specified. That is not to deny that a *latent* conception of the self – construed as a sense of "me," i.e., an integrated purposeful person – ultimately orders the narrative story that emerges in analysis.[19] Even though such an *implicit* identity never appears as a governing status in Freud's writings, the analysand does adopt some version of self-identification along these lines. Yet from a formal point of view, the analysand is not construed beyond the ordinary pronominal agent.

Freud used the word, "self" (*Selbst*), only once in his writings (fourth paragraph of *Civilization and its Discontents* [1930]). He freely uses *das Ich, the I,* (mis-translated as *ego*) as opposed to *Selbst*, but the Freudian ego does not equate with "the self." When *self* rarely appears in the *Standard* [English] *Edition*, it is misappropriated. Indeed, selfhood considered in any formal sense eclipsed Freud's interest. That he never explicitly referred to a self, but only employed the pronominal – s/he, you, and "the I" – attests to a deliberate decision.[20]

So, we might fairly ask, *who* is this agent of inquiry? And who is the *object* of analysis? Freud offers a deafening silence: *Ich* is simply *I* or *me*, a self-reflexive, self-conscious, interpreting *person*. This is a phenomenological identity; the self as some essential or totalizing entity never appears, and to the extent pursued, *Selbst* simply vanishes upon any attempt to define such an entity. Yet, Mr.

---

19 Ilham Dilman, *Freud and the Mind* (Oxford: Blackwell, 1984), 106.

20 Alfred I. Tauber, "The Psychoanalytic *das Ich*: Lost in Translation," in The *Routledge Handbook of Psychoanalysis and Philosophy,* eds. Aner Govrin and Tair Caspi (London: Routledge, 2023), 359–373. Early post-Freudians introduced ego psychology and Heinz Kohut promoted an explicit "psychology of the self" in the 1970s. As a member of the object relations school of psychology, he sought to extend psychoanalysis to a more holistic consideration of the individual, namely one whose identity becomes a focus of concern. Yet, and this represents an irony, Kohut made no attempt at defining "the self" and simply acknowledged an implicit understanding based on empirical observations (what he called, "psychological manifestations"): 'My investigation contains hundreds of pages dealing with the psychology of the self – yet it never assigns an inflexible meaning to the term self, it never explains how the essence of the self should be defined … Demands for an exact definition of the nature of the self disregarded the fact that "the self" is not a concept of an abstract science, but a generalization derived from empirical data.' See, Heinz Kohut, *The Restoration of the Self* (New York: International Universities Press, 1977), 310–311.

Analysand lays on the couch, pays his bill, and asserts his "I-ness" freely. On this pragmatic view, the "I" serves as a useful point of reference, but no more. The same lesson was already presented by Kant in the *First Critique*, where the ego is formulated as only a transcendental function, i.e., a placeholder for providing the conditions through which cognition must occur. There is no entity as such.[21]

By avoiding the identity question, Freud found passive support from the key philosophers of his period. Nietzsche naturalized the subject into a medley of competing drives, where consciousness becomes a conceit, conventional morality a disguised egoism, and identity an assumed masquerade.[22] Indeed, for Nietzsche, das Ich 'has become a fable, a fiction, a play on words.'[23] And Wittgenstein delegated any attempt to objectify the self as misplaced philosophical "nonsense" of "poor grammar" and a defunct metaphysics,[24] while Heidegger's Dasein's "receptivity" and integration within the world replaced the self-conscious ego altogether.[25] Freud joined this illustrious company in the sense of dispensing with the ego as an entity, nevertheless, an implicit understanding of agency operates throughout his opera. He invokes the authority of individuals to probe their inner-emotion and thought, and, as a result of this introspection, a new understanding of that experience conferred by a more acute self-consciousness opens the possibility of a therapeutic outcome. Moreover, the reflexive component of psychoanalytic self-consciousness becomes the means of achieving a revised sense of personal history and identity through a process that putatively generates options and choices arising from insight and reconstruction.

3 Stories of Me

By-passing the self, Freud shrewdly protected his conception of the psyche. The self "existed" only when invoked by a third-party (e.g., the philosopher referring

---

21 The Kantian character of Freud's thought is presented in Alfred I. Tauber, 2009. "Freud's dreams of Reason: The Kantian Structure of Psychoanalysis," in *History of the Human Sciences* 22, no. 4 (2009): 1–29. See also Tauber, *Freud*, chapter 4 and Tauber, *Requiem for the Ego*, Introduction and chapter 1.

22 Walter Kaufmann, *Nietzsche, Heidegger, and Buber: Discovering the Mind, Vol. 2* (New Brunswick: Transaction Publishers, 1992), 47–166.

23 Friedrich Nietzsche, *The Anti-Christ, Ecce Homo, Twilight of the Idols*, eds. A. Ridley and J. Norman, trans. J. Norman (Cambridge: Cambridge University Press, 2005), 178 (in the section, "The Four Great Errors:" #3. "Error of false causation").

24 Tauber, *Requiem for the Ego*, chapter 7.

25 Ibid., chapter 4.

to agency or "the knowing subject"). The interlocutor could be another or the inner voice of self-consciousness ... it made no substantive difference. And perhaps more saliently, in "real life" one lives in the world essentially unaware of such a conception as a *self*. Persons evidently *are* and simply *do*. In the attempt to define the self as an entity one does so by a process of self-reflection that yields an objectified construct – a subject construing an object (albeit itself). Certainly, constructs are useful, but the lessons of analytic psychology support postmodern conclusions.[26] There is no homunculus, a core ego, an essence of some sort. Such a conception perhaps serves the autobiographies one tells to order mental lives and to create useful coherence. This is, of course, no small task and certainly a worthy one for psychological health, but the circumspective philosophical dissection leaves even the story-telling suspect.

Taking various forms, such narratives characterize something called *me* or *I* as a projection of what seems self-justifying to oneself and explanatory to others. These tales are crucial for grounding behavior by establishing goals, conferring responsibility, bestowing reasons for choices and actions, etc. However, their consistency, comprehensiveness, and veracity are very much in doubt. How does one accurately represent an inner state, an emotion, a memory? Obviously representational language is the means, but capturing such subjectivity is only an approximation. After all, it is only a *re*-presentation with inescapable distortions and lacunae.

The most intimate of uncertainties is memory. The refinements of retrospection are inescapable. The attempt to be self-critical hopefully corrects, at least partially, the distortions imposed by time and the bias that grows from changing "sentiments." What is important today may have had minimal, if any, significance in the past. The reflexive tale is both a hermeneutical treatise and a work of art in the sense that memory has,

> a knack for selection, the taste for detail. ... Memory contains precisely details, not the whole picture; highlights if you will, not the entire show. The conviction that we are somehow remembering the whole thing in a blanket fashion, the very conviction that allows the species to go on with its life, is groundless.[27]

More, the protagonist of memory is notoriously unstable; the story of *myself* is always in flux; the narrative freezes the moving present. And as one's self-image

---

26   Ibid., chapter 6.
27   Joseph Brodsky, "In a room and a half," in *Less than One: Selected Essays* (New York: Farrar, Straus, Giroux, 1986), 447–501, 489.

changes in time, emotional elements shift and here temperament comes to the foreground.

How one reviews the choices made and interpretations derived cannot escape the power of the present that inescapably frames the recount. After all,

> memory betrays everybody, especially those whom we knew best. It is an ally of oblivion, it is an ally of death. It is a fishnet with a very small catch, and with the water gone you can't use it to reconstruct anybody ... Presumably the whole point is that there should be no continuum: of anything. That failures of memory are but proof of a living organism's subordination to the laws of nature. No life is meant to be preserved. Unless one is a pharaoh, one doesn't aspire to become a mummy.[28]

Of course, memory is radically fragmented and incomplete. Nodal points of objectivity hardly suffice to reconstruct a life and thus minimalist reconstructions must suffice.

Given such limitations, *the I* emerges in varying degrees through the articulation of self-consciousness and the narration of personal history. Freud explained the psychology of reconstructing the past as the workings of "screen memories." These are what is recalled in the present to shield or to hide traumas that have been repressed or at least softened. Freud eloquently described the intractable lost reality of childhood:

> It is perhaps altogether questionable whether we have any conscious memories *from* childhood: perhaps we have only memories *of* childhood. These show us the first years of our lives not as they were, but as they appeared to us at later periods, when the memories were aroused. At these times of arousal the memories of childhood did not *emerge*, as one is accustomed to saying, but *were formed*, and a number of motives that were far removed from the aim of the historical fidelity had a hand in influencing both the formation and the selection of the memories.[29]

Yet a story is told, indeed, must be told. Out of the complexities and noise of the everyday and the chaos of the disruptive, one imposes sequences and linkages to build coherence. And then from that ordering, given the selection and partial recall, how is the exposition to be judged?

---

28 Ibid., 492–493.
29 Sigmund Freud, "Screen memories," in *The Uncanny*, trans. D. McLintock (London: Penguin Books, 2003), 3–22; 21.

The stories others tell about you and the stories you tell about yourself: which ones come closer to the truth? ... But, actually, that is not the question on my mind. The true question is: In such stories – is there, as a matter of fact, a difference between true and false? ... Is the soul a place of facts? Or are the alleged facts only the deceptive shadows of our stories?.[30]

A most reasonable question, for within the domain of the personal, truth assumes varying "valences." Indeed, we allow latitude for the subjective account and so one can only claim best intentions to capture that which is now gone.

In the end, although Freud sought to free the conscious *I* from the shackles of the unconscious, the question of identifying the true *me* is never resolved. And here Freud's seminal contribution to characterizing the postmodern subject appears in full relief: We are strangers to ourselves. But more, the entire attempt to discern our inner life as an objectification is futile.

4 James

Perhaps on the Worcester stroll, James suggested to Freud that instead of the putative positivist position psychoanalysis assumes with its conceits of objectification, a more developed phenomenological orientation might profitably have been considered. This was hardly a novel option. After all, as a university student, Freud had studied with Franz Brentano, whose views Freud both resisted and incorporated.[31] Phenomenology literally means the description of appearances; the word "appearances," like "phenomena," attempts to describe what actually happens in human consciousness in connection with the "objective" world. The phenomenological psychologists began with the premise that the mind did not see the object "as is," but through a complex integration of related perceptions. A total experience was thus constructed from

---

30 Pascal Mercier, *Night Train to Lisbon*, trans. Barbara Harshav (New York: Grove Press, 2008), 142. Quoted by Wolfgang Prinz, *Open Minds: The Social Making of Agency and Intentionality* (Cambridge, MA: MIT Press, 2012), v.

31 Tauber, *Freud*, 16, 29–30, 40. The key early phenomenological texts are Franz Brentano's *Psychology from an Empiricist Point of View*, trans. A. C. Rancurello, D. B. Terrell, and L. McAlister (London: Routledge, [1874], 1973); Ernst Mach's *Analysis of Sensations*, trans. C. M. Williams and S. Waterlow (Chicago: University of Chicago Press [1886], 1914), and William James's *Principles of Psychology* (Cambridge, MA: Harvard University Press, 1983).

imperfect and piecemeal data. A correcting mind formed the conscious image, for perception was based on an 'interactive relationship between subject and object: the object was, in effect, partially "created" by the act of seeing it.'[32] Brentano went further: The object did not exist except with reference to the act of seeing, and conversely perception existed only in reference to its object. He called this relationship, "intentional," and it served as the origin of twentieth-century phenomenology as expounded by Husserl and his followers.[33]

On the phenomenological account, the self "exists" as a functioning, convenient, practical entity (recognized retrospectively) conceived as an abstract construct in which ever-changing sense impressions cohere and take on meaning. That meaning, established in the very act of attention, is thus framed by the mind's *intention*, and is experienced in consciousness as the fleeting bundle of perceptions (whether interior or exterior) that Hume had described in the mid-18th century. James called consciousness a "selecting agency," "the very hull on which our mental ship is built," forming the "nucleus of our inner self."[34] This is the central motif of his *The Principles of Psychology* (1890) and constitutes the basis of viewing the mind as active and selective, whose volition is dictated by attention: "[E]ach of us literally chooses, by his ways of attending to things, what sort of a universe he shall appear to himself to inhabit."[35] The selective attending of consciousness is simply the extension of the cognitive expression of an active organism in its environment, and it is manifest from the simplest responses to the most complex interactions.

Selection and ordering of perceptions are pre-requisites for experience. Most inputs are ignored so thinking requires choice based on practical or aesthetic importance. Experience is thus arrested upon certain objects, whose conceptualization in turns demands isolating and distinguishing some

---

32 Judith Ryan, *The Vanishing Subject: Early Psychology and Literary Modernism* (Chicago: The University of Chicago Press, 1991), 11.
33 This constructivist orientation began with Kant, but with the new-found optimism of a scientific approach, a strong empirical element entered the philosophical discussion. The phenomenological critique recalls an earlier philosophical issue that in many ways deals with the same problem but formulates it differently: 'In the end, after an honest effort, we will probably find ourselves agreeing with the philosopher [Kant] who asserts that no idea is fully congruent with experience, although he admits that idea and experience can and must be analogous.' Johann Wolfgang von Goethe, "Doubt and Resignation," in *Goethe: Scientific Studies*, ed. and trans. D. Miller (Berlin: Suhrkamp Verlag, 1988), 33–34. There are obviously complex Romantic antecedents to this view as exemplified by Goethe's epistemological project. See Alfred I. Tauber, "Goethe's Philosophy of Science: Modern Resonances," *Perspectives in Biology and Medicine* 36 (1993): 244–257.
34 James, *The Principles of Psychology*, 142, 423, 640.
35 Ibid., 401.

perceptual aspects, excluding others, and ordering reality not by hard and fast divisions, but by active, selective processing. Experience, then, enters as bare or raw data, and then integrated and organized according to the intentions of the experiencing individual, who manipulates sensory data to serve personal needs. In human terms, that cohesive "self" becomes an inviolate "me," a self-defining, unique individual.

Note, consciousness ironically becomes another "object" of consciousness. This intentional "object," "self" is not consciousness itself. As an object, consciousness somehow resides separate, albeit close to one's true self, but always distinct. Consciousness is the stream of thoughts (James coined the term, "steam of consciousness") that, when contemplated as an object, must then be displaced by another core sense of selfness that unforgivingly retreats.[36] The self then cannot be purely experienced but is represented by the 'sum total of all that he *can* call his.'[37] These, of course, include emotional, spiritual, and material elements of identity beyond bodily sensations, but the embodiment reactions (according to James) serve as the foundation of consciousness and, more fundamentally, selfhood. Since consciousness is world-directed, it is defined in terms of its objects, including the recognition of its own body as its "self." And, of course, consciousness is only known in retrospect: '[I]t is not one of the things experienced at the moment; this knowing is not immediately known. It is only known in subsequent reflection.'[38] Consciousness, then, is *process*, the function of objectification, but it is irretrievably distinct from its ontological source, its "selfness." And, on this view, the self simply eclipses comment and is left as some intentional activity.

From a third-party perspective, there is a *self* in its selecting and doing, but selfness is not definable from the subject's own vantage. Simply, the organization of the world phenomenologically cannot define the self, but the composite array of behavior points to that nebulous coherence. Indeed, how does the subject define itself? Its boundaries are only described in its bumping into "reality," in its meeting with the other. For James, the self serves as an integrating conception, an inclusiveness of being (perceiving, knowing, feeling,

---

36 'But it must be remembered that all writers who have described the Cogito have dealt with it as a reflexive operation ... a consciousness which takes consciousness as an object. ... But the fact remains that we are in the presence of two consciousnesses, one of which is conscious *of* the other ... Thus, the consciousness which says I *think* is precisely not the consciousness which thinks.' See, Jean-Paul Sartre, *The Transcendence of the Ego: An Existentialist Theory of Consciousness*, trans. Forrest Williams and Robert Kirkpatrick (New York: Hill and Wang, 1991), 44–45.

37 James, *The Principles of Psychology*, 279. Emphasis in original.

38 Ibid., 290.

remembering); it entails the whole of an inner presence and mediates that core identity with respect to both the body and the environment. The self in its world is ever-changing and thus contingent, but the prevailing theme of its historical development is its persistence and representation as a holistic construction, forever appearing a manifestation of one faculty or another, but nevertheless remaining somehow coherent and intact. There is no such *thing* as a self.

James defaulted in postulating how mind functioned, having "grown up in ways of which at present we can give no account."[39] The nature of the experienced *I* is also left an open question, remaining as a description of an interactive process of that consciousness with the world. But the key element of these early phenomenological accounts is the view of the mind in a forceful and energetic engagement with the environment, where the self – the abstracted agency of the mind – selects and constructs its world from the bewildering complexity of the surrounding plenum and thereby differentiates itself. It does so only by active engagement. And by focusing on the act of perception, on the act of recognition, on the act of reaction, the subject is defined in action. In this sense, there is no self residing as some preexisting and specified ontological entity. Underlying this conception of agency is an implicit sense of freedom of choice, an active aggrandizement that James would later build into a moral philosophy.

Freud joined his own theory to James's general agnosticism about personal identity. And in a sense, one might construe psychoanalysis as a method of discerning intention, unconscious and a-rational. And in a larger framework, the psychodynamics depicted in the Freudian universe follow phenomenological integrative behaviors, now organized to fulfill fantasy and desire. Each of these parallels (and others) might profitably be followed to illuminate the underlying conceptual structure of psychoanalysis.[40] However, the deeper philosophical resonances shared by Freud and James reside in a different domain.

---

39   Ibid., 1280.
40   For example, Maurice Merleau-Ponty, "Phenomenology and Psychoanalysis: Preface to Hesnard's *L'Oeuvre de Freud. Review of Existential Psychology & Psychiatry*" 18, no. 1–3 (1982–1983): 67–72; Marilyn Nissim-Sabat, "Psychoanalysis and Phenomenology: A New Synthesis," *Psychoanalytic Review* 73, no. 3 (Fall 1986): 273–299; Alessandro D'Agostino, Milena Mancini, and Mario Rossi Monti, "Phenomenology in Psychoanalysis: Still and Open Debate?" *Psychopathology* 52, no. 2 (2019): 104–109.

5   Moral Agency

Beyond the limits of articulation and the distortion of memory, the psychoanalytic report is *always* both incomplete and adjusted to fit within the circumstances of the present. Freud's abiding importance resides in how he bequeathed persistent insecurity about self-knowledge. After all, if one's deepest motivations are not objectively discerned, then autonomous agency is always in doubt. And precisely because the psyche is immune to objective appraisal, true knowledge is in principle unobtainable. Here, the restrictions of hermeneutics strike at the heart of the psychoanalytic enterprise. Psychoanalysis is not science, but rather a way of understanding human subjectivity. One "knows" oneself better, in a particular way, but without the assurances of objectivity, the uncertainty generated by even this most intimate analysis of the psyche jeopardizes the ethical order. If I do not know *who-I-am*, then how can *I* be responsible? Practical demands impose moral imperatives, but the philosophical uncertainty is not thereby resolved. Here we find the heart of Freud's humanist conception of human potential and the full moral dimension of psychoanalysis, in which the evolution from patient to liberated soul constitutes both a psychological project and an ethical venture. On this basis, psychoanalysis is a moral enterprise.

Moral refers to the entire panoply of human life existing within a stratification of values. Actions, choices, relationships, self-understanding fall upon the coordinates of importance, worthiness, costs, and consequences. And *value* is the métier of the moral universe. In terms of lived experience and the relevance of the topic, Charles Taylor asserts (in the form of a question) the key point: 'Is there a sense in which the human agent is responsible for himself which is part of our very conception of the self?'[41] Yes. Why? And here a great assumption or belief orients all that follows:

> the human subject is such that the question arises inescapably, which kind of being he is going to realize. He is not just de facto a certain kind of being, with certain desires, but it is somehow "up to" him what kind of being he is going to be ... [W]e have the notion that human subjects are capable of evaluating what they are, and to the extent that they can shape themselves on this evaluation, are responsible for what they are in a way that other subjects of action and desire (higher animals for

---

41   Charles Taylor, "Responsibility for Self," in *The Identities of Persons*, ed. Amelie Oksenberg Rorty (Berkeley: University of California Press, 1976), 281–99, 281–282.

instance) cannot be said to be. It is this kind of evaluation/responsibility which many believe to be essential to our notion of the self.[42]

Taylor is building on a long line of existential thinkers (Kierkegaard, Nietzsche, Sartre, Camus), who have made human choice – the whom-I-want-to-be – the central characteristic of one's humanity.[43] Whether one is free to so act is another question. However, the assertion that one *might* act by choice is the freedom that already sets the course of the road one must travel. And on that basis the key component of the identity issue emerges in the postmodern context: The existential challenge for one who makes choices, whether "free" or only imagined as independent, becomes the determinative element setting one's life-course. Simply, those selections establish one's identity. And the result of that line of reasoning resets the anchor of identity: *The agent viewed through the moral prism is irreducible.*

What one cares about and identifies with, what values are embraced, which choices are made and behaviors enacted, define *me*. *Who-am-I?* embeds identity as an agent of responsibility, whose constancy in relationships and character traits determines expectations and reciprocity. Self-knowing identifications largely determine choices that have both immediate and future effects and thus constitute the practical aspects of ethics. Here, moral inquiry is considered in the most general sense of "knowing" *who-I-am* in the context of the fallibilities of self-knowledge.

Although Freud refrained from defining personal agency with explicit coordinates or foundations, psychoanalysis nevertheless serves *das Ich*, who (with guided interpretations) effectively introspects to exercise rational self-responsibility and thus assert moral authority. On this view, self-appraisal leads to personal liberation, not a final escape from one's fate (as determined by personality and past experiences), but in strengthening the sense of establishing

---

42 Ibid., 281–282.
43 As Nietzsche espoused, we are ultimately responsible for establishing and following the values guiding our moral decisions. Taylor cites a key passage in Heidegger's *Being and Time*, where *Dasein* is defined as having the option of choosing its authenticity: 'Dasein is mine [self-determined] to be in one way or another. Dasein has always made some sort of decision as to the way in which it is in each case mine. That entity which in its Being has this very Being as an issue, comports itself towards its Being as its own most possibility ... Dasein *is* its possibility, and it "has" this possibility, but not just as a property, as something present-at-hand would. And because Dasein is ... essentially its own possibility, it *can*, in its very Being, "choose" itself and win itself; it can also lose itself.' See Martin Heidegger, *Being and Time,* trans. John Macquarrie and Edward Robinson (New York: Harper & Row, 1962), 68. Emphasis in original.

a point of view for expressing *the* fundamental moral question: *who-am-I?* A paradox lies at the base of the entire enterprise: We are determined (by unconscious psychic dynamics) and yet we must make moral decisions as best we can. Those decisions are based on Reason (just as Kant professed), but unlike Kant, Freud recognized the weakness of rationality; how rationalization may work as a defense mechanism; how illusion nurtures fantasy; how denial obscures psychic realities, and so on. Simply, the voice of reason is quiet, but it is all humans possess to assess themselves and maintain some potential on their ethics.

Freud presents an irresolvable paradox: choice is based on notions of free will, in the face of psychic determination. Knowing the resistance to such a claim, he repeatedly admonished any resistance to accepting the reality of psychic determinism, a claim that lay at the very foundations of psychoanalysis: "You nourish the illusion of there being such a thing as psychical freedom, and you will not give it up. I am sorry to say I disagree with you categorically over this."[44] And

> you nourish a deeply rooted faith in undetermined psychical events and in free will, but that is quite unscientific and must yield to the demand of a determinism whose rule extends over mental life. I beg you to respect it as a fact ... I am not opposing one faith with another. It can be proved.[45]

Despite the obstacles such a view held for emotional liberation from repression, psychoanalysis provided a schema in which to undertake the search for self-knowledge. That project has had a tormented history and I need not review the judgments of seemingly endless commentary other than to note that irrespective of prevailing doubt, one need not endorse Freudianism to accept its cardinal message: Exploring the deeper reaches of motivations and desires, excavates one's own identity. Self-reflection never ends, for the inquiry is, by its very nature, ceaseless. In many respects, Freud displayed the Sisyphusian character of moral inquiry, which is the basis of defining moral agency. In sum, although we are strangers to ourselves, just posing the *who-am-I?* question constitutes the initial step in moral cognizance.[46]

---

44 Sigmund Freud, *Introductory Lectures on Psycho-analysis, Part I & II*, in *The Complete Psychological Works of Sigmund Freud, Vol XV* (London: The Hogarth Press, 1963), 49.
45 Ibid., 106.
46 Alasdair MacIntyre, *After Virtue* (Notre Dame, IN: University of Notre Dame Press, 2007).

6 On Reason

It is a truism that people hardly reason impartially, nor are they immune from idiosyncratic inclinations or feelings. Hume, as mentioned, is the great skeptic of reason's role in moral circumspection. In *A Treatise of Human Nature*, he wrote: 'In order to shew the fallacy of all this philosophy [the superiority of reason over passion], I shall endeavour to prove first, that reason alone can never be a motive to any action of the will; and secondly, that it can never oppose passion in the direction of the will.'[47] He reconfigured the relative roles of reason and emotion, proposing that reason was only a tool for deliberation and hardly could suffice as the source of moral choice and motivation. Moreover, he maintained that preferences or desires cannot be motivated by reason alone, and that reason can only help direct our choice: 'A belief, desire, feeling, or action may be rationally required, rationally permitted, or rationally proscribed, [so that] unless they derive from false beliefs, they are all rationally permissible.'[48] From this perspective, goals are determined by a complex array of psychological and cultural factors, of which rational order may play only a small part. In what has become a famous hyperbole, Hume asserted, 'Tis not contrary to reason to prefer the destruction of the whole world to the scratching of my finger.'[49] No wonder Kant was outraged! The essential disagreement between Kant and Hume is over the putative role of reason in moral decision making. For Kant, reason is the sole arbiter of self-governance. Hume was skeptical of reason's hegemony, because he believed that the sentiments fix the agent's ultimate ends and reason is left to determine the best way of achieving those goals.

Adhering to Hume's suspicion of the rationality of such decisions, i.e., rationalized and ultimately self-serving, how can one be sure of motivations? The short answer, one cannot. Instead of certainty, *per* James, we must *create* (and then assert) the basis for action through self-reflection and rigorous scrutiny of one's own psychic dynamics. This hardly consoles the perplexed, but we have

---

47 Hume, *Treatise of Human Nature*, 413.
48 Richard Lindley, *Autonomy* (London: Macmillan, 1986), 30.
49 Hume, *Treatise of Human Nature*, 416. For a rigorous analytical defense of The Humean Theory see, Mark Schroeder, *Slaves of the Passions* (Oxford: Oxford University Press, 2007), which argues that 'all reasons for action are ultimately explained by desires. It is the view not that Reason is beholden to the passions, but that *reasons* are' (Schroeder, *Slaves*, vii). Schroeder's title draws from Hume's assertion in the *Treatise* that 'Reason is, and ought only to be the slave of the passions, and can never pretend to any other office than to serve and obey them.' See Hume, *Treatise*, 415.

little recourse than to follow philosophy's original dictum, *know thyself.* And that means that the inquiry, *who-am-I?* is *the* fundamental moral enterprise.

Indeed, demurrals abound. Much of twentieth-century criticism, as well as psychoanalytic tenets, concerning freedom of choice belies this ambidextrous position. Not only is rationality often considered a conceit and incapable of assuring moral responsibility, but to even believe that ethical actions are reducible to one's rationality ignores the complex array of social, existential, historical, and emotional factors that go into play in any reasoned decision. Indeed, Freudian skepticism can hardly claim originality in this regard, nor postmodern critics for their rebuttals, for the history of such doubt dates to early modernity itself. Hume, long preceding Freud, argued that ethics are grounded in human need, emotion, and caprice that are rationalized into moral justifications. His essential insight highlighted reason's heterodox variations – not everyone has to reason in the same way, and consequently individuals might arrive at divergent choices, each of which may be reasonable within their own frame of reference. Arguments based on austere logic did not necessarily coincide with a rationality framed by diverse mores and values. In other words, something more than *reason* is "rational."

Yet Freud remained steadfastly reliant on fallible reason despite the obvious effects of biased judgment and rationalized emotion. He did so as a moral choice, for his epistemology failed to establish a science of the mind based on his interpretive methods.[50] Freud's analytic extensions, in which assessing subjective states and memories might be processed with the same effective rationality applicable to other kinds of cognition, proved to be a far-reaching supposition with little basis in fact. After all, as Freud himself acknowledged, selective memory and self-appraisal are weak tools for objective accounts, not to speak of deeper philosophical obstacles. The scientific pretensions of its methods and the tortured attempts to prove its efficacy lingered far longer than an argument about scientific merited. After all, as a scientific enterprise, psychoanalysis failed the standards of Freud's day and even more so the gauntlet of later critics.[51] Given Freud's own prediction, we are left with an ironic

---

50   Tauber, *Requiem for the Ego,* chapter 1.
51   Psychoanalysis is 'the starting point of a new and deeper science of the mind' Sigmund Freud, *An Autobiographical Study,* in *The Complete Psychological Works of Sigmund Freud, Vol. XX* (London: The Hogarth Press, 1959), 47. But Freud patently failed to fulfill the criteria that would establish psychoanalysis as a "science of the mind" – his own putative ambition, and later crippling critiques had settled the *scientific* merits of clinical psychoanalysis for me. See, for example, Adolf Grünbaum, *The Foundations of Psychoanalysis: A Philosophical Critique* (Berkeley: University of California Press, 1984); Hans J. Eysenck, *The*

verdict: 'Psycho-analysis makes a basic assumption, the discussion of which is reserved to philosophical thought but the justification for which lies in its results.'[52]

On this view, Freud's signal accomplishment has been to present psychic reality in terms of re-defining agency defrocked of rational pretensions. The normative floats on the surface of a deep cultural sea that undulates beneath conceptions of mind and the agent who thinks. Freud, despite acknowledging the precarious status of the rational ego, still endorsed the exercise of reason as the sole resource for rescuing the future from human self-destructiveness.

> The voice of the intellect is a soft one, but it does not rest till it has gained a hearing. Finally, after a countless succession of rebuffs, it succeeds. This is one of the few points on which one may be optimistic about the future of mankind, but it is in itself a point of no small importance. And from it one can derive yet other hopes.[53]

And here Freud emerges as a social philosopher, a cautious utopian thinker who ultimately embraced human freedom or choice, which, despite the force of post-humanist criticism and the shredding of its scientific conceits, remains at the core of his vision, one from which we continue to develop.[54] However, he leaves the matter of choice unsettled. James offered a release from the imbroglio.

    Decline and Fall of the Freudian Empire (New York: Viking, 1985); Frank Cioffi, *Freud and the Question of Pseudoscience* (Peru, IL: Open Court, 1998); Richard Webster, *Why Freud Was Wrong: Sin, Science, and Psychoanalysis* (New York: Basic Books, 1995); Malcolm Macmillan, *Freud Evaluated: The Completed Arc* (Cambridge: MIT Press, 1997). And the most recent, Fredrick Crews, *Freud: The Making of an Illusion* (New York: Henry Holt, 2017), which may be the last word.

52   Sigmund Freud, *An Outline of Psycho-analysis*, in *The Complete Psychological Works of Sigmund Freud, Vol. XXIII* (London: The Hogarth Press, 1964), 144.

53   Sigmund Freud, *The Future of an Illusion*, in *The Complete Psychological Works of Sigmund Freud, Vol. XX* (London: The Hogarth Press, 1959), 53.

54   Alfred I. Tauber, "Freud's Social Theory: Modernist and Postmodernist Revisions," *History of the Human Sciences* 25, no. 4 (2012): 41–70; Alfred I. Tauber, "Freud and Social Theory," in *Encyclopedia of Modern Political Thought, Vol. 1*, ed. Gregory Claeys (Thousand Oaks, CA: Sage Publications, 2013), 321–325. Note, Freudianism joins the same general promise of rationality that undergirds all modern political philosophies from classical liberalism to the totalitarian and all in between. See Isaiah Berlin *Two Concepts of Liberty* (Oxford: Oxford University Press, 1958), 144.

7   Introducing Chance[55]

The moral question concerns the degree to which humans exercise choice in their psychic and social force fields. Freud and his heirs embraced psychic determinism and at the same time asserted analytic insight as the only conduit to the free will afforded by self-knowledge. This Spinozist position makes moral agency coincident to the inquiry itself, namely, introspection (the preliminary step in moral cognizance) leads to ethics. James took this logic a step further.[56] He drew two startling conclusions: First, in science and the facts derived from its workings, the currency of reality is not logically assembled by certain rules and abiding standards of evidence. How those facts are gathered and placed into models and theories is the result of drawing lines of causation that he assumed often fell well beyond simple logic and scientific standards of evidence. Echoing Hume, he rejected the idea of necessity. Instead, James embraced chance as the underlying metaphysics that governed nature. This orientation is far from the linear Newtonian mechanics of Freud's depiction of psychic force fields governed by push-pull dynamics.

For James, *chance* was another word for *freedom* – freedom of will, freedom of choice. While "chance begets order," that order, as exemplified by statistical mechanics of gases, is a depiction of the disorder and the chance interactions of myriad particles.[57] In the spirit of Emersonian self-reliance and the guiding American assertion of manifest destiny (personal and national), James developed the notion of chance – as opposed to determinism – as the conduit to his central dogma, the "will to believe." As he declared in the self-willed escape from a debilitating depression, 'My first act of free will shall be to believe in free will.'[58]

---

55 Adapted from Tauber, *James and Freud*, chapter 6.
56 James was a key member of a group of thinkers at Harvard in the 1870s, who assembled to informally discuss philosophy. Led by Chauncey Wright, they called themselves "The Metaphysical Club," which included the luminaries that would eventually be regarded as the early authors of pragmatism (besides Wright and James, Charles Peirce, and Oliver Wendell Holmes, Jr.). Louis Menand, *The Metaphysical Club: A Story of Ideas in America* (New York: Farrar, Straus and Giroux, 2001). See also Philip Weiner, *Evolution and the Founders of Pragmatism* (Cambridge, MA: Harvard University Press, 1949); Edward H. Madden, *Chauncey Wright and the Foundations of Pragmatism* (Seattle: University of Washington Press, 1963).
57 Charles S. Peirce, "Evolutionary Love," in *The Essential Peirce: Selected Philosophical Writings Vol. 1 (1867–1893)*, ed. Nathan Houser and Christian Kloesel (Bloomington, IN: Indiana University Press, 1992), 358.
58 Quoted by Robert D. Richardson, *William James. In the Maelstrom of American Modernism* (Boston: Houghton Mifflin, 2006), 120. Every biographer of James I have read highlights

'Properly speaking there is no certitude; all there is men who are certain.' Rather than see doubt and uncertainty as troublesome or negative, Renouvier, with James right behind, recognizes that what we call freedom in human affairs rests on and grows out of what in physics is called chance – that is, not determinism. Just as the possibility of there being such a thing as a chance occurrence is what we mean by the word "freedom," so doubt, instead of meaning a lamentable loss of certainty, meant for James, the positive possibility of certainty.[59]

In this sense, certainty is a definition of the uncertain. And in uncertainty, lies freedom.

In one direction, the *will* points to the spiritual and all that lies outside scientific investigation, and, following another tack, the *will* refers to the freedom of choice required for assuming responsibility that grounds moral agency. This required a leap of faith (or in another parlance, acceptance) that found its basis in the rejection of a deterministic universe. *Freedom* is not necessarily a spiritual leap á la Kierkegaard, but rather the dimension in which one fulfills the moral imperative of accepting responsibility for making choices. This is, in the spirit of James, an act of will, because the strictures of self-knowing leave, in principle, no lines of causation by which one can track with confidence the basis for making an ethical decision.

Here we find the point at which Freud and James might have met. They each held that belief in free will remains *necessary* despite the evidence arrayed against its exercise. This Spinozean vision is not readily mortgaged, much less, forsaken. On this view, the lasting influence of Freud's work rests squarely on the meliorism derived from the effort to achieve insight, explanation, and a new equilibrium. Accordingly, Freud's "choice" serves a larger agenda. Whether formalized in psychoanalysis or conducted *ad hoc*, deliberate self-reflection is the beginning of asserting personal responsibility constitutive to agency. Responsibility is embedded in self-analysis and self-evaluation, for the search for identity is itself a moral procedure where the self-interrogation itself becomes the *who-I-am*. So, despite the distrust of self-knowledge and its conceits, Freud rightfully claims the title, Last (humbled) Defender of Reason. As a moralist, he insisted on the exercise of self-analysis and self-correction and irrespective of the success of achieving some idealized psychic balance, the exercise itself constitutes the basis of agency.

---

the influence of Charles Renouvier (1815–1903), who embraced Kant's notions of autonomy and freedom.

59   Ibid., 177, 247.

8   Conclusion

Discrediting Freud's clinical claims and fully acknowledging the lethal philosophical flaws of psychoanalytic theory are matters settled long ago. However, he nevertheless holds the pre-eminent title of architecting contemporary notions of identity, namely, the skepticism of self-knowledge and its conceits. On this basis, Reason cannot be relinquished despite its tenuous standing. Moral agency requires self-conscious exploration of those reaches of the psyche beyond ordinary rationality and logic, for otherwise one abdicates *any* attempt to fulfill the human mandate to do right. Accordingly, self-appraisals constitute the beginning of moral behavior in the process that ends with choices and responsibility assumed for those decisions.

To the extent one deliberates, the exercise of self-reflection, limited and inescapably biased, comprises the wellspring from which the "right" is determined. Following Freud's moral lead, we have no recourse as social, ethical subjects other than to relentlessly scrutinize oneself and then follow insights as best one can. Such attempts to attain self-knowledge ultimately leads to moral self-definition. And here we find Freud's deepest lesson: Even defrocked of certain conceits, one continues to struggle against one's Oedipal fate – not necessarily the primal family drama, but rather to answer *who-am-I*? Psychoanalysis thus taps into a foundational notion of personal identity that still has a powerful hold on Western culture. Freedom consists of self-knowledge, albeit flawed, incomplete, and confused by unconscious desire. On this reading, psychoanalysis, in terms of its circumscribed commitment to reason and the capacity for self-reflection, holds to a moral imperative with full acknowledgement that inevitable skeptical conclusions set the stage for postmodern uncertainties.

Admitting postmodern dismissals, Freud's staunch adherence to the ethical venture remains salutary. He attempted to renew the humanist project and despite the powerful critiques levelled against him, his effort to assert personal responsibility remains an enduring contribution. As for the truth claims he made, well, that is another story.[60] Nevertheless, Freud's cardinal message holds: Following his own pervasive pessimism, we must still employ a rationality whose weaknesses have been revealed in full embarrassment. As social, moral subjects one has no other option than to relentlessly scrutinize Reason … and then follow its dictates as best one can. Indeed, what choice does one

---

60   I referred to this truncated understanding as "Freud without Oedipus," namely, Freudianism without the clinical explanations and psychic structures he proposed. See, Alfred I. Tauber, "Freud's Philosophical Path: From a Science of the Mind to a Philosophy of Human Being." *The Scandinavian Psychoanalytic Review* 32, no. 1 (2009): 32–43.

have? And in closing this discussion, Freud drew from the resources developed as a scientist to put such faith in reason. Despite the incredulity of the more radical postmodern critics, science – even the most constructivist understanding of its enterprise – affirms the irreducibility of the *rational* subject.[61] Freud's conception of freedom, of self-knowing, is affirmed precisely by the objectivity marking science's success. So even when self-understanding is heard as only a faint echo of a scientific standard of knowledge, science at least provides a model of a reliable rationality. Indeed, through critical analysis, the uncertainty of self-knowledge is revealed and from that understanding, further insight may be attained. Whatever its demerits and failings, when applied to the moral or subjective, reason still offers a wedge to break the hold of the a-rational and to counter the anarchic skepticism unleashed by Freud's own insights. From this position, a revamped moral panorama opens: Freedom resides in recognizing our state, the Spinozist paradox – we are determined yet we are free. On this view, self-awareness is the basis of moral self-consciousness to become agency's grounding.

Bibliography

Ames, Roger T., and Wimal Dissanayake. *Self and Deception: A Cross-cultural Philosophical Inquiry*. Albany: State University of New York Press, 1996.
Berlin, Isaiah. *Two Concepts of Liberty*. Oxford: Oxford University Press, 1958.
Brentano, Franz. *Psychology from an Empiricist Point of View*. Translated by A. C. Rancurello, D. B. Terrell, and L. McAlister. London: Routledge, 1973.
Brodsky, Joseph. "In a room and a half." In *Less than One: Selected Essays*. New York: Farrar, Straus, Giroux, 1986.
Butler, Judith. *Gender Trouble: Feminism and the Subversion of Identity*. New York: Routledge, 1990.
Carruthers, Peter. *The Opacity of Mind. An Integrative Theory of Self-knowledge*. Oxford: Oxford University Press, 2011.
Cassam, Quassim, ed. *Self-knowledge*. Oxford: Oxford University Press, 1994.
Chalmers, David. "Facing up to the Problem of Consciousness." *Journal of Consciousness Studies* 2, no. 3 (1995): 200–219.
Cioffi, Frank. *Freud and the Question of Pseudoscience*. Peru, IL: Open Court, 1998.
Crews, Fredrick. *Freud: The Making of an Illusion*. New York: Henry Holt, 2017.

---

61   Alfred I. Tauber, *The Triumph of Uncertainty: Science and Self in the Postmodern Age* (Budapest: Central European University Press, 2022).

D'Agostino, Alessandro, Milena Mancini, and Mario Rossi Monti, "Phenomenology in Psychoanalysis: Still and Open Debate?" *Psychopathology* 52, no. 2 (2019):104–109.

Dilman, Ilham. *Freud and the Mind*. Oxford: Blackwell, 1984.

Eysenck, Hans J. *The Decline and Fall of the Freudian Empire*. New York: Viking, 1985.

Fingarette, Herbert. *Self-Deception*. Berkeley: University of California Press, 2000.

Flanagan, Owen. *The Really Hard Problem: Meaning in a Material World*. Cambridge, MA: MIT Press, 2007.

Freud, Sigmund. "An Autobiographical Study." In *The Complete Psychological Works of Sigmund Freud*, Vol. XX. London: The Hogarth Press, 1959.

Freud, Sigmund. "The Ego and the Id." In *The Complete Psychological Works of Sigmund Freud*, Vol XIX. London: The Hogarth Press, 1961.

Freud, Sigmund. "Introductory Lectures on Psycho-analysis, Part I & II." In *The Complete Psychological Works of Sigmund Freud*, Vol XV. London: The Hogarth Press, 1963.

Freud, Sigmund. "New Introductory Lectures on Psycho-analysis." In *The Complete Psychological Works of Sigmund Freud*, Vol XXII. London: The Hogarth Press, 1964.

Freud, Sigmund. "Screen memories." In *The Uncanny*. Translated by D. McLintock. London: Penguin Books, 2003.

Gertler, Brie. *Self-Knowledge*. London: Routledge, 2011.

Goethe, Johann Wolfgang von. "Doubt and Resignation." In *Goethe: Scientific Studies*. Edited and Translated by D. Miller. Berlin: Suhrkamp Verlag, 1988.

Griswold, Charles L. *Self-Knowledge in Plato's Phaedrus*. New Haven: Yale University Press, 1986.

Grünbaum, Adolf. *The Foundations of Psychoanalysis: A Philosophical Critique*. Berkeley: University of California Press, 1984.

Guthrie, W.K.C. *Socrates*. Cambridge: Cambridge University Press, 1971.

Heidegger, Martin. *Being and Time*. Translated by John Macquarrie and Edward Robinson. New York: Harper & Row, 1962.

Hume, David. *Treatise of Human Nature*. Edited by L. A. Selby-Bigge and P. H. Nidditch. Oxford: Oxford University Press, 1978.

James, William. *Principles of Psychology*. Cambridge, MA: Harvard University Press, 1983.

James, William. *Psychology: The Briefer Course*. Mineola, NY: Dover Publications, 2001.

Jopling, David A. *Self-knowledge and the Self*. New York: Routledge, 2000.

Kant, Immanuel. *Critique of Pure Reason*, edited by Paul Guyer and Allen W. Wood. Translated by Allen W. Wood. Cambridge: Cambridge University Press, 1998.

Kaufmann, Walter. *Nietzsche, Heidegger, and Buber: Discovering the Mind*, Vol. 2. New Brunswick: Transaction Publishers, 1992.

Kohut, Heinz. *The Restoration of the Self*. New York: International Universities Press, 1977.

Kriegel, Uriah. *Subjective Consciousness: A Self-Representational Theory*. Oxford: Oxford University Press, 2009.

Lindley, Richard. *Autonomy*. London: Macmillan, 1986.
Longuenesse, Béatrice. *I, Me, Mine: Back to Kant, and Back Again*. New York: Oxford University Press, 2017.
Mach, Ernst. *Analysis of Sensations*. Translated by C. M. Williams and S. Waterlow. Chicago: University of Chicago Press, 1914.
MacIntyre, Alasdair. *After Virtue, 3rd ed*. Notre Dame, IN: University of Notre Dame Press, 2007.
Macmillan, Malcolm. *Freud Evaluated: The Completed Arc*. Cambridge: MIT Press, 1997.
Madden, Edward H. *Chauncey Wright and the Foundations of Pragmatism*. Seattle: University of Washington Press, 1963.
Mauss, Marcel. "A Category of the Person: Anthropology, Philosophy, History, the Notion of Self." In *The Category of the Person: Anthropology, Philosophy, History*, edited by Michael Carrithers, Steven Collins and Steven Lukes, 1-25. Cambridge: Cambridge University Press, 1985.
McLaughlin, Brian P. and Amélie Oksenberg Rorty, eds. *Perspectives on Self-Deception*. Berkeley: University of California Press, 1988.
Mele, Alfred R. *Self-Deception Unmasked*. Princeton: Princeton University Press, 2001.
Menand, Louis. *The Metaphysical Club: A Story of Ideas in America*. New York: Farrar, Straus and Giroux, 2001.
Mercier, Pascal. *Night Train to Lisbon*. Translated by Barbara Harshav. New York: Grove Press, 2008.
Merleau-Ponty, Maurice. "Phenomenology and Psychoanalysis: Preface to Hesnard's L'Oeuvre de Freud." *Review of Existential Psychology & Psychiatry* 18, no. 1-3 (1982-1983): 67-72.
Morris, Brian. *Anthropology of the Self: The Individual in Cultural Perspective*. London: Pluto Press, 1994.
Nietzsche, Friedrich. *The Anti-Christ, Ecce Homo, Twilight of the Idols*, edited by A. Ridley and J. Norman. Translated by J. Norman. Cambridge: Cambridge University Press, 2005.
Nissim-Sabat, Marilyn. "Psychoanalysis and Phenomenology: A New Synthesis." *Psychoanalytic Review* 73, no. 3 (Fall 1986): 273-299.
Onians, R.B. *The Origins of European Thought About the Body, the Mind, the Soul, the World, Time and Fate*. Cambridge: Cambridge University Press, 1951.
Paton, H.J. *In Defense of Reason*. New York: Hutchinson's University Library, 1951.
Pierce, Charles S. Charles S. "Evolutionary Love." In *The Essential Pierce, Selected Philosophical Writings* Vol. 1 (1867-1893). Edited by Nathan Houser and Christian Kloesel, 352-371. Bloomington, IN: Indiana University Press, 1992.
Pippin, Robert B. *Hegel's Idealism: The Satisfactions of Self-Consciousness*. Cambridge: Cambridge University Press, 1989.

Prinz, Wolfgang. *Open Minds: The Social Making of Agency and Intentionality.* Cambridge, MA: MIT Press, 2012.

Richardson, Robert D. *William James: In the Maelstrom of American Modernism.* Boston: Houghton Mifflin, 2006.

Ricoeur, Paul. *Freud and Philosophy: An Essay on Interpretation.* New Haven: Yale University Press, 1970.

Roland, Alan. *In Search of Self in India and Japan: Toward a Cross-cultural Psychology.* Princeton: Princeton University Press, 1988.

Rosenzweig, Saul. *The Historic Expedition to America (1909): Freud, Jung, and Hall the Kingmaker.* St. Louis: Rana House, 1994.

Ryan, Judith. *The Vanishing Subject: Early Psychology and Literary Modernism.* Chicago: The University of Chicago Press, 1991.

Sartre, Jean-Paul. *The Transcendence of the Ego: An Existentialist Theory of Consciousness.* Translated by Forrest Williams and Robert Kirkpatrick. New York: Hill and Wang, 1991.

Schroeder, Mark. *Slaves of the Passions.* Oxford: Oxford University Press, 2007.

Scott-Bauman, Alison. *Ricoeur and the Hermeneutics of Suspicion.* London: Continuum, 2009.

Smithies, Declan, and Dabuek Stoljar, eds. *Introspection and Consciousness.* Oxford: Oxford University Press, 2012.

Tauber, Alfred I. "Freud and Social Theory." In *Encyclopedia of Modern Political Thought*, Vol. 1, edited by Gregory Claeys, 321–325. Thousand Oaks, CA: Sage Publications, 2013.

Tauber, Alfred I. *Freud: The Reluctant Philosopher.* Princeton: Princeton University Press, 2010.

Tauber, Alfred I. "Freud's dreams of Reason: The Kantian Structure of Psychoanalysis." *History of the Human Sciences* 22, no. 4 (2009):1–29.

Tauber, Alfred I. "Freud's Philosophical Path: From a Science of the Mind to a Philosophy of Human Being." *The Scandinavian Psychoanalytic Review* 32, no. 1 (2009): 32–43.

Tauber, Alfred I. "Freud's Social Theory: Modernist and Postmodernist Revisions." *History of the Human Sciences* 25, no. 4 (2012): 41–70.

Tauber, Alfred I. "Goethe's Philosophy of Science: Modern Resonances." *Perspectives in Biology and Medicine* 36 (1993): 244–257.

Tauber, Alfred I. "The Psychoanalytic das Ich: Lost in Translation.," In *The Routledge Handbook of Psychoanalysis and Philosophy*, eds. Aner Govrin and Tair Caspi , 359–373. London: Routledge, 2023,.

Tauber, Alfred I. *Requiem for the Ego: Freud and the Origins of Postmodernism.* Stanford: Stanford University Press, 2013.

Tauber, Alfred I. *The Triumph of Uncertainty. Science and Self in the Postmodern Age: A Philosophical Romance.* Budapest: Central European University Press, 2022.

Tauber, Alfred I. *William James and Sigmund Freud on the Mind. Saving Subjectivity*, London: Routledge, 2025.
Taylor, Charles. "Responsibility for Self." In *The Identities of Persons*, edited by Amelie Oksenberg Rorty, 281–299. Berkeley: University of California Press, 1976.
Thiel, Udo. *The Early Modern Subject: Self-consciousness and Personal Identity from Descartes to Hume*. Oxford: Oxford University Press, 2011.
Webster, Richard. *Why Freud Was Wrong: Sin, Science, and Psychoanalysis*. New York: Basic Books, 1995.
Weiner, Philip. *Evolution and the Founders of Pragmatism*. Cambridge, MA: Harvard University Press, 1949.

CHAPTER 13

"No One Believes in His Own Death." On More and Less Necessary Illusions

Ulrike Kistner

1   War and Death as Signs of the Times

War gives rise to thought on death. That this is more than trivially pertinent, is borne out by Sigmund Freud's writings of the first three decades of the twentieth century, most explicitly in the essay "Thoughts for the Times on War and Death," penned around March-April 1915, some six months after the start of World War I. It combines "The Disillusionment of War" (section I) with "Our Attitude Towards Death" (section II). Freud turns to war and death again in his essay *Beyond the Pleasure Principle* in March 1919, in the context of the immediate aftermath of war, revolution, and the disintegration of the Austro-Hungarian Empire. While the signs of the times embedded in Freud's 1920 *Beyond the Pleasure Principle* clearly point to World War I and the upheavals of the immediate post-war period, they attain psychically-structural dimensions in this meta-psychological essay.[1] A third explicit thematization of war and death, this time taking up Eros and the "death instinct" (manifesting itself in aggression, destructiveness, and war) articulated in the second version of the *Beyond*-essay again, is to be found in the exchange between Albert Einstein and Sigmund Freud on the topic "Why War?"[2] Once again (albeit in a different context), this text itself is embattled from the outset. At the time that the exchange was published – in March 1933 – Hitler had assumed dictatorial powers in Germany, and two months later, Freud's books were among many others burning in Berlin. Being banned from public view in Germany, the correspondence with Einstein was published in Paris.

The connection between war and thought on death thus seems to be scripted by the signs of the times. But what I would like to show in this chapter

---

1 Sigmund Freud, *Beyond the Pleasure Principle*, in *The Complete Psychological Works of Sigmund Freud* (Standard Edition, Vol. 18), ed. James Strachey et al. (London: The Hogarth Press, 1955), 7–64.
2 Sigmund Freud, "Why War," in *The Complete Psychological Works of Sigmund Freud* (Standard Edition, Vol. 22), ed. James Strachey et al. (London: The Hogarth Press, 1964), 199–215.

is a deeper connection, a philosophical connection, between war and (un)thought on death. To this end, I will take a closer look at the three texts mentioned, and others that shed light on the enigma of the psychic registrations of life and death, and of their relation – and the changes that this apparently eternal theme undergoes in its conceptualizations.

2   Psychoanalytic Thought on War and Death

Any expectation of finding a consistent and coherent account of war and death in psychoanalysis is bound to be disappointed. Psychoanalytic thought on war and death is itself beset with snags. It sets itself up to confront illusions with reality, and gets ensnared in yet more rounds of illusions in the process; it makes a compelling case for taking death seriously, while having to acknowledge an anthropological basis for the denial of our own death.[3] It is drawn into the black hole of the impossibility of imagining our own death even unconsciously, while insisting (in the first version of the *Beyond*-essay) that we are each driven unconsciously toward death – along with all living organisms, each instinctually and immanently seeking its own way of dying.[4] This, however, could turn out to be yet another illusion in the search for the representability of death.[5] Thought on war and death plays itself out between the observation of play involving repetition with the aim of mastery, and repetition compulsion in the grip of the death drive.

3   Ambivalence, Guilt, and Illusions

In what is to follow, I will attempt to unravel some of these conundrums. Starting with the last one of those I have just mentioned, I would venture to say that developing an attitude to death is and is not child's play. Similar to the sexual theories of children sparked by the arrival of a sibling, the death of a close person 'forced [primaeval man] to reflection and thus became the starting-point of all speculation.'[6] Thus, it is the birth of another and the death

---

[3] Sigmund Freud, "Thoughts for the Times on War and Death," in *The Complete Psychological Works of Sigmund Freud* (Standard Edition, Vol. 14), ed. James Strachey et al. (London: The Hogarth Press, 1973), 280, 284–285.
[4] Freud, *Beyond the Pleasure Principle*, 39–40.
[5] Ibid., 45.
[6] Freud, "Thoughts for the Times on War and Death," 292–293.

of another that set off the drive for research. But Freud hastens to correct the 'philosophers thinking too philosophically' in assuming that it is 'the enigma of life and death' that sparks such reflection. Instead, the drive for reflection is a matter primarily of a "vital exigency" (*Lebensnot*), and secondarily of a properly speaking psychological ambivalence.[7] Ambivalence sparked by an encounter with death is evoked by an internal conflict: 'the conflict of feeling at the [birth or] death of loved yet alien and hated persons,' which (in the case of the death of another) at the same time, under the impact of a sense of guilt, conjures up religious tropes of life after death, and of the division into a mortal body and an immortal soul.[8]

Thus, the very conditions that give rise to the drive for research, can also produce illusions (if not delusions) driven by wishful thinking. The cessation or suppression of the drive for research, internally conditioned or externally imposed, is as ontogenetically consequential in the case of children's curiosity about "where babies come from" as the disavowal of death is socio-culturally consequential. In both cases, it generates psychic conflict typically finding expression in neurotic symptoms,[9] and/or intellectual blunting, variously evinced in the adoption of illusions of different kinds, to which I will return in the concluding remarks.[10]

4 Child's Play (Kinderspiel) and Staged Play (Schauspiel)

An outcome for dealing with "vital exigencies" that is more favorable than that of holding onto illusions is provided by another route – and surprisingly, we can see a parallel of the most sublime and culturally valued of human creations with those of children. Freud initially (that is, in his short reflection on "Psychopathic Characters on the Stage" of 1906) thinks of child's play as a way of obtaining relief through "blowing off steam," as well as an imitation of

---

[7] In the case of childhood sexual theories, Freud sees their origin in the 'necessities of the child's psychosexual constitution.' Sigmund Freud, "On the Sexual Theories of Children," in *The Complete Psychological Works of Sigmund Freud* (Standard Edition Vol. 9), ed. James Strachey et al. (London: The Hogarth Press, 1959), 215.

[8] Ibid.; and Freud, "Thoughts for the Times on War and Death," 293–294.

[9] Freud, "On the Sexual Theories of Children," 214, 225.

[10] Freud suggests that it might be 'precisely religious education which bears a large share of the blame for [the] relative atrophy [by which the radiant intelligence of the child is turned into the feeble intellectual powers of the average adult].' Sigmund Freud, "The Future of an Illusion," in *The Complete Works of Sigmund Freud* (Standard Edition, Vol. 21), ed. James Strachey et al. (London: The Hogarth Press, 1961), 47.

"what grown-ups do."[11] This view, foregrounding dynamic and identificatory processes in child's play, is taken up again in the second chapter of *Beyond the Pleasure Principle*, but there it is set alongside another, more prominent observation on child's play: the play of the child repeats a distressing experience – the absence of the mother – as a game. Being inserted in the chapter describing traumatic and war neuroses characterized by fixation to trauma and repetition of passively experienced trauma in dreams and obtrusive reminiscences, the observation of a child at play seems incongruous; but its placement in that chapter becomes explicable in light of the fact that child's play adds a different dimension of repetition (one that is to be taken up in the second version of Freud's text, with the re-orientation of repetition towards Eros). Here, repetition functions as re-enactment, this time with the child assuming an active role, with the aim of mastering the distressing experience. Actively working an unpleasurable experience over in the mind and mastering it yields pleasure.[12]

The same difference between unpleasurable and pleasure-yielding repetition surfaces in the analogy of imitative child's play with the play staged in the theatre (*Schau-Spiel*). In his early formulation of the analogy of child's play and adult spectatorship of a play on stage, Freud combines the functions of identification and mastery (albeit, in the case of *Schau-Spiel,* mastery of a different kind – that of surviving the downfall of the tragic hero as the demise of an other, and as protagonist in what is "only" a game, a play).[13] Like children at imitative play doing what adults do, the spectator of a play, and the reader of literary fiction, identify with the protagonist(s) and become "great" with them.[14] In identifying with the hero, adult spectators can enjoy the grandeur of their hero/ine – classically a hero/ine in tragedy – while being spared the pain and suffering that befalls him/her. However, and herein lies the difference between children at play and the adult spectator or reader identifying with the hero/ines in their tribulations: in play, children attain mastery through re-enactment, that is, by taking an active role, whereas adult spectators are dis-interested onlookers, as a condition for the representational mechanism to take hold. 'Accordingly, [this] enjoyment is based on an illusion,' says Freud, the status of which is known to the spectator: '[the spectator's] suffering is mitigated by the certainty that, firstly, it is someone other than himself who is

---

11   Sigmund Freud, "Psychopathic Characters on the Stage," in *The Complete Works of Sigmund Freud* (Standard Edition, Vol. 7), ed. James Strachey et al. (London: The Hogarth Press, 1953), 305.
12   Freud, *Beyond the Pleasure Principle*, 22.
13   Sigmund Freud, "Psychopathic Characters on the Stage."
14   Ibid., 305.

acting and suffering on the stage, and, secondly, that after all it is only a game, which can threaten no damage to his personal security.'[15]

5 Changing the Game: The Unconscious and the Problem of Death

Nine years later, in "Thoughts for the Times on War and Death" (1915b), Freud once again takes up the attitude toward death mediated through the perspective of the reader or spectator – of literature and theatre, respectively:

> We ... seek in the world of fiction, in literature and in the theatre compensation for what has been lost in life. There we still find people who know how to die – who, indeed, manage to kill someone else. There alone too the condition can be fulfilled which makes it possible for us to reconcile ourselves with death: namely, that behind all the vicissitudes of life we should still be able to preserve a life intact ... In the realm of fiction we find the plurality of lives which we need. We die with the hero with whom we have identified ourselves; yet we survive him, and are ready to die again as safely as with another hero.[16]

Once again, the condition for representation of dying is the derealization facilitated by the space of the theatre, or by the genre of fiction. But under the impression of "the times," the "thoughts on war and death" are articulated far less assuredly than before. Entailed in the passage just quoted are statements suggesting that death has been lost in life and to life, that we do not know how to die (any more).[17] Opening the section "Our Attitude towards Death" are statements to the effect that we tend to eliminate death from life, for good or bad reason: 'It is indeed impossible to imagine our own death'; 'at bottom no one believes in his own death'; 'in the unconscious every one of us is convinced of his own immortality'; 'our unconscious is ... inaccessible to the idea of our own death';[18] 'the unconscious seems to contain nothing that could give any

---

15 Ibid., 306.
16 Freud, "Thoughts for the Times on War and Death," 291.
17 The intimations of a sense of loss of the power of wishful thinking in the formulation 'in the world of fiction, in literature and in the theatre ... we *still* find people who know how to die' and in the implication that we don't know how to die *any more*, recall the opening of Grimm's fairy tale, *Der Froschkönig* (The Frog King): '*In den guten alten Zeiten, in denen das Wünschen* noch *geholfen hat*' (emphasis added). The sense of loss entailed in the disillusionment itself is consigned to fairy tales.
18 Freud, "Thoughts for the Times on War and Death," 289, 296.

content to our concept of the annihilation of life. ... nothing resembling death can ever have been experienced'[19] The big question raised by these remarks is, 'What ... is the attitude of our unconscious to the problem of death?' If what we call our "unconscious" consists of 'the deepest strata of our minds, made up of instinctual impulses,' as Freud asserts, including drives rushing toward death (as the first version of the *Beyond*-essay stipulates), how can it be that 'there is nothing in us which responds to a belief in death'?[20]

6 Ways of (Un)Knowing Ways of Dying

One possible answer to this question is to be gleaned from the different ascriptions to life and death drives in the two different versions of the *Beyond*-essay, which do not get harmonized into a consistent account, as Ulrike May and Michael Schröter have shown in detail.[21] Another possible answer could be garnered from the dualism of the drives whose terms do not correspond to each other in their antithetical relation. Yet another possible response to this question can be found in the elaboration of the paradoxical notion of "unconscious feelings" in the 1915 meta-psychological essay on "The Unconscious."[22] Here, Freud explicitly raises this question: can there be 'unconscious instinctual impulses, emotions and feelings?'[23] His initial answer is unequivocal: 'An instinct can never become an object of consciousness – only the idea that represents the instinct can. Even in the unconscious, moreover, an instinct cannot be represented otherwise than by an idea.'[24] In the absence of an idea attached to it, the drive (translated as "instinct") could not become known.[25]

---

19 Sigmund Freud, *Inhibition, Symptoms, and Anxiety,* in *The Complete Psychological Works of Sigmund Freud* (Standard Edition, Vol. 20), ed. James Strachey et al. (London: The Hogarth Press, 1959), 129–130.
20 Ibid.
21 Ulrike May and Michael Schröter, "Sigmund Freud – *Jenseits des Lustprinzips.* Kritische Edition von Ulrike May und Michael Schröter." *Luzifer-Amor. Zeitschrift zur Geschichte der Psychoanalyse* 26, no. 51 (2013): 7–91.
22 Sigmund Freud, "The Unconscious," in *The Complete Psychological Works of Sigmund Freud* (Standard Edition, Vol. 14), ed. James Strachey et al. (London: The Hogarth Press, 1963), 166–204.
23 Ibid., 177.
24 Ibid.
25 Ibid.

We could thus say that death as drive ("instinct") is unconscious, but not *in* the unconscious.[26]

But even if we can at most be "spectators" of death, as Freud characterizes the conventional treatment of death, there are still some provisos for assuming that position. For there are certain conditions under which it is *not* possible to take up the position of spectator. Freud's early observations on this subject, as well as those articulated in the first version of the *Beyond*-essay, indicate the limits of representability and binding. Physical injury or illness, or pre-established full-blown psychopathology presented on stage is not the stuff of heroism or aesthetic pleasure, unless there is an aspect of the illness that 'make[s] psychical activity possible.'[27] The example provided in the footnote, namely the play by Austrian novelist and playwright Hermann Bahr entitled *Die Andere* (The other Woman), and staged in Vienna at the end of 1905, is instructive. The footnote informs the reader that the plot 'turns upon the dual personality of its heroine [interpreted by Freud at the time as 'an unfamiliar and fully established neurosis,'][28] who is unable, in spite of every effort, to escape from an attachment (based on her physical feelings) to a man who has her in his power.'[29] Upon a closer look at the plot, it emerges that the protagonist, violinist Lida Lind, gets involved with a certain Professor Heinrich Hess, in order to get over a previous relationship with her agent Amschl. Just as she thinks she has succeeded, the previous lover returns, and she leaves with him. In making her way back to the professor, she is suddenly afflicted with a mysterious illness and dies thinking of her first love.

Two aspects about this play, trashed by the critics at the time as failed drama,[30] are noteworthy, also with regard to the attention that the play solicited from Freud: firstly, the plot displays an instance of repetition compulsion *beyond* pleasure, that is, of the kind later mentioned in the third chapter of the first version of Freud's *Beyond*-essay, namely a passive repetition of the same unpleasurable experience, thus defying the pleasure principle as fundamental

---

26 See also Freud's dictum that 'death is an abstract concept with a negative content for which no unconscious correlative can be found.' See Sigmund Freud, "The Dependent Relations of the Ego," in *The Complete Works of Sigmund Freud* (Standard Edition, Vol. 19), ed. James Strachey et al. (London: The Hogarth Press, 1961), 58.
27 Freud, "Psychopathic Characters on the State," 307–308.
28 Ibid., 310.
29 Ibid., n. 1.
30 Hanns von Gumppenberg, "Rezension Hermann Bahr *Die Andere*." *Das literarische Echo. Halbmonatsschrift für Literaturfreunde* (hrsg. v. Dr. Josef Ettlinger). 8. Jg. (Oktober 1905 – Oktober 1906), 358.

principle of mental functioning;[31] and secondly, the fact that the demise of the protagonist is not due to an inner (psychic) conflict, but to a sudden fatal illness.

7 'Destruction of Illusion by Reality' – Destruction of Reality by Illusion

A sudden fatal illness, just like war, amounts to 'the destruction of illusion by reality,' the latter of which Freud variously designates with the name of one of the Greek primordial deities Ἀνάγκη – goddess of inevitability, compulsion, and necessity and, in latter-day adaptations, natural necessity. Ἀνάγκη asserts itself in the death of Sophie, of which her distraught father notifies his friend Oskar Pfister in 1920:

> we received the news that our sweet Sophie in Hamburg had been snatched away by influenzal pneumonia, snatched away in the midst of glowing health, from a full and active life as a competent mother and loving wife, all in four or five days, as though she had never existed. Although we had been worried about her for a couple of days, we had nevertheless been hopeful; it is so difficult to judge from a distance. And this distance must remain distance; we were not able to travel at once, as we had intended, after the first alarming news; there was no train, not even for an emergency. *The undisguised brutality of our time* is weighing heavily upon us.[32]

At the beginning of the sixth chapter (newly inserted at the beginning of 1920) in the second version of the *Beyond*-essay, Freud ostensibly alludes to Sophie's death, but this time in slightly different terms, indicating an attempt to draw "the sublime ἀνάγκη," "the remorseless law of nature" into the internal causes of death. But that attempt appears as yet another possible illusion held by those looking on, as opposed to accidental death, which now harbors that unbearable gravity:

> If we are to die ourselves, and first to lose in death those who are dearest to us, it is easier to submit to a remorseless law of nature, to the sublime

---

31   Freud, *Beyond the Pleasure Principle*, 22.
32   Sigmund Freud, *Letters of Sigmund Freud 1873–1939*, ed. by Ernst Freud. Trans. by Tania Stern and James Stern (London: The Hogarth Press, 1961), 327–328. Emphasis added.

ἀνάγκη [Necessity], than to a chance which might perhaps have been escaped. It may be, however, that this belief in the internal necessity of dying is only another of those illusions which we have created 'um die Schwere des Daseins zu ertragen.' It is certainly not a primal belief. The notion of a "natural death" is quite foreign to primitive races; they attribute every death that occurs among them to the influence of an enemy or of an evil spirit.[33]

Thus initially, Freud seems inclined to ascribe sudden deadly illness to ἀνάγκη as natural necessity, and as part of the "undisguised brutality" that is the reality of the time – as the notices of Sophie's death sent to his mother and to his friend indicate. But then (at more or less the same time, in the reworked version of the *Beyond*-essay, that is, in its newly inserted sixth chapter), he recasts deadly illness as internal necessity of death (here the focus shifts from the spectator to the afflicted organism itself). This would require some explanation, which Freud had supplied in meta-psychological terms in the fourth and fifth chapters of his *Beyond*-essay: In the case of overwhelming stimuli from without, the organism beset with sudden deadly illness mobilizes all defenses from other systems, leaving it inadequate to the task of binding incoming amounts of stimulus; as a result, the pleasure principle is put out of action.[34] In redirecting the move towards death to a process internal to the organism, however, Freud implies the possibility of psychic binding.[35] But the hope of a possibility of psychic binding and mastery is shattered: The idea of "natural death" is an illusion acquired later in human history. Beneath the conventional attitude towards death, a primaeval attitude towards death lies dormant in every human being: a friend-enemy scheme of a special kind, resulting from the ambivalence toward death of a loved, yet alien and hated person; and from the split between the putative impossibility of one's own annihilation while at the same time wishing for the annihilation of the enemy (or stranger).[36]

8 The Destruction of an Illusion ...

The impossibility of psychic binding in events of war and (mass) death entails the destruction of an illusion by reality, completing a double *denouement:* not

---

33 Freud, *Beyond the Pleasure Principle*, 44.
34 Ibid., 29.
35 Ibid., 34.
36 Freud, "Thoughts for the Times on War and Death," 291–293, 296.

only does war shatter the illusion of "a remorseless law of nature" circumscribing the internal necessity of death; it also shatters the illusion of 'chance [event] which might perhaps have been escaped.'[37] As Freud notes in "Thoughts for the Time on War and Death" (published five years earlier):

> war is bound to sweep away [the] conventional treatment of death. Death will no longer be denied; we are forced to believe in it. People really die; and no longer one by one, but many, often tens of thousands, in a single day. And death is no longer a chance event. ... the accumulation of deaths puts an end to the impression of chance.[38]

But even a preparedness to 'give death the place in reality and in our thoughts which is its due' borders on an illusion to the extent that it makes life amid war and death more tolerable. This illusion to the third degree is justified, however, as it is a vitally necessary illusion,[39] giving life its due.

While insisting that there cannot be such a thing as the eradication of evil, enmity, strife, and war, Freud also acknowledges the role of illusions that transform primal impulses through erotism, diverting the sexual drive towards socially valued aims (among which can be counted even the "sublime ἀνάγκη" we had encountered earlier). It is particularly in intellectual and artistic productions (literature, drama) that our unconscious seeks to find an attitude towards death (even as mass death in war and genocide would exceed its grasp).

9 ... and "The Future of an Illusion"

While the vitally necessary illusion and the ludic illusion, aiming at identification and mastery in the case of child's play and involving sublimation in the case of artistic production[40] and scientific inquiry, can go in search for wish-fulfilment without disavowing reality,[41] the wishful illusions entailed in

---

37 Freud, *Beyond the Pleasure Principle*, 44.
38 Freud, "Thoughts for the Times on War and Death," 291.
39 Ibid., 300.
40 In the case of artistic creativity involving fantasy and imagination, it is understood that it was exempted from reality-testing from the start and by definition (see Freud 1930a SE 21, 81).
41 Sigmund Freud, *Civilization and its Discontents*, in *The Complete Psychological Works of Sigmund Freud* (Standard Edition, Vol. 21), ed. James Strachey et al. (London: The Hogarth Press, 1961), 81.

religious doctrines tend to distort, disavow, displace, or replace the demands of reality. Religious doctrines[42] are impervious to verification and proof, and on that account, are comparable to delusions,[43] even mass delusions.[44] Instead of allowing the drives to be inflected by intelligence, dogmatic religion seeks to direct them through prohibitions on and inhibitions of thought, thus weakening the intellect.[45] To the extent that religious doctrines demand intellectual sacrifices, they foster ignorance, from which 'no right to believe anything can be derived.'[46]

Responding to the assertion that religion responds to human needs by holding out wish-fulfilment and consolation, Freud postulates the primacy of the intellect, however tenuous and uncertain its status and its findings may be. In assigning external reality to Ἀνάγκη, Freud is calling upon Greek mythology to make his case. The counterpart of Ἀνάγκη is Reason, Λόγος (Logos).[47] Plato's *Timaeus* describes the interaction between Reason and Necessity in producing the visible world: 'Reason overruled Necessity by persuading her to guide the greatest part of the things that become towards what is best.'[48] While Freud did not share in the view of the triumph of Reason over Necessity, he adduces the pair of Λόγος and Ἀνάγκη adapted by one of his favorite writers (on whom he bestowed the epithet of one of the greatest philosophers of his time), Eduard Douwes Dekker, also known by the pen name of Multatuli.

However, the dualistic casting of the reality principle, with Λόγος as counterpart to Ἀνάγκη, is short-lived. In *Civilization and its Discontents* (published three years later), it is Ἔρως (Eros) – referenced to Plato's *Symposium* – that is instated in that role. It is now Ἔρως that sets the task instigated by Ἀνάγκη.[49]

---

42   With "religion" as "illusion" Freud here designates, as he qualifies it later in *Civilisation and its Discontents*, 'what the common man understands by his religion ... the system of doctrines and promises which on the one hand explains to him the riddles of this world with enviable completeness, and, on the other, assures him that a careful Providence will watch over his life and will compensate him in a future existence of any frustrations he suffers here.' It amounts to an 'attempt to procure a certainty of happiness and a protection against suffering through a delusional remoulding of reality.' Sigmund Freud, *Civilization and its Discontents*, 73, 81.

43   Freud, *The Future of an Illusion*, 31.

44   Freud, *Civilization and its Discontents*, 81, 84.

45   Freud, *The Future of an Illusion*, 47; Freud, *Civilization and its Discontents*, 84.

46   Freud, *The Future of an Illusion*, 32.

47   'Not even the gods fight against Ἀνάγκη,' Greek lyrical poet Simonides of Coes (556–468 BCE) is cited as saying, acknowledging a power mightier than the gods. Cecil Maurice Bowra, *The Greek Experience* (New York: W.P. Publishing Company, 1958), 61.

48   Plato, *Timaeus*, in *Plato's Cosmology. The Timaeus of Plato*, trans. Francis MacDonald Cornford (Indianapolis and Cambridge: Hackett Publishing Company, 1997), 160.

49   Freud, *Civilization and its Discontents*, 140.

The attenuation of Λόγος under the ascendance of Ἔρως renders illusions – deflections and substitutive satisfactions, particularly in the form of mass delusions – less objectionable constructions.[50] Under the impact of the third formulation of the drive theory first presented in the second version of *Beyond the Pleasure Principle*, the dualism of the drives plays itself out between *Eros* and the death drive, not only ontogenetically, but in the life of the human species.[51] Death and aggression are pitted against Eros and Ananke: 'Eros and Ananke have become the parents of human civilization ... The first result of civilization was that even a fairly large number of people were now able to live together in a community.'[52]

The drive for research under the impact of ambivalence sparked by an encounter with death that we had encountered earlier, in the "Thoughts for the Times on War and Death," is being placed wholly under the sign of 'the eternal struggle between love and death' (the death drive in its later formulations understood to be expressed in hate, hostility, aggression, and destruction).[53] Guilt at the aggression towards the father, and love towards and identification with the father, set up the agency of the super-ego. These factors find their correspondence phylogenetically in the cultural role of religious belief, for which the disbelief in our own death becomes structurally salient.[54] Yet we can *know* what belief and disbelief do – that is, what epistemological status they occupy – and that presupposes that knowledge is distinct from belief as a set of collective perceptions and symbolics of fundamental truths.

Bibliography

Freud, Sigmund. "Psychopathic Characters on the Stage." In *The Standard Edition of the Complete Psychological Works of Sigmund Freud.* (Standard Edition, Vol. 7), edited and translated by James Strachey et al., 303–310. London: The Hogarth Press, 1953.

Freud, Sigmund. "On the Sexual Theories of Children." In *The Standard Edition of the Complete Psychological Works of Sigmund Freud.* (Standard Edition, Vol. 9), edited and translated by James Strachey et al., 209–226. London: The Hogarth Press, 1959.

Freud, Sigmund. "Thoughts for the Times on War and Death." In *The Standard Edition of the Complete Psychological Works of Sigmund Freud.* (Standard Edition, Vol. 14),

---

50   Ibid., 75.
51   Ibid., 122.
52   Ibid., 100.
53   Ibid., 132.
54   Ibid.

edited and translated by James Strachey et al., 275–300. London: The Hogarth Press, 1973.

Freud, Sigmund. "The Unconscious." In *The Standard Edition of the Complete Psychological Works of Sigmund Freud.* (Standard Edition, Vol. 14), edited and translated by James Strachey et al., 166–204. London: The Hogarth Press, 1973.

Freud, Sigmund. *Beyond the Pleasure Principle.* In *The Standard Edition of the Complete Psychological Works of Sigmund Freud.* (Standard Edition, Vol. 18), edited and translated by James Strachey et al., 7–64. London: The Hogarth Press, 1955.

Freud, Sigmund. "Group Psychology and the Analysis of the Ego". In *The Standard Edition of the Complete Psychological Works of Sigmund Freud.* (Standard Edition, Vol. 18), edited and translated by James Strachey et al., 69–143. London: The Hogarth Press, 1955.

Freud, Sigmund. "The Economic Problem of Masochism." In *The Standard Edition of the Complete Psychological Works of Sigmund Freud.* (Standard Edition, Vol. 19), edited and translated by James Strachey et al., 159–170. London: The Hogarth Press, 1961.

Freud, Sigmund. *Letters of Sigmund Freud 1873–1939,* edited by Ernst Freud. Translated by Tania Stern and James Stern. London: Hogarth Press, 1961.

Freud, Sigmund. "Inhibitions, Symptoms and Anxiety". In *The Standard Edition of the Complete Psychological Works of Sigmund Freud.* (Standard Edition, Vol. 20), edited and translated by James Strachey et al., 87–172. London: The Hogarth Press, 1959.

Freud, Sigmund. "The Future of an Illusion". In *The Standard Edition of the Complete Psychological Works of Sigmund Freud.* (Standard Edition, Vol. 21), edited and translated by James Strachey et al., 5–56. London: The Hogarth Press, 1961.

Freud, Sigmund. "Civilization and Its Discontents" In *The Standard Edition of the Complete Psychological Works of Sigmund Freud.* (Standard Edition, Vol. 21), edited and translated by James Strachey et al., 64–145. London: The Hogarth Press, 1961.

Freud, Sigmund. "Why War?" (Letter to Albert Einstein, September 1932). In *The Standard Edition of the Complete Psychological Works of Sigmund Freud.* (Standard Edition, Vol. 22), edited and translated by James Strachey et al., 203–215. London: The Hogarth Press, 1964.

May, Ulrike and Michael Schröter. "Sigmund Freud – *Jenseits des Lustprinzips.* Kritische Edition von Ulrike May und Michael Schröter." *Luzifer-Amor. Zeitschrift zur Geschichte der Psychoanalyse* 26, Nr. 51 (2013): 7–91.

Plato. "Timaeus". In *Plato's Cosmology. The Timaeus of Plato.* Translated and commented on by Francis MacDonald Cornford. Indianapolis and Cambridge: Hackett Publishing Company, 1997.

Simonides Fr. "4.20 Diehl." In Cecil Maurice Bowra. *The Greek Experience*. Cleveland and New York: W. P. Publishing Company, 1958.

von Gumppenberg, Hanns. "Rezension Hermann Bahr *Die Andere*." *Das literarische Echo. Halbmonatsschrift für Literaturfreunde* (hrsg. v. Dr. Josef Ettlinger). 8. Jg. (Oktober 1905 – Oktober 1906): 357–59.

CHAPTER 14

Killing in the Name of the Father: Freud and René Girard on the Question of Desire

Clint Jones

1   In the beginning

To understand the continuing relevance of Freud's work in a critical theory context it is necessary to examine his contributions and influences not to note his one-time significance but rather to demonstrate how his theories remain foundational and useful for the ongoing development of social critique. Toward that end the focus of this essay is on the conceptualization of the origin of social institutions. While Freud's work in this regard can easily fit him into a history of social contract theory, what makes this type of approach unique is that it places the onus of societal development on *desires* rather than *needs as such*. In Freud's analysis of early human society, we find the groundwork for a critical theory of social development that attempts to outline the driving force behind violence and the overarching social need to control it.

The locus of this violence, for Freud, is the father-son relationship. Freud develops his critique of the father-son relationship, and the resulting violence it bears out, across several of his most enduring works. However, there is an important influence at work on Freud in the construction of this theory and that is the social critique of Friedrich Nietzsche. A brief detour through some of those formative ideas will help sharpen and clarify Freud's approach to developing his theories on the origin of society; especially important will be the ideas in Nietzsche's work that culminate in his claims about the death of God.[1] Drawing on Freud's works, it is possible to construct a well-built theory

---

1   While Freud's denial that he read Nietzsche is well-known there is ample evidence in his personal correspondence and published works to suggest this is not true. To say nothing of the fact that Freud moved in social circles that were also a part of Nietzsche's social life. Perhaps most indicative of this overlapping is the relationships Nietzsche and Freud enjoyed with Lou Andreas-Salomé. There are plenty of scholarly attempts to uncover this influence as well as those arguing whether or not Freud plagiarized some of Nietzsche's ideas. I am going to bypass that entire quagmire by positing that Nietzsche anticipated many of the themes central to psychology, Freud was aware of Nietzsche's work and drew inspiration from it, but that the ideas Freud advances are his own and should be read in light of multiple influences

about the inherent frailty of the human character and how the organization of society is arranged to control human desires. This essay will, of necessity, argue that Freud was correct is designating the foundation of civilization in an originary act of violence: a murder.

The theory of a "founding murder" was picked up by René Girard, further developed to account for gaps and potential missteps in Freud, and presented, again, as the most accurate theory of society's origin. Because Girard treats Freud's work as critical to an understanding of human psychology, which would result in such a heinous act as patricide, both the work of Freud and Girard ought to be considered central to any critical theory of society. However, neither theorist enjoys their proper place in popular critical theory. My argument is that, while seemingly rudimentary, Freud's theory was correct, as Girard argues, in surmising that unchecked desire was the foundation of civilization. Further, I believe that Girard's use and development of Freud can be employed to strengthen theories that engage Freud directly, like Herbert Marcuse, and sometimes do so derisively, here specifically, I am thinking of John Rawls.[2] Through this demonstration of the continued relevance of Freud I hope to make clear the importance of his theories to contemporary social critique.

2   Laying the Groundwork

Early in his career Nietzsche struggled against the prevailing influences that were at work shaping his thought, namely the philosophy of Arthur Schopenhauer and the socio-cultural influence of Richard Wagner. As Nietzsche began to break away from these influences and develop his own ideas regarding morality, culture, and society, he also began to interrogate aspects of moral psychology and the resulting expression of moral attitudes in society; from *The Birth of Tragedy* (1872) through *The Gay Science* (1882) and *Thus Spoke Zarathustra* (1883–5), ultimately culminating in *On the Genealogy of Morality* (1887). Nietzsche would build a powerful critique of social mores that would come to bear a strong influence on Freud's social theory. It must be remembered that when Nietzsche was publishing his analysis of the human

---

and judged on their own merit. In this way I am treating Nietzsche as an influence on Freud the same way I would interpret Nietzsche as an influence of, say, Jacques Derrida.

2   In *A Genealogy of Social Violence: Founding Murder, Rawlsian Fairness, and the Future of the Family* (Burlington, VT: Ashgate Publishing, 2013) I develop a sustained criticism of John Rawls's *Theory of Justice* and indicate how I think a richer account of Freud and Girard can bolster Marcusean social critiques.

condition psychology was not a discipline unto itself and, in Nietzsche's hands, it retained its explicit connection to philosophy.[3] The emergence of psychology as a discipline during the publication period of Freud's most productive efforts saw a distancing of the two disciplines but never a separation of them.

When Nietzsche set out to develop his own thoughts on the human condition he perceptively noted at the beginning of *Human, All Too Human* that philosophers have failed to properly understand the human condition because they treat humankind as an "eternal truth" rather than something that is the product of dynamic social, cultural, and biological evolutionary processes. Nietzsche claims, 'everything *essential* in the development of mankind took place in primeval times, long before the four thousand years we more or less know about.'[4] By asking how society formed and what kind of event could have motivated the social institutions and mores found in the oldest cultures Freud was clearly engaging with the question of humankind in precisely the way Nietzsche thought necessary to develop any coherent understanding of "modern man." Pushing the point further, Nietzsche argues that for humanity to progress it must overcome the belief that religion can accurately articulate how every person ought to act. If humanity is to avoid self-destruction through an adherence to such universal rule, then, 'it must first of all attain to a hitherto altogether unprecedented *knowledge of the preconditions of culture* as a scientific standard for ecumenical goals.'[5]

Attempting to parse out the circumstances and conditions that prevailed in human communities prior to the formalization of cultural norms is, as Nietzsche indicates, a difficult task. Many early social theorists merely posited hypothetical conditions that fit their contemporary arguments for the nature of humanity. For instance, Thomas Hobbes understands human nature as inherently aggressive, egoistic, and capable of great violence. In his formulation of the social contract, then, he posits a pre-social condition of perpetual war, a war of all against all, and extrapolating from this justifies *both* his explanation for how society formed into a justifiable monarchy *and* the belligerence between modern states. Nietzsche is arguing for something more systematic, in his terms *scientific*, and Freud, relying on a psychologically

---

3   See Richard Schacht's introduction to Friedrich Nietzsche's *Human, All Too Human*, trans. R.J. Hollingdale (Cambridge: Cambridge University Press, 1996), xviii.
4   Nietzsche, *Human, All Too Human*, 12. This quotation is located in aphorism 2 and the emphasis is in the original.
5   Nietzsche, *Human, All Too Human*, 25. The quotation is in aphorism 25 and the emphasis is in the original. Nietzsche declares this to be the "tremendous task" facing the great spirits of the future.

grounded philosophical anthropology, attempts to develop just such an explanation. It is not at all surprising, then, to see overlaps between the two projects: examinations of Oedipus, the focus on inner drives, the role of ego, the importance of dreams, the relevance of customs, the role of mythology, and even the notion of discontent. Though examining these parallels would require more space than what is available, there is one connection between the two that does require closer scrutiny: the death of God.

Nietzsche is undoubtedly most popular for his claim that God is dead. This theme in Nietzsche's thought is often poorly understood and rarely developed in the context of his larger project. In fact, Nietzsche makes this claim several times and in each instance the claim is connected to additional content that renders the oft cherry-picked claim something of a deliberate misreading. In the "Prelude in Rhymes" that begins *The Gay Science*, Nietzsche writes, 'God loves us, *because* we are made by *him*. // "But man made God!" say the refined. // Should he not love what he designed?'[6] The idea that humans invented God is the culmination of ideas developed in the works preceding *The Gay Science* wherein Nietzsche argues that morality exists in society as an extension of the belief in a metaphysical world that undergirds this one and is administered by a law-giving deity. Nietzsche is derisive of this idea, comparing it in a famous passage of *Daybreak* to the undertaking of alchemists. There he states, 'I deny morality as I deny alchemy, that is, I deny their premises: but I do *not* deny that there have been alchemists who believed in these premises' and from this comparison it is clear Nietzsche takes the premises of morality to be wrong-headed as well.[7]

Establishing the introduction of morality as an expression of social formation Freud will parallel these ideas in Nietzsche. Subsequently, René Girard, refining Freud's work, will do the same. As will be shown below, Freud posits the creation of God via the deification of the murdered father and, consequentially, the instantiation of moral taboos becomes a kind of social alchemy aimed at the transfiguration of the individual into a civilized being. If, as Nietzsche claims in his "Prelude," man created God, then what does it mean to say that God is dead? In the opening aphorism of Book III of *The Gay Science*, Nietzsche first claims that God is dead, *but* he continues we still have to vanquish his shadow.[8] Later, in aphorism 125 titled "The Madman,"

---

6 Friedrich Nietzsche, *The Gay Science*, trans. Walter Kaufmann (New York: Vintage Books, 1974), 57. The quotation appears in the poem "The Pious Retort," emphasis in the original.
7 Friedrich Nietzsche, *Daybreak*, eds. Maudemarie Clark and Brian Leiter (Cambridge: Cambridge University Press, 2011), 60. The quotation is drawn from aphorism 103 with emphasis in the original.
8 Nietzsche, *The Gay Science*, 167. The quotation is drawn from aphorism 108.

Nietzsche's madman exclaims 'Wither is God? ... I will tell you. *We have killed him* – you and I. All of us are his murderers.'[9] Given Nietzsche's scathing criticisms of religion and his arguments in Book III leading up to this passage, one can deduce that Nietzsche is talking about the decoupling of moral values and religion. More generally, we might claim Nietzsche is concerned about what effect science is having on our ability to believe in the metaphysical and what that means for the socially contrived notions of moral values. It is precisely this concern that exists in much of Freud's work concerning the value and role of religion in society.

In this formulation of the death of God we have a future-oriented concern. Freud will take the premise of God's death and work backwards, inverting the concern, so that the death of God becomes the basis for religion and social mores. Beginning with the Nietzschean concern that understanding the primeval conditions that generated society is of paramount importance, Freud interrogates the possibility that God is dead, and we are his murderers, as the foundation of society. From this formulation we get the basis for understanding human society at its core instinctual motivations. In his "untimely meditation" on *Schopenhauer as Educator* Nietzsche writes, 'How can man know himself? He is a thing dark and veiled ... it is a painful and dangerous undertaking thus to tunnel into oneself and to force one's way down into the shaft of one's being by the nearest path.'[10] It is, perhaps, from this point that we can say Freud begins the process of developing a disciplinary psychology in an attempt to answer this fundamental question that has, in the formulation "know thyself," been a philosophical admonishment since Socrates.

3 Building the Foundation

In her attempt to explain the origins of war, Barbara Ehrenreich dismisses Freud's thesis in *Totem and Taboo* as an unfashionable "just-so" hypothetical story, and claims instead to be interested in cultural "antecedents," like hunting, that explain the socio-cultural urge to engage in warfare.[11] This rendering

---

9   Nietzsche, *The Gay Science*, 181. The quotation is drawn from aphorism 125 with the emphasis in the original.
10   Friedrich Nietzsche, *Untimely Meditations*, ed. Daniel Breazeale (Cambridge: Cambridge University Press, 2011), 129.
11   Barbara Ehrenreich, *Blood Rites* (New York: Metropolitan Books, 1997), 21. Curiously, on the same page, she brings Girard's analysis of violence into her discussion of the sacralization of war and says her account is a search for *why* that is the case. Stunningly, as with Freud, she seems to miss the point of Girard's argumentation in *Violence and the Sacred*,

of both Freud's and her project seems to miss a very important point, namely, that Freud is also searching for an antecedent in a plausible fashioning of humanity's formative years. The difference between the two is that Ehrenreich, like many other contemporary theorists that dismiss Freud's work, is seeking an antecedent to warfare in culture, whereas Freud is seeking the antecedent to culture. The importance of accurately framing Freud's project cannot be understated. Not only does he allow for the limitations of his theory and the possibility of future developments that may prove it incorrect, but he begins by centering the mysteriousness of totemism as a way of structuring primitive society and the persistence of taboos as a means for directing individual behavior in the context of a subsequent civilized life. In the preface to the collected volume of essays that comprise *Totem and Taboo,* Freud claims,

> The analysis of taboos is put forward as an assured and exhaustive attempt at the solution of the problem [regarding a lack of focus on the issue]. The investigation of totemism does no more than declare that 'here is what psycho-analysis can at the moment contribute towards elucidating the problem of the totem.' The difference is related to the fact that taboos still exist among us. Though expressed in a negative form and directed towards another subject-matter, they do not differ in their psychological nature from Kant's 'categorical imperative,' which operates in a compulsive fashion and rejects any conscious motives. Totemism, on the contrary, is something alien to our contemporary feelings – a religio-social institution which has been long abandoned as an actuality and replaced by newer forms. It has left only the slightest traces behind it in the religions, manners, and customs of the civilized peoples of to-day and has been subject to far-reaching modifications even among the races over which it still holds sway. The social and technical advances in human history have affected taboos far less than the totem.[12]

---

which is an explanation for the sacralization of war and other types of social violence. To be fair to Ehrenreich, she wants to locate the religious nature of our relationship to war in a context of hunting, and more specifically, being hunted by more able predators, and she may well be correct, but her story is not as compelling as Girard's. Given her breezy dismissal of Freud, I think it is obvious why that is the case.

12   Sigmund Freud, *Totem and Taboo,* ed. James Strachey (New York: W.W. Norton and Company, Inc., 1989), xxviii. I have left the punctuation in Freud's work as it appears in the text.

The oversight in Ehrenreich's work does not diminish the contribution of her scholarship but it does put it in a weaker position than either Freud's or Girard's, precisely because she makes a mistake common to theories of this nature. That is, the assumption that primeval human *communities* are synonymous with human *culture*, which Freud's arguments makes clear is not the case in the story he is trying to tell. Ehrenreich may be on to something important in her argumentation that hunting provides both the necessary skills and technologies to make warfare possible, and she is likely correct that early humans repressed their innate fear of being hunted. However, before we can examine the *sacralization of war* in cultures, as she does, we must examine not only *why* culture exists, but more importantly why *this* type of culture exists – *a culture capable of sacralization in the first place*. To that end Freud remains a vital source for attempting to understand the impulse to form a civilization out of a human community. Freud's analysis of a probable explanation for the organization of society fits him squarely in the tradition of social contract theory and his insights still resonate within contemporary contractarian theories. When we too quickly or too easily brush aside Freud's work on this score the resulting theory is weaker than it could have otherwise been.

By seeking to explain the possible origins of taboos in society, Freud identifies two that seem to be present in every primitive culture: prohibitions against murder and incest. Surely it must be the case that prohibitions existed for individuals in primeval human communities most especially at the level of children's behavior being shaped by the "do's and don'ts" proscribed by their parents. Taboos, as Freud understands them, are significantly different because they rise to a level of societal imposition. He explains, 'taboo is a primeval prohibition forcibly imposed (by some authority) from outside and directed against the most powerful longings to which human beings are subject.'[13] It seems obvious that a society would have a prohibition against murder because without it society would likely self-destruct in a short time. Murder, unlike mere killing, is a specific thing in human society and we, like Freud,

---

13   Freud, *Totem and Taboo*, 44. Again, I have left the punctuation of the text as it appears in the original. Freud will go on to claim, 'Our assertion that taboo originated in a primeval prohibition imposed at one time or other by some external authority is obviously incapable of demonstration' (45). But this is precisely why psychology is helpful in determining a likely explanation for how these prohibitions arose in society. Again, Freud is not insensitive to the reality that this is a pioneering theory and subsequent research and evidence might significantly alter or undermine his theory. But given what psychology had uncovered in the human condition at the time Freud believed he could accurately describe the possible conditions that led to the instantiation of these foundational prohibitions of human civilization.

must wonder why there exists a prohibition against murder that prevails in all cultures. More bluntly, it stands to reason that at some point in the formative history of human society there was an event, a specific act of killing, that was substantially different from other types of killing known to and experienced by early humans such that it changed the way humans understood the act itself and reconfigured their understanding of participation in community.

It is this insight that will lead Freud to formulate what we know as the "founding murder," but what is missing here is the relevance of the other foundational taboo: incest. A prohibition against incest must be linked in some way to prohibition of murder precisely because, like murder, it is common to all cultures. We must be careful when developing such postulates that we do not engage in anachronistic ascriptions of rationale to primitive peoples. This is not to say that they were not capable of rational thought, but rather that they would be unlikely to have had access to the information necessary to inform such judgements. For instance, the realization that inbreeding among animals can produce an enfeeblement of the species over time would have required observations across generations in an agricultural setting, but the prohibition against incest assuredly pre-dates such knowledge, and as such we are obliged to look elsewhere for its roots. On the point of incest, Freud, citing James Frazer, with whom he claims to be in total agreement, says, 'The law only forbids men to do what their instincts incline them to do; what nature itself prohibits and punishes, it would be superfluous for the law to prohibit and punish. Accordingly, we may always safely assume that crimes forbidden by law are crimes which many men have a natural propensity to commit.'[14] Subsequently, we may draw the conclusion that a natural aversion to incest does not exist even if human communities were to discover later that there were *additional* reasons to shun the practice of incest.

Hence, we must again look for an action taking place in a primitive human community that struck the community members as being an egregious violation of belonging to the community; but which is nevertheless understood as deriving from previously accepted or at least tolerated behaviors. Again, more simply, like killing, which must have been well-known to primitive peoples, incest must have been known and experienced, so something specific and unique must have happened to warrant the creation of a taboo at the social level that prohibited it. For Freud, the two taboos can be interpreted as linked. Having fashioned an explanation for the possible origin points of the taboos on murder and incest, Freud puts forward a theory regarding the hypothetical

---

14   Freud, *Totem and Taboo*, 153.

unfolding of events that produced the realization within the community that these taboos were needed.[15]

4 Theorizing an Origin

Although it is often put forward that the individual is the building block of society, in truth, it is the family.[16] This insight was given its most well-known treatment by Jean Jacques Rousseau in the development of his own social contract theory. Generalizing a similar starting point, Freud assumes the existence of a familial unit as the basis of pre-civilized human communities. In Freud's language, this "primal horde" consisted of a dominant male figure (the father), a harem of women taken to wife by this male, and their offspring. In Freud's formulation there is no distinction between methods of acquiring the women of the harem; they could have been traded for, captured, bought, gifted, or matched through a mutual love of each other. How the women came to form the harem is of little interest to Freud, and beyond that, he pays no attention to a hierarchy among the women if, indeed, any existed. The shape of this primaeval family was a patriarchal arrangement and Freud treats the women in this situation primarily as sex-objects, or, more generally, objects of desire.

Because of the dominance of the male figurehead, who possesses all the women, his sons, as they come of age, are prohibited access to the harem.[17] Eventually this arrangement will lead to tension between the father and sons and they will be disinherited; that is, the father will banish them from the family unit. Ostensibly, this decision is one driven by jealousy regarding his

---

15 It is interesting to note here that well before either Nietzsche or Freud, Scottish philosopher David Hume would also utilize parricide and incest as testing grounds for his moral theory and one could, quite easily, draw a direct line between Hume's project and Freud's own work even if Freud never did so himself. See Hume, *A Treatise of Human Nature* (New York: Penguin Books, 1985), 518–521.

16 Freud constructs this narrative in several of his key works addressing issues bound up in the theory of the founding murder. What follows is a recreation of that basic narrative Freud draws upon. Freud provides this narrative in *Totem and Taboo*, *Group Psychology and the Analysis of the Ego*, as well as allusions in *The Future of an Illusion*, and *Civilization and Its Discontents*.

17 Here, by "coming of age," we merely need to acquiesce to the assertion that as the boys matured they would naturally desire the women of the harem and these could include mothers, sisters, aunts, etc., because what is important to Freud's story is that the young men were sexually frustrated by the imposition of the prohibition against having sex with the women in their father's harem. Obviously, as the sons went through puberty, they would naturally be inclined to desire sexual gratification.

women, although there could have been any number of factors at play in the decision; Freud merely postulates that jealousy on one end and desire on the other is sufficient to carry the narrative forward. The sons, having been banished from the safety of the family unit and simultaneously prevented from accessing the women, begin to plot against the father. This conspiracy will ultimately result in the murder and cannibalization of the father and the rape of the harem. This is a rather shocking conceptualization of the origins of human civilization. We might easily, at this juncture, join Ehrenreich in surmising that hunting has provided for the sons both the tools and skills necessary to successfully overthrow the father, but again, Freud's theory is antecedent to any such postulate.

The success of Freud's theory regarding the sons' actions hinges on our willingness to accept such violence on three separate scores: murder, cannibalism, and rape. Why should these be the actions that follow from the sexual frustrations and anger directed at the father? Murdering the father does seem to follow from the conspiratorial impulse of the disinherited sons since the sons would have a need to remove the obstacle preventing them from accessing the women of the harem. Although it does seem obvious that "killing" would have been known to the sons through conflict with other families, extended communities, or through hunting, the act of killing the father would have met the requirements of being unique as an act of killing because it would have transcended other types of killing by virtue of being directed at another member of the family unit. Because the reason driving the sons to act was their desire to possess the women of the harem explicitly (in Freud's formulation) as sex objects following the murder of the father the violence would have culminated in the incestuous rape of the harem, and potentially, the murder of some of the women as well. These two facets of the violence seem to follow from Freud's conceptualization of the founding murder. We are left to address the cannibalism attributed to the sons' savagery.

Cannibalism is a necessary component because it maps onto the subsequent establishment of the totem animal, its sacralization with respect to the family-clan, as well as the subsequent deification of the father. Following Freud, it is entirely possible these early humans were already practicing cannibalism in some form to some extent. As Freud says in his own construction of the fateful event, 'cannibal savages as they were, it goes without saying that they devoured their victim as well as killing him ... in the act of devouring him they accomplished their identification with him'[18] Freud also allows for

---

18   Freud, *Totem and Taboo*, 176.

the fact that cannibalism seems to be the only universally proscribed activity in human society, that is, the only facet of the founding murder scenario that we have fully surmounted, at least to the non-psychoanalytic view.[19] The consumption of the totem animal in primitive cultures referenced by Freud and his contemporaries parallels similar consumption habits in classical society, such as the consumption of sacrificial animals in Dionysian festivals, and, more relevantly perhaps, the consumption of the Eucharist in Christian traditions. Per this relationship between the sacred and its celebration, Freud concludes that cannibalistic tendencies must have been present during the sons' violent unleashing of their frustrated desire along with murder and incestuous rape, elsewise the ability to explain the need to consume the totemic or sacrificial animal is inexplicable.[20]

Only in the aftermath of this orgy of violence are the sons forced to confront the heinousness of their actions. Following this, the two taboos central to the development of human civilization will develop as a method of preventing similar future outcomes. Realizing what they have done, the surviving sons seek to protect themselves from similar violence, both between themselves and from their own future offspring. Slaying the father brings about the taboo on murder as the guilt and remorse experienced by the sons result in the deification of the father, and subsequently his association with a sacred animal whose life will be sacrificed *in memoriam,* thus fixing the totem animal within primitive society as the primary organizing principle of kinship. The taboo on incest will take shape as the cultural force that redirects sexual desire outside and away from the family. However, the family in this context is organized around totemic kinship rather than strict blood relations because the women of the harem were not all blood relations to the sons but rather existed in a matrix resembling a modern conception of an extended family. However, their position in the harem rendered them objects of desire for the sons and as such the taboo developed to prevent a recurrence of the son's violence against the father must account for that larger relationship matrix. Kinship in this arrangement extends to all persons identified with a particular totemic animal, and it

---

19 Freud, *The Future of an Illusion*, 13.
20 It bears noting here in defense of Freud's characterization of early humans that there is, especially today, ample and substantial evidence to support the view early hominids were engaged in cannibalism. However, it also bears noting that these acts were not always carried out as acts of desperately hungry people. Rather, there may have been numerous motivations for the consumption of human flesh. Freud's characterization may strike us as shockingly unsympathetic, but it does, nevertheless, have some truth to it.

is prohibited to kill either the animal or anyone identified with it. Similarly, sexual relationships are prohibited among members of the totemic kin.

Generated within society, then, in the aftermath of this "originary crime," is the foundation for religion and the elevation of prohibitions to social imposition, or law, and human civilization develops along these fault lines. A critical component to Freud's rendering of taboos is that he explicitly denies they are neuroses, and that they are merely representative of neuroses, but rather that by virtue of being social impositions they become substantially different and form the foundational guidelines for the development of civilization.[21] Because the veneration of the father after his murder alters the spiritual landscape of the remaining human community, Freud will later claim that 'man has, as it were, become a kind of prosthetic God.'[22] Here, Freud is referencing the effort that people expend in attempting to overcome their natural limits, but this striving is set in contrast to the divine, which is just a cultural ideal, yet nevertheless acts as a measure for the development of humanity. Put differently, our efforts to overcome nature and bring the earth to heel represent a desire for a "godlike" character. In this insight Girard will pick up the narrative because the desire to be both man and god is the contradiction at the heart of the world.

5   Refinement in Critique

René Girard's first major work, *Deceit, Desire, and the Novel*, is an attempt to refashion Freud's concept of desire at the heart of the founding murder. However, Girard approaches the problem differently by focusing on novelizations of that desire-as-mechanism that exists between two people longing for the same thing. This early work by Girard reconfigures the question of an originary conflict by examining it through the lens of desire first rather than violence. Using novels by Proust, Dostoyevsky, Stendhal, Cervantes, and others, Girard demonstrates that the common thread running through these various stories – and by extension the relationship these storytellers are interested in – is what he will call "triangular desire."

Triangular desire represents a generalization of Freud's theoretical relationship in the primal horde between the father, son, and the women of the harem. Of course, Girard does not make this explicit in his work on these novelists. By generalizing the relationship and reducing it to variables, Girard indicates that

---

21   Freud, *Totem and Taboo*, 89.
22   Freud, *Civilization and Its Discontents*, 89.

the mechanism of desire not only exists but prefigures the ordering principle of social violence. In his theory, Girard implies that we can replace the father with a more general "model" and the son with the non-descript "disciple" while the mother figure who occupied the harem in Freud's theory is reduced to the status of object.[23] Here, however, it is critical to delineate this objectification as not necessarily being sexual in nature; that is, rather than reducing the mother, or female, in Freud's story to a mere sexual object, Girard is replacing the person of the female with *any* object of desire. By shifting the focus of Freud's psychoanalytic theory to these more general terms, Girard can showcase how the relationship of triangular desire occupies the center of human relationships.[24]

Girard highlights this in each of the novels he examines, and while it is not necessary to examine each in turn here, it is important to note that in his critical analysis of these novels, Girard does tease out the elements of what will become his theory of mimetic desire. By generalizing the agents in the theory of triangular desire, Girard is able to update Freud's theory without having to entangle himself in the arguments surrounding applications of psychoanalytic theory to literature. Avoiding these entanglements allows Girard to point out that the same literary device is present in these various stories relying on different objects to generate an eerily similar interpersonal development between the main characters of a given tale: the model and disciple. Girard claims the relationship between model and disciple begins when the disciple surrenders the fundamental prerogative of the individual, namely, to choose that which they desire.[25] Allowing someone else to determine what we will desire places us in a triangular relationship with that person – real or imagined; Girard goes a step further than this and argues that the mediator's desire for the object may also be imagined. Therefore, it is possible to enter a triangular relationship

---

23 At this point in the development of his theory, Girard also uses the terms "mediator" and "subject" interchangeably with "model" and "disciple" respectively.

24 It is interesting that Girard only mentions Freud once in the entirety of *Deceit, Desire, and the Novel* (Baltimore, MD: The John Hopkins University Press, 1976), and then only in a footnote that acknowledges the correctness of critiques of psychoanalysis from a literary criticism perspective, but also, attempts to salvage Freud's theories about Oedipus at the same time. For instance, Girard claims, 'Attempts to dismiss literature through a summary psychoanalytic diagnosis have been justly ridiculed. But these attempts were not representative of the best psychoanalytic thought. From a Freudian viewpoint, the original triangle of desire is, of course, the Oedipal triangle. The story of "mediated" desire is the story of this Oedipal desire, of its essential permanence beyond its ever changing (sic) objects ... One of the tasks facing criticism is the establishment of a genuine dialogue with Freud.' (186–87).

25 Girard, *Deceit*, 1.

wherein the model and their desire are both imagined, but the effects of mimesis are no less real as a result.

A fundamental shift away from Freud becomes immediately apparent in Girard's formulation of the triangular relationship. Girard explains, 'The triangle is no *Gestalt*. The real structures are intersubjective. They cannot be localized anywhere; the triangle has no reality whatever; it is a systematic metaphor, systematically pursued.'[26] That shift is the move away from something mechanical and potentially logical residing concretely within human relationships toward something that is apprehendable, but primarily metaphysical in nature. Triangular desire transforms the object in the tension created between the model and disciple. This transformation makes the object seem concrete, but in reality, it is an abstraction, we might identify it as an existential longing: love, power, chivalry, vanity, reputation, and so on. What is central for Girard in this formulation is that the disciple *does not choose* the objects of their desire but has them implanted in them by the model *whom they do freely choose*.

The model mediates desire for the disciple by indicating *what* is desirable and also stipulating *why* it is desirable. By desiring the same thing and striving to acquire it through similar means, the identity between the two rivals – model and disciple – becomes harder to distinguish. The important distinction made here by Girard is that the model may or may not *actually* want the object in question, but the disciple does want the object but *as a means* for accessing, or becoming, like the model. He stipulates, 'The mediator's prestige is imparted to the object of desire and confers upon it an illusory value.'[27] Subsequently, Girard clarifies, 'The object is only a means of reaching the mediator. The desire is aimed at the mediator's *being*.'[28] At this point in his analysis of triangular desire, Girard has all the component pieces necessary to give a fuller, more complete, account of Freud's founding murder narrative. Having already recognized the need for a serious engagement with Freudian theory, in his next major work, *Violence and the Sacred*, Girard sets out to do just that.[29]

When Girard turns his attention to Freud, he positions his own theoretical commitments to mimesis outside the scope of Freud's psychoanalytic origin point by approaching the problem of founding-murder-as-social-beginning by examining numerous mythologies. Girard contends, '[a]nger is never without antecedents; it is always preceded and determined by an initial outburst.

---

26   Girard, *Deceit*, 2. Emphasis in the original.
27   Girard, *Deceit*, 17.
28   Girard, *Deceit*, 53. Emphasis in the original.
29   See footnote 23 above.

Even that initial anger is never truly the original anger. In the domain of impure violence, any search for origins leads back to myth.'[30] By analyzing various myths, Girard is able to demonstrate that Freud's initial hypothesis, rooted in psychoanalytic assumptions, does bear out in the origin stories cultures tell about themselves much as it does in the novels he focused on in *Deceit, Desire and the Novel*. Girard's operating assumption here, much like Freud's, is that society originated from a violent act. Where Freud must stipulate this as a function of his psychoanalytic investigations, Girard demonstrates it by showing that the origin stories of cultures are built around a violence that stems from the triangulation of desire: mimetic violence as a rupture that occurs between two individuals locked in a model-and-disciple relationship oriented toward a particular object. The important thing to remember here is that the characters of the myth and the object of their desire may prove to be fanciful inventions, but the story they are created to tell is one of the utmost and serious consequences.

One may, for example, consider the following narrative as exemplary of a Girardian interpretation of how mimesis develops in a relationship. A father and son are surveying a pasture populated by various horses. The father prefers a particular type of horse – size, build, certain number of hands high, etc. – and in his evaluation of the available horses he teaches his son how to distinguish a desirable horse from the less desirable one. Over time, the son learns to evaluate horses in just this way, and, as he matures in the tribe or clan, he finds himself in competition with his father for the very same horses. If one's prestige in the community is linked to one's prowess as a warrior, or hunter, or horseman, then the son's desire to imitate his father morphs, via the competition for particular horses, into rivalry. The son no longer wants to merely imitate his father but to supplant him, to overtake him, and, in doing so, by cultivating his desire on this score, will eventually find himself, his father, and their mutual desires locked into a triangular mimetic struggle that will, eventually, turn violent. Girard notes that humans, unlike all the other animals, lack a critical breaking mechanism where violence is concerned and, so, we may confidently assume the violence between the rivals will become deadly at some point.

While Freud's theory is limited in its ability to tell such a story precisely because Freud is determined to make the mother and father figures central to his theory, he has nevertheless developed the structural components

---

30   René Girard, *Violence and the Sacred* (Baltimore, MD: The John Hopkins University Press, 1979), 69.

necessary for Girard's theory to develop. More importantly, while Girard can explain a relationship like the one above, he can also more convincingly tell Freud's story while preserving Freud's initial penetrating insights. Girard does not abandon Freud or Freud's core ideas regarding the mimetic relationship. Rather, highlighting Freud's attraction to the Oedipus story as exemplary of his theory, Girard claims, 'the admirable thing about Freud is his refusal ever to renounce anything.'[31] 'It is hopeless,' he continues,

> to attempt to isolate the three elements of mimetic desire: identification, choice of object, and rivalry. That Freud's thought was never free of the influence of mimetic preoccupations can be proved by the irresistible conjunction of these three elements; wherever any one of them appears, the other two are sure to follow.[32]

What is clear in Girard's approach to mimetic desire and violence is that he is not trying to disprove Freud's theory nor is he trying to develop a competing theory parallel to Freud's own speculations on the matter. Rather, Girard is clearly attempting to refine and develop Freud's ideas in such a way that Freud's theory remains integral to the ability of mimesis to articulate how society is organized. If Girard's theory is recognizably an intentional extension of Freud's theory, then it is reasonable to assert that Freud's continuing relevance to critical theory is embodied in Girard's obvious importance to critical theory.

6   Final Thoughts

Although Girard's work will continue to refine and develop his own mimetic theory by adding key details, new concepts, and demonstrations of the vitality of his ideas via the application of his analysis to increasingly varied myths, stories, and historical events, he never abandons his theoretical inheritance from Freud. It is also the case that he does not try to diminish the importance of understanding Freud's theory as a necessity for a deep and thorough understanding of his own mimetic ideas. By attempting to develop a non-hypothetical approach for articulating how civilization developed as an organizing principle, Freud created the possibility of using a critical approach

---

31   Girard, *Violence and the Sacred*, 180.
32   Ibid.

to social problems that not only makes it possible to analyze these issues in important and relevant ways, but also allows us to consider new ways of addressing societal ills. As both Freud and Girard make clear in their diagnosis of society, if we want to address systemic or institutional problems we have to begin by asking *why* these systemic problems and institutions exist and *why they exist in just the way they do*, before we can adequately, or successfully, begin to redress the problems they generate, buffer, and perpetuate in society today.

Freud and Girard have developed a theoretical framework that makes it possible to reevaluate approaches to justice, religion, marriage, economics, entertainment, and other areas of our social life that are designed to alleviate the pressures of mimesis, redirect our desires to avoid mimetic struggles, or adjudicate the fallout of mimetic rivalry. How we do this is still, in many ways, and further, in many important ways, still an open question. Girard has pushed Freud in new directions and to new heights of relevance for critical analysis, but Girard is not without his own problems, pitfalls, and shortcomings. As such, there remains work to be done both on refining Girard's mimetic theory and in developing Girard's ideas so that they are more easily and accurately applied to a critical analysis of society especially as a way of identifying potential solutions to contemporary problems. Yet, it remains true that our ability to do this requires that we have a robust understanding of Freud's original insights and, as such, it is clear that Freud remains a central figure in developing, using, and understanding critical social theory today.

Bibliography

Ehrenreich, Barbara. *Blood Rites.* New York: Metropolitan Books, 1997.
Freud, Sigmund. *Totem and Taboo*, edited by James Strachey. New York: W.W. Norton and Company, Inc., 1989.
Girard, René. *Deceit, Desire, and the Novel.* Baltimore, MD: The John Hopkins University Press, 1976.
Girard, René. *Violence and the Sacred.* Baltimore, MD: The John Hopkins University Press, 1979.
Hume, David. *A Treatise of Human Nature.* New York: Penguin Books, 1985.
Jones, Clint. *A Genealogy of Social Violence: Founding Murder, Rawlsian Fairness, and the Future of the Family.* Burlington, VT: Ashgate Publishing, 2013.
Nietzsche, Friedrich. *Daybreak*, edited by Maudemarie Clark and Brian Leiter. Cambridge: Cambridge University Press, 2011.

Nietzsche, Friedrich. *The Gay Science*. Translated by Walter Kaufmann. New York: Vintage Books, 1974.

Nietzsche, Friedrich. *Untimely Meditations*, edited by Daniel Breazeale. Cambridge: Cambridge University Press, 2011.

Schacht, Richard. "Introduction." In Friedrich Nietzsche, *Human, All Too Human*. Translated by R.J. Hollingdale. Cambridge: Cambridge University Press, 1996.

PART 6

Freud, Neo-freudians, and Beyond

∴

CHAPTER 15

Psychoanalysis and the American Intellectual

Eli Zaretsky

1 Introduction

What do we mean when we speak about the American intellectual? Can we even speak of intellectuals in a democratic society in which, as Gramsci taught us, everyone is an intellectual? Are intellectuals a critical force, for example, in relation to capitalism? Above all, can we frame the problem of the American intellectual historically, so that we can illuminate the situation of the intellectual today?

Understanding the intense although sometimes fraught relations between American intellectuals and psychoanalysis, especially between the 1920s and the 1970s, provides a vantage point to at least begin to address these questions. To be sure, Freudianism was not the dominant outlook among intellectuals in those years; that honor belongs to pragmatism, when considered broadly to take in the social sciences, jurisprudence, and philosophy. Nor was Freudianism typically part of the "adversary culture" of the period, which was rooted in Marxism and other forms of leftism, and which was generally skeptical of psychoanalysis. Nonetheless, for many, as I will show, Freudianism was a prominent part of their intellectual vocation, shedding light on intellectuals more broadly.

Correspondingly, situating American psychoanalysis in the context of the history of intellectuals opens a path for understanding the peculiarities of American psychoanalysis. Freudianism was embraced by American intellectuals with a passion and near-unanimity that the intellectuals of very few other countries shared. Yet after a few decades it was rejected with an even greater passion, and as the carrier of the very same societal malignancy – Puritanism – the intellectuals had imported it to cure. A flip flop of that magnitude cries out for an explanatory historical frame, which the broader history of the US intellectual may supply.

By an intellectual I mean an individual who employs symbols of general scope and abstract reference to a significantly greater degree than is required in practical life. In my view, an intellectual should never be considered alone but only in relation to society, or to relevant social groups, such as academia, the scientific community, or the public. Is there a general model for describing the relations of intellectuals to society in the modern world? In this paper I will propose such a model for the United States, using psychoanalysis as a test case.

In his *Group Psychology,* Freud provided a suggestive starting point, albeit substituting the poet for the intellectual. In "The Group and the Primal Horde," he wrote, 'no impulses whatever came into existence except collective ones; there was only a common will, there were no single ones.'[1] The murder of the father led to an 'advance from group psychology to individual psychology.' In the era that followed,

> some individual, in the exigency of his longing, [i.e., for the primal father] may have been moved to free himself from the group and take over the father's part. He who did this was the first epic poet; and the advance was achieved in his imagination ... The poet who had taken this step and had in this way set himself free from the group in his imagination, is nevertheless able ... to find his way back to it in reality. For he goes and relates to the group his hero's deeds which he has invented.[2]

Freud's "scientific myth" suggests that wish-fulfillment and identification play an important role in the relations between the intellectuals and the group, but it neglects the conflictual aspects of the relationship. We can see the problems of maintaining a "philosophic" life in the ancient world (which does not seem to have had the concept of "the intellectual") in the case of Socrates. Athens, then a democratic society, put Socrates to death. His student, Plato, wrote *The Republic* to investigate whether it was even possible for philosophy to survive in the polis. While the modern intellectual has many sources, historians often ascribe the birth of the modern intellectual to the Dreyfus Affair (1894–1906). The reason is that while there were intellectuals on both the nationalist and the liberal sides of the question of the captain's guilt or innocence, "the intellectual" was someone who stood up to physical bullying, crowd intimidation, or the loss of livelihood, i.e., the Dreyfusard. Edward Said took this point one step further when he claimed that the "true intellectual" is 'always an outsider, living in self-imposed exile, and on the margins of society.'[3] This, however, goes too far. It was not even true of Said, much less of all intellectuals.

---

1 Sigmund Freud, "The Group and the Primal Horde," in *Group Psychology and the Analysis of the Ego* (New York: Boni and Liveright, 1922), 91.
2 Freud, *Group Psychology,* 112–113.
3 See Jeremy Jennings and Tony Kemp-Welch, "The Century of the Intellectual: From Dreyfus to Salman Rushdie," in *Intellectuals in Politics: From the Dreyfus Affair to Salman Rushdie* (London: Routledge, 1997), 100–110.

In modern America, the most important factor mediating the relation between intellectuals and society may well be capitalism. Antonio Gramsci distinguished between traditional intellectuals, such as writers or clergymen, who were integral to such institutions as the church or the court, and organic intellectuals, such as engineers, copywriters, or schoolteachers, who are integral to the capitalist system.[4] The role of the traditional intellectual was to supply cultural legitimacy to power, although many traditional intellectuals were critics or heretics. The organic intellectuals, by contrast, emerged because knowledge and the manipulation of symbols had become forces of production. While Gramsci's distinction between traditional and organic is helpful, I would not necessarily call a person performing a specialized function under capitalism an intellectual. There are many working-class intellectuals, and most managers, engineers, and accountants, not to mention academics, are not intellectuals. The intellectual component in my view transcends or exceeds the societal function.

With these considerations behind us, the model for the relations of psychoanalysis I have in mind for American intellectuals in their experience of psychoanalysis is based on Puritanism. By Gramsci's definition, the Puritans were traditional intellectuals, but they were also modern if not "organic," in their focus on freedom. In Perry Miller's words:

> [The Puritans] were endeavoring to mark off an area of human behavior from the general realm of nature, and within it to substitute for the rule of necessity a rule of freedom. They were striving to push as far into the background as possible the order of things that exists by inevitable equilibrium, that is fulfilled by unconscious and aimless motions, that is determined by inertia and inexorable law, and in its place set up an order founded by voluntary choice, upon the deliberate assumption of obligation, upon unconstrained pacts, upon the sovereign determinations of free will.[5]

The Puritans were, in fact, the first American intellectuals of any sort, and Miller took them as his paradigm for American intellectuals.

The Puritan precedent does indeed have great consequences for the idea of the intellectual. In the medieval church, one gained salvation through the

---

4 Antonio Gramsci, *The Antonio Gramsci Reader: Selected Writings 1916–1935*, ed. David Forgacs (New York: New York University Press, 2000), 300–322.
5 Perry Miller, *The New England Mind: The Seventeenth Century* (Cambridge, MA: Harvard University Press, 1939/1953), 398–399.

church, and especially through good works as recognized by the church. For the Calvinist wing of the Reformation, by contrast, salvation and damnation were predestined; therefore, one's fate could not be known though empirical observation. It could only be discerned through a personal reckoning, which required self-scrutiny, interpretation, and scrupulous honesty. In pursuing this path, Puritans rejected not only intuition but all direct, unmediated responses to stimuli. No event, no matter how powerful – not sexual love, not the death of a child, not the sight of a flower – should provoke a direct response. Rather, experience had to be "weaned" – attenuated so it could be understood in the context of God's will. Accordingly, the Puritans rejected both external, behaviorist solutions to the problem of salvation, on the one hand, and solutions based on direct experience or inner conviction, on the other.

This established a difficult standard for the Puritan, and for the intellectuals that followed in their path. Max Weber spoke of the "deep spiritual isolation" of the Puritans. Referring to predestination, Weber wrote: 'In what was for the man of the age of the Reformation the most important thing in life, his eternal salvation, he was forced to follow his path alone to meet a destiny which had been decreed for him from eternity.'[6] The Puritans were defending an unfamiliar, stringent, and difficult practice even as they were deeply engaged with the masses, especially through education, religion. and politics. Not surprisingly, they faced strong "resistances" to their message. These resistances took two different forms.

---

6   Max Weber, *The Protestant Ethic and the Spirit of Capitalism* (New York: Routledge, 1992). Weber's essay was originally published as a two-part article in 1904–1905 in the *Archiv für Sozialwissenschaft und Sozialpolitik*, of which Weber was an editor. A revised version appeared as the opening study in Weber's *Gessamelte Aufsätze zur Religionssoziologie* (Collected Essays on the Sociology of Religion) published in 1920–21, just after Weber's death. In 1930 Talcott Parsons translated the latter version, along with the introduction to the *Gessamelte Aufsätze,* and this remains the authoritative English version. A second essay of Weber's, "The Protestant Sects and the Spirit of Capitalism," largely devoted to the relations of Protestantism and capitalism in the United States, is often included in discussions of Weber's thesis. It can be found in Hans Gerth and C. Wright Mills, *From Max Weber: Essays in Sociology* (New York: Oxford University Press, 1946). The page numbers in the text and all other references are to the Routledge 1992 republication of Parsons's translation. It is also worth noting that Weber's thesis is among the most commented upon, and the most controversial, in the history of social science. Social theorists who have engaged importantly with it include Robert Bellah, Clifford Geertz, Michael Walzer, Robert Merton, Daniel Bell, Jürgen Habermas, and Erich Fromm. Historians include Henri See, Richard Tawney, Christopher Hill, Henri Pirenne, Perry Miller, E. P. Thompson, Eric Hobsbawm, and Le Roi Ladurie. I will not enter into the many controversies surrounding it here.

The first was Arminianism, which returned to the original belief that Protestantism had rebelled against, namely, salvation through works. The growth of the market, as early as the first half of the seventeenth century, encouraged Arminianism since the rich naturally wanted to be seen as saved, and to be leaders within the churches as well as in society at large. By the 1660s, church membership was determined by the "halfway covenant," which allowed individuals to enter the church by virtue of birth, without evidence that they had been saved. Since economic success was taken as a sign of salvation, this expedience quickly led New England to be governed by inherited wealth. Eventually, Arminianism, expressed in such ideologies as the "self-made man," the "can-do spirit," and America's self-definition as a "land of opportunity," replaced the Puritan idea of a calling because it converged with the American preoccupation with economic life. In this form, Arminianism was a successor to Max Weber's original Protestant Ethic (as Weber showed in his analysis of Benjamin Franklin's autobiography).[7]

The second form that resistance took was antinomianism, the claim to know God through direct experience. Given the anxieties associated both with Puritanism, and with the success ethic that succeeded it, the country veered regularly into antinomian periods, "Great Awakenings," radical upsurges, and periods of communal aspiration that renewed and revised the Arminian tradition, feeding it, so to speak, from the well of primary narcissism. As with Arminianism, antinomianism caught individuals up in a powerful group process, but also covered over the narrow path the Puritans had opened between "gut" feeling, on the one hand, and behaviorism, on the other. By the time of the American Revolution, if not much earlier, the original Puritan impulse was spent. However, the Puritan moment cast a shadow over the country's identity, in the form of a collective ego ideal or super-ego, so that even centuries later, when psychoanalysis was imported to the US, there was an uncanny sense of repetition. The narrow path seemed unblocked again, but the warnings and criticisms that lined it also loomed.

The Puritans, then, created a template for American intellectuals. The path of the intellectual – I will call it sublimation – was a narrow one, ultimately resting on disciplined self-knowledge, especially when devoted to psychological, social, and cultural questions. Once on that path, the intellectual was menaced from two sides. On one side, stood supposedly free-standing, objective methods that could guarantee the success of ideas such as falsifiability, operationalism, pragmatism, the cash value of an idea (William James), behaviorism,

---

7   See Chapter II, "The Spirit of Capitalism," in *The Protestant Ethic*.

quantification, or probability. On the other side, stood the regression to primary narcissism or to mysticism, as in transcendentalism, the reliance on intuition, the mass psychology of nationalism, or "gut feeling." This template was well-established by the 1920s, when psychoanalysis exploded among US intellectuals.

There is a coda to this template: Freud described the difficulty of achieving insight, which is the therapeutic counterpart to intellectuality, as "resistance," which meant both the individual's resistance to being cured, and societal resistance to psychoanalytic ideas. But what is the source of the resistance to intellectuality? A problem arises from the pressure or the demands of something inexpedient, something 'running counter to the flow of life,' according to Freud.[8] At the same time, we build up defenses, "under the sway of preferences deeply rooted within," which complicate, supplement and otherwise infect the problem.[9] The resistance doesn't come from the original pressure or demands. Rather it comes from the defenses, which are centered in the higher strata of the mind, i.e., the intellectual strata, and, in society, among the intellectuals themselves. The same forces that make the intellectual also block him or her.

2 Freud

Like Puritanism, the original Freudianism was neither pragmatic nor results-oriented, as an Arminian approach would have demanded; nor did it rest content with releasing the instincts from excessive, "civilized" demands, as antinomianism would have urged. Rather Freud counseled *sublimating* the instincts. Sublimation, for Freud, required "abstinence" (a favorite term, echoing the Puritan "weaned") or delayed gratification in order to transform sexual and aggressive energies into desexualized insight or non-instrumentalized rationality.

While Freud's emphasis on abstinence or sublimation was present in his work from the first, it increased when he came to realize how easily the analytic process could be subverted. In 1910, Freud condemned the anarchist Otto Gross, a forerunner of Wilhelm Reich, for reducing psychoanalysis to instinctual release. In this Freud agreed with Max Weber, who scorned Gross's

---

8 Sigmund Freud, "Civilization and Its Discontents," in *The Standard Edition of the Complete Psychological Works of Sigmund Freud,* ed. and trans. James Strachey (New York: Norton, 1976), 21:85, 101.

9 Sigmund Freud, *Beyond the Pleasure Principle,* in Pelican Freud Library, Vol. 11 (London: Penguin, 1984), 333.

"psychiatric ethic": 'admit to yourself what you are like and what you desire.'[10] It was especially World War I that led Freud "beyond the pleasure principle," in other words, beyond the striving for instinctual release. That "beyond" is reflected in his postwar distinction between the id, which does indeed strive for the release of buried instincts, impulses, and memories, and the ego, which defers or resists that release, sometimes for defensive or "neurotic" reasons – i.e., to serve the resistance – but also, sometimes, to turn instinctual energies toward self-knowledge. Freud's slogan, "Where id was there shall be ego," can be restated as, "Where release was, there shall be sublimation."[11]

The reason Freud was invited to Clark University in 1909 was that he was seen as an opponent of the great, antinomian upsurge that had erupted in the 1890s along with consumerism and urban life. Interest in "mind cure," "New Thought," "mental science," and Christian Science had grown exponentially, while the highly influential Emmanuel movement, founded in 1906, brought together dissenting doctors, clergy, and lay reformers in pursuit of what William James called an "anti-moralistic" method: release from the demands of that unceasing clockwork, the super-ego. Freud's hosts, far from partaking in this therapeutic of release, with its affinity to the lower classes and to a dawning mass culture, hoped Freud would counter antinomianism through supposedly scientific behaviorist techniques. In other words, they were Arminians, who wanted to harness psychoanalysis to the project of social control.

Heirs to the Arminian Puritans, New England Progressives, such as G. Stanley Hall and James Jackson Putnam, wanted to take psychotherapy out of the hands of "un-credentialed, female amateurs" and build what Harvard psychologist Hugo Munsterberg called 'a conscious social program of symbol-building and communal reintegration led by professionals.'[12] Putnam was typical in this respect. He did not believe that individuals could change for the sake of insight alone. Instead, he wanted psychoanalysts to introduce a transcendental, i.e., Kantian/Emersonian ethic into their practice. Ironically, then the first American Freudians were advocates of sublimation in the sense of a "higher" level of ethical behavior on the part of immigrants and a burgeoning working

---

10 Max Weber, *Max Weber: Selections in Translation*, ed. W. G. Runciman, trans. Eric Matthews, (New York: Cambridge University Press, 1978), 383ff. See also Marianne Weber, *Max Weber: A Biography* (New York: Wiley, 1975), 375ff.
11 See the discussion in Freud, "The Ego and the Id," in *The Standard Edition*, 19:18.
12 Hugo Munsterberg, *Psychotherapy* (New York: Moffat, Yard and Co., 1909), x; Nathan G. Hale, *Freud and the Americans* (New York: Oxford University Press, 1971), 127, 140. Munsterberg himself was an opponent of psychoanalysis, but the general point holds.

class. That was sublimation in the sense of uplift, as a Victorian like Matthew Arnold understood it, but not what Freud meant at all.

The narrow caste of Harvard professors, reformers, and doctors who invited Freud to Clark were traditional intellectuals, meaning clergy, college professors, and doctors, promoting the Calvinist values of domesticity, propriety, and hard work even as mass consumption was dawning. In contrast, the young intellectuals of the twenties who first embraced Freudianism were organic intellectuals in the sense that they were performing newly specialized social functions integral to the capitalist mode of production as it was entering its mass consumption phase: in other words, managers, technicians and engineers, social workers and supervisory personnel, salesmen, advertisers, and public relations specialists. By the twenties, this class had spawned a "culture industry," which included what Gilbert Seldes called in 1924 the "seven lively arts": film, radio, popular music, and comics among them.[13] Unlike the traditional intellectuals, the organic intellectuals of the twenties emerged amid a torrential onrush of commercialism, mass culture, and mass politics, all aimed at gratification and release.

Christopher Lasch termed the organic intellectuals of the 1920s "the new radicalism in America."[14] What was new about this radicalism was its social basis, which I've called personal life, the experience of having an identity distinct from one's place in the family or in the social division of labor. In one sense, the possibility of having a "personal life" is a universal aspect of human life, but that is not the sense I have in mind. Rather, I mean an historically specific experience of singularity and interiority, sociologically grounded in industrialization, urbanization, and the history of the family.

Previously, the family was the primary locus of production and reproduction; as a result, the individual's sense of identity was rooted in the family. In the nineteenth century, however, the separation (both physical and emotional) of paid work from the household, which is to say the rise of industrial capitalism, gave rise to new forms of privacy, domesticity, and intimacy. At first, these were experienced as the familial counterparts to the impersonal world of the market. Later, they became associated with the possibility and goal of a personal life distinct from and even outside of the family. Personal identity became a problem and a project for individuals, as opposed to something given to them by their place in the family or the society. Psychoanalysis was a theory and practice of this new aspiration for a personal life. Its original historical telos

---

13 Gilbert Seldes, *The Seven Lively Arts* (New York: Harper & Bros, 1924).
14 Christopher Lasch, *The New Radicalism in America* (New York: Knopf, 1965).

was "defamilialization," the freeing of individuals from unconscious images of authority originally rooted in the family.

Personal life was the social basis for the intellectual's retrieval of the project of disciplined introspection of sublimation. This can be seen through the effects of Freudianism on the Progressive movement (1890–1917). Progressivism had three core ideals: the Enlightenment ideal of the independent, "objective," bipartisan, informed, public-spirited citizen; the Protestant ethic of self-restraint and diligence; and the public/private division, which assigned to women moral responsibility and high cultural value. All three ideals were rendered obsolete by the social transformations of World War I, while Freudianism supplied an alternative.

First, the Great War undercut the ideal of the rational citizen by demonstrating the power of propaganda, the ease with which democratic liberties were suspended, and the near-futility of rational will-formation, especially in the face of war. Freudianism became important because of its insights into mass irrationality. Second, the expansion of mass production capitalism undercut the Protestant ethic, by fostering spending instead of saving, and the release of labor from direct engagement in material production. Freudianism encouraged a new spirit of capitalism, in other words based on a healthy narcissism as opposed to asceticism, disciplined introspection as opposed to compulsivity, and directness as opposed to hypocrisy. Finally, the cult of true womanhood and gentility gave way to the Freudian emphasis on sexuality and the unconscious. This was a true Copernican revolution, leading to the view that every individual, regardless of race or gender, was the site of a unique, idiosyncratic intra-psychic life characterized by what Freud called his or her 'special individuality in the exercise of the capacity to love.'[15]

Behind the enthusiasm for Freudianism lay the debate among American intellectuals concerning their place in the nation. Van Wyck Brooks's *America's Coming of Age* (1915), which coined the expressions "highbrow" and "lowbrow," was central in precipitating this debate. According to Brooks, the center of gravity in American life was shifting 'from the plane of politics to the plane of psychology and morals.' Emerson's 'really equivocal individualism,' Brooks elaborated, 'asserted the freedom and self-reliance of the spirit as easily as of the business man.'[16] Waldo Frank's 1919 *Our America* restated Brooks' critique in

---

15 Sigmund Freud, "The Dynamics of Transference," in *The Standard Edition of the Complete Psychological Works of Sigmund Freud*, ed. and trans. James Strachey, in collaboration with Anna Freud, assisted by Alix Strachey and Alan Tyson (New York: Norton, 1976), 12:99. I have followed the translation in Philip Rieff, ed., *Sigmund Freud: Collected Papers* (New York: Collier, 1963).

16 Brooks Van Wyck, *America's Coming of Age* (New York: B.W. Huebsch, 1915), 168, 45.

Freudian terms. American life, Frank argued, had been characterized by "endless exteriorization," meaning labor and self-denial. 'Whole departments of psychic life had been repressed, categories of desire inhibited, reaches of consciousness lopped off.'[17] The inner life, which alone could sustain an intellectual and artistic culture, had been neglected in favor of a vacuous Emersonian "oversoul." Here was not only a call for sublimation in its Freudian sense, but a welding of the intellectuals to the cause of the American nation.

The "new radicalism" drew on Freud to radicalize two related areas of life: the family and culture. The traditional view of the family as a private sphere, a "haven in a heartless world," associated it with the "higher things of life."[18] Freudianism, the avatar of personal life, encouraged a youth revolt, a loosened attitude toward sexuality, bobbed hair, short skirts, and jazz, which supplied a foil to the genteel tradition. The Freudian "new woman," who rebelled against her Victorian and Progressive predecessor by forthrightly claiming her sexuality was in the vanguard of the change associated with personal life. New women, like Rheta Childe Dorr, stopped reading Charlotte Gilman, and turned to Margaret Sanger's writings on birth control and Marie Stopes's manual, *Married Love,* which extolled heterosexual love. The flapper, the *New York Times* enthused in 1922, could 'take a man's view as her mother never could.'[19] That men revolted against their fathers was not new, but that women would turn to men to free themselves from overbearing, "smothering," and sexually policing mothers was.

Closely related to the change in the family were the "New Negroes" of the 1920s, who based their claim to equality on the production of culture (i.e., music, literature, painting, sculpture, dance, and the like). While the anthropological usage of the term "culture" dates back to the nineteenth century, Freudianism gave the 1920s usage its connotation of internal depth and its grounding in a theory of the unconscious mind as linguistic, stratified, and polychronic. In 1965, Lionel Trilling described the new, Freudian-inflected idea of culture,

> The idea of culture, in the modern sense of the word, is a relatively new idea. It represents a way of thinking about our life in society which developed concomitantly with certain new ways of conceiving of the self. Indeed, our modern idea of culture may be thought of as a new sort of

---

17   Waldo David Frank, *Our America* (New York: Boni and Liveright, 1919), 45, 19.
18   "Haven in a heartless world" borrowed from the title of Christopher Lasch's 1977 book.
19   *New York Times,* July 16, 1922, quoted in Ann Douglas, *Terrible Honesty: Mongrel Manhattan in the 1920s* (New York: Farrar, Straus and Giroux, 1995), 245–247.

selfhood bestowed upon the whole of society. [Indeed,] the unconscious of society may be said to have been imagined before the unconscious of the individual.[20]

Around this new idea, Freudian intellectuals transformed literary criticism, cultural anthropology, advertising, film, celebrity culture, office psychotherapy, the stream of consciousness novel, experimental theatre, and the idea of a sexual revolution. They encouraged the move away from mimetic descriptions of social reality and toward the associative flux of symbols and images unfolding within the individual consciousness. They sanctioned "primitivism," which linked the magical power of sculpture in Oceania and Africa with an awareness of the power of the sexuality and the instincts. Whereas this insight had led the Progressives to a racist politics, the "New Negro" of the 1920s associated Afro-American distinctiveness with dignity and a refusal to submit to Jim Crow.

Nevertheless, most intellectuals resisted the difficult analytic ideal of sublimation, seeing it as an obstacle to their real goal: personal liberation. In 1928, Margaret Mead's *Coming of Age in Samoa* largely invented today's ideal of cultural pluralism, by devising what became the widespread charge that Freudianism was culture-blind. The extended Samoan family, Mead explained, 'seems to ensure the child against the development of the crippling attitudes which have been labelled Oedipus complexes, Electra complexes, and so on.'[21] Mead went further by redefining the meaning of the cultural revolution of the 1920s, not in terms of sublimation, but in terms of diversity and the recognition of difference. The value of learning about different cultures, she argued as World War II approached, is that it teaches us that cultures cannot be judged by a single standard. This lesson was especially valuable for a "multicultural" society like the United States. What 'America needed most,' she later added, was '"education for choice," preparing its young ones to recognize and embrace the unprecedented varieties of lifestyles available to them.' By 'accepting the downfall of a single standard,' and educating for choice, we will achieve 'the highpoint of individual choice and universal toleration which a heterogeneous culture alone can attain.'[22]

---

20   Lionel Trilling's definition of culture appears in *Freud and the Crisis of Our Culture* (Boston: Beacon Press, 1955), 34–35.
21   Maureen Molloy, *On Creating a Usable Culture: Margaret Mead and the Emergence of American Cosmopolitanism* (Honolulu: University of Hawaii Press, 2008), 64.
22   Peter Mandler, *Return from the Natives: How Margaret Mead Won the Second World War and Lost the Cold War* (New Haven: Yale University Press, 2013), 12.

With the Depression, American intellectuals moved to the Left. In 1966, Lionel Trilling wrote, 'the importance of the radical movement of the thirties cannot be overestimated. It may be said to have created the American intellectual class as we now know it in its great size and influence.'[23] This did not mean that psychoanalysis faded. The significance of the concept of personal life, as opposed to such concepts as "modernity," "the culture of the new," or "post-traditional" society, was that it tied individual freedom to capitalism, both as enabling condition and as an obstacle to freedom. Personal life was the complement to alienated labor, even as it also pointed beyond it. Hence, in the late thirties and during World War II, many intellectuals espoused the formula of Marx *and* Freud. Accordingly, psychoanalysis became integrated into a wide discourse concerning the preconditions for democratic society in such areas as family life, education, and political culture. Increasingly, psychoanalysis became Arminian, as Freud's hosts at Clark University had wished. Even so, the narrow path of sublimation did not disappear. In 1939 and 1953, the Puritans were reinterpreted, not as the iron guard of repression but as the pioneers of sublimation in Perry Miller's *The New England Mind*. Miller called special attention to the Puritan appreciation of the snares of narcissism, which Miller termed "self-hood."[24]

That the problem of maintaining the ideals of sublimation and disciplined introspection was not restricted to America, was apparent in Freud's last completed book, *Moses and Monotheism* (1939). There he used the transformation of Judaism into Christianity to illustrate the dilution and vulgarization that occurs when a difficult elite doctrine assumes a popular form. Freud praised the old, Mosaic Judaism for what he called *Geistigkeit* (i.e., Sublimation). Often translated as intellectuality or spirituality, the best English equivalent for *Geistigkeit* may be "inwardness" or "subjectivity." *Geistigkeit*, Freud believed, was a difficult human achievement, which went against the instinctive drive for sensory satisfaction. At the same time he wrote, 'it would be wrong to break off the chain of causation with Moses and to neglect what his successors, the Jewish prophets, achieved ... From the mass of the Jewish people ... there arose again and again men who ... did not rest until the lost cause was once more regained.'[25]

---

23   Lionel Trilling, "Young in the Thirties," *Commentary* 41, no. 5 (1966): 47.
24   Miller, *The New England Mind*.
25   'It is proof of a special psychical fitness in the mass which became the Jewish people that it could bring forth so many persons who were ready to take upon themselves the burden of the Mosaic religion.' Freud, *Moses and Monotheism*, in *The Standard Edition*, 23:176.

Thus, the first wave of American psychoanalysis conforms to the Puritan template. As a unique expression of the power of the mind, Freudianism electrified young intellectuals. Soon, however, it merged with the two great rivers of absorption: Arminian pragmatic benefits, on the one hand, and antinomian narcissism, a fascination with the self, without considering its relation to social production, on the other. The result was a great repression of the knowledge of the unconscious, accomplished neither by the masses, nor by a repressive state, or by an official church, but rather by the intellectuals themselves. For this they marshalled not so much mass passions (except for anti-Communism) as carefully formulated, but ultimately repressive, ideas.

3   Social Change

The next – and to some minds final – phase in the relations between psychoanalysis and American intellectuals was precipitated by the upheavals of the 1960s: civil rights, antiwar activism, and feminism. For our purposes, I will treat these upheavals as one continuous movement, with flows and counter-flows, with different groups and issues taking center stage at different times, all responding to the changed character of US capitalism. Taken as a whole, the upheavals were antinomian, constituting the third Great Awakening in American history, after the Great Awakening of the 1740s, which gave us the nationalism that fueled the American Revolution, and the Great Awakening of the 1830s, which gave us anti-slavery, the women's rights movement, and the full range of progressive reform. What role did psychoanalysis play in the Great Awakening of the 1960s-70s?

The Civil Rights movement set the Awakening in motion. During World War II, at the newly dug graves on Iwo Jima, Rabbi Roland B. Gittelsohn eulogized: 'Here lie officers and men, Negroes and whites, rich and poor together. Here no man prefers another because of his faith or despises him because of his color.'[26] Only in death could this claim be made. American society rested on unconscious racist assumptions. Whereas Blacks were degraded and associated with the profane, white women were desexualized, and placed on a pedestal, but in a way that denied them full citizenship, and infantilized them psychologically. W.E.B. DuBois criticized himself for assuming that race

---

26   Roland B. Gittelsohn, "The Purest Democracy" (speech, Dedication of 5th Marine Division Cemetery on Iwo Jima, March 21, 1945), full text available from the Marine Corps University, https://www.usmcu.edu/Research/Marine-Corps-History-Division/Frequently-Requested-Topics/Historical-Documents-Orders-and-Speeches/The-Purest-Democracy/.

prejudice was based on ignorance. He had not been 'sufficiently Freudian,' he said, 'to understand how little human action is based on reason.'[27] Richard Wright and Frantz Fanon were two great psychoanalytic thinkers of the 1960s. Growing up in the South, Wright consciously negated every message that society directed at him.[28] 'In what other way had the South allowed me to be natural, to be real, to be myself except in rejection, rebellion, and aggression?' he asked.[29]

The second wave of the Great Awakening of the 60s began in 1965, with the first SDS anti-war movement. Behind it lay the shift from an industrial society, devoted to goods production, to a post-industrial society, producing ideas and services. On the one hand, the organic intellectuals of the twenties had morphed into a new professional (or professional-managerial) class, largely because of the expansion of education, science, and technology. This class – also known as the Baby Boomers – was composed of (1) workers concerned with social reproduction (e.g., teachers, social workers, psychologists, health care workers), (2) creators of the new, mass culture, (entertainers, writers of advertising copy and TV scripts, etc.), (3) engineers and technical workers, and (4) middle level administrators and managers. On the other hand, the older working class, already threatened by deindustrialization, responded to African American gains with the idea that Blacks were receiving special favors and by giving salience to the law-and-order issue, especially after Martin Luther King Jr.'s slaying in 1968. A fireman who lost his son in Vietnam expressed a widespread sentiment.

> I'm bitter. You bet your goddam dollar I'm bitter. It's people like us who give up our sons for the country. ... Let's face it: if you have a lot of money, or if you have the right connections, you don't end up on a firing line in the jungle over there, not unless you want to. [My son] had no choice. He didn't want to die. He wanted to live. They just took him – to 'defend democracy,' that's what they keep on saying. Hell, I wonder.[30]

---

27 W.E.B. DuBois, "My Evolving Program," quoted in Claudia Tate, *Psychoanalysis and Black Novels: Desire and the Protocols of Race* (Oxford: Oxford University Press, 1998), 51.
28 Abdul R. Janmohamed, "Negating the Negation: The Construction of Richard Wright," in *Richard Wright: Critical Perspectives Past and Present,* eds. Henry Louis Gates and Anthony Appiah (New York: Amistad, 1993).
29 Richard Wright, *Black Boy* (New York: Harper and Row, 1945), 284.
30 Robert Martin Coles, *The Middle Americans* (Boston: Little, Brown, & Co., 1971), quoted in Christian G. Appy, *The Working-Class War: American Combat Soldiers and Vietnam* (Chapel Hill, NC: University of North Carolina Press, 1993), 42.

Finally, between 1950 and 1998, the proportion of women working outside the home in America rose from 33.9 to 59.8 percent. The number of married women with young children at work rose from 12 percent in 1950 to 40 percent in 1990. The increase reflected the decline of industry, and the rise of services, finance, and the consumer economy. The emancipation of women from the home converged with marketization, which broke down the "natural" i.e., patriarchal, family, as well as such conservative obstacles to meritocracy as nepotism and the "old boy's network." While white women had worked outside the home before, they had mostly done so as a response to national emergencies, especially wars. The changes of the sixties, however, entailed the creation of new form of family life, partly based on the expansion of classical liberal values, to include abortion rights and equal rights for gays and transsexuals, and partly on new ideals of empathy and the recognition of vulnerability.

While psychoanalytic ideas affected the entire society, they were especially prominent in the post-industrial, professional class (which of course included women and Blacks.) During World War II, every doctor in the military had been trained in the fundamentals of psychoanalysis. After the war, school psychologists, guidance counsellors, urban planners, therapists, juvenile court justices, and religious advisors joined doctors in expanding the sway of psychoanalysis. Their advice took the form of the maturity ethic, which stressed the strength and adaptability of the ego in the market-based world, while also maintaining that the deeper experiences of post-war life were to be found in the private realm. Maturity entailed a new intimacy between men and women in the family, supplanting the gender-based world of "mates" and "women's networks" that characterized the industrial working class. Its essence was its rejection of "utopian," i.e., left-wing, politics of the sort that had characterized the United States during the New Deal.

The maturity ethic reflected the Arminian analytic currents launched in the thirties. However, what gave a new centrality to psychoanalysis was the antinomianism of the Awakening. As a charismatic source of meaning, Freudianism embodied powerful sexual and other emancipatory currents that socializing institutions, above all the family, could not contain. As antinomian upsurges – beats, hippies, the New Left – overflowed the boundaries of administered society, activists developed what might be called the theory of the two Freuds. One Freud was an apolitical, sexist medical doctor. The other was a theorist of suppressed longings, utopia, and desire. One Freud authorized straight-male domination based on the theory of penis envy. The other encouraged the liberatory explosions of the 60s.

Herbert Marcuse's *Eros and Civilization* (1955) was the Bible for the liberatory (i.e., antinomian) Freud. Marcuse criticized the "pseudo-individuation" of the maturity ethic and espoused the "late Freud" (often linked to the "early Marx"), whose accounts of an original oneness with the mother were the basis of revolt. Exalting the antinomian loss of ego boundaries, Marcuse described the ego as an 'aggressive, offensive subject ... a subject against an object' and portrayed the artist, the mystic and the homosexual as the dramatis personae of the new society.[31] Above all, the drive toward the antinomian was visible in the blurring of sexual boundaries, the be-ins, the huge crowd formations for civil rights and for peace in Vietnam, the demotic music and art, communes, the scorn for property, new art forms like happenings, Newsreel and Living Theatre, and "altered states of consciousness" (drugs). The highpoint of the crowd experience occurred at the moment the ego dissolved, the antinomian moment, which abstracts the individual from his or her social context. Kristin Ross has called this New Left moment "dis-identification," writing,

> May '68 had little to do with the social group – students or "youth" – who were its instigators. It had much more to do with the flight from social determinants, with displacements that took people out of their location in society, with a disjunction that is, between political subjectivity and the social group.[32]

This moment reflects the hovering in the New Left between a revised theory of revolution and an adjustment to post-industrial capitalism, with its stress on networking and intersubjective sensitivity.

What tipped the balance toward the latter outcome was the eruption of feminism within the New Left. Ever since Dora (Ida Bauer) dismissed Freud as her therapist, many feminists saw Freud as a Victorian thinker who accepted the backward ideologies of his day, such as innate aggression, the patriarchal family, and women's inferiority. In the early seventies, radical feminists like Kate Millett and Shulamith Firestone largely defined themselves through attacks on Freud. In the course of the decade, feminists went through three conflicting but overlapping phases in working out their relation to Freud. In the first, psychoanalysis was rejected tout court as an enemy, or even the enemy. In the second, it was redescribed as "feminist theory *manqué*," a flawed theory of patriarchy that had to be reconstructed by feminists. In the third, which persists even now, Freudianism was revised again in a relational or "self-object" form.

---

31 See Douglas Kellner, "Marcuse and the Quest for Radical Subjectivity," *Counterpoints* 168 (2003): 67–83.

32 Kristin Ross, *May '68 and Its After-Lives* (Chicago: University of Chicago Press, 2002), 2–3.

This revision converged with the neoliberal turn and with the consolidation of a new spirit of capitalism, spearheaded by the professional class. Critical to the shift was the division between the older industrial working class and the newer professional class, set in motion by the war in Vietnam. In the event, class gave way to gender as a master signifier of oppression. Second-wave feminism's explosive redefinition of the women's community, motivated by the idea of the "woman-identified woman," whether overtly as in lesbianism or in the sublimated form of women's loyalty to women, precipitated the shift. Loosening the ties that bound women to men, feminists strengthened the ties that bound women to one another. The result was a joyful reunion among mothers and daughters, or sisters and sisters, the intense feelings of pleasure released indicating the lifting of a repression, especially in the form of "consciousness-raising" groups.

This was the outcome of the politics of personal life set in motion by Mead and others in the 1920s. It was epitomized by the shift from the language of sexuality to that of identity. Whereas New Left antinomianism had generated "dis-identification," a "shattering of social identity," the emotional drive in the seventies lay in *identification,* the earliest tie with another person, the trigger for group formation, and the basis for the building up of the self. Identity politics – the creation of groups based on sameness – was the triumph of narcissism in its group-psychological form. What appeared from one perspective as solidarity based on difference was, from another perspective, self-assertion for the individual members of the group. In the early 1970s Cathy Cade, a documentary photographer, wrote, in the civil rights and anti-war movements, 'I had been fighting for someone else's [freedom] and now there was a way that I could fight for my own freedom.' For Mimi Feingold, 'women couldn't burn draft cards and couldn't go to jail so all they could do was to relate through their men and that seemed to me the most really demeaning kind of thing.'[33] Another feminist collective proclaimed, 'the most profound and potentially the most radical politics come out of our own identity, as opposed to working to end somebody else's oppression.'[34]

Bucking the social-democratic tide of the New Deal era, a small group of "neoliberals," as they called themselves, centered on the Mont Pelerin Society, and including Walter Lippmann and Friedrich Hayek, sought to extend the

---

33 Sara Evans, *Personal Politics: The Roots of Women's Liberation in the Civil Rights Movement and the New Left* (New York: Vintage, 1980), 205, 182.

34 Combahee River Collective, as quoted in Mary Louise Adams, "There's no place like Home: On the Place of Identity in Feminist Politics," *Feminist Review* 31, no. 1 (March 1989): 22–33.

market, not only into regulated or publicly owned areas of the economy, but even into previously sacrosanct areas, such as the family. Their efforts remained marginal for decades, given the achievements of the New Deal, and the understandable desire to protect society from the market. In the 1970s, Keynesianism ran into the economic difficulties known as "stagflation," leading to the embrace of monetarism and deregulation. However, economic factors alone could never have precipitated neo-liberalism's massive success in transforming society. Only when the neo-liberal project of universal marketization merged with identity politics could such a counter-intuitive project penetrate into the soul. Thus was "progressive neo-liberalism" born.

As the Great Awakening of the 1960s ended, the American intellectual class fractured. One current of intellectuals broke with the classic alliance of liberals with the Left and joined the older industrial working class in a new, aggressive theory of neo-conservatism. Feminist intellectuals, artists, performers, etc., created a genuinely new current of thought. Most intellectuals reverted to their default preference: pragmatism, which, given American realities, could only serve as a lubricant for corporate power. A handful, such as Daniel Ellsberg and Noam Chomsky, empowered by the anti-war movement, create America's own version of the heroic Dreyfusard. Finally, psychoanalysis lost its intellectual content and was reduced to a therapeutic practice.

The most authoritative account we have of the intellectual revolution of the 1970s is Daniel Rodgers' 2011 book, *The Age of Fracture*.[35] Rodgers' theme is the recession of concept of society in American thought. On the one hand, he traces the "rediscovery of the market," as shown in the return of pre-Keynesian neo-classical economics, the rational choice revolution in political science and sociology, and the reduction of psychoanalysis to cognitive psychology and neurobiology. On the other hand, he traces the postmodern attack on suspect wholes or totalities, such as those of gender, class, and nation. The result is evident in the dispersion, fissuring, "fracture," hybrid or performative character of identities and the valorization of the local and the particular, the "little platoons," idealized by Edmund Burke in his assault on the French Revolution, and resurrected by Michael Walzer as an ersatz option for the Left.[36] In Rodgers' book, rational choice and disaggregated identities each go their own way, and what is lost is the older sense that society had a unified core.

But if we look at the cultural and intellectual revolution of the 1960s and 70s with the Freudian picture of the unconscious in mind, we can begin to see

---

35   Daniel Rodger, *The Age of Fracture* (Cambridge, MA: The Belknap Press of Harvard University Press, 2011).
36   Ibid.

how the vanished signifier "society" might be resurrected. Rodgers' "rediscovery of the market" – the neo-liberal redefinition of the subject in egoistic or economic terms – was a surface phenomenon. Beneath the embrace of egoism lay the validation of narcissism. Foucault's term "productive power" – dispersed, centrifugal, mercurial, self-generated, and self-managed – was also a surface grid. Neither Rodgers nor Foucault understood that productive power required a libidinal basis. This it found not only in the secondary narcissism of self-assertion, which motivates the instrumental rationality a reified society requires, but even more deeply in the primary narcissism of identity politics, which motivates consumerism and nullifies political radicalism.

Finally, let us consider the fate of the original model for, but also enemy of, the American intellectual: Puritanism. Here, in light of cancel culture, censorship, and political correctness, we might give Christopher Lasch's 1979 *Culture of Narcissism* a second look.[37] According to Lasch, the social changes of the 60s and 70s did not abolish the super-ego but rather released its primitive elements. Lasch used Joseph Heller's novel *Something Happened* (1974) as an example. Heller's father-hero, an advertising man plagued by impulses to kick or otherwise harm his fellow workers, is regularly provoked by his adolescent daughter. For example, she leaves her diaphragm around. 'Refusing to be maneuvered into administering punishment, he wins psychological victories ... by giving in to her wishes.' His daughter, like his son, to whom he has always sought to be "best friend," unconsciously regards him as a tyrant. He muses: 'I don't know why my son feels so often that I am going to hit him when I never do; I never have; I don't know why both he and my daughter believe I used to beat them a great deal when they were smaller, when I don't believe I ever struck either one of them at all.'[38]

4 Conclusion

Together, the warm welcome originally extended to psychoanalysis, and the angry, hostile expulsion that followed, represent a major episode in American intellectual history. The ambivalence American intellectuals showed toward psychoanalysis reveals an important feature. During eras of crisis or transition the country produces amazing bursts of original thought, and engages in very real self-questioning. Examples include the early Puritans, the Civil

---

37 Christopher Lasch, *The Culture of Narcissism: American Life in An Age of Diminishing Expectations*, (New York: W.W. Norton & Co., 2018).

38 Ibid., 180.

War and Reconstruction, the twenties and the sixties, Vietnam, the current rewriting of the history of slavery and Jim Crow, and perhaps the present rebirth of socialism. Impressive as such moments are, however, they have proved short-lived, insufficient to generate a continuing body of reflection. More often, American intellectuals have been servants of power, lacking independence both in thought and as a societal force. The related experiences of the Puritans and psychoanalysis offers a clue as to why. American thought has vacillated between two mass psychological currents: the market, which generates pragmatism, scientism and rational choice, and antinomian upheavals, characterized by quasi-mystical experiences of merger. The path between them is a narrow one and hard to follow, but it is the only one that can shed real light.

Bibliography

Adams, Mary Louise. "There's no place like Home: On the Place of Identity in Feminist Politics." *Feminist Review* 31, no. 1 (March 1989): 22–33.

Appy, Christian G. *The Working-Class War: American Combat Soldiers and Vietnam.* Chapel Hill, NC: University of North Carolina Press, 1993.

Coles, Robert Martin. *The Middle Americans.* Boston: Little, Brown, & Co., 1971.

Douglas, Ann. *Terrible Honesty: Mongrel Manhattan in the 1920s.* New York: Farrar, Straus and Giroux, 1995.

Evans, Sara. *Personal Politics: The Roots of Women's Liberation in the Civil Rights Movement and the New Left.* New York: Vintage, 1980.

Frank, Waldo David. *Our America.* New York: Boni and Liveright, 1919.

Freud, Sigmund. *Beyond the Pleasure Principle* in Pelican Freud Library, Vol. 11. London: Penguin, 1984.

Freud, Sigmund. "Civilization and Its Discontents." In *The Standard Edition of the Complete Psychological Works of Sigmund Freud,* edited and translated by James Strachey. New York: Norton, 1976.

Freud, Sigmund. "The Dynamics of Transference." In *The Standard Edition of the Complete Psychological Works of Sigmund Freud,* edited and translated by James Strachey. New York: Norton, 1976.

Freud, Sigmund. "The Group and the Primal Horde." In *Group Psychology and the Analysis of the Ego.* New York: Boni and Liveright, 1922.

Freud, Sigmund. "Moses and Monotheism." In *The Standard Edition of the Compete Psychological Works of Sigmund Freud Vol. 23,* edited and translated by James Strachey. New York: Norton, 1976.

Gerth, Hans, and C. Wright Mills, eds. *From Max Weber: Essays in Sociology.* New York: Oxford University Press, 1946.

Gittelsohn, Roland B. "The Purest Democracy" (speech, Dedication of 5th Marine Division Cemetery on Iwo Jima, March 21, 1945), full text available from the Marine Corps University, https://www.usmcu.edu/Research/Marine-Corps-History-Division/Frequently-Requested-Topics/Historical-Documents-Orders-and-Speeches/The-Purest-Democracy/.

Gramsci, Antonio. *The Antonio Gramsci Reader: Selected Writings 1916–1935,* edited by David Forgacs. New York: New York University Press, 2000.

Hale, Nathan G. *Freud and the Americans.* New York: Oxford University Press, 1971.

Janmohamed, Abdul R. "Negating the Negation: The Construction of Richard Wright." In *Richard Wright: Critical Perspectives Past and Present,* edited by Henry Louis Gates and Anthony Appiah. New York: Amistad, 1993.

Jennings, Jeremy, and Tony Kemp-Welch. "The Century of the Intellectual: From Dreyfus to Salman Rushdie." In *Intellectuals in Politics: From the Dreyfus Affair to Salman Rushdie.* London: Routledge, 1997.

Kellner, Douglas. "Marcuse and the Quest for Radical Subjectivity." *Counterpoints* 168 (2003): 67–83.

Lasch, Christopher. *The Culture of Narcissism: American Life in An Age of Diminishing Expectations.* New York: W.W. Norton & Co., 2018.

Lasch, Christopher. *The New Radicalism in America.* New York: Knopf, 1965.

Mandler, Peter. *Return from the Natives: How Margaret Mead Won the Second World War and Lost the Cold War.* New Haven: Yale University Press, 2013.

Miller, Perry. *The New England Mind: The Seventeenth Century.* Cambridge, MA: Harvard University Press, 1939/1953.

Molloy, Maureen. *On Creating a Usable Culture: Margaret Mead and the Emergence of American Cosmopolitanism.* Honolulu: University of Hawaii Press, 2008.

Munsterberg, Hugo. *Psychotherapy.* New York: Moffat, Yard and Co., 1909.

Rieff, Philip, ed. *Sigmund Freud: Collected Papers.* New York: Collier, 1963.

Rodger, Daniel. *The Age of Fracture.* Cambridge, MA: The Belknap Press of Harvard University Press, 2011.

Ross, Kristin. *May '68 and Its After-Lives.* Chicago: University of Chicago Press, 2002.

Seldes, Gilbert. *The Seven Lively Arts.* New York: Harper & Bros, 1924.

Tate, Claudia. *Psychoanalysis and Black Novels: Desire and the Protocols of Race.* Oxford: Oxford University Press, 1998.

Trilling, Lionel. *Freud and the Crisis of Our Culture.* Boston: Beacon Press, 1955.

Trilling, Lionel. "Young in the Thirties." *Commentary* 41, no. 5 (May 1966): 43–51.

Van Wyck, Brooks. *America's Coming of Age.* New York: B.W. Huebsch, 1915.

Weber, Marianne. *Max Weber: A Biography.* New York: Wiley, 1975.

Weber, Max. *Max Weber: Selections in Translation*, edited by W. G. Runciman, translated by Eric Matthews. New York: Cambridge University Press, 1978.

Weber, Max. *The Protestant Ethic and the Spirit of Capitalism.* New York: Routledge, 1992.

Wright, Richard. *Black Boy.* New York: Harper & Row, 1945.

CHAPTER 16

A Freudian Analysis of the Competing Groups on Uncorroborated Allegations of Child Sexual Abuse

Michael Naughton

1   Introduction

It was just over twenty years ago when I was a second year PhD student that I first started to think about, and question, why certain academic colleagues opted to take a side in debates or a biased or overtly one-sided political stance in their researches. There seemed to be an apparent inability or unwillingness by such colleagues to consider, not only their apparent blindness to other points of view or alternative perspectives, but, most crucially, the inherent injustice in their choice of camp or tribe and the harm that it can cause when they are wrong in the beliefs which underpin their thinking and forms of social action. It has puzzled me ever since.

The first time that this happened was at a postgraduate conference where I was giving a work-in-progress paper on a chapter of my thesis that started to categorize the different causes of miscarriages of justice that can be identified in analyses of successful appeal against criminal conviction cases. Things were going well when I talked about successful appeal cases that highlighted how vulnerable suspects can give false confessions and admit to crimes that they did not commit, that police officers can fabricate evidence against innocent suspects or how prosecutors can fail to disclose evidence that is favorable to the defense, and so on. But there was a palpable change of atmosphere when I talked about successful appeal cases where the criminal conviction was overturned because a child (overwhelmingly young girls) who said that they were sexually abused or a woman who has claimed that she had been raped were shown to have lied. Female peers who identified as feminist and who had previously been friendly with me, personally, and supportive about my research, generally, changed tack and started to treat me and my research as if I and/or it was on an opposing "side" of a political debate and as an enemy to be openly attacked. I remember vividly being told that it was 'impertinent' to even mention that girls and women can tell lies when they claim that they were sexual abused or raped. I was told that it was something that I should not speak of as there were far too many child sexual abusers and/or rapists who were getting away with it and it was that side of the debate and that type of injustice that I should be concentrating on and not giving ammunition to the "other side." It was as if the injustice and harm of the wrongful conviction of innocent victims of false allegations of child sexual abuse or rape did not matter when compared against the injustice and harm to victims of child sexual abuse or rape, as if we were to only look at one type of victim of injustice and harm and totally neglect another.

I have received this kind of mixed response and reaction to my work, and by extension to my person, on established and alleged miscarriages of justice ever since: aspects of my researches seem acceptable to certain groups if they are perceived to be supportive of the political aims of the group, whilst others are seen as supporting the "other" camp that the group is fighting against. As indicted, if my work highlights police or prosecution misconduct it is embraced and endorsed by those anti-police or anti-prosecution campaigners who see my research as supporting their cause. Similarly, if I show how prisoners maintaining innocence are discriminated against in prisons and at a disadvantage in parole hearings compared to those prisoners who acknowledge their guilt and comply with their sentence plans, anti-prison activists see value in my research. Yet, if I highlight how not all prisoners maintaining innocence are innocent, which is cited by those who deny even the possibility that some prisoners are innocent, that girls or women can make false allegations, which is utilized by the false allegations community, or how criminal appeal lawyers can fail their clients, which is embraced by pretty much all alleged innocent victims of wrongful convictions, then, anti-miscarriages of justice, anti-rape, anti-child sexual abuse advocates and pro-criminal appeal lawyer groups see it appropriate to criticize my research, as well as me personally.

Reflecting on these experiences, I think it would be fair to say that my academic career has been a rather isolated and somewhat isolating experience. I say this as I have not found it possible to be involved with academic groups or societies, nor groups or organizations in civil society that might appear on face value or on the surface to be aligned with my research interests and/or findings. I just do not, and cannot, it seems, fit into groups with one-sided or biased views of the world? which set themselves in political opposition to some identified "other" groups who they see as their adversaries and who they treat with hatred and want to destroy.

This is not to somehow paint myself as a victim, nor a person of particular personal outstanding integrity. Rather, it is to draw attention to, and emphasize, the divides in a society that exist, both within academia, specifically, and a civil society, more broadly, that is increasingly structured along adversarial lines: you are either on this side or that side; in or out; one of us or one of them; a comrade or an enemy. It is as though my workplace environment and civil society, more generally, are not suited to an objective scientific approach to research, or a personal subjectivity, that is concerned only with the truth of whether alleged victims of wrongful convictions did or did not do what they were convicted of, which I think is the only path to true justice.

Most recently, when I was researching the substantive focus of this chapter, the competing discourses or groups on uncorroborated allegations of child sexual abuse (UACSA), I had lunch with a prominent feminist scholar to talk about my draft article and work-in-progress findings. She is among a very small number of people within academia that I would say was a friend. She has been to my house. I have been to hers. We have had coffee and talked about work and ideas and personal things. We have had lunch and dinner together and talked about our research and our families, and so on.

When I told her about my research on the opposing discourses on UACSA and how the child protection camp can cause and exacerbate the harm to innocent victims who were falsely accused when they believe without question an allegation of child sexual abuse (discussed further below), she got very angry with me, in almost exactly the same way that the postgraduate feminist colleague did in the example above. She said that she would not, and could not, accept that girls tell lies about being sexually abused. When I said that it is documented in successful appeal cases that girls can tell lies about being victims of child sexual abuse; that it is a social and legal fact that is indisputable; and, that I could not understand why, as an academic, she would be so hostile to that reality, she shouted through clenched teeth: 'I am an activist first, and an academic second.'[1] As I said, we had been quite good friends prior to this meeting, but, sadly, we have not met or spoken since.

In response to such reactions, my first response is usually from the perspective of academic objectivity. I try to assuage the criticisms of my findings or me,

---

[1] I should say here that I do not believe that such a stance or subjectivity is possible. The conscious choice at the heart of such an assertion to be an activist first, interpreted as denying the reality of certain types of harm and injustice in favor of forms of harm and injustice felt to be more important, means that, to my mind at least, you cannot be an academic at all. Indeed, an academic approach, in my view, is the objective pursuit of truth and to be fully transparent with any research findings, however uncomfortable or inconvenient they may seem. A political positioning as an 'activist first', as the one in question, therefore, nullifies the ability to be an academic at all. I could say more here about the increasing number of such colleagues within academia and how they utilize the guise of being an academic seemingly in attempts to strengthen their inherently political discourses, but this is neither the place nor the time and I must concentrate on the matters in hand.

personally, on the basis of scientific neutrality. I say that I agree, because I do agree and have written about it, that convictions for child sexual abuse against young girls and convictions for men who rape women were notoriously low, but that was an altogether different issue to my research on false allegations of child sexual abuse; the two things are not related.[2] I say it is unacademic and asociological to try to ignore socio-legal phenomenon, such as the wrongful conviction of innocent victims, on the grounds of allegiance to a political cause that works counter to an inclusive academic approach that seeks the truth as a precursor to justice. I say that it is unethical, unjust and an exacerbation of the harm and injustice caused to innocent victims that is engendered by wrongful convictions to deny that innocent individuals can be, and are, wrongly convicted when allegations of child sexual abuse or rape are false (discussed further below). And, I say that I believe that forms of counter discourse against rape or child sexual abuse are strengthened, rather than weakened, by more holistic critical analyses that contextualize the difficulty in obtaining criminal convictions against men who sexually abuse children or who rape women within a broader analysis that also considers the reality that some children and women do say that they were sexually abused or raped when they were not. I explain that my reasoning here is that I think it is better to engage with any potential or perceived limitations or weaknesses of one's argument or position; to concede in the present example that it has been known on relatively rare occasions for girls and/or women to falsely claim to be victims of child sexual abuse or rape, but the greater problem in terms of both numbers and injustice and harmfulness is the failure of a criminal justice system that is structured and operates along patriarchal lines to deliver justice for women and girls who are victims of rape and /or child sexual abuse. This has had little or no impact whatsoever in terms of bridging apparent divides. On the contrary, in my experience it has always had the opposite effect of angering and entrenching still further those who identify with a particular tribe that they think my work or I stand against.

It is against this background that I was grateful to the Editors, Dustin J. Byrd and Seyed Javad Miri, for the opportunity to research this intrinsically psychological phenomenon that has emerged both in reactions to my work, generally, and more specifically, in response to the socio-philosophical research that I conducted on UACSA with reference to the work and ideas of Sigmund Freud. Indeed, it is from Freud (1922) that we can learn much about group psychology

---

2 See Michael Naughton, "Rethinking the Competing Discourses on Uncorroborated Allegations of Child Sexual Abuse." *The British Journal of Criminology* 59, no. 2 (2019): 461–480.

and the causal factors that underpin why individuals feel the need to join a group, what they obtain from that choice, what they give up as individuals as a consequence of it, and, hopefully, what, if anything, might be done to reduce the existing forms of injustice and harm that the competing groups on UACSA currently inflict on to innocent victims on the opposing side.³ It has genuinely baffled me why people choose to join groups and be on sides that are so apparently problematical and which can cause identical forms of injustice and harm that they claim to stand against. It is in this context that I welcomed the possibility to research this phenomenon for a chapter in this book from a Freudian lens.

To these ends, the remainder of this chapter will be structured into two broad parts. In terms of the order of the parts, I follow Freud's (1922) approach and method to describe, firstly, the phenomenon that I then want to try to explain through the lens of his thesis on group psychology and other relevant work.⁴ To this end, I will begin by providing an overview of my previous research (Naughton 2019) Footnote here to: Naughton, "Rethinking the Competing Discourses" or just Footnote and delete "(Naughton, 2019)"? . on the competing groups on UACSA to identify and highlight the opposing factions, which I designate as Child Protection Discourse (CPD) versus False Allegations Discourse (FAD). This first part will also consider the question of who the victim is in cases of UACSA cases to draw out and highlight the problematical nature of the so-called forms of 'victimology' that the competing discourses construct and deploy in conflicts with one another. This part will call into question any notion that either child sexual abuse (CSA) or false allegations of CSA can be quantified from uncorroborated allegations: We simply cannot know the extent of a phenomenon where any given allegation may be truthful or false. It will also emphasize why it is crucial to know who the victim is in UACSA cases. And it will highlight the epistemic blind spots of the warring factions on UACSA and how this links with the causation of a range of collateral forms of injustice and harm in the fight between CPD and FAD to genuine victims of CSA and innocent victims of false allegations, alike. Then, in the second part of the chapter, I will turn to Freud's thesis on group psychology and other key and core Freudian texts and concepts as they bear on the following interrelated questions: Why do individuals choose to join groups such as CPD or FAD; what, if anything, do they gain or lose from that choice; and, what, if anything, can

---

3 Sigmund Freud, *Group Psychology and the Analysis of the Ego*, translated by James Strachey (London & Vienna: The International Psycho-Analytical Press, 1922).
4 Ibid.

be done to reduce or prevent the forms of injustice and harm inherent in the opposing groups that have emerged in response to UACSA?

2 The Competing Groups on Uncorroborated Allegations of Child Sexual Abuse

The first thing to say is that child sexual abuse (CSA) is a repulsive crime that can have permanent harmful effects on a victim's life. Conceived widely as an abuse of power,[5] CSA is mostly committed by persons known to, and trusted by, victims and can affect mental and physical health, as well as social, sexual and interpersonal functioning.[6] More specifically, CSA occurs where an individual or group takes advantage of an imbalance of power to coerce, manipulate or deceive a child or young person under the age of 18 into sexual activity.[7]

On the other hand, false allegations of CSA is an equally abhorrent crime, which can, and does, also cause irreparable forms of damage and harm to victims. False allegations of CSA can ruin careers and reputations, for instance, and there can be permanent and ongoing social stigma, psychological trauma and forms of cultural and financial harm to direct victims and their families when the label "child abuser" is falsely applied.[8] Crucially, allegations of CSA conflates those who may be or are innocent with those who may be or are

---

5 Stephen J. Rossetti, "Child Sexual Abuse and Power," *The Furrow* 46, no. 12 (1995): 684–688; Vera Baird, "Sexual Abuse is about Power – and the Powerful shouldn't be Protected," *The Guardian*. April 29 2014; David Finkelhor, "Current Information on the Scope and Nature of Child Sexual Abuse," *The Future of Children* 4, no. 2 (1994): 31–53, 33; Gerrilyn Smith, "Child Sexual Abuse: The Power of Intrusion," *Adoption & Fostering* 10 no.3 (1986): 13–18, 13.
6 Judy Cashmore and Rita Shackel. "The Long-Term Effects of Child Sexual Abuse," *Child Family Community Australia* 11 (2013): 1–29, 2; Elizabeth Oddone Paolucci, Mark L. Genuis, and Claudio Violato. "A Meta-Analysis of the Published Research on the Effects of Child Sexual Abuse." *Journal of Psychology* 135, no. 1 (2001): 17–36; Jocelyn Brown, Patricia Cohen, Jeffrey G. Johnson, and Elizabeth M. Smailes, "Childhood Abuse and Neglect: Specificity of Effects on Adolescent and Young Adult Depression and Suicidality," *Journal of the American Academy of Child and Adolescent Psychiatry* 38, no. 12 (1999): 1490–1496.
7 HM Government 2015. "Working Together to Safeguard Children: A guide to Inter-agency working to Safeguard and Promote the Welfare of Children." (2015), 93; World Health Organization (WHO). "Preventing Child Maltreatment: A Guide to Taking and Generating Evidence." Geneva: World Health Organization (WHO). (2006), 10.
8 Nik Greene, *False Accusations: Guilty Until Proven Innocent*. Houston, TX: Strategic Book Publishing & Rights Agency, LLC, 2011; Paul Gambaccini, *Love, Paul Gambaccini: My Year under the Yewtree* (London: Biteback Publishing, 2015); Simon Warr, *Presumed Guilty: A Teacher's Solitary Battle to Clear His Name* (London: Biteback Publishing, 2017).

guilty,[9] which can be devastating for genuinely innocent victims and their families, as well as society as a whole in terms of the climate of suspicion and diminished trust that allegations of CSA can cause.[10]

The obvious evidential challenge with uncorroborated allegations of CSA (UACSA) is that in so called 'he said, she said' cases only the accused and the accuser have the potential to know whether the allegation is true or not.[11] This problem is compounded further by the propensity of children to make false allegations of CSA against teachers[12] or by parents to one another during child custody battles.[13] As such, there is always uncertainty surrounding UACSA in terms of whether the accuser is a genuine victim or, alternatively, the perpetrator of a false allegation against an innocent individual who is the real victim.

Despite the inherent uncertainty of whether UACSA are truthful or not, the existing discourses are highly polarized, falling into one of two groups. On the one hand, what I term "Child Protection Discourse" (CPD) leaves no room for false or untruthful allegations, working on the rather simplistic and problematic basis that all alleged victims of CSA are telling the truth.[14] CPD sources include governmental,[15] third

---

9   David Jones, *No Smoke, No Fire: The Autobiography of Dave Jones* (Chichester: Pitch Publishing Limited, 2011); Michael Naughton and Gabe Tan, *Claims of Innocence: An Introduction to Wrongful Convictions and How they might be Challenged* (Bristol: University of Bristol, 2011), 70–71.

10 Michael Naughton, "How the Presumption of Innocence Renders the Innocent Vulnerable to Wrongful Conviction," *Irish Journal of Legal Studies* 2, no. 1 (2011): 40–54, i.

11 I say 'potential to know' as mental health can mean that accusers can be mistaken when they say that they were sexually abused as children and may make false allegations that they believe to be truthful unintentionally.

12 Elizabeth M. Anderson, and Murray Levine, "Concerns about Allegations of Child Sexual Abuse against Tachers and the Teaching Environment," *Child Abuse & Neglect* 23, no. 8 (1999): 833–843.

13 Leona M. Kopetski, Deirdre Conway Rand, and Randy Randy, "Incidence, Gender, and False Allegations of Child Abuse: Data on 84 Parental Alienation Syndrome Cases," in *The International Handbook of Parental Alienation Syndrome*, ed. Gardner, R. A., Sauber, S.R. and Lorandos, D. (Springfield, IL: Charles C. Thomas Publisher Limited, 2006); Arthur H. Green, "True and False Allegations of Sexual Abuse in Child Custody Disputes," *Journal of the American Academy of Child Psychiatry* 25 (1986): 444–456; Lee Coleman, and Patrick E. Clancy. "False Allegations of Child Sexual Abuse: Why is it Happening, What Can We Do," *Criminal Justice* 5, no. 3 (1990): 14–47; Kathryn Kuehnle, and Mary Connell. eds. *The Evaluation of Child Sexual Abuse Allegations: A Comprehensive Guide to Assessment and Testimony* (Hoboken, NJ: John Wiley and Sons, 2009).

14 Naughton, "Rethinking the Competing Discourses".

15 Alexis Jay, "Independent Inquiry into Child Sexual Exploitation in Rotherham (1997–2013)," 2014; Independent Inquiry into Child Sexual Abuse, "Report of the Internal

sector,[16] journalistic[17] and third sector and governmental collaborations.[18]

In the opposing camp, what I call "False Allegations Discourse" (FAD) works on the equally problematic basis that those who claim to be victims of false allegations of CSA must always be treated as though they might be innocent.[19] Paying strict adherence to the legal principle of the presumption of innocence, the discourse underpinning this position, FAD also derives from a diverse range of academic,[20] legal practitioner,[21] and journalistic sources.[22] Third sector versions of FAD[23] go further, however, in continuing to support alleged innocent victims of false allegations in cases of UACSA who continue to say that they are innocent after conviction and/or after failing in an appeal but who are making or "planning" to make an application to the Criminal Cases Review Commission (CCRC),[24] also working on the basis that they might be innocent.

Review," 2016a; Independent Inquiry into Child Sexual Abuse, "Truth Project. Experiences shared: Victims and Survivors Speak Out," 2016b.

16 NSPCC 2013, "Child Sexual Abuse: An NSPCC Research Briefing," 2013; Dan Roan, "FA Abuse Inquiry Chief Receives Counselling after Hearing Victims' Stories," 2017; The Offside Trust, "Who are we," 2018.

17 Gaby Hinsliff, "'It Never Stops Shaping You': The Legacy of Child Sexual Abuse – and How to Survive it," *The Guardian*. June 28, 2018.

18 David Gray, and Peter Watt, "'Giving Victims a Voice': A joint MPS and NSPCC report into Allegations of Sexual Abuse made against Jimmy Savile under Operation Yewtree," 2013.

19 Naughton, "Rethinking the Competing Discourses".

20 Carolyn Hoyle, Naomi-Ellen Speechley, and Ros Burnett. "The Impact of Being Wrongly Accused of Abuse in Occupations of Trust: Victims' Voices," 2015; Ros Burnett, ed. *Wrongful Allegations of Sexual and Child Abuse* (Oxford: Oxford University Press, 2016); Ross Burnett, "Why it is too easy for Innocent People to be Wrongly Accused of Sexual Abuse." *The Justice Gap*. 13 March; Dennis Eady, "What to do about the Epidemic of Historical abuse Cases?" *The Justice Gap*. 2017.

21 Richard Henriques, "Report – Independent Review of Metropolitan Police Service's handling of non-recent sexual offence investigations," 2016; Barbara Hewson, "False Allegations, Emotional Truths and Actual Lies," *The Justice Gap*. 2016; Mark George, "Why the Policy of 'believe the complainant' was behind the Failure of Disclosure in the case of Liam Allan," 2017.

22 Charlotte Rowles, "They can't all be making it up," *The Justice Gap*, 2015; Jon Robins, "Hogan-Howe finally Apologies for Disastrous Operation Midland," The Justice Gap, 2016; Allison Pearson, "Alison Saunders must Stand Down – or be Sacked," *The Telegraph*. December 19, 2017.

23 FACT 2022. "What we do," 2022; Unfounded: Alliance Against Unfounded Accusations of Abuse. "Who are we," 2018.

24 With the establishment of the CCRC, the criminal appeals system is, effectively, never ending. That is to say, there is no limit to the number of applications that alleged victims of false allegations of UACSA (or any other crime) can make to the CCRC in their attempts to challenge their alleged miscarriages of justice (see Elks 2008).

3   Pseudo Victimologies

The crucial question relating to UACSA is who is the victim: Is it the person making the allegation or an innocent individual who is falsely alleged to have committed the offence? A major problem with the discourses on either side of the CPD versus FAD group divide is that the underpinning epistemic assumptions means that neither group can claim to constitute a robust victimology in the strict sense of that term.

To be sure, the Oxford English Dictionary defines a "victim" as 'a person harmed, injured, or killed as a result of a crime, accident or other event or action.'[25] Evaluated from this definition, the so-called "victimologies" of CPD and FAD both fail in an epistemological sense due to the method employed in the construction of the knowledge at the heart of their respective discourses. That is to say, a genuine victimology cannot be based on the word alone of an alleged victim of CSA or an alleged victim of a false allegation of CSA. On the contrary, to be regarded as a genuine victim, the person who is claiming to be offended against, has to have been, actually, in fact, been offended against. As things stand, then, neither CPD nor FAD can claim or prove that an alleged victim is a genuine, truthful, victim in any given case or allegation.

Looked at from this perspective, the competing discourses on UACSA are, therefore, better understood as competing forms of "pseudo-victimology": they are discursive inventions that have weaponized the inherent uncertainty of UACSA for their competing discursive and programmatic ends. Indeed, in cases where there is no evidence other than an uncorroborated allegation of either CSA or a false allegation of CSA there is no way of knowing for certain if the person is a victim or a victimizer.

In response to this epistemic failing, all existing forms of knowledge/discourse relating to either CPD or FAD; to alleged victims in cases of UACSA, or to alleged victims of false allegations in cases of UACSA, must be approached with extreme caution. This applies, too, to the foregoing references to research undertaken and deployed by both CPD and FAD camps, alike. In consequence, the true nature and scale of either social phenomenon, CSA and/or false allegations of CSA, is simply not knowable.

---

25   Oxford English Dictionary 2022. "Victim."

4   The Inherent Injustice and Harmfulness of CPD and FAD

However, the question of who is the victim is in cases of UACSA is not only about methodology in the production of knowledge and the representativeness, reliability, validity, or otherwise of the forms of knowledge that underpin the competing discourses of CPD versus FAD. It is crucial when making a victim claim that the claim is truthful and genuine. If an alleged victim is not genuine then justice can be miscarried and any policy or legislative reform attempts to diminish or prevent CSA or false allegations of CSA can also be misdirected. This is, precisely, the position that we find ourselves in. It is simply not possible to claim with any certainty who the victim is in cases of UACSA. There is, therefore, what might be termed a "justice impasse," with no sound basis in any given case whether to act in one way or the other, whether to adopt a CPD or a FAD approach.

Yet, this situation does not seem to have any effect on group members of either CPD or FAD. On the contrary, the way that the competing groups are constituted sees them acting as though they are in a symbiotic relationship as they clearly see the epistemic failings or blind spots of their opponents but fail to see their own. This locks them in a seemingly never-ending discursive battle within which they seem trapped. At the heart of the exchanges between CPD and FAD is an apparent cognitive dissonance, whereby the members of the opposing camps seem to be unable to see or comprehend the obvious flaw in their discursive stance to believe alleged victims, of either CSA or false allegations of CSA, based only on their word or allegation. Yet, each camp can see the failure of the opposing camp to see their inherent epistemological failings.

As this plays out on the CPD side, there is a deafening silence on the reality of genuine false allegations of CSA. This translates to the group as a collective denial that not all alleged victims of CSA are truthful, which serves to provide further fuel for its adversaries in the FAD camp. Correspondingly, the FAD side makes no mention of the equivalent reality that not all those claiming to be victims of false allegation of CSA are telling the truth.[26] As already indicated, FAD attempts to explain away allegations, charges or convictions for CSA as a product of a system that can convict on the word of complainants without corroboration which are further encouraged by a compensation culture.[27] This

---

26   Michael Naughton, *Rethinking Miscarriages of Justice: Beyond the Tip of the Iceberg* (Basingstoke: Palgrave Macmillan, 2007); Michael Naughton, "Factual Innocence versus Legal Guilt: The Need for a New Pair of Spectacles to view the Problem of Life-Sentenced Prisoners Maintaining Innocence," *Prison Service Journal* 177 (May 2008): 32–37.

27   Burnett, "Why it is too easy."; Eady, "What to do about the Epidemic".

may well be true, and I have written about such issues previously myself, but rather than unsupported discursive assertions, it requires supporting evidence in the form of a significant number of cases in which genuinely innocent individuals were subjected to false allegations by individuals who made the allegation because of the lure compensation.[28]

But CSA and false allegations of CSA are not purely about the potential for injustice. They are also inherently about harm; about harm prevention or redress for harms caused, with both CPD and FAD claiming to stand against the harm of CSA or the harm of false allegations. As we have seen, however, this claim is undermined as it is impossible to know with any certainty whether allegations of CSA are true or false. In consequence, we do not know whether alleged victims are genuine victims who have been harmed, or fake "victims" who are causing harm when they say that a genuine victim of CSA is not telling the truth, or when a false allegation of CSA is made against an innocent victim.

In consequence, the existing discourse constructions and operationalizations of the competing groups on CPD versus FAD means that they inflict the same types of injustice and harm upon one another, which their opponent exists to reduce or prevent altogether.

This can be represented as follows:
- CPD causes forms of injustice and harm to innocent victims of false allegations when it believes an alleged victim of CSA who is not genuine;
- CPD causes forms of injustice and harm to genuine victims of CSA when it makes no distinction between them and alleged victims of CSA who are not telling the truth;
- FAD causes forms of injustice and harm to genuine victims of CSA when it believes a child sexual abuser in a claim of innocence that is not genuine;
- FAD causes forms of injustice and harm to genuinely innocent victims of false allegations of CSA when it makes no distinction between them and those claiming to be victims of false allegations who are not innocent.

Indeed, it is crucial that the fight for supremacy between CPD and FAD for power over how society thinks and feels about UACSA and what to do in response is not seen through a merely discursive or theoretical lens. The forms of injustice and harm in the forgoing bullet points have real, material consequences too.

To give just one example on the CPD side of the equation, Frances Andrade was reported to have committed suicide the day after her alleged CSA offender,

---

28 Michael Naughton, *The Innocent and the Criminal Justice System* (Basingstoke: Palgrave Macmillan, 2013), 69; Michael Naughton, *Rethinking Miscarriages of Justice: Beyond the Tip of the Iceberg* (Basingstoke: Palgrave Macmillan, 2007), 61.

Michael Brewer, gave evidence at his trial saying that she was a liar and a "fantasist." Brewer was later found guilty of five charges of indecent assault against her.²⁹ An example on the FAD side is Graham Smith. He also committed suicide, which was attributed to the "mental trauma" of being accused of an historic CSA offence despite a police investigation 'clear[ing] him of any wrongdoing.'³⁰

The inherently unknowable nature of UACSA cases or what is commonly referred to as "he said, she said" cases means that the truth in such cases, and, therefore, the justice or injustice and harmful consequences in such cases may never truly be known.

5 A Freudian Analysis of CPD and FAD

Armed with the foregoing description of CPD and FAD, the way that the opposing groups conflict over UACSA, and the consequences of those conflicts in terms of injustice and harmfulness, we are now in a position to be able to turn to Freud to see what sense, if any, his thinking can make of it.

It is important to state at the start of this analysis, however, that what follows will be an application of Freud's thesis on group psychology and other core ideas where it is thought to be relevant to understanding the problematic identified and described rather than a critical evaluation of it.

Before turning to Freud's thesis on group psychology, however, it is, first, necessary to consider some of his core operating concepts developed in some of his other major works to allow a meaningful consideration of his application of those ideas to the specific case study of the psychology of groups.³¹

6 Freud's Core Concepts

Freud's core concepts that we must consider as a precursor to engaging with his thesis on group psychology are contained in his psychoanalytic theory, which saw him structure the psyche into three distinct, yet overlapping, separate parts: id, ego and super-ego.³² We must also understand the force or psychic

---

29 Peter Walker, "Frances Andrade Killed Herself After Being Accused of lying, Says Husband," *The Guardian*, February 10, 2013.
30 Martin Robinson, "Father, 56, Leapt to his Death from the Humber Bridge After Being Falsely Accused of Abusing Child," *Mail Online*, November 13, 2013.
31 Freud, "Group Psychology".
32 Sigmund Freud, *The Ego and the Id*, trans. Joan Riviere (London: The Hogarth Press, 1923).

energy at play in the functioning of our mental lives that molds individuals together in the groups that they form from a Freudian perspective, to which I will now turn.

7   Libido or Psychic Energy

Those with only a nominal familiarity with Freud and his work will likely have heard of his concept "libido," which is his favored term for the underlying force or power behind our thoughts, feelings, and actions. It may surprise many, however, that it is not simply to be understood as it is common parlance as "sex drive." Indeed, British culture is awash with what we might call *Freudisms*, that may cause those who have never read a single page of his work to have a sense that he was obsessed with sex. The fact that references to the Oedipus complex, "castration anxiety," and "penis envy" are enduring tropes in contemporary British culture gives support to such a view.

This way of thinking about Freud is strengthened if the analysis is restricted only to his earlier work on what he called the five stages of psychosexual development, which espoused a rather simplistic view of libido that seems to dominate how British society continues to see the man and his work.[33] In this early work, Freud saw life as built around pleasure and tension, with libido conceptualized entirely in terms of sexual energy, where tension is attributed to a buildup of libido and pleasure to a discharge of it.[34] Yet, Freud's thinking on libido was not a static concept, but rather a concept that developed over the course of his research and practice and therefore should not be limited to being seen as a mere drive for sex. It is also an expression for a multidimensional source of energy present in a multiplicity of relationship types and forms.

In the present analysis, I have neither the space nor the inclination to engage critically with Freud's earlier thoughts on how he conceived of libido and the role or function that in played in the sexual development of children. As already stated, my purpose here is to determine any possible relevance in a Freudian explanation of why individuals choose to join the CPD or FAD group despite the obvious and very apparent limitations of the wholesale adoption of either camp.

---

33   Sigmund Freud, *Three Essays on the Theory of Sexuality*. In *The Standard Edition of the Complete Psychological Works of Sigmund Freud, Vol. VII*, trans. James Strachey (London: Hogarth Press, 1905).
34   Ibid.

With this in mind, I want to jump straight to what Freud said in *Group Psychology* about his continued usage of the concept of libido, notwithstanding what turns out to be widespread misunderstandings and misinterpretations of what he meant by the term and what he was trying to convey by using it.[35] In a more expansive mode, Freud went far beyond a reductive and rather restrictive notion of libido as mere sex drive or lust by grounding it in the theory of emotions and the concept of "love," which is also not to be restricted to sexual love.[36] Indeed, for Freud, the dominant usage or understanding of the concept "love" may relate to sexual love, but it is a concept also used for love of self, parents, children, friends, to humanity, generally, or even to abstract ideas, e.g., I love Karl Marx's theory of commodity fetishism, or material objects, e.g., I love my car, my new shoes, dark chocolate, and so on.[37]

In his discussion of this wider sense and usage of the concept of love, in *Group Psychology* Freud cited Plato's concept of "Eros" in terms of a "love force" with wide applicability, and also Saint Paul the Apostle's letter to the Corinthians, wherein he praises love above all else, which also referred to love in a much wider sense than mere lust or sexual drive.[38] Reflecting on this, Freud acknowledged that his previous work and psychoanalysis, generally, has tended to give these "love instincts" 'the name of sexual instincts, *a potiori*,' a "nomenclature" that has been regarded by '[t]he majority of "educated" people' as insulting.[39] He then concedes that he 'might have ... spared [himself] much opposition had he used the more "genteel" expression of "eros," for instance, "from the first" 'but [he] did not want to.'[40] His reasoning for retaining the concept libido, rather than that of love instincts or eros, was as follows:

> I like to avoid concessions to faintheartedness. One can never tell where that road may lead one; one gives way first in words, and then little by little in substance too. I cannot see any merit in being ashamed of sex; the Greek word "Eros," which is to soften the affront, is in the end nothing more than a translation of our German word Liebe [love].[41]

---

35   Sigmund Freud, *Group Psychology*.
36   Ibid.
37   Ibid., 23.
38   Ibid.
39   Ibid.
40   Ibid.
41   Ibid., 24.

Applying this wider way of thinking about love or emotional energy at the heart of the psychology of groups, Freud averred that 'love relationships (or, to use a more neutral expression, emotional ties) also constitute the essence of the group mind.'[42] For Freud, this claim is supported on the basis of the following two grounds:

> First, a group is clearly held together by a power of some kind: and to what power could this feat be better ascribed than to Eros, which holds together everything in the world? Secondly, that if an individual gives up his distinctiveness in a group and lets its other members influence him by suggestion, it gives one the impression that he does it because he feels the need of being in harmony with them rather than in opposition to them—so that perhaps after all he does it "ihnen zu Liebe" [literally meaning "for love of them"].[43]

If we apply this aspect of Freud's thesis on group psychology to CPD and FAD, we can say that a Freudian perspective would see the members of the opposing camps joining together on a psychological level on which they have a certain love of, or emotionality for, their fellow group members. That is to say that Freud might say that the members of the opposing groups share a common love or libidinal bond or libidinal admiration for one another, with libido here understood in a wider sense than mere sexual lust. Moving from the type of power or force that binds individual group members, the question arises as to what makes an individual attracted to members of one side or the other in the push and pull between CPD and FAD. In an attempt to answer this question from a Freudian approach, we now turn to his notions of the id, ego, and super-ego.

8 The Id and the Ego

To help clarify the nature and role of the id in his tripartite structure, it is helpful to discuss the relationship between the id and the ego, as Freud himself did.[44] Indeed, for Freud, individuals are to be seen entirely as 'a psychical id, unknown and unconscious, upon whose surface rests the ego.'[45] More specifically, for

---

42 Ibid.
43 Ibid.
44 Freud, *The Ego and the Id*.
45 Ibid., 23.

Freud, the id represents the part of our minds where unconscious thoughts, feelings, and desires reside. In this sense, the id can be described as the primal and instinctual part of the mind; It is where our default psychic settings are located.[46] It is the core of who we are from birth, being inherited biologically from our parents and previous generations.

In terms of its functioning, the id is an amoral organism for Freud; we might even say a premoral force, which is not controlled by pragmatic societal moral notions of right versus wrong or good versus evil.[47] Rather, the id contains the source of our bodily needs and wants, emotional impulses, our passions and sexual and aggressive drives, and where our repressed memories are located. It is driven by a desire for pleasure and instant gratification and the avoidance or dispelling of pain.[48]

The job of the ego, for Freud, is to try to resist and repress the id or the unconscious in such a way that the individual character of the individual is formed to act appropriately within the setting or society that they find themselves in.[49] An analogy given by Freud for the ego as it tries to control the id was that of a rider on a horse 'who has to hold in check the superior strength of the horse.'[50] In distinguishing, further, between the id and the ego, Freud posited that:

> the ego is that part of the id which has been modified by the direct influence of the external world ... Moreover, the ego seeks to bring the influence of the external world to bear upon the id and its tendencies, and endeavours to substitute the reality principle for the pleasure principle which reigns unrestrictedly in the id. For the ego, perception plays the part which in the id falls to instinct. The ego represents what may be called reason and common sense, in contrast to the id, which contains the passions.[51]

In preparation for this task, Freud asserted that the most important step in the development of the ego is the transition from the "pleasure principle" to the

---

46   Freud, *Group Psychology*; Freud, *The Ego and the Id*; Sigmund Freud, *Introductory Lectures on Psychoanalysis*, in *The Standard Edition of the Complete Psychological Works of Sigmund Freud, Vol. XV & XVI*, trans. James Strachey (London: The Hogarth Press, 1963).
47   Freud, *The Ego and the Id*.
48   Freud, *Group Psychology*; Freud, *The Ego and the Id*; Freud, *Introductory Lectures*.
49   Freud, *The Ego and the Id*, 25.
50   Ibid.
51   Ibid.

"reality principle."⁵² In its experience and encounters with the real world or social reality, the ego comes to learn that it cannot simply cede to the demands of the id and its unconscious and irrational demands for instant gratification and pleasure. Rather, it must seek to postpone obtaining pleasure, learn to accept a certain amount of unpleasantness and even give up the hope of ever achieving certain types of pleasure as it strives to not be entirely governed and controlled by the id. Such an ego, for Freud, has educated itself from its real-world encounters to the extent that it serves the reality principle, which also seeks pleasure, but pleasure that is assured through taking account of reality.⁵³ An example to illustrate this point could be the pleasure of owning a new car. Whist the id would simply see a car and want to take it, an educated and appropriately developed and functioning ego would try to get a job and save up the money to buy the car: that is, the pleasure and gratification would be deferred, rather than demanded immediately.

9 The Ego and the Super-ego or Ego Ideal

As with the discussion of the id and the ego, it is helpful to understanding Freud's concept of the super-ego if it is discussed alongside the ego.⁵⁴ As indicated, for Freud, the ego can be described as the part of the id that has been transformed by the influence of the external reality, but Freud sees a differentiation between the egos of individuals in terms of what he labelled the super-ego or ego ideal, which along with the ego also play a part in molding a person's character.⁵⁵ It is the super-ego that incorporates the values and morals of the society we find ourselves in, which we learn from forms of authority, starting with our parents, but also involving religion or other belief systems, school, influences from wider society, and so on.

In essence, then, the super-ego or ego ideal, for Freud, contains our moral conscience and the ego is the realistic part that mediates between the desires of the id and the super-ego.⁵⁶ Moreover, for Freud, the super-ego rewards us for behavior or deeds thought to be good by making us feel good or proud, but punishes us for behavior or acts thought to be bad or wrongful in the form of guilt and shame.⁵⁷ This adds a further dimension to the pleasure principle as

---

52 Freud, *Introductory Lectures*, 402.
53 Ibid.
54 Freud, *The Ego and the Id*.
55 Ibid., 28.
56 Ibid.
57 Ibid., 35–37.

the super-ego applies an altogether different pressure on the ego to abide by its standards. For this reason, Freud's saw the ego as having an incredibly difficult job in trying to contain and satisfy the id and the super-ego or ego ideal. Indeed, for Freud, the ego is: 'a poor creature owing service to three masters and consequently menaced by three dangers: from the external world, from the ... id, and from the severity of the super-ego.'[58] We can also see here that the super-ego, for Freud, is partly conscious in terms of its effect on the behavior of the ego, yet playing an unconscious part as well, as it is a product of forms of cultural power that both determine and shape this predominantly unconscious aspects of the psyche of individuals. As Freud said:

> Whereas the ego is essentially the representative of the external world, of reality, the super-ego stands in contrast to it as the representative of the internal world, of the id. Conflicts between the ego and the ideal will, as we are now prepared to find, ultimately reflect the contrast between what is real and what is psychical, between the external world and the internal world.[59]

The ideas of the inherent unconscious nature of the id, how it functions in relation to the pleasure principle, and how the reality principle governs the workings of the ego alluded to here, are useful in making some sense of why individuals elect to either align themselves with CPD or FAD from a Freudian lens. In a Freudian sense, their choice of which side or group to join can be interpreted as a product of an idinal or unconscious drive from which they derive pleasure to the detriment or sacrifice, it seems, of rationality or the reality that opting to join the CPD group or the FAD group inherently, and unescapably, inflicts injustice and harm to innocent victims of CSA or false allegations of CSA.[60] Such a choice for Freud is based on deep rooted psychological feelings that give pleasure to the id or unconscious of the individual.[61] This may explain why the group members of CPD versus FAD seem impervious to objective logical reflection or adaptation when the inherent injustice and harmfulness of the group to which they belong in the conflict over how to see or respond to UACSA is brought to their attention.

Moreover, we can also make a provisional application of the role of the super-ego or ego ideal in Freud's work to the opposing groups that have taken

58   Ibid., 56.
59   Ibid., 36.
60   Freud, *Introductory Lectures*.
61   Freud, *The Ego and the Id*.

sides in response to the problematic of UACSA.[62] Indeed, from a Freudian perspective, we might say that a determining factor in the choice of which side to join, as opposed to joining no side at all; staying neutral on an issue wherein it is not possible to know the truth of (as a third party), may relate to the strength or power of the individuals super-ego or ego ideal towards child protection, on the one hand, or the presumption of innocence and due process rights of those accused of CSA where there is no corroboration, on the other.[63] Whatever the reason for the choice of group to join, however, and whatever perverse pleasure that they may obtain, neither side is innocent in the infliction of forms of injustice and harm to innocent victims on the side of their adversary that they claim to stand against.

10 The Key Features of Group Psychology

Now that we are equipped with an understanding of Freud's core operating concepts, we can turn, specifically, to his thesis on group psychology to illuminate its key features in the context of CPD and FAD.[64] This will be discussed under the following three subheadings: The inter-relationship between individual and group psychology; The group mind and its consequences; and Identification: Why individuals join the groups they chose.

11 The Inter-relationship between Individual and Group Psychology

It is significant that the first idea that Freud engages with in his book dedicated to evaluating and understanding group psychology, *Group Psychology and the Analysis of the Ego* (*Group Psychology*), is to emphasize that to make a distinction between individual psychology and group psychology would be a folly. On the contrary, for Freud, 'from the very first, individual psychology is at the same time group psychology as well,' as it is only rarely, and under exceptional circumstances (which will not be part of this analysis) that individuals are in a position to be able to disregard their relations to others.[65] Here, Freud is highlighting how individuals are fundamentally social beings, and how in the psychological minds of all individuals 'someone else is invariably involved, as an

---

62 Ibid.
63 Ibid.
64 Freud, *Group Psychology*.
65 Ibid., 7.

object, as a helper, as an opponent.'[66] That is to say, our thinking is always to be understood as a creation or product of a response or a reaction, positive or negative, however those terms are to be defined or interpreted, to an engagement with others.

Put simply, individual psychology is, therefore, best seen as forged in relationships with others, that is, within groups within any given society, which presents a challenge to any notion of thinking about individual psychology in isolation of the relationships that have created it. At our earliest age, this will be relatively small groups with as little as two members, such as with our parent(s) or sibling(s), with group size and complexity growing as we get older to include other individuals at school, at church, at work, and so on. As we grow, Freud sees our sphere of relationships extending to a greater number of other individuals with whom we form different types of groups for different purposes: social or sports clubs, political parties, professional societies, and the like. In so doing, Freud bridges individual and group psychology and locates individual psychology firmly within a context within which the social actions of individuals as members of groups are to be understood. As he said, group psychology is, therefore, concerned with the individual only so far as they are a member of a nation, a social class, an ethnic group, a profession, an institution, or as a 'component part of a crowd of people who have been organized into a group at some particular time for some definite purpose.'[67] Crucially, for Freud, individual psychology *is* group psychology, with neither the individual nor the group being able to understand without reference to the other.

In thinking about what Freud might term the indivisibility of individual and group psychology, then, we might say that it is in the very nature of human beings from a Freudian perspective to be both formed by groups and then to form groups with others. Freud owes this part of his thesis in *Group Psychology* to a critical evaluation of Gustave Le Bon's pioneering contribution to analyzing and understanding group psychology in his 1896 book, *The Crowd: A study of the Popular Mind*.[68] Citing Le Bon directly, Freud asserted that although individual and group psychology are intrinsically related, when individuals mold into a group they form 'a sort of collective mind that makes them feel, think, and act in a manner quite different from that which each individual of them would feel, think and act if they were in a state of isolation.'[69]

---

66   Ibid.
67   Ibid.
68   Gustav Le Bon, *The Crowd: Study of a Popular Mind*. New York: The Macmillan Co, 1896.
69   Freud, *Group Psychology*, 9.

As this relates to the groups or oppositional camps that we are concerned with in this chapter, CPD versus FAD, Freud might say that they act as an individual unit with a "group mind," which has significant consequences for the psychology of both individuals and groups.[70]

12 The Group Mind and its Consequences

For Freud, the groups formed by individuals and the collective minds that they adopt are always 'very simple and very exaggerated,' 'knowing no doubt nor uncertainty' 'as to what constitutes truth or error.'[71] Moreover, for Freud, the collective minds of groups have never been concerned about nor worried about the truthfulness or otherwise of their position.[72] Rather, they operate in the realm of the unconscious and to the tune of the pleasure principle, 'constantly giv[ing] what is unreal precedence over what is real; they [groups] are almost as strongly influenced by what is untrue as by what is true. They have an evident tendency not to distinguish between the two.'[73] It was in this sense that Freud saw the mind of the group as synonymous with the minds of primitive people where 'the most contradictory ideas can exist side by side and tolerate each other, without any conflict arising from the logical contradiction between them.'[74]

Taken together, these key and core traits of the psychological functioning of groups in Freud's analysis serves to unshackle and absolve individuals from any responsibility or conscience for the actions of the groups that they form a part to the following effect:

> when individuals come together in a group all their individual inhibitions fall away and all the cruel, brutal, and destructive instincts, which lie dormant in individuals as relics of a primitive epoch, are stirred up to find free gratification.[75]

The implications of this part of Freud's thesis on group psychology involves both potential gains and losses for individuals, depending on how one looks

---

70 Ibid., 24.
71 Ibid., 13.
72 Ibid., 14.
73 Ibid.
74 Ibid., 8.
75 Ibid., 13.

at it. In losing their conscience and sense of responsibility, individuals are free to act according to the unbridled whim of their unconscious passions and instincts, which? Freud asserted is a place where 'all that is evil in the human mind is contained as a predisposition.'[76] On the other hand, the price to pay, if the foregoing is not enough, in giving up our moral conscience and sense of individual responsibility for our actions can be conceived in terms of the loss of our very selves and our unique individuality.

This aspect of Freud's thesis on group psychology speaks directly to the problem that I have encountered in response to my work that was discussed in the introduction to this chapter. Feminist colleagues, for instance, who claim to be academics, who might see themselves as academics, and who want others to see them as academics, appear to undermine any notion that they are academics when the tension between their individual and group psychology is exposed. At such times, the psychology or mind of the group to which they align themselves is seen to dominate their individual psychology, which certainly seems to be the case in my own personal experiences of reactions to my research on UACSA.

But this phenomenon appears to apply, equally, to group members of CPD and FAD who show understanding of the inherent injustice and harmfulness of the group that they oppose, but not of the group or side that they belong to, that they are a part of. To be sure, they not only have a blind spot on how the group they are a part of can cause forms of injustice and harm that they claim to stand against, the recognition of the injustice and harm that their opposing group causes, which it seems oblivious to, acts to spur them on further in their cause. In my previous research, my analysis identified this phenomenon as a form of cognitive dissonance.[77] However, an application of a Freudian perspective substantially deepens the analysis by linking it to the unconscious minds of individuals bound together in groups that operate on principles of pleasure, rather than rationality, objectivity and/or logic.[78]

13 Identification: Why Individuals Join the Groups They Chose

My question here not only relates to the relationship between individuals and groups and the way that the minds of groups merge together to act in unison, but also, what makes individuals choose the groups they join? In answer to this

---

76 Ibid., 11.
77 Naughton, "Rethinking the Competing Discourses".
78 Freud, *Group Psychology*.

question, Freud's concept of "identification" seems helpful.[79] For Freud, identification is the earliest expression of an emotional connection with another person, which, as already indicated, can form the simplest type of group. The process of identification, for Freud, relates to when individuals are growing up and show a strong desire either to be like their Fathers or other forms of authority figures.[80] In essence, for Freud, identification 'endeavors to mold a person's own ego after the fashion of the one that has been taken as the "model."'[81]

Freud conceived two additional features of identification, which are also useful to this discussion. Identification, for Freud, functions in terms of a form of love energy, as described above, which acts in a repressive way on the egos of the individual who join together to form a group and a group psychology or mind.[82] Moreover, not only can identification 'arise with any new perception of a common quality shared with some other person,' 'the more important the common quality is, the more successful may this partial identification become, and it may thus represent the beginning of a new tie.'[83]

If we link these defining characteristics of group psychology with the foregoing discussion of Freud's conceptualization of the id and the super-ego, we might say that Freud makes a direct link between individual group members in terms of the compatibility of their ids, which are biologically inherited, as well as their super-egos, which are products of social factors that determine the higher moral values pertaining to the particular society and/or epoch that an individual is born into.

If this theory is applied to group membership of either CPD or FAD, we can argue that a Freudian analysis would suggest that the individuals who opt to take a side in the debate about UACSA do so because they identify strongly with others who they join with to form such groups or with whom are already members of the group they decide to join. That is to say, such individuals mold with likeminded others to form or join the groups in question where there is compatibility between their ids and super egos or ego ideals. Moreover, in a Freudian sense, the choice to be members of CPD or FAD is largely, if not entirely, unconscious. By this I mean that it is a choice made by idinal instincts and feelings, which are enhanced and strengthened by social factors, which formed the person's super-ego, rather than along lines of rationality, objectivity, and logic. Such members would be "rewarded" on both the level of the id

---

79   Ibid., 34–38.
80   Ibid., 34.
81   Ibid., 35.
82   Ibid., 27.
83   Ibid.

and the super-ego in the sense that they are satisfying their unconscious urges and also their sense of morality in thinking that they are on the side of a vulnerable victim group in a fight against a foe that means them harm.

In such circumstances, a Freudian approach might say that it seems little wonder that attempts to reason with members of CPD or FAD, suggesting that their position is inherently problematical in terms of the way that each group inflicts forms of injustice and harm on innocent victims in the adversary group, falls on deaf ears, which has potentially profound implications in terms of what might be done in response (to be discussed in the conclusion below). To be sure, a Freudian perspective may further say that the pleasure principle can be conceived as at its strongest and most potent when the ids and super egos of the individuals who mold together in groups are in alignment to such a degree that mere reality (the role of the ego) seems unable to disrupt or dislodge it.

14   Conclusion

From the foregoing application of some of Freud's core concepts and his specific theorizing in *Group Psychology*, it should be clear that it can be stated without equivocation that Freud does appear to have some contemporary relevance, certainly so in terms of shedding some light on the problem that I posed when I began this project from a close reading and application of his theories: Why do individuals choose to join groups such as CPD or FAD; what, if anything, do they gain or lose from that choice; and, what, if anything, can be done to reduce or prevent the forms of injustice and harm inherent in the opposing groups that have emerged in response to UACSA?

Indeed, if we deconstruct the interrelated questions that I set myself and take them in chronological order, we might say from a Freudian perspective that individuals choose to join either CPD or FAD because the group that they join aligns, perfectly, with their ids and super egos; that it is largely an unconscious drive that propels certain individuals to elect to take a side in such debates; to join either CPD or FAD.[84] Moreover, a Freudian analysis might suggest, further, that it permits those individuals who become members of such groups to satisfy the passions and desires of their unconscious ids as they merge with compatible compatriots on the level of the super ego, too.[85] Overall, such group

---

84   Freud, *Group Psychology*; Freud, *The Ego and the Id*.
85   Ibid.

members can be conceived from a Freudian perspective to share a moral quest that gives pleasure to their ids and their super-egos as they (appear to) stand up for the (so-called) victims that they claim to represent, and fight against a clearly identifiable enemy that wants to crush them and who they, likewise, want to destroy.[86] The obvious loser in this war for superiority between CPD and FAD combatants are the egos of the opposing individual group members, which Freud described as a "poor creature" on the basis that he saw it as 'owing service to three masters and consequently menaced by three dangers: from the external world, from the ... id, and from the severity of the super-ego.'[87] As this relates to those individuals who join CPD and/or FAD, the egos of the individuals involved can be said, again from a Freudian perspective, to have failed in this critical task of holding their ids and super-egos in check as the reality of the injustice and harm that the group that they have subscribed to is sacrificed in favor of satisfying an unconscious idinal and super-ego craving for instant pleasure and gratification.

In terms of the question of what do individuals gain or lose by joining a group like CPD or FAD, a Freudian analysis might argue that the question is invalid.[88] That is to say, a Freudian analysis can be conceived as not about attributing value to how individuals or groups act, but rather describing how they act and explaining why they act in the way that they do. This being said, I think that it is worth conceptualizing here what members of groups such as CPD or FAD gain or lose by joining such a group, noting up front that it depends on how gain and loss is defined. To think about what such individuals might lose by joining CPD or FAD, from the perspective of individual integrity, scientific objectivity, and truth and justice, I would conceptualize the loss of individual autonomy and responsibility for thoughts and actions as a loss, as a loss of self. On the other hand, I can also see also that it could just as easily be seen as a gain to merge with a group of compatible others and form a group mentality in the interests of feeling good and obtaining pleasure, such that the burden of individual responsibility for thoughts and deeds is offloaded, as appears to be the case with members of CPD and/or FAD.

But what does this mean for the final part the question that I set myself: What, if anything, can be done to reduce or prevent the forms of injustice and harm inherent in the opposing groups that have emerged in response to UACSA? The simple answer is that I am not sure if anything can be done about it at all from

---

86 Ibid.
87 Freud, *The Ego and the Id*, 56.
88 Freud, *Group Psychology*; Freud, *The Ego and the Id*.

a Freudian perspective.[89] Indeed, as discussed above, for Freud the groups formed by individuals and the collective minds that they adopt are always 'very simple and very exaggerated,' 'knowing no doubt nor uncertainty' 'as to what constitutes truth or error.'[90] Moreover, for Freud such groups functions with a singular mentality that sees the world in black and white and neither concern themselves with, nor worry about, the truthfulness of their position.[91] Rather, for Freud, they operate in the land of the unconscious and march to the drum of the pleasure principle, 'constantly giv[ing] what is unreal precedence over what is real; they [groups] are almost as strongly influenced by what is untrue as by what is true.'[92]

Looked at from this perspective, groups that function along unconscious feelings and unrestrained passions and desires, and where rationality and truth have no bearing, are unlikely to be able to be reformed by attempts to educate group members to snap them back into reality. It is fair to say that this does seem to correspond with my own experiences. I have often felt exasperated and frustrated at the apparent inability of those who subscribe to groups such as CPD or FAD to see the problematic nature of their position in terms of the potential, and reality, to inflict injustice and harm on innocent victims, and who can become even deeper entrenched in such positions if they are challenged by that reality. Freud expressed this tendency in the following terms:

> In the psycho-analytical theory of the mind we take it for granted that the course of mental processes is automatically regulated by the "pleasure-principle": that is to say, we believe that any given process originates in an unpleasant state of tension and thereupon determines for itself such a path that its ultimate issue coincides with a relaxation of this tension, i.e., with avoidance of "pain" or with production of pleasure.[93]

An apt analogy might be the law of physics, which dictates that energy will always flow along the path of least resistance. It seems appropriate, too, when thinking about how a Freudian analysis might explain the apparent intransigence of group members of CPD and FAD.[94] The energy (or forms of power)

---

89 Ibid.
90 Freud, *Group Psychology*, 13.
91 Ibid., 14.
92 Ibid.
93 Sigmund Freud, *Beyond the Pleasure Principle,* trans. James Strachey (London: Hogarth Press, 1920).
94 Freud, *Group Psychology*; Freud, *The Ego and the Id.*

that binds such groups together appears to also flow along the path of least resistance and take little or no notice whatsoever about the forms of injustice and harm that they cause to the "other" side as they act in the interests of avoiding such a painful reality in favor of the pursuit of uninhibited pleasure.

The final thing to say in closing this chapter is the caveat that the analyses undertaken and presented here were applications of Freud's core concepts and specific theory on group psychology. That is to say, it neither problematized, nor critiqued, the works by Freud that were utilized in the analysis by reference to competing or conflicting alternative perspectives, which might have produced an altogether different outcome if I had. This is not to somehow detract from the analyses that were conducted. Rather, it is to merely emphasize the parameters of the task that I set for myself and to flag up that had other theorists been brought into the exercise, then, the outcome might have been different.

But such is the caution that must be placed on any analysis produced from the perspective of a single theorist, which can only ever provide an insight into a problem from the perspective of that particular way of looking at things. As this relates to this chapter, then, the analysis is to be received as from a strict Freudian perspective, and a particular interpretation and application of a Freudian perspective at that. It is not definitive, nor exhaustive. And, if the same problem were evaluated from the lens of a different theorist, the analysis would likely be different and the conclusions different, too.

Bibliography

Anderson, Elizabeth M., and Murray Levine. "Concerns about Allegations of Child Sexual Abuse against Tachers and the Teaching Environment." *Child Abuse & Neglect* 23, no. 8 (1999): 833–843.

Baird, Vera. "Sexual Abuse is about Power – and the Powerful shouldn't be Protected." *The Guardian*. April 29, 2014.

Brown, Jocelyn, Patricia Cohen, Jeffrey G. Johnson, and Elizabeth M. Smailes. "Childhood Abuse and Neglect: Specificity of Effects on Adolescent and Young Adult Depression and Suicidality." *Journal of the American Academy of Child and Adolescent Psychiatry* 38, no. 12 (1999): 1490–1496.

Burnett, Ros. ed. *Wrongful Allegations of Sexual and Child Abuse*. Oxford: Oxford University Press, 2016.

Burnett, Ros. "Why it is too easy for Innocent People to be Wrongly Accused of Sexual Abuse." *The Justice Gap*. March 13, 2017. http://thejusticegap.com/2017/03/easy-innocent-people-wrongly-accused-sexual-abuse> Accessed: August 26, 2022.

Cashmore, Judy, and Rita Shackel. "The Long-Term Effects of Child Sexual Abuse." *Child Family Community Australia* 11 (2013): 1–29.

Coleman, Lee, and Patrick E. Clancy. "False Allegations of Child Sexual Abuse: Why is it Happening, What Can We Do." *Criminal Justice* 5, no. 3 (1990): 14–47.

Eady, Dennis. "What to do about the Epidemic of Historical abuse Cases?" *The Justice Gap*. 2017 http://thejusticegap.com/2017/05/ccrc20-epidemic-historic-sex-abuse-cases> Accessed: August 26, 2022.

Elks, Laurie. *Righting Miscarriages of Justice? Ten Years of the Criminal Cases Review Commission*. JUSTICE. 2018.

FACT 2022. "What we do." https://factuk.org/about-us/what-we-do> Accessed: August 26, 2022.

Finkelhor, David. "Current Information on the Scope and Nature of Child Sexual Abuse." *The Future of Children* 4, no. 2 (1994): 31–53.

Freud, Sigmund. *Beyond the Pleasure Principle*. Translated by James Strachey. London: The Hogarth Press, 1920.

Freud, Sigmund. *The Ego and the Id*. Translated by Joan Riviere. London: The Hogarth Press, 1923.

Freud, Sigmund. *Group Psychology and the Analysis of the Ego*. Translated by James Strachey. London & Vienna: The International Psycho-Analytical Press, 1922.

Freud, Sigmund. "Introductory Lectures on Psychoanalysis". In *The Standard Edition of the Complete Psychological Works of Sigmund Freud, Volumes XV and XVI*. Translated by James Strachey. London: The Hogarth Press, 1963.

Freud, Sigmund. *Three Essays on the Theory of Sexuality*. In *The Standard Edition of the Complete Psychological Works of Sigmund Freud, Vol. VII*. Translated by James Strachey. London: Hogarth Press, 1905.

Gambaccini, Paul. *Love, Paul Gambaccini: My Year under the Yewtree*. London: Biteback Publishing, 2015.

George, Mark. "Why the Policy of 'believe the complainant' was behind the Failure of Disclosure in the case of Liam Allan." 2017. https://gcnchambers.co.uk/policy-believe-complainant-behind-failure-disclosure-case-liam-allan> Accessed: August 26, 2022.

Gray, David, and Peter Watt. "'Giving Victims a Voice': A joint MPS and NSPCC report into Allegations of Sexual Abuse made against Jimmy Savile under Operation Yewtree." 2013. https://www.nspcc.org.uk/globalassets/documents/research-reports/yewtree-report-giving-victims-voice-jimmy-savile.pdf> Accessed: August 26, 2022.

Green, Arthur H. "True and False Allegations of Sexual Abuse in Child Custody Disputes." *Journal of the American Academy of Child Psychiatry* 25 (1986): 444–456.

Greene, Nik. *False Accusations: Guilty Until Proven Innocent*. Houston, TX: Strategic Book Publishing & Rights Agency, LLC, 2011.

Henriques, Richard. "Report – Independent Review of Metropolitan Police Service's handling of non-recent sexual offence investigations." 2016. http://news.met.police.uk/documents/report-independent-review-of-metropolitan-police-services-handling-of-non-recent-sexual-offence-investigations-61510> Accessed: August 26, 2022.

Hewson, Barbara. "False Allegations, Emotional Truths and Actual Lies." *The Justice Gap*. 2016. http://thejusticegap.com/2016/04/false-allegations-emotional-truth-actual-lies> Accessed: August 26, 2022.

Hinsliff, Gaby. "'It Never Stops Shaping You': The Legacy of Child Sexual Abuse – and How to Survive it." *The Guardian*. June 28, 2018.

HM Government 2015. "Working Together to Safeguard Children: A guide to Inter-agency working to Safeguard and Promote the Welfare of Children." 2015. https://www.gov.uk/government/uploads/system/uploads/attachment_data/file/592101/Working_Together_to_Safeguard_Children_20170213.pdf> Accessed: August 26, 2022.

Hoyle, Carolyn, Naomi-Ellen Speechley, and Ros Burnett. "The Impact of Being Wrongly Accused of Abuse in Occupations of Trust: Victims' Voices." 2015. https://www.law.ox.ac.uk/sites/files/oxlaw/the_impact_of_being_wrongly_accused_of_abuse_hoyle_speechley_burnett_final_26_may.pdf> Accessed: August 26, 2022.

Independent Inquiry into Child Sexual Abuse. "Report of the Internal Review." 2016a. https://www.iicsa.org.uk/key-documents/935/view/IICSA%20Review%20Report_Final_alt_v4_ACCESS.pdf> Accessed: 26 August 2022.

Independent Inquiry into Child Sexual Abuse. "Truth Project. Experiences shared: Victims and Survivors Speak Out." 2016b. https://www.iicsa.org.uk/key-documents/923/view/truth-project-experiences-shared.pdf> Accessed: August 26, 2022.

Jay, Alexis. "Independent Inquiry into Child Sexual Exploitation in Rotherham (1997–2013)." 2014. http://www.rotherham.gov.uk/downloads/file/1407/independent_inquiry_cse_in_rotherham> Accessed: August 26, 2022.

Jones, David. *No Smoke, No Fire: The Autobiography of Dave Jones*. Chichester: Pitch Publishing Limited, 2011.

Kopetski, Leona M., Deirdre Conway Rand, and Randy Randy. "Incidence, Gender, and False Allegations of Child Abuse: Data on 84 Parental Alienation Syndrome Cases." In *The International Handbook of Parental Alienation Syndrome*, edited by Gardner, R. A., Sauber, S.R. and Lorandos, D. Springfield, IL: Charles C. Thomas Publisher Limited, 2006.

Kuehnle, Kathryn, and Mary Connell. eds. *The Evaluation of Child Sexual Abuse Allegations: A Comprehensive Guide to Assessment and Testimony*. Hoboken, NJ: John Wiley and Sons, 2009.

Le Bon, Gustav. *The Crowd: Study of a Popular Mind*. New York: The Macmillan Co, 1896.

Naughton, Michael. "Confronting an Uncomfortable Truth: Not all Alleged Victims of False Accusations will be Innocent." *FACTion* 3 no. 10 (November 2007): 8–11.

Naughton, Michael. "Factual Innocence versus Legal Guilt: The Need for a New Pair of Spectacles to view the Problem of Life-Sentenced Prisoners Maintaining Innocence." *Prison Service Journal* 177 (May 2008): 32–37.

Naughton, Michael. "How the Presumption of Innocence Renders the Innocent Vulnerable to Wrongful Conviction." *Irish Journal of Legal Studies* 2, no. 1 (2011): 40–54.

Naughton, Michael. *The Innocent and the Criminal Justice System*. Basingstoke: Palgrave Macmillan, 2013.

Naughton, Michael. "Rethinking the Competing Discourses on Uncorroborated Allegations of Child Sexual Abuse." *The British Journal of Criminology* 59, no. 2 (2019): 461–480.

Naughton, Michael. *Rethinking Miscarriages of Justice: Beyond the Tip of the Iceberg*. Basingstoke: Palgrave Macmillan, 2007.

Naughton, Michael, and Gabe Tan. *Claims of Innocence: An Introduction to Wrongful Convictions and How they might be Challenged*. Bristol: University of Bristol, 2011.

NSPCC 2013. "Child Sexual Abuse: An NSPCC Research Briefing." 2013. https://www.nspcc.org.uk/globalassets/documents/information-service/research-briefing-child-sexual-abuse.pdf> Accessed: August 26, 2022.

Oxford English Dictionary 2022. "Victim." https://en.oxforddictionaries.com/definition/victim> Accessed: August 26, 2022.

Paolucci, Elizabeth Oddone, Mark L. Genuis, and Claudio Violato. "A Meta-Analysis of the Published Research on the Effects of Child Sexual Abuse." *Journal of Psychology* 135, no. 1 (2001): 17–36.

Pearson, Allison. "Alison Saunders must Stand Down – or be Sacked." *The Telegraph*. December 19, 2017.

Roan, Dan. "FA Abuse Inquiry Chief Receives Counselling after Hearing Victims' Stories." 2017. http://www.bbc.co.uk/sport/football/41645807> Last accessed: August 26, 2022.

Robins, Jon. "Hogan-Howe finally Apologies for Disastrous Operation Midland." *The Justice Gap*, 2016. http://thejusticegap.com/2016/11/hogan-howe-finally-apologies-disastrous-operation-midland> Accessed: 26 August 2022.

Robinson, Martin. "Father, 56, Leapt to his Death from the Humber Bridge After Being Falsely Accused of Abusing Child," *Mail Online*, November 13, 2013. http://www.dailymail.co.uk/news/article-2506252/Father-56-leapt-death-Humber-Bridgefalsely-accused-abusing-child.html> Accessed: August 26, 2022.

Rossetti, Stephen J. "Child Sexual Abuse and Power." *The Furrow* 46, no. 12 (1995): 684–688.

Rowles, Charlotte. "They can't all be making it up." *The Justice Gap*, 2015. http://thejusticegap.com/2015/11/they-cant-all-be-making-it-up-investigating-historic-abuse-claims> Accessed: August 26, 2022.

Smith, Gerrilyn. "Child Sexual Abuse: The Power of Intrusion." *Adoption & Fostering* 10 no. 3 (1986): 13–18.

The Offside Trust, "Who are we." 2018. http://www.theoffsidetrust.com> Accessed: September 21, 2018.

Unfounded: Alliance Against Unfounded Accusations of Abuse. "Who are we." 2018. http://www.unfounded.org.uk/who-we-are> Accessed: August 26, 2022.

Warr, Simon. *Presumed Guilty: A Teacher's Solitary Battle to Clear His Name*. London: Biteback Publishing, 2017.

Walker, Peter. "Frances Andrade Killed Herself After Being Accused of lying, Says Husband." *The Guardian*, February 20, 2013. https://www.theguardian.com/uk/2013/feb/10/frances-andrade-killed-herself-lying> Accessed: 26 August 2022.

World Health Organization (WHO). *"Preventing Child Maltreatment: A Guide to Taking and Generating Evidence."* Geneva: World Health Organization (WHO), 2006. http://apps.who.int/iris/bitstream/10665/43499/1/9241594365_eng.pdf> Accessed: August 26, 2022.

CHAPTER 17

No Heart to Feel, No Soul to Steal: Necrophilia and Mass Shootings in America

Joan Braune

1   Introduction

The past several years in the United States have been marked by a rising tide of violent hate attacks and fringe political violence, alongside forms of seemingly "random," nihilist mass violence, including some mass shootings that have been hard to explain. The rise in these "extreme" forms of violence has occurred alongside violence in the form of institutional policies (including targeting immigrants, refugees, and vulnerable minorities) and practices (police violence against Black, indigenous, and other people of color populations), a coup attempt at the U.S. Capitol that occurred with apparent support by the departing President, Donald J. Trump, and smaller scale hate crimes instigated by far-right social movements. Psychoanalysis has been underutilized to make sense of these developments, with some limited exceptions.[1]

Sigmund Freud's theory of the death instinct seems immediately relevant to the rise of mass shootings and related violence, but I suggest that these phenomena are better understood through Erich Fromm's modification of Freud's death instinct, in Fromm's preferred category of "necrophilia." According to Fromm, necrophilia is characterized by a malignant fascination with what is dead, mechanical, and easily controlled, may manifest in the desire to dismember and torture, and can contribute to extreme forms of violence.

Fromm's concept of necrophilia builds upon Freud's concept of the death instinct but also challenges and amends it. In *The Anatomy of Human Destructiveness*, Fromm praises the later Freud for moving past the limitations of a focus on physical desires for sex and survival, to the more developed

---

1   E.g., Claudia Leeb, *The Politics of Repressed Guilt: The Tragedy of Austrian Silence* (Edinburgh: Edinburgh University Press, 2019); Federico Finchelstein, *A Brief History of Fascist Lies* (Oakland: University of California Press, 2020); Lauren Langman and George Lundskow, *God, Guns, Gold and Glory: American Character and Its Discontents* (Chicago: Haymarket Books, 2016).

concepts of "Eros" and "Thanatos."[2] However, Fromm was also critical of the way that Freud naturalized the death instinct, which Fromm saw as tied to Freud's nationalism and conformity, including Freud's support of the First World War. In *Sigmund Freud's Mission*, Fromm calls Freud a rebel as opposed to a revolutionary.[3] Freud's rebelliousness against his father's authority never extended to rebellion against Austrian nationalism and the state.[4] Although Freud related the death instinct to the forces of war, Fromm goes much further in his social analysis and leads to more radical conclusions, seeing how necrophilia is related to particular historical and cultural moments and structures, including modern industrial capitalism.

In this chapter, I suggest a new understanding of the mass shooter might draw from Fromm's theory of necrophilia. I first define and explore what I call "fascistic mass shooter culture," which is a broader category than shooters holding a conscious allegiance to fascist political movements. I then discuss a number of cases, focusing at some length on a case study of a 2019 mass shooter in Dayton, Ohio.[5] I conclude that rather than providing an individualized "profile" for which we should be on the watch, the theory of necrophilia contributes to social theory an understanding of what needs to change in society to reduce the threat of nihilistic mass violence.

2 Fascistic Mass Shooter Culture

Increasingly in the public mind, the mass shooter in America is often imagined to be a white supremacist or fascist ideologue, or at least an exponent of some related far-right ideology, like misogynist male supremacist movements.[6] We think for example of the mass shooters who, within the last five years,

---

2 Erich Fromm, *Anatomy of Human Destructiveness* (Greenwich: Fawcett Publications, 1973), 29.
3 Erich Fromm, *Sigmund Freud's Mission: An Analysis of His Personality and Influence* (New York: Harper & Brothers, 1959), 60.
4 Ibid., 61.
5 The names of mass shooters have been omitted where possible, in line with the recommendation of the No Notoriety campaign, since mass shootings can be partly inspired by the "notoriety" shooters expect to receive, a theme I will discuss later in this chapter.
6 A series of mass shootings have been inspired by male supremacist movements, such as the incel ("involuntary celibate") and MGTOW (Men Going Their Own Way) movements. Scholars increasingly suggest that male supremacy is a better term, as opposed to inaccurately lumping all male supremacist mass shooters into the "incel" category, as is often done in the mass media and popular discourse.

targeted a synagogue in Pittsburgh, mosques in New Zealand, Latino shoppers in El Paso, and Black shoppers in Buffalo; the mass shooters in all those cases expressed support in online writings for the "Great Replacement" conspiracy theory that sees white people as endangered by an "invasion" of dark-skinned migrants or faster-reproducing people of color, whose increasing demographics the shooters attributed to a secret Jewish conspiracy.

Other mass killings appear to have been motivated at least in part by prejudice or hate, even if the killers' ideologies may have been less clearly or less consciously expressed in writing or public statements than in other cases. For example, the killing of Asian women workers in multiple massage parlors in Atlanta, Georgia, was carried out by a right-wing Christian man who had recently received religious "treatment" for his "sex addiction" and who saw Asian women sex workers as temptations. Although not convicted of a hate crime, the massage parlor spree killer's words and actions seemed to many to play upon racist stereotypes of Asian women as seductive, and occurred at a period of renewed heights of anti-Asian prejudice stirred up by demonization of Chinese people and others in the midst of the COVID-19 pandemic. Similarly, although no "manifesto" has yet been made available to the public if it exists, as of this writing, the mass shooter targeting LGBTQ+ people and allies attending a drag show at Club Q in Colorado, likely faces bias/hate crime charges, and his act occurred in a context of rising homophobic and transphobic prejudice, including protests and intimidation of drag shows by fascist and far-right activists.

Despite the prevalence of hate-motivated mass shootings, a number of mass shooters are difficult to categorize. This seems to be the case, for example, with the 2019 mass shooter in Dayton, Ohio, and the 2022 mass shooter in Highland Park, Illinois. Neither had written a "manifesto." In fact, the Dayton shooter considered himself left-wing, supported either Elizabeth Warren or Bernie Sanders for President, and praised antifascist struggle, making him a particularly complicated case that, as I will show, led to him being mislabeled by some as a "leftist accelerationist" bent on killing for political motives. Meanwhile, the Highland Park shooter, while ostensibly a Trump supporter, also did not seem to have a clear political motive. Yet neither incident should be viewed in abstraction from larger social forces. The Dayton shooter abused women and enthusiastically showed his girlfriend a video of a mass shooting at a synagogue, for example, while the Highland Park shooter spent time in internet spaces filled with Nazis and participated in the trend of "schizoposting," an internet meme activity particularly promoted by Nazis and the far-right to encourage people to be paranoid, angry, and isolated, to "go schizo," and to commit mass shootings. Both the Dayton and Highland Park shooters had a long-running fascination with violence and with spaces of the internet consumed by violent despair.

"Fascistic" mass shooters are aware of online circulation of imagery and videos of mass shootings, and they may even encounter the iconographic memes made by Nazis depicting mass shooters with haloes and referring to them as "the Saints."[7] They also become aware of the mass shooter as a potential identity and one that holds the key to immortality – to fame and to being "remembered." The mass shooter in Parkland, Florida, for example, had stated that he wanted to become a "professional school shooter."[8] Although it may be the case that such shooters as the Dayton or Highland Park shooter may not have identified as white nationalists or may not even been narrowly "politically motivated," dismissing such cases as the Dayton and Highland Park shootings as "apolitical" or "non-ideological" misses the mark.[9] More must be done to explain and understand such cases than relying only on the shooters' professed political allegiances.

I consider such shooters as the Dayton and Highland Park shooters to be *"fascistic,"* even if they are not explicitly or consciously "fascist." This distinction between fascistic and fascist stems from an attempt to distinguish different senses of the term "fascism." The word "fascism" often is used to refer to three different things. First, it is used to refer to a worldview and the social movements that consciously support that worldview. For example, a neo-Nazi group is "fascist." Secondly, the term "fascism" is used to refer to states. In this sense of the term, one asks questions such as, "Is the United States fascist? Is Italy? India?," and political scientists and historians debate the stages by which a nation becomes "fascist" and the markers of fascist rule. It is in neither of these senses – conscious ideological belonging, nor possession of or a road to state power – that I am describing the Dayton and Highland Park shooters as "fascistic." Rather, I refer to a different and third sense of the term, in which actions and institutions may be reasonably criticized as "fascist" on the grounds that they are fascist-*ish* or fascistic, namely that they are *doing the*

---

7 Graham Macklin, "'Praise the Saints': The Cumulative Momentum of Transnational Extreme-Right Terrorism," in *A Transnational History of Right-Wing Terrorism: Political Violence and the Far Right in Eastern and Western Europe Since 1900*, ed. Johannes Dafinger and Moritz Florin (London: Routledge, 2022), 225.

8 Moonshot Team, "Mass Shooterism and the Need for Online Interventions and Bystander Resources," GNET, August 3, 2022. https://gnet-research.org/2022/08/03/mass-shooterism-and-the-need-for-online-interventions-and-bystander-resources/.

9 Joan Braune, "Experts Who Study Far-Right Mass Violence Must Center the Communities Affected," RANGE, July 26, 2022. https://www.rangemedia.co/highland-park-ideology-mass-shooting/.

work of fascism. To be clear, this third sense is not a catch-all: fascism is not just a word for things we do not like, whether disliked by the left or the right. But it is not inappropriate to use the term "fascism" to refer to people, activities, or institutions that are behaving in a way consistent with fascist ideology or fascist state power.

For example, horrifying footage was recently released of Border Patrol officers on the Texas/Mexico border riding horses and swinging whips at Haitian migrants on the ground beneath them. This imagery of white figures (or representatives of white power) on horses, whipping the Black figures beneath them, is so obviously reminiscent of the horrors of American enslavement of Black humans. So many markers of a fascist worldview are there: racism, hierarchy, violence, authoritarianism, and a hardcore nationalist "defense" of the national border against defenseless human beings seeking only the basics of human dignity. Someone who exclaimed that this action was "fascist," or used that language in a protest against this violation of human rights and dignity, would not be saying something inaccurate, nor would the protester have to believe the Border Patrol officers in question belonged to a hate group (although they certainly might).

Although I prefer the looser term "fascistic," what I am discussing here also has close relationship to the idea of "Microfascism," a term in the work of Gilles Deleuze and Felix Guattari, and very well developed and explicated in light of current recent developments by Jack Bratich's new book *On Microfascism: Gender, War, and Death*.[10] Although I am not relying on the framework of Deleuze and Guattari in this chapter, Bratich's theory of Microfascism especially as it relates to gender, is influential on my work here. Bratich points out that fascism shows up in various cultural phenomena, including in violence in interpersonal relationships. In line with fascists' and far-right theorists' emphasis on the "metapolitical," the idea that "politics is downstream of culture" (a saying of Andrew Breitbart frequently quoted by Steve Bannon), we can understand that fascism as a social movement seeking power and always already connected to sources of power, relies and depends upon fascistic or microfascist practices and activities to expand and resurge.

Defining fascism is a fraught space of debate, but fascism may be best defined not in a standard lexical manner but along the lines of what philosopher Ludwig Wittgenstein called "family resemblances," as is also suggested

---

10   Jack Z. Bratich, *On Microfascism: Gender, War, and Death* (Brooklyn: Common Notions, 2022).

by Umberto Eco in his famous essay on "ur-fascism."[11] One might point to a list of characteristics, such as racist and sexist prejudices, conspiracy theories, scapegoating, genocidal ambitions, an emphasis on an "us" and a "them," a cult of violence, authoritarianism, the privileging of a "movement" or "people" over the rule of law, nostalgia for a past social order, apocalyptic visions of the future destruction of the present social order, the use of armed paramilitary forces, and the belief that a natural hierarchy has been upended and must be restored. How many elements may need to be present for something to be "fascist," may be unclear, but a "laundry list" approach gets us to a level of familiarity with the concept.

Perhaps the fascistic mass shooter might show even fewer of these characteristics than a consciously fascist one would be likely to do. For example, perhaps the merely fascistic mass shooter does not see himself as belonging to a clear "us" positioned against a "them" – perhaps he sees himself as a lone individual cast against a sea of faceless, dehumanized others who simply menace his individuality and creativity and repress his power. He may have no sense of belonging to a movement. Perhaps, in fact, he sees himself as a kind of force of nature, uniting with the brutality of the world that he sees as the real essence of the universe.

The merely fascistic (as opposed to consciously fascist) mass shooter generally does not, I would suggest, participate in Freud's "primal horde." He is not whipped up by primal enthusiasms of group belonging and adherence to a leader. Rather, he proceeds coldly, icily, to his aim, spreading his own deathlike essence out into the world, rendering the external world increasingly akin to his inner deadness. Without a leader or even a clear cause to which he can give authoritarian submission, he seeks simply to destroy a world from which he feels radically disconnected. Nevertheless, he is influenced by a wider *fascist milieu*. This can include spending time in internet spaces that celebrate violence, deliberately desensitize, and promote fascism and hate. It also includes societal manifestations of hate, cruelty, and violence, including misogyny and militarism. I argue that, drawing on Fromm and seeing the fascistic mass shooter as necrophilic or having necrophilous tendencies, transcends a narrowly political paradigm (classifying each mass shooter according to who they voted for, for example) but simultaneously reckons with the ideological implications of mass shootings.

---

11   Umberto Eco, "Ur-Fascism," *The New York Review of Books*, June 22, 1995. https://www.pegc.us/archive/Articles/eco_ur-fascism.pdf.

3   Necrophilia

Fromm's category of necrophilia is primarily addressed in *The Heart of Man* (1964) and again in *The Anatomy of Human Destructiveness* (1973), although it does occur elsewhere, including an antiwar pamphlet he wrote for the American Friends Service Committee.[12] Necrophilia in Fromm's vocabulary denotes a mode of relatedness to others and the world that is blighted by intense disconnection from life and an attraction to what is lifeless, mechanical, and easier to control. It does not merely denote a sexual attraction to corpses, but manifests more broadly in the desire to dismember and torture, contributing to severe forms of violence. More to the point, Fromm sees necrophilia as an expression of "malignant aggression"; one that lacks any rational or life-affirming basis, and is rooted in the character structure of the severely damaged individual, involving "the pure passion to destroy."[13] The necrophilous person not only likes dead things but actually prefers things to be dead or deathlike, and embraces violence or force, seeing force as the "first and last solution for everything."[14] The necrophile prefers "law and order" to the unpredictable, uncontrollable nature of social life. Not necessarily seeing himself as a disrupter, he may self-deputize to support the power structure by means of deadly violence. I think here, for example, of far-right militias that appoint themselves to act as police at antiracist protests or as border guards harassing migrants. Wisconsin teenager Kyle Rittenhouse, who shot three people and killed two after entering an antiracist protest armed to allegedly protect local businesses, fits this pattern of right-wing paramilitary violence in defense of "law and order."

Necrophilia's only model for achieving connection or understanding resides in taking things apart and includes a fascination with the dismemberment of living beings.[15] It understands through dissection, or through torture ("putting nature on the rack," in the words of Francis Bacon's famous scientific dictum); it believes the truth is uncovered not through love but through forcing nature to reveal its secrets. The necrophile's passion for destruction also extends to beautiful objects that are disjunctive with the necrophile's inner dead and controlled condition, such as beautiful works of art or architecture, and beyond that, the necrophile himself, who may seek his own destruction.[16]

---

12   Erich Fromm, *War Within Man: A Psychological Enquiry into the Roots of Destructiveness* (Philadelphia, PA: American Friends Service Committee, 1963).
13   Fromm, *Anatomy of Human Destructiveness*, 366.
14   Ibid., 376.
15   Ibid., 366–367.
16   Ibid., 375.

Unlike the Freudian death instinct, necrophilia as Fromm understood it is not a part of our instinctual equipment, or something that exists naturally in all people. Rather, it has social causes, and its prevalence in a society depends on various conditions. The necrophile is often characterized less by the constant expression of rage, and more by a kind of boredom and disconnection. Their ability to connect with machines rather than people is rooted in their bored and disconnected condition, and this alienation is rooted in capitalism itself. Capitalism contributes to the growing passivity of modern society, turning our free time into passive consumption and our labor time into a controlled period of production, deadening our productive/creative capacities and translating them into the quantitative framework of profit.[17]

According to Fromm, the necrophile is chronically bored and thus boring, having the effect of "deadening" any conversation or project in which they engage.[18] The necrophile's boredom stems from a profound passivity – an inability to act and perceive change in the world as the result of one's actions. Fromm also links necrophilia to the deadening impacts of the domination of technology over human life and values, which also contributes to this passivity and inner deadness – it is not merely the presence of technology, but its dehumanizing power over us in a system that disempowers people.[19] The necrophile experiences a desire to merge with the mechanical, and to transform what is alive into something mechanical, which can only be done through killing it. In Fromm's lifetime, the problem of nuclear warfare in particular as well as growing ecological collapse suggested a triumph of the mechanical over the living. Today, we find a resignation in the face of growing deadness that must be overcome if humanity is to survive; we are faced more acutely than ever with the choices Fromm articulated and the necessity of choosing a more humane society.

Fromm links necrophilia and fascism, and devotes a chapter of *The Anatomy of Human Destructiveness* to analyzing Hitler's necrophilia. Fromm sees necrophilia in the "Futurist Manifesto" of the fascist Marinetti, who wrote:

> We will sing the love of danger ... [T]he beauty of speed. A racing car ... is more beautiful than the "Victory of Samothrace." ... No work [of art] without an aggressive character can be a masterpiece. Poetry must be conceived as a violent attack by unknown forces ... We will glorify

---

17 Erich Fromm, *The Sane Society* (New York: Henry Holt & Co, 1955).
18 Fromm, *Anatomy of Human Destructiveness*, 377.
19 Erich Fromm, *The Revolution of Hope: Towards a Humanized Technology* (New York: Harper & Row, 1968).

war – the world's only hygiene – militarism, patriotism, the destructive gesture ... and scorn for woman. We will destroy the museums, libraries, academies of every kind, will fight moralism, feminism... [20]

I am being deliberately selective in my use of ellipses here, showing how the document emphasizes the embrace of danger (as opposed to safety); the rejection of women and feminism and the idealization of the car, a lifeless mechanical invention that is experienced sexually; and an aesthetic of mechanical speed, power, violence, war, and misogyny. The connection of necrophilia with fascism does not mean that every necrophile is a fascist. However, it does suggest that necrophilia may be fostered in a society with an increasing openness to fascism.

To explore the connection between necrophilia and the fascistic mass shooter, I will examine the case of a 2019 mass shooting in Dayton, Ohio in some depth. The shooter was misclassified as a "leftist accelerationist," but was deeply misogynistic and necrophilic.

4 The "Leftist Accelerationist" that Wasn't

August 4, 2019: A twenty-four-year-old man opened fire on a crowd at the entrance to the Ned Peppers Bar in Dayton, Ohio. He killed nine people that day, their ages ranging from 22 to 57, including the shooter's own brother, who had recently come out to friends as transgender.[21] Dozens of others were injured. The shooter fired continually for less than thirty seconds, until he was shot and killed by police.

The shooter had clearly planned and come prepared, wearing "a bulletproof vest, mask, and ear protection."[22] A week before in Gilroy, California, another mass shooter had worn similar gear, as the Dayton shooter likely knew.[23] The Dayton shooting occurred one week after the mass shooting at the Gilroy Garlic Festival, and one day after a mass shooting at a Walmart in El Paso, Texas. But

---

20   Fromm, *Anatomy of Human Destructiveness*, 382–383.
21   Nina Golgowski, "These Are the Victims of the Dayton, Ohio Mass Shooting," *Huffington Post*, August 9, 2019. https://www.huffpost.com/entry/dayton-shooting-victims-identified_n_5d46eeb4e4b0aca3411f48e6.
22   Inside Edition, "Body Armor Worn by Ohio Gunman is Shockingly Easy to Purchase," August 5, 2019. https://www.insideedition.com/body-armor-worn-ohio-gunman-shockingly-easy-purchase-55003.
23   Ibid.

there appeared to be a substantial difference. The Gilroy and El Paso shooters appeared to have been inspired by far-right racist ideology, while the Dayton shooter, by contrast, was left-wing. The Gilroy, California shooter expressed hatred for "mestizos and Silicon Valley white twats" (expressing both racist and misogynist motives) and promoted the late nineteenth-century white supremacist book *Might is Right*.[24] Similarly, the El Paso shooter expressed his desire to murder Latinos and trumpeted his admiration for the white nationalist who had killed fifty-one people in an attack on mosques in New Zealand several months earlier.[25]

At a time of rising racist and far-right violence, right-wing media leaped on the story of the Dayton shooter, presenting him as an extremist whose leftist politics drove him to mass murder. *Fox News* pointedly noted that the shooter supported gun control,[26] while *Breitbart* added that he had shared tweets by progressive presidential candidates Bernie Sanders and Elizabeth Warren.[27] Journalist and provocateur against antifascist protesters Andy Ngo, noting that the shooter had tweeted support for antifascism, wrote an article headlined, "Dayton Shooter ... May Be Antifa's First Mass Killer."[28]

For some police, security analysts, and counterterrorism think tank staffers, the Dayton shooter's act seemed like a timely reminder that "extremism" and violence could come from anywhere on the political spectrum. In a period when a number of mass shootings in the United States were carried out by white supremacist and antisemitic mass shooters, the Dayton shooter seemed to be a relevant exception proving that it was not any specific ideological commitments, but rather any kind of "extremism" that can lead to mass violence.

---

24 Amir Vera, "Garlic Festival Shooter Died from Self-Inflicted Gunshot Wound," CNN, August 2, 2019. https://www.cnn.com/2019/08/02/us/gilroy-garlic-festival-shooter/index.html; David Futrelle, "Might Is Right: Inside the Gilroy Shooter's Borrowed Manifesto," *We Hunted the Mammoth*, July 29, 2019. https://wehuntedthemammoth.com/2019/07/29/might-is-right-inside-the-gilroy-shooters-borrowed-manifesto/comment-page-1/.

25 Jacob Ware, "Testament to Murder: The Violent Far-Right's Increasing Use of Terrorist Manifestos," *International Centre for Counter-terrorism – The Hague*, March 2020. https://icct.nl/app/uploads/2020/03/Jaocb-Ware-Terrorist-Manifestos2.pdf.

26 Danielle Wallace, "Dayton Gunman Was Pro-Gun Control, Friend Says," *Fox News*, August 6, 2019. https://www.foxnews.com/us/dayton-gunman-anti-2nd-amendment-not-conservative-right-leaning-left-tweets-conner-betts-will-el-fakir.

27 Joel B. Pollak, "CNN Confirms: Dayton Shooter Had 'Extreme' Left-Wing Views; Backed Warren, Sanders," *Breitbart*, August 5, 2019. https://www.breitbart.com/the-media/2019/08/05/cnn-confirms-dayton-shooter-left-wing/.

28 Andy Ngo, "Dayton Shooter Connor Betts May Be Antifa's First Mass Killer," *New York Post*, August 6, 2019. https://nypost.com/2019/08/06/dayton-shooter-may-be-antifas-first-mass-killer/.

Intelligence analyst Jade Parker classified the Dayton shooter as an "accelerationist" alongside the Gilroy and El Paso shooters. Parker wrote, "Throughout 2019, [the] socialist and self-identified antifascist ... tweeted about accelerationism. He grew impatient with incremental political solutions and sought a socialist revolution."[29] As evidence of the shooter's accelerationist tweets, Parker cited an article that identifies such tweets from the shooter as, "I want socialism, and i'll [sic] not wait for the idiots to finally come round to understanding"; a tweet encouraging people to cut down fences around immigration detention centers; and a retweet of someone's tweet that, "Millenials [sic] have a message for the Joe Biden generation: hurry up and die."[30]

Parker's designation of the Dayton shooter, who was a self-identified leftist, as an "accelerationist" might seem puzzling. In the mass media, the term "accelerationist" typically describes a dangerous international network of Nazi insurgents, often called "the skullmasks," belonging to a set of amorphous and loosely linked organizations known by names like Atomwaffen Division and The Base. However, there is no evidence that the Dayton shooter belonged to that network or had any contact with it. That network is known for its rejection of "normalizing" strategies pursued by some other white nationalist groups (such as members of the white nationalist "Groyper" movement of Nick Fuentes, which has worked publicly with some Republican members of Congress; Fuentes also met with Trump in Mar-o-Lago in 2022).[31] By contrast, the skullmasks embrace acts of violence such as mass shootings, bombings, and destruction of infrastructure, as well as using disinformation to spread conflict. The white nationalist shooters in Gilroy and El Paso may have been influenced by this accelerationist network through its online propaganda, but there is no evidence that the Dayton shooter was particularly influenced by or in contact with this network, though he was aware of and fascinated by fascist violence.

The use of the term "accelerationist" to describe the Dayton shooter reflects a widespread trend in counter-extremism research that sees disparate ideological movements converging, caring more about overthrowing the government

---

29 Jade Parker, "Accelerationism in America: Threat Perceptions," *Global Network on Extremism & Technology*, February 4, 2020. https://gnet-research.org/2020/02/04/accelerationism-in-america-threat-perceptions/.

30 Yaron Steinbuch, "Dayton Shooter Connor Betts May Have Had Far-Left Twitter Account," *New York Post*, August 6, 2019. https://nypost.com/2019/08/06/dayton-shooter-connor-betts-may-have-supported-leftist-ideas-on-shadow-twitter-account/.

31 Matthias Christopher, "Paul Gosar Spoke at a White Nationalist Conference. The GOP Doesn't Care," *Huffington Post*, March 5, 2021. https://www.huffpost.com/entry/paul-gosar-white-nationalist-republican_n_60415a1ec5b60208555d4f60.

and inspiring chaos than implementing a particular political program. Terms like "salad bar extremism"[32] and "coalitional accelerationism"[33] are used to describe this nebulous alleged convergence. In addition, it is suggested that counterposed "extremist" movements (fascists and antifascists; ISIS and Islamophobic street brawlers; etc.) are mutually co-constitutive, a theory often known as "cumulative extremism"[34] or "reciprocal radicalization."[35] In my view, these frameworks downplay fundamental differences between movements. There are very real tactical alliances, use of shared symbols and resources, and escalations of conflict, but these do not amount to long-term coalitions, a loss of ideological differences, or mutual causation between differing movements.

The Dayton shooter identified as a leftist and an antifascist, but that is different from his final act being a politically strategic or tactical action in a political movement or program. There does not seem to be evidence that the shooting was intended to function in that way. He did not leave behind a "manifesto" or other writings expressing the intent of his actions, nor did he demonstrate an extensive or long-term involvement in, or even intellectual curiosity about, leftist political movements or strategy. Rather, the most consistent patterns in his life leading to the shooting, as we shall see, appear to be misogyny and an obsession with violence, expressed in a series of threats and acts of physical violence, as well as in his fantasies and musical aesthetic.

5 Dayton Shooter's Misogyny and Obsession with Violence

If he wasn't trying to start a socialist revolution, and if the frameworks of the counter-extremism industry are insufficient to explain his actions, what did motivate the Dayton shooter? More relevant perhaps are the shooter's history of violence, threats, and violent fantasies; the shooter's misogyny; and his impatient and personally entitled (rather than socially humanitarian) outlook.

---

32   Hicham Tiflati, "The Extremism Market and Salad Bar Ideology," *European Eye on Radicalization*. https://eeradicalization.com/the-extremism-market-and-salad-bar-ideology/. Accessed October 8, 2022.

33   Brian Hughes and Cynthia Miller-Idriss, "Uniting for Total Collapse: The January 6 Boost to Accelerationism," *The Combating Terrorism Center at West Point*, April/May 2021. https://ctc.usma.edu/uniting-for-total-collapse-the-january-6-boost-to-accelerationism/.

34   Roger Eatwell, "Community Cohesion and Cumulative Extremism in Contemporary Britain," *The Political Quarterly* 77, no. 2 (April-June 2006): 204–216.

35   Julia Ebner, *The Rage: The Vicious Circle of Islamist and Far-Right Extremism* (London: I.B. Tauris, 2017).

Several of the shooter's personal acquaintances told media or law enforcement after the act that he had made violent threats for many years and provided some context:

- In middle school, he "told a female classmate he fantasized about slitting her throat,"[36] leading the girl's parents to contact the school.
- In high school, he had a "kill list" of male classmates he wanted to kill and a "rape list" of female classmates he wanted to rape.[37]
- One of the shooter's ex-girlfriends described him as being obsessed with violence and revenge. She told the media that he showed her a video on their first date of a mass shooting targeting a synagogue; that on another occasion he drove her to another ex-girlfriend's house and "sought to leave a threatening note" (this must have been very intimidating to the present girlfriend!); that he called her up when he was drunk and said he wanted to kill a lot of people;[38] and that on another occasion he put a gun in his mouth.[39]
- A former high school classmate said that the shooter had held a gun to the former classmate's head several months before the shooting.[40] The former classmate also said that the future shooter had been "getting violent with pals" and "surveyed bars as good places to do 'damage.'"[41]

This brief history suggests that the shooter, since he was twenty-four at the time of the shooting, had been threatening people and fantasizing about doing violence for at least ten years leading up to the shooting and that numerous people were well aware of his tendencies towards violence. It also suggests that he had a pattern of violence and intimidation towards women, and the ex-girlfriend's account suggests that he may have been violent or threatening towards women who broke up with him or rejected him (a claim repeated by former classmates, whose remarks will be examined momentarily). If he was fascinated enough by the synagogue shooting to show a video of it on a first date, he was probably also fascinated by the shootings in El Paso and Gilroy

---

36 Danielle Wallace, "Dayton Gunman Was Pro-Gun Control, Friend Says," *Fox News*, August 6, 2019. https://www.foxnews.com/us/dayton-gunman-anti-2nd-amendment-not-conservative-right-leaning-left-tweets-conner-betts-will-el-fakir.
37 Ibid.
38 Morgan Phillips, "Dayton Shooter's Ex-Girlfriend Says He Showed Her Footage of a Mass Shooting on Their First Date," *Mediaite*, August 6, 2019. https://www.mediaite.com/news/dayton-shooters-ex-girlfriend-says-he-showed-her-footage-of-a-mass-shooting-on-their-first-date/.
39 Jessica McBride, "Connor Betts: 5 Fast Facts You Need to Know," *Heavy*, August 12, 2019. https://heavy.com/news/2019/08/connor-betts/.
40 Wallace, "Dayton Gunman Was Pro-Gun Control, Friend Says".
41 Ibid.

that immediately preceded his own act, which may have contributed to spurring him to act at that time.

Another topic that was much discussed in relation to the shooting was the shooter's band – I warn the reader that my description in this paragraph will contain some graphic language from the music genre. The shooter belonged to a "goregrind" or "pornogrind" metal band called "Menstrual Munchies." The pornogrind genre has lyrics that depict violence and rape, and aims to depict dehumanization and objectification. The band produced albums with names like "6 Ways of Female Butchery" and "Preteen Daughter Pu$$y Slaughter," with songs like "Cunt Stuffed with Medical Waste – Sexual Abuse of a Teenage Corpse."[42] Lyrics and images on the albums included glorification of rape, necrophilous sex, and coprophagia.[43] The band "often performed naked, wearing nothing but Santa Claus hats and beards, or an executioner's hood."[44]

After the shooting, his band denounced him and removed online videos in which the shooter had performed. One of his bandmates told the media that the band's lyrics were a joke and asked in horror, "It's like, Jesus Christ, how much of this was like real life for him?"[45]

A musician from the metal band Neckbeard Deathcamp tweeted in all caps: "OH TURNS OUT THE DAYTON SHOOTER WAS LITERALLY [SHOOTER'S FIRST NAME] FUCKING [SHOOTER'S SURNAME].[46] I DON'T KNOW IF I WOULD USE THE TERM LEFTIST TO DESIGNATE ONE OF THE DUDES IN MENSTRUAL MUNCHIES. ANTIFASCIST SURE. BUT NOT GREAT WITH WOMEN. JUST ANOTHER DIME A DOZEN OHIO GRIND DUDE WHO CAPED PROGRESSIVE POLITICS WHILE TREATING WOMEN LIKE SHIT."[47]

---

42   Vince Neilstein, "Op-Ed: Unpacking Dayton Shooter Connor Betts' Connection to Metal and Pornogrind," *MetalSucks*, August 5, 2019. https://www.metalsucks.net/2019/08/06/op-ed-unpacking-dayton-shooter-connor-betts-connection-to-metal-and-pornogrind/.

43   Rod Dreher, "Connor Betts and 'Pornogrind,'" *The American Conservative*, August 5, 2019. https://www.theamericanconservative.com/dreher/connor-betts-pornogrind-dayton-murder/.

44   Tim Wyatt, "Dayton Shooting Suspect Connor Betts Sang About Raping and Killing Women in 'Pornogrind' Metal Band," *The Independent*, August 6, 2019. https://www.independent.co.uk/news/world/americas/dayton-shooting-connor-betts-suspect-pornogrind-band-murder-rape-a9040981.html.

45   Daniel Newhauser, "EXCLUSIVE: Dayton Shooter Was in a 'Pornogrind' Band That Released Songs about Killing and Raping Women," *VICE*, August 5, 2019. https://www.vice.com/en/article/j5yekp/exclusive-dayton-shooter-was-in-a-pornogrind-band-that-released-songs-about-killing-and-raping-women.

46   As mentioned earlier, I am omitting names of mass shooters where possible in accord with the No Notoriety campaign.

47   Ibid.

Comments from former high school classmates on social media and their statements to reporters repeat the theme that the future shooter was dangerous, especially to women, and that this had been known for a long time. Many also pushed back against a narrative in the media that he had been bullied in school and classified him as a bully rather than a victim. Here are some of the comments:

- "Before the Media portrays this full grown man as an innocent kid who was damaged in high school due to bullying I want to set the record straight right now. [The shooter] had a history of serious harrassment [sic] towards fellow female students. Some of which were my friends or siblings of friends. He had a notebook with detailed information on how he wanted to hurt … female students."[48]
- "He loved scaring people. He thought it was funny and got off on it. He scared my sister so bad once, I think he held her in his car against her will. She started crying and he laughed at her. He was sick."[49]
- "He loved to look at you and pretend to shoot with guns, guns with his hands."[50]
- "A real scumbag who threatened to kill women and attack the school. he WAS NOT BULLIED in school; he was a classic glorifier of violence and an all-around unpleasant person who had threatened many of my friends in the past.

  You can blame bullying (which would be lying) you can blame media (which would be extremely untruthful) or you can blame a society where threats against women that are bad enough to get you kicked out of High School are simply forgotten and allowed to ferment for almost a decade so he can kill 9 people.

  His violence was simply ignored as a 'Boys will be boys' rhetorical/willfully ignorant cop out to protect that status quo. A lot of blame all around, he had access to guns, he was a toxically masculine asshole, the cops did nothing about his threats. the list goes on."[51]
- "This isn't a mystery to me. I'm furious."[52]

---

48   Jessica McBride, "Connor Betts: 5 Fast Facts You Need to Know," *Heavy*, August 12, 2019. https://heavy.com/news/2019/08/connor-betts/.
49   Ibid.
50   Ibid.
51   Emilee Coblentz, "Connor Betts Had a Hit List, Ex-Classmates Say," *Heavy*, August 21, 2019. https://heavy.com/news/2019/08/connor-betts-had-a-hit-list-ex-classmates-say/.
52   Ibid.

- "[The shooter] is nothing but a case study on how consistently our society fails to call a perpetrator for what they are. He was not bullied; he was a bully. A bully towards women, including myself. A bully towards everyone he deemed below him. I knew [him] for over 10 years, and to pretend that he has ever been any other way, to pretend that he wasn't capable of this level of violence, is nothing but willful ignorance. It does a disservice to those he finally had the opportunity to [exercise] his power over to believe he was ever otherwise."
- "He was the bully. He used to make fun of me on the bus, talk about my weight, make me feel bad about myself. He would laugh and think it was funny, joke about it. We thought it was a normal thing."[53] (This female student later learned she was on the shooter's hit list.)
- "The news says he was remembered as 'being bullied,' which is interesting, because I just remember him as someone who enjoyed making people afraid. [He] seriously threatened to hurt women who rejected him, myself included."[54]
- "No one should be surprised. No one should be shocked. He made a rape list, and a hit list, and threatened the school with a bomb threat and was kicked out. He was not 'odd' he was not bullied he was not an outcast; he was dangerous and he scared us."[55]

These comments suggest that many people knew the future shooter posed a threat. It seems that the shooter was not simply prone to violence that expressed itself in one situation (the shooting), perhaps due to drugs as some suggested,[56] but rather that his act was the culmination of a long-developing characterological tendency towards violence and control, and that he seemed to delight in scaring others.

Another recurrent theme in the classmates' remarks is the shooter's hatred of women. Although men were also killed in the shooting, the shooter particularly threatened women, made lists of women he wanted to rape, intimidated and threatened girlfriends and ex-girlfriends, and expressed angry entitlement towards women who rejected him. That his brother, who was assigned female

---

53   Associated Press, "Connor Stephen Betts, Identified as Dayton Suspected Shooter, Once Kept 'Hit List,' 'Rape List,' Classmates Say," *ABC7 Chicago*, August 6, 2019. https://abc7chicago.com/ohio-shooting-dayton-connor-stephen-betts-shooter/5442328/.
54   Coblentz, "Connor Betts Had a Hit List, Ex-Classmates Say".
55   Ibid.
56   Connor Mannion, "Dayton Shooter was on Cocaine, Alcohol During Massacre, Coroner Reveals," *Mediaite*, August 15, 2019. https://www.mediaite.com/news/dayton-shooter-was-on-cocaine-alcohol-during-massacre-coroner-reveals/.

at birth and had recently come out to friends as transgender, was among the victims – the shooter drove to the bar with his brother and the shooter's best friend, both of whom he shot – is also likely relevant.

Misogyny often fuels physical violence, but misogyny is undertheorized by those who study hate, the far-right, or political violence broadly. As Alex DiBranco of the Institute for Research on Male Supremacism points out, misogyny is sometimes referred to as a "gateway drug" to extremism or the far-right, and she notes that this rhetorical practice can downplay the degree to which misogyny directly inspires acts of violence.[57] That is, hatred of women is sometimes spoken of as a *stage* on the way to "radicalization," or an *indicator of vulnerability* to "radicalization," rather than itself a form of hate that could motivate violence. In fact, some criticize the use of terms like "extremism" and "radicalization" as well, in part because this terminology tends to depict movements like white supremacist movements as a fringe, criminal element – *something weird over there that we gawk at,* maybe a topic for a reality television show or a tabloid – rather than expressions of *mainstream* attitudes and behaviors, in a society where racism and other oppressions are embedded in everyday ordinary interactions and widespread social policies.[58] Characterizing misogyny as a "gateway drug" or an indicator of potential *future* "radicalization," partly acknowledges how normal misogyny is (i.e., not yet rare enough to be considered "extreme"), but also fails to acknowledge its inherent

---

57   Alex DiBranco, "Male Supremacist Terrorism as a Rising Threat," *International Centre for Counter-Terrorism – The Hague,* February 10, 2020. https://icct.nl/publication/male-supremacist-terrorism-as-a-rising-threat/.

58   The limitations of the "extremism" or "radicalization" framework have been challenged by numerous writers researching the far-right, Critical Terrorism Studies, or insurgency. Concerns include not only the way it can make far-right violence and hate seem disconnected from mainstream policies and practices, but also the way the left and right get lumped into single overarching categories that lack specificity and can lead to surveillance or crackdowns on activists for emancipatory social change, as well as the way that "extremism" and "radicalization" theories have been mobilized to fuel Islamophobia, among other concerns. See, for example, these insightful critiques: Chip Berlet and Matthew Lyons, "Repression and Ideology: The Legacy of Discredited Centrist/Extremist Theory," *Political Research Associates,* April 15, 1998. https://www.politicalresearch.org/repression-and-ideology-legacy-discredited-centristextremist-theory; Liz Fekete, *Europe's Fault Lines: Racism and the Rise of the Right* (London: Verso, 2019), 44–47; Arun Kundnani, *The Muslims Are Coming! Islamophobia, Extremism, and the Domestic War on Terror.* (London: Verso, 2015), 55–88, 115–152; Nimmi Gowrinathan, *Radicalizing Her: Why Women Choose Violence* (Boston: Beacon Press, 2021), 9–29; Aurelien Mondon and Aaron Winter, *Reactionary Democracy: How Racism and the Populist Far Right Became Mainstream* (London: Verso, 2020), 57–68.

violence and its political nature by distancing it from classification under categories associated with political violence.

Surely necrophilia and misogyny are connected, although Fromm does not draw this connection as explicitly as I would like. It becomes most apparent in the links between sadism and necrophilia. According to Fromm, the sadist believes that there are fundamentally two kinds of people: the powerful, strong winners, and the weak, bad losers.[59] Sadism is fostered by the dependence of societies on exploitation and the oppression of marginalized groups.[60] Fromm also gives a compelling example of necrophilous tendencies in the man who seems to be more in love with his car than his wife, who washes his car tenderly and gives it cute little nicknames, but who is cold and distant in his relationships with human beings.[61]

It should be noted here that some critics believe Fromm underemphasizes the role of misogyny in necrophilia and correspondingly places too much blame on the role mothers play in the causality of necrophilous tendencies.[62] This is a rather complex point, as women function both symbolically and as individual cases. When Fromm suggests as a "hypothesis" a possible connection of cold, distant mothers to the development of the necrophile, he may be inferring too much from some necrophiles' own conceptual associations of "the mother" in the abstract, with soil, nation, tradition, destruction, and death.[63] Perhaps this association of the mother with death shows more clearly that the necrophile is unable to see a truly creative principle, such as birth, without linking it to powers of destruction – the necrophile's only conception of real possibility of change in the world lies in destruction. It should be added here that linking the mother to death, while it can be done in a tone of awe – "mother" as a sort of Jungian archetype or goddess representing both creation and destruction – may in fact express a related dehumanization of women even while imbuing them with seemingly mythic, cosmic powers. Seeing the other as an ominous bringer of death or somehow already dead or deathlike, can not only underlie prejudice but can contribute to the forms of dehumanization that make genocidal politics possible. Although Fromm is close to drawing out the deep linkages between necrophilia and misogyny, it remains for others to further unfold them, especially for the contemporary context.

---

59 Fromm, *Escape from Freedom*, 190.
60 Fromm, *Anatomy of Human Destructiveness*, 331.
61 Ibid., 381.
62 Mary Daly, *Gyn/Ecology*, cited in Bratich, 132.
63 Fromm, *Anatomy of Human Destructiveness*, 401.

Misogyny is beginning to be taken more seriously by researchers on far-right violence, in part because the "incel" (involuntary celibate) community has inspired several mass shootings in the past couple of decades.[64] Although the term has different origins, today the term "incel" refers mainly to men belonging to a far-right online social movement, who are united by their belief that they are incapable of having consensual sex with a woman because they believe no woman would want them. They direct their anger towards feminism and women in general. To return to the Dayton shooter, there is no evidence that he was involved in misogynistic internet spaces like incel forums or other openly misogynistic social movements, and the label of "incel" is sometimes too broadly applied by counter-terrorism researchers to include any misogynist mass violence. This results in a tendency to ignore the ways in which misogynist violence is "normal," not merely perpetrated by an "extreme."[65]

"Mainstream" misogynist violence is reflected in how more "extreme" acts of violence are carried out. According to Every Town for Gun Safety, most of the mass shootings in the United States between 2009 and 2020 took place in a domestic setting (*unlike* the Dayton bar), and in 53% of all cases, a current or former intimate partner or relative was shot (like the Dayton shooting, where the shooter's brother was killed).[66] Almost all of the shootings were carried out by men. That the shooter killed his transgender brother, perhaps taking vengeance in some way on his brother's inability to perform a certain kind of femininity but here we can only speculate, seems to reflect this trend. But more crucially, we see that mass shootings, while conceived as "random," terrifying in their attacks on public locations in the manner we often imagine "terrorism" to be carried out, are generally more domestic; here the "extreme" act of the mass shooting is carried out in perhaps the leading "mainstream" locale of violence, the home.

I raise these questions to demonstrate the complexity involved in distinguishing acts of violence such as the Dayton shooting, between being "extremist" actions or acts of hate on the one hand, or simply "ordinary" or "mainstream" forms of mass violence on the other. The Dayton shooter's act

---

64 Alex DiBranco, "Male Supremacist Terrorism as a Rising Threat," *International Centre for Counter-Terrorism – The Hague*, February 10, 2020. https://icct.nl/publication/male-supremacist-terrorism-as-a-rising-threat/.

65 Julia R. DeCook and Megan Kelly, "Interrogating the Incel Menace: Assessing the Threat of Male Supremacy in Terrorism Studies," *Critical Studies on Terrorism* 15, no. 3 (December 2021): 706–726.

66 Every Town for Gun Safety, "Mass Shootings in America," *Everytown Research and Policy*, June 4, 2021. https://everytownresearch.org/maps/mass-shootings-in-america-2009-2019/.

is certainly not the norm (despite the horrific prevalence of mass shootings in the United States), but it emerged out of social conditions that are quite normal or prevalent in U.S. society.

If indeed we wish to theorize mass shootings in light of gender, we come back to the adage that the personal is political. When dehumanization of any group is normalized in society, in the form of misogyny or anti-Black racism and other prejudices, it expresses itself not only in illegal activity but in ordinary daily, interactions and in law and social policy. Not only does the Dayton shooter not seem to have been motivated by an "extremist" ideology; his action seems to be a particularly vivid expression of the widespread violence and misogyny of U.S. American culture, the reality of which is often denied.

The social character of America, including its obsession with guns and violence as expressing the nature of masculinity and upholding the values of freedom, no doubt plays a role here.[67] Lauren Langman and George Lundskow, in their study of the American social character building on Fromm's work, explore the example of Chris Kyle, the subject of the film *American Sniper* – the racist soldier with the highest "kill count" in Iraq, who spoke about enjoying killing.[68] Charles Thorpe, in his study of American necrophilia, notes National Rifle Association spokesman Charlton Heston's necrophilous insistence that his guns could only be taken by Al Gore "from my cold dead hands."[69] Figures like Kyle and Heston represent not a "fringe" or "extremist" kind of violence, from the standpoint of social norms – in fact, both are widely held up as exemplars of the American character. Understanding the fascistic mass shooter requires understanding how American society itself continues to propagate notions of masculinity and individual freedom as tied to violence and weapons.

Certainly, while mass shootings are becoming more common, they are fortunately still not socially acceptable. Yet U.S. militarism is broadly accepted in U.S. society. As a teenager, for example, the Dayton shooter belonged to his high school ROTC military training program.[70] His father was a successful engineer for a military contractor,[71] and the shooter's best friend, who drove the shooter

---

67 Langman and Lundskow, *God, Guns, Gold and Glory*.
68 Ibid., 170–177.
69 Charles Thorpe, *Necroculture* (New York: Palgrave MacMillan, 2016), 221.
70 Jonah Walters, "We Need to Get the U.S. Army Out of High Schools," *Jacobin*, August 13, 2019. https://www.jacobinmag.com/2019/08/jrotc-army-recruitment-high-schools-connor-betts-dayton-shooting.
71 Jessica McBride, "Connor Betts: 5 Fast Facts You Need to Know," *Heavy*, August 12, 2019. https://heavy.com/news/2019/08/connor-betts/.

to the bar and was shot, worked for weapons manufacturer Raytheon.[72] The largest employer in Dayton, Ohio is the local military base.[73] A few weeks after the shooting at the Ned Peppers bar, a white Dayton man shot at three Black teenagers he encountered on his property, killing two of them.[74] It is important to locate the August 4 shooting within a wider context of militarism, imperialism, and racist and sexist violence.

In addition, male violence both in the form of mass shootings and of intimate partner violence, is undergirded by attitudes of male entitlement that our broadly misogynistic society encourages. In a coauthored article on school shooters, Rachel Kalish and Michael Kimmel refer to "aggrieved entitlement" as an influential factor in spurring mass shootings by young males particularly.[75] Aggrieved entitlement combines a sense of having been wronged by society with the sense that vengeance is justified and that others should be made to feel the same suffering as the aggrieved person.[76] Surely aggrieved entitlement is not an unusual attitude among young white U.S. American men, and in fact reflects "normal" attitudes that, while increasingly being challenged, are still commonplace, such as the attitude that men are entitled to dates or sex with women, or the widespread right-wing belief that jobs are being "stolen" by dark-skinned undocumented immigrants.[77] There is a conversation to be had about the Trump campaign's and the North American and European far-right's mobilization of aggrieved entitlement and how misplaced narratives about a forgotten "white working class" are used to spur reactionary social movements by capitalizing on that aggrievement. The existence of aggrievement does not mean that members of the violent far-right have "legitimate grievances" or "have a point." The person who takes on an attitude of aggrieved entitlement no doubt has some source of suffering in their life, but they may misdiagnose their problems and blame scapegoats or the world at large. These

---

72   Laura Collins, "EXCLUSIVE: Man who drove with Dayton mass shooter and sister before massacre was his best friend – who Connor Betts then shot and is now cops' best hope of finding motive for murders," *Daily Mail*, last updated August 14, 2019. https://www.dailymail.co.uk/news/article-7324839/Connor-Betts-shot-best-friend-mass-shooting-driving-Dayton.html.

73   Ibid.

74   David K. Li, "Homeowner Shoots Dead Two Teens Allegedly Trespassing on his Property in Ohio," *NBC*, August 29, 2019. https://www.nbcnews.com/news/us-news/homeowner-shoots-dead-two-teens-allegedly-trespassing-his-property-ohio-n1047686.

75   Rachel Kalish and Michael Kimmel, "Suicide by Mass Murder: Masculinity, Aggrieved Entitlement, and Rampage School Shootings," *Health Sociology Review* 19, no. 4 (2010): 454.

76   Ibid.

77   Kate Manne, *Down Girl: The Logic of Misogyny* (New York: Oxford University Press, 2019), 106–120.

misdiagnoses are often wrongly treated as "legitimate grievances" by some in the counter-terrorism field and political commentators.

6   The Dayton Shooter and Necrophilia

The Dayton shooter's music tastes, "rape list," internet searches, and expressed threats and fantasies, suggest a fascination with corpses, violence including sexual violence, and dismemberment. Furthermore, while his father was a productive and successful engineer, the Dayton shooter was relatively unsuccessful in school and was living at home while studying psychology at the local community college; his sense of stifled potential and rage must have found expression in a variety of technical means – he googled mass shootings and terms like "absolute carnage" to consume violence on the internet; he trained with the high school ROTC; he trapped a woman in a car; he carried out a mass shooting with a military-style weapon. His fascination with violence allowed him to construct what Fromm calls "mini-Colosseums"[78] to observe violence and find release for his sadistic desires, and pornogrind music was surely one of these outlets. Guitar, gun, car. Each must have been a source of technical control, an arena for exerting power. Even the fact that the shooter once scrawled his high school hit list on the wall of a bathroom stall is telling: Fromm writes that the necrophile is drawn to feces and to "smelly toilets"; the necrophile believes that he has uncovered the truth of the world on some level, that really everything is to some degree excess and waste, to be managed and controlled, or to be destroyed.

In his book *Necroculture*, Charles Thorpe relies heavily on Fromm to argue that contemporary American society is deeply necrophilous. Thorpe includes a chapter on pornography and a chapter on gun culture, both arenas in which Thorpe sees technical power used to enforce dehumanization and where Thorpe sees necrophilia at work.[79] Necrophilia is present in the denigration of women into mere tools of satisfaction and the gun as the means by which the sovereign individual, generally conceived as male, defends his lifeless property and expands its limits through colonial and imperial war. According to Thorpe, Silicon Valley reactionaries also express a necrophilous impulse in their embrace of "transhumanism," seeing the human body as outmoded and in need of replacement by a new, mechanized, invulnerable, and

---

78   Fromm, *Anatomy of Human Destructiveness*, 278.
79   Thorpe, *Necroculture*.

immortal self. A similar exploration of these destructive tendencies in the American social character, also drawing on Erich Fromm, is Lauren Langman and George Lundskow's aforementioned book *Gold, God, Guns, and Glory*. Thorpe, Langman, and Lundskow all link these death-dealing forces to capitalism as well.

7   A Warning about Profiling

Necrophilia is a theoretically fecund category for understanding not only the shooting itself but the wider social conditions that contribute to mass shootings in contemporary society. This is the concept's greatest contribution, rather than – it seems important here to stress – for building some kind of profile of "the mass shooter," presumably in order to prevent future shootings by identifying potential shooters with "necrophilous" tendencies. First, even if all "necrophiles" were going to commit violence, which may not be true, it would be difficult to identify a necrophile on the basis of Fromm's criteria. Certainly, only a highly trained humanistic psychoanalyst could make such a diagnosis of a patient, not law enforcement or the media. Attention to symptoms such as fascination with corpses or graveyards would be superficial measures that could not be relied upon, because there are many healthy (or biophilic, in Fromm's terms) reasons for fascination with death or corpses: including scientific, philosophical, or historical interests; religious or cultural beliefs and practices; artistic expression; or what we might call a creative nostalgia that yearns to find and recover something beautiful from the past that appears to have been lost to the present (the moody romantic or "goth"). Even art that revels in death in graphic or offensive ways, can have a multitude of meanings other than necrophilia. (I will return momentarily to the matter of the shooter's "pornogrind" band.) Such fascination with the dead could also involve healthy psychological processes of grieving and remembering. In the case of technology, a delighted fascination with technical or mathematical challenges in the case of attachment to technology does not express necrophilia, as Fromm would readily acknowledge, given his distinction between humanistic and "idolatrous" ways of relating to technology;[80] intense (biophilic) interest would be distinguished from the kind of cruel boredom that gives rise to destructiveness. Nor would one wish to rely on Fromm's vivid but difficult to use descriptions of necrophilous individuals as having dead-looking faces, appearing "dirty-faced,"

---

80   See Fromm, *The Revolution of Hope: Towards a Humanized Technology*.

or seeming to be always sniffing.[81] Seeking to identify potential violent actors on the basis of isolated symptoms would be harmful and unhelpful, and this was not Fromm's intention.

It is also important to carefully distinguish disabilities such as autism from necrophilia, which Fromm was not able to do adequately, not yet understanding the science of autism and relying on the research then available by Leo Kanner, who originated what became known as the "refrigerator mother" theory that attributes autism to coldly distanced parenting. Unlike autism, which we now know is a genetic condition, necrophilia is partly socially caused by widespread violence and dehumanization in society, and necrophilia involves the "character" of the individual, including involving their agency in choosing what kind of person to be.[82] Someone who has a disability such as autism that could make some kinds of social interaction harder for them or that could predispose them to technical skill and a fascination with machines, can have deep humanitarian concern and can certainly be biophilous as opposed to necrophilous. This caveat is particularly important because current targeting of autistic people for potential recruitment into the violent far-right has led to problematic profiling of individuals with disabilities as vulnerable to "radicalization."

A profile of the necrophile would hardly have been needed in the case of the Dayton shooter anyway. One of the most striking things about the Dayton shooting (and often others as well) is the multitude of warning signs. One gets the impression that many people knew he was likely to carry out a mass shooting and were not sure what to do about it. As we have seen, people who knew the shooter responded after the fact with comments like, "No one should be surprised," and "This isn't a mystery to me."

Rather than using necrophilia to build a "profile" of potential killers, we should employ the theory of necrophilia as Critical Theorists informed by

---

81 Fromm, *Anatomy of Human Destructiveness*, 378.
82 Fromm, writing in the 1970s when very little was known about autism, falsely links autism to necrophilia (*Anatomy of Human Destructiveness*, 392–393). Avoiding seeing autistic people as biologically preconditioned to belong to violent far-right movements is very important today, as ableist profiling of potential "extremists" is already a problem. As some researchers and activists point out, the reason that there appears to be a high rate of autistic people engaged in fascist movements today may be because of the way fascists target vulnerable people for recruitment, as well as because ableism in society creates conditions of alienation that prime autistic people for recruitment. (Further study: Autism Against Fascism, "Why Have Fascists Found a Home in the Autism Community?" June 26, 2021. https://autismagainstfascism.wordpress.com/2021/06/26/why-have-fascists-found-a-home-in-the-autism-community/; Esther Warwick, "Autism and the Alt-Right," Presentation, Autistics Present).

the psychoanalytic tradition, not simply as clinicians, reflecting on what the Dayton shooter's apparent necrophilia has to say about the causes of the shooting and about society more broadly. We should also use such analysis to push past reductive answers, such as seeing the Dayton shooter as a "socialist revolutionary," as suggested by one counter-terrorism analyst.

8 Beyond the "Violent Music" Argument

Similarly, in avoiding profiling or fearmongering, we should also avoid reducing the "inspiration" for the shooting to the shooter's pornogrind band. Concerns about "violent music" (as well as, similarly, video games) have often followed mass shootings. Following the Columbine high school shooting in 1999, much attention was given to rocker Marilyn Manson. In his film exploring the shooting, *Bowling for Columbine*, Michael Moore gave Manson a chance to defend himself. Manson described himself as a "posterchild for fear," identifying himself as a convenient scapegoat for a society with broader social ills such as consumerism and war.[83] As Manson and Moore point out in their discussion, the day of the Columbine shooting was also the day of the most intense U.S. bombing of Kosovo of the conflict there to date.[84] (The Columbine shooting was also carried out on Hitler's birthday, by the shooters' choice, and in the midst of an intensification of far-right militia organizing in Colorado, where the shooting took place.[85] In fall 2022, Colorado yet again was a site of national grief and ongoing reckoning following the mass shooting targeting LGBTQ + patrons of a drag show at Club Q).

Blaming Marilyn Manson for the Columbine shooting was an extension of the Satanic Panic, a period of widespread conspiracy theories about alleged harm to children in secret Satanic rituals, a set of conspiracy theories that are partly the forerunners of QAnon today, which also has roots in a variety of other conspiracy theories, including antisemitic "blood libel." The Satanic

---

83 Although later allegations suggest Manson raped over a dozen women, this does not legitimate the reductive arguments of his late '90s critics. (Jenna Amatulli, "Marilyn Manson Sued by Ex for 'Malevolent Behavior,' Human Trafficking," *Huffington Post*, July 1, 2021. https://www.huffpost.com/entry/marilyn-manson-accuser-sexual-abuse_n_60ddcae9e4b0e2e21cbeb7fb).

84 *Bowling for Columbine*, directed by Michael Moore (United States: Metro-Goldwyn-Mayer, 2002).

85 Guerry Hoddersen, "The High Price of Ignoring Teenage Fascists," *Freedom Socialist Party*, April 20, 1999. Last updated August 2018, https://socialism.com/fs-article/the-high-price-of-ignoring-teenage-fascists/.

Panic led to a number of abuses and harms, including the false convictions in 1994 of the West Memphis Three, three teenage boys in Arkansas who, as social outsiders in a small town, were wrongfully accused of murdering three young boys in a Satanic ritual. Scares like the Satanic Panic, often animated by conspiracy theories, themselves lead to violence, scapegoating, bullying, suspicion, and profiling of those perceived as "different" for their outsider status, their rebellious persona. The presumption that the threat of violence is located in the extreme, the edgy, or the macabre, as opposed to being rooted in centers of power and normalcy, continues to do harm. A love of heavy metal or death metal music and black clothing is not itself a warning sign that someone is a necrophile, nor is every angry outsider a threat to be feared – like the "radicalization warning signs" that have led to surveillance or over-policing, these assumptions can perpetuate stereotypes, oppression, or exclusion.

Pornogrind music did not cause the Dayton shooting. The shooter's acts of violence, threats, and fantasies of mass murder long preceded his involvement in the band. That said, his participation in the band and his love of the genre are not irrelevant to the question of his character. For another individual, involvement in a pornogrind band could indicate something different about their character, such as primarily indicating antiauthoritarian nonconformity through aesthetic transgression of social norms. But for the Dayton shooter, the band fits neatly into his fascination with death, violence, and misogyny. The shooter even died in a sweatshirt bearing lyrics from one of his favorite bands, seeming to express the necrophile's inner deadness: "No heart to feel, no soul to steal."[86] (The particular band his hoodie quoted, Acacia Strain, released a statement expressing their horror at the shooting and promising to offer support to victims.)[87]

9 Transcending the Dominant Framework

In contrast to many of the reigning categories of the counter-terrorism industry, Erich Fromm's concept of necrophilia is a better and less depoliticizing way of understanding mass shooters who do not meet the ideal type of the white nationalist/fascist mass shooter. As compared to terms like coalitional

---

86 Brian Dugger, "Tweet: Dayton Gunman's Hoodie Referenced Metalcore Group Lyrics," *WTOL11*, August 4, 2019. https://www.wtol.com/article/news/crime/not-for-publicat ion-until-confirmation-dayton-gunmans-hoodie-referenced-metalcore-group-lyrics-no -heart-to-feel-no-soul-to-steal/512-facb9e86-be32-41f8-8615-8b22c909e830.

87 Ibid.

accelerationism,[88] necrophilia does not suggest either a devolution of ideological boundaries or a convergence of diverse ideologies into one single threat against the status quo, which might suggest that the solution lies in political compromise with everyone meeting in the safety of the moderate, status quo, "center." Instead, Fromm's analysis, drawing upon but critiquing Freud's theory of the death drive, shows how necrophilic desire is fostered by capitalism itself and expressed in its fascistic tendencies, but also does not equate necrophilia with narrow political allegiances.

Fromm's work shows how psychoanalysis contributes to Critical Theory, as well as the necessity of a Critical Theory of society that takes an interdisciplinary approach to understanding the root causes of social problems. While necrophilia does not provide a "profile" that can be used to prevent future mass shootings, as a social theoretical framework it helps us do something more important: explore the root causes of mass violence and find the mechanisms in the wider society and within the "American character" itself that continue to give rise to fascistic violence.[89] Only by understanding and addressing these root causes can this threat ultimately be reduced or ended. Eliding these questions leads to reductive explanations (blaming "drugs," "music," "mental illness," etc., in the abstract) that will leave us constantly failing to understand and to some degree recapitulating the social conditions that give rise to fringe violence by presuming the health and sanity of the status quo.

Bibliography

Amatulli, Jenna. "Marilyn Manson Sued by Ex for 'Malevolent Behavior,' Human Trafficking." *Huffington Post*, July 1, 2021. https://www.huffpost.com/entry/marilyn-manson-accuser-sexual-abuse_n_60ddcae9e4b0e2e21cbeb7fb.

Associated Press. "Connor Stephen Betts, Identified as Dayton Suspected Shooter, Once Kept 'Hit List,' 'Rape List,' Classmates Say." *ABC7 Chicago*, August 6, 2019. https://abc7chicago.com/ohio-shooting-dayton-connor-stephen-betts-shooter/5442328/.

Autism Against Fascism. "Why Have Fascists Found a Home in the Autism Community?" June 26, 2021. https://autismagainstfascism.wordpress.com/2021/06/26/why-have-fascists-found-a-home-in-the-autism-community/.

Berlet, Chip, and Matthew Lyons. "Repression and Ideology: The Legacy of Discredited Centrist/Extremist Theory." *Political Research Associates*, April 15, 1998.

---

88 Hughes and Idriss, *Uniting for Total Collapse*; Parker, *Accelerationism in America*.
89 Langman and Lundskow, *God, Guns, Gold and Glory*.

https://www.politicalresearch.org/repression-and-ideology-legacy-discredited-centristextremist-theory.

Bratich, Jack. Z. *On Microfascism: Gender, War, and Death*. Brooklyn: Common Notions, 2022.

Braune, Joan. "Experts Who Study Far-Right Mass Violence Must Center the Communities Affected," RANGE, July 26, 2022. https://www.rangemedia.co/highland-park-ideology-mass-shooting/.

Coblentz, Emilee. "Connor Betts Had a Hit List, Ex-Classmates Say." *Heavy*, August 21, 2019. https://heavy.com/news/2019/08/connor-betts-had-a-hit-list-ex-classmates-say/.

Collins, Laura. "EXCLUSIVE: Man who drove with Dayton mass shooter and sister before massacre was his best friend – who Connor Betts then shot and is now cops' best hope of finding motive for murders." *Daily Mail*, last updated August 14, 2019. https://www.dailymail.co.uk/news/article-7324839/Connor-Betts-shot-best-friend-mass-shooting-driving-Dayton.html.

DeCook, Julia R. and Megan Kelly. "Interrogating the Incel Menace: Assessing the Threat of Male Supremacy in Terrorism Studies." *Critical Studies on Terrorism* 15, no. 3 (December 2021): 706–726.

DiBranco, Alex. "Male Supremacist Terrorism as a Rising Threat." *International Centre for Counter-Terrorism – The Hague*, February 10, 2020. https://icct.nl/publication/male-supremacist-terrorism-as-a-rising-threat/.

Dreher, Rod. "Connor Betts and 'Pornogrind," *The American Conservative*, August 5, 2019. https://www.theamericanconservative.com/dreher/connor-betts-pornogrind-dayton-murder/.

Dugger, Brian. "Tweet: Dayton Gunman's Hoodie Referenced Metalcore Group Lyrics," WTOL11, August 4, 2019. https://www.wtol.com/article/news/crime/not-for-publication-until-confirmation-dayton-gunmans-hoodie-referenced-metalcore-group-lyrics-no-heart-to-feel-no-soul-to-steal/512-facb9e86-be32-41f8-8615-8b22c909e830.

Eatwell, Roger. "Community Cohesion and Cumulative Extremism in Contemporary Britain." *The Political Quarterly* 77, no. 2 (April-June 2006): 204–216.

Ebner, Julia. *The Rage: The Vicious Circle of Islamist and Far-Right Extremism*. London: I.B. Tauris, 2017.

Every Town for Gun Safety. "Mass Shootings in America." *Everytown Research and Policy*, June 4, 2021. https://everytownresearch.org/maps/mass-shootings-in-america-2009-2019/.

Fekete, Liz. *Europe's Fault Lines: Racism and the Rise of the Right*. London: Verso, 2019.

Finchelstein, Federico. *A Brief History of Fascist Lies*. Oakland, CA: University of California Press, 2020.

Fromm, Erich. *The Anatomy of Human Destructiveness*. Greenwich: Fawcett Publications, 1973.

Fromm, Erich. *Escape from Freedom*. New York: Avon Books, 1969.

Fromm, Erich. *The Heart of Man: Its Genius for Good and Evil*. New York: Harper and Row, 1964.

Fromm, Erich. *The Revolution of Hope: Towards a Humanized Technology*. New York: Harper & Row, 1968.

Fromm, Erich. *The Sane Society*. New York: Henry Holt & Co., 1955.

Fromm, Erich. *Sigmund Freud's Mission: An Analysis of His Personality and Influence*. New York: Harper & Brothers, 1959.

Fromm, Erich. *War Within Man: A Psychological Enquiry into the Roots of Destructiveness*. Philadelphia, PA: American Friends Service Committee, 1963.

Futrelle, David. "Might Is Right: Inside the Gilroy Shooter's Borrowed Manifesto." *We Hunted the Mammoth*, July 29, 2019. https://wehuntedthemammoth.com/2019/07/29/might-is-right-inside-the-gilroy-shooters-borrowed-manifesto/comment-page-1/.

Golgowski, Nina. "These Are the Victims of the Dayton, Ohio Mass Shooting." *Huffington Post*, August 9, 2019. https://www.huffpost.com/entry/dayton-shooting-victims-identified_n_5d46eeb4e4b0aca3411f48e6.

Gowrinathan, Nimmi. *Radicalizing Her: Why Women Choose Violence*. Boston: Beacon Press, 2021.

Hoddersen, Guerry. "The High Price of Ignoring Teenage Fascists," *Freedom Socialist Party*, April 20, 1999. Last updated August 2018. https://socialism.com/fs-article/the-high-price-of-ignoring-teenage-fascists/.

Hughes, Brian and Cynthia Miller-Idriss. "Uniting for Total Collapse: The January 6 Boost to Accelerationism." *The Combating Terrorism Center at West Point*, April/May 2021. https://ctc.usma.edu/uniting-for-total-collapse-the-january-6-boost-to-accelerationism/.

Inside Edition. "Body Armor Worn by Ohio Gunman is Shockingly Easy to Purchase." August 5, 2019. https://www.insideedition.com/body-armor-worn-ohio-gunman-shockingly-easy-purchase-55003.

Kalish, Rachel, and Michael Kimmel. "Suicide by Mass Murder: Masculinity, Aggrieved Entitlement, and Rampage School Shootings." *Health Sociology Review* 19, no. 4 (2010): 451–464.

Kundnani, Arun. *The Muslims Are Coming! Islamophobia, Extremism, and the Domestic War on Terror*. London: Verso, 2015.

Langman, Lauren and George Lundskow. *God, Guns, Gold and Glory: American Character and Its Discontents*. Chicago: Haymarket Books, 2016.

Leeb, Claudia. *The Politics of Repressed Guilt: The Tragedy of Austrian Silence*. Edinburgh: Edinburgh University Press, 2019.

Li, David K. "Homeowner Shoots Dead Two Teens Allegedly Trespassing on his Property in Ohio." *NBC*, August 29, 2019. https://www.nbcnews.com/news/us-news/homeowner-shoots-dead-two-teens-allegedly-trespassing-his-property-ohio-n1047686.

Macklin, Graham. "'Praise the Saints': The Cumulative Momentum of Transnational Extreme-Right Terrorism." In *A Transnational History of Right-Wing Terrorism: Political Violence and the Far Right in Eastern and Western Europe Since 1900*, edited by Johannes Dafinger and Moritz Florin, 215o240. London: Routledge, 2022.

Manne, Kate. *Down Girl: The Logic of Misogyny*. New York: Oxford University Press, 2019.

Mannion, Connor. "Dayton Shooter was on Cocaine, Alcohol During Massacre, Coroner Reveals." *Mediaite*, August 15, 2019. https://www.mediaite.com/news/dayton-shooter-was-on-cocaine-alcohol-during-massacre-coroner-reveals/.

Matthias, Christopher. "Paul Gosar Spoke at a White Nationalist Conference. The GOP Doesn't Care." *Huffington Post*, March 5, 2021. https://www.huffpost.com/entry/paul-gosar-white-nationalist-republican_n_6o415a1ec5b6o208555d4f6o.

McBride, Jessica. "Connor Betts: 5 Fast Facts You Need to Know." *Heavy*, August 12, 2019. https://heavy.com/news/2019/o8/connor-betts/.

Mondon, Aurelien and Aaron Winter. *Reactionary Democracy: How Racism and the Populist Far Right Became Mainstream*. London: Verso, 2020.

Moonshot Team. "Mass Shooterism and the Need for Online Interventions and Bystander Resources," *GNET*, August 3, 2022. https://gnet-research.org/2022/o8/o3/mass-shooterism-and-the-need-for-online-interventions-and-bystander-resources/. Accessed October 8, 2022.

Moore, Michael, dir. *Bowling for Columbine*. United States: Metro-Goldwyn-Mayer, 2002.

Neilstein, Vince. "Op-Ed: Unpacking Dayton Shooter Connor Betts' Connection to Metal and Pornogrind." *MetalSucks*, August 5, 2019. https://www.metalsucks.net/2019/o8/o6/op-ed-unpacking-dayton-shooter-connor-betts-connection-to-metal-and-pornogrind/.

Newhauser, Daniel. "EXCLUSIVE: Dayton Shooter Was in a 'Pornogrind' Band That Released Songs about Killing and Raping Women." *VICE*, August 5, 2019. https://www.vice.com/en/article/j5yekp/exclusive-dayton-shooter-was-in-a-pornogrind-band-that-released-songs-about-raping-and-killing-women.

Ngo, Andy. "Dayton Shooter Connor Betts May Be Antifa's First Mass Killer." *New York Post*, August 6, 2019. https://nypost.com/2019/o8/o6/dayton-shooter-may-be-antifas-first-mass-killer/.

Parker, Jade. "Accelerationism in America: Threat Perceptions." *Global Network on Extremism & Technology*, February 4, 2020. https://gnet-research.org/2020/02/04/accelerationism-in-america-a-threat-perceptions/.

Phillips, Morgan. "Dayton Shooter's Ex-Girlfriend Says He Showed Her Footage of a Mass Shooting on Their First Date." *Mediaite*, August 6, 2019. https://www.mediaite.com/news/dayton-shooters-ex-girlfriend-says-he-showed-her-footage-of-a-mass-shooting-on-their-first-date/.

Pollak, Joel B. "CNN Confirms: Dayton Shooter Had 'Extreme' Left-Wing Views; Backed Warren, Sanders." *Breitbart*, August 5, 2019. https://www.breitbart.com/the-media/2019/o8/o5/cnn-confirms-dayton-shooter-left-wing/.

Steinbuch, Yaron. "Dayton Shooter Connor Betts May Have Had Far-Left Twitter Account." *New York Post*, August 6, 2019. https://nypost.com/2019/08/06/dayton-shooter-connor-betts-may-have-supported-leftist-ideas-on-shadow-twitter-account/.

Thorpe, Charles. *Necroculture*. New York: Palgrave MacMillan, 2016.

Tiflati, Hicham. "The Extremism Market and Salad Bar Ideology" *European Eye on Radicalization* https://eeradicalization.com/the-extremism-market-and-salad-bar-ideology/. Accessed October 8, 2022.

Vera, Amir. "Garlic Festival Shooter Died from Self-Inflicted Gunshot Wound." *CNN*, August 2, 2019. https://www.cnn.com/2019/08/02/us/gilroy-garlic-festival-shooter/index.html.

Wallace, Danielle. "Dayton Gunman Was Pro-Gun Control, Friend Says." *Fox News*, August 6, 2019. https://www.foxnews.com/us/dayton-gunman-anti-2nd-amendment-not-conservative-right-leaning-left-tweets-conner-betts-will-el-fakir.

Walters, Jonah. "We Need to Get the U.S. Army Out of High Schools." *Jacobin*, August 13, 2019. https://www.jacobinmag.com/2019/08/jrotc-army-recruitment-high-schools-connor-betts-dayton-shooting.

Ware, Jacob. "Testament to Murder: The Violent Far-Right's Increasing Use of Terrorist Manifestos." *International Centre for Counter-terrorism – The Hague*, March 2020. https://icct.nl/app/uploads/2020/03/Jaocb-Ware-Terrorist-Manifestos2.pdf.

Warwick, Esther. "Autism and the Alt-Right," Presentation, Autistics Present.

Wyatt, Tim. "Dayton Shooting Suspect Connor Betts Sang About Raping and Killing Women in 'Pornogrind' Metal Band." *The Independent*, August 6, 2019. https://www.independent.co.uk/news/world/americas/dayton-shooting-connor-betts-suspect-pornogrind-band-murder-rape-a9040981.html.

CHAPTER 18

Freud as a Mythmaker, Scientist, and Critical Social Theorist

Francesco Ranci

In 1932, a seventy-six-year-old Sigmund Freud wrote back to Albert Einstein, who was then fifty-three, just about twenty-three years younger than him. Einstein had chosen Freud as the one person in the whole world who would be able to throw some light on how to free mankind from war. The International Institute for Intellectual Cooperation (IIIC) had initiated this exchange of views the year before, by asking Einstein to identify a pressing problem of interest to the international community, and a suitable intellectual to engage in a public debate with.

The IIIC was set up in the 1920s, by the League of Nations, forerunner of our contemporary United Nations. After World War II its mission and archives were incorporated by the United Nations Educational, Scientific, and Cultural Organization (UNESCO). Rather than promoting public exchanges of views between prominent scholars, however, UNESCO puts forward official declarations of its own device, over matters of international concern. Michel Foucault suggested that "whether or not the IIIC methodology was more effective, it was certainly more entertaining."[1]

The exchange of letters between Einstein and Freud was immediately published in Paris, by the IIIC, and its existence is well known today. At times, however, it is quoted in a way that might suggest the two men were friends, which was not the case. For example, these two letters are the only ones they ever wrote to each other. What they wrote in them makes it clear enough, for the purpose of this paper, that both men considered each other as nothing less and nothing more than fellow *scientists*.

In Einstein's words, they were both 'men who, absorbed in the pursuit of science, can see the world-problems in the perspective distance lends.'[2] It is also

---

[1] Michel Foucault, "What is Enlightenment?" in *The Foucault Reader*, edited by P. Rabinow (New York: Pantheon Books, 1984), 32. (https://foucault.info/documents/foucault.whatIsEnlightenment.en).

[2] Albert Einstein and Sigmund Freud, "Why War," in *The Standard Edition of the Complete Psychological Works of Sigmund Freud,* ed. James Strachey, vol. XXII, (London: Hogarth Press, 1964), 199.

important, from the very limited point of view of this paper, to take into proper consideration a problem that may be raised by Einstein's use of the word *distance*, on this occasion. Einstein is not possibly suggesting that an actual, physical distance be taken from the *world-problems*. He is rather using the word in a metaphorical sense, which is well established and meant to put the scientist somehow above the fray.

It is commonly understood, Einstein says to Freud, that "civilization as we know it" is under a deadly threat because of "the advance of modern science." Apparently, the Great War (known today as World War 1), had left its mark. People were already dreading the possibility of another and even greater adventure of reciprocal destruction, by the supposedly most civilized nations. So far, all attempts at solving this problem seem to have failed, Einstein continues, and he points to "certain psychological obstacles" whose "existence the layman in the mental sciences can only surmise."[3] Thus, Einstein asks Freud to bring the light of his "far reaching knowledge of man's instinctive life" to bear upon the problem of war. He is convinced that Freud will be able to suggest "educative methods" that would "eliminate those obstacles."[4]

In other words, Einstein, who is representing here a supposedly shared set of beliefs, sees the future of what we might refer to as "modern civilization," for good and for bad, as depending on a scientific assessment of its own psychological problems. At stake does not seem to be yet the future of mankind. However, since nuclear weapons did not exist yet in 1932, and maybe more importantly, since both Einstein and Freud seem quite sure they are living in the most civilized part of the world.

Einstein wants an assessment that is to be based on the best knowledge available but does not feel any need to explain why he chose Freud, as opposed to another psychologist, or philosopher, as his source of this knowledge. 'As for me (Einstein says), the normal object of my thought affords no insight into the dark places of human will and feeling.'[5] But, I would say surprisingly, while offering his own advice, in his reply Freud suggests that any science, including Einstein's own "Physics," to be sure, entails a mythology.[6]

Freud's suggestion to Einstein, who was probably not supposed to continue this public exchange of views, and as a matter of fact he did not, could mean to us simply that Freud took Einstein's invitation as a chance to publicly respond to circulating criticism toward his own science. Psychoanalysis was at this

---

3 Einstein and Freud, "Why War," 199.
4 Ibid.
5 Ibid.
6 Einstein and Freud, "Why War," 211.

point known to the public (even Hollywood's romance with Freud had already begun, in the 1920s, and was growing in the 1930s), by redirecting the accusation of selling myths for science towards no less the most celebrated scientist in the world at the time (and possibly even today).

Freud was probably aware that Einstein's physics, especially his theory of general relativity, was being questioned by many of his colleagues, by philosophers, and by public intellectuals at large. Including the French philosopher Henry Bergson, who was also the Chairman of the International Institute for Intellectual Cooperation (IIIC).

Einstein himself acknowledged to some extent that what he was offering were theories – conceptual constructions of his own – that were used to better understand our solar system and the universe beyond that, not to be confused with a mythical (we might say) *existing* world, supposedly waiting *out there* to be discovered, once and for all, by a sort of (again, mythical or metaphorical) Christopher Columbus. Einstein was probably well aware that the real Columbus always believed he had traveled from Europe to India, and that his ignorance about the American continent was not shared by every other human being, just as much as the ignorance about Europe by the peoples we call today native Americans – very lucky for them, up to that point in time -, widespread as it was, did not mean that Europeans did not exist at all before Columbus landed in the Caribbeans.

Thirty years after this exchange of letters over the scourge of war between a physicist and a psychologist who turned their respective academic disciplines upside down with their theories, Thomas Kuhn's book *The Structure of Scientific Revolutions* (1962) unleashed yet another debate among philosophers of science, and intellectuals at large, by questioning the possibility of actually separating science from myth.[7] As a side effect of this book, we can still recognize a widespread – and quite vague – use of the word *paradigm*, which entered our colloquial language back then – when Kuhn used it in practically every page of his 1962 book. Kuhn essentially argued that any definition of science must be tied to a social and historical context, since what a scientific revolution does, by establishing a new paradigm, is to modify the very concept of *science* itself, together with the world scientists believe they live in.[8] Other examples of this debate over the concept of scientific knowledge (which one may say is certainly a work in progress) can easily be found both in the so-called Western philosophical tradition and, as much as they have not been

---

7   Thomas Kuhn, *The Structure of Scientific Revolutions* (Chicago: University of Chicago Press, 1962).
8   Ibid.

destroyed by it, in the so-called non-Western philosophical traditions, albeit a suitable criteria for distinguishing Western from non-Western philosophical or scientific traditions still being itself a matter of debate. And the history of psychoanalysis provides no fewer debates of this kind than that of any other school of thought: from theoretical issues, like how can pathologies be properly identified and treated, to more practical ones, like the truthfulness (or untruthfulness) of Freud's and others' accounts of their research practices. Not to mention the themes of development, and internal consistency of Freud's theoretical propositions, and of the overlap or conflict that may be found with other thinkers,' or schools of thought, sets of explicit and implicit statements.

It is thereby somehow surprising that Louis Menand takes such a widespread but controversial distinction – that between science and myth – for granted. Without defining these terms, however, he labels Freud as a mythmaker in his 2005 *Introduction* to Freud's classic book *Eros and Civilization* (1930). Which is a book that according to Menand himself became a staple of Cold War intellectual debates.

The term *mythmaker* is by itself problematic since a myth is rarely if ever single handedly manufactured by an individual. However, taken by itself, it is not necessarily a disparaging term. Depending on context it can mark the designee in a positive or negative light. It can be appreciative if the person who is called that way is engaged in fiction (like a poet, or novelist), while the opposite is usually the case if that author is engaged in nonfiction (like an historian, or a scientist). Like so many other terms, it can also be applied favorably or unfavorably depending on one's political views. And Menand takes another questionable step by claiming that Freud's words are bound to be interpreted at will, depending on the political views of their interpreters: 'radicals and conservatives (says Menand) have read Freud the way they wanted to, because it is the fate of all mythmakers to be revised,' thereby making Freud pay for his interpreters' politically motivated readings of his work.[9]

As Max Weber pointed out, the fate of scientists is actually to be revised much sooner than mythmakers are.[10] We still talk about *Prometheus*, for example, and not so much about *Phlogiston,* anymore. Even though the former name is thousands of years old, while the latter name is only a few centuries old. The use of fire by hominids, to be sure, has nothing to do with it, since it goes back to over a million years ago. Menand's argument turns out to be puzzling, at

---

9   Louis Menand, "Introduction," in *Civilization and Its Discontents*, by Sigmund Freud (New York: W.W. Norton & Company, 2005), 32.
10 Max Weber, "Science as a Vocation," in *From Max Weber: Essays in Sociology*, ed. and trans. H.H. Gerth and C. Wright Mills, 77–128 (New York: Oxford University Press, 1946).

this point. What he means is probably that the fate of mythmakers is to be *arbitrarily* revised, since mythologies are not bound to follow the methodological requirements that sciences are bound to follow. However, as we have seen, according to thinkers like Weber, Kuhn, Einstein and Freud, actually, and just to name a few of them, to figure out the difference between science and myth is not such a clear and simple matter at all. A term like *phlogiston*, for example, used to belong to science, while it belongs to myth now – the reason for this being that, as noted before, the fate of scientists is to be revised much sooner than mythmakers are.

Without providing any historical evidence, Menand also reports that Freud's psychoanalysis was outlawed both in Nazi Germany and in the Soviet Union. If left at that, such a statement can be considered, at least to some extent, a myth. Psychologists continued to practice *psychoanalysis* in Nazi Germany. They were allowed to do so as long as they were not labeled as Jews. It is the same officially established Nazi criteria – so to speak, considering its logical flaws – following which Freud's books were not allowed to circulate in Germany, just like Einstein's and scores of other authors' books. In the Soviet Union, on the other hand, psychoanalysis was flourishing throughout the 1920s and Menand has nothing to say about Stalin's change of mind about it, during the 1930s. He seems to suggest that there was a sudden conversion to *Anti-Semitism* by Stalin, but even if that was the case, it still would not settle the matter, just as it doesn't in Hitler's case.

Menand does not question the scientific *bona fide* of psychoanalysis as a whole, and has to concede that, as everyone knows, Freud always claimed to be a scientist, not a mythmaker. Whatever the distinction between a scientist and a mythmaker means to Menand, as evidence for his claim according to which Freud was a manufacturer of myths, he puts forward the following piece of news: in a conversation with the Italian writer Giovanni Papini, Freud defined himself as "a poet and a novelist" at heart.[11]

Neither entering into further details nor providing any sources for this piece of news, Menand gives full credibility to what, as we will soon see, is a prank, or a spoof, by Papini. If believed, it does fit well with Menand's categorization of Freud as a mythmaker. But to knowingly sell a spoof for a fact does amount to committing a fraud. So, we would rather assume he believed it.

Before we deal with Papini's *fictional interview*, however, let's take into consideration that as Foucault pointed out, Kant defined the Enlightenment in a "negative way," as an *Ausgang* (exit), a "way out" of humankind's state of

11   Menand, "Introduction," 9.

"immaturity." Which is to say, Kant defined the Enlightenment not so much as an historical epoch, but in terms of a personal decision.[12] In short, it is a personal decision to stop believing what one doesn't really know, and instead – as Kant famously stated -, to find the courage to know.

1   The Problem of Negative Definitions: From Kant to Foucault to Freud

What Kant proposed to Frederick II, in scarcely veiled terms, says Foucault, was a contract between "rational despotism" and "free reason."[13] His proposal to the King of Prussia was to maintain that authorizing "the public" the "free use of autonomous reason" would give any king "the best guarantee of obedience." On the condition, however, that the "political principle," which was to be obeyed, would itself also be in "conformity with universal reason."[14] In other words, Kant probably assumed that the free use of autonomous reason would necessarily deliver conformity with universal reason.

The purpose of this contract (a way out of political and military troubles), was to replace the early modern European doctrine of *cuius regio, eius religio* (whose land, their religion) with the ideal (the myth, Foucault implicitly argues) of *universal reason*. Foucault argues that this way out was presented by Kant in a rather ambiguous manner, as it was left to be determined how such a *conformity to reason* could be verified, and by whom (by either the king or the philosopher, or possibly by both – but it seems that no one else needed to be involved, even though Kant does mention the *public* use of reason as a requirement).

In order to avoid Kant's ambiguity, Foucault's proposal is to assume that *criticism* is no longer to be practiced in the search for formal structures, endowed with universal value. Criticism, argues Foucault, should rather be conceived as a historical investigation into the events that have led us to constitute ourselves the way we do now. We know from experience, says Foucault, that 'the claim to escape from the system of contemporary reality so as to produce the overall programs of another society, of another way of thinking, another culture, another vision of the world, has led only to the return of the most dangerous traditions.' We should forget, says Foucault, about all alternative "worldviews" and focus our inquiries only on how we came to think what we

12   Foucault, "What is Enlightenment?"
13   Ibid., 32.
14   Ibid.

think today.[15] As we know now, he said that just a few years before the collapse of the Soviet Union.

The questions we should ask ourselves, according to Foucault, are the following: (1) How are we constituted as subjects of our own knowledge? (2) How are we constituted as subjects who exercise or submit to power relations? (3) How are we constituted as moral subjects of our own actions? However, the "critical ontology of ourselves," which according to him we would obtain by answering such questions, 'has to be considered not, certainly, as a theory, a doctrine, nor even as a permanent body of knowledge that is accumulating.'[16]

The answers to these questions are supposed to come from the study of what Foucault defines as *modes of problematization*, that is, of what is 'neither an anthropological constant nor a chronological variation.'[17] This study is described by him as the way to 'analyze questions of general import in their historically unique form.'[18] However, notwithstanding his critique of Kant's negative definition of the Enlightenment, Foucault apparently relies here on plenty of negative definitions too. It remains to be seen what a study of something that is neither an anthropological constant nor a chronological variation looks like. Nevertheless, his remedy to the ambiguity of Kant's definition of the Enlightenment, he quite vaguely argues, 'has to be conceived as an attitude, an ethos, a philosophical life.'[19]

An especially cryptic remark wraps up the way in which the Enlightenment, or *criticism* as he says, should be conceived according to Foucault. He concludes by saying that 'the critique of what we are is at one and the same time the historical analysis of the limits that are imposed on us, and an experiment with the possibility of going beyond them.'[20] No less than three issues: (1) the critique of ourselves, (2) the historical analyses of our limits, and (3) the experiment of our possibility of going beyond them, are to be considered at one and the same time. A set of instructions allowing one to actually pursue such a seemingly self-contradictory task (dealing with three problems at one time) is not surprisingly missing. Furthermore, it remains to be clarified how such limits are so surely *imposed* on us, as opposed to being *self-imposed*, especially since we are talking about an inquiry that was initially concerned with how we constitute ourselves.

---

15   Ibid.
16   Ibid.
17   Ibid.
18   Ibid.
19   Ibid.
20   Ibid., 50.

Foucault argues that notwithstanding Kant's hopes, 'many things in our experience convince us that the historical event of the Enlightenment did not make us mature adults.'[21] We have not reached that stage yet, says Foucault, and we may add, more than two centuries after Kant and four decades after Foucault, that things may even be getting worse at times, and there is no way to know what the future will bring. However, Foucault is talking now about the Enlightenment in terms of an historical event, not in terms of a personal decision, anymore.

By "immaturity," as Foucault reports, Kant famously meant 'a certain state of our will that makes us accept someone else's authority to lead us in areas where the use of reason is called for.'[22] We would be in a state of immaturity when a book takes the place of our understanding, or when a spiritual director takes the place of our conscience, or when a doctor decides for us, for example, what our diet is going to be.[23] Thinking about Freud, what our mental health is like and what we should do about it, would also be up to us as patients, and not to our doctor. On this point, as we will see, sociologist Erving Goffman parted ways with what he called the *Freudians*, even though not necessarily with Freud himself.

Kant's examples of our immaturity, even though the term is defined in a negative, and in a rather metaphorical way, given that we human beings are not vegetables, may in the end still be worth considering, is Foucault's conclusion concerning the Enlightenment, side by side with Foucault's own suggestions of avoiding universal claims, and alternative worldviews – but this is no less than a self-contradictions in terms. Kant's ambiguity seems now to have been forgotten by Foucault, and to it – to the optimistic view of the relationship between free use of autonomous reason and universal reason – he adds his own recipe. A way of doing things which (supposedly without involving any *theories,* or even any accumulation of knowledge) would consist of providing ourselves with historical contexts in which our questions – questions about how we constitute our-selves, as subject of our own knowledge, and so on – could be "critically found, examined, and answered."[24]

By taking into consideration Papini's spoof at Freud's expense, we will be primarily concerned with demonstrating that it was a prank. However, we will also try to address the main question of *criticism*, to some extent following Foucault's suggestions, but without necessarily sharing all his assumptions. We

---

21 Ibid.
22 Ibid.
23 Ibid.
24 Ibid.

will freely use our own autonomous reason, as Kant suggested, however without assuming (as he possibly did) that by doing so our result will be a *universal reason* – meaning by that an impossible *one and the only way out of immaturity*. It goes without saying that the "unconscious," as Freud defined and described it, also seems to tragically run into the problem of negative definitions.

2   Freud, or Rather Menand, as a Mythmaker

Menand does not say, but it is possible to find out, that in June 1934 the British journal *Colosseum: A Quarterly Review of Critical Thought*, published Papini's account of the conversation he had with Freud, who told him he was a "scientist" by necessity, and not by vocation. By this account, Freud claims to have tried to make his vocation clear all along and complains that no one understood him. 'Everybody thinks that I stand by the scientific character of my work and that my principle scope lies in curing mental maladies (says Freud), but this is a terrible error that has prevailed for years, and I have been unable to set it right.'[25] Freud also felt that it was too late to rock the boat, and at the end of the conversation asked Papini to keep quiet about this terrible secret. 'Luckily you are not a writer or a journalist,' he says, to someone who was both.[26]

Papini had been invited to write for the second issue of *Colosseum* and to add to the new journal his name, which was the name of a highly polemic and controversial writer. However, 'I am sure you will not share my secret,' Freud supposedly told him. Papini gives the final touch to his prank, ending his article by saying that 'I reassured him – and sincerely; these notes are not destined for the press.'[27]

Founded and edited by the conservative Catholic intellectual Bernard Wall, *Colosseum* had promised on its very first issue to fight against social ills such as Capitalism, Bolshevism, and Fascism. There was also Freudism in this list, which was the only target built around the name of an individual, and in all likelihood worked as a proxy for a more standard target of those times, the so-called "Jewish problem," which was not listed.

Not surprisingly, there is nothing in Papini's piece that sounds in any way credible, while every bit of information he gives is absurd, unless his reader understands that his interview is not to be taken as reality. The reader is not

---

25   Giovanni Papini, "A Visit to Freud (8 May 1934)," in *Freud as we Knew Him*, ed. Hendrik M. Ruitenbeek (Detroit: Wayne State University Press, 1973), 99.
26   Ibid., 102.
27   Ibid.

asked by Papini to imagine a conversation between him and Freud, but rather to recall what the reader already knows about Freud and psychoanalysis, and to get a good laugh at it.

Papini begins by claiming to have bought a statue of Narcissus, and to have sent it to Freud as a birthday present with a note that said, 'To the discoverer of Narcissism.'[28] This alleged gift makes the whole story a plain mockery at Freud's expense, supporting the dismissal of his work for selling an old myth as if it was a new scientific finding. It seems quite unlikely that Freud would have been flattered by receiving, as Papini describes it, a 'lovely marble statue, Greek, of the Hellenistic period, which according to the archeologists, represents Narcissus,' while being addressed at the same time as the discoverer of Narcissism.[29] The contrast Papini devises and subsequently ties to the word "discovery," is striking (here is your discovery, Dr. Freud). However, Papini, or so he says, promptly received in return an invitation to Freud's home.

It is a matter of record that Freud's birthday falls on May 6th. But even if Papini's title is *A Visit to Freud (8 May 1934)*, and his claim is to have met Freud right after his birthday, it obviously does not make the interview any more credible. What is to be verified is that the meeting, not the birthday, actually took place. When Papini pretends to have just come back from Freud's house, and to want to jot down the essential parts of their conversation, implying that he is very much in a hurry, after traveling all the way to Vienna, and then maybe back to Florence, before writing his account of his meeting with no less than Freud, he is just mimicking and trashing anyone who might be in awe of the supposedly great thinker (not so great, obviously, in Papini's view).

A sentence like 'now at last I can speak freely to you' is ascribed by Papini to Freud, and it sounds completely absurd, given any conceivable context, and furthermore, one featuring Papini as its listener.[30] The Italian intellectual is at the same time treated like an anonymous admirer. And, oddly enough, he is allegedly welcomed into Freud's home the day after his 77th birthday (not the second day after his birthday – this is Papini's sense of humor at work, once again) – finding him, or so he says, exhausted and depressed.

Besides sentences like *no one knows or has ever guessed the real secret of my work*, also absurd and insulting to Freud personally are the words 'your visit is a great consolation. You are neither a patient, nor a colleague, nor a disciple, nor a relative.'[31] Duly implementing the *Colosseum* agenda, Papini attacks here the

---

28   Ibid.
29   Ibid.
30   Ibid.
31   Ibid.

entire psychoanalytic movement (Freudism). Freud complains that he lives 'all year round surrounded either by hysterical or obsessed people,' by 'doctors who despise me or are jealous of me,' and by 'disciples who can be classed either as chronic parrots or ambitious schismatics.'[32]

However, surprisingly enough, Papini's spoof is taken as 'an interesting glimpse into Freud's own feelings about friends, pupils, and colleagues' in 1973 by Ruitenbeek, even though contrary to Menand, Ruitenbeek does point out that 'this paper is virtually unknown in psychoanalytic literature,' and that 'Jones does not mention it.' All Ruitenbeek has to say about it, however, which is not nearly enough, and not supported by any piece of evidence, is that 'its veracity has been questioned.'[33] This paper was probably never questioned: it was either understood for what it is or misunderstood as a real interview.

In Papini's article, Freud acknowledges that France had a decisive influence on the development of his ideas, but 'not so much for what I learned from Charcot,' it was rather that in France 'the literary life in those days was rich, prosperous, and active,' as 'Symbolism raised its banner against Naturalism.'[34] Clearly, what Papini is offering here, in mocking terms, is his own assessment of the background of Freud's theories.

Funny or not funny, interesting or not, Papini's prank is better understood by looking at one of his previous publications. In 1930, Papini published a novel, both in Italian and in English (1931). Its main character, named Gog, short for Goggins, was an American millionaire born into poverty, and now rich but suffering from depression. As a narrative device, Papini says he met Gog by chance in Florence's asylum, while he was paying a visit to another patient. Traveling the world in search of the meaning of life, Gog had met people like Lenin, Gandhi, Einstein, and Freud. From Gog's notes, Papini says, he assembled his text, the novel is thereby also a mockery of the social sciences, which were becoming a prominent feature of the academic world in those years.

Gog's encounters all revealed how those celebrities deserved only to be laughed at. Lenin, for example, is made to declare that his real objective is to exterminate all the peasants in Russia; they will have to choose between becoming industrial workers or die because a Marxist revolution does not know what to do with peasants. Freud, in his turn, is made to explain that he is not a scientist at all, contrary to what everyone thinks of him, and to

---

32 Ibid.
33 Hendrik M. Ruitenbeek, ed., *Freud as we Knew Him* (Detroit: Wayne State University Press, 1973), 98.
34 Papini, "A Visit to Freud (8 May 1934)," 98.

rhetorically challenge Gog to find any instructions on how to replicate his own results (as any scientific methodology requires) in any of his books.

Papini's attack of Freud (in *Gog*) was easily understood by Italian psychoanalysts, who responded in 1933 on the newborn *Rivista Italiana di Psicoanalisi*.[35] It seems quite possible that Freud knew of the reply, by his own first followers in Italy, to Papini's novel. If so, this fact would not be compatible at all with the belief that Freud talked to Papini in 1934 the way Papini said he did.

Gog sold well in Italy, but was not well received in America, which makes one think that Papini was trying to capture attention for its English version via the British public. It is also possible that he responded to the *Colosseum*'s invitation by recycling a paper he had already written. What matters here is only that based on the contents and context of his 1934 article for the *Colosseum*, it is absurd to believe the words Papini ascribes to Freud to be from anyone other than Papini himself, contrary to what Menand, as we have seen, does in 2005.

Menand is picking up the story from someone else, as a sort of psychoanalytic *vox populi*. Ruitenbeck's position is similar, to some extent, to what Eissler argued a few years later: 'proofs abound that Freud could never have told Papini what the latter reported, (but) whether or not he had ever met Freud, (Eissler says) Papini may have intuitively estimated correctly significant elements in Freud's unconscious.'[36]

Just a few more considerations are due at this point. On the one hand, the commodification of higher culture may have something to do with the wide circulation of unverified information and baseless accounts, like Papini's paper being offered without any references, or like ascribing to someone like Papini, who clearly makes fun of psychoanalysis, a superior ability to grasp Freud's unconscious. On the other hand, Papini's satire may have hit upon some flaws within psychoanalysis as a scientific theory, making it suitable to be ignored by Freud, and by almost every one of his followers, but also making it suitable to be exploited by other psychoanalysts, who decided to categorize Freud as a poet and novelist, and who brought it to Menand's attention.

To be sure, when Papini makes Freud say that his family was poor and living under an antisemitic monarchy, so that for a Jewish boy like him hoping to become a novelist was not allowed, he is not at all far from the truth. Freud himself would probably have agreed up to this point if they ever had met (and talked about his life experiences as a Jewish boy in Vienna, who had to find a

---

35 Giorgio Granata, Israele Zoller, and Emilio Servadio, "Varia," *Rivista Italiana di Psicoanalisi* 2 (1933): 49–57.

36 K. R. Eissler, "Creativity and Adolescence—The Effect of Trauma in Freud's Adolescence," *Psychoanalytic Study of the Child*, 33 (1978), 461.

way to make a living fairly quickly). A possibility which, however unlikely, still can't be denied from a strictly historical point of view. In other words, Papini surely knew about Freud, while Freud probably also knew about Papini, and both were on the international market as writers at the same time, so that other individuals may be found that met both Freud and Papini, albeit separately and on different occasions.

Likewise, when Papini makes Freud say that in any country, artists and novelists have shown more interest in his work than scientists did, this may also be true, for what it means (it might be true for Einstein as well). It's even possible that, as Papini says, Freud's childhood hero was Goethe, even though others say it was actually Napoleon, and this information might even be considered important to reach an understanding of Freud's unconscious, but it is hard to consider that anyone would prefer to get this information from Papini, instead of finding it in Freud's extensive autobiographical work – and, of course, in the historical record.

In other words, depending on the argument one is making, the use of Papini's prank as evidence can be damaging with respect to the argument that it supposedly supports. Once the prank is exposed for what it is (Freud never met Papini, and, thereby, never told him that he was a poet and a novelist at heart) some other piece of evidence is going to be needed to make the argument that he actually was a poet, and a novelist, or a "mythmaker." Freud's above-mentioned reply to Einstein, for example, might be taken into consideration for this purpose, but it brings into focus what Freud tells Einstein about science, thereby calling into question Menand's simplistic separation of science from myth.

For psychoanalysts who are not willing to address the issues involved in the alleged or denied scientificity of their discipline, it may turn out to be useful just to believe that Freud told Papini what Papini says he told him, that he never really wanted to be a scientist. However, from a methodological point of view, the matter can only be settled by coming up with some theory about how one can distinguish scientific knowledge from mythologies. Papini invokes an established criterion, that of delivering instructions about how to replicate one's results. Freud implicitly and explicitly subscribed to that basic criterion. Otherwise, to put it bluntly, he would not have written about a new therapy and would not have dared charging his patients for a physician's services. But, as we have seen, Freud's view was also that at the end of the day, such instructions can't be fully separated from some kind of arbitrary beliefs, and one may even call them myths.[37]

---

37   Kuhn, *The Structure of Scientific Revolutions.*

Myths are understood as beliefs that can't be reached by following a set of instructions but must rather be either accepted or rejected without embarking oneself into a process of verification, which is assumed to be impossible to describe in terms of an intersubjectively sharable methodology (but at any given point in time this problem will play out differently, as Foucault, for one, would point out). According to Freud, even though any science may at the end of the day reveal a lurking mythology, there is still room for science. What is meant by that is exactly Papini's operational criteria, but instead what Freud calls 'the detached and rational perspective of the unworldly theoretician' in his enlightened and enlightening exchange of views with Einstein (who, as we have seen, defined science in a similar fashion in his own letter to Freud).[38]

The scientist's job is commonly understood to be that of coming up with a somehow validated knowledge; for example, in our case, that Freud did not meet Papini, as far as we can tell by reading Papini's article. What Freud does, in his reply to Einstein, is only to raise a question about what science is, or how it works, when a suitable criterion for validating a piece of knowledge seems to be missing. Yet, one can't just give up the piece of knowledge in question without compromising the whole theory. It is clear that, for example, Foucault's historically unique forms are still the result of the work of historians. However, as we have seen Foucault maintains as valid the myth that they are already there, waiting to be found.

A quick look at the political context in 1934 confirms the quite unlikely status of Papini's interview as an actual historical event and offers a glimpse on how Freud followed the political struggles of his times. In 1930, the police headquarters in Rome had issued a warrant and he was to be arrested if he ever traveled in Italy again, as he had done several times before. For the Italian writer not to mention it, and not to hear about it from Freud – who loved going to Italy – is, once again, to say the least, quite hard to believe.

In January 1933, Hitler became Chancellor of Germany. In February, the Reichstag was burned by Nazi terrorists, and by May 1934 (when the alleged interview took place), Freud's books had already been publicly burned in what had become Nazi Germany. Papini obviously knew all that, and his readers also knew it very well. One may wonder if he is adding insult to injury by portraying Freud the way he does, or if he is trying to somehow defend him by making him seem less of a dangerous fellow, or maybe he does not care about Freud in the least (thanks to Mussolini's favor, the following year Papini became a University Professor in Bologna). In any case, what remains clear is that in a

---

38   Freud, "Why War," 213.

real interview, in a real piece of journalism, some attention to current events would have to have been given.

On June 16, Freud wrote a letter to Ernest Jones which stated that 'one does not enjoy life' because 'the foundations are rocking.' At that very moment, he says, 'the intriguer M. in Venice is selling us to the captain of the thieves H.' Mussolini and Hitler are into their first meeting (which was held in Venice), and Freud is following their actions while having reached his conclusions about the two heads of State. 'I will be happy to see you (and your wife?) with us in the summer,' he writes to Jones, before adding 'but what will it look like here then?'[39] One month later, on July 25, Austria's Catholic-Fascist dictator Engelbert Dollfuss, who had shut down Parliament and outlawed all opposition parties in Vienna the year before, was killed during an insurrection of Nazi activists.

Three years after the Italian arrest warrant, in April 1933, Freud sent a written message to Mussolini himself. To some commentators this is to be interpreted as an infatuation for the Italian strong leader. However, as we have just seen, Freud calls Mussolini in a way that does not square much with this interpretation. The fact is that Mussolini opposed Hitler's attempts to invade Austria, in 1934, so in 1933 Freud might have been still hopeful that Mussolini and Hitler would not manage to get along. Freud's message reads: 'To Benito Mussolini, respectfully, from an old man who sees the hero of civilization in the one who governs.'[40] It is written on a copy of the above-mentioned exchange of letters between him and Einstein (their joint attempt to spare Europe World War II, one might say, retrospectively), which the Institute for International Intellectual Cooperation had just published in German, French and English (but not in Italian, and was not allowed to circulate in Nazi Germany, or it would have been burnt, obviously). This gift was elicited by a Fascist politician, close enough to Mussolini, whose daughter was undergoing psychoanalysis under one of Freud's Italian associates. The three of them did pay a visit to Freud – unlike Papini – in 1933. Shortly after the delivery of this gift, it appeared in Mussolini's newspaper, *The People of Italy*, an article accusing Freud of being close to the Bolsheviks. This article, probably written by Mussolini himself, repeated the accusations already printed by the *Osservatore Romano* in Vatican City. Under such circumstances, once again, Papini's article can only be confirmed for what it clearly appears to be, if one reads it.

---

39   Sigmund Freud, "Letter to Ernst Jones, June 16, 1934," in *The Complete Correspondence of Sigmund Freud and Ernest Jones 1908–1939* (Cambridge, MA: Harvard University Press, 1993), 736–737.
40   Roberto Zapperi, *Freud e Mussolini* (Milano, Franco Angeli, 2013).

In 2005, Menand sold to his readers an unchecked piece of information, thereby turning himself (not Freud) into a "mythmaker." Ironically, twelve years beforehand, in 1993, Papini's spoof had already been exposed on the pages of *The New York Review of Books,* thanks to three of its readers who had read *Gog* and independently pointed it out to Frederick Crews. Crews looked at the fictional source of information (Papini's novel) and concluded that Freud's 'supposed confidences to Papini should be struck from the record.'[41] Notice that Crews did not waste any time on the alleged interview which, however, considering that Papini was quite an unpredictable character, and that he was also a journalist, could have been authentic (in principle).

In the very same journal, at the very same time in 1994, Menand complained that another author's work was not 'a useful contribution to the debate' because, Menand argued, 'I found Mr. Bernstein's reporting selective and one sided and his conclusions tendentious.'[42] Surely Menand's own 2005 treatment of Papini's report can be categorized in a similar manner, to say the least.

It is hard to think of a more basic tenet of the scientific method than that of checking what the text being quoted actually says, which is something that can be done only by reading it. Only by doing that can one apply Kant's principle of autonomous reason, Foucault's questions about how we are (by ourselves) constituted, and the rational detachment Freud and Einstein maintained a scientist must show.

However, to offer a quotation of the text you are referring to (Menand did not even do that) so that others can verify your analyses of it does come close to being an even more basic tenet of the scientific method. In other words, only by sharing your information with others can the belief in the possibility of a public debate, on humanity's large or small problems, be sustained. And fostering a debate in which anyone who is interested can make up their mind, and thereby have their say, is not only the scientifically correct way of doing things, it is also, one may argue, what distinguishes critical thinkers from mythmakers.

3   Freud as a Scientist, or Philosopher?

Scholarship abounds on Freud, including sloppy controversies, as we have seen. However, Freud gets credit at times for his groundbreaking attempts at

---

41   Frederick Crews, "Footnote to Freud," *The New York Review of Books*, December 16, 1993, and "The Unknown Freud. An Exchange," February 3, 1994.

42   Richard Bernstein in response to Louis Menard, "The Culture Wars: An Exchange," *The New York Review of Books,* November 3, 1994.

bringing mental activities under the domain of scientific procedures, while at other times, like in Menand's case, that credit seems to be thoroughly denied. Or maybe such credit is unduly based on premises that were not Freud's, like that of a supposedly therapeutic value of entertaining the victim of a mental illness (however identified as such) with a novel, myth, or some other kind of fiction.

Freud tried to address the domain of mental processes from the functional, as opposed to the organic, side, without forgetting neither the principles of the scientific method nor his concern for the body supporting those functions, their "biological base."[43]

Like most of his contemporaries, and our contemporary scientists, Freud maintained that mental activity is to be considered a function of the brain and given the accumulation of neuroscience's results since his own times, one may consider his analyses as outdated today. Robert Sapolsky recently argued, for example, that a *transition to automaticity* seem to happen so that when people get good at sports, or music, for example, it's because their mental functions are 'transferred from the cortex to the cerebellum, or other peripheral regions of the brain,' as the process of learning takes its course.[44]

Freud embraces a philosophically realistic take on perception, i.e., a fellow creature is perceived – as a set of *stimuli* – by virtue of the fact that it is already *there*. What he calls at times perceptual complexes arise seemingly on their own, regardless of any active *categorization* process – something that is much harder to ignore, but also to understand, for neuroscientists today. Sapolsky, for example, illustrates the meaning of the term category with the metaphoric image of a "bucket of explanation," apparently without speculating on its possible biological base at all.[45] Likewise, the process of self-identification (the turning point in the development of consciousness), supposedly originates from a comparison, between stimuli and memories, that must be accomplished by the *ego*. Freud's model, however, seems to require the *ego* to be already active but still not self-conscious, at first, and then active and self-conscious, but still to be called the *ego* as if, instead of modeling a function of the brain, it was to be considered a sort of entity, or myth.

Like many others, Silvio Ceccato pointed out that Freud's work was a major contribution in bringing everyday experiences like dreams, temporary memory losses, slips of the tongue, children's interests in sexuality, and more, within the

---

43   Sigmund Freud, "Why War," 203.
44   Robert Sapolsky, *Behave: The Biology of Humans at our Best and Worst* (New York: Penguin Books, 2017), 50.
45   Ibid., 5.

domain of mainstream scientific research.[46] As a therapist, however, Ceccato argued, Freud's need for a dynamic approach brought his theorizing into conflict with the traditional theory of knowledge, which offers only a metaphorical definition of the min, a mind which is conceived as an immaterial set of static entities, or ideas, somehow duplicating features of a supposedly already existing external world. To Ceccato, who draws from the *critical* philosophical line of Hume, Berkeley, and Kant, the traditionally realistic theory of knowledge hides a logical impossibility, which was already pointed out by Socrates, and to which Plato and Aristotle failed to adequately respond.[47]

At times mistaken for an Italian promoter of Wiener's Cybernetics, Ceccato rejected Wiener's notion of information (as an element of the physical world). His drastic critique of the Greek philosophical tradition, or the dominant part of it to be precise, was inspired in the late 1940s by the operational methodologies of physicists like Dingler and Bridgman. Only from the early 1950s did Ceccato became a cybernetician. As a physician, Ceccato argues in 1970, Freud had to conceive the mind as a set of functions to be ascribed to the brain as their most plausible organic counterpart. Much like contemporary neuroscientists, however, because of his assumptions, and more generally his limited involvement with the issues raised by the traditional theory of knowledge, or by philosophy strictly speaking, Freud struggled to find a satisfactory criterion of analysis of the mind, thereby ending up multiplying the fictional subjects he ascribed to such functions. To the Ego he added the Id and the Super-ego, while also ascribing multiple tasks to each, including having to manage presumed instinctual forces (like those of love, or *Eros*, and *Thanatos*, the death instinct). Devising the dynamisms he needed in order to deal with his patients came at the dear price of having to talk about a quite unstable arrangement of characters and their reciprocal relationships. Once taken this road, Ceccato concluded, Freud – not a philosopher by training – was bound to the endless multiplication of these supposedly active, but ill-defined agents, thereby falling into the *homunculus* fallacy (as the multiplicity of things, supposed to be already in the world, before anyone can see them, had to be somehow, statically or dynamically, duplicated by, or at any rate somehow within the mind). As a result, for Ceccato, we find in Freud's speculations an ever-growing plurality of alleged functions that have however lost their potential to lead to the identification of the organs which are supposed to perform them.

---

46 Silvio Ceccato, "Freud oggi: Considerazioni di indole metodologica," *Archivio di Psicologia, Neurologia e Psichiatria* 31, no. 4 (1970): 330–351.

47 Silvio Ceccato, "Il Teocono," *Methodologia* 1 (1949): 1–13. https://www.methodologia.it /testi/teocono/teocono.pdf.

An inquiry based on the names listed in the Index of contemporary primatologist and neurologist Robert Sapolsky's recent book, *Behave: The Biology of Humans at Our Best and Worst* (2017), makes one believe, at first, that neuroscience does not rely at all on the work of Sigmund Freud, as Ceccato predicted. The reader is referred at first to page 222, where Sapolsky just points out that 'Freud, Bowlby, Harlow, Meany, from their differing perspectives, all make the same fundamental and once-revolutionary point: that childhood matters.'[48] The other suggestion leads one back to the times when, supposedly, 'the Freudians and the behaviorists hooked up,' in order to explain why 'infants become attached to their mothers.'[49]

There is no need to explain why infants do that, Sapolsky claims, thereby in his view dismissing Freudians and behaviorists, because even rodents need a mother to be there for them when they are little. Otherwise, as contemporary scientific results show, they develop into pathological adults, affected by elevated glucocorticoid levels and poor cognitive skills.[50]

However, Sapolsky also says, 'well into the twentieth century, most experts didn't think so,' hence the now infamous child rearing techniques that were used 'by the wealthy in the West.' Leading experts like Luther Holt of Columbia University, for example, considered it as nothing less than vicious behavior, what Sapolsky describes as 'picking up a crying child.'[51] One is made to wonder if Freud really had anything to do with such a change of attitudes, at least by the wealthy in the West. One also finds that the main insight of Sapolsky's book is best summarized, according Sapolsky himself, by 'Freud's quote emphasized by Elie Wiesel,' the 1986 Nobel Peace Prize winner and a concentration camp survivor, which states that 'the opposite of love is not hate; it's indifference.'[52] Notice that this occurrence of Freud's name is not even included in the index of the book, presumably because Wiesel did not quote Freud when he stated his principle, even though Sapolsky does. In other words, Sapolsky acknowledges that one of Freud's main insights is guiding his own mindset and is being confirmed by current research.

Freud's first contributions to science are to be found in the areas of comparative zoology; his first publication being a painstaking and anti-Aristotelian search for the elusive testes of eel, and of neurophysiology. He put forward assumptions that are not far from the current neuron doctrine, which was

---

48   Sapolsky, *Behave*, 222.
49   Ibid., 188–189.
50   Ibid.
51   Ibid.
52   Ibid., 19.

being established by others at the time, namely Camillo Golgi and Santiago Ramon y Cajal, who were presented with the Nobel Prize for it in 1906. At the very end of his life (and while running for his own life, in 1938) we find him putting forward the following basic psychoanalytic assumptions:

(1) 'mental life is the function of an apparatus, to which we ascribe the characteristics of being extended in space and of being made up of several pieces – which we imagine, therefore, as being like a telescope or microscope or something of the sort.'[53]

(2) 'this general pattern of a mental apparatus may be supposed to apply equally to the higher animals which resemble man mentally. A superego must be presumed to be present wherever, as in the case of man, there is a long period of dependence in childhood. The assumption of a distinction between ego and id cannot be avoided.'[54]

Freud takes note that 'animal psychology has not yet taken in hand the interesting problem which is here presented.'[55] He assumed, and at least in his early scientific production he also helped demonstrate, that we are made of the same biological components of all other animals. With respect to the necessity of a model of the mind in order to make any scientific progress, we find him stating that 'we know two things concerning what we call our psyche or mental life – while everything between these two things, is unknown to us.'[56]

The two things we know about our mental *apparatus* are (1) 'its bodily organ and scene of action, the brain (or nervous system),' and (2) 'our acts of consciousness, which are immediate data and cannot be more fully explained by any (other) kind of description.'[57] Even if 'a direct relation between the two endpoints of our knowledge, says Freud, existed, it would at the most afford an exact localization of the processes of consciousness and would give no help towards understanding them.'[58]

When it comes to his methodology, Freud explains that 'we have arrived at our knowledge of this apparatus of the mind by studying the individual development of human beings,' thereby putting forward an argument that is symmetrically the opposite with respect to the one used by contemporary neuroscience, namely that the 'oldest portion of the mental apparatus remains the

---

53   Sigmund Freud, *An Outline of Psycho-Analyses,* trans. James Strachey (London: The Hogarth Press and the Institute of Psycho-Analysis, 1959), 1.
54   Ibid., 4.
55   Ibid.
56   Ibid., 1.
57   Ibid.
58   Ibid.

most important throughout life.'[59] Contemporary neuroscientists like Sapolsky do not mind using the concept of "super-ego" when characterizing our neocortex, which for them is the most important part of the brain.' Says Freud, 'to the oldest of these mental provinces or departments we give the name of id,' and he claims that 'it contains everything that is inherited, that is present at birth, that is fixed in the constitution – above all, therefore, the instincts originating in the somatic organization, which find their first mental expression there in forms unknown to us.'[60] The *id*, he claims, was 'the first subject of the investigations of Psycho-Analysis,' and he characterizes the object of study of the newly founded discipline as the oldest part of the brain – even though, as he said before, 'an exact localization of the processes of consciousness, would give no help towards understanding them.'[61]

A logical, or methodological reflection on these assumptions follows quite smoothly: the metaphor of a telescope reaffirms Freud's philosophical realism, stigmatized by Ceccato as being logically inconsistent (Sapolsky, for one, also usually brings about the metaphor of getting closer, which is of course the opposite of that ability scientists allegedly display, according to the letters exchanged by Einstein and Freud in 1932, of taking a look at things from a distance).

Even though Freud denied that an act of consciousness could be understood in terms of biology, he nonetheless ascribed different functions, however vaguely described, to different areas of the brain. The criteria for giving importance to a particular area of the brain, which is identified by Freud, and by Sapolsky, as its older or newer status – both in phylogenetic and ontogenetic terms – are different from each other, although in both cases seem to refer mainly to ontological development. Freud's pointing to an innate structure of personality (*Id*) is not easily squared with the importance his theory gives to ontological development, while Sapolsky's pointing to the ability to fully understand the social context one has to deal with (the super-ego, it is posited, would come to fruition at a much later point in one's life, with cortex coming fully online at age 25) is not easily squared with Sapolsky's own emphasis on a *transition to automaticity*, from cortex to cerebellum, which would accompany, as we have seen, the process of learning.

---

59   Ibid., 2.
60   Ibid.
61   Ibid., 1.

4 Freud as a Critical Social Theorist

Freud analyzed social arrangements and offered his proposals aimed at improving the human predicament, in terms of our awareness of how they came about – both in terms of the evolution of our species, and in terms of our daily lives (or, in other words, our ontogenetic development). By this criterion, he can be considered a critical social theorist.

Such a broad criteria as to identify a critical social theorist by the fact that he criticizes any given social arrangement, however, would force one to make room for possibly anyone who cared about putting forward a theory about social life – granted that such an effort will always start from questioning a previous theory, namely, the socially accepted one at the time. Sir Francis Galton and his *eugenic* project, for example, would also fit such a broad definition. Galton employed the statistical correlation of variables to argue, among other things, that prayers are a waste of time because believers who do pray do not live longer (on average) than non-believers, or believers who do not pray. Galton's eugenics then played a prominent part in Freud's historical context, having become, when Freud came about, a mainstream view. In what was possibly his first publication about religion, Freud offered a different kind of analysis of it. He was "struck," he says, by the resemblance between what were called "obsessive acts" in neurotics, at times also called ceremonies in ordinary language, and 'those religious observances by means of which the faithful give expression to their piety.'[62]

What Freud wanted to verify was if 'an insight into the origin of neurotic ceremonial may embolden us to draw by analogy inferences about the psychological processes of religious life.'[63] In other, more current terms, while Galton employed a quantitative methodology, Freud was pursuing a qualitative one. Both were critical of the established social arrangement and its religion, characterizing it as delusional (Galton) and, possibly, in its origins, similar to pathological behavior (Freud). Galton's methodology can be (and has been, more recently) turned around and used to make even the opposite claim (that people who pray do live longer), Freud's contributions involve instead a more direct confrontation with the problem of meaning, and of our awareness (or lack of awareness) of it.

---

62 Sigmund Freud, "Obsessive Acts and Religious Practices," in *Collected Papers of Sigmund Freud,* ed. and trans. Joan Riviere (5 Vols.) (London: Hogarth Press and the Institute of Psycho-Analysis, 1948–1950), Vol. II, 25–50.

63 Sigmund Freud, "Obsessive acts and religious practices," 25–50.

A critique of human social arrangements is not necessarily implied in any quantitative or qualitative sociological research. However, when a social theory or analysis provides support for a new dogma, it defeats its own purpose, which is instead to provide a way to replace dogmas with analysis, thereby allowing for the replacement of the old (and often embarrassing) dogma, in favor of a procedural view of the problem, and of its alternative solutions. Hence the necessity to avoid the pitfall of a critical analysis that ends up offering a new *ipse dixit*, supposedly produced by a genius. Hence the necessity to adopt instead a methodological point of view, in other words a commitment to put all of one's cards on the table without indulging in misleading metaphors and in negative definitions (like, for example, the use of the word barbarians – meaning at first *stutterers*, in Ancient Greece).

The necessity is to describe how one's conclusion is reached, and to do so in such a way that the reader is allowed to independently follow the path leading to that conclusion, thereby being able to autonomously decide if the analyses will be repeated in the future or not. This is what Papini claimed Freud did not offer. The crucial point of an assessment of Freud as a critical social theorist is the clarification of to what extent he did, or in other words, to what extent he was not a mythmaker. Weber wrote about this problem in his reflections on objectivity as far as the cultural sciences are concerned. In Freud's psychoanalysis, it may correspond to the principle of honesty, when it comes to the relationship between the therapist and the patient – and especially to the right, which only the patient has, to consider herself (or himself) healed (as Kant, as we have seen, stated).

The alleged retrieval of a previously forgotten traumatic event, thanks to the therapeutic intervention of the psychoanalyst, may entitle the latter to monetary compensation, to be sure. But only the patient can say if the psychoanalytic treatment is helping or has been successful. However, such a principle was not upheld by the institutionalized version of psychoanalysis, and Freud himself did not consistently apply it throughout his life, acting rather as a patriarch of the psychoanalytic movement. Habermas addresses this issue with his notion of *communicative rationality*, which requires participants in the process of communication to openly share their views until an agreement, or at least a mutual understanding of the nature of the reciprocal disagreement, is reached, no matter how long it takes.

We don't have to choose between Hobbes and Rousseau, or the popularized scarecrow versions of their opposite ideas of human nature: human nature does not have to be conceived as existing before and after an alleged first social contract – and, in fact, keeping an eye on its biological *base,* it can't be conceived that way. As we have seen, for Freud 'a super-ego must be presumed to be present wherever, as in the case of man, there is a long period of dependence in childhood,' and 'the assumption of a distinction between ego and id cannot be avoided,' not even in animals, let alone human beings.[64] As Erving Goffman puts it, 'if a particular person or group or society seems to have a character all of its own, it is because its standard set of human-nature elements is pitched and combined in a particular way.'[65]

In 1952, in one of his first publications, Goffman offers an analysis of how a con mob takes care of their victim even after taking his or her money: the final part of any confidence game scheme, Goffman argues, is that in which 'the mark is given instruction in the philosophy of taking a loss.'[66] This way, the very basic social story of blaming victims for their own alleged failures repeats itself, over and over again, as the process of cooling the mark out is meant to make sure that the fraud will neither be exposed for what it was, nor punished.

Unlike a con mob, Goffman points out that an institution must pacify its marks. For example, this is what the functional specialization of complaints departments (nowadays called "customer service") is about, within all sorts of organizations and bureaucracies. Borrowing an example from Max Weber, Goffman argues that in traditional societies this process came to fruition more smoothly than it does in modern society. In Medieval China, for example, 'anchoretic withdrawal apparently gave to persons of quite different stations a way of retreating from the occupational struggle while managing the retreat in an orderly, face-saving fashion.'[67] In modern society, however, and this is the main point of Goffman's essay, the burden of cooling the mark out – thereby preserving the social order – seems to fall mainly on the families and friends of the victim, or as a last resort on the professional psychologist (if not on the police, one may add, but Goffman clarifies that the reason why the con mob cares so much about cooling the mark out is precisely that they do not want the police to get involved, unless of course the police has been already bought by the con mob).

Freud, says Goffman too, like Ceccato, and many others, played a major part in the process of expanding the domain of the natural sciences by suggesting that a mental (or functional) pathology may be identified before establishing any organic dysfunction. By focusing on everyday social behaviors like a slip of

---

64 Sigmund Freud, *An Outline of Psycho-Analyses*, 4.
65 Erving Goffman, "On Face-Work: An Analysis of Ritual Elements in Social Interaction." *Psychiatry: Journal for the Study of Interpersonal Processes* 18 (1955): 231.
66 Erving Goffman, "On Cooling the Mark Out. Some Aspects of Adaptation to Failure," *Psychiatry: Journal of Interpersonal Relations* 15, no. 4 (1952): 451–63.
67 Ibid.

the tongue, or *lapsus*, for example, Freud suggested they might be caused by unconscious self-censorship, due in turn to a forgotten – but not completely erased – traumatic experience.

While Freud's insight was read by Goffman (and many others, including Freud himself) as questioning and blurring the dichotomy between healthy and mentally sick people, it was taken by professionals of mental health as a sort of green light allowing them to consider any socially improper behavior as a symptom of a mental illness, thereby stigmatizing any form of disagreement, or dissent, as pathological (a process often referred to as the *medicalization* of deviance by sociologists). This interpretation of Freud's main insight is criticized by Goffman both as methodologically incorrect and as useful only for those who are given the task to cool the mark out in modern society – in other words, of giving the mark lessons in the philosophy of taking a loss, or blame the mark for his own supposedly ill mental processing – instead of helping the mark to properly deal with the fraudulent behavior he is complaining about.

Weber's reflections on the role played by charismatic individuals in the history of Western and non-Western civilizations, such as Luther or Confucius, for example, were not of great interest to Goffman. Rather than memorable turning points in world history, he brought into focus everyday interactions, within the context of "Anglo-Saxon, middle-class" social environments.[68] However, in the Presidential Address to the American Sociological Association, which he wrote at the end of his relatively short life, in 1982, he mocks the American hippies (by this point in time already well integrated into bourgeois society), by comparing them unfavorably to Fox's disciples, who were in Goffman's view the 'real great terrorists of contact forms.'[69] He goes on to praise 'that sturdy band of plain speakers,' who should 'always stand before us as an example of the wonderfully disruptive power of systematic impoliteness, reminding us once again of the vulnerability of the interaction order.'[70]

Any ambiguity ascribable to Goffman's position with respect to the alternative between supporting or upsetting the established social order vanishes if only one takes into due consideration his concluding remarks, in that last speech to the American Sociological Association, which he prepared for delivery while dying of cancer. What is needed from sociologists, he told his colleagues, is an analysis that does not cave to the pressure of "well-placed persons," among which he listed priests and psychologists, together with white,

---

68   Erving Goffman, *The Presentation of Self in Everyday Life* (New York: Anchor Books, 1959).
69   Erving Goffman, "The Interaction Order. American Sociological Association, 1982 Presidential Address." *American Sociological Review* 48, no. 1 (1983): 1–17.
70   Ibid.

males, and so on, as long as they are 'in a position to give official imprint to versions of reality.'[71]

Goffman's position can be easily compared to Max Horkheimer's position, even besides Horkheimer's characterization of modern society as a "racket society," to which certainly both Veblen and Marx would certainly have also subscribed, and which can be found even in Freud himself, for example, by looking at how he characterized not only Hitler and Mussolini, as we have seen, but also Woodrow Wilson. Horkheimer stated that 'the critical attitude of which we are speaking is wholly distrustful of the rules of conduct with which society as presently constituted provides each of its members.'[72] A statement that can be easily categorized as pathological, even as a paradigmatic case of mental illness, by psychiatrists in general, even today, including the mainstream Freudian psychiatrists criticized by Goffman.

Both Goffman and Horkheimer call for a critical review of the way the society in which they lived defined itself, taking for granted that in all societies such collective self-definitions are largely the result of unaware self-interest of the powerful. In both cases, social inquiry must begin with a rejection of the most basic assumptions concerning the supposedly shared social reality.

Metaphorically speaking, the need for a new standpoint arises when one is down, or, in proper terms, it arises when a process does not unfold as expected, and not in a good way – that is for Goffman the situation of the mark, or that of the "stigmatized" person, which more specifically interested him.[73] The need for a critical review of the previously made assumptions comes to the fore and sparks a more or less exhaustive inquiry. As a result, new expectations may replace the ones that were not fulfilled in the first place, but the likelihood of success, in overcoming such a critical juncture, will depend both on the awareness resulting from this critical work and on the strength of the reaction coming from the supporters of the *status quo ante*. Freud's work can be considered here, following Goffman, as an attempt to forge an alternative, or a way out, from the traditional philosophy of taking a loss, which could be made available to the mark, but has been turned by mainstream Freudians into a modern, or psychiatric, philosophy of taking a loss.

The opening sentence of Rousseau's *Social Contract*, 'man is born free and everywhere he is in chains,' is another example of an attempt to put forward a

---

71　Ibid.
72　Max Horkheimer, "Traditional and Critical Theory," in *Critical Theory: Selected Essays* (New York: Continuum, 1972), 243.
73　Erving Goffman, *Stigma: Notes on the Management of Spoiled Identity* (New York: Touchstone, 1963).

critical social theory, such as Rousseau's may be considered, insofar as he criticized Hobbes' notion of mankind's state of nature. From such a critical standpoint as Rousseau's, Freud's psychoanalysis cannot be easily categorized as a critical social theory, given Freud's own refusal to take a stand in favor of a radically different kind of society, which Freud, talking about the Bolsheviks, calls an "illusion."[74] Freud's concept of human nature is closer to the Hobbesian version even though, while *Eros* is introduced as the main force sustaining life, and given its name by Freud, *Thanatos* remains in his writings unnamed. It is introduced as a force, which somehow may correspond both to the irreversibility of thermodynamic processes, and to the second term of the polarity of attraction and repulsion (two very different kinds of phenomena, hence rightful accusations of *irrationalism* to Freud).

Freud is explicit in his offering of no consolation, while pointing out shortcomings of social arrangements. Room must be made for *Eros,* he claims, in terms of our awareness of it, and of its importance for the survival of civilization. Freud's attention to everyday phenomena related to memory and language, dreams, or the way children learn about their bodies, at the time neglected by Victorian science, also put him on the side of critical social theorists, at least to some extent, as Wilhelm Reich's enthusiasm for his main ideas, for example, also shows.

Before Rousseau's critique of the notion of progress, which was on the rise at the times of his writing, Michel de Montaigne tried to demonstrate 'how we must be careful about clinging to common opinions,' and how we must judge them 'not by popular report, but with the eye of reason.'[75] A call which Freud, like Kant and so many others thinkers, including of course Habermas, subscribed to, and substantiate with their social theories.

Montaigne begins his essay on cannibalism by telling the story of king Pyrrhus, moving across the sea into Italy, and 'scouting out the organization of the army which the Romans sent out against him.'[76] King Pyrrhus, according to Montaigne, 'observed, "I do not know what sort of barbarians these are" (for the Greeks used to call all foreign nations by that name) "but the formation of this army I am looking at has nothing barbarous about it."'[77] According to Terence Cave, Montaigne presented cannibalism as part of a 'complex and balanced set of customs and beliefs,' which he described as 'attached to a powerfully positive morality of valor and pride,' and which he contrasted with the 'modes

---

74 Einstein and Freud, "Why War".
75 Terence Cave, *How to Read Montaigne* (London: Granta Books, 2007), 81–82.
76 Ibid.
77 Ibid.

of behavior in the France of the wars of religion,' such as torture, and barbarous methods of execution, which he found 'even less attractive.'[78] Montaigne also claimed that Chrysippus and Zeno, leaders of the Stoic school, thought that there was "nothing wrong" with cannibalism, and claimed that "our ancestors," the Gauls, when besieged by Julius Caesar in the town of Alesia, 'resolved to stave off the hunger of this siege with the bodies of old men, women, and other people useless in combat.'[79] His critical review of common opinions was not framed, as one may think, as a comparison between a (supposedly) Native American way of life and his own, the French one (at the time).

Using what Montaigne metaphorically calls the eye of reason to scrutinize common opinions may lead one to embarrassment, and to even worse, even deadly ones at times, outcomes. The embarrassment arises, as a Freudian analysis based on a monolithic notion of the super-ego will fail to appreciate, but as the Freudian duality of the basic drives of the id will suggest, from a contradiction regarding those values on which the rules are based that regulate our social interactions, including putting someone to death, given that in any society even a homicide may end up falling under the domain of someone's legitimate behavior in the appropriate context. Our most solemn rituals are planned to avoid embarrassment, as Freud's analysis often suggested, which makes them paradoxically even more vulnerable than everyday rituals to intentional, as well as involuntary, disruptions, as Goffman (following Freud's leads) pointed out.

In the early paragraphs of the speech given by Frederick Douglass in 1852, on the 4th of July celebrations, we find a reference to his own embarrassment, a reference that must have caused some degree of embarrassment in his audience, too. Douglass explains having gone from being a Black slave to being invited to celebrate White America's freedom, and his answer is to put *that* on the table. He exposes his own situation and demands *consistency* – if they want to consider him an American, they must abolish slavery. He does not cave, to use Goffman's phrase, to *the philosophy of taking a loss*. His own embarrassment is a symptom of a social pathology that he is exposing, not of a pathology that can be pinned on him.

Embarrassing contradictions constantly arise in the social world, and there are very few ways to deal with them. Native Americans who do not celebrate Thanksgiving exemplify the *critical thinking* that arises every year on Columbus Day, relative to the statues dedicated to the man respectfully called

---

78 Ibid.
79 Ibid.

"the Admiral" even by Bartolomeo De Las Casas, one who did not locate himself as an outsider with respect to Christianity and was not located as an outsider, like Douglass was, with respect to the "white space."[80] De Las Casas exposed the genocide of the native inhabitants of the Americas, by the Spanish Empire, as well as the fact that it was perpetrated in the name of the highest ideals of the time, being considered instrumental in bringing the Holy Land under the Papacy. De Las Casas, like Douglass, did not cave to social pressure and kept up his loud opposition fighting against that genocide throughout his life.

5 Conclusion

A social issue arises when supposedly accepted values and norms fall short of delivering advantages, in their own experience, to the people who are supposed to benefit from supporting them. Hence their demands of a thorough review, based on evidence formerly denied or neglected by the mainstream sense of reality. Implicit in this breakaway effort is both a rejection of old ideas and a search for new ones, which must be based on positive criteria in order to generate a different set of assumptions and expectations. This is what a charismatic leader does according to Max Weber. In Rousseau's case, a new paradigm was ascribed to human nature as it originally was, albeit its discovery was claimed as something new and accredited to the awakening of a genius, at least by Rousseau and his followers. Freud's intellectual and mundane journey can be considered a good example of this very basic social story. Likewise, De Las Casas and Douglass, Montaigne, and, to some extent at least, even sociologists like Goffman and Habermas have provided intellectual and political leadership in their own lifetime, and beyond.

According to Goffman's biographer, Gary Jaworski, 'genius always has a social location, but it must clear a path for creativity'; in other words, 'as Rousseau notes somewhere, the prime mark of genius is refusal to imitate.'[81] Jaworski agrees with Winkin, another of Goffman's biographers, who writes that 'Goffman conducted his dissertation research on a tiny island in the Shetlands in order to escape from the influence of his teachers and give full play to his own natural talent.'[82] That early geographic escape, says Jaworski, 'symbolizes

---

80   Elijah Anderson, *Black in White Space: The Enduring Impact of Color in Everyday Life* (Chicago, University of Chicago Press, 2022).
81   Gary Jaworski, "Erving Goffman: The Reluctant Apprentice," *Symbolic Interaction* 23, no. 3 (2000), 305.
82   Ibid.

his lifelong efforts to escape the influence of his past.'[83] To his former professor and life-long friend Everett Hughes, in a long letter, Goffman wrote that he looked only forward. And he did so to justify himself, Jaworski explains, since it was from Hughes, his father figure, that he publicly concealed his indebtedness, to make room for his own creative genius. Based on this claim, that Goffman publicly concealed his indebtedness to Hughes, Jaworski defined him as *The Reluctant Apprentice*.[84] Goffman was, Jaworski argues (clearly evoking a standard Freudian concept), neither parricide nor partner, but a radical innovator, albeit full of respect for his own roots. Jaworski's conclusion is that if we can appreciate this fertile tension in Goffman's work, the tension between originality and tradition, then we will be able both to understand and to build on his legacy. However, given the allegations he makes, the kind of respect for his own roots that Jaworski grants to Goffman is quite limited. Apparently, he should be forgiven of his failure to quote his master – a sin often called plagiarism – because of his need to make room for his own creative genius. To elevate someone to such heights, however, does run the risk of preparing the ground for a sound rejection, and a brutal downfall, of the previously worshiped personality. To be sure, it is unconvincing to say that Goffman had to escape from the influence of his teachers. He might have wanted to do his required fieldwork on Shetland Isle for a host of other reasons, including being close to the newly created Department of Anthropology at the University of Edinburgh, whereas he later reported he *almost met* Radcliffe-Brown. More importantly, it is also unconvincing to say that he did not properly acknowledge his intellectual debt to Hughes. Allegedly, he did so by quoting, in his first book, Hughes, but only just like he quoted any of his other sources. As anyone can check, however, in his first book Goffman gives Hughes unique consideration by quoting his work a dozen times, and referring to him like a pupil does to a master. By analyzing their private correspondence, Jaworski does show in great detail how the relationship played out, but to claim that the master-apprentice relationship was hidden in Goffman's text goes beyond that. Goffman even quotes an unpublished manuscript by Hughes, which is quite the opposite of *concealing his indebtedness* to him.

Do we really need another genius? Maybe, or maybe not. Papini's spoof has been taken for real both by "Freudolatrists" and by Freud-bashers. It is very easy to understand why, among the latter camp, someone like Crews, for example, did not find it hard to fall for it. Freud was not a scientist at all,

---

83   Ibid.
84   Ibid.

according to Crews' information, and as Papini's interview also shows he very well knew it. But how is it that a psychoanalyst like Eissler decided not to press the issue, and accept Papini's prank as the best evidence one can find concerning Freud's *id*? This is the crucial point. Once Freud – or Einstein, or Goffman, or others – is considered a genius, it seems like he or she must be kept in that categorization, whatever happens afterwards. If his ideas turn out to be not so convincing to the mainstream, the critical or uncritical *followers* (including those not so eager to claim that they are uncritical followers, like Sapolsky) will continue to worship his name and his words, while giving other meanings to them.

Bibliography

Anderson, Elijah. *Black in White Space: The Enduring Impact of Color in Everyday Life*. Chicago: The University of Chicago Press, 2022.

Bernstein, Richard in response to Louis Menard. "The Culture Wars: An Exchange." *The New York Review of Books*. November 3, 1994. https://www.nybooks.com/articles/1994/11/03/the-culture-wars-an-exchange/.

Cave, Terence. *How to Read Montaigne*. London: Granta Books, 2007.

Ceccato, Silvio. "Freud oggi: Considerazioni di indole metodologica." *Archivio di Psicologia, Neurologia e Psichiatria* 31, no. 4 (1970): 330–351.

Ceccato, Silvio. "Il Teocono." *Methodologia* 1 (1949): 1–13. https://www.methodologia.it/testi/teocono/teocono.pdf.

Crews, Frederick. "Footnote to Freud," *The New York Review of Books*, December 16, 1993. https://www.nybooks.com/articles/1993/12/16/footnote-to-freud/.

Crews, Frederick. "The Unknown Freud." *The New York Review of Books*, November 18, 1993. https://www.nybooks.com/articles/1993/11/18/the-unknown-freud/.

Eissler, K. R. "Creativity and Adolescence—The Effect of Trauma in Freud's Adolescence." *Psychoanalytic Study of the Child* 33 (1978): 461–517.

Foucault, Michel. "What is Enlightenment?" In *The Foucault Reader*, edited by P. Rabinow, 32–50. Pantheon Books, 1984. https://foucault.info/documents/foucault.whatIsEnlightenment.en/.

Freud, Sigmund and Albert Einstein. "Why War?" In *The Standard Edition of the Complete Psychological Works of Sigmund Freud*, edited by James Strachey, London, Hogarth Press, 1964.

Freud, Sigmund. "Letter from Sigmund Freud to Ernest Jones, June 16, 1934." In *The Complete Correspondence of Sigmund Freud and Ernest Jones 1908–1939*, edited by R. Andrew Paskauskas. Cambridge, MA: Harvard University Press, 1993.

Freud, Sigmund. "Obsessive Acts and Religious Practices." In *Collected Papers of Sigmund Freud*, edited and translated by Joan Riviere (5 vols). London: The Hogarth Press and the Institute of Psycho-Analysis, 1948–1950.

Freud, Sigmund. *Civilization and Its Discontents*. Translated by James Strachey. New York: W.W. Norton and Company, 2005.

Freud, Sigmund. "An Outline of Psycho-Analyses." Translated by James Strachey, *International Journal of Psycho-Analyses* 21, no. 1 (1940): 27–82.

Freud, Sigmund. *"An Outline of Psycho-Analyses."* Translated by James Strachey. London: The Hogarth Press and the Institute of Psycho-Analysis, 1959.

Granata, Giorgio, Israele Zoller, and Emiliio Servadio. "Varie." *Rivista Italiana di Psicoanalisi* 2 (1933): 49–57.

Goffman, Erving. "On Cooling the Mark Out. Some Aspects of Adaptation to Failure." *Psychiatry: Journal of Interpersonal Relations* 15, no. 4 (1952): 451–63.

Goffman, Erving. "On Face-Work: An Analysis of Ritual Elements in Social Interaction." *Psychiatry: Journal for the Study of Interpersonal Processes* 18 (1955): 213–231.

Goffman, Erving. *The Presentation of Self in Everyday Life*. New York: Anchor Books, 1959.

Goffman, Erving. "The Interaction Order. American Sociological Association, 1982 Presidential Address." *American Sociological Review* 48, no. 1 (1983): 1–17.

Goffman, Erving. *Stigma: Notes on the Management of Spoiled Identity*. New York: Touchstone, 1963.

Horkheimer, Max. "Traditional and Critical Theory." In *Critical Theory: Selected Essays*. Translated by Matthew I. O'Connell. New York: The Continuum Publishing Company, 1972.

Kuhn, Thomas. *The Structure of Scientific Revolutions*. Chicago: University of Chicago Press, 1962.

Jaworski, Gary. "Erving Goffman: The Reluctant Apprentice." *Symbolic Interaction* 23, no. 3 (2000): 299–308.

Menand, Louis. "Introduction." In *Civilization and Its Discontents*, by Sigmund Freud. New York: W.W. Norton & Company, 2005.

Papini, Giovanni. "A Visit to Freud (8 May 1934)." In *Freud as we Knew Him*, edited by Hendrik M. Ruitenbeek. Detroit: Wayne State University Press, 1973.

Ruitenbeek, Hendrik M., ed. *Freud as we Knew Him*. Detroit: Wayne State University Press, 1973.

Sapolsky, Robert. *Behave: The Biology of Humans at our Best and Worst*. New York: Penguin Books, 2017.

Schimek, J., James Hopkins, Herbert S. Peyser, David D. Olds, Marian Tolpin, et al. "The Unknown Freud: An Exchange." *The New York Review of Books,* February 3, 1994. https://www.nybooks.com/articles/1994/02/03/the-unknown-freud-an-exchange/.

Weber, Max. "Science as a Vocation." In *From Max Weber: Essays in Sociology*, edited and translated by H.H. Gerth and C. Wright Mills. New York: Oxford University Press, 1946.

Zapperi, Roberto. *Freud e Mussolini.* Milano: Franco Angeli, 2013.

CHAPTER 19

Psychodynamics and the Public Spheres: Class, Identity, and the Political

Lauren Langman

1   Introduction

With the rise of bourgeois modernity, the hitherto peripheral masses of rural peasants and artisans were incorporated into the political sphere by the rising bourgeoisie, initially as allies in their struggles against the aristocracies. But with industrial capitalism, and the peasantry-turned-urban proletariat, it was soon evident that class interests conflicted; the working classes might become agents of resistance, e.g., socialists. Nevertheless, through a variety of strategies, including economic benefits and entitlements, and/or nationalism and consumerism, resistance eroded. A long tradition of the Marxist scholarship has noted how ideologies were shaped by the ruling class. As Gramsci argued, hegemonic discourses normalized domination as normal, natural, and "beneficial to all," and thus produced "willing assent" to domination by shaping identities, values, and insinuating "false needs." Citizenship as a national identity erased class consciousness, while the privatized hedonism of consumerism fostered a withdrawal from social concerns to enhance personal selfhood via possession, often in competition with others. The primary consequence of citizenship and consumerism, and perhaps religion as well, reproduced class relations. One of the primary sites for this transformation has been the public sphere. That said, at moments of legitimation crises of today, the pluralization of virtual public spheres has become a major factor in fostering class conflicts, often contested in cultural terrains. This has been clear in the proliferation of various alt-right, authoritarian populisms, and/or religious ethno-nationalisms, which have been critical – indeed oppositional – to both mainstream political elites as well as subaltern classes below, especially racial, ethnic, religious, or gendered minorities.

Craig Calhoun offers us some preliminary definitions of civil society, the realm of sociability that emerged apart from the family and/or the state.[1] The

---

1   Craig Calhoun, "Civil Society and the Public Sphere," *Public Culture* 5, no. 2 (Winter 1993): 267–280.

bourgeois public sphere became spaces wherein intellectual, philosophical, and political discussions led to the rise of "public opinion" as a political force advancing the interests of the bourgeoisie.[2]

> The closely related concepts of civil society and public sphere developed in the early modern era to refer to capacities for social self-organization and influence over the state. Civil society usually refers to the institutions and relationships that organize social life at a level between the state and the family. Public sphere is one of several linked terms (including 'public space,' simply 'public,' and the German *Öffentlichkeit*, or publicness) that denote an institutional setting distinguished by openness of communication and a focus on the public good rather than simply compromises among private good.[3]

2 Civil Society: Sociability Apart from Family or State

With the rise of a market society and expanded trade came a growing merchant class with increasing economic power that soon overtook the feudal economies based on land ownership and agricultural commodities along with exceedingly small numbers of produced products. The trade-based money economy, dependent on rational calculation, as clearly seen in accounting/double entry bookkeeping and the emergence of the "joint share" organization, was the forerunner of the corporation. At this time, the Gutenberg brothers created moveable type, which eventually led to the spread of print capitalism that disseminated "common languages," enabling nations as "imagined communities."[4]

At the same time, the Italian merchant classes sought to establish a distinct identity apart from the bloodlines of nobility, and clearly differentiated from the peasant farmers. The discovery of the Greek or Roman texts in philosophy, literature, poetry, and science, prompted the Renaissance, the rebirth of "lost" knowledge that became the elements of a new identity, resurrecting

---

2   Jürgen Habermas, *The Structural Transformation of the Bourgeois Public Sphere: An Inquiry into a Category of Bourgeois Society*, trans. Thomas Burger (Cambridge, MA: The MIT Press, 1991).
3   Calhoun, Craig, "Civil Society/Public Sphere: History of a Concept," in *International Encyclopedia of the Social and Behavioral Science* (Amsterdam: Elsevier, 2001), 1897.
4   Benedict Anderson, *Imagined Communities: Reflections on the Origin and Spread of Nationalism* (London: Verso Books, 2016).

elements of Greco-Roman culture. This was seen in the rise of humanism. While embraced by some clerics, humanism nevertheless challenged the dominant understandings of the Church/State elite. Moreover, within the writings of Plato and Aristotle were the discussions of Athenian democracy and the Roman Republic, which kindled alternative ideas of legitimate governance. Such alternative governance would have to await the growing numbers and powers of the bourgeois. With growing urbanization, and larger numbers of people interacted via commerce and leisure outside of kinship networks. There were increasingly such public spaces where people mixed with each other, not just theaters but also marketplaces, coffee houses, streets, and squares. Urban life was basic to the Renaissance.[5]

Eventually, a realm of sociability emerged, civil society, which was a social location that was quite separate from the "natural" ties of family and state. This new sociability, often involving strangers that might become friends, was tied to shared cultural interests, music, theater, as suggested by Montesquieu. Such ties also developed at work and commerce through networks and organizations larger than family enterprises. For Hegel, this is where the needs of all are met and where I make my particular contribution in a pro-market economic vision that accepts a natural division of labor.[6] Civil society created the conditions and spaces for the public sphere that in turn created the rise of "public opinion," which became a major force within governance.

3 The Rise of Public Sphere

Following the Renaissance, and the humanism of Erasmus and Pico Della Mirandolo, came growing intellectual/philosophical critiques of feudal/clerical domination as several secular intellectual perspectives began questioning – if not challenging – aristocratic rule based on land ownership, which was legitimated by the Church. Desire grew amidst the educated bourgeoisie for philosophical tracts critical of dynastic rule, which offered alternative visions of society, such as Thomas More's *Utopia,* written in 1516. For Habermas, the rise of mercantile capitalism and urbanization led to civil society, with the development of postal systems, printed newspapers, pamphlets, letters, etc.

---

5 Craig Calhoun, "Civil Society and the Public Sphere," in *The Oxford Handbook of Civil Society. Oxford Handbooks in Politics & International Relations*, ed. Michael Edwards (Oxford: Oxford University Press, 2011): 311–323.

6 Georg W.F. Hegel, *Elements of the Philosophy of Right* (Cambridge: Cambridge University Press, 1991), 198.

The early 18th century gave rise to the public spheres, theoretically open to all, where people might gather to discuss current events, debate political perspectives, and perhaps most importantly, within what he would later call "ideal speech situations," people might engage in "undistorted communication," where rational debates over ethics and morality, including visions of the social/political, might achieve consensus. Salons, pubs, and opera lobbies became the meeting places for what Sennett would call "public" man.[7] In such contexts, the growing bourgeoisie, informed by social critics and philosophers, might freely and rationally discuss, and debate these newer ideas.

Rousseau:	'Man is born free, but he is everywhere in chains'; through the general will (*volonté générale*) common laws would promote the general good.
Hobbes:	'War of all against all' anticipating social Darwinism and the nature of capitalist markets.
Locke:	"Popular sovereignty" by equal peoples; ownership of property necessary for freedom.
Montesquieu:	Separation of legislative, executive, and judicial powers to promote liberty.
Smith-Ricardo:	Free the market from aristocracy; invisible hand generally ensures prosperity for all.
Kant:	Enlightenment as freedom from self-imposed ignorance; living in peace not war.
Hegel:	Civil society, telos of history towards Absolute knowledge; "right" as freedom for self-actualization.
Mill:	Individuals need freedom to realize themselves.

Although in theory the public spheres were open to all, in practice these were primarily gatherings of an educated bourgeoisie. The free, open, and rational communication within the public spheres gave rise to public opinion, which became a political force that would secure support from other sectors of society and eventually, together, challenge dynastic rule, i.e., 1776 or 1789. While thwarted in 1848, eventually electoral democracies and rational legal governance, political parties would become the dominant political features of modern and of late modernizing societies.[8]

---

7   Richard Sennett, *The Fall of Public Man* (New York: W.W. Norton & Co., 2017).
8   Today, even many dictatorships use highly rigged elections and legislative bodies to appear legitimate, i.e., Putin's overwhelming support in the recent Russian 2024 election.

But the bourgeois public sphere itself eroded; its legitimating values became the new hegemonic ideologies, which were universalized. In the face of the commodification of information, new communication technologies, especially film, radio, photographs, and eventually television, and in the last two decades the internet, have enabled the proliferation of the "culture industries," which provides commodified entertainment as deception and propaganda disseminating capitalist ideology. Mass culture rents eyeballs to advertisers and public relations firms in order to influence voters and encourage consumption. A long tradition of media critics and scholars have shown that mainstream sources of news, striving to be "objective," have been far from it. For much of the history of mass communication, most newspapers, radio stations, and television stations have been private corporations. As such, to entice listeners and readers, and to gain interviews with "important people," as well as to secure advertising revenues, mass media served whitewashed pablum, typically devoid of either in-depth analysis or any genuinely critical perspectives.

Bourgeois logic and rationality, as well as the instrumental reason valorized by the media, have subverted the capacity for the working classes to become conscious of themselves as historical agents capable of resistance.[9] Eventually, mass mediated "one-dimensional thought" intertwined with "repressive desublimation" to manipulate public opinion in general. It transforms citizens into audiences seeking escapism, and consumers who value "having over being" in accordance with images of the "goods life."[10] Yet, in the process, subtle forms of domination fostered alienated inauthentic selfhood while privatized hedonism withdraws cathexis from society. Society becomes transformed into audiences and fandoms. What Karl Marx had seen as the alienation of the proletariat (estrangement of self, dehumanization, fragmentation of the social) had become the general condition of late capitalist society.[11]

4   The colonization of Identity

There have been endless debates over human nature, i.e., are we products of nature or nurture; are we instinctively aggressive or communitarian; are we inherently selfish or charitable? The Frankfurt School's Critical Theory has

---

9   Georg Lukács, *History and Class Consciousness: Studies in Marxist Dialectic* (Cambridge, MA: The MIT Press, 1972).
10 Herbert Marcuse, *One-Dimensional Man* (Boston: Beacon Press, 1965).
11 Karl Marx, *The Economic and Philosophical Manuscripts of 1844 and the Communist Manifesto* (New York: Prometheus Books, 1988).

generally suggested that while there are certain human universals, such as language, communication, tendencies for attachments, as well as hostility, agency, for the most part, character, in the psychoanalytic sense, the totality of what is conscious and unconscious, the nature of desire and repression, and the range of emotional experiences, *is largely shaped by historical factors*. Moreover, within each historical era, *there are significant differences in social character that vary by class*. That said, while the typical social character may change over time, most iterations of character have been shaped within the contexts of systems of domination, surely ever since the times of advanced horticulture, antiquity, feudalism, early capitalism, consumer capitalism and today, neoliberal, and globalized capital. As Fromm put it, people are socialized to "want to do" or social systems require that they "must do."[12] Every society has its own demands and fosters a "social character" that adapts to those demands.

It should be further noted that while "social character" encompasses the totality of individual/collective subjectivity, a significant moment of that character is identity, what Erikson called "ego identity," the more or less conscious notions of who one is, a narrative of one's self past, present, and imagined future.[13] Our identity, a reflexive narrative of values, beliefs, and memories, tells us who we are, how we act with other people, and what are our basic values. Identity is a basic sense of self, and aspect of the ego, an enduring aspect of subjectivity and organizing principle of our "collective identity," i.e., who we are based on group membership, which gives us a sense of "we-ness" and belonging.

Identities are not simply verbal statements or self-reflexive cognitive scripts about oneself, but rather, are anchored by social character with powerful, often unconscious, desires and defenses that shape understandings, emotional reactions, and impel actions. Moreover, identities are closely intertwined with aspects of status and myriad gratifications that accrue from forms of status, as well as fears and anxieties. Otherwise said, esteem, individually or collectively, is a salient aspect of subjectivity. For Erikson, while adolescence is the crucial period in the life cycle when people form a more or less stable identity, the social context and experiences can impact a generation's identity, and differ cohorts may have different, indeed clashing identities.[14]

---

12   Erich Fromm, *Escape from Freedom* (New York: Henry Holt & Co., 1994).
13   Erik Erikson, *Identity and the Life Cycle* (New York: W.W. Norton & Co., 1994).
14   For example, as has been shown, the Z generation, the largest and most progressive generation in American history, is far less racists, sexist, homophobic than their older cohorts. Few attend churches, most strongly support a woman's right to define her own body and sexuality. They prefer cohabitation to marriage. A slight majority support supports socialism over capitalism. Their national vote in 2018 and 202 supported the Democrats, saved

In so far as economic factors are mediated through character, the perceptions and interpretations of events and subsequent actions depend on the identities of actors and the extent to which those identities provide myriad gratifications and/or the reactions to events that may range from "our" team winning, to the major political issues of the day. In many societies, one's status is dependent upon economic standing and economic conditions. Contradictions and crises of legitimacy can engender a great deal of anxiety and uncertainty, what has been called "status anxiety," which often leads to various grievances and anger. Among these groups are those who statuses are based on certain essentialist notions of identity with inherent notions of hierarchy, such as racial identities, gender identities/patriarchy, ethnic identities, heteronormative, for many, religious identities, and most important for our discussion, political identities.

Clashes of identity and values evoke strong emotional responses. Thus, political clashes between groups typically reflect different political identities, group loyalties, lifestyles, and in turn they elicit reactions to change or crisis. For those embodying authoritarian identities, economic uncertainties, legitimation crises, and/or certain social change, fosters perceived challenges to their racial status, gender status, ethnic status, as well as their religious morality and values, etc. For conservatives, especially those without college education, the growth of minorities, often immigrants, and their greater acceptance into the mainstream is perceived as threatening jobs, identities, and status. Subaltern others are seen as a danger, as dragging the society down by seeking a godless, multicultural, multiracial society of parasites demanding expensive social benefits. Multiculturalism, derided as "woke," rests upon a highly mistaken perception that minorities have prospered while hard working "real Americans," i.e., White men, have been left behind.[15] To be clear, this position articulates a politics of identity in so far as various social/political actions can be seen as collective attempts to defend certain aspects of identities, lifestyles, and values that groups fear are being challenged and undermined, perhaps most distinctly articulated by the 2017 Charlottesville, Virginia, *Unite the Right* rally, wherein marchers chanted "Jews will not replace us."

The uncertainty of economic conditions and the reality of progressive social changes, which have challenged identities based on status, have fostered three

---

the Senate in 2022. The outcome of the 2024 election will largely be determined by their vote. See John Della Wolpe, *Fight: How Gen Z is Channeling Their Fear and Passion to Save America* (New York: St. Martin's Press, 2022).

15 Samir Gandesha, "Understanding Right and Left Populism," in *Critical Theory and Authoritarian Populism*, ed. Jeremiah Morelock. London: University of Westminster Press, 2018.

enormously powerful emotional reactions: (1) Nietzschian *ressentiment*; (2) the fear of death; (3) necrophilia. *Ressentiment* is a particular expression of authoritarian sadomasochistic aggression aimed at the self-serving corrupt elites, who are believed to be responsible for the rise of the nation's adversaries. Such elites need to not only be replaced, but severely punished for the "evils" they have inflicted on the "real people." At the same time, some of that aggression is directed toward the interlopers from below who might challenge esteem granting status based on race, gender, gender identity, ethnicity etc. These are typically racial minorities, immigrants, queers, and on most lists, Jews. Central to reactionary thought and action is the fear of the demise of their identities, values, lifestyles, and status. This mobilizes what may be the most powerful human motive: the fear of death, i.e., "replacement" – ontological anxiety when faced with challenges and potential demise of identities, values, lifestyles, and status. In a meritocratic society, when structural factors over which the individual has no control such as factories closing, businesses failing, etc., many people are likely to feel shame as if they are personally responsible, and gravitate towards aggression to cover that shame.[16] Finally, as Erich Fromm has argued, those who are thwarted in their self-fulfillment turn to necrophilia, the "love of death and destruction" as compensatory form of the lack of agency.[17]

A long tradition in political sociology has argued that the experience and even fear of losing status, i.e., "status anxiety," disposes the embrace of conservative if not authoritarian politics that would preserve status-based identities and/or restore a lost "golden age." These psycho-cultural factors have triggered protective ethno-racial nationalisms, policies hostile to minorities, immigrant outgroups, and opposition to globalization and the globalist elites (Jews) seen as responsible for the erosion of economic security and traditional identities, as well as the economic decline of the nation and wasteful taxation supporting the "undeserving." Reactionaries seek to restrain, if not reverse, progressive social/political changes and mobilize political action to retain their hierarchical identities based on imputed status, valorizing the strong and powerful.

Progressives typically embrace inclusive cosmopolitan values and identities and support various social justice movements that promote greater toleration, inclusion, and equality. They support the expansions of group-based rights, economic as well as cultural, to secure equality, dignity, and recognition for subordinated racial minorities, women, or LGBTQ. Progressives are also likely

---

16   Thomas J. Scheff, "Social–emotional Origins of Violence: A Theory of Multiple Killing," *Aggression and Violent Behavior* 16, no. 6 (November–December 2011): 453–460.
17   Erich Fromm, *The Anatomy of Human Destructiveness* (New York: Holt, Rinehart and Winston, 1973), 325–368.

to oppose war and the vast amounts of money that go for military spending and strongly support environmental causes.

At the same time, the general trend of most advanced societies has been toward more liberal and inclusive social values embracing racial and ethnic inclusion, feminism, gay rights, and empathy, along with generosity toward the various underprivileged, including the handicapped etc. This has been due to several reasons, not the least of which has been the changes in child-rearing patterns, in no small part due to the influence of Freudian theory on pediatric advice, beginning in the 1940s with Dr. Spock. At the same time, the postwar years provided a degree of economic security and promises of social mobility, along with a major surge of higher education. This caused many people to be more tolerant of human differences as was seen in the Civil Rights bills. Similarly, sexual repression diminished with the advance of feminism, which together brought on the sexual revolution, although the empirical research shows that it was much more a revolution of discussion and openness than actual behavior. Last but not least, a growing number of college students (the beatnik generation), who were exposed to such currents of thought, including existentialism, along with critical sociologists like Gouldner and Mills, and even some popular Marxist writings, especially Erich Fromm and Herbert Marcuse, began to decry the shallowness of consumerism, the stifling conformity of corporate America, the military industrial complex, and the degradation of the environment. These trends culminated in the various social movements of the 1960s, which initiated challenges to the identities and values of the status quo – that which fosters conservative political responses. In the last several decades, the country has become far more socially liberal, but the nature of the American political system, shaped by legacies of racism, has limited fundamental political change.

The Family: For several generations after the general movement from rural to urban society, from agricultural to industrial economies, authoritarian patterns of child-rearing tended to be reproduced for several generations beyond the economic conditions that first engendered them.[18] As Wilhelm Reich argued, that authoritarian child-rearing, especially when sexually insinuated dispositions to submit to authority both working classes whose labor produced commodities (and surplus value), as well as white-collar managerial/technical work to produce and manage innovation, regulate production, distribution within hierarchical organizations.[19] Managerial work and other

---

18   Max Horkheimer, "Authority and the Family," in *The Essential Frankfurt School Reader,* ed. Andrew Arato and Eike Gephardt (London: Bloomsbury Academic, 1982).

19   Wilhelm Reich, *The Mass Psychology of Fascism,* trans. Vincent R. Carfagno (New York: Farrar, Straus, and Giroux, 1980).

forms of symbolic labor provided more autonomy and more abstract notions of authority. Nevertheless, the labor in such organizations primarily consists of routinized forms of record-keeping and/or salesmanship at several levels, which gave rise to the "marketing character," a distinct form of social character in which selfhood itself became a commodity to be bought and sold. The lower middle class, squeezed between the more politically powerful working classes and the upper-middle-class that it could never join, was especially fearful of its problematic relationship to capital; it tended to be highly fearful and thus gravitated toward authoritarianism.

Schooling: Working within the shadow of Marx on ideology and Gramsci on hegemony, the long tradition of Marxist educational critics, from Paulo Freire and the "banking model" of education, to Bowles and Gintis on curriculum and class reproduction, or Henry Giroux on schooling as instilling ideology, has systematically examined how schools reproduce class relationships. As Anderson has argued, nations as "imagined communities" are based on mediated ties between those with recently constructed national identities, which are initially instilled by the curricula of social studies and history classes that exalt the nation and present its "glorious" history, ignoring for example, its inglorious "dark sides" of imperialism, colonialization, and/or genocide, racism, sexism, etc.[20] The socialization of citizenship, honoring flags, participating in national holidays, serves to foster an inclusive community of citizens, united by a common culture, language, and goals, obscuring class differences, and indeed, ignoring histories of resistance. Thus, most schools will advance "board approved" curricula that "normalize" if not obscure class differences, especially rendering the working classes and histories of resistance invisible.

Moreover, not only is there a clear hierarchy of educational institutions, public or private schools, or cash-starved urban schools, for minorities, but within most schools, there tends to be hierarchies of youth cultures headed by highly inclusive "popular kids," down to jocks, nerds, punks, and gang members. The social arrangements of students reproduce social hierarchies that tend to become normalized.

Churches: There is a wide range of variations in American religion: progressive Unitarians who border on atheism; Evangelical Protestants with literal interpretations of scripture and believe in biblical inerrancy, which socializes submission to structures of power that are often tied to the ruling classes. Such religions demand sexual repression, which as Reich noted, is fundamental to

---

20 Benedict Anderson, *Imagined Communities: Reflections on the Origin and Spread of Nationalism* (London: Verso Books, 2016).

authoritarian socialization, as it instills the tendencies to submit to superior authority and to dominate subordinates. Moreover, these doctrines sacralizes the domination of men and subordination of women and children as "God ordained." If necessary, they believe that sparing the rod spoils the child. Similarly, onanism (masturbation), as well as homosexuality, are considered sinful and worthy of extreme punishment if not death.

While most religions emphasize community, sharing, generosity (even to outsiders), Evangelicals have noticeably clear boundaries of inclusion and exclusion – the "worthy" and the "unworthy" – the basis of which is often race, as non-Whites are deemed dangerous heathens.

The Culture Industries: The proliferation of the "culture industries," which initially eroded the public sphere, have been reborn and have become the dominant context for the socialization of character, especially the shaping of desire. This was already evident when Edward Bernays had "high-class debutantes" publicly smoke cigarettes, i.e., "torches of freedom" – symbols of phallic power of course – during an Easter Sunday parade in 1929. Within a year, the number of cigarette smokers doubled, as did lung cancer. It is at this point that we can begin to see the intersection of psychodynamics and Gramsci's notion of hegemony, as far as the dominant cultural perspectives, crafted by literate segments of the elites, render social arrangements normal, natural, and "common sense." Thus, any critique of the dominating social arrangements is easily dismissed as abnormal, bizarre, or even pathological. For Gramsci, one of the main institutions for the securing of "spontaneous consent" was the hierarchically organized and highly authoritarian Church, which demanded obedience to authority and the subjugation of individual freedom, all secured by sexual repression, as previously noted by Reich.

Had Gramsci been able to read Freud while in prison, he would've better understood how hegemonic discourses not only become internalized as frameworks of perception and understanding, but shaped desire in such ways as to secure conformity to power arrangements, primarily through fear of punishment, and in this case, the most severe form of punishment is isolation; separation anxiety taps into a very deep fear: the fear of death, or "necrophobia."[21]

Nevertheless, with the explosion of post-World War II consumerism, there were fundamental changes in the socialization of character, in part due to the influence of Freudian theory on child-rearing advice, especially among more educated populations. Particularly, Dr. Spock encouraged more democratic socialization that emphasized empathy and self-fulfillment. Lakoff has

---

21   Ernest Becker, *The Denial of Death* (New York: Free Press, 1997).

suggested that empathic, democratic socialization disposes the youth towards progressive politics, while strict father orientation, often punitive, disposes more conservative politics.[22] At the same time, general economic growth, and subsequent economic security, at least for white men, had a considerable impact on the changing nature of character and identity.[23] This change was clear in the work of Marcuse, who initially echoed Reich, arguing that authoritarian socialization patterns foster "surplus repression."[24] In other words, authoritarianism as a repressively strict super-ego was a necessity to socialize workers in order to produce/manage surplus value. Yet, a funny thing happened on the way to the shopping malls, the existence and numbers of which exploded in the 1950s. It became necessary to relax the constraints of the super-ego to enable impulse buying. Eleven years later for Marcuse, there was a "relaxation" of sexual repression, intertwined with growing feminism and the sexual revolution.[25] But capitalism colonized sexual desire for the sake of consumption. Buying certain things, clothes, cars, home décor, or even particular appliances, etc., promised some form of erotic gratification. For men, this might mean "muscle cars," tall, erect tailfins advertising "testicular" power, while the facial expressions of women driving cars in TV adverts were indistinguishable from their orgasmic faces.

But alas, as philosophers from Plato and Aristotle onward have told us, the possession of things does not bring happiness. Mass culture was superficial, conformist, stifling, and Puritanism was a drag. Thus, by the 1950s, we begin to see several cultural critiques of consumerism and character; philosophically there was a growing interest in existentialism and the absurdity of life; the beatnik generation found drugs, sex, and jazz, as forms of cultural resistance, as well as literature and poetry. With the changes in socialization and social context came changes in social character, especially among college students – typically arts and social science types – in the 1960s.

The Colonization of Consciousness: One of the most important concepts coming from Freudian theory is the notion of repression and defense: the systematic ways that people avoid dealing with unpleasant memories, repressed desires, etc., including denial, rationalization, projection, sublimation, etc.

---

22 George Lakoff, *Moral Politics: How Liberals and Conservatives Think*, Third Edition (Chicago: University of Chicago Press, 2016).
23 Ronald Inglehart, *The Silent Revolution: Changing Values and Political Styles Among Western Publics* (Princeton: Princeton University Press, 2015).
24 Herbert Marcuse, *Eros and Civilization* (Boston: Beacon Press, 1953), 54.
25 Herbert Marcuse, *One-Dimensional Man: Studies in the Ideology of Advanced Industrial Society* (Boston: Beacon Press, 1964).

As the Frankfurt School tradition has shown, authoritarianism is not simply a characterological trait emphasizing domination, subordination, and projection of aggression towards out groups, but also a factor shaping beliefs, modes of consciousness, and understandings of the world that were ego-syntonic, as was clearly seen in the role of Nazi propaganda, e.g., *Triumph of the Will,* or *The Eternal Jew*.[26] As various reactionary, indeed fascist, agitators have argued, seemingly using all the same script, speaking to actual fears and grievances, "discontents" amplify a danger to the "people" by selecting particular scapegoats by virtue of race, ethnicity, gender, gender orientation, and often religion, who are constructed as being an impending catastrophe, which quickly evolves into a moral panic. The agitator directs anger (and encourages aggression) toward the "opponents" responsible for real grievances and discontents. Jews have been favored targets for centuries, more recently followed by communists, feminists, liberals, queers, etc. Reactionary leaders claim that they and they alone can lead the battle against such enemies that need to be ostracized, punished, and even eliminated, by whatever means necessary.[27]

We might begin to note that the authoritarian personality study showed that authoritarians were more intolerant of ambiguity, had a limited ability to understand nuance, and tended towards more simplistic, rigid, either/or, black/white, and good/evil thoughts and understandings of the world.[28] Authoritarian agitators, leaders, and orators, intuitively understand the power of emotional provocations conjoined with explanatory simplicity to explain the "causes" of grievances and discontents, and in response, provide clear, simple solutions, which are erroneous at best and dangerous at worst. One need only consider how the Nazi scapegoating of Jews culminated in the Holocaust.

One of the legacies of authoritarianism research has been the advancement in our understanding of social psychology, which clearly speaks to the impact that authoritarianism has had on consciousness. Studies have shown that those high in authoritarian tendencies are more fearful, as they perceive more danger than do low authoritarians. Several neuropsychologists, many using MRIs, have pointed out the vital role of the prefrontal cortex and limbic

---

26   One might recall Plato's critique of democracy and that how a powerful, charismatic orator, perhaps a tyrant, might arouse powerful emotions to sway a crowd. Shakespeare seemed to note this when Mark Anthony came "not to praise but to bury Caesar".

27   Leo Löwenthal and Norbert Guterman, *Prophets of Deceit: A Study of the Techniques of the American Agitator* (New York: Verso, 2021). One of the January 6th insurrectionists, who was later sentenced to prison, was wearing a "Camp Auschwitz" shirt at the time.

28   Theodor W. Adorno et al, *The Authoritarian Personality* (New York: Verso, 2019).

system, showing significant differentiation between progressives and authoritarians regarding fear and disgust:

> Unconsciously generated emotions selectively favor emotionally congruent decisions, and that cognitive rationalizations are recruited to support them in order to achieve overall consistency. The neuroanatomical facts that descending fibers from the cortex to the amygdale are few and that ascending fibers are many, further supports the dominance of emotions over cognitions.[29]

As we well know, authoritarians mobilize anger and grievance. They encourage fear of the Other and are more likely to feel intense, visceral disgust, especially toward queers, transgender individuals, gender-fluid individuals, and all other variations that challenge essentialist notions of gender identity.

Dogmatism: One of the earliest research studies inspired by authoritarian personality research was the study of dogmatism, which demonstrated a cognitive pattern of open versus close-mindedness. Rokeach defines dogmatism as:

> (a) a relatively closed cognitive organization of beliefs and disbeliefs about reality, (b) organized around a central set of beliefs about absolute authority which, in turn, (c) provides a framework for patterns of intolerance and qualified tolerance toward others. A cognitive organization is considered to be closed to the extent that there is (a) isolation of parts within the belief system and between belief and disbelief systems, (b) a discrepancy in the degree of differentiation between belief and disbelief systems, (c) dedifferentiation within the disbelief system, (d) a high degree of interdependence between central and peripheral beliefs, (e) a low degree of interdependence among peripheral beliefs, and (f) a narrowing of the time perspective.[30]

Rokeach has carefully noted that dogmatism can be characteristic of either the left or the right. It is quite clear today that most of the members of the Alt-Right, authoritarian populists, and religious ethno-nationalist groups tend to be highly dogmatic, and that dogmatism tends to be associated with other cognitive/emotional tendencies.

---

29 Warren W. Tryon, *Cognitive Neuroscience and Psychotherapy: Network Principles for a Unified Theory* (Amsterdam: Academic Press, 2014).
30 Milton Rokeach, "The Nature and Meaning of Dogmatism," *Psychological Review* 61, no. 3 (1954): 194–204. https://www.all-about-psychology.com/dogmatism.html.

Motivated reasoning/confirmation bias: One of the main legacies of psychoanalytic theory is that it has shown us how emotional factors shape how we perceive (or indeed misperceive) events, understandings, and ourselves. People are motivated by unconscious wishes and feelings; therapy attempts to make our unconscious feelings/desires conscious, revealed through transference: "where Id is, ego shall be." In so many words, therapy would allow one to overcome defenses and enable people to make decisions more rationally, especially about themselves, their identities, and their values, thus escaping their self-destructive behaviors, understandings, and relationships.

People tend to accept congruent information that confirms pre-existing biases that sustain self-esteem (and collective identities) and select information that would seem to convince others of the validity of their beliefs. Contrary information quite often leads to a doubling down on one's biases and perceptions. The Marxist critique of ideology, further developed by Gramsci's notion of hegemony, has argued that the dominant culture shapes people's political-economic decisions, which are based on their identities and values and sustain power relationships that ultimately do harm to themselves. People who voted for pro-life politicians reaped the results: factories closed, tax cuts favored the wealthy, and thus educational performances declined, infrastructures deteriorated, and jobs are lost.

Cognitive dissonance: For the American Psychological Association, cognitive dissonance is "an unpleasant psychological state resulting from inconsistency between two or more elements in a cognitive system," and that inconsistency must be resolved by contrary evidence.[31] This was abundantly clear when the Church rejected Galileo and Copernicus, as a scientifically based worldview was inconsistent with Church theology at that time. More recently, a sizable number of Americans, primarily the MAGA Republicans, strongly believe that Trump won the 2020 election, without any compelling evidence whatsoever. Yet, they accept theories that somewhere between Hugo Chavez and the People's Republic of China, voting machines were hacked via internet connected thermostats in polling places. The Q-Anon followers strongly believe that about 100,000 or so children are kidnapped every year, tortured, raped, and murdered to obtain their life preserving Adenochrome. This is about three times the figure that the Federal Bureau of Investigation (FBI) reports, and most of those "missing" children tend to either be runaways or caught in the middle of custody conflicts.

---

31   American Psychological Association, "Cognitive Dissonance," https://dictionary.apa.org/cognitive-dissonance.

Linguistic Codes: Little cited today, the linguistic research of Basil Bernstein compared the linguistic patterns of the less educated using "restricted codes" with limited descriptive ranges, and limited vocabularies that tend to be more typical informal contacts within a relatively narrow range of group membership and limited diversities of identity emphasizing a shared, if limited linguistic universe based on collective identities and group membership, as opposed to more complex elaborations, with the assumption that the other person shares the same, limited linguistic/cognitive universe, with little elaboration needed.[32] Elaborated codes, with a wider range of alternatives, including subordinate clauses, adjectives, nuances, tend to be more often used in more formal situations among the more educated. The primary point is that in general more educated people can deploy and understand a greater degree of verbal complexity and thus tolerate uncertainty, while those with less education, especially those with an authoritarian orientation, tend toward more simplistic, rigid either/or, black/white, good/evil understandings of the world. Such modes of thinking tend to be "one-dimensional." Bernstein has shown that among working-class families, socialization tends to focus on concrete specifics 'don't hit your little brother or I'll whoop you,' 'or help mom do the dishes.' Among the more educated families, the imperative is not only a bit more complex but provides a short explanation, e.g., 'It's not nice to hit someone because it hurts, would you like anyone to hit and hurt you,' or 'could you be a nice little boy or girl or person and help mom or perhaps dad with the dishes.' Notice the complexity of the language, the level of abstraction, nuance, and the encouragement of empathy regarding the consequences of one's actions. And if Jewish, the parent might add, 'haven't I done enough for you.'

The Dunning Kruger Effect: In an advanced technological society, a variety of jobs require a certain degree of training-based expertise, such as automotive repair, commercial law, and neurosurgery. But a fundamental problem is that people without any formal knowledge or expertise often have strong opinions about topics where they know almost nothing, otherwise said, uninformed people are too uninformed to know that they have no basis for judging various "truth claims." Nevertheless, this lack of information often has little influence on beliefs; consider only how many people have been misinformed about the nature of COVID-19. They have refused masks, refused vaccines, refused to social distance, and quite often, in the final days of their lives, refused to believe that they had contracted COVID-19. We can say similar things about global climate change; people without any training whatsoever in climatology know for sure it

---

32   Basil Bernstein, *Class, Codes, and Control Vol. 1* (London: Routledge, 1973).

is a hoax, even as rivers dry up, massive floods become frequent, and hurricanes more devastating.

5 The Public Spheres Redux

By the end of the 20th century and beginning of 21st, two crucial technological innovations were evident, the internet and the cell phone, which eventually became interconnected. Initially rooted in the military needing a form of networked communication that could endure a nuclear attack, the earliest internet was largely used by scientists and academics connected to universities. However, the development of technologies, including the mouse, were adapted by a variety of progressive organizations, which resulted in a numerous "virtual public spheres," where analyses of social adversities called for recruitment, planning, and organizing resistance, led to the emergence of several "internetworked" global justice movements.[33] This was evident in the Zapatista movement of Chiapas, Mexico, soon followed by the anti-World Trade Organization (WTO) protests that students spread around the world. Soon, advances in transmitting images and documents, and online pay walls (pioneered by porn sites) eventually led to the explosion of the internet, which now includes hundreds of thousands of informational websites on every topic one could imagine. We have now seen the rise of the enormous power and reach of social media, most notably Facebook, X (formallyTwitter), Instagram, Tik-Tok, and the lesser-known war political sites such as 8Chan and Gab. This recent technology has enabled a vast explosion of "virtual public spheres" providing political "information" and spaces for group discussions, but the "democratic" nature of the internet is such that no standards of evidence or credulity can substantiate claims. Does George Soros command a fleet of Jewish flying saucers with energy beams to start wildfires? Worst yet, are school shootings just hoaxes? The most dangerous has been the claim that the 2020 American election was stolen, although none of this "undeniable" evidence ever withstood legal scrutiny.

---

[33] Lauren Langman, "From Virtual Public Spheres to Global Justice: A Critical Theory of Internetworked Social Movements," *Sociological Theory* 23, no. 1 (March 2005): 42–74.

6   The Politics of Identity

As was first noted, the emergence of public spheres was bourgeois in nature. It was dependent on print, literacy, and the cognitive/conceptual ability to read and understand social philosophical texts, along with the verbal skills for engaging in rational debate within "ideal speech situations," wherein groups could find consensus. While the rising bourgeoisie were initially able to mobilize support from other classes in their struggles against dynastic rule, as was clear in 1776 and 1789, with the emergence of industrialization, when capitalist wealth depended on appropriating the surplus value of proletariat labor, the "amity" of classes returned to enmity, or, as Marx put it, history was a history of class conflict. Nevertheless, what Marx did not articulate was the significant role that collective identity would play in such class conflict, which as such was underpinned by social character, which partially determines the nature of class struggles or even inter-class cooperation.

While economic, political, or cultural crises of systemic legitimacy may be the triggers, such crises migrate into the lifeworld of subjectivity, identity, and emotion, where people might experience fear, anger, shame, and anxiety. The reactions will be mediated through social character and collective identities as cultural frameworks of interpretation of a particular group. Additionally, as we have seen, that character's socialization has been shaped by social institutions, such as family, schools, churches. But what is now important today, has been the vital role of the culture industries, which includes the vast number of "virtual public spheres" providing unprecedented amounts of "information," some of it relatively accurate, such as the weather reports provided by well-trained meteorologists, or COVID-19 hospitalizations based on records submitted to the Center for Disease Control (CDC). But what is salient is the extent to which the fragmented and segmented nature of the internet and its many social media sites have become the source of alternative political and/or "scientific" knowledge, which, given limited censorship, has no meaningful standards or limits. One can find the extraordinary claim that all "Mainstream Media" (MSM) is "fake news," school shootings are staged, vaccines are dangerous, etc., all of which promotes the critique of so-called "elites," i.e., experts, causing a drastic withdrawal of loyalty from the dominant system. Many such sites offer alternative visions of the possible, which for many is a white, patriarchal, illiberal, Christian nationalism, intolerant, indeed hostile to minorities, foreigners, immigrants, queers, or "uppity women."

7 Class Politics

There is no single factor that can explain the rise of authoritarianism, often in the form of reactionary movements and parties, in the last two decades. We should note that in an analysis of 150,000 voters via the American Voter Survey, the most salient predictive value was based on a five-item measurement of authoritarianism; the presence of authoritarian characteristics in individuals predicted support for Trump, regardless of class, education, or region.[34] The relationships between the dynamics of class position, authoritarian character, and collective identities are quite complex. A crucial factor is the attention paid to specific internet public spheres for information and/or confirmations [or sometimes denigrations] of lifestyles, identities, and values.

A starting point of course would be the material conditions of neoliberal globalized capitalism as a response to the crises of Keynesianism and the declining rate of profit. The subsequent discontents and mobilizations as resistance were foreshadowed by the Zapatista movement and their demand for autonomy from the Mexican government, whose growing embrace of neoliberal policies had devastating effects on the *campesinos,* the peasant population. Neoliberalism, privileging the "free market," financialization (casino capitalism), import substitution, etc., aided by technological innovations, have led to vast profits for the few. Simultaneously, the many faced an explosion of inequality, precarity, privatization and/or retrenchments of government services and benefits, environmental despoliation, etc. The crucial moment however was the collapse of the housing market and subsequent implosion of the world financial markets in 2008, followed by businesses closing and skyrocketing unemployment: the great recession.[35] To prevent a total economic collapse, governments, especially the US government, printed trillions of dollars to bail out the banks and financial institutions. Then came the election of Barack Obama, whose election aroused the fears and anger of the more conservative, authoritarian, indeed racist, segments of American society, outraged that an African American, seen as either a witch doctor or a communist, was President of the United States. Then came the rise of the Tea Party, an Astroturf reactionary movement, primarily of lower middle class, mostly exurban or rural evangelical Christians, whose rural economies were in decline as their church membership receded. History, and decades of political sociology, have shown

---

[34] D.N. Smith and E. Hanley, "The Anger Games: Who Voted for Donald Trump in the 2016 Election, and Why?" *Critical Sociology* 4 (2018): 195–212.

[35] David McNally, *Global Slump: The Economics and Politics of Crisis and Resistance* (New York: PM Press, 2010).

that when some people face economic and/or cultural changes and hardships, to paraphrase Erich Fromm, many attempt to "escape" the alienation of social fragmentation, powerlessness, and meaninglessness, and willingly submit to "superior" powers, ideologies, or leaders, who would not only dominate the subordinates, but would also express and/or enact actual aggression against the scapegoats "responsible" for the masses' adversity (yet, other segments of society are more likely to embrace more democratic, progressive policies and leaders). Opposition to "socialized medicine," for example, was rooted in racism. "Socialized medicine" would provide "undeserving" racial minorities, i.e., "parasites," with unearned benefits. Such leaders and ideologies promise incorporation into a greater collectivity providing a pseudo-*gemeinschaft* (community) for the socially isolated, illusory empowerment for the powerless, and frameworks of "explanation." Such visions of a "better" futures are typical when ideologies fail. Many such reactionary groups were funded and given organizational aid by affluent right-wing organizations, and even libertarians like the Koch brothers, who could not care less about abortion or prayer in the schools, let alone stopping the advancement of homosexual rights, knew that supporting such organizations kept taxes low and thwarted attempts at regulation.

At times of legitimation crises, given anxiety, fear and uncertainty, people seek out interpretations of reality consistent with their underlying character, collective identities, and frameworks of understanding. They may join online discussion groups that often leads to joining actual groups. As has been suggested, social character and political identities vary by class location; a politics of identity is clearly tied to social class, beginning with socialization within and without the family, life experiences, and how larger events are experienced and interpreted. Consider for example a 60-year-old factory worker who loses their job as the company closes the factory and opens one in low-wage Mississippi or lower wage Thailand. The reaction might include anger at the company, anxiety over survival without a job, a blow to their identity and self-esteem as a "good employee," and frequently depression, and some cases drug addiction or even suicide, i.e., "deaths of despair."[36] Quite often, they may then gravitate to one of the reactionary websites that will "explain" their victimization and grievances: the plant closed because of either greedy globalists (code for Jews) or "dangerous" immigrants. Voilà! They soon show up at a MAGA rally. Meanwhile, the vice president of operations is absolutely elated that their stock went up by ¼ million dollars so that they can buy a decent boat or vacation

---

36 Anne Case and Angus Deaton, *Deaths of Despair and the Future of Capitalism* (Princeton, NJ: Princeton University Press, 2021).

home. But to the manager, the plight of the worker, a thousand miles away, is invisible, just a number on the spreadsheet.

To bring these various moments together, to perhaps oversimplify, in advanced societies today, we can suggest that the majority of the politically engaged population might be considered (1) Working-class, by which we mean primarily with less than a college education and more likely engaged in production, construction, or service jobs, most having family incomes of roughly $40,000 to about $120,000 a year; (2) Lower middle classes, are primarily petty bourgeois, small business owners, some artisans and lower echelon state employees in agencies of coercion, most with no more than high school educations, middle incomes.[37] (3) Upper middle bourgeoisie consists of managers, professionals, and various intellectuals e.g., the professoriate, writers, and journalists, especially opinion writers, whose incomes range from about $120,000 to $175,000 a year, which puts them into the top 10% earners. The top 1% average around $850,000 a year; a handful of elites, and the top .01% make about $35 million a year.

Let us note at the outset that however we define class, whether by Marx as sources of income (wages, profits, or rents), honorific status of lifestyle per Weber-levels of education, cultural tastes, and perceived occupational status, amounts of income, or the apolitical American sociological composite of income, education, occupational status, and residence, classes are not homogenous groupings. Within each category one will find a range of social characters, political identities, and differential access to the "virtual public spheres" of the contemporary internet, selecting and interpreting information and acting upon that information.

What is interesting to note however is that while at times class conflict has been the basic structural relationship between workers and owners, many workers nevertheless support the domination of the bourgeois classes. The hegemonic discourses of the elites convince many workers that they do better under capitalism than they would under socialism, while at the same time the ruling classes of been remarkably successful at dividing workers by race and ethnicity to thwart collective resistance.

---

37 It should be noted the major differences between the working-classes and lower middle-classes is that the lower middle-class tend to be more entrepreneurial and may own small businesses. In many cases, ambitious blue-collar workers, especially in various repair or maintenance services or construction work, decided to become owners/managers, and many are quite successful. Small businesses typically include car dealerships, real estate agencies, construction firms, and various franchises, some of which achieve very high incomes.

8 The Working Classes

In general, working classes are socialized to comply with hierarchical authority or assume a limited degree of managerial work as supervisors, or direct supervisors of service providers such as domestic services, repairs/maintenance services, etc. But as we noted, socialization and family, schools, churches, and even work, provides little space for creativity or innovation outside of increasing the efficiency of labor. Nevertheless, we should remember that at various times, labor unions have been progressive forces fighting to improve working conditions, salaries, and benefits. Yet so too did many unions discriminate against minorities and women.

We might begin to note that for journalists, the "deciding factor" for the 2016 election of Trump where the white working classes who were unemployed or underemployed, especially in the rust belts and small industrial towns. Interview after interview, aggrieved blue-collar voters supported Trump because of his promise to revitalize dying industries, to stop the immigration of low-wage workers, and the perceived preferences for minority groups. A convincing story, but unsubstantiated. Careful analysis of the voters however showed that a slight majority of the working classes, who actually faced various hardships, voted for Clinton and later Biden. The more affluent workers, especially in highly rural states, and in the smaller towns of the South, were more likely motivated by racism, sexism, ethnocentrism, xenophobia, and homophobia. Otherwise said, progressive challenges to essentialist identities evoke fear and anxiety. Given the convenient "explanations" provided by right-wing internet sites and recruitment channels, many of the aggrieved expressed their anger at progressive social change.

9 Lower Middle Classes

Ever since Marx noted the support for the Louis Bonaparte coup by the peasant farmers, the lower middle classes, long the bearers of reactionary politics, find themselves in an awkward position, squeezed between the working classes, whose incomes are quickly subjected to the vagaries of the economy, and the growth of large capitalist enterprises, but without the security of large savings accounts or investment portfolios. Moreover, for many, every day business requires a pleasing demeanor, even with unpleasant customers and often equally unpleasant employees. Nevertheless, they must repress their anger and smile, while that anger boils over from within. As Fromm pointed out, the legacy of the humiliation of Versailles joined with the economic crisis and unemployment/hyperinflation, had devastating effects on the lower middle class, whose economic fortunes were problematic, as was their self-esteem, leading to anxiety and powerlessness. Consequently, this morphed into support for fascism and Hitler, who appealed to their authoritarian need for a powerful leader, who promised both the restoration of pride – *Deutschland wieder groß machen* – and prosperity for followers, as well as exclusion, if not punishment, for the weak who were the unworthy and the traders within: Jews and Communists.[38]

To be sure, the conditions of Germany in the 1920s were far worse than recent years, and many lower middle-class businesses including heretofore successful franchises, have succumbed to economic adversities compounded by challenges to hierarchical identities, eliciting the same kinds of fears and anxieties. Given the authoritarian characteristics of many, often including membership in authoritarian churches, this class has remained a staunch supporter of reactionary causes. Consider for example the sudden growth of QAnon, a generator organization of millions, initiated by Q, a mysterious figure who claims to be an insider within the government, who advised followers that the election of Trump was the "will of God," and that Trump was fighting to end the massive kidnapping, torturing, and slaying of children by liberals and celebrities to extract the adenochrome that would give them eternal lives. No, these people are not mentally ill, but membership in QAnon provides a sense of community for people that have been highly isolated, and it provides a worthy goal (saving the lives of children). To accomplish this goal, they will support authoritarian politics to the point where many joined the January 6th, 2021, insurrection. Reactionary segments of the lower middle-classes perceive the ruling-classes, the capitalists and their bought off political allies, and civil servants, i.e., the "deep state," as the fundamental enemy of the real people; they are responsible for economic uncertainty and hardship, and they embrace "woke" politics, which challenges the essentialist identities of "real Americans."

It is clear for those who have studied this group that while their economic and cultural hardships are the consequences of neo-liberal capitalism, much like the Tea Party that preceded them, they garner support from the reactionary elements of the elites since their votes for authoritarian candidates keep taxes low, limit environmental action, and suppress worker rights and wages. While this merely repeats what Marx said 150 or so years ago, today, we would simply point out the salience of identity, and the politics of identity as essential moments of structural reproduction.

---

38   Erich Fromm, *Escape from Freedom* (New York: Farrar & Rinehart, 1941).

10   Upper Middle-Class and Beyond

It was already noted that the bourgeois classes spearheaded the moves toward "life, liberty, and the pursuit of happiness," or *liberté, égalité et fraternité*. Of course, when they finally assumed power, these progressive values became elements of their hegemony, as the working-classes were subject to domination, inequality, alienation, and immiseration.

By virtue of overtly more democratic empathic socialization encouraging creativity and care, quality education, and subsequent levels of education typically college or beyond, comfortable incomes and often more than ample savings accounts/investment funds, the upper middle classes of managers, professionals, entrepreneurs, etc., are typically economically secure. Given how their occupational roles require complexity of thought, capacity for innovation, and control over their work process, etc., that should be among the most liberal segment in the society, and indeed many are. But as has been noted, notwithstanding similarities and social positions and economic assets, there are variations within this group, especially by occupations. Thus, many professionals, especially those that may be working in the corporate sector, and even many self-employed, are likely to gravitate toward conservative politics.

As Robert Pape indicated, almost half of those arrested participating in the January 6th insurrection had come from the privilege classes, few of these were members of the more typically working or lower middle-class militias or hate groups.[39] They had come from blue states not just red states, urban areas not just rural, as the reported demographic evidence showed. Most of those arrested were living in upscale neighborhoods as would surely be expected, but these neighborhoods, had in recent years seen a growing influx of "successful" racial minorities, immigrants, and even queer families. Pape suggested that this growing economic power of minorities represented a challenge to the "superiority" of white identities, and as has been argued, such challenges raise fear that one's identity-based status is problematic; it evokes powerful emotions and perhaps in this case the most powerful of all emotions: the fear of death, or in this case the demise of white, hyper-masculine authoritarian identities.

Over most of the history of capitalism, there has been a fundamental class conflict between the bourgeoisie and the working classes, but as we have seen, the provision of benefits and entitlements has dulled class consciousness.

---

39   Robert Pape, "American Face of Insurrection: Analysis of Individuals Charged for Storming the US Capitol on January 6, 2021," *Chicago Project on Security and Threats*. January 5, 2022. https://cpost.uchicago.edu/publications/american_face_of_insurrection/.

A form of nationalism that renders everyone "equal" citizens, along with the explosion of consumerism, has further obscured class differences. Nevertheless, the secure conditions of upper-middle-class life have meant that many have supported a variety of democratic causes and institutions. Moreover, most journalists, editorialists, and writers have typically embraced progressive values. The forces for racial integration (surely dating back to the days of slavery), feminism since 1848, and more recently the struggle for LGBTQ rights, have pushed forward legislation and practices promoting greater equality, expansions of rights, and of singular importance in the United States, the separation of church and state. Although many may be religious, progressives tend to worship at more inclusive congregations, such as the Unitarian Church, Episcopalian Church, and Reform Judaism, etc. The fundamental point here is that these values challenging traditional, authoritarian, and essentialist identities, have not only been a factor in mobilizing a variety of reactionary agendas, but some of this class, including elements of corporate America that made appeals toward an inclusive multiculturalism, are seen as the "woke" enemy.

11 Conclusion

To address a social/political problem, we need to fully understand its basis in order to think about appropriate strategies of amelioration. One of the major problems of the world today is the assent of various authoritarian populists and reactionary social movements. Indeed, there have been several countries where they have achieved political victories, often "illiberal democracies" as seen in Brazil, Turkey, India, Poland, Hungary, post-Brexit UK, and of course Trump's America. While the causes are many, as this paper attempts to understand, it becomes imperative to consider the psychosocial dimensions, beginning with a psychoanalytic understanding of self and identity, as expressions of underlying social character, most typically authoritarian. Such a perspective is all too often ignored or rejected out of hand.

At the same time, one of the major contemporary factors that has facilitated authoritarian populism has been the access to the internet, which acts in much the same way as did the printing of books, pamphlets, and newspapers in earlier times, but at a much faster rate. Whereas the initial bourgeois public spheres extolled ideologies of democracy, equality, economic, personal, and political freedom, often not practiced, many of the contemporary "virtual public spheres" valorize authoritarian leadership, accept hierarchical relationships as "normal," reject notions of universal human rights and the rule of law, and believe that these leaders and their mobilizations can restore a lost Golden

Age. As far as this perspective is deeply anchored within an authoritarian character, it should be clear at the outset that rational debate, facts, and evidence is quite unlikely to temper or assuage the deeper unconscious feelings of shame, fear, anxiety, anger, and aggression articulated as *ressentiment* toward the rich and disdain of subordinates. Rational debate, facts, and evidence will not dampen ontological anxiety over the very future of essentialist identities, nor will it turn millions away from the embrace of necrophilia and its death and destruction. What is to be done?

The most important thing that can be done for those of us who believe in equality, democracy, social justice, and freedom is to avoid cynicism, defeatism, and the despair that things cannot change. Indeed, garnering far less attention, but the last several decades have seen unprecedented progressive social mobilizations that have challenged, often successfully, various authoritarian leaders and their agendas. If we embrace a Hegelian-Marxist position in which history moves via dialectical negation, it seem as if the forces of reaction have now reached the point where they have engendered myriad expressions of resistance and counter-reactions, i.e., the #MeToo movement, support for Black Lives Matter, 350.org, resurgent feminist activism, etc. Yet, every historical era fosters a particular type of social character. It seems as if we are now in one of those periods where, to paraphrase Gramsci, the older, more authoritarian character is dying out, but the newer, more democratic, humanistic, egalitarian character is not yet dominant. In this transitional time, what Gramsci called an "interregnum," morbid symptoms flourish.

There is widespread evidence that the present youth, the Z generation of those between 18 and 30, is a leading edge of what Karl Mannheim called the generational mediation of social change through "cohort flow." As a generation comes of age, it continues the values shaped by the earlier historical context as it exits the scene of world history. These contemporary youth are the most progressive generation in history, and many are involved in a variety of movements for social change, racial/ethnic equality, feminism, environmentalism, LGBTQ, and indeed close to half of these youth reject binary notions of sexual identity.[40] Furthermore, over half prefer socialism to capitalism, even if their understanding of socialism is limited.

As the power and numbers of these progressive youths grow, there will be unintended consequences. As we well know, the distributions of character patterns in a population are more like bell curves than either/or. As was noted,

---

40   John Della Wolpe. *Fight: How Gen Z is Channeling Their Fear and Passion to Save America* (New York: St. Martin's Press, 2022).

at times of crisis, fear leads many people toward more authoritarian perspectives. But at the same time, understanding the human capacity for what Erich Fromm called "dynamic character change," as progressive character structures proliferate, and progressive identities become more typical, one consequence is to impact larger populations to move leftward and embrace progressive stances. Is this possible? We can note that so many of the positions embraced by radicals not so long ago, reflecting a character change toward greater democracy, flexibility, and toleration/inclusion, including racial, gender, LGBTQ and ethnic equality, sexual freedom, have moved from deviant positions deemed radical to acceptable for many and are now generally embraced by most, notwithstanding the reactionary mobilizations to thwart such changes. Even amidst the rise of various authoritarian movements, progressives should know that history is on their side, and that the general move has been toward greater inclusion, freedom, and democracy. Yet, at the same time, change is dialectical and does not proceed in a smooth linear fashion. But as the tradition of Fromm, Marcuse, and Bloch have argued that we must never let the tragedies of the moment stifle our optimism of the will. So, what can we do? Educate, organize, and mobilize. To paraphrase Kant, let our tolerant democratic, egalitarian, characters, undergirding our progressive collective identities, become the models for all humanity, and may the internet help us in this quest. The alternative is unthinkable.

Bibliography

Adorno, Theodor W., et al. *The Authoritarian Personality*. New York: Verso, 2019.

American Psychological Association, "Cognitive Dissonance," https://dictionary.apa.org/cognitive-dissonance.

Anderson, Benedict. *Imagined Communities: Reflections on the Origin and Spread of Nationalism*. London: Verso Books, 2016.

Becker, Ernest. *The Denial of Death*. New York: Free Press, 1997.

Bernstein, Basil. *Class, Codes, and Control Vol. 1*. London: Routledge, 1973.

Calhoun, Craig. "Civil Society and the Public Sphere." *Public Culture* 5, no. 2 (Winter 1993): 267–280.

Calhoun, Craig. "Civil Society and the Public Sphere." In *The Oxford Handbook of Civil Society. Oxford Handbooks in Politics & International Relations*, edited by Edwards, Michael, 311–323. Oxford: Oxford University Press, 2011.

Craig, Calhoun. "Civil Society/Public Sphere: History of a Concept." In *International Encyclopedia of the Social and Behavioral Science*, 1897–1903. Amsterdam: Elsevier, 2001.

Case, Anne, and Angus Deaton. *Deaths of Despair and the Future of Capitalism.* Princeton, NJ: Princeton University Press, 2021.

Erikson, Erik. *Identity and the Life Cycle.* New York: W.W. Norton & Co., 1994.

Fromm, Erich. *The Anatomy of Human Destructiveness.* New York: Holt, Rinehart and Winston, 1973.

Fromm, Erich. *Escape from Freedom.* New York: Farrar & Rinehart, 1941.

Gandesha, Samir. "Understanding Right and Left Populism." In *Critical Theory and Authoritarian Populism.* Edited by Jeremiah Morelock. London: University of Westminster Press, 2018.

Habermas, Jürgen. *The Structural Transformation of the Bourgeois Public Sphere: An Inquiry into a Category of Bourgeois Society.* Translated by Thomas Burger. Cambridge, MA: The MIT Press, 1991.

Hegel, G.W.F. *Elements of the Philosophy of Right.* Cambridge: Cambridge University Press, 1991.

Horkheimer, Max. "Authority and the Family." In *The Essential Frankfurt School Reader,* edited by Andrew Arato and Eike Gephardt. London: Bloomsbury Academic, 1982.

Inglehart, Ronald. *The Silent Revolution: Changing Values and Political Styles Among Western Publics.* Princeton: Princeton University Press, 2015.

Lakoff, George. *Moral Politics: How Liberals and Conservatives Think, Third Edition.* Chicago: University of Chicago Press, 2016.

Langman, Lauren. "From Virtual Public Spheres to Global Justice: A Critical Theory of Internetworked Social Movements," *Sociological Theory* 23, no. 1 (March 2005): 42–74.

Löwenthal, Leo, and Norbert Guterman. *Prophets of Deceit: A Study of the Techniques of the American Agitator* New York: Verso, 2021.

Lukács, Georg. *History and Class Consciousness: Studies in Marxist Dialectic.* Cambridge, MA: The MIT Press, 1972.

Marcuse, Herbert. *Eros and Civilization.* Boston: Beacon Press, 1953.

Marcuse, Herbert. *One-Dimensional Man: Studies in the Ideology of Advanced Industrial Society.* Boston: Beacon Press, 1964.

McNally, David. *Global Slump: The Economics and Politics of Crisis and Resistance.* New York: PM Press, 2010.

Pape, Robert. "American Face of Insurrection: Analysis of Individuals Charged for Storming the US Capitol on January 6, 2021." *Chicago Project on Security and Threats.* January 5, 2022. https://cpost.uchicago.edu/publications/american_face_of_insurrection/.

Reich, Wilhelm. *The Mass Psychology of Fascism.* Translated by Vincent R. Carfagno. New York: Farrar, Straus, and Giroux, 1980.

Rokeach, Milton. "The Nature and Meaning of Dogmatism." *Psychological Review* 61, no. 3 (1954): 194–204. https://www.all-about-psychology.com/dogmatism.html.

Scheff, Thomas J. "Social–emotional Origins of Violence: A theory of Multiple Killing." *Aggression and Violent Behavior* 16, no. 6 (November–December 2011): 453–460.

Sennett, Richard. *The Fall of Public Man,* New York: W.W. Norton & Co., 2017.

Smith, D.N., and E. Hanley. "The Anger Games: Who Voted for Donald Trump in the 2016 Election, and Why?" *Critical Sociology* 4 (2018): 195–212.

Tryon, Warren W. *Cognitive Neuroscience and Psychotherapy: Network Principles for a Unified Theory.* Amsterdam: Academic Press, 2014.

Wolpe, John Della. *Fight: How Gen Z is Channeling Their Fear and Passion to Save America.* New York: St. Martin's Press, 2022.

Index

Adler, Alfred 33, 242
Adorno, Theodor W. 9, 43, 48, 53, 56–59, 71–93, 95, 97, 99, 101–103, 105, 107, 109, 111, 113, 115, 117, 119, 121–123, 125, 127, 129, 188–189, 240–242, 245–263, 270, 283–288, 297–319
Aeschylus 97–98, 120
Akhenaton 35
Alienation 1, 49, 68, 81, 225, 228, 285, 288, 302, 413, 445, 461, 506, 521, 525
Ananke 232, 361
Andrade, Frances 417
Andreas-Salome, Lou 3
Anschluss 2, 46
Antinomianism 389–391, 401
Anti-Semitism 96, 473
Apophatic Theology 57–59
Aquinas, Thomas 61
Aristotle 120, 151, 201, 219, 233, 486, 504, 513
Arminianism 389–391, 396–397, 399
Arnold, Matthew 392
Arroyo, Raymond 97
Aryan Psychology/Aryan Psychoanalysis 29, 46, 101
Aschaffenburg (Battle of) 96
Atheistic Theology 149
Audubon Ballroom 176
Aufhaben/Aufhebung 8, 142
Autarky 233

Bachofen, Johann Jakob 107, 115
Bahr, Hermann 356
Bannon, Steve (Stephen K.) 442
Baraka, Amiri (Leroi Jones) 177
Barot, Rohit 14
Barros, Tomas Zicman de 195, 196
Bauer, Ida (Dora) 400
Bauer, Otto 187
Baum, Gregory 111
Beard, Matthew 2
Benedict XVI (Pope) 119
Benjamin, Walter 43, 240
Bergen Belsen 93
Bergson, Henry 243, 246, 251, 253, 254, 259, 471

Bernays, Martha 23
Bernfeld, Siegfriend 246
Beyond the Pleasure Principle 31, 33, 49, 72, 83, 109–112, 216, 218, 227, 228, 274, 275, 277, 279, 289–292, 297, 308–316, 350, 353, 356–361, 391, 422–424, 427, 428, 430, 432
Biden, Joseph R. 104, 118, 448, 523
Bilderverbot (Image ban) 57–59
Binswanger, Ludwig 241
Black Arts Movement (BAM) 177
Black Lives Matter 527
Black Power Movement 162–179
Block, James 211
Bolshevism 477
Bonaparte, Louis 523
Bourgeois Coldness 297, 307, 309, 310, 315
Braun, Eva 97, 111
Brecht, Bertolt 111
Breger, Louis 45
Bratich, Jack 442
Breitbart (News) 447
Breitbart, Andrew 442
Brentano, Franz 332
Breuer, Josef 2, 3
Brewer, Michael 418
BREXIT 199, 526
Broder, David 191
Brooks, Van Wyck 393
Burke, Edmond 402

Cade, Cathy 401
Calhoun, Craig 502
Calvinism 37, 388, 392
Camus, Albert 337
Cannibalism 141, 373–374, 495–496
Capitalism 6, 73, 76, 77–79, 82, 103–105, 223–228, 229, 231, 261, 282, 284, 312, 385, 387, 388, 392, 393, 396, 397, 400, 401, 439, 445, 464, 477, 502, 503, 504, 507, 513, 520, 522, 524, 525, 527
Carmichael, Stokely 164–166, 176
Castoriadis, Cornelius 232
Castration 110, 166, 169, 170, 175, 419
Cataphatic Theology 57

Categorical Imperative   369
Cathexis   113, 114, 229, 506
Catholicism   106, 124
Ceccato, Silvio   485–487, 489, 492
Cervantes, Miguel de   375
Charcot, Jean-Martin   2, 479
Child Protection Discourse (CPD)   411–421, 424–432
Child Sexual Abuse (CSA)   409–418, 424–431
Chomsky, Noam   402
Christianity   2, 27, 46, 47, 50, 61, 64, 66, 95, 102, 105, 106, 117, 118, 119, 163, 396, 497
Ciezskowski, August von   219
Civilization and its Discontents   11, 15, 25, 43, 49, 135, 137, 145, 269, 277, 278, 284, 328, 359, 360, 372, 375, 390, 472
Clark University   391, 396
Class Consciousness   187, 189, 502, 525
Clegg, Claude   166, 171
Clift, Montgomery   3
Cold War   59, 472
Colonization   6, 244, 506, 513
Columbia University   94, 487
Commodity   71, 73, 77, 78, 80, 225–227, 231, 237, 420, 511
Commodity Fetish   77, 225, 227, 420
Communicative Rationality   491
Communism   95, 96, 103, 397
Conjunctive Capacity   217, 218, 222
Constantine (Roman Emperor)   64
Copernican Revolution   393
Cornelius, Hans   240, 241, 247–253, 255, 260
COVID-19   15, 116, 440, 517, 519
Crews, Frederick   23, 24, 150, 498, 499
Criminal Case Review Commission (CCRC)   414
Critical Psychoanalysis   209, 231, 297, 298–305
Curtis, Adam   3

Dark Charisma   4
Darwin, Charles   120, 170, 244, 505
Death Instinct. *See* Thanatos
Deaths of Despair   521
Debs, Eugene   296
De-Reification   212, 228–237
Der Trafikant (film)   2
Descartes, René   321, 323

Dialectical Religiology   94, 99, 100
DiBranco, Alex   454
Dollfuss, Engelbert   483
Dorr, Rheta Childe   394
Dostoevsky, Fyodor   147, 159, 160
Drewermann, Eugen   124–128
Dreyfus Affair   386
Driesch, Hans   244–245, 253
DuBois, W.E.B.   397
Dunning-Kruger Effect (The)   517
Durkheim, Émile   21, 33
Dyson, Michael Eric   176

Eckhart, Meister   120
Eco, Umberto   443
Ehrenreich, Barbara   368–370, 373
Einstein, Albert   350, 469–473, 479, 481–484, 489
Eliade, Mircea   101
Elias, Norbert   186
Ellsberg, Daniel   402
Emerson, Ralph Waldo   342, 391, 393, 394
Engels, Friedrich   95
Enlightenment (The)   13, 47, 48, 52, 56, 57, 60, 61, 62, 63, 68, 88, 104, 118, 120, 209, 210, 223, 230, 243, 303, 313, 326, 393, 473–476, 505
Erasmus of Rotterdam   504
Erikson, Erik   507
Eros   31, 110, 111, 121, 160, 216–218, 222, 225, 226, 230, 270, 274–278, 280, 290–292, 350, 353, 360–361, 399, 420, 421, 439, 472, 486, 495
Eroticism   276
Eternal Word Television Network (EWTN)   97, 118
Ethnomasochism   8
Evil   24, 26–29, 34, 116, 210, 358–259, 422, 428, 509, 514, 517

False Allegations Discourse (FAD)   411, 414–419, 421, 424–425, 427–432
False Consciousness   284, 319
False Totality   77–82, 83–84
Fanon, Frantz   398
Fascism   86, 96, 101, 260–261, 303, 312, 441–447
Feingold, Mimi   401

INDEX

Fenichel, Otto   245
Feuerbach, Ludwig   43, 52, 219, 220
Fichte, Johann Gottlieb   120, 219, 251
Firestone, Shulamith   400
Fliess, Wilhelm   23
Foucault, Michel   200, 202, 403, 469, 473, 474–476, 482, 484
fox News   97, 447
Frankfurt School   4, 8, 12, 43–68, 71–86, 93–127, 240–263, 286, 297–299, 300–320, 506, 514
Frank, Waldo   393
Frankl, Viktor   1, 60–61
Frazer, James   371
Freud, Anna   46
Freud, Sophie   357–358
Freud's Last Session (film)   1, 2
Freudian Left   185–186, 199, 204
Fromm, Erich   1, 12, 43, 55, 62, 82, 93, 94, 102, 108, 285, 388, 438, 439, 443–445, 455, 457, 459, 460, 461, 463, 464, 507, 509, 510, 521, 523, 528
Fuentes, Nick   448
Future of an Illusion (The)   11, 25, 35, 43, 47–51, 135–138, 140–141, 144, 146–160, 352, 359–360, 372, 374

Galton, Sir Francis   490
Ganz, Bruno   2
Garvey, Marcus/Garveyism   166
Gay, Peter   22–23
Geistigkeit (Subjectivity)   35, 396
Gerald, Carolyn   177
Germany   8, 9, 93, 94, 96, 117, 126, 243, 244, 245, 263, 350, 473, 482, 483, 524
Gestalt Psychology   247, 255
Giddens, Anthony   14
Gilman, Charlotte   394
Girard, René   364–380
Gittelsohn, Rabbi Roland B.   397
Goethe, Johann Wolfgang von   93, 110, 246, 292, 481
Goffman, Irving   14, 476, 492–499
Goldman, Peter   173–174, 176, 177
Goode, Matthew   2
Gore, Al   457
Gramsci, Antonio   193, 385, 387, 502, 511, 512, 516, 527

Great Awakening   30, 389, 397, 398, 402
Great Replacement   440
Groddeck, Georg   36
Gross, Otto   390
Group Psychology   4, 23, 25, 28, 33, 71, 185–204, 372, 386, 410, 411, 418, 420–422, 425–433
Grünbaum, Adolf   150

Habermas, Jürgen   43, 48, 64, 67, 388, 491, 495, 497, 504
Hayek, Friedrich   401
Hegel, Georg Wilhelm Friedrich   10, 56, 59, 73, 80, 93–95, 102–106, 111, 112, 115–117, 120, 142, 159, 209, 219, 234, 280, 282, 504, 505, 527
Hegemony   157, 190, 193–198, 339, 511, 512, 516, 525
Heidegger, Martin   101, 122, 242, 322, 329, 337
Hall, G. Stanley   391
Herodotus   116, 120
Herz, Otto O.   58
Hess, Heinrich   356
Himmler, Heinrich   96
Hinduism   95
Historical Materialism   59, 94, 103
Hitchcock, Alfred   3
Hitler, Adolf   97, 101, 104, 111, 122
Hobbes, Thomas   34–36, 50, 51, 269, 278, 366, 491, 495
Hobsbawm, Eric   187, 388
Holocaust   8–9, 60, 96, 312, 514
Holt, Luther   487
Holy Inquisition   120, 121
Hopkins, Anthony   2
Horkheimer, Maidon   93, 126
Horkheimer, Max   43, 48, 52–53, 58, 64, 74, 93–99, 102–127, 133, 240, 299, 302, 494
Horney, Karen   82–84, 86, 89, 120, 285
Howard University   164, 165, 173
Hume, David   322–324, 333, 339, 340, 342, 372, 486
Husserl, Edmund   240, 333
Hysteria   108

Ibn ʿArabī   147, 149
Idolatry   57, 59, 104
Incels   439, 456

Islam   45, 95, 105, 167
Islamophobia   449, 454

Jafari, Allama Muhammad Taghi   155
James, Willliam   321, 332, 334, 342, 389, 391
Jesus of Nazareth   61, 95, 99, 100, 111, 118, 124, 125, 162–163
Jim Crow   395, 404
Johann Wolfgang von Goethe Universität   93, 110
Johnston, Adrian   270, 279
Joseph, Peniel E.   163–164, 166
Jouissance   192, 194–196
Judaism   44, 45, 46, 47, 57–58, 61, 95, 105, 106, 125, 396, 526
Judas Iscariot   100
Jung, Carl Gustav   3, 28, 29, 33, 46, 51, 62, 67, 101, 102, 124, 242, 245, 455
Jünger, Ernst   242

Kanner, Leo   461
Kant, Immanuel   89, 93, 95, 103, 105, 111, 120, 148, 209, 210, 219, 223, 224, 234, 240, 244, 246, 247–249, 250, 251–254, 262–263, 280, 282, 287, 321, 322, 324–325, 327, 329, 333, 338, 339, 343, 369, 391, 473–477, 484, 486, 491, 495, 505, 528
Kehl, Albin   103
Kierkegaard, Søren   240, 322, 337, 343
King Jr., Martin Luther   173, 398
Klages, Ludwig   241, 243, 244, 253
Knight, Etheridge   177
Koffler, Chaim   45
Kozin, Sergey   15
Kuhn, Thomas   201, 471
Küng, Hans   111
Kyle, Chris   457

Lacan, Jacques   3, 4, 185, 186, 190, 194–196, 198, 199, 200–204
Laclau, Ernesto   185, 190–198, 203, 204
Ladyman, James   14
Lahouri, Iqbal   14
Landauer, Karl   93
Lanzer, Ernest "Rat Man"   26–28
Laplanche, Jean   269, 275, 289
Lasch, Christopher   392, 403
Le Bon, Gustav   426

Lebensnot (Vital exigency)   352
Lebensphilosophie (Life philosophy)   242, 243
Leytner, Nikolaus   2
Lewis, C.S.   2
Liberalism   75, 76, 79, 80, 82, 96
Libido   13, 71, 83, 216, 223, 230, 263, 277, 290, 419–421
Lichtman, Richard   229
Liebnitz, Gottfried Wilhelm   75
Lippman, Walter   401
Lipps, Theodor   243
Little, Ella   167
Locke, John   209, 210, 321, 322, 505
Logotherapy   1, 60
Löwenthal, Leo   43, 58, 85
Lukács, György (Georg)   77, 78, 231
Lundskow, George   457, 460
Luther, Martin   61

MacCulloch, Diarmaid   66
Machiavelli, Niccolò   51, 194
Make America Great Again (MAGA)   4, 516, 521
Male Supremacism   439, 454
Mannheim, Karl   527
Människosyn   156
Manson, Marilyn   462
March, Meredith   164
Marcuse, Herbert   68, 93, 102, 281, 282, 283, 299, 302, 365, 399, 400, 510, 513, 528
Marinetti, Filippo Tommaso   445
Mariology   106
Marx, Karl   10, 21, 33, 43, 52, 53, 56, 57, 58, 62, 77, 80, 93–95, 97, 99, 101–105, 119, 120, 122, 126, 127, 187, 189, 190, 108–237, 281, 282, 297, 299, 300, 385, 396, 400, 420, 479, 494, 502, 506, 510, 511, 516, 519, 522, 523, 524, 527
Masochism   8, 124, 189, 273, 276
Mass Psychogenic Delusion   65
Maurer, Jürgen   3
Max Plank Institute   103
May, Ulrike   355
McLennan, Gregor   14
Mead, Margaret   395
Menand, Louis   472–473, 477, 479, 480, 481, 484, 485

INDEX 535

Messiah   144–145, 152
Metz, Johannes Baptist   111
Micah (Prophet)   99
Michigan State University   10
Millet, Kate   400
Mimesis   123, 377, 378, 379, 380
Mirandolo, Pico Della   504
Misogyny   443, 446, 449, 454–457, 463
Mitscherlich, Alexander   93, 227
Mitscherlich, Margaret   93
Monad   75–76, 78, 79, 81
Montesquieu   35, 504
Moore, Michael   462
Moral Agency   314, 321–345
More, Thomas   504
Mortensen, Viggo   3
Moses and Monotheism   11, 25, 35, 43, 45, 170, 396
Mouffe, Chantal   191, 197
Muhammad, Elijah (Poole)   162, 166–167, 171–175, 178
Muhammad, Warith Deen   174
Munsterberg, Hugo   391
Mussolini, Benito   482–483, 494
Musto, Marcello   190

Narcissism   30, 32, 33, 34, 64, 67, 217, 218, 274, 290, 389, 390, 393, 396, 397, 403, 478
Nation of Islam   167
National Association for the Advancement of Colored People (NAACP)   173
Nazism   8, 29, 37, 46, 50, 64, 93, 96, 97, 126, 188, 245, 440, 441, 448, 473, 482, 483, 514
Nebuchadnezzar   99
Necrophilia   438–464
Negative Dialectics   59, 78, 88, 303, 306
Neo-Liberalism   11, 82, 402, 520
Netanyahu, Benjamin   8
New Deal   399, 401–403
New Left   399, 400, 401
Nietzsche, Friedrich   3, 43, 61–62, 64, 119, 121, 241, 243, 244, 246, 251, 261, 321, 322, 329, 337, 364, 365–368, 372
Non-Identical   45, 79, 284, 303, 306
Nyman, Alf   242

Oedipus complex   43, 48, 65, 97, 98, 102, 108, 109, 112, 113, 115, 121, 134, 163, 166, 167, 169, 170, 171, 178, 257, 262, 367, 376, 379, 395, 419
Orexis   219

Papini, Giovanni   473, 476–484, 491, 298, 299
Parapraxis (Magazine)   5, 6
Parker, Jade   448
Peripeteic-Dialectics   67
Peter (Apostle)   100
Pettazzi, Carlo   240
Phantasy   24, 35, 72, 223, 228
Plato   28, 120, 150, 216, 234, 254, 326, 360, 386, 420, 486, 504, 513, 514
Pleasure Principle   31, 32, 33, 49, 72, 83, 109, 216, 218, 227, 228, 274, 275, 277, 278, 289, 290–292, 297, 308–310, 313–315, 350, 353, 356, 358, 359, 361, 391, 422–424, 427, 428, 430, 432
Popper, Karl   150
Populism   4, 67, 118, 185–207, 502, 526
Positivism   124, 153, 243, 246, 262, 302–305
Post-Truth   185, 199–207
Price, Robert   177
Primal Horde   12, 178, 372, 375, 386, 443
Proust, Marcel   375
Psalm   91 126
Psychoid   245
Psychosis   49, 152, 153
Puritanism   385, 387, 389, 390, 403, 513
Putnam, James Jackson   391

QAnon   462, 516, 524
Qur'ān   95, 162

Rawls, John   299, 365
Reagan, Ronald   104
Reality Principle   48, 51, 72, 102, 109, 150, 153, 211, 227–228, 275, 301, 257–360, 422–424, 432
Reich, Wilhelm   93, 262, 390, 495, 510, 511, 512, 513
Reification   73, 77–86, 90, 103–104, 211–212, 213, 225–231
Ressentiment   509, 527
Revel, Jean-Francois   157
Ricard, Matthieu   157
Ricoeur, Paul   212–214, 226, 230

Rittenhouse, Kyle   444
Robinson, Paul   186
Rodgers, Daniel   402–403
Roe vs. Wade   118
Rolland, Romain   1, 34, 46
Romeo, Nick   5
Rokeach, Milton   515
Rorty, Richard   35
Ross, Kristin   400
Rousseau, Jean Jacques   372, 491, 494, 495, 497
Russia   8, 15, 67, 95, 117, 121, 190, 479, 505
Rustin, Bayard   164, 165, 166

Sadomasochism   509
Said, Edward   386
Sanders, Bernie   191, 440, 447
Sanger, Margaret   394
Sapolsky, Robert   485, 487, 489, 499
Sartre, Jean-Paul   334
Schmitt, Carl   101, 242
Schopenhauer, Arthur   49, 52, 110, 111, 116, 121, 251, 317, 365, 368
Schröter, Michael   355
Scientism   154, 157, 159, 245, 404
Seldes, Gilbert   392
Shakespeare, William   66, 109–110, 514
Shariati, Ali   14
Sheehi, Lara   6
Sheehi, Stephen   6
Shoah. See Holocaust   8, 9, 60, 96, 101, 312, 514
Silberstein, Eduard   23
Smith, Graham   418
Smith, Robertson   169
Social Order   81, 137–143, 158, 159, 160, 196, 198, 211, 213, 260, 261, 306, 443, 492, 493
Socrates   61, 326, 368, 386, 486
Sophocles   97–98, 108, 120
Soros, George   518
Southern Christian Leadership Council (SCLC)   173
Soviet Union   63, 97, 120, 473, 475
Spengler, Oswald   244, 253, 259, 261
Spinoza   209, 210, 214, 223
Spock, Dr. Benjamin   510, 512
Springer, Kimberly   164

St. Germain, Mark   1
Stalin, Joseph   120–121, 187, 473
Stendhal   375
Stopes, Marie   394
Student Nonviolent Coordinating Committee (SNCC)   165, 174
Sublimation   49, 195, 196, 198, 227, 270, 273, 279, 288, 290, 291, 293, 359, 389, 390, 391, 392, 393, 394, 395, 396, 513
Sulloway, Frank   23
Super-Ego   50, 89, 96, 109, 110, 111–113, 118, 119, 211, 237, 291, 361, 389, 391, 403, 418, 421, 423, 424, 425, 429, 430, 431, 486, 489, 491, 496, 513

Tallis, Frank   2, 8, 13
Taylor, Charles   336
Thanatos/Todestrieb   65, 95, 109, 110–111, 121, 236, 270, 274, 276–278, 280, 291, 439, 486, 495
Thorpe, Charles   457, 459
Thucydides   116, 120
Tillich, Paul   94
Totem and Taboo   11, 25, 28, 29, 30, 43, 44, 49, 134, 168–170, 368–375, 380
Transference   29, 122–124, 224, 279
Triebregungen (drives-impulses)   289
Trilling, Lionel   394, 396
Troupe, Quincy   178
Trump, Donald J.   4, 33, 199, 438, 440, 448, 458, 516, 520, 523, 524, 526

Ukraine   8, 117
Uncanny   30–33
Uncorroborated Allegations of Child Sexual Abuse (UACSA)   409–418, 424–425, 428–431
University of Frankfurt   71, 93, 240, 263
University of Olivet (The)   11
University of Oxford   8, 10
University of Vienna   46
Utopia   59, 102, 110, 269–270, 287–288, 293, 341, 399, 504

Vatican   97, 483
Vergangenheitsbewältigung (Working through the past)   8

Vergegenständlichkeit
   (Objectification)   223
Victimology   411, 415
Vienna Blood   2

Walzer, Michael   388, 402
Warren, Elizabeth   440
Weber, Max   21, 210, 388, 389, 390–391, 472,
   473, 491, 492, 493, 497, 522
Wettik, Theresa "Resi"   44
Whitebook, Joel   218
Wiesel, Eli   487
Williams, Evelyn   175
Wish Fulfillment   43, 56, 63, 146, 152, 386
Wittgenstein, Ludwig   322, 329, 442
World War I (WWI)   107, 350

World War II (WWII)   93, 94, 97, 107, 305,
   395, 396, 397, 399, 469, 483, 512
Wright, Richard   398

X, Jeremiah   176
X, Malcolm   162–179
Xenophobia   9, 523

Young, Whitney   174
Yovel, Yirmiyahu   213–214

Zapatista Movement   518, 520
Zeavin, Hannah   3
Zionism   45
Žižek, Slavoj   4, 94
Zoophobia   108–109

www.ingramcontent.com/pod-product-compliance
Lightning Source LLC
Chambersburg PA
CBHW070603030426
42337CB00020B/3689